Course	Shively Vol. 1
Course Number	**Power & Choice:** **An Introduction to Political Science**
	Virginia Tech

http://create.mcgraw-hill.com

ISBN-10: 1308027273   ISBN-13: 9781308027272

Contents

Credits

International Politics 405

Examples and Boxed Features

PREFACE

This book provides a general, comparative introduction to the major concepts and themes of political science. For a number of years, I had taught a course that attempted to accomplish this aim, and that experience showed me how badly we need a text that is conceptually alive and that engages students with concrete examples of analysis without losing them in a clutter of definitional minutiae. That is what I aimed for when I first wrote this book, and I've been very pleased at the response it has elicited.

The title of the book, Power & Choice, indicates a subsidiary theme that recurs at intervals. We may view politics as (1) the use of power or (2) the production of a public choice. Often one or the other is heavily emphasized in approaching the subject. Marxism emphasizes politics as the use of power, while pluralism and much formal modeling work emphasize the emergence of public choices. For our present purpose, I have defined politics as the use of power to make common decisions for a group of people, a definition that obviously demands that one hold both perspectives simultaneously. At various stages of my presentation, I note instances in which an emphasis on just one of the two halves of the definition may yield a distorted interpretation.

Behind this subsidiary theme lies a broader theme that remains largely implicit—it is best if we conduct political analysis eclectically, rather than straitjacketing ourselves into a single approach. My own research is squarely in the behavioral realm, for instance, but I found as I was working on this book that necessities of exposition and understanding pulled me toward a greater emphasis on policy and institutions than I had originally intended. Similarly, the state as an organizer of politics thrust itself more to the fore than I had anticipated. Distinctions that provide useful boundaries for research proved unhelpful in my efforts to build an understanding of politics among students. I think this is a healthy sign.

I present the material in the book topically rather than on a country-by-country basis. However, in order to add the sort of detailed contextual grounding that students gain from a country presentation, I have included within each substantive chapter a couple of extended examples from countries that particularly display the conceptual material of that chapter. For instance, Chapter 3, which deals with the state, concludes with detailed sections on the establishment and maintenance of the Nigerian state and on the European Union. Similarly, Chapter 16, "Bureaucracy and the Public Sector," gives detailed treatment to France and a comparison of bureaucratic cultures in Europe and Africa.

✦ New to the Fourteenth Edition

Over the decades since I first wrote this book, the world has proved to be a strange and wonderful place—even more than I realized at that time. The book has seen the joy and light of the young people who pulled down the Berlin Wall in 1989 and the darkness of the suicide attackers who destroyed the World Trade Center in 2001. As it has evolved across a number of editions during this time, very little that it started out with has remained unchanged. Its mood has also varied from time to time, but one thing that has been constant is my faith in people's capacity to shape their futures through politics.

In this fourteenth edition there is, of course, a great deal of updating. When a book deals with all the states of the world, much changes over even a couple of years. I have updated the fallout from the 2008–2009 worldwide economic crisis, Russia, the Arab Spring, new elections in Mexico and other states, and many other topics.

More substantial changes include:

- a new section on media and political socialization
- reorganization of the global politics chapter
- a new example: Egypt and the Arab Spring
- new treatment of the principal-agent problem
- new treatment of soft power

I long wrestled with what might seem like a small matter, but is not: what to call states that are not democracies. "Non-democracy" is clunky. "Authoritarian system" risks confusion with "authoritarian democracy," which is too important a concept to omit. In past editions I have used "autocracy" as a compromise, though it is not literally accurate. Starting with the thirteenth edition, I decided I really had to make a choice, and opted for "authoritarian system." I hope this works for you.

✦ Supplements

For the Instructor

Instructor's Online Learning Center. This password-protected, Web-based supplement offers access to important instructor support materials and downloadable supplements. Visit www.mhhe.com/shively14e for a comprehensive Instructor's Manual, Test Bank, Computerized Test Bank, and PowerPoint lecture slides.

✦ ACKNOWLEDGMENTS

I have been very pleased by the response to this book. It is a wonderful experience to run into people who have used it and feel that it has helped them. I benefited greatly from comments by the reviewers of the fourteenth edition, who will notice many of their suggestions have been incorporated.

W. Phillips Shively

The Idea of Politics

PART I

The Idea of Politics

CHAPTER 1

POLITICS: SETTING THE STAGE

Everyone knows something about politics, and many people know a great deal about it. It is an interesting, amusing, and moving spectacle that sometimes even supplants professional sports in the public eye. Political scientists, however, study politics and analyze it. This involves doing pretty much the same sorts of things that other people do who follow politics: we read the newspapers, listen to press conferences, and take part in political campaigns. However, we also do some things differently. We usually try to see both sides of any question and to keep our emotions in low key, because emotions can cloud judgment. We borrow deliberately from other disciplines—such as economics, history, sociology, psychology, and philosophy—to help us understand what is going on politically. Above all, as you will see later in this chapter, we try to be precise about the meanings of the words we use. Many words having to do with politics—such as "liberal," "represent," and even "politics"—are quite complex, but most people use them unthinkingly. Political scientists are careful to analyze the varied meanings of such words and to use them precisely, partly because it is important to know exactly what we mean by the words we use and partly because careful examination of a richly complex word may teach us a lot about the things it describes.

What do political scientists study? Over the years, we have seen work in which political scientists:

- Measured just how much it actually costs a country to lose a war.
- Devised a new system of voting in primaries that might have led to a different set of candidates for most presidential elections.
- Analyzed and explained the various styles that members of the U.S. Congress adopt in dealing with their constituents.
- Studied the spread of stem-cell research laws across the states.

2   PART I   THE IDEA OF POLITICS

- Showed that the roots of successful government may go back to social institutions several centuries ago.
- Showed why most nations ignore warnings about surprise military action by hostile nations.
- Studied why democracies almost never wage war on other democracies.

These are the sorts of things in which political scientists engage. This book introduces you to the broad principles of what we have learned about politics, especially about the politics of democracies like the United States. I hope the study will sharpen and enrich the more general understanding of politics that you already have.

This first chapter, in particular, involves the precise definition of several words with which you are already somewhat familiar. We must examine these definitions because you should start your study with some basic terms in place. You may also find it intriguing to see complexity in words, such as politics, that have probably not struck you before as particularly complicated.

✦ POLITICS

What is **politics**? What is it that makes an act political? Consider the following questions, all of which involve politics. What do these have in common?

- How was Hitler able to take power through a series of supposedly democratic elections?
- Why does the U.S. Congress so often disagree with the president in framing energy policies?
- Why should workers sort letters the way their boss directs if they know a more efficient way?
- Why were southern blacks denied the vote and placed in segregated schools throughout the 1950s while at the same time their housing was not as segregated as that in the North?
- Should homosexuals be barred from the military?
- Should fascists be banned from teaching in the schools?
- Why does the United States have only two major political parties when most democracies have more?
- Should state and local governments have the right to force landholders to sell them land that they need for public purposes?
- Was Harry Truman right to bomb Hiroshima and Nagasaki?
- Why do people so often feel guilty about not doing what their parents want them to do?

These questions deal with politics. The questions about bosses and parents may not have looked to you as if they belonged in this group, but their connection with politics should become clearer by the end of this chapter.

What is it that these questions have in common? There are two main things, and scholars have often used both as the defining characteristics of politics. First, all the questions involve making a common decision for a group of people, that is, a uniform decision applying in the same way to all members of the group. Second, all involve the use of power by one person or a group of people to affect the behavior of another person or group of people. Let us look at both of these in more detail.

⤳ POLITICS AS THE MAKING OF COMMON DECISIONS

Any group of people must often make decisions that will apply to all of them in common, as a group. A family must decide where to live, what sorts of rules to set for children, and how to balance a budget. A class in a college or university (including the instructor as part of the "class") must decide on the required reading material, how to grade students, and the brightness of lights in the classrooms. A country must decide where to locate parks, what allies to seek out in war, how to raise revenue by taxing its citizens, how to care for the helpless, and many other things. Each of these requires setting common policy for the group, a single decision that affects all members of the group.

Not all human actions, of course, involve making a common policy for a group. When one brother teases another, he is not making a family policy, nor is a family member who decides to write the great American novel. A student who decides to read extra material on one section of the course (or, perhaps, to skip a bit of the reading) is not making a policy of the class. A person's decision to build a new house is not part of any common national policy, although the country may have policies—on interest rates, the regulation of building, land use, and zoning that affect this person's decision. Ford Motor Company's decisions on new-car styling are not part of a common national policy.

Those actions that contribute to the making of a common policy for a group of people constitute politics, and questions about those policies and the making of those policies are political questions. The political/nonpolitical distinction is not always easy to draw. The Ford Motor Company example above is tricky because Ford is so large that its decisions verge on being common policy for the whole United States, even though the company has no formal role in the nation's government. In other words, one might argue that because the U.S. government tolerates the concentration of our automobile industry among a few giant corporations and because (as a result of this) the decisions of any one of them bulk large in American life, those decisions have a quasi-public character and are "sort of" political.

Another tricky aspect of the political/nonpolitical distinction is that it is also a matter of perspective. Ford's design decisions are not (except via Ford's quasi-public nature) political decisions for the United States; but they are political decisions for Ford's stockholders, managers, and workers, because they set a common policy for the company. A family's decision to build a house is not a political decision for the country, but it is a political decision for the family as a group inasmuch as it involves a common policy for the family. "Company politics" is involved in Ford's decision, and "family politics" is involved in the family's decision. Neither, however, is a national political decision. Society consists of groups within groups within groups. Ford Motor Company is a group within the United States, and a family may be a group within the larger group of those dependent on Ford. Politics exists within any of these groups whenever they make a decision that will apply to all the members of the group. Depending upon which group you are thinking of, you may treat a given decision—the decision of the Clauski family to build a house—as either political or nonpolitical. The Clauski decision is political for the family as a group but not political for the country.

✦ POLITICS AS THE EXERCISE OF POWER

A second characteristic of politics, one that runs through the questions at the start of this chapter, is that politics always involves the exercise of power by one person or persons over another person or persons. **Power** is the ability of one person to cause another to do what the first wishes, by whatever means. Politics always involves this: one person causing others to do what that person wants. Looking back at the questions, we note that Hitler rose to high office by convincing many Germans to vote for him; the U.S. Congress disagrees with the president so often about energy policy because the president does not have much power either to force or to convince Congress to go along with his wishes in that area; and so on. In such ways, each of these questions involves the power of one person or persons over others.

The two defining characteristics of politics, then, are that (1) politics always involves the making of common decisions for groups of people and (2) those decisions are made by some members of the group exercising power over other members of the group. Power can consist of a wide variety of tools that help one person affect the actions of another. Power may be stark, as when a police officer stops a demonstrator from marching up the street; or it may be subtle, as when a group of poor people, by their very misery, elicit positive governmental action on their behalf.

We may exercise power as coercion when we force a person to do something he or she did not want to do, as persuasion when we convince someone that that is what she or he really wishes to do, or as the construction of incentives when we make the alternative so unattractive that only one reasonable option remains. The ability to exercise any of these forms of power may be based on all sorts of things—money, affection, physical strength, legal status (the power of a police officer to direct traffic, for instance), the possession of important information, a winning smile, strong allies, determination, desperation (which helped North Vietnam to defeat the United States in the 1970s), and many more. Any of these can help some people convince other people to act as they wish.

It is not necessary to learn the specific bases of power I have listed here. They are meant to provide a sense of the variety and complexity of power, not as an exhaustive list of its important sources. The point is that all politics involves the use of power, and such power may take varied forms.

Implicit and Manifest Power

Power need not consist of any observable link at all between the people or groups involved. Scholars distinguish between **manifest power** and **implicit power**. Manifest

CHAPTER 1 POLITICS: SETTING THE STAGE 5

power is based on an observable action by A that leads B to do what A wants. A police officer's signal that causes a driver to stop and wait is an example of manifest power. In the case of implicit power, B does what A desires not because of anything A says or does but because (1) B senses that A wants something done and (2) for any of a variety of reasons B wishes to do what A wants done. Many examples of implicit power are found in families, whose members are so attuned to one another that there is often no observable communication between members who yet manage to "read" and comply with one another's wishes. A father may toss the car keys to his daughter on Saturday morning completely unprompted except by his knowledge of her habits and his desire to comply with her wishes. As she drives, the daughter may obey the 55 miles-per-hour speed limit because she knows that her parents feel strongly about it. In neither case is there any overt signal from one family member to the other.

A famous example of implicit power in a broader sphere of politics comes from the reign of King Henry II of England. The king had been involved in a series of disputes with Thomas à Becket, the Archbishop of Canterbury. Henry exclaimed one day, "Will no one rid me of this man?" Four of his knights overheard what the king said and proceeded to murder Becket. Historians still dispute whether the king really wished to have Becket killed.

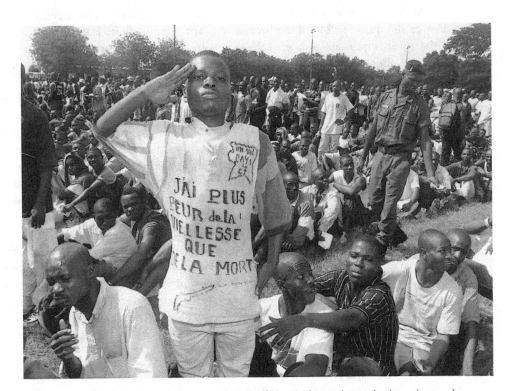

Politics as power: a child-soldier abducted and forced to fight. His shirt reads, in either bravado or pathos, "I fear old age more than death."
©AP Photo/Boris Heger

What is most important and interesting about implicit power is that an observer would have a hard time deciding whether or not power has been exercised in any particular instance. The source of implicit power may lie far away from its exercise. To understand why the daughter drives 55 miles per hour, for instance, we might have to look back to her early childhood. We can analyze power easily in the case of one country telling another, "Cede the province Anemone to us or we'll invade you." We cannot so easily analyze it if the resources on which it is based are varied and complex, as in the power of a defeated Iraq to draw economic aid from the United States, or if it is in whole or in part implicit, as in the king's muttered remark in the presence of his soldiers.

An Example of the Difficulty of Analyzing Power

Both because power is important to politics and because it is difficult to measure precisely how and when power is exercised, there are recurrent disputes within political science about how much power various groups have. A famous dispute of the 1950s and 1960s centered on American cities, about which scholars asked: "Is there a small group of people [the "downtown people," the political bosses, or what have you] who run things in American cities?" This might seem like a simple question, but it was difficult for political scientists to answer, and we still do not have a clear answer to it. In a broader form, the dispute has continued to this day.

The dispute started when in a study of Atlanta, Georgia, Floyd Hunter attempted to answer the question by asking journalists, officials, business leaders, and others who the most important people in the city were.[1] When his varied sources named roughly the same set of leaders, he concluded that Atlanta was run by a small group of insiders.

In response, however, Robert Dahl observed that Hunter's respondents might all be mistaken, but mistaken in the same way; they might think that the downtown corporate elite ran Atlanta because that idea was part of the conventional wisdom about the city, but they might be wrong. That the downtown people had a reputation for power did not prove to Dahl's satisfaction that they really had power; rather, he said, we must actually see power being used. As a response to the earlier Atlanta study, he performed a new study of his own based on New Haven, Connecticut.[2] He chose a set of major issues that faced the community which included education and urban renewal, and recorded who participated in making decisions on each type of issue. He was restricting himself to observable power; therefore, he had to ignore the possibility of implicit power. Other than that, his procedure was straightforward. He found that quite different groups of people were active on the different issues. Parents and "society people" were especially involved in education, for example, while downtown people were especially involved in urban renewal. He concluded that New Haven was not run by a single group of insiders but that all sorts of groups were involved, moving in and out of participation depending on what issue was up for decision.

---

[1]Floyd Hunter, *Community Power Structure* (Chapel Hill: University of North Carolina Press, 1953). Note that the politics of Atlanta today is very different from that which Hunter described in 1953. The most obvious difference is that Atlanta has now had black mayors for many years. The power structure Hunter described was all white.
[2]Robert Dahl, *Who Governs?* (New Haven: Yale University Press, 1961).

Still a third position was then staked out in the dispute. Peter Bachrach and Morton S. Baratz criticized Dahl's study of New Haven, noting that it is not enough just to see who has been active in various kinds of decisions but that we must also investigate why particular issues get raised in the first place.[3] Perhaps the most important decision is the one that governs which issues will be brought before the public. For instance, during the period Dahl studied, New Haven did not consider any policies for taking over utilities and running them publicly, for breaking up the residential racial segregation of the city, or for cutting taxes. An ability to influence or control the public agenda in this way gives one great power over public policies. Who has this ability? Political leaders? The media? Teachers and professors? Bloggers? At this level, decisions may or may not be controlled by a small "power elite"; we simply cannot tell from a study designed as Dahl designed his.

This question of which issues enter public debate is crucial to politics. Larry Bartels notes, for example, that the American people value economic equality and think of equality as one of the characteristic virtues of American society. Yet, economic inequality is greater in the United States than in almost any other prosperous, advanced economy in the world, and has increased sharply since 1980.[4] How is it, then, that economic inequality has not become a major issue in the press or in popular opinion? Bartels shows that the failure to bring this issue to the fore has affected American politics profoundly.

Beyond the complexity that such control of agendas adds to the concept of power, Peter Digeser, drawing on the work of Steven Lukes, has suggested a "third face of power." Taking Bachrach and Baratz beyond the notion of an elite controlling the agenda of discussion about different groups' needs and wants, Digeser points out that the process they describe might consist of an elite controlling ideas and public opinion such that it does not even occur to some groups to want the things they should want: "Lukes contended that power could be exerted even if B consciously wants to do what A desires. Lukes claimed that if B acts contrary to her objective, real interest then power is being exercised."[5] In other words, an elite might exercise power not just by preventing discussion of proposals it does not want to see on the table, but by influencing what people want so that inconvenient proposals never occur to them in the first place. The test for Digeser (based on Lukes) is not whether people have proposals that never reach the table, but whether the things people want are contrary to their real interests. Such a disjunction between people's wants and their real interests, for Digeser, is the footprint of elite power. That is to say, the elite maintains its power by controlling communications and ideas, such that people do not want (do not realize they need) things that threaten the elite. Of course, this becomes remarkably difficult to analyze, because it requires us to identify what people really need as distinct from what they merely think they need. Academics, who have very distinctive values of our own, are not always in a good position to judge other people's "true" needs.

---

[3]Peter Bachrach and Morton S. Baratz, "The Two Faces of Power," *American Political Science Review* 56 (1962): 947–53.
[4]Larry M. Bartels, *Unequal Democracy: The Political Economy of the New Gilded Age* (Princeton, NJ: Princeton University Press, 2008).
[5]Peter Digeser, "The Fourth Face of Power," *Journal of Politics* 54 (November 1992), p. 980. The reference to Lukes is Steven Lukes, *Power: A Radical View* (London: Macmillan, 1974).

Notice how complex the question of power in American cities has become. Hunter gave us a very straightforward assessment of Atlanta. Dahl complicated the issue by pointing out that in New Haven different types of people had dominant power with respect to different kinds of issues. Bachrach and Baratz reminded us that we must also consider who controls which issues will even come up for discussion. And Digeser added the consideration that this control might operate at an unconscious level, in elite control of how people form their very desires. In the end, it is difficult to say anything general and conclusive about the concentration of power in our cities because it is difficult to study what might have been—what issues might have entered public discussion but did not. This series of studies illustrates clearly the inherent complexity of power.[6]

Although these studies certainly show that there are few blanket truths about power, one should not therefore conclude that power is impossible to study. Rather, an understanding of the complexity of power and the difficulty of measuring it can lead us to detailed examinations of very specific instances of power. In response to the Bachrach and Baratz article, for instance, several interesting studies appeared on the setting of agendas in American politics. These were a direct result of the argument that the most important power is that which decides what issues will be up for debate.

Despite the complexity and elusiveness of power, we can say that all politics is based on some form of power and that its sources may be highly varied. For most questions about politics, it is not necessary to specify in detail exactly what sort of power is involved. It is always helpful to bear in mind that you are dealing with power of one sort or another; but that realization may often serve rather as a background or setting for your analysis. We can address most of the questions posed at the opening of this chapter without conducting precise analyses of the power relationships that form contexts for the questions.

Interpreting Politics as Choice of a Common Decision

Although power is difficult to pin down in observations, conceptually it is rather simple: One person manages, by some means or another, to get another person to do (or not do) what the first one wants. We have seen above that identifying the "some means or another" can be difficult, but the concept itself is fairly simple.

When we seek to interpret politics as a "choice," however, we find that the concept itself is a bit hard to get our minds around. Just what do we mean by choice? When we view a political outcome as a matter of choice, we explain the outcome by the fact that it was needed, either by society as a whole or at least by some politically significant figures. That is, the result came about because, to a significant set of people (possibly all of the people) it should have happened. On the face of it, this sounds mystical. We know that causation must always work forward in time, but here we say that the need for something brought about the actions that would produce it!

---

[6]Digeser goes on to describe still another approach to power (this is his "fourth face")—that of Michel Foucault, who develops a rich but elusive concept in which our definition of ourselves and of our very interests results from others' exercise of power over us. That is, the elite can maintain hegemony not only over what people want, but also over how they define themselves. At this point, analysis becomes difficult—some would say it collapses—because nothing is anchored.

The choice interpretation, however, is really a shorthand for many factors that led various people to act, all of which had to do with the fact that they felt the need to bring something about.

Thus, you will see in Chapter 3 that one explanation (the "choice" explanation) for why powerful governments developed in the fifteenth to eighteenth centuries in Europe was that modern large-scale commerce and industry arose in Europe at about that time, and powerful governments holding sway over broad territories were necessary if the commerce and industry were to operate efficiently. This does not mean that in some mystical way the need called forth the strong governments. Rather, kings could extend and deepen their power because large, significant groups in the society (merchants, factory owners) felt they would benefit from a strong king and supported him in extending his power. In other words, the need for strong governments brought them about—but not in some mystical way. Rather, many individual exercises of power brought about the "choice" outcome.

As another example, you will see in Chapter 14 that parliamentary government works most smoothly when prime ministers can control tightly how individual members vote. As a result—in a "choice" interpretation—most parliamentary systems have developed tightly disciplined parties. This does not mean that the need, in some mystical way, produced the disciplined parties. Rather, over a number of years and by trial and error, prime ministers found that their lives were easier if their political parties were tightly disciplined, and they devised all sorts of rewards and punishments to keep their party members in line.

In principle, each of these examples could have been reduced to a large number of relatively small individual power transactions. However, that would almost certainly have meant missing the forest for the trees. The central process running through all the individual power transactions was that patterns of behavior were reshaped to meet the needs either of society as a whole or of significant and powerful parts of society. A "choice" interpretation captures that truth in a way that analyzing thousands of small power transactions could not.[7]

We see that "choice" actually involves "power," because it is through power events that we reach the "choice" outcome. The "choice" perspective has some advantages, however. First, as we have seen above, it is sometimes more efficient than power in helping us to see the big picture. Second, it emphasizes that politics meets needs. From a purely power perspective, we can easily lose the role of needs in shaping politics.

✦ POWER AND CHOICE

Politics, then, consists of making common decisions for a group through the use of power. Although the concept involves some complexity, it will usually be clear to everyone concerned whether a given action is or is not political in this sense. From the two parts

---

[7]A choice interpretation in political science is analogous to the statement of an evolutionary biologist that a certain tree has developed sweet fruit buds to reward and attract ants that will keep its leaves free of caterpillars. No one believes that the tree thinks this through in that way, of course. Rather, the end result is the culmination of millions of events of natural selection in the species over the years. The biologist's statement gives a true understanding that would be lost in an enumeration (even if that were possible) of all the selection events.

"Because this family isn't ready to hold democratic elections—that's why!"

of our definition there stem two basic ways of looking at the making of such common policies, and people often emphasize one or the other of these in evaluating any particular political action. In so doing, they may fail to consider how their viewpoint colors their conclusions. The two alternative viewpoints are as follows:

1. We may interpret political action as a way to work out rationally the best common solution to a common problem—or at least a way to work out a reasonable common solution. That is, politics consists of public choice. (Even though this perspective emphasizes the cooperative aspect of decisions, power will still be involved in the making of choices, as I noted above; if nothing else, the power to persuade will be involved; and of course some of the "public" will undoubtedly have had more power than others and will have tipped things in favor of their needs.)

2. We may interpret political action as a process through which some people are dominated by other people. That is, politics consists simply of the use of power. Here we often think of power as power through coercion.

In other words, two people who observe the same political action from these opposing viewpoints might have different ideas of what is happening. For instance, a person operating from the choice viewpoint might look at the large number of people who fail to vote in American presidential elections and conclude that this is a reasonably healthy situation, because if such a large number of people have chosen not to bother voting, they must be tolerably satisfied with things as they are. Someone else, operating from the "power" viewpoint, might look at that same large number of nonvoters and conclude that American elections are a sham, that they are meant to give the appearance of popular choice without providing the voter with significantly different options (i.e., many voters do not bother to vote because their choices have been restricted).

Most often, both viewpoints are partly accurate. Politics generally involves considering at least the broad needs of the group for whom policy is made: Pure tyranny is rare and is difficult to maintain. At the same time, making a common policy generally means that one part of a group is dominating another part to at least some extent. In the previous presidential voting example, both characterizations probably have some truth to them.

It is good to bear these two perspectives in mind, because we may then be able to avoid misjudging a particular political situation as all one or the other. For example, a college or university class is a group for which common policies must be made and in which a single person (the instructor) is formally charged with responsibility. Thus, the group's politics will largely consist of domination of the students by the instructor, based on the authority of her role as professor. However, the class is not solely or simply a system of domination, because there are a number of informal mechanisms by which students participate in decision making. In short, the politics of a classroom also includes aspects of a rational working out of solutions to common problems. Such questions as the timing of tests, whether or not to close doors or leave the lights on, or the nature of special projects and examinations are often decided by the instructor in consultation with the students. In less direct ways, students—by their expressions of interest—often influence the content or pace of a class. (Never underestimate the effect of paper shuffling two minutes before the end of a class.) Thus, although the politics of a classroom consist primarily of domination, there is also some element of a common search for solutions to common problems. We might overlook this if we were not alert to the two sides of politics.

An example of this problem is raised by Terry M. Moe, who argues that a popular theory (rational choice theory, which we will discuss in Chapter 5) emphasizes "choice" too much at the expense of "power." One of the concerns of this body of theory is the question of why institutions like Congress, the Presidency, bureaucracies, and the like are set up as they are. The theory emphasizes voluntary choice in setting up such institutions; it sees them as evolving in order to solve problems of coordinating varied people's actions to obtain coherent policies. This is clearly a "choice" perspective, in that it explains the way institutions are set up by a need for coherent policy making. But as Moe points out, while this benign view may be part of the story, institutions are also shaped by powerful political figures to get things they want. The absence of such a "power" perspective is a serious flaw in the theory.[8]

It is especially important to bear in mind these two points of view when we consider political actions about which we have strong feelings and about which we may

---

[8]Terry M. Moe, "Power and Political Institutions," *Perspectives on Politics* 3 (June 2005), p. 214.

expect to be prejudiced. Until the opening up of democratic elections in the Soviet Union, for instance, Americans tended to dismiss elections in communist countries as simple fraud, since voters could only vote for a single candidate, with no electoral competition for their votes. However, there was also evident in those elections a surprising element of broad participation in a search for common action. For instance, even during the period of noncompetitive elections, with only a single candidate on the ballot, 28 percent of Soviet citizens reported that they had at one time or another attempted to persuade others to vote as they did; 19 percent had contacted a state or national government official about some problem.[9] "The weeks preceding the election see the formation of countless study circles, discussion groups, campaign meetings, door-to-door canvassing, rallies, demonstrations, and speeches."[10] There appears to have been something more to the Soviet Union's uncontested elections than we were able to see at the time.

Another example of emotions leading us to think of politics not as an interplay among power and choice, but just as one or the other, is furnished by Iraq at the time of the second Gulf War in 2003. The U.S. government focused so strongly on Saddam Hussein as a brutal dictator, ruling by the power of coercion, that they assumed victorious American troops would be greeted by jubilant crowds of grateful Iraqis. In their intense dislike of Saddam Hussein, they forgot that although he did indeed maintain his regime by unspeakable violence, the basis of his rule was more complex than that. He was not only a brutal dictator, but at the same time a focus of national unity and nationalism; some parts of the country had been favored by his regime (although others had suffered); and he was seen as having maintained order in a potentially violent territory. The resulting mixed reaction to American troops—relief at the end of Saddam Hussein's oppression, but anger at the breakdown in security and the presence of a foreign army of occupation—caught the U.S. government by surprise, and left it unprepared for the rise of a crippling insurgency.

Bearing in mind that there is almost always more to any political choice than just the exercise of power, or just the provision of a collective choice, helps us to remain alert to more varied possibilities even when we know we are strongly prejudiced about a subject.

To summarize this section of the chapter: Politics consists of making a common decision for a group of people through the use of power. We may view any act of politics from two perspectives, either as a search for an answer to common problems or as an act by which some members of a group impose their will on other members of the group. It is important to remember that generally both viewpoints have at least some validity. It is especially important to remember this when we might be prejudiced about the subject at hand, because keeping both viewpoints in mind can help us to avoid thinking about the subject in narrow, prejudiced ways. Power and choice, the two major themes by which we organize our views of politics, have provided the title of this book. They will recur in succeeding chapters as we examine various aspects of politics.

---

[9]Richard D. Little, "Mass Political Participation in the U.S. and the U.S.S.R.," *Comparative Political Studies* (January 1976), p. 439.
[10]Ibid.

The Concentration of Power in Leaders

The use of power is surprisingly universal, even in determining common decisions for very large groups of people. People around the world do not vary much in physical strength and intelligence. They are more or less equal in their basic talents. Yet millions of them will fear and obey another person whose intrinsic capacities are little superior to theirs.

It is understandable that this should be so within families because of the weakness and inexperience of children. The adult members of a family are stronger than the children, and it is perhaps natural that they should be able to control them. However, it is astounding that large numbers of adults will grant this sort of control over their own actions to a military officer, a member of Congress, a dictator, or a religious leader. How is it that political power is so universal and often so concentrated in small numbers of people?[11]

Simply posing the question in this way demonstrates once again that the bases of power must be varied and complex. Physical compulsion alone would not be sufficient to ensure the obedience that people all over the world give to their political leaders.

Authority and Government

The thing that makes it possible to concentrate power in this way is **authority.** A person (or a group of people) has authority if there is general agreement among those involved that she has the right to control certain decisions and that her decisions in those areas should be complied with. Various individuals or groups in a society have limited sorts of authority that extend over specific ranges of behavior. A parent has authority to tell children of a certain age when they should go to bed or with whom they should play, but as children grow older the range of activities over which a parent has authority dwindles until it disappears. A teacher in a classroom has the authority to tell students how they should prepare for classes, but the teacher does not have the authority to tell them whom they may date or what political candidate to support. A General Motors supervisor has the authority to tell an assembly-line worker which bolts to tighten, but he cannot tell the worker how to spend coffee breaks; and when the worker resigns, the supervisor has no authority at all.

In contrast to such groups, a **government** is a group of people with ultimate authority within a territory. It is unique in society in that all of its power involves authority, and at least potentially, there is no limit to the range of activities over which it may exercise authority. Most governments themselves impose some limits on their authority; for instance, the U.S. government, in its Constitution, rules out the exercise of authority over what religion people are to follow or what people are to say to each other. However, these limitations are self-imposed and not necessarily "natural" to governments. Many governments around the world, at one time or another, have claimed authority to tell people what religion they should follow, what they should or should not say to one another, what sort of sexual activity was permitted, what they might eat or drink, or the sports and recreation in which they could take part. It is safe to say that there is no area of human activity over which some government or another has not at some time exercised authority.

---

[11]R. M. MacIver, *The Web of Government* (New York: Macmillan, 1967), chap. 1.

Authority is so pervasive and important because it is an efficient way to exercise power. It provides a "standard operating procedure" for power, in which a decision does not require any direct use of force, making of arguments, or construction of incentives. Authority allows smooth day-to-day decisions on many questions with minimal spinning of wheels. It may be backed up ultimately by the threat of coercion (the police will haul you off and punish you physically if you do not do what those in authority tell you to do), or it may be backed up ultimately by persuasion (if you keep your well clean, as the government tells you to do, you will be sick less often). However, if people do what the government tells them to do, without having to be coerced or persuaded, everything goes more smoothly and—at least from the government's point of view— more satisfactorily. In general, authority does not require the actual use of coercion or persuasion to any great extent. No one has to stand at street corners to force cars to stop at red lights, and no one has to stand there to persuade them to do so. One of the things that makes a government so important to politics is that it has authority and therefore can ensure that people will comply with its commands with a minimum of expensive and time-consuming coercion or persuasion.

People do obey governmental authority. Actions against authority are by definition "outlaw" behavior and therefore extraordinary, so we can think of many vivid examples of refusals to obey authority—burglary, speeding on the highways, or tax evasion. The startling thing, however, is that few people steal things even when it would be safe to do so, most people drive at or near speed limit even though only a sprinkling of police are available to monitor what they are doing, and most people pay the taxes they owe. It is authority that makes this system of commands and obedience work as smoothly as it does, and this makes the modern state appear to us to be the most natural form of political organization.

Authority is not a simple thing that is either present or absent. Rather, it is a matter of degree. Remember that authority exists because it is "generally agreed on"; that is, most people believe it exists. There will probably never be a government for which every person agrees on the existence and range of the government's authority. Sometimes when a government issues commands, a portion of the people do not accept its authority to do so. If enough people deny the authority of the government, there is a problem. In the early part of the twentieth century, the government of the United States attempted to command people not to drink alcohol. So many people denied the authority of the government in this area that enforcement proved impossible and the law was eventually abandoned. More seriously, in the 1860s, the whole southern region of the United States denied that the national government had any authority over it at all. The states in that region set up their own new government instead, and it took a long and bloody Civil War to reestablish the authority of the U.S. government over them.

Legitimacy and Authority

The crux of government then, and of its ability to function effectively, is the government's wide-ranging authority to organize the lives of its people. Paradoxically, this authority exists only because the people believe it to exist and that it is appropriate. If authority were to fail, it might still be possible for a government to organize its people by coercion and persuasion but at such great cost that this approach could probably not be sustained. A pure tyranny, existing without the benefit of at least some degree of authority, probably could not last long.

It is crucial to a government that large numbers of its people should believe not only that it has authority, but that it properly *should* have that authority. We call the existence of this sort of feeling, to the extent that it does exist, the **legitimacy** of the government. Legitimacy, like authority itself, is a matter of degree. Not everyone in a state will necessarily always agree that its government is legitimate or that a given type of governmental act is legitimate. Much of the violence of politics in Afghanistan, for instance, is a result of a failure to agree on what sort of government is legitimate.

Sources of Legitimacy

How does a government achieve a reasonable degree of legitimacy? There are many ways by which the people's allegiance may be bound to a government so that it is considered legitimate.

1. *Legitimacy by Results.* First and foremost, a government may gain and retain legitimacy with its people by providing for them the things they most want: security against physical assault, security of their country's borders against invasion, pride in their nation, and economic security. If the government can provide these things, its legitimacy will be greatly strengthened. If it cannot, its legitimacy is likely to be called into question.

A good example of "legitimacy by results" is the rule of Adolf Hitler in Germany in the 1930s. In 1933, Hitler took power through dubious maneuvers and with at most a bare majority of support. The highest number of votes the Nazi party had received in a fully free election was 37 percent—enough to make it the largest party in the country but not a mandate for dictatorship. Once in power, Hitler could initially count on the free support of only about one-third of the Germans, and powerful forces were arrayed against him—the labor unions, the Catholic Church, much of the army's general staff. Hitler was a monster, but what solidified his hold on Germany and gave him a degree of legitimacy by the end of the 1930s were the results of his early policies. He reduced unemployment by large-scale deficit spending; by some audacious bluffs, he outmaneuvered France and England and reestablished Germany as a great power; he built the autobahn system of superhighways; he even pioneered the Volkswagen "beetle" automobile. In spite of his suppression of free speech, his oppression of Jews, and his crude party comrades, these accomplishments brought him widespread support from the German people. By the late 1930s, it probably would have been impossible for anyone to seek to overthrow his rule. It was not until 1944, when he had obviously lost World War II, that a group of generals were able to muster sufficient strength to try to depose him; even then, the attempt failed.

2. *Legitimacy by Habit.* Once a government has existed for a while, people become accustomed to obeying its laws. People expect to operate under some government or other, and so whatever government is in place and has been obeyed in the past is likely to be regarded as legitimate—unless a particular crisis arises or some force (another state, perhaps) intervenes from outside. In other words, once a particular government has been in place for a while, and people have developed the habit of obeying it, it no longer has to perpetually justify its existence. Rather, the burden of proof lies with whoever would propose an alternative government. The existing government remains

Legitimacy by results: Adolf Hitler dedicates his latest project, the Volkswagen; Fallersleben, Germany, 1938.

© Underwood & Underwood/Corbis

legitimate unless and until a compelling alternative comes along. We should not underestimate the importance of habit in maintaining governments in power.[12]

3. *Legitimacy by Historical, Religious, or Ethnic Identity.* Many governments enhance their legitimacy by the ties that exist between themselves and the people because of the government leaders' past accomplishments (their historic role) or because of the religious and/or ethnic similarity between the government leaders and the people.

This may be especially important when a government has not yet been in place long enough for the people to have developed the habit of treating it as legitimate and in which the many economic and social problems that plague most new countries make it difficult for the government to achieve legitimacy by results.

Many new governments are able to buy time by virtue of the status they acquired in leading the country into independence in the first place. George Washington was revered as the "father of his country" after his success as commander of the Revolutionary Army. He and his associates enjoyed a couple of decades in which the people of the United States regarded them as their natural government, and this allowed them

---

[12]Also, a government that is in place is usually able to foster a supportive mythology. See, for example, Barry Schwartz, *George Washington: The Making of an American Symbol* (New York: Free Press, 1982), and Lisa Wedeen, *Ambiguities of Domination: Politics, Rhetoric and Symbols in Contemporary Syria* (Chicago: University of Chicago Press, 1999).

to get the Constitution into place and establish among the people the habit of obeying it. Similarly, the Labor Party in Israel, the Congress Party in India, the party of Julius Nyerere in Tanzania, and the National Liberation Front in Algeria had a breathing space in which the people accepted their governments because they had led the independence movements that established their states in the first place. A government may also use religious or ethnic ties to enhance its legitimacy. In Iran, the regime used its ties to the dominant Shiite Muslim sect and has played on antagonisms between the Persian majority in the country and the Arab populations in the rest of the Mideast to strengthen its legitimacy. Similarly, South Africa's former, white-dominated government long used whites' fears of blacks to strengthen its legitimacy among the white population.

4. *Legitimacy by Procedures.* Finally, a government may strengthen its legitimacy by following certain procedures in setting itself up—procedures in which many people have confidence, so that they will start off with a fund of trust for any government that has been established along these lines.

The best example of this is democracy—a system in which the citizens participate in selecting their leaders and perhaps also in determining the country's policies. Typically, democratic governments are chosen by competitive elections in which citizens vote to decide which of various alternative leadership teams are to govern. Since the resulting government has won broader support than any alternative, it gains a strong base of legitimacy. It is the government "of the people."

The procedures of democratic election are what give such a government a good part of its legitimacy. One may dislike particular leaders or think their policies unwise, but it is hard to argue with their right to govern as long as they have been selected by the proper procedures.

Democratic government is the preeminent example of legitimacy by procedures— so preeminent that dictatorships often imitate democratic procedures through staged elections. At other times, other procedures have served as the basis for legitimacy; all that is important is that the procedure be accepted as appropriate. Until a few centuries ago, for instance, and still in a few countries, it was accepted that political leadership was most properly passed on by inheritance. One king ruled; when he died, his heir became the new king. This procedure was so important as a basis of legitimacy that great care was taken to lay out precise rules of inheritance; if no clear heir was available, the result was sometimes civil war.

✛ POLITICS OF THE STATE

One thing that has probably seemed odd to you in this chapter, right from its inclusion of family and workplace in the set of questions on page 2, is that I have defined some things as politics that we do not always think of under that heading. There is some variation in common usage of the word. We do not often think of family, workplace, or place of worship as political places, but we sometimes think of them that way. When we refer to "office politics," "campus politics," and "church politics," we mean activities that fit under the definition of politics presented in this chapter: the use of power to make common decisions for groups of people.

This broad use of the word politics fits the general definition presented in this chapter, but a much more common use of the word is narrower. If we say, "Frank went into politics," or "I'm fascinated by politics," we are not thinking of the family or corporation or place of worship. In this sense of the word we are referring only to the kind of politics that has to do with government of the state.

State has a special meaning in political science. It is not the same thing as the states of the United States; instead, it is what we commonly call a country. The United States is a state in this sense, as are France, Russia, Algeria, and Mexico. Political scientists prefer the word "state" to the more usual "country" because it is more precise. Except for the minor confusion of "states" in the United States, the word means just one thing. "Country," on the other hand, can mean a state like France or Canada; a region or type of place ("cattle country"); or the opposite of urban ("I live in the country").

We will look at the state in more detail in Chapter 3, but for now it is enough to note that the state is a particular kind of social group. Over the last few centuries, people have focused increasingly on the state of which they are citizens, and the state has determined more of what goes on in our lives. Several centuries ago, most people were almost unaware of the state in which they lived; they noticed it only if the king's soldiers marched through their fields. At that time, many large geographic areas could hardly be said to have been organized as states at all. Gradually, states have become more thoroughly organized and have demanded more from us. First, states became the prime focus of peace and war, maintaining peace within their borders and waging war with other states. Then, states also became the organizers of commerce and industry within their borders, regulating prices and the quality of products, and constructing roads and canals. Only for the last several decades has the state generally been expected by its citizens to maintain stability in the economy, guarantee employment, and keep the value of currency stable. A couple of centuries ago, events in the economy were treated as "acts of God," and the state was not much involved in them, but today the state is generally held responsible for economic conditions. The responsibilities of the state continue to grow. In the future might the weather, now treated as an "act of God," become part of the state's responsibility?

For better or worse, the state has become critically important to us, and its politics has taken on great importance. When we say "politics," we usually mean "politics of the state." Political science shares this general preoccupation with politics of the state. Although we will occasionally look at other sorts of politics in this book, we will direct most of our attention to the politics of the state. Remember the more general meaning of politics, however, and remember that in dealing with the state we will be looking at politics only in one of its forms, albeit its most important and most complex form.

✦ Political Science

Political science is the academic field that takes as its sole and general task the analysis of politics, especially the politics of the state. There has been continuing debate over how "scientific" political science should be. Some political scientists think that politics is so complex and involves such basic personal values that we should not try to pin it down to exact regularities. Rather, we should interpret each political event and idea more or less in and of itself, in a personal, subjective way. Such political scientists would model themselves upon historians, who interpret a particular sequence of events more or less in and of itself, seeking to retain the richness of its detail while making a general patterned interpretation of what process unfolded through the events. Or, upon anthropologists, who interpret a particular society and culture more or less in and of itself, seeking to retain the richness of its detail while making a general patterned interpretation of it.

Other political scientists think that their discipline should be more scientific, seeking out the basic essence of regularities across a whole set of events, even though this means sacrificing some of the rich detail with which each single event is laden. They think that the only way we will be able to explain and predict what happens in politics is to emphasize the underlying processes that a number of disparate events may have in common. These political scientists would model themselves on other social scientists such as economists, who analyze events simply as instances of general processes, which they treat in the abstract. Economists, for instance, prefer to deal at a general level with supply-and-demand theories rather than analyze specifically what happens in a given used car lot.

The first type of political scientists are sometimes called "interpretivists" (or often "qualitative"), the latter "behavioralists" (or "quantitative"). **Interpretive political scientists** are most likely to deal in historical and philosophical aspects of politics and to seek detailed, nonnumerical information on a few cases. **Behavioralists** lean more toward looking for broad patterns across cases and using statistical analyses of numerical information. They find numerical information especially attractive because it distills a set of complex details down into something very simple and basic—a number. Therefore, because behavioralists are looking for simple descriptions of basic processes, they see it as more useful to summarize party competition in many congressional districts with a single index number for each district than to try to digest masses of biography, newspaper accounts, and other sources from a few congressional races.

Do not view this picture as black and white. Political science does not consist of two warring camps, and most political scientists combine some element of "interpretivism" with some element of "behavioralism." However, there are different degrees of these among political scientists, which adds greatly to the variety of materials available in the field.

Whatever their preferred way of gathering information about the political world, all political scientists tend, in their thinking about politics, to emphasize broad generalization and abstraction. Political scientists pursue generalization through theory.

A **theory** is a statement linking specific instances to broader principles. **Empirical theories** are theories describing how things work in the world we observe. They are usually explanatory; that is, they have to do with why things happen as they do. This means they consist of causal statements of the form "X causes Y." (For more on causation, see the discussion in the appendix, pp. 423–425.) An example of an empirical theory addressing one of the questions from page 2—why does the United States have only two major political parties—would be: "Single-member-district-plurality (SMDP) electoral systems, by disadvantaging small parties, tend to reduce the number of political parties to two; since the United States has an SMDP electoral system, that tends to lead to a two-party system in the United States." You will meet the single-member-district-plurality electoral system in Chapter 10. For now, the point is that this is a causal statement (SMDP causes two-party systems) and it links the specific case (the United States, which has an SMDP electoral system) to a general principle.

Normative theories involve making a judgment about the world, not describing how it works. They address the question: "What should X be or do?" Again, these theories link specific cases to general principles. An example would be, "What sort of public health care plan should the United States have?" Normative theorists would answer this question by applying general principles, such as "governments should intervene as little as possible in people's lives" or "societies are good to the extent that everyone has equal chances in life," to the specific policy question.

The important thing to note here is that both of our major kinds of theory—normative and empirical—are statements that deal with specific instances by linking them to general principles. Our relatively strong reliance on theory is what sets political scientists apart from others, especially historians, who also deal with politics as a subject. Theories are the building blocks of political science, and you will find them throughout this book.

For practical purposes of curriculum and organization, the field of political science in the United States is divided into subfields according to the subjects in which political scientists specialize. The major subfields are:

- *American political behavior:* The study of individuals and nongovernmental organizations involved in politics and of why they do what they do. Studies of public opinion, elections, interest groups, and political parties fall under this heading.

- *American political institutions:* The study of national governmental bodies, the Congress, the presidency, the bureaucracy, and—in part—the courts.

- *American public law:* The study of legal reasoning and of why courts hand down the decisions they do.

- *American public policy:* The analysis of the product of politics—the policies that are laid down.

- *American state and local politics:* The study of all of the above, but at the level of "states" (such as California or Minnesota) and localities rather than the country as a whole.

- *Comparative politics:* The study of all of the above in any place but the United States. To lump together all aspects of politics outside of the United States is parochial, but that is what usually happens. Political scientists in other countries are as bad. For example, Swedish political scientists have many subdivisions of the study of Sweden, as do the French for France, and the Japanese for Japan.

- *International politics:* The study of politics between states—the making of common decisions for a group of states, for example, through wars and diplomacy.[13] "International politics" is the only subfield that does this; all of the previously listed subfields deal with politics within states, not between them.

- *Political theory:* The history of ideas about politics, and critical discussion of political values.

---

[13]International politics also includes other actors that operate beyond the state, such as the United Nations, international professional organizations, and humanitarian groups like Amnesty International. Such actors are growing in importance in international politics.

This book reviews the general findings of political science but blends U.S. politics and "comparative politics," treating the politics of all parts of the world (including the United States) comparatively.

✦ THE PLEASURES OF POLITICS

I have led you through some rather dry material in this chapter because it was necessary to start you off with clarity on a number of concepts. Frequently throughout this book you will find that we are working toward greater precision than we find in everyday language; this usually requires abstraction and may also seem a bit dry. I hope, however, that as we do this, you will remember—and I can communicate—what a fascinating and dramatic thing we are studying.

"The use of power to reach collective choices"—think what this phrase means. We are talking about struggles for the souls of nations. The "use of power" has meant eighteenth-century American author Henry David Thoreau going to prison to protest the United States' invasion of Mexico; underground resistance by the Catholic Church and the Communist Party against Nazi occupation troops in the Second World War; students braving police dogs and murderous assaults to integrate American businesses and public facilities in the 1960s; Mikhail Gorbachev and Boris Yeltsin juggling political coalitions to create democracy in the Soviet Union, where it had never been seen before; indigenous people in the mountains of Mexico confronting the government and the army to assert their rights. "Collective choices" have included the invention of democracy as a way to accomplish government by the people; the development of public education, park systems, public health—and also such horrors as the Nazis' murder of millions of Jews and other "undesirables."

I try in this book to write dispassionately about politics, because it is easier to keep a clear head that way, but a love of politics lies behind all of it. I switched from an English Literature major to political science in the 1960s because I was excited by John Kennedy's call for public service. I have remained a news "junkie" and sometime participant in politics ever since. The things we will be analyzing in the pages that follow involve real people devoting their energies to things in which they believe. While you will learn how to analyze what is happening in these events and to deal with the events dispassionately, I hope you will not forget the humanity that is moving through them.

KEY TERMS

politics
power
manifest power
implicit power
authority
government

legitimacy
state
political science
interpretive political
    scientists
behavioralists

theory
empirical theories
normative theories

FURTHER READING

Politics and Power

Dahl, Robert. *Modern Political Analysis.* 5th ed. New York: Prentice-Hall, 1990, chaps. 3 and 4.

Jones, Bryan D., and Baumgartner, Frank R. *The Politics of Attention: How Government Prioritizes Problems.* Chicago: University of Chicago Press, 2005.

MacIver, R. M. *The Web of Government,* rev. ed. New York: Free Press, 1965.

"Power." In *The International Encyclopedia of the Social Sciences.* David L. Sills, editor. New York: Macmillan, 1968.

Political Science

Annual Review of Political Science (Palo Alto, CA: Annual Reviews, serial) is a series that presents each year a collection of essays in which leading scholars review research and theory in their areas of political science.

Boix, Carles, and Stokes, Susan C. *The Oxford Handbook of Comparative Politics.* New York: Oxford University Press, 2007.

Goodin, Robert E., and Klingemann, Hans-Dieter, eds. *A New Handbook of Political Science.* New York: Oxford University Press, 1997.

Stepan, Alfred. *Arguing Comparative Politics.* New York: Oxford University Press, 2001.

 # BROAD WEBSITES OF GENERAL USE IN POLITICAL SCIENCE

Political Resources on the Net–Canada, myriad links to sites on Canadian politics and Canadian political science:
www.politicalresources.net/canada/canada.htm

The CIA's *World Factbook*, with assessments and data on every country of the world:
https://www.cia.gov/library/publications/the-world-factbook

The Library of Congress country studies:
http://lcweb2.loc.gov/frd/cs/cshome.html

The Center for the American Woman and Politics:
http://www.cawp.rutgers.edu/

Journalist Ron Gunzberger's grab bag of news, candidate biographies, and Web links:
http://www.politics1.com

BBC online news:
http://www.bbc.co.uk

The International Herald Tribune (an excellent newspaper):
http://global.nytimes.com/?iht

intute: social sciences. Links, articles, resources:
http://www.intute.ac.uk/social sciences/

A good page on political resources, based in Britain:
http://www.psr.keele.ac.uk/

CHAPTER 2

Modern Ideologies
and Political Philosophy

Most people approach politics through an **ideology**—an organized set of related ideas that modify one another. For instance, one person may believe that everyone is basically selfish, that politicians are all crooks, that a citizen owes nothing to the state, that it is all right to cheat on one's taxes, and that gun control is a bad thing because it keeps us from protecting ourselves. This is an ideology—a set of ideas about politics, all of which are related to one another and that modify and support each other. For example, the belief that everyone is basically selfish helps provide a justification for the need to carry a gun, or the wish to cheat on taxes helps make one comfortable in the belief that the citizen owes nothing to the state, and vice versa. Another person may believe that individual freedom is very important, that government should regulate people as little as possible, that the United States should try to protect any people whose government is oppressing them, and that the U.S. government should not tell people whether they may carry guns. This is also an ideology, an organized set of ideas that modify and support each other. In this second example, the high value placed on individual freedom supports both a wish to protect human rights around the world and a reluctance to have the government regulate gun ownership.

Ideologies are useful to people, both for their own personal ease and satisfaction and for their public political activities. From the personal point of view, an ideology helps us to make sense reasonably easily and quickly of the varied political questions that come to our attention. In any given week, the newspaper will raise questions about issues such as the control or deregulation of oil prices, the busing of school-children to improve racial balance, the level of support for retired people in the Social Security system, the size of the military budget, or federal acquisition of land for parks and wildlife refuges. If we had to consider each of these issues anew, we would have an awesome task. However, if we approach each from the standpoint of a general ideology that we have developed over time, the job is much simpler. Most issues will turn out to be instances of more general principles, and we can quickly settle them by applying the principles.

The new issue may also modify our ideology, because an ideology is not graven in stone. For instance, devout Catholics who believe that the government should regulate people as little as possible may find themselves torn over the issue of legalized abortion and may modify some of their more general ideas about politics in light of the new issue. An ideology, then, while it is an organized set of ideas about politics that helps us to make sense of the myriad of political questions that face us, is not static. An ideology organizes ideas, but as it absorbs new ideas it evolves, too, and is slowly modified.[1]

An ideology also has public uses. In politics, we are typically concerned to convince others that a policy we favor is the right one. We usually have personal reasons for favoring the policy (we may want taxes to be cut because we are wealthy, oppose gun control because we like to collect guns, or favor national health insurance because we are poor), but these personal reasons are not usually good public reasons. People distrust a self-interested argument. Also, arguing for a policy by giving one's personal reasons for it would not win many allies; only those who are also rich could be convinced by the argument "I'm wealthy, therefore I want to see taxes cut." In political argument, we usually try to attract as many allies as possible to our position, and so personal reasons will not make good arguments. Ideologies, however, can serve this purpose very well. The wealthy person who argues, "Government spending and taxation hamper individual initiative," may appeal to a great many people who for various reasons favor individual initiative.

Thus, we develop and maintain ideologies because of their usefulness to us in responding to events and their utility in public political argument. This is not a conscious, cynical process in which we deliberately frame an ideology so as to enlist allies in some cause or another. Rather, we are all comfortable with ideology and generally, over time, work out ideologies that fit our particular needs. Ideologies tend to take on a life of their own and guide their holders' political views in unanticipated ways. A business leader who feels that government should regulate as little as possible (for what we may think are obvious reasons) may find that this ideology also leads to positions—not particularly connected to self-interest—on the censorship of books in public libraries or the regulation of handguns.

An ideology helps us make sense out of politics for ourselves and gather allies for public argument. We develop our ideologies in such a way that they fit our needs and predispositions, reflecting what we want; but they also take on a life of their own and guide our decisions.

----

[1]See Michael Billig, Susan Condor, Derek Edwards, Mike Gane, Daniel Middleton, and Alan Radley, *Ideological Dilemmas: A Social Psychology of Everyday Thinking* (Beverly Hills, Calif.: Sage, 1988); Teun A. Van Dijk, *Ideology: A Multi-Disciplinary Approach* (Beverly Hills, Calif.: Sage, 1988); and Stanley Feldman, "Values, Ideology, and the Structure of Political Attitudes," in David O. Sears, Leonie Huddy, and Robert Jervis, eds. *The Oxford Handbook of Political Psychology* (New York: Oxford University Press, 2003).

↝ AMERICAN IDEOLOGIES

All of us have some sort of ideology, in the sense that our various ideas about politics bear some sort of relationship one to another. However, not every ideology is equally neat and tidy, nor is every ideology worked out in equally full detail. Americans' ideologies tend to be more loosely organized than those of other peoples. In fact, Americans tend to admit exceptions and inconsistencies into their ideologies rather cheerfully.

Two main ideologies are found among Americans: **American liberalism** and **American conservatism.** As we shall see, both of these ideologies are variants of a more general and well-worked-out ideology known as liberalism. American liberalism and American conservatism are simply differing versions that have sprung up in a predominantly liberal society. As you will see when we look at more established ideologies below, we usually determine ideologies by an intellectual structure—a core value or values, from which we can derive a number of disparate policy positions by deduction. For instance, you will see that the core value of liberalism in its general (not American) sense is that all individuals should be able to develop their capacities to the fullest; from this it is possible to deduce arguments for issues such as the defense of free speech, for democracy, and for minimizing regulation. Since American political thought was dominated from the start by a general liberalism in this sense, Americans did not sort themselves out politically by competing deductive systems. Rather, ideologies in America have evolved as rival coalitions operating within a common intellectual structure.

American liberalism, for instance, has developed as a rather loosely held sense of support for underdogs. As a result, concerns for economic equality are strong in American liberalism (the poor as underdogs), as is support for the interests of ethnic minorities, women, and gays. Support for environmental protection is also part of American liberalism. And so is support for a fairly radical defense of freedom of expression, as exemplified by the American Civil Liberties Union.

American conservatism has traditionally emphasized more keeping governmental regulation of people's lives to a minimum, in order to allow ample room for individual self-reliance. This has led to such positions as support for the right to own guns without regulation, the right of consumers to make their choices free of government oversight, and the right of businesses to operate with a minimum level of governmental regulation. In recent decades American conservatism has added to these concerns a desire to maintain common values of morality and spirituality, and opposition to legalized abortion.

American liberalism and American conservatism are not tidy ideologies. It is sometimes hard to see logical connections among the various attitudes detailed. It frequently happens that an American political figure is "liberal" on some of these issues and "conservative" on others. American labor unions, for example, have generally been quite concerned about issues of equality but have not been equally concerned about an issue such as abortion rights. There are many other complexities as well. As one more example, American conservatives generally favor free trade but are also concerned about the repression of religion in China. This leaves them to grapple with the question of what sort of trade relations the United States should maintain with China.

Both ideologies are therefore mixtures, representing marriages of political convenience, and it is difficult to find strict internal coherence among the various parts of either one.

The two American ideologies have been shaped as coalitions partly by the American two-party system. As you will see in Chapter 10, the American system of elections forces Americans into a system of two large parties; small parties find it very difficult to establish themselves. As a result, Americans with a wide variety of ideas on different questions find themselves squeezed together into one or another of the two parties, along with a large number of people who may have different concerns. American ideologies are shaped by this process of squeezing into coalitions, at least as much as by an intellectualized process of deduction. One indication that this is what happens is the fact that sometimes an issue migrates between ideologies.

It is probably the case, for instance, that at the time of the Supreme Court decision legalizing abortion, more American liberals than American conservatives opposed the decision. (Simply from historic patterns of immigration, there were more Irish, Italian, and Polish Catholics in the Democratic Party at that time than in the Republican Party.) Democratic Party gatherings at the time were often split about evenly on the issue. Strikingly, Senator Ted Kennedy—who would be a leading pro-choice figure by the mid 1970s—favored protecting the unborn in 1971, on the eve of the Supreme Court decision.[2] However, there was another part of the American liberal constellation of interests that could not easily coexist with a pro-life position—the feminist movement. The presence of both positions within American liberalism proved untenable. Over the ensuing decade or two, large numbers of those opposing abortion drifted away from American liberalism, until eventually opposition to abortion lodged on the right and became one of the defining issues separating the two ideologies.

Similarly, protection of the environment was at least as much an issue of American conservatives in the 1950s as it was of American liberals. As conflicts between businesses and environmentalists intensified in the 1960s and 1970s, environmentalism partially migrated to American liberalism, although there is still a significant minority of environmentalist conservatives. In this case, it was never entirely clear which way things would go: business interests associated with American conservatism experienced conflicts with environmentalism, but so did trade unions associated with American liberalism. Key issues do tend to sort themselves out to one side or the other, however, and this is what happened to environmentalism.

Foreign policy issues are especially fluid. A cynic might say that American liberals trend internationalist when a Democrat is president, and isolationist when a Republican is president—and that American conservatives trend internationalist when a Republican is president and isolationist when faced with a Democrat. Thus Republicans opposed (Democratic) President Clinton's military intervention in former Yugoslavia, and spoke scathingly of his "nation-building." But after 2000, with a Republican president, it was the Democrats who opposed George Bush's interventions. With a change in party control in 2008, liberal opinion shifted again; liberals' opposition to continuing

---

[2]Anne Hendershott, "How Support for Abortion Became Kennedy Dogma," *The Wall Street Journal,* January 2, 2009, p. W11.

CHAPTER 2   MODERN IDEOLOGIES AND POLITICAL PHILOSOPHY   27

"I keep my core beliefs written on my palm for easy reference."

the war in Afghanistan now softened because a Democratic president, Barack Obama, was leading the war effort. Positions on foreign policy seem to flip freely back and forth between American liberalism and American conservatism.[3]

American ideologies may be a bit untidy, but they still have real influence. American labor leaders have probably been more concerned than they might otherwise have been with freedom of expression because this issue was linked to redistribution of income through American liberalism. Americans concerned about high taxes have probably also become more concerned about traditional social values because traditional social values and low taxes are linked through American conservatism.

Over the last few decades, the intensity of ideological debate has strengthened markedly in the United States. I have described American ideologies as "untidy mixtures," but they are still ideologies. We can see the intensity of ideology today in the very strong reactions (positive and negative) to President George W. Bush in the 2000s and in the Tea Party movement in 2010; we can see it in the contemporary sharp contestation over judicial appointments in the Senate, that would have been almost pro forma in the 1960s and 1970s; and we can see it in the proliferation of ideologically based interest groups and think tanks.

It is not obvious why we should have come to feel so much more strongly about our loose ideologies in the twenty-first century than we did in earlier decades. In part, it may be because of new techniques and technology (direct mailings, focus groups, polling,

---

[3]Consistent with this interpretation of American ideologies, Paul Goren finds that American voters' party attachments shape their ideologies, rather than their ideologies determining which party they identify with. ("Party Identification and Core Values," *American Journal of Political Science* 49 (October 2005): 882–897).

e-mail) that have made it easier for ideologues to raise money and fire up their troops. In part, it may be because of the involvement of the newly active religious right, who have brought some of the emotion of religious belief into the political sphere. In part, it may be the addition to the political realm since 1973 of a new issue, abortion, which excites deep emotion and on which compromise is at best exceedingly difficult. And in part, it may be the partisan realignment of the 1960s and 1970s in which the conservative South moved to the Republican Party, leaving the two parties more cleanly divided along ideological lines than they had been and thus adding the emotion of partisanship to conflicts over ideology. But in the end, it is also because these ideologies do articulate real conflicts between real groups in the population. They may be primarily coalitions rather than intellectual systems—less neat systems of ideas than the more general liberalism, conservatism, and socialism that I will describe in the next sections. But as systems of conflict, they are just as real as those more tightly knit intellectual systems. In short, there are real differences between "American conservatives" and "American liberals."

An interesting Website at which to examine your own ideology, and see what mix of American liberalism and conservatism shapes your views, is http://www.politicalcompass.org/. From a survey you fill out, giving your views on various issues, the program places you on a two-dimensional ideological grid, and allows you to compare your position with that of various world leaders.

→ LIBERALISM

The two American ideologies are actually variants of **liberalism,** one of the three great ideologies that developed in Europe in the eighteenth and nineteenth centuries. These three ideologies—liberalism, conservatism, and socialism—have provided the framework for most political debate throughout the world since then.

To understand their development, we must remember that the medieval social order in Europe was one in which people were bound together in patterns of rather strict domination, with mutual responsibilities between those who were dominated and those who dominated them, between "top dogs" and "bottom dogs." Farmers often lived in a condition of near-slavery, subject to a local church official or a member of the nobility. A farmer paid heavy taxes to his local patron and had to provide him with specified periods of labor for road building, or service in war. In many parts of Europe, the farmer was not allowed to leave his land and move elsewhere without the permission of his patron. Furthermore, farmers were required to offer the patron formal social respect and deference. In return, the patron was supposed to provide his farmers with protection and with help in times of illness or want. Such industry as existed was organized in guilds, which laid down strict rules as to how an item was to be manufactured, how many such items were to be produced, and what was to be charged for them. Trade in many items was subject to ancient rules: The king might have a monopoly on trade in a commodity such as salt, for instance, or a particular town might have the enduring right to receive all imports of some specific item. Jews were a pariah group, banned from many occupations and generally forbidden to own land. The Roman Catholic Church maintained a stern control over proper belief (a striking example of this occurred when, in 1616, the church forced the great astronomer Galileo to state, contrary to his true convictions, that he did not believe the earth orbited around the sun). To transport goods from one end of a country to another could be a complex affair in which the carrier of the goods was required to pay taxes, fees, and tributes to various local personages at all stages of the journey. Politics was the province of the king, the nobility, and the church.

For our present purposes, two things are important about these arrangements: (1) people were bound to each other in complex and cumbersome systems of domination; and (2) the arrangements were static, difficult to change. Ownership of the land, feudal privileges, the rights of the church, the political role of the king and nobility, the power of the guilds—all were granted in perpetuity and could only evolve slowly.

Onto this setting—faintly in the fifteenth and sixteenth centuries, in crescendo through the seventeenth and eighteenth centuries, and with a deafening crash in the nineteenth century—came modern large-scale commerce and industry. The new commercial and industrial leaders chafed under the static restrictions of medieval society. To carry on large-scale trade and manufacture, it was often necessary to move commodities over great distances; laborers had to be gathered at large factories, which often involved moving people from one end of the country to another; canals and roads had to be built, which would run through many different patrons' domains; prices and the nature of goods often had to be adjusted to reflect changing needs and technology; and science and invention had to be free to pursue truth wherever they found it, regardless of orthodoxy. These requirements collided with the organization of preindustrial medieval society. The new and increasingly powerful commercial and industrial elite cast about for ways to make society more fluid and manageable. One helpful solution, as we shall see in Chapter 3, was the invention of the modern state as a way to organize politics and government. Another was the appearance of liberalism.

Liberalism was not introduced by the commercial and industrial leaders themselves. Rather, it was invented by intellectuals who were moved by the general artistic and scientific restlessness of the age. However, it suited the new economic leaders, and they warmed to it. It gave them a view of politics that could make sense to them in light of their needs, and it allowed them to argue for their causes in ways that were less crass than simply saying, "We wish to limit the power of the nobility, the guilds, and the church because we want to make money."

Liberalism posits as the highest good of society the ability of members of that society to develop their individual capacities to the fullest. That is, in a good society, all individuals should be able to develop their minds, musical talents, athletic abilities, or any other gift as much as possible. This requires, according to liberalism, that people be responsible for their own actions, rather than having someone else do things for them or tell them what to do. It is only by acting and feeling the consequences of such action that we can develop our capacity to act.

This is the central assumption of liberalism, from which a number of consequences flow. For instance, in his essay "On Representative Government," John Stuart Mill based his argument in favor of democratic government on liberal premises, as follows: The chief end of politics is to allow people to become responsible and mature. They can do this only if they take part in decisions affecting their own lives. Therefore, even though a wise and benevolent despot or monarch might make better decisions on behalf of the

John Stuart Mill and Liberalism

John Stuart Mill (1806–1873) was a major figure in liberal thought. His father, James Mill, an important figure in the history of British philosophy, educated young John himself, following an incredible regimen: John was reading Greek at age three, and by the time he reached maturity he probably knew more of science and literature than anyone else in Britain. He spent his adult years in a sinecure with the British East India Company, which allowed him plenty of time to write. His main contribution to liberal thought was to reconcile individual freedom with the general good of society, in a fairly tight logical system. Unusually for his time, John Stuart Mill was a strong feminist and advocated women's suffrage. Some believe the logic of liberalism pushed him to this conclusion, while others have ascribed it to the influence of his wife, Harriet Taylor Mill.

people than they can make for themselves, democracy is better, because under it the people make their own decisions, mistakes and all. In this way they develop their political capacities. Therefore, some form of democracy is the best kind of government.

By the same sorts of argument, the following elements follow from the basic liberal premise; together, they constitute the liberal ideology:

- Democracy is the proper form of government.

- People should have full intellectual freedom, including freedom of speech, freedom of religion, and freedom of the press. (They should have responsibility for their own values, so that they will develop the ability to judge values.)

- Government should remain minimal and should regulate people's lives very little. (As few decisions as possible should be made for people so that they learn to make decisions for themselves.)

- In particular, people should be free to regulate their own economic activity.

- Power of one person over another is a bad thing; hence, government should be organized to guard against abuses of power. (Again, one person should not make decisions for another.)

Liberalism flourished especially in Great Britain and its colonies, perhaps because Britain was the first country to industrialize. In Britain, liberal forces first gained control of the House of Commons and the cabinet in 1832; through the nineteenth century, political control of the country seesawed between liberals and conservatives. (See the section on "The Conservative Reaction" for a discussion of conservatism.) In the United States, the new Constitution of 1789, with its precautions against a concentration of power in any one part of the government and its guarantees of various individual freedoms, clearly signified the ascendance of liberalism. On the continent of Europe, liberalism was a potent force throughout the nineteenth century, but it was nowhere as strong as in Britain and its former colonies. Most Western European countries had established liberal constitutions by the end of World War I, but by that time liberalism was fading quickly.

As we noted earlier, "liberalism" in American politics is not the same as liberalism in the general sense that we have described in this section. **Libertarianism,** however, is another ideology espoused by a small but influential number of Americans. (It helped to provide some of the impetus for the Tea Party movement in 2010, and Senator Rand Paul of Kentucky is a libertarian.) Libertarianism is a relatively pure version of classic liberalism. To examine its tenets, check out the home page of the Libertarian party, http://www.lp.org/.

With regard to the distinction between the "choice" and "power" perspectives, liberals will strongly favor a view of politics as choice. To liberals, power is a bad thing that we should limit as much as possible. Power allows some people to force choices on others, which violates liberal principles. To a liberal, politics should properly consist of public choices, in the making of which each person shares equally and without undue influence from others. We should keep as many choices as possible private. That is, we should limit the sphere of politics itself.

✦ THE CONSERVATIVE REACTION

When liberalism arose to challenge the existing social arrangements, the defenders of those arrangements needed an ideology to counteract the persuasive power of liberalism. **Conservatism** developed in response to this need.

Conservatism in the European sense is unfamiliar to Americans because it is distinctly different from American conservatism. Defenders of existing arrangements in Europe pointed out quite properly that liberalism is an individualistic doctrine; that is, liberalism looks on society as consisting of the individuals constituting it. To liberals, the whole of society equals the sum of its component parts, so that a society is happiest when the total of individuals' happiness is greatest. This is implied in the basic premise of liberalism: we are to judge the goodness of a society by the extent to which its members individually are able to develop their capacities.

In opposition to this, conservatism holds that societies and other groups of people are more than just the sums of their parts; that a group of people creates greater happiness through its existence and maintenance as a group than its members could individually produce for themselves. Liberalism, conservatives say, is a lonely and selfish philosophy whose ultimate result would be a group of people resolved to better themselves with no regard for the people around them.

Conservatives regard it as important that their society should have order and structure and that this structure should be stable enough to let people know where they stand with regard to each other. Most important, an ordered group develops and maintains religion and standards of morality. People gain greater happiness as members of a family, members of a church, and members of society than they could possibly gain individually. This is what conservatives see as the highest good of society: the maintenance of ordered community and of common values.

In such a society, it is silly to try to keep one person from doing things for another or to keep one individual from exercising power over another. The whole point of "community" is that people are important as members, not as individuals. What matters is how they fit into the web of mutual responsibilities.

32   PART 1   THE IDEA OF POLITICS

 Edmund Burke and Conservatism

Edmund Burke (1729–1797) is perhaps the most important figure in the development of conservative thought, at least in Britain. He was born and educated in Dublin, Ireland, the son of a lawyer. Although he was a professional politician and a great orator in the House of Commons, he was too intellectual and independent to rise to a major position in his party. As a philosopher, he was not abstract and did not deal in logical systems. Rather, he drew pragmatically from experience. What was already a well-developed conservative ideology was sharpened for him by what he saw as the excesses of the French Revolution.

The structure of the community should be relatively stable and predictable so that all may easily fit into their place in it; therefore, there is nothing wrong with assigning power to people by even such arbitrary devices as heredity if those people can be expected to use their power wisely. Patterns of domination that have evolved gradually should not be changed casually, because what has grown slowly is at least familiar to us and must have had some virtue to have lasted so long. Conservatism is an ideology that accepts and welcomes power; conservatives believe that appropriate arrangements for power will ensure good treatment for everyone.

It is obvious why this philosophy based on ordered community was useful to the aristocracy, the established church, and others who were trying to maintain their positions against the liberal challenge. However, ideologies take on a life of their own, and conservatism stresses another theme that might not otherwise have come so naturally to the defenders of the status quo: the responsibilities of power. Where liberalism is suspicious of power and seeks to limit it, conservatism sees power as binding and shaping its holder in good ways. Conservatives do not see a powerful monarch or president as one who is in a position to treat people capriciously. Rather, they see such an official as one who is in a position of awesome responsibility, with generally little choice as to courses of action. Conservatism stresses the responsibility of the powerful in a community to help the weak, a position opposed to the view of liberals that the weak should be given responsibility for their own affairs. European conservatives, because of this side of conservatism, have not been especially reluctant to help the poor or to develop the welfare state. In the late eighteenth century in Britain, under the conservative regime, there was already a system of guaranteed minimum income for anyone in Britain—a floor below which no one was allowed to fall. Abolishing this system, on the grounds that people should have responsibility for their own affairs, was one of the first tasks of the liberals when they took power in 1832. To take another example, Otto von Bismarck, the conservative chancellor of Germany from 1871 to 1890, introduced the world's first systems of unemployment insurance, workers' compensation, and social security. He obviously did not find these incompatible with his conservative philosophy of politics.

Conservatism in this sense is unfamiliar to Americans. This is because, to the extent that the early immigrants had any ideas about politics at all, America was founded by liberals and populated largely by liberals. Most of the early settlers were trying to escape the rigidities of the old order in Europe. Also, our more fluid society has had few ordered systems of domination; conservatism, a defense of such systems, has therefore been largely irrelevant.[4]

In the last quarter of the twentieth century, however, one of our few ordered systems of domination came under liberal questioning, and something rather like conservatism arose as a defense. The feminist attempt to eliminate men's domination of women was a classic statement of liberal argument. Women should be free to take on all sorts of responsibility, feminists said, so that they could develop their capacities to the fullest. Protective laws (e.g., limiting the hours women may work, barring them from certain dangerous jobs, and protecting them from combat in the armed forces) were wrong because protecting people from unpleasantness made them weak and dependent. Feminists did not want women "put on a pedestal."

Opponents of feminism often responded in ways that were akin to conservatism. The traditional family is a good thing in its own right, they said. It is the family we should be thinking of, not the individuals who comprise it. Families work better, children are raised better, everyone is in the end happier, if there is a clear structure of authority in the family rather than a situation in which each member is striving individually. This has clear echoes of European conservatism.

Conservatism was a strong force throughout Europe in the nineteenth and early twentieth centuries. With the massive changes brought by World War II and its aftermath, European conservatism changed. The nobility were generally destroyed or discredited, the church was in ferment, and most countries had introduced a sweeping expansion of taxation and social services, the "welfare state," to make people more equal. After the huge destruction of the war, it was not always clear that there was a social order for conservatism to defend.

However, conservatism adapted fairly rapidly to these changed circumstances. Conservatives' traditional emphasis on the responsibility of the powerful to help the poor and weak, together with a willingness (in contrast to the position of liberals) to see power concentrated, made it fairly easy for conservatives to accept the welfare state. Also, conservatism welcomes active encouragement of religion by the state, whereas liberalism is suspicious of it. Large numbers of Europeans after the war felt a need for a stability of values offered by religion, although among recent generations religious practice has now dropped off sharply. While liberalism declined in Europe throughout the twentieth century, conservatism has lived on healthily. Its adherents accepted the welfare state but urged that it be built in ways that were consistent with traditional moral values and that it should not lead to a leveling of society. In other words, conservatives felt that some structure should remain by which one part of society can lead the rest. In Britain, the Liberal Party declined during the 1920s and 1930s, but the Conservative Party remained as the chief opponent of the new Labour Party. When Labour introduced the welfare state in 1945, the Conservatives accepted it within a few years and went on to dominate British politics for the next forty years. On the continent of Europe, after the war, Christian Democratic parties arose in many countries; these adhered to an established church but were flexible and pragmatic with regard to taxes and social programs. They were especially strong in Italy

---

[4]Louis Hartz, *The Liberal Tradition in America* (New York: Harcourt Brace, 1955).

and Germany, while a somewhat similar movement, the Gaullist movement, dominated French politics from 1958 to 1981. In fact, the ambitious and highly regulated welfare state of France was introduced and developed after World War II not by socialists, but by conservatives. One can safely characterize the politics of most west European states since World War II as having consisted of a conflict between socialism (described in the section on "The Socialist Alternative") and a modified conservatism.

In the Third World, liberalism outside of Europe and North America has generally been weak (countries that are trying to develop their economies apparently find that they cannot afford to limit and restrain concentrations of power) and conservatism is rather strong. Traditional religious leaders and the aristocracy, as in Saudi Arabia and Iran, or new elites of business leaders, as in Japan or Brazil, can often maintain a strong political movement to keep the political leadership of the state in their hands. And frequently, the two groups join forces.

A major exception to the general weakness of liberalism in the Third World (the poor states of the world) has appeared in recent years, as part of the worldwide rise of "neoliberalism" (see p. 41). This has involved reduced regulation by governments, privatization of government-run industries, and a general reliance on open markets for economic decisions. It picks up on the economic aspects of liberalism but not necessarily on any others. Under this impetus, a number of states of the Third World have reduced governmental involvement in the economy, while not particularly "liberalizing" their societies in other ways.

About now, you might be asking, "Why are we looking at this ancient history? These are obviously things that were fought out a century or two ago. How about today's issues?" The answer is that the general frameworks of liberalism and conservatism (and the ideology dealt with in the next section, socialism) still live on in European and American societies, if somewhat subconsciously. In order to understand contemporary politics of these countries we must understand the foundational ideological traditions on which they are built.

Why is it that the United States is the only advanced industrial country in which gun ownership is only lightly regulated? Our overwhelmingly liberal tradition might have something to do with this.

Or, consider another example. Socialist parties in Scandinavia built pervasive, cradle-to-grave welfare states after the Second World War. (In Sweden, at one point in the 1990s, 68 percent of all spending in the country was done by government programs.) In the last few decades, however, most of the Scandinavian countries have alternated socialist governments with center-right coalitions; as of this writing, two of the five countries had a non-socialist prime minister. But non-socialist cabinets have continued to support the welfare state about as much as their Socialist predecessors did. Why is there relatively little opposition to the massive welfare states of Scandinavia? Could it be because liberalism (with its opposition to governmental involvement in people's lives) never took much of a hold there? Instead, conservatism provided the Scandinavian alternative to socialism, and conservatism does not have a problem with welfare states.

If you tried to explain American gun regulation or the Scandinavian welfare state without knowing the ideological background of politics in these countries, you would be reduced—as many journalists and pundits seem to be today—to saying, "Well, Americans are like that; they love guns," or "Oh, those Swedes!"

✦ THE SOCIALIST ALTERNATIVE

When liberalism first arose to challenge the established order, it drew considerable support from the "working class," the workers and their families who were beginning to congregate in the growing cities. Workers welcomed the assumption that all people were equal and should have an equal opportunity to develop their talents. They especially liked the liberal doctrine of democracy, which would recognize them as having full and equal citizenship rights. In 1848, a wave of attempted revolutions by liberals swept across the continent of Europe; in most of these, skilled workers played a leading part, along with shopkeepers and other small businessmen. In Britain, the leaders of most labor unions were active in the Liberal Party as late as 1900.

However, through the latter part of the nineteenth century, the enthusiasm of the working class for liberalism weakened. Liberalism implied not only that people should be politically equal but that they should be regulated and helped by the government as little as possible. Workers were in a weak position socially and economically, and they often found that they needed help from the government in ways that were inconsistent with liberalism. Governmental protection against unemployment and sickness, governmental regulation of working hours and safety in the factories, governmental prohibition of child labor—these and similar wishes of labor were inconsistent with liberal principles. Naturally, compromises and accommodations could be reached within the movement, and labor was not left totally out in the cold, but the fact remained that labor often found that it had to buck the basic philosophy of the movement of which it was a part. When a new ideology appeared that was more congenial to labor, workers moved to it fairly readily. This ideology was **socialism.**

Socialism retained the assumption of liberalism that all persons deserve equal treatment by the state and should have equal opportunities to develop themselves; but unlike liberalism, it did not posit that people could develop individually, and it was not as suspicious as liberalism of the concentration of power and of positive action by the state. Karl Marx (1818–1883) was the greatest socialist writer, and all socialism since Marx has been heavily influenced by his views. Marx thought that society consisted not of individuals but of **classes.** A class is a group of people who share the same relationship to the means of production and who therefore develop a distinctive view of themselves and of the world. Marx thought that the most important thing about us is our work. Our work creates for us most of our view of the world, and thus people who share similar work (a similar "relationship to the means of production") form the natural basis for a class. The aristocracy had been such a class, intellectuals were such a class, the industrialists were such a class, and now a new class—the working class—was appearing in Europe. To Marx, people did not develop themselves individually in a vacuum, but of and through the class to which they belonged. According to this view, individuals do not form their own values, their own ideas about politics, their own sense of their needs; rather, they and the people with whom they associate form these things communally in ways that are difficult to specify. A person may contribute to these values and ideas, but so do the other members of his or her class. Each member draws much more from the class than any single member contributes to it.

For Marx, then, the basic unit of concern was the class. As he saw it, the working class was oppressed; it was made to give up its members' labor to feed the rich capitalist class.

Karl Marx and Socialism

Karl Marx (1818–1883) was raised at first in Bonn, Germany, and later in Berlin. After graduating from the university, Marx and his close friend Friedrich Engels (1820–1895) worked as journalists. In 1848 they wrote the *Communist Manifesto* and they were forced to flee Germany in the aftermath of unsuccessful liberal revolutions there. They settled in London, where Engels's family had connections and Engels could take care of Marx. Marx did not return to Germany until shortly before his death. In London he worked as a correspondent for the *New York Tribune* and wrote his massive, major work, *Das Kapital*. Marx combined a sweeping view of history with an astonishing appetite for the minutiae of economics. At its most basic level, his theory of politics, as of all other human activity, was that it is determined solely by economic processes and can be understood by economic analysis.

This was wrong, he said, because the working class were numerically much larger than the capitalist class and their oppression bred great misery. Therefore, the working class should take over control of the government and the government should take over industry, so that the workers, through their government, would control the industries in which they worked. This would ensure fair treatment for everyone.

The writings of Marx and other socialists derived their energy and moral force from the writers' awareness of the truly miserable conditions under which workers lived in the nineteenth century. Marx's friend and collaborator Friedrich Engels, in his study of the living conditions of English workers, quoted an Anglican priest's account in 1844 of conditions in his parish:

> It contains 1,400 houses, inhabited by 2,795 families, comprising a population of 12,000. The space within which this large amount of population are living is less than 400 yards square, and it is no uncommon thing for a man and his wife, with four or five children, and sometimes the grandfather and grandmother, to be found living in a room from ten to twelve feet square, and which serves them for eating and working in. . . . There is not one father of a family in ten throughout the entire district that possesses any clothes but his working dress, and that too commonly in the worst tattered condition; and with many this wretched clothing form their only covering at night, with nothing better than a bag of straw or shavings to lie upon.[5]

Engels goes on to describe his own investigation of the living conditions of the working class in the city of Manchester:

> One walks along a very rough path on the river bank, in between clothes posts and washing lines to reach a chaotic group of little, one-storied, one-roomed cabins. Most of them have earth floors, and working, living and sleeping all take place in the one

---

[5]Friedrich Engels, *The Condition of the Working Class in England*, tr. by W. O. Henderson and W. H. Chaloner (Oxford, England: Basil Blackwell, 1958), pp. 35, 36.

Karl Marx, architect of socialist ideology.

© Hulton–Deutsch Collection/Corbis

room. In such a hole, barely six feet long and five feet wide, I saw two beds—and what beds and bedding!—which filled the room, except for the fireplace and the doorstep. Several of these huts, as far as I could see, were completely empty, although the door was open and the inhabitants were leaning against the door posts. In front of the doors filth and garbage abounded. I could not see the pavement, but from time to time, I felt it was there because my feet scraped it.[6]

Marx developed a theory of history arguing that a revolution of the working class was not only appropriate but inevitable. According to Marx's theory, all history has consisted of a successive unfolding of domination by one group, leading to revolution against that group, followed by domination by a new group (the group that had led the successful revolution), leading to yet another revolution, and so on. Currently the capitalist class (which had earlier overturned the rule of the aristocracy) dominated the working class, but according to his theory the working class would eventually overturn them—either at the ballot box, or by revolution. This theory of history and revolution was powerfully attractive to workers. It told them that their unhappy plight was not their own fault as individuals but rather a condition imposed on them as a class by the working out of a broad historical process. Furthermore, it prophesied that they must, in the end, prevail over the capitalists because that is the way history works. Finally, it assured them that once they had prevailed, a brave new world would be created in which the cycle of revolutions was no longer necessary.

Socialism burst explosively on Europe. In 1850, there were only a few socialists on the continent. By the early 1900s, the Social Democratic Party was the largest party in Germany and was growing fast, and socialism was growing just as rapidly in other Western European countries.

⤖ COMMUNISM AND SOCIALISM

In 1917, a key event occurred in the development of socialism when Lenin's Bolsheviks succeeded in seizing control of the Russian Empire and transformed it into a socialist state renamed the Union of Soviet Socialist Republics (U.S.S.R.). Marx and Engels had never fully settled whether they thought the working class should take control of the

---

[6]Ibid., p. 61.

state peacefully through electoral victory or violently through revolution. Many social-ists thought revolution was the only answer, while others believed deeply in democ-racy. Lenin's successful revolution galvanized those who wanted to take the route of revolution, and over the years after 1917 they tried to dominate the socialist movement. They argued that the one state that had now successfully become socialist, the U.S.S.R., should lead all socialists in the world. The attempt to commit socialism to a revolution-ary strategy led to a split in the socialist movement in the 1920s. The revolutionists set themselves up as **Communist** parties, while the democratic socialists continued to call themselves Socialist or sometimes **Democratic Socialist** parties.

The split has endured, so that there are two branches of socialism, although outside of a few places such as Cuba, communism has been in broad retreat for the last couple of decades. Communists have generally held to a revolutionary strategy, although with the passage of time they have grown a good deal less emphatic about it. Socialists have been much more willing to settle for a portion of power within an only partially socialist system, and they have generally worked within a democratic framework. Socialists have also been more willing than communists to settle for partial improvements for workers, rather than holding out for a total change. In fact, socialists in Europe and many other parts of the world are hard to distinguish from the left wing of the Democratic Party in the United States. They still bear the mark of their history as revolutionary movements, but have evolved into left-of-center stalwart supporters of democratic politics. Almost all European states, for example, have been governed at one time or another by demo-cratic socialist parties that have pursued policies of a broad welfare state, gender and ethnic equality, and protection of the environment.

In the period after World War II, most of Eastern Europe was governed by com-munists, with military help from the U.S.S.R. By 1989, communism in Eastern Europe and the Soviet Union had become more of a bureaucratic sink than a shining ideol-ogy, and over the next two years these communist regimes collapsed. The Eastern European states tend now to look to democratic socialism, combined with free markets, as a model; the remnants of the Soviet Union have made stabs at economic change, but many have also been occupied with working out ethnic and nationalistic conflicts. Communism and socialism have been strong forces in the Third World. China, Cuba, Vietnam, and North Korea still have more or less communist governments today, while a number of Third World states have socialist governments.

→ Fascism

In the 1920s and 1930s, there arose a political movement, **fascism,** which did not hang together well as ideology, but was more a style of politics and a popular movement. Adolf Hitler in Germany, Benito Mussolini in Italy, and Francisco Franco in Spain established fascist regimes at this time. Fascists did not generally write elaborations of their theory, because among other things, they despised intellectualism and ideology. Accordingly, most analysts of fascism as an ideology have looked mainly at what fascists did. The essence of fascism seems to have been a rejection of most institutions of mod-ern life, combined with a national rebirth focused on a charismatic, dictatorial leader.

Fascists were antisocialist, generally anticapitalist, and (at least in Hitler's and Mussolini's cases) hostile to the church. They tended to glorify instead a mythical war-based society of the past—for Mussolini the ancient Roman Empire, for Hitler the Teutonic knights of the Middle Ages and German composer Richard Wagner's dreamy stories about the old Germanic gods.

Their political style was opportunist. All used violence and terror to advance their movements. Somewhat paradoxically—remember, they despised modern institutions—they were also "up to date" and presented themselves as forward-looking. Hitler was the first German politician to campaign from an airplane, for instance, and the Fascists cleverly designed their propaganda and rallies in the modern-looking art deco style.

Fascism appealed particularly to those who felt left out in the modern age. In Spain and Italy, these were mostly the traditional elites, who felt threatened by modern industrial managers and by socialist workers. In Germany, the "left out" were mainly the middle class, small farmers, and shopkeepers. The uprooting of European civilization in the First World War helped prepare the ground as well, adding to the sense of loss among the disinherited of modern life.

The details of fascism actually varied a good deal from one place to another. The Nazi party of Germany attacked the existing social system, including the churches, more actively than most. It had a strong element of anti-Semitic racism that was not present in Italian or Spanish fascism and that ultimately led to the murder of millions of Jews. Spanish fascism identified with conservative church leadership and supported the church. Italian fascism was marked by an attempt to reorganize the economy into "corporations"—guilds of employers and workers in each industry. Such variations in fascist policy again underscore that fascism was, and is, more a political style than a system of ideas.

The defeat of the fascist powers in World War II ended most organized fascism; but since then, when established sets of people have felt their positions threatened by modern change—especially by new racial or ethnic claims, or by immigration of new groups into the country—echoes of fascism have often been heard. The American Nazi party and white power movements, and anti-immigrant movements in Europe, often involve a dramatic leader, violence, and a denial of modern change in ways that show kinship with the old fascist movements.

→ IDEOLOGIES IN THE TWENTY-FIRST CENTURY

With the long period of general peace in Europe and among other industrialized states since World War II, some of the edge has worn off the conflict among the great modern ideologies. As modern society has become more firmly established, the old grievances do not seem to move people as strongly as they once did. With the decline of religion (at least in Europe) and with the poor economic performance of communist states, there has been a resurgence of liberalism—but a liberalism modified by considerable governmental support for the weak.

Many leaders of parties, especially parties that hold responsibility for the government of a state, have begun to modify their ideologies in light of practical experience.

The most dramatic example of this is the collapse of the communist regimes of Eastern Europe and Russia. Many states of this region have become liberal democracies, and all have abandoned their old, ideologically based communist systems.

Other leaders, too, have shown a more compromised blend of ideologies. Britain's Margaret Thatcher was for fifteen years the leader of the Conservative Party, which among other things had emphasized ties to the Anglican Church and the monarchy. However, her personal ideology combined these conservative elements with a set of very liberal economic policies that called for shrinking the state's role in the economy, often through the privatization (sale to private owners) of many government enterprises. On the other side of the spectrum, some socialists such as Tony Blair, the Labour Party prime minister of Britain from 1997 to 2007, so blended their socialism with concerns for efficiency and stable economic growth that it was scarcely recognizable as a doctrine of conflict between classes. Italy's former Communist Party, with even the word Communist now removed from its name, emerged in the mid-1990s as the Democratic Party of the Left, a left-of-center, democratic party—and it has evolved through mergers with other parties to be one of the leading parties of post–Cold War Italy.

However, ideological conflict is not dead in the twenty-first century. In Europe, new "green" parties have raised over the past few decades a set of issues that established leaders, accustomed to the old ideologies, found hard to absorb into their debates. These issues, labeled "postmaterial issues" by Ronald Inglehart, have included feminism, protection of the environment, and open and spontaneous styles of life.[7] In part, they have been represented by totally new parties (among others, the Greens); in part, they have found their way into established democratic socialist parties where they have often represented a minority voice. At the other end of the spectrum, anti-immigrant parties, such as France's National Front, have raised issues of race and nationalism that had been thought dead since the Second World War. Outside of Europe, militant Islam, with its claims for a religious state, has raised a qualitatively different kind of challenge in many states of North Africa, the Mideast, and South Asia. Faith-based politics, based on divine will, is intense and difficult to compromise. This has proved true of both militant Islam and the religious strand of American conservatism. We will explore the political impact of fundamentalist religion in more detail in the next section.

History, and the development of ideologies, does not stop. The great modern ideologies were a product of the tension between Europe's industrialization and the static institutions Europe had inherited from its feudal past. As that tension recedes, other sources of ideological development have come to the fore, in a sometimes confusing mix of forces and tensions. These include the practical economic experiences of the United States, Europe, and Japan; the increasing problem of degradation of the environment; the resurgence of militant Islam; the discovery of youth and women as classes, even though Marxist socialism saw classes as based solely on economic position; and the division of interests between rich and poor parts of the world.

---

[7]Ronald Inglehart, *Culture Shift in Advanced Industrial Society* (Princeton, N.J.: Princeton University Press, 1990).

Perhaps most notably, in a new mood of **neoliberalism,** in the 1990s many states cut back on governmental regulation of the economy, privatized state-run businesses, made their central banks more independent of direction from the government and opened business in their state to international competition by lowering trade barriers. In effect, these governments adopted the economic part of liberalism, although not necessarily the full ideology. (Many of these states established democracy at the same time, but some carried out "neoliberal" reforms without any of the other parts of liberalism; a good example is China, whose communist government maintains tight control over politics and speech but has hugely opened up the economy.)

The impetus for this neoliberal tide seems to have been not so much ideology as a practical desire to operate economies more efficiently. It was heightened especially by the economic success of the United States in the 1990s, which was taken by many states as a model to imitate. The tide was also encouraged by the International Monetary Fund and U.S. foreign policy, which generally tied economic help in times of crisis to reforms along neoliberal lines.

Neoliberalism also benefited from the growth of "globalization," in which states can no longer control the flow of ideas or goods across their borders as well as they once could. Since it is increasingly difficult for a state to control its affairs by itself, it must be able to connect with the states around it. The openness that this requires fosters "neo-liberal" competition with businesses beyond the state's borders.

The worldwide economic crash of 2008–2009 called into question the success of unregulated markets, however, and the tide of neoliberalism has now to at least some extent receded. Especially in East Asia, which weathered the crash of 2008–2009 better than Europe or the United States, leaders are beginning to develop new models of state intervention in the economy.

✦ RELIGION, POLITICS, AND POLITICAL PHILOSOPHY

Religion is an important part of politics and political philosophy, even though religious practice and belief have diminished somewhat in the last few decades in Europe and America (see pp. 187–188). Two of the most intractable issues in American politics, for instance, are based on religious doctrine: abortion and gay marriage. Elsewhere, violent politics often has had its roots in religious differences: Catholics and Protestants in Northern Ireland; Sunni and Shiite Muslims in Iraq; anti-Western attacks by Muslims, especially Muslims living in Europe; and others.

Religions are belief systems—organized sets of ideas that modify each other—so they are in fact a kind of ideology. But they are set apart from other ideologies by their origin in divine inspiration. This makes them so different from other ideologies that it is only in a technical sense that we would call them "ideologies." Their divine core makes them more difficult to argue about, because one either believes in the divine basis of a religion or does not believe in it. Two who share that belief may argue about important differences of interpretation within the religion, but a believer and a nonbeliever just have to agree to disagree. This is a very different discourse than what we usually think of as ideological argument.

The degree to which religious discourse differs from other ideological discourse depends in part on how fundamentalist the believer is. Fundamentalist believers take it that every word of their God-given scripture, be it the Bible or the Qur'an, is true because it came from God. Less fundamentalist believers, noting that in every religious book there are inevitable contradictions and ambiguities, see the documents of their faith as having a central core of principles, but believe they are interpretable as to exact prescriptions. These more interpretive believers may not compromise on the Golden Rule, for instance, but may consider God's words on homosexuality more open to discussion. Interpretive belief often leaves a good deal of room for blending with elements from other ideologies like liberalism, socialism, or conservatism, and so discourse about such belief is in the end somewhat more like other ideological discussion than is discussion based on fundamentalist belief. But to the extent that understandings of God's truth are part of the discussion, any religious discourse always has a special character.

Religion (like its modern cousin nationalism, which we will discuss in the next chapter) appears able to tap deep emotions of love and hate more easily than other ideologies, and this contributes to its immense impact on politics. Its place in politics comes partly from the fact that a religion is an **identity group**—a group of people who share an identity that they (and others) think defines them and sets them apart from others. Since politics often involves questions of various groups' power and rights, this involves religion in politics in a way that is different from adherents of other ideologies.

Yet a religion is also a belief system. In this aspect, religions function in politics much like other ideologies, though with the differences in discourse that I mentioned above.

The fact that a religion is both an identity group and a belief system leads it to function in two very different ways in politics. These two aspects of religion have different implications for politics, and they can be easily confused, which makes it difficult to analyze the role of religion in politics and understand how to respond to it. The political role of Islam is an excellent case in point. As a belief system, Islam emphasizes generosity and doing good for others. Historically, Islamic empires were notably tolerant of other religions. While it is true that many versions of Islam distinguish how believers and nonbelievers may be treated (wars may generally only be fought against nonbelievers, for instance), it is primarily a peaceful and generous religion.[8]

However, in various parts of the world, Muslims are involved as an identity group in conflicts that have excited emotions deep enough to inspire acts of political violence even up to suicide attacks. In the Mideast, Muslims are confronted with the ongoing, identity-based conflict between Israel and the Palestinians. In other parts of Africa and Asia, however, that conflict has not in the past inspired as much emotion, and there we have not generally seen politics waged as intensely as in the Mideast.[9]

Muslim immigrants in Europe find themselves largely ghettoized and marginalized in society—without much access to jobs, citizenship, or a regular role in society.

---

[8]It is, of course, very traditional in questions of sex and family.
[9]The advent of 24-hour news coverage, however, has made the Palestinian conflict more immediate and intense for Muslims everywhere than it used to be.

This has shaped their identity as separate from other Europeans, and has bred much alienation and bitterness. These in turn have spawned a good deal of violence: riots in France, terrorist attacks in Britain and Spain. European Muslims organized the terrorist attack on the World Trade Center and the Pentagon on September 11, 2001.

In contrast, Muslim immigrants in the United States are relatively well integrated. (A surprising 59 percent of adult Muslims are college graduates, compared with only 29 percent of all adult Americans.[10]) There has been very little terrorist activity or support from among Muslims living in the United States.

Depending on the situation, then, identity-based Muslim politics can vary widely. This contrasts with the effect of Islam as a belief system, which generally inclines its adherents toward very traditional values on abortion, homosexuality, and the family, and to generous programs for the poor, but does not vary so greatly from one region to another.

Islam as a belief system, the identity-based politics of Muslims in the Mideast, the different identity-based politics of European Muslims, and the still different situation of American Muslims—all these get badly muddled in the public mind, and in governments' policies.

In the United States, religions do not serve very strongly as identity groups, but at times identity conflict does have some resonance. While it has disappeared in the United States, the mutual hostility of Catholics and Protestants was still strong enough fifty years ago that it was a major factor in the 1960 Presidential election; many Republican Catholics switched that year to vote for John F. Kennedy, and many Protestant Democrats switched to vote against him. In the 2012 Presidential election campaign, significant numbers of voters told pollsters they could not support Mitt Romney because he was a Mormon.

By and large, though, the impact of religion on politics in the United States stems more from the differing belief systems of different religions that lead to differing policy choices and votes. For instance, in a study of evangelical Protestants (almost all of whom described themselves as "born-again Christians"), variations in the nature of the born-again experience had important political ramifications. The evangelical Protestants were sorted into a small group who said they were not born again; a group who said being born again was a result of Christ's Church nurturing them throughout their life; a group who said it was a gradual experience that occurred over time; a group who said it was a condition that they enjoy by profession of faith in Jesus; and a group who said it was a specific, memorable, "born-again" moment in their life. These groups greatly varied in their views on both religion and politics, as seen in Table 2.1. Differences in belief systems produced these varying political choices.

In summary, religions are belief systems, so they are technically ideologies. To the extent that participants consider religious beliefs God given, thus not susceptible to compromise, these beliefs cannot be discussed as ideologies usually are. Even so, religions as belief systems often blend with other ideological discussion and enter politics

[10]Paul M. Barrett, "They're Muslims, and Yankees, Too," *BusinessWeek*, January 15, 2007, p. 1.

TABLE 2.1

Various Types of Evangelical Protestants Compared

	Percent Believing Every Word of the Bible Is True	Percent Believing Abortion Can Never Be Justified	Percent Republican
Not born again	20%	3%	22%
Nurtured in faith	54	8	46
Gradual experience	70	13	53
Profession of faith	73	16	61
Specific experience	85	20	74

SOURCE: Adapted from Table 10.3 of Ted G. Jelen, Corwin E. Smidt, and Clyde Wilcox, "The Political Effects of the Born-Again Phenomenon," in David C. Leege and Lyman A. Kellstedt, *Rediscovering the Religious Factor in American Politics* (Armonk, N.Y.: M. E. Sharpe, 1993), p. 211.

in a normal way. Religions as identity groups, however, evoke such strong emotions that it is difficult for politics to deal with them. Most of the role of religion in American politics has been as belief systems, not identity groups.

✦ POLITICAL PHILOSOPHY IN OTHER HISTORICAL ERAS

In all of these discussions of ideology, it should be clear that ideologies develop in response to the dominant problems and dilemmas that people face at a given time. Liberalism, conservatism, and socialism all arose out of the changed world of the Industrial Revolution, and today's ideologies are being shaped by conflicts over the environment, gender, religious values, and identity politics.

What sorts of concerns drove political thought and ideology over the longer play of Western history before the challenge of industrialization? The scope of this book does not allow space enough to deal fully with this rich history of political thought; I will just sketch some of the major strands for you here in order to place the presentations of this chapter in their broader context. I also hope this may whet your appetite to dig more deeply. Political philosophy of earlier eras is worth reading partly for its own sake, to see how intelligent people dealt with the problems they faced. But it also often applies, by analogy, to problems we face today. Thomas Hobbes, for example, struggled in the sixteenth century with the problem of what obligation and obedience he owed to the king of England. Today, we have kings only in a few countries, but we do have governments, and what obedience we owe to governments, whether deliberate disobedience of a government's laws is legitimate, are live political questions.

The Greeks were the first great political philosophers, especially the Greeks of Athens, a few centuries before the birth of Christ. These were a people who valued speech and argument highly, and incorporated debate and rhetoric into their daily, practical lives. From that tradition of debate there sprang an extraordinary burst of questioning and thought around 400 to 300 B.C., which eventually laid the basis for virtually all Western thought in all areas. The Greeks were especially concerned with how we know what we know and how we can reason. They developed the basis for rationalism, a reliance on reason as the sole basis for truth, including religious truth. This in turn led to the development of mathematics, of esthetics as we know it, and of the natural sciences. In the realm of morality and politics, they were especially concerned with the nature of justice and with the question of what sort of constitution would produce the best political community. Plato (428–347 B.C.) was perhaps the greatest of the Athenian philosophers. In *The Republic*, he describes a utopian political community in which good, gifted people are selected as infants to be the leaders ("guardians") and are carefully trained (their reading censored, their minds honed by the study of mathematics) so that they will be able to rule wisely and autocratically and thus produce a just state. His was an ideal world, not likely to be accomplished in fact. It is reminiscent of modern conservatism.

While Plato sought for the ideal, Aristotle (384–322 B.C.), another great Athenian, restricted himself more to observations of the world around him. Aristotle thought that if people could be trusted to rule unselfishly, the best constitution was one in which a single person ruled; the next best was aristocracy, the rule of the few; and the least good was rule by a large number of people. In practice, however, people were selfish, and Aristotle argued that—because the perversion of the best leads to the worst—selfish rule by a single person was worse than selfish rule by a large number. Therefore, in the end he argued for something like democracy.

With their concerns about the proper role of citizens, about the nature of justice, and about what sort of constitution produces a good community and good people, the Greeks laid the foundation for Western political philosophy that followed. With the coming of the Christian church in the first centuries after Christ a new period of activity began. The development of a church that claimed allegiance from people all over Europe brought to the forefront the question of just what obligation people bore to their earthly rulers. If they were ruled by God in Christ, why should they do what their king told them to do? What should they do, for instance, if ordered by their king to do something that was a sin?

Much of the development of political philosophy for a thousand years or so centered on this question, and the answers shifted as the relative power of the church and of secular rulers waxed and waned. Early Christian writers, perhaps reflecting the weakness of the young church, claimed a rather modest role for the church in the affairs of this world. The greatest of these writers was Saint Augustine (354–430), who argued that government was made necessary by humanity's sinfulness and that only once we were without sin could we be ruled by God. To Augustine, government was a necessary evil (made necessary by evil), which at least produced internal order for sinful humanity.

As the church grew in power, popes sought to assert more authority over secular rulers. By the Middle Ages, Saint Thomas Aquinas (1225–1274) was asserting that the church was responsible for people's spiritual well-being and rulers were responsible for their physical well-being; since the spiritual was more important than the physical, however, rulers must be guided by the church whenever the church held that spiritual needs were involved.

Analytic Political Philosophy

Much work in the study of political philosophy is of the sort presented in this chapter— a history of the development of political ideas, with critical commentary on them. An alternative way of approaching the study draws its inspiration from the modern school of "analytic philosophy," which concerns itself especially with the meaning of words.

This approach, called "analytic political philosophy," does not primarily concern itself with the history of political ideas or with critical argument about them at a general level. Rather, its practitioners feel that they can contribute most to our understanding of politics by clarifying the language we use when we talk about politics. Certainly, a problem of muddled language lies behind many political arguments. The United States calls itself a "democracy," and so did the Soviet Union throughout the post–World War II period until its dissolution. The two meant quite different things by the word, but this was often forgotten in red-faced arguments along the lines of "We're a democracy!" "Are not!" "Are!" "Aren't!"

Some questions commonly dealt with by analytic political philosophers are, What is the state? And, more importantly, what are our obligations to the state? What is the "public interest"? What should be considered "rights," as in "human rights"? What should be meant by "equality"?

One excellent example of work in the mode of analytic political philosophy is Hannah Pitkin's study, *The Concept of Representation*, in which the author examines the varied ways in which, over the last several centuries, the word representation has been used in order to make clear what general, central meaning it has.[11]

[11] Hannah Pitkin, *The Concept of Representation* (Berkeley: University of California Press, 1967).

The church was not without opposition in this thrust, of course, especially as it weakened in later centuries. A curious and famous response to it was that of Niccolo Machiavelli (1469–1527), who wished to help kings resist the church and wrote *The Prince*, a primer of how to be a successful king, to help them. In it he argued that a king should be ruthless and pragmatic, not swayed by sentiment or morality.

Toward the end of the Middle Ages, and as Europe entered the modern period, kings grew stronger and the church weakened. This became particularly clear during the Reformation, when the historic Catholic Church was replaced in much of northern Europe by local Protestant churches established by local kings. The pendulum of political philosophy swung back against the church, as in the writings of Martin Luther (1483–1546), who returned to Saint Augustine's doctrine that government is a necessity to which even faithful Christians should submit.

As kings became more powerful, questions of political philosophy shifted to what obligations people in general bore to them. This question was brought to a head in the English Civil War (1647–1649), in which a diverse group of opponents to the king succeeded in deposing him and set up a republic that lasted for a bit over a decade.

This successful challenge to royal authority focused attention on the question of the duties owed to kings and eventually led to the development of liberalism, discussed previously.

One particularly important writer who participated in this debate was Thomas Hobbes (1588–1679), author of *Leviathan*, a strangely modern defense of authority. (Hobbes does not specify whether that authority must be vested in a king.) His argument is as follows: All people are selfish; in the absence of authority they will turn on each other, and life will be "solitary, poor, nasty, brutish, and short." To avoid this, people voluntarily band together into states and contract to give their rights to a sovereign, who will rule autocratically to provide peace and order for all. Hobbes's theory was intended primarily to justify the rule of kings, but it could be used to justify any sort of government. Of their free wills, by a cooperative decision, the people set up a power to dominate them for the common good.

With the questioning of royal authority at this time, the stage was set for the development of liberalism and of the other modern ideologies responding to liberalism; the bulk of this chapter has dealt with these ideologies. But while these ideologies have dominated political discourse in this century, they do not represent some kind of final stage of philosophical development. Ideologies are always rooted in the social challenges of their time, and at the beginning of the twenty-first century numerous new questions of political philosophy face us. Chief among these are a number of issues having to do with identity: feminist political theory, theories of politics based on a religion such as Islam, and theories of multiethnic politics. Emerging problems in the environment also stimulate philosophical discussion, especially regarding the question of what one generation owes the next.

The one sure thing is that as the new discourse develops, it will build on and absorb the old, just as liberalism, conservatism, and socialism did over the past couple of centuries.

KEY TERMS

ideology	conservatism	fascism
American liberalism	socialism	neoliberalism
American conservatism	classes	identity group
liberalism	communism	
libertarianism	democratic socialism	

FURTHER READING

Ball, Terence, and Bellamy, Richard, eds. *The Cambridge History of Twentieth-Century Political Thought*. New York: Cambridge University Press, 2003.

Berlin, Isaiah. "Does Political Theory Still Exist?" In *Philosophy, Politics, and Society*, 2d series, ed. P. Laslett and W. G. Runciman. Oxford, England: Basil Blackwell, 1962.

Calhoun, Cheshire, ed. *Setting the Moral Compass: Essays by Women Philosophers*. New York: Oxford, 2003.

48   PART I   THE IDEA OF POLITICS

Dryzek, John S., Honig, Bonnie, and Phillips, Anne, eds. *The Oxford Handbook of Political Theory*. New York: Oxford University Press, 2006.

Ebenstein, Alan, Ebenstein, William, and Fogelman, Edwin. *Today's Isms*, 11th ed. Upper Saddle River, NJ: Prentice-Hall, 2001.

Hirschmann, Nancy J. *Gender, Class, and Freedom in Modern Political Theory*. Princeton, NJ: Princeton University Press, 2008.

Honig, Bonnie. *Democracy and the Foreigner*. Princeton: Princeton University Press, 2001.

Rawls, John. *Political Liberalism*. New York: Columbia University Press, 1993.

———. *A Theory of Justice*. Cambridge, MA: Belknap, 1971.

Shapiro, Ian. *The State of Democratic Theory*. Princeton, NJ: Princeton University Press, 2006.

Strauss, Leo. "What Is Political Philosophy?" *Journal of Politics* 19 (August 1957), pp. 343–68.

Wolff, Jonathan. *Why Read Marx Today?* New York: Oxford University Press, 2002.

Wolin, Sheldon S. *Politics and Vision: Continuity and Innovation in Western Political Thought*, revised and expanded ed. Princeton: Princeton University Press, 2004.

The State and Public Policy

PART II

The State and Public Policy

CHAPTER 3

THE MODERN STATE

In this book, I will focus on the politics of the *state*—rather than on "office politics," or politics in the family, or politics in other groups—simply because the state has come to play such a central role in modern politics.[1]

The extent to which the state has come to dominate our attention is evident even in the way we treat individuals. When we think about a person who comes from a different country, we are likely to think of him or her primarily in terms of this—to the exclusion of other characteristics that may actually have more to do with what the person is like. If you knew a Danish engineer named Ole, for instance, and were asked to say quickly, in one word, what Ole is, you would likely say "a Dane." The other likely answer would be "a man"; gender has not given way even to the state in the amount of attention we give it. Ole is an engineer, and that speaks volumes about him; but not many people would choose that over his nationality as a label for him. He may be a Lutheran or a Jew, pious or apathetic, tall or short, a charmer or a clod; still, most people who know him would characterize him first as a Dane. This does not make much sense because almost all the other things that I mentioned would have told you more about Ole's personality or person than does the fact that he is a Dane. It is a result not of logic but of our modern fixation on nationality and the state.

If you have ever lived abroad, you will have noticed this phenomenon in a particularly striking way. Most of us do not ordinarily think of ourselves in terms of the state to which we belong. However, let us reside in a different state, and suddenly our native state becomes a most important aspect of our identity. Canadians living in the United States or Europe begin to think of themselves much more as Canadians than they ever have before; Nigerians studying or working in the United States suddenly begin to think of themselves as Nigerians; and Americans living in Europe or Asia suddenly feel

---

[1]As noted in Chapter 1, the word *state* in this context does not refer to a place like California or Pennsylvania. Rather, it means approximately what is often called a "country," such as Canada, Nigeria, or the United States of America.

58 Shively - Vol. 1

50   PART II   THE STATE AND PUBLIC POLICY

© Sidney Harris/*The New Yorker Collection*/www.cartoonbank.com.

themselves to be vividly American. I myself, when I lived abroad at one time in my life, discovered a hitherto unsuspected taste for peanut butter! (and American television, and American political news.) When everyone you meet responds to you as a Nigerian or an American, it is hard not to start feeling that way about yourself.

Our fixation on the state goes almost beyond what reason would dictate. We have seen that we could say more about Ole if we characterized him as tall or university educated than merely as a Dane. Another paradoxical result of our fixation on the state is that most people pay a good deal more attention to the central government, which is remote and inaccessible to them, than they do to their relatively more accessible local governments. In America, politics and attention to politics reach a peak every four years at the election of a new president. This national event so seizes our attention that enrollment in political science courses at American universities generally follows a four year cycle, rising 10 percent or so in a presidential election year, and Americans turn out to vote in considerably larger numbers at presidential elections than at local elections.

One can reasonably argue that the policies of local government are just as important as the policies of the national government. It is true that foreign policy and issues of war or peace, the state of the national economy, and the broad issues of social policy—all the purview of the national government—are extremely important to people's lives. But so are the public schools, the condition of the street in front of your house, the purity and taste of your drinking water, how you are treated by police officers—all of which your local government decides. How odd, then, that most people pay so much more attention to their national than to their local government. This is just further evidence that our focus on the state and its operations goes beyond the demands of reason.

The people of the world have not always been so thoroughly organized into states. In the remainder of this chapter, we shall look at the history of how the modern system of states arose; we shall then consider the relationship between the modern state and "nationalism"; finally, we shall look at contemporary challenges to the state and emerging political forms that might serve as alternatives to the state.

✦ THE DEVELOPMENT OF THE MODERN STATE

The invention of this thing to which we pay so much attention, the state, is fairly recent. Six or seven hundred years ago, people did not think of themselves as belonging to a state or nation as we know it. Most people lived on subsistence farms, intimately concerned with the village in which they lived but not caring much about the world beyond. Armies sometimes raided the village, but it did not make much difference to the villagers whether the army was hired by the king of France, by the pope, or by the Inca king. Barbara Tuchman's picture of today's "France" as it existed in the fourteenth century depicts a geographic region carved into various political divisions that might be controlled by the English king or by the French, and whose populations did not seem to care much which of these was their ruler.[2]

In the fourteenth and fifteenth centuries, as European kings began to claim greater powers and to tighten their control over large territories, these shifting political divisions began to coalesce into states. Even in Europe, however, it was not until the early nineteenth century that states were well established in the form we know.

Throughout the early period of state building in Europe, populations continued to be largely indifferent about the state to which they belonged. During the early stages of its formation, for example, the state of Prussia was spread in smears and droplets all over the map of northern Europe (see Figure 3.1), and this did not especially concern the Prussians. Some of these regions had been acquired for the crown by royal marriages, others by settlements of war or debt, and the people living in them were transferred like property from one ruler to another.

If ordinary people did not care much about the state, the leaders and the educated elite also saw it more as a convenience than as something special. This was particularly true early in its formation, but to some extent it remained true even as late as the eighteenth century. At the beginning of the period of state building, most members of the elite, if they could write, wrote in Latin rather than in their local tongue. Although daring writers such as Dante were breaking out in their local languages by the fourteenth

---

[2]Barbara W. Tuchman, *A Distant Mirror: The Calamitous Fourteenth Century* (New York: Knopf, 1978).

FIGURE 3.1   Prussia in 1789. As recently as this, a state did not need to be contiguous. Prussia splashes all across northern Europe.

century, most writers still tended to think of themselves well into the seventeenth century as belonging primarily to a cosmopolitan, European literary world rather than to a local English, French, or Spanish community.

The kings who were creating these new states often had family ties or other interests that took priority over their state. As late as 1714, a German line of kings whose members could not even speak English for the first generation came to power in England. In contrast, during World War I (after Britain and Germany had evolved into modern states), it would prove an embarrassment to the British royal house that the kaiser of Germany was their cousin—so much so that they changed their name from Hanover to Windsor.

Even military affairs were not as clearly divided by state through much of this period as they were at the end. Foreign mercenaries were an important part of most wars: Bands of English soldiers could be hired by the French king to fight the English, and vice versa. In the American Revolution, the king of England hired German troops (the Hessian soldiers) to do some of the fighting in America.

It was not until the early nineteenth century that we could see the state as we know it—a relatively large territory with stable boundaries, whose people were bound together by intricate political ties and who thought of themselves distinctively in terms of the state to which they belonged.

Historians mark the invention of modern states in Europe with Napoleon's work from 1800 to 1815. In France, he created a well-organized, broad political entity with an active and efficient bureaucracy and army. The resulting state was nearly invincible and succeeded in conquering most of Europe. The modern state had finally emerged. Even after Napoleon eventually overreached himself and was defeated at the Battle of Water-loo in 1815, things could never be the same. He had demonstrated what a full-fledged state could accomplish, and the new or remaining states that emerged after 1815 tried, some eagerly and some with more hesitation, to emulate his method of organization.

Although the modern state had finally been invented in Europe and North America by the early nineteenth century, most other peoples of the world still lived under a variety of other arrangements. However, a great surge of European colonial expansion during the eighteenth and nineteenth centuries had divided the rest of the world into colonies organized somewhat as subsidiary states. When European power waned in the twentieth century as a result of two disastrous world wars, these colonies were able to break away and establish themselves as independent. Then their new leaders, almost all of whom had been educated in Europe and to whom the state seemed a natural way to organize things, adopted the state as their own form of political organization. Even some regions that had never been conquered by Europeans, such as Ethiopia and Thailand, found that they needed to organize as states in order to defend themselves and participate in international commerce. The modern state became the universal form of political organization.

You should not underestimate how novel this new way of organizing people's lives and efforts was. As Joel Migdal puts it (somewhat slyly):

> Unlike most premodern political structures, the state has aimed to impose uniform and ultimate conformity on social life within far-reaching (but still circumscribed) boundaries: Its leaders have sought obedience in even the most personal realms of social interaction, from whom one might sleep with to how one must bury the dead. Compliance to these sorts of social norms was not new, but the claims of a single centralized organization to enforce such norms over huge territorial expanses were novel almost everywhere they were made. And, indeed, one can point to real cases in which this kind of microregulation has been successfully achieved. Astonishingly, some states have been able to garner from people's yearly earnings a share equivalent to all their work performed through April or May or, sometimes, even June of that year and to sequester their children for 30 or so hours a week in a state institution. Premodern political leaders could not have imagined such audacious goals.[3]

→ THE ORIGIN OF STATES: POWER OR CHOICE?

What was it that led to the invention of the state over the last several centuries? Perhaps an exploration of this question will help us to better understand the nature of the state. There has long been a vigorous debate among scholars as to why states developed in

---

[3]Joel Migdal, "Studying the State," *Comparative Politics: Rationality, Culture, and Structure*, ed. Mark Irving Lichbach and Alan S. Zuckerman (Cambridge, England: Cambridge University Press, 1997), p. 209.

Europe.[4] However, one thing is clear: The modern state developed there along with the coming of industry and of complicated commercial arrangements. Large-scale industry and commerce could be carried on most easily among large populations whose members could be held together with minimal difficulty and who were willing to have their economic activities coordinated. If most economic activity consisted of subsistence farming, cottage weaving, and coastal fishing from small boats, almost any form of political organization would do. However, as larger-scale, more complicated economic operations developed, something like the state offered important advantages.

With the development of the state, merchants and industrialists could draw on a large, uniformly treated population as their pool of laborers, and they could sell their products across a large market subject to a single set of laws. Goods could be transported readily, without being subject to special taxes or duties as they passed from one part of the state to another. On the greater scale made possible by the modern state, large factories and ships could be built, and these could be involved in complex nets of transactions. Industry and commerce thus benefited from the development of the state.

In this sense, then, modern industry and commerce *needed* something like the state, and this partly explains why it developed when it did. However, modern industry and commerce also made the state *possible* by providing the hardware, the technology, and above all the ease of communication by which an army could readily control a large, widespread population. Before the coming of modern communications, it was difficult for the government of a state of even moderate size to control the population with any exactness. As late as the early nineteenth century, it took a stagecoach three days to cross southern England. Under those circumstances, the government's control was necessarily loose. With the coming of the railroad and the telegraph in the nineteenth century, however, governments could keep an instantaneous check on what was happening throughout their realm and could move troops rapidly to any trouble spot. Add to these the development of gunpowder, cannons, and large warships, and we can see that by the nineteenth century, kings had acquired unprecedented power to provide uniform government across large territories.

Thus, we can interpret the relationship between the modern state and modern commerce and industry in two ways. On the one hand, commerce and industry needed something like the state, and so the state was invented. It emerged because it was an appropriate choice. On the other hand, modern commerce and industry made it easier to control people and seize taxes from them, and so the state was able to develop. Governments were able to spread their power more widely. Probably both explanations carry part of the truth. These interpretations embody "choice," and "power," the two sides of politics which I introduced in Chapter 1. To the extent one believes that the state emerged because the modern economy made it necessary, its invention represents politics as choice. To the extent one believes that it developed because people could now be controlled more easily, it represents politics as power. Different scholars will lean

---

[4]This theme and the theme of the next paragraph are well developed in Charles Tilly, *Coercion, Capital, and European States, A.D. 990–1992* (Cambridge, MA: Blackwell, 1992). In general, recent studies of the establishment of states in early modern Europe have emphasized the new possibilities for coercion in the 1500s much more than the new needs of society, so I am something of an outlier in my interpretation above. Two other good examples are Perry Anderson, *Lineages of the Absolutist State* (London: N.L.B., 1974); and Thomas Ertman, *Birth of the Leviathan* (New York: Cambridge University Press, 1997).

The Marxist Theory of the State

In this chapter, I have interpreted the state partly as being made possible by modern military technology and communications and partly as required by modern commerce and industry. Another way of interpreting the rise of the state is offered by Marxist socialism. (See the fuller treatment of Marx and socialism offered in Chapter 2.)

Marx thought that modern society consisted of one class (the capitalists) dominating another (the workers). The workers had to be controlled because of the tensions caused by this domination, and this necessitated the state. The state keeps the workers under control partly by repression (the police) and partly by integrating them into the prevailing system by convincing them, in school and by other means, that their current situation is good.

Marx thought that eventually the workers would revolt and set up a socialist system in which one class would no longer dominate another. Then the state would have become unnecessary and would wither away through disuse.

This theory sees the state solely as an instrument of power and it does not analyze public choice. As you saw in Chapter 2, this is generally true of Marxist theory, which interprets politics solely as a matter of power.

Further readings in the Marxist theory of the state are Ernest Mandel, *Late Capitalism* (London: NLB, 1975), chap. 15; and V. I. Lenin, "State and Revolution," in *Sources in Twentieth-Century Political Thought*, ed. Henry Kariel (New York: Free Press, 1964).

more to one or another of these points of view. In extreme cases, such as that noted in the box headed "The Marxist Theory of the State," some may hold that one of the viewpoints explains everything; but to go wholly one way or another is probably a distortion.

→ THE STATE AS A DEVICE TO PROVIDE PUBLIC GOODS

Another explanation for why states might exist is offered by the problem of *public goods*. This is a basic problem for all human societies, and it turns out that the state is a good device for solving it. A **public good** is something that benefits all members of the community but that no one can be prevented from using; every member of the community can enjoy the benefits of it whether that person has helped pay for it or not. Some examples of public goods are national defense, medical research, the space program, and public health programs to control the spread of disease. It is impossible, for instance, for the United States to defend its borders without defending me where I live in Minnesota; therefore, if the United States provides defense at all, it cannot avoid defending me. Public goods like defense are benefits that the government cannot turn on for some citizens and off for others.

Plenty of things that governments do, of course, are *not* public goods, because they could in principle be given selectively only to those who would pay for them. For instance, the government could in principle set up toll roads rather than offer free roads to all with funds generated from tax revenues, or could sell education rather than provide it free to all children. The test of a public good is whether it is impossible to deny it to any member of the group; if a public good is available to any, it is necessarily available to all.

Thus, all members of the community benefit from public goods, whether or not they have helped pay for them—and this is what makes public goods a problem. An army, for instance, cannot defend just those people who have helped pay for it; it defends a territory and unavoidably defends everyone within that territory. Left to purely voluntary action, such public goods would be very difficult to finance. Each individual could quite sensibly think, "If I don't pay my share, the army will still be there, and I'll get all the benefits of it. Why should I pay? I'll let someone else do it." In other words, everyone would try to be a free rider on all the others. As a result, no one would pay to finance the army, there would be no army, and all would lose out.[5] States provide one way to prevent such paradoxical failures. Faced with the need for a public good, a state can decide not to rely on volunteers. Instead, it can force the people to pay taxes, and then use those taxes to provide the public good that all (or most) desire.

A good example of the painful dilemma of producing public goods through voluntary choices is familiar to anyone who watches public television in the United States. Every few months, everyone watching public television has to sit through excruciating sessions in which the station's staff run on in a staccato patter to try to encourage viewers to help pay the costs of running the station by becoming members. They appeal to guilt: "Only one in ten of you who watch this station is a member." They appeal to greed: "For the basic $35 membership, we offer this lovely ceramic mug, embossed with the logo of the station." Perhaps the most effective pitch was made a few years ago in Minnesota, when the Twin Cities station staff promised that if they reached their goal early, they would cut off the fund drive (and its painful staff solicitations) before its scheduled conclusion. Contributions flooded in!

Public television stations are caught in the classic bind of those who produce public goods. Since they broadcast on open bands, they cannot restrict watching their shows only to those who have contributed (as pay-per-view television providers can), and so they can offer no incentive to force anyone to contribute. As a result, only about one in ten viewers sends in a contribution. This is actually a fairly generous response, but it still makes life difficult for the station.[6]

The problem of providing public goods can only be solved by the use of power— not necessarily coercion, but power in some form: coercion, persuasion, shaming, and so on.[7] The state turns out to be a very effective way to organize power; not the only way, but a very effective way. And so, the problem of public goods, by providing an important reason to have states, serves as an additional explanation for why we see states so dominant today. Certain public goods are so important, especially the defense of territory, that they provide a powerful motivation to organize power in a way that

---

[5] The basic statement on the problem of public goods and free riders in politics is Mancur Olson's *Logic of Collective Action.* See the box on page 282.

[6] Actually, about one-fourth of the operating costs of public television comes from government subsidies. But for the marginal dollar, which makes or breaks the station, public television relies on membership contributions.

[7] The public television station tries all of these except coercion, which of course is not available to it; it does not have the power to levy taxes or apply thumbscrews.

allows coercion to be institutionalized—in other words, the state.[8] The state can solve the public goods problem of defense (or any other public good it decides to provide) by using its coercive power to gather money from the citizens in the form of taxes, and then using that money to provide for defense.

The problem of public goods will arise at various points throughout this book. We have discussed it here in relation to the state, but for any sort of collectivity—the state, a family, an interest group—providing public goods without everyone trying to be a free rider is a central problem of politics. When we look at interest groups, for instance, we will see that the lobbying function of an interest group is a public good; if a farmers' interest group succeeds in getting a tax break for farmers, all farmers will get the break whether they have contributed to the group or not. How to get potential members to contribute is a central problem of interest groups.

However, for our purposes in this section, our conclusion is that the need for a vehicle to coerce the production of important public goods is yet another explanation for the existence of the modern state. Notice, by the way, that this is a "choice" explanation, not a "power" one: the existence of the state is explained by the need for a coercive mechanism to provide public goods.

✦ "STATE," "NATION," AND THE "NATION-STATE"

Up to this point we have not defined the word *state* precisely, although we have considered the modern state, its development, and its characteristics at some length.

We will now distinguish between **nation** and **state**. People often use these terms loosely as synonyms, along with the more common word *country*, and they are clearly related. As one example of the relationship between the two, we will later in this chapter label as "nationalism" a passionate identification with the state. In fact, in ordinary conversation, most people use the words *state*, *nation*, and *country* interchangeably.

However, *nation* and *state* have more precise meanings for political scientists. A nation is *a large group of people who are bound together, and recognize a similarity among themselves, because of a common culture; in particular, a common language seems important in creating nationhood.* Beyond language, many other factors may lead a group to identify in common as a nation. A shared history has apparently been important in welding what were originally diverse linguistic groups of immigrants into a single nationality in the United States. A shared religion blended speakers of various languages into a national identity in Israel. Various aspects of people's lives and circumstances may figure in their formation of a shared identity—but a shared language appears usually to be the most compelling of such bonds.

A state, on the other hand, is a *political unit that has ultimate* **sovereignty**—*that is, a political unit that has ultimate responsibility for the conduct of its own affairs.* France is a state, Brazil is a state, the United States of America is a state. The Jewish people do not make up a state, since they are not a political unit, but Israel is a state. General Motors and

---

[8]One of the main reasons why the thirteen independent colonies resolved to unite into a single state, the "United States of America," was that they found it impossible to "provide for the common defense" as long as they were not organized in a single, unified state.

Exxon are not states, though they are large organizations. Chicago is not a state, although it is a political unit. It lacks sovereignty (the ultimate responsibility for the conduct of its own affairs) because another government, represented by the Supreme Court and the U.S. Army, has the right to intervene and force decisions on Chicago should that be necessary. Sovereignty was first established as the basic defining characteristic of states in the treaties of Westphalia (1640) that ended a series of religious wars in Europe. They established that sovereigns ruled territories, and they should not be interfered with by other sovereigns. The development of modern states is often thought to have started with these treaties.

A nation is a *cultural* and especially a linguistic grouping of people who feel that they belong together; a state is a *political* unit with sovereignty. Although we have this straight for our purposes, I must admit that the mixing of the terms in everyday use does cause confusion. Some of that confusion will be unavoidable even in the rest of this book. The United Nations is an organization of states, for example, not of nations. We will still call it the United Nations, however, because that is what it calls itself.

One reason *state* and *nation* tend to commingle in common use is that leaders of states have almost universally tried to link the two in order to harness the emotional attachment of people to their nation and use that attachment to build support for the more abstract, legal entity—the state. If a state can coincide with a nation, then the state's leaders can more easily obtain acquiescence in the laws of the state and can build positive support in willingness to serve in the armed forces, or pay taxes. It is striking and somewhat disturbing to see how much the modern state has been able in this way to enlist its people to its cause.

Figure 3.2 shows a linguistic map of Europe. Some apparent nations spread across the boundaries of states. For instance, the German language and culture spread well beyond the boundaries of Germany. Austria, a large part of Switzerland, and a small part of Italy are German, and there is a pocket of Hungarian population in Romania. The Basques are spread across north-central Spain and southwest France. Switzerland encompasses a variety of linguistic groups that might qualify as nations.

Correspondence between nation and state is particularly loose in Africa and Asia. The boundaries of many African and Asian states are left over from the older colonial era, when they were drawn by the colonizing powers to suit their own convenience.[9] Thus, a crazy quilt of boundaries was superimposed on the land, with little regard for the culturally coherent groups of people living there. Once they regained their independence, of course, those people inherited these peculiar boundaries. The map of Nigeria in Figure 3.3 illustrates the loose correspondence between nation and state that exists in much of Africa today. In the Mideast, Turkey, Iraq, and Iran are home to parts of the Kurdish people, who are a minority in each of these countries and have from time to time made attempts to break away and form their own unified state. India includes fifteen official linguistic groups. Many other former colonies exhibit similar mismatches of state and nation.

With the modern importance of nationalism, we have come to think it a right of people, if they feel that they have a common nationality, to have a state to match

---

[9]The correspondence between state and nation is reasonably close in South and Central America, for an unhappy reason: Here, except for a few states such as Bolivia and Peru, the native population was either exterminated, to be replaced by a reasonably coherent population of settlers from Europe, or over a period of centuries absorbed culturally in a *mestizo* blend of natives and Europeans. As a result, the populations of these states are relatively homogeneous.

FIGURE 3.2 Linguistic map of Europe: Note that languages tend to coincide with states' borders, but the matchup is by no means perfect.

SOURCE: From Kingsbury, *An Atlas of European Affairs*. Copyright © 1964 by Praeger Publishers. Reproduced with permission of ABC-CLIO, LLC.

that nationality. This "right" has become a constant source of political tension and conflict for two reasons. First, as just pointed out, many state boundaries do not coincide with the geographic distribution of nations. Second, the sense of nationhood is a subjective thing. Persuasive leaders may stimulate or lay to rest a "feeling" on the part of a group of people, so the sense of nationhood is liable to change. Even if state boundaries could ever at any one time be brought into a perfect fit with the distribution of nations, this benign situation could not last, because new nations would gradually be invented and some old ones would fade and be forgotten. The small black nationalist movement in the United States is just one example of an

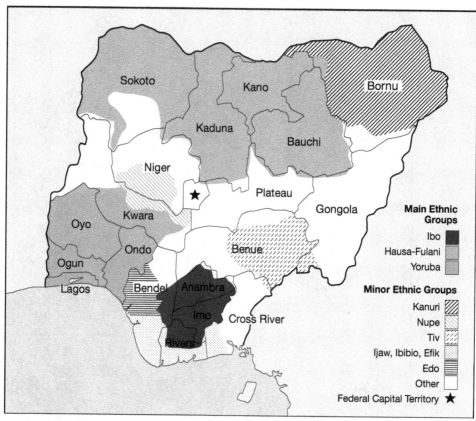

FIGURE 3.3 Ethnic map of Nigeria.

SOURCE: Reproduced with permission from the *Wilson Quarterly*, Winter 1980. Copyright © 1980 by the Woodrow Wilson International Center for Scholars.

attempt to arouse a "nation" (the nation of blacks) among a people who had not generally thought of themselves as belonging to a separate nation. Another good example is Belgium, where the French- and Dutch-speaking regions of the state coexisted without much notice for a long time but then became agitated about their separate nationalities in the 1970s. Today, hostility between the two nationalities is intense, and they operate with such autonomy that they have almost become separate states within the state of Belgium.

Figure 3.4 offers a good example of how malleable national identity can be. It shows the dramatic rise from 1969 to 1997 in the proportion of French-speaking residents of Quebec who thought of themselves as Quebecers, rather than as Canadians or French Canadians. Over those three decades the percent thinking of themselves as Quebecers grew from about 20 percent to a bit over 60 percent.

At any given time, then, the system of states will not coincide with the system of nations. Points at which state and nation fail to coincide are likely to be hot spots politically; indeed, many of the most intense political struggles in the present era have resulted from such situations. The movement to separate Quebec from the rest

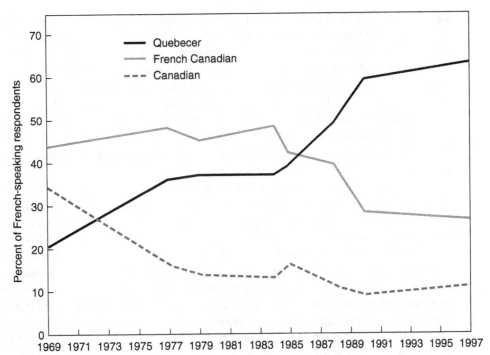

FIGURE 3.4   Collective identification among French-speaking Quebecers, 1970–1997.

SOURCE: By permission of Oxford University Press, Inc. Human Development Report 1998 by The United Nations Development Programme (1998) Fig.5.11.

of Canada; the war between East and West Pakistan, which resulted in the formation of a new state, Bangladesh; the Basque nationalist movement in Spain, which killed an estimated 31 people and injured 125, in 36 attacks from 1995 to 2003; the conflict between French- and Dutch-speaking Belgians; the activities of the Palestine Liberation Organization, which embodies the desire of Palestinians for a state of their own; the chronic unrest among Kurds in Iraq, Iran, and Turkey; the attempt by the region of Chechnya to secede from Russia; talk of eastern Bolivia seceding from the rest of the country; the bloody ethnic wars of the 1990s in Bosnia, Croatia, and Kosovo; the disastrous conflict between the Darfur region of Sudan and the central government of that state; and the difficulty of getting the three regions of Iraq to function together as a state—these are only some of the hot political conflicts occasioned by a disparity between states' boundaries and peoples' sense of nationhood.[10]

One striking, and sometimes disturbing, reality about the modern state is the way it has been able to enlist its people in its cause. Citizens of a state generally identify themselves strongly with it and will defend it with passion. This passionate identification with a nation, or with a state riding on the coattails of nation, is called **nationalism**,

---

[10]Source on Basque nationalist attacks: International Policy Institute for Counter-Terrorism (Israel), *www.ict.org.il.*

and like any passion, it can make people either noble or base.[11] Some have performed great acts of courage and self-sacrifice under the influence of this sentiment, and others have carried out cowardly assassinations and brutal massacres. Whether it makes people noble or ignoble, nationalism is undeniably convenient for governments. It predisposes a large and varied population to obey the single government of the state; and if the state is attacked from outside, nationalist passion makes the defending soldiers a more formidable force than they would otherwise be. Therefore, all governments try to encourage nationalism—not necessarily a hatred of others, but at least a national pride—by holding parades, using national symbols such as the flag, or presenting the state's history to school-children.[12]

Benedict Anderson points out that nationalism (even though it is an "ism") is more akin in many ways to a religious identity than to an ideology like conservatism or socialism.[13] It obviously reaches deeply into people's psyches, because men and women have often been willing to die for their nation. Anderson argues that political ideologies, which mostly address the distribution of power and rewards among different groups of people, leave out an important part of people's lives—the deep, cyclical mysteries of death, procreation, birth, and a continuity that extends beyond our own lives. For many centuries, religion met these needs, and when religion began to decline in the latter part of the eighteenth century in Europe, nationalism arose (or was created) to take its place. Like religion, nationalism offers an identity that takes us beyond ourselves and builds something that lasts across generations.

We have always been ambivalent about nationalism. Consider the two sides in the following quotations. The first is Sir Walter Scott's celebration of it in his *Lay of the Last Minstrel*:

> *Breathes there the man, with soul so dead,*
> *Who never to himself hath said,*
> *This is my own, my native land!*
> *Whose heart hath ne'er within him burned,*
> *As home his footsteps he hath turned,*
> *From wandering on a foreign strand!*
> *[Such a man] concentered all in self,*
> *Living, shall forfeit fair renown,*
> *And, doubly dying, shall go down*
> *To the vile dust, from whence he sprung,*
> *Unwept, unhonoured, and unsung.*[14]

---

[11]An alternative word is *patriotism*, which is actually more directly associated with the state than *nationalism* (since it does not have any other referent, as nationalism has the nation). *Patriotism* has a bit of an old-fashioned ring to it, since it stems from the root *pater*, or "father"—embodying a sense of the state as the fatherland.

[12]There is a large literature on what causes nationalism and how nationalist sentiments are maintained. See, for instance, Hugh Seton-Watson, *Nations and States: An Enquiry into the Origins of Nations and the Politics of Nationalism* (Boulder, CO: Westview Press, 1977); Tom Nairn, *The Break-up of Britain* (London: Verso, 1977); E. J. Hobsbawm, *Nations and Nationalism Since 1780* (Cambridge, England: Cambridge University Press, 1990); Benedict Anderson, *Imagined Communities*, 2nd ed., revised (London: Verso, 1991); and David Laitin, *Identity in Formation: The Russian-Speaking Populations in the Near Abroad* (Ithaca, NY: Cornell University Press, 1998).

[13]Benedict Anderson, *Imagined Communities*, 2d ed. (London: Verso, 1991).

[14]Walter Scott, *The Lay of the Last Minstrel*, canto 6, 1807.

The second gives the view of a cynical spy, portrayed in a novel by Eric Ambler:

> Love of country! There's a curious phrase. Love of a particular patch of earth? Scarcely. Put a German down in a field in Northern France, tell him that it is Hannover, and he cannot contradict you. Love of fellow-countrymen? Surely not. A man will like some of them and dislike others. Love of the country's culture? The men who know most of their countries' cultures are usually the most intelligent and the least patriotic. Love of the country's government? But governments are usually disliked by the people they govern. Love of country, we see, is merely a sloppy mysticism based on ignorance and fear. It has its uses, of course. When a ruling class wishes a people to do something which that people does not want to do, it appeals to patriotism. And, of course, one of the things that people dislike most is allowing themselves to be killed.[15]

The idea of "nation" has been so adapted to modern states for their own use, especially to tap into the emotion of nationalism that is associated with it, that we often refer today simply to **nation-states**. This use recognizes that every state in the world tries to promote feelings of common nationhood among the people living within its boundaries. There is not a state in the world that is not to some degree a nation-state, and political scientists simply recognize that the basic units with which we deal are a combination of state and nation. At the same time, it is good to keep the concepts "state" and "nation" clear because competing claims of nationhood continue to provide one of the strongest challenges to states.

While state leaders would like to enforce a one-to-one correspondence of state and nation, and while this is close enough to being the usual case that we often use the term *nation-state* to describe the basic political unit, nations do not always or necessarily coincide with the political boundaries of states. When they do not, politics is likely to be hot.

✦ STATE-BUILDING

Most of the European states with which I introduced this chapter developed rather slowly, some over a few centuries. The process of establishing a state may have seemed rather natural to you in these examples, even if I did try to emphasize the use of power by those who constructed the state. But states do not just "happen." A state is a structure of rules and institutions, and a set of expectations by people as to how collective actions will be performed. Constructing a state from scratch, or **state-building**, is a complicated thing.

This may not be so evident in the European examples, because they have been softened by the passage of time. However, it is obvious when we look at current examples in which someone has tried to build or transform a state. One of the most dramatic current examples is Iraq, where the victorious United States forces eliminated almost all aspects of the regime of Saddam Hussein in 2003 and set to work to build a new state apparatus untainted by any association with his old Ba'athist Party. This proved to be a very difficult job, as rivalries between the three main ethnic/religious groups in Iraq prevented any easy marshalling of the whole society in a new state structure. Even building the skeleton of the state—the police and military—proved difficult.

---

[15]Eric Ambler, *Journey into Fear* (New York: Knopf, 1943; rpt. Bantam), p. 166.

Many other new or reconstructed states have faced similar problems—Japan after the Second World War, Russia after the fall of the Communist Party in 1991, newly freed colonies since the 1960s, Iraq and Afghanistan in the last few years. Some of these efforts have simply failed, and the regions have descended into what we call **failed states**, geographic entities with no effective central state apparatus. In a failed state such government as there is, is unable to project military force across the territory of the state to maintain security and safety for its people; its laws are not obeyed, and it is unable to provide public services. Much of the territory of the state is controlled by various warlords and gangs in loose and fluid relationships with one another. International terrorist groups like al Quaeda often find it easy to insert themselves into the vacuum of power in failed states, and use them as a home base.

Failed states are rare, but Somalia is a good example, as was Afghanistan in the 1990s. More often, states under construction stumble between varying forms of government for what may be a fairly long time, unless a strong leadership group (the original movement for independence, for instance, in the case of a former colony; the United States occupation forces, in the case of Japan after World War II) is able to establish a firm direction from the start.

Foreign Policy magazine and the Fund for Peace maintain an annual ranking of states according to how high the danger is that they will become failed states. Their rankings can be found at http://www.foreignpolicy.com/failedstates. For 2012, Somalia topped the list, followed by the Democratic Republic of Congo, Sudan, and Chad.

✦ Government and the State

Who is the state? In the section on "'State,' 'Nation,' and the 'Nation-State,'" I referred to "the state" acting in various ways; for example, I wrote, "One striking, and sometimes disturbing, reality about the modern state is the way it has been able to enlist its people in its cause." Who is acting here? If the people are the state, what does it mean to say that they enlist themselves to their cause? We defined the state above as a geographical unit of people who have the legal right to make and enforce rules within their boundaries. This definition implies that we can think about the state in two ways:

- as everyone living in a given territory (the idea of the nation-state, for instance, emphasizes this usage), or
- the governing apparatus that makes and enforces rules.

In the latter vein, when we say "Egypt called for new peace talks in the Mideast," we do not mean that all 84 million Egyptians issued this call; it was the government of Egypt that did so. When we are referring to the *actions* of a state, it is the government we are talking about, because it is the government that acts for a state. This legal right to make and enforce rules is such a central part of our basic definition of *state* that for many purposes, we simply equate the repository of that right (the government) with the state itself. When we use the word in this way, by state we mean the government and bureaucracy.

Thus, the *government* is a key part of the state. As we saw in Chapter 1, the government of a state is a group of people who have the ultimate authority to act on behalf of the state. The government is a unique group in the state; only that group has the right to make decisions that everyone in the state has a duty to accept and obey. When we speak of a state acting—as in the previous example, or as in "Greece asked the International Monetary Fund for help in its 2010 crisis"—it is the government to which we refer.

An influential current of thought in political science has sensitized us to the fact that governments and their bureaucracies are often self-starters in questions of policy—that they actively develop problems and seek solutions to them, rather than waiting for the population to come to them with problems. To understand politics properly, according to this current of thought, we must think of the government and bureaucracy itself as a participant and claimant in politics, rather than as a passive adjudicator over a political process that comes from the population. We often refer to this as the theory of the **autonomous state**.[16] The idea is that the state often participates autonomously in political conflict and decision making.

There is a creative ambiguity here, because this theory requires us to speak of the government and the bureaucracy as the "state," while treating them as autonomous of the rest of what we also call "state." In effect, we use *state* to mean both a territory and its people as well as the government that acts on behalf of those people. This should not be too difficult. In other circumstances, for instance, we are used to saying "the White House" to signify both a building and the presidency that is headquartered in that building. Recognizing the creative ambiguity of our usage helps us address an inherent vagueness in our notion that the "state" acts—that it does things. In the example of the state "enlisting its people to its cause," for example, the actions of the state in fostering nationalism come largely from government and bureaucracy (in outlawing burning of the flag, for instance) but also to some extent from a broader group including television announcers, religious leaders, teachers, and writers (as in the quotation from Sir Walter Scott). The theory of the autonomous state helps sensitize us to this problem, but it cannot answer it finally, because there is an inherent ambiguity in whom we mean when we refer to the state as acting.

Another good thing about the theory of the autonomous state is that it emphasizes for us that the government and bureaucracy may often participate in politics directly, as claimants on their own behalf.[17] Especially in new states where diverse populations have been thrown together into a state and where there is little consensus about proper directions to take, the state apparatus may be forced to (or find itself free to) govern in an authoritarian way.[18] Under these circumstances, free from the constraint of shared traditions and norms, governments may pursue policies benefiting their own personal or class interests in a fairly direct way, which adds to the problems of the new state.

---

[16]P. B. Evans, D. Rueschmayer, and Theda Skocpol, eds., *Bringing the State Back In* (Cambridge, England: Cambridge University Press, 1985).
[17]This is especially relevant to the discussion of "pluralism" in Chapter 12, and to the discussion of institutional interest groups in that chapter.
[18]Here is another nice contrasting example of alternative "choice" and "power" interpretations of a political situation. In this sentence, I was uncertain whether to characterize the government as "forced" to govern in an authoritarian way (which would suggest that they were seeking the best public outcome and that circumstances forced them into authoritarian rule: a choice perspective) or to characterize them as "free" to govern in an authoritarian way (which would suggest that they were self-seeking and took advantage of the chance that was available to them to initiate authoritarian rule: a power perspective).

This is part of what is going on in the example of Nigeria at the end of this chapter. Another example would be the Philippine government's charge that Ferdinand Marcos stole several billion dollars from the government during his rule.[19] Some governments have even savaged the people of their state to further their own ends. Between 1975 and 1979, the government of Cambodia killed about 3 million people (out of a population of 9 million) in its effort to establish a new socialist society. From 1991 to 1994, Haiti's military government encouraged systematic terrorizing of the democratic opposition by troops and thugs. From 2003 to 2006, the government of Sudan turned loose terror to subdue the Darfur tribe in its western region.

Thinking of the government (and associated bureaucracy, media, public institutions, etc.) as "the state" is also useful because it allows us to draw a distinction between "state" and "society." As we have seen, the state is a set of legal arrangements involving sovereignty and embodied in a government. However, the people of the state have a *society* of personal, social, and economic interactions that is partially independent of the people's organization into a state. For instance, from 1989 to 1993, Czechoslovakia was organized as a single state. In 1993, it split into two states: the Slovak Republic and the Czech Republic. Before and after the split, the people of Czechoslovakia were involved in families, friendships, clubs, and economic arrangements (jobs, investments, etc.) that were only indirectly affected by the nature of state organization. A family that was spread across the new border did not cease to function as a family merely because of the new state arrangements.

There is usually some tension between society and state. Some often believe that if "society" is too strong—that is, if pressure groups and special interests can easily force their views on the government—the state will be ineffective and will not be able to make clear decisions. Critics cite this as the reason the United States has difficulty setting clear economic policies and energy policies, for example. A reverse problem is that totalitarian states sometimes seek total control of society (this is why they are called "totalitarian"). Hitler's Germany abolished many private clubs and all labor unions, setting up instead its own organizations; it tried to undermine the family by drawing children away from their parents and into the Hitler Youth organizations.

In the relationship between state and society, an important subset of the overall society is **civil society**. The civil society is the part of society that is organized and active, but is neither controlled by the government nor focused on private concerns such as the family or economic activity. It consists, therefore, of organizations that deal with public questions, but that are not controlled by the government. It is often defined simply as the set of all organizations that are not directly or indirectly part of the government, that are not families, and that are not set up for economic activity. Civil society includes religious organizations, hobby groups, political movements, and professional societies.

What makes civil society important is that it is the natural counterweight to government in the affairs of the state. A diverse and vigorous civil society is important to the healthy functioning of democracy and to the defense of basic human rights.

---

[19]In 2003 the Philippines Supreme Court awarded the government $650 million in Marcos' Swiss bank accounts, all that could be found of his fortune.

Furthermore, civil society is often an important factor when spontaneous movements oppose governmental policies in either democratic or non-democratic systems (see the discussion of such movements in Chapter 13).

This subtle distinction between state and society is a central concern in many theories of democratization and of economic policy making. We will see it again in Chapter 5, for instance, in our analysis of the economic progress of Ghana and South Korea. The distinction is hard to express other than through the theory of the autonomous state.

✦ CHALLENGES TO THE STATE

The state may have evolved over the last few centuries to be the dominant form of political organization, but today it is under strong challenge both from above and below.

Above the state, world leaders are groping for structures that would replace many functions of states and operate over a wider geographic range than the state. This has developed especially in economic matters. In Europe, a European Union established by twenty-seven states is in the process of taking over much of its member states' control of their own economies (I discuss the European Union in the example at the end of this chapter). The United States, Canada, and Mexico have established a free trade zone within which governments will not tax trade. Worldwide, states accepting loans from the

German Soccer fans celebrate their team's victory over Costa Rica with waving flags. The sea of flags was controversial because many Germans are ambivalent about nationalism, given their state's history during the Hitler period.

©AP Photo/Fabian Bimmer

International Monetary Fund (IMF) must shape their financial policies to conform with its requirements. In the area of environmental regulation, many cross-state bodies have been formed through which states relinquish, for instance, their individual control of migratory species of wildlife or the production of pollutants. The challenge from above is not only in the areas of economic policy or the environment. Across North Africa, the Middle East, and southern Asia, militant Islam—the most dynamic religion in the world—seeks to replace the secular states of the postwar period with religious political structures in which the state plays a relatively minor role, state boundaries would (ideally) fade, and the Islamic community would be ruled throughout by its religious leaders.

The state is also under attack from below. Far from fading away with the development of modern economies, as most scholars of all stripes thought they would do, ethnic and regional separatist movements have grown explosively. From the Walloons in Belgium to Tamil separatists in Sri Lanka, to French Canadians in Quebec, to the Croatians and Slovenians in former Yugoslavia, to the Eritreans in Ethiopia, to the Baltic republics in the former Soviet Union—the list could include dozens of other examples—regional or ethnic aspirations, which many years ago were quiet, built up after the 1980s into serious political movements capable at the least of paralyzing their states.

What has been happening? Why the challenges to the state? One way to look at it is to note ways in which the state may have become less valuable in meeting societies' needs. This could help explain the challenge from "above" and the challenge from "below." From above, a series of environmental problems have appeared that are clearly going to become even more pressing in future years and are not readily dealt with by individual states. Swedish trees are dying because of pollution from industry in Britain, Germany, and other states; the chimney swift, which breeds in Canada and the United States but winters in eastern Peru, may cross the boundaries of eleven states in its annual migration; "greenhouse" gases warm every state in the world, regardless of whether they helped to produce them. These are problems that need broader, more overarching political structures than a single state can provide.

Economically, the appropriate scale of industry increased in the twentieth century. Few small states were ever able to develop an automobile industry, for instance. There is no Norwegian auto company or Dutch auto company; auto companies developed mostly in such large states as the United States, Britain, France, Italy, and Japan. Such dynamic industries as nuclear technology, the aircraft industry, and space technology require an even larger scale to work economically. Is it any wonder that states are banding together?

From the other end, the experience of the latter half of the twentieth century was that centralized states are rather clumsy structures for fine-tuning responses to varying local needs such as housing, education, and health care. This helped to fuel pressures for local and regional autonomy. Perhaps, too, with a waning of the symbols of nationalism in a world in which most states cannot control their own destinies militarily, ancient local symbolic attachments or religious symbolic attachments have risen more to the fore and have come to satisfy people's yearning for symbolic identity. Thus, from "above"—problems too big for states to deal with—and from "below" at the local level, states find themselves challenged.

The previous paragraphs give rather a "choice"-oriented explanation of challenges to the state: Other structures can meet some of the people's needs better than the state, I have argued, and so they have begun to rival the state. However, one could also develop a "power"-based explanation: The state really evolved as a military structure; the one thing that defined a state—that still defines *sovereignty*—was that the state wielded a military force that could protect its people against invasion from outside its boundaries and could put down any internal challenge to the government's authority as well. Two developments in the latter half of the twentieth century, both born in the Second World War, have weakened this claim by the state to a monopoly of military power. First, nuclear weapons were invented. In the nuclear age, no government can protect its people against destruction from abroad. It may be able to reply in kind, but it cannot prevent its own destruction; nuclear weapons are too devastating for that. From the other end, guerrilla warfare came into its own in the Second World War. Techniques for local, sustained military effort against superior central forces were developed that insurgent local forces use today in dozens of places around the world, most recently in Afghanistan. Militarily, the ability of states to control their destinies against other states and against internal insurgency has diminished.

Whether we can better understand this from a "choice" or a "power" perspective, it is clear that the state is seriously challenged. We will see in Chapter 18 how some new structures are evolving that might eventually replace some functions of the state.

 ## EXAMPLE

State-Building in Nigeria

No state's experience has been "typical," but it is useful to look at some examples to flesh out the concepts and analyses you have read so far in this chapter. In this section, we will take a brief look at how the Nigerian state was established; in the next section, we will consider the European Union and how it is drawing a number of European states into something new, which is beginning to look like a new, much broader "state."

Nigeria is a populous state on the west coast of Africa, with a population of 170 million. One out of six Africans lives in Nigeria, and its gross national product is second on the continent only to that of South Africa. The country is rich in oil, but it has so many people to feed that the average Nigerian is not especially well-off; the average annual income is $2,600 per person.

In the example that follows, notice especially the difficulties posed for state-building by ethnic and regional tensions, by the presence of armed forces that are not restrained by a strong government, and by the possibilities for corruption that undermine people's faith in the process.

70   PART II   THE STATE AND PUBLIC POLICY

Until 1960, Nigeria was a British colony. Like most colonies, it was not constructed for internal coherence but rather for the administrative convenience of the British. Over 250 different languages and dialects are spoken within its borders, and there is also an important religious split, as the north is primarily Muslim and the south is primarily Christian. After World War II, Britain experimented with various ways of handling this diversity. The plan that it eventually adopted was a decentralized system under which Nigeria was divided into three regions, each centered on one of the three main ethnic groups (see Figure 3.3): (1) the northern region, based on the Hausa-Fulani, (2) the western region, based on the Yorubas, and (3) the eastern region, based on the Ibos. These regions were administratively distinct, each having its own budget.

This arrangement continued in the initial democratic structure set up in 1960. The central government of the new state left many functions under the control of regional governments, in what is called a "federal" system. The situation was unstable, however, because tensions soon developed among the regions. The democratic procedures that were written into Nigeria's constitution favored the north, because it was the most populous region, and the north quickly established political control under the first prime minister, a northern Muslim named Abubakar Balewa.

However, the Ibos in the eastern region—a restless, economically active, and well-educated minority—felt stifled by the political domination of the north. Ibos all over Nigeria were disproportionately urban and held many technical and administrative positions. Three-quarters of Nigeria's diplomats were from the eastern region, as were about half the students who graduated from Nigerian universities in 1966.[20]

In 1966, a coup by Ibo officers toppled the democratic government and put an Ibo general at the head of the state. Six months later, Muslim soldiers struck back, and a new government under Yakubu Gowon, a northerner but a Christian, was installed. At this point the eastern region seceded from Nigeria and proclaimed itself the state of Biafra. The federal government refused to accept Biafra's right to secede, and there followed a bloody civil war lasting two and a half years in which over a million people died. Eventually, the Ibos were starved out and had to give up on secession. Gowon wisely followed a generous, conciliatory policy toward the defeated province and its leaders, one calculated to make it easy for them to rejoin the rest of the country.

Since that time Nigeria has alternated between military rule and democracy. From 1966 to 1979 a series of military governments ruled, replacing each other by armed coups. A brief attempt at democracy from 1979 to 1983 failed because the government was so corrupt that it built no popular support, and it was not mourned when it fell to yet another military coup. From 1983 to 1999, once again the country had a succession of military rulers—who proved just as corrupt as their democratic predecessors, but were more difficult to eliminate. Finally in 1999, when the dictator at that time died, Olusegun Obasanjo—a general but one who had not been implicated in the recent, corrupt regimes—took over and engineered a return to democracy. Obasanjo was elected president in the first election in 1999 and reelected in 2003. He was generally popular, viewed as an honest man who had moved cautiously to weed out some of the most corrupt generals and officials, but he was barred by the constitution from running for a third term in the election of 2007.

---

[20]Pauline H. Baker, "Nigeria: Lurching Toward Unity," *Wilson Quarterly* 4 (Winter 1980), p. 76.

Obasanjo considered flouting the constitution and working out an arrangement by which he could run, but when he realized this would not work he arranged the nomination of a weak and unknown successor, Umaru Yar-Adua. Yar-Adua was an ineffective president, partly because of serious health problems from which he eventually died in 2010. He was succeeded by his deputy president, Goodluck Jonathan, who has turned out to be a rather popular president, making some efforts to restrain corruption. Jonathan was elected President in his own right in 2011, but is opposed by many in the North because he is a Southerner.

Democratic government is hampered in Nigeria by the religious, ethnic, and regional divisions between the north and the south. Southerners believe that the Muslim north will never allow them to gain power. Northerners, in turn, fear that because the south has the oil and most of the economic activity of the state, they will be left with nothing if they give up political power to the south. Religious tensions were fed in 2012 by a wave of church burnings and assassinations in the north led by a militant Islamic group, Boko Haram.

Economic weakness has also hurt Nigeria. Despite its rich oil resource, weak political leadership has left it struggling economically. The military interlude from 1983 to 1999 was especially damaging in this regard. The generals of this period were adept at corruption and holding onto power, but were competent at little else.

However, friends of Nigeria hold on to the hopeful note that the election of 2007, flawed though it was, represented the first successful democratic transition of power from one leader to another in the history of the country, and that the 2011 election was probably the cleanest and least distorted election in the country's history.

Two websites on which you can follow Nigerian affairs are: http://nigeriaworld .com, and http://www.newnigerianpolitics.com.

EXAMPLE
State-Building in the European Union

The **European Union (EU)** is an association of twenty-seven states in Europe that have agreed to coordinate much of their economic policy and some other policy areas; toward this end, they have set up a governmental structure that has limited but increasing power over the governments of the member states. The Union is of particular interest to political scientists because it represents the most serious experiment to date in getting states to give up some of their sovereignty voluntarily.

In the example that follows, notice especially how the European Union has gradually taken on many of the characteristics of a state itself. But notice also how unwieldy the state-like structure is, since it has grown only by accretions of power that the member states have been willing to relinquish to it voluntarily. It lacks the central authority of a real state.

The first real push to unify Europe came after World War II. Many people thought that France and Germany, which had twice in the century fought disastrously against one another, should be bound together in such a way that war between them would be inconceivable. Also, the advantages of operating as a large economic unit, with a single free market open to all, were obvious to those who were trying to rebuild Europe after the war. So with encouragement and some pressure from the American side, what would grow into the European Union was established in 1956. Initially, only six states were members—West Germany, France, Italy, the Netherlands, Belgium, and Luxembourg.

The main economic agreement among the initial members was that all trade would flow freely within their borders. That is, no member could place a tariff on imports of a product from another member to discourage local people from buying it. All the combined populations of the six member states were freely available as customers to any producer in any member state. Also, the member states soon coordinated their agricultural policy, giving up control of most agricultural policy within their borders to the governmental structure of the Union. It is the Union government that decides how high price supports will be for a given commodity, or what will be charged for that commodity abroad. The Common Agricultural Policy was a breakthrough in regional integration, although it proved in practice to be cumbersome and expensive, leading to large production surpluses and to high prices for consumers.

For about thirty years, the Union gradually built somewhat greater institutional power but remained held in check by strong nationalist sentiments on the part of some member states. During this relatively stagnant time, the entrance of Britain, Ireland, Denmark, Portugal, Greece and Spain was probably the biggest change to occur in the Union. Starting in 1985, however, the Union entered a period of intense reform and institution-building that continues today. Many internal barriers to trade were eliminated; decision-making rules that had protected the special interests of member states were relaxed; and finally in 1999, the member states adopted a single common currency to replace the separate currencies of twelve of the then-fifteen member states. (Britain, Denmark, and Sweden decided to opt out.) These changes were significant, and difficult to achieve; the new treaties barely survived a referendum in France, and it took two tries to pass them in a referendum in Denmark. But pass they did, and the end result is that much of Europe now has something like a single economy; and politically, it is approaching something like a state.

Another huge change in the Union was its expansion in 2004 and 2006, when twelve mostly poor states from Eastern Europe and the Mediterranean joined the Union. These states increased the population of the E.U. by about 30 percent but only increased gross domestic product (GDP) by about 4 percent. They need substantial help in developing to the economic level of older members, and their disparate political and economic interests are likely to complicate decision making in the Union.

The European Union has an unwieldy governing structure. The two most important parts of the Union government are the Commission and the European Council, which make most of the rules and carry out executive functions. Two other parts are the Parliament and the Court of Justice. These have lesser powers but are still important.

The European Commission consists of twenty-seven appointed commissioners who head a staff of 55,000 people, including 6,000 translators. Home governments select their commissioners for a term of five years, but they must swear an oath to act on a European

TABLE 3.1

European Union Compared with the United States

	Total Population	Total Armed Forces	Total Gross Domestic Product (billions of dollars)	Defense Expenditures (billions of dollars)
U.S.A.	313,847,465	1,569,000	$15,040	$739.0
E.U.	503,824,373	1,660,574	$15,390	$266.5

SOURCES: International Institute for Strategic Studies, *The Military Balance 2012* (London: Routledge, 2012); CIA, *CIA WorldFactbook online* (revised June, 2012).

basis rather than in the interests of their home country. In practice, the commission has been the focal point of pan-European interests, as opposed to national interests. In this it has been cheered on by its thousands of bureaucrats, whose lives and careers are bound up in the Union. The Commission has a great deal of power. It dominates the setting of most of the Union budget ($163 billion in 2012) and sets regulations for member states in a wide range of areas. As the only permanent part of the executive branch of the Union's government, it also takes the lead in initiating new proposals for policy.

The other part of the executive is the European Council, which represents national interests. It consists of the foreign ministers of the member states, who meet several times a year to consider proposals from the Commission.[21] The Council must approve any major policy proposal before it can go into effect. The Council votes on proposals, with large states getting extra votes.

The Union also has a parliament, which is still the weakest of the big three institutions, though it has been expanding its power in recent years. Its members are elected in Union-wide elections every five years, so it is the only part of the governing apparatus that is directly accountable to the public. This gives it added legitimacy. In recent years the Parliament has gained the right to veto the budget, and it also approves new commissioners after they have been nominated by the government of their state. A number of laws now require the approval of the Parliament, but in many areas, including such important topics as agriculture, economic policy, immigration, police cooperation, and transport, the Commission is only required to consult with the Parliament before it sets the law; the Parliament's consent is not required. Further, a vast number of regulations are set directly by the Commission without ever requiring a vote or consultation with the Parliament.

The fourth institution is the European Court of Justice, which rules on disputes over the treaties the states signed on joining the union. The Court has expanded its powers to include many policies that go beyond those treaties, however. (The European Court of Justice is discussed in detail in Chapter 17.)

Together, the members of the Union have great strength. Table 3.1 shows that, combined, the E.U. has a population greater than that of the United States; its members

---

[21]In addition, four times a year the Council consists of the prime ministers or presidents of the twenty-seven states. Important questions are saved for these "summit" meetings.

have more men and women under arms, and their combined gross domestic products are slightly larger than the gross domestic product of the United States. If they had a unified foreign policy and a unified military command, with a full-scale nuclear force, they would be a superpower similar to the United States.

There is general recognition that a governmental structure that was originally designed for just six countries cannot work for a Union of twenty-seven, or at least not work very well. If nothing else, twenty-seven commissioners are surely too many. And should Malta (with its population of 409,836) have one commissioner, the same as Germany (with over 87 million people)? Also, many broad policies such as the large agricultural subsidies should have changed with the addition of large, poorer countries like Poland, but have never really been adjusted to take into account the expansion of the EU.

Problems with the loosely organized institutional structure of the EU were further highlighted in 2010, when as a result of the worldwide crisis of 2008–2009, several poorer states (Greece, Ireland, Portugal and Spain) came close to economic collapse and required financial aid from the rest of the Union. The Union eventually worked out a package of aid, but only after months of dithering. The EU has a unified economy, but politically it does not have a unified structure to set basic economic and security policies. Germany, for example, has been reluctant to tax its people to provide economic help that would flow to citizens of other European states because of the EU's unified economy. It is as if Pennsylvania had to decide whether to pass an economic aid package to benefit people in other parts of the United States.

To address the problem of weak institutions, the EU established a committee in 2004 to write for the first time a formal constitution for the Union. The vast majority of political leaders favored the new constitution, but it was not broadly popular—not so much for the terms of the constitution itself, as for the "European project" it embodied. When the constitution faced referendums for approval in various countries, it passed in Spain, but then was resoundingly defeated in both France and the Netherlands in May 2005.

In response to this setback, EU leaders developed a stripped-down version of the proposed constitution, and wrote it into a treaty that parliaments could pass rather than requiring a vote by national electorates. It went into effect in 2009, making modest changes in the preceding arrangements (especially, setting a single person to serve as president and spokesperson for the European Council, and weighting the votes of states in the Council more directly on the basis of their populations), but it does not really solve the basic problem of a unified economy tied to a relatively weak and divided political structure.

How close is the European Union to being something like a state? The member states have relinquished considerable sovereignty to the Union. The Union has independent taxing powers, collecting a tax of about 1 percent of each state's income to finance its operation. It sets members' tariff and trade policies and their policies on agricultural price supports, and it regulates many other areas of daily life. The European Court of Justice has successfully imposed surprisingly strong political judgments on member states. On the other hand, military control is the real core of statehood; in that area, the Union has not developed any control over its members, although it has taken some small steps in that direction, establishing its first common military force, a small mobile unit of 60,000 soldiers, in 2003. Just what the EU will become is still open to the tides and chance of time. Today it illustrates nicely the gray area in which it may become difficult to distinguish clearly just when a state is a state.

A well-organized guide to the multifarious websites of different parts of the European Union governance structure is: http://europa.eu/.

KEY TERMS

public good	nationalism	autonomous state
nation	nation-state	civil society
state	state-building	European Union
sovereignty	failed state	

FURTHER READING

Anderson, Benedict. *Imagined Communities: Reflections on the Origin and Spread of Nationalism*, rev. ed. New York: Verso, 1991.

Evans, P. B., Reuschmayer, D., and Skocpol, Theda, eds. *Bringing the State Back In*. New York: Cambridge University Press, 1990.

Hobsbawm, E. J. *Nations and Nationalism Since 1780: Programme, Myth, Reality*. New York: Cambridge University Press, 1990.

Lelieveldt, Herman, and Princen, Sebastiaan. *The Politics of the European Union*. New York: Cambridge University Press, 2011.

Migdal, Joel. *Strong Societies and Weak States: State-Society Relations and State Capabilities in the Third World*. Princeton: Princeton University Press, 1988.

Roeder, Philip G. *Where Nation-States Come From*. Princeton: Princeton University Press, 2007.

Rotberg, Robert I., ed. *When States Fail*. Princeton: Princeton University Press, 2004.

Spruyt, Hendrik. "The Origins, Development, and Possible Decline of the Modern State," *Annual Review of Politics* 5 (2002), pp. 127–49.

Tilly, Charles. *Coercion, Capital, and European States, A.D. 990–1992*. Cambridge, MA: Blackwell, 1992.

CHAPTER 4

POLICIES OF THE STATE[1]

In Chapter 3, we saw that the modern state is a relatively recent invention. It developed gradually over the last several centuries and is still developing as people come to expect the state to take care of more aspects of their lives and as military operations—the special purview of the state—become more complex and expensive. In this chapter, we shall survey some of the most important policies of modern states to consider the variety of things the state does today.

Figure 4.1 charts the growth of overall state activity since the nineteenth century for Sweden, Great Britain, and the United States.

During the latter part of the nineteenth century and into the early twentieth, all three countries devoted a stable and relatively small percentage of their wealth to the government: approximately 8 to 10 percent of all economic activity. Beginning about the time of World War I, however, governmental spending began to take up more and more of the economy, until by the first years of the twenty-first century, it accounted for 38 percent (United States) to 52 percent (Sweden) of all economic activity.

The two world wars contributed to this growth. Britain showed great jumps in the government's role in the economy during both wars, while the United States surged during the Second World War. (The United States entered World War I only near the end of the war.) When the governments' roles subsided again after the wars, they generally did not return to the same levels as before. This pattern is more pronounced in the British case, but it is evident in both. The lasting expansion of government as a result of these wars is probably due not only to the actual expenditures in the wars but also to the fact that in the "total warfare" of the twentieth century, governments became accustomed to controlling the lives of their people: rationing the goods they could buy, for instance, and telling them what jobs they could do. After the wars, the governments continued to

---

[1] I am indebted to Professor Robert Grey for very insightful suggestions about this chapter.

a: Sweden

b: Great Britain

c: United States

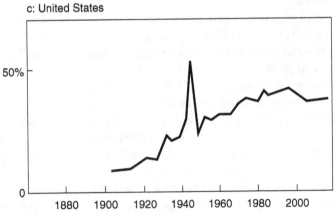

FIGURE 4.1   Government expenditures as a percentage of gross domestic product.

SOURCE: U.S. Department of Commerce, *Historical Statistics of the United States;* Peter Flora ed., *State, Economy, and Society in Western Europe, 1815–1975* (London: MacMillan, 1983); International Monetary Fund, *Government Finance Statistics Yearbook 2007.*

intervene actively in people's lives and extended this intervention to a range of other policies as well.

Sweden was neutral during both wars, and so the conflicts did not have the same effect on Sweden as they had on Britain and the United States; but even neutral Sweden shows a modest spike in governmental activity around 1940. After the war, Sweden, too, left behind the stable, low level of expenditure that had characterized its public sector in the earlier part of the period and, with a socialist government, began a steady increase in the government's share of the economy. By the 1960s, this had brought Sweden up to the same levels as the other two countries, and over the following decades, Sweden surpassed both.

Circumstances (the two world wars, for instance) are a major factor in the development of governments, but ideology also plays a role. Remember from Chapter 2 that the United States has a strongly liberal tradition, and never had a strong socialist movement. Britain also has had stronger liberal traditions than the other countries of Europe; its socialist movement developed later than in other European states, and alternated with Conservative Party governments throughout the post-war period. Sweden, on the other hand, did not have as strong liberal traditions as the other two states, and its strong Social Democratic Party ruled with only occasional interruptions throughout the post-war period. (Britain's social democratic Labor Party governed for only thirty of the eighty years following the Great Depression; Sweden's Social Democratic Party governed for sixty-three of those eighty years.) We can see the effect of liberalism's emphasis on a government that leaves as much as possible up to individuals in the relatively smaller size of government in the United States, somewhat greater size in Great Britain, and still greater size in Sweden. To some extent in Great Britain, and to a much greater extent in Sweden, social democratic governments in Europe built extensive welfare states with national health care systems, free higher education, aid to families, and similar measures unlike the United States.

A strong governmental role in society is typical of industrialized democracies today. When we note that 38 percent of the U.S. gross national product consists of governmental expenditures, for instance, this means that well over one-third of all purchasing of goods and services is done by the government, or by people to whom the government granted money. Ideology moderates the degree to which government grows, but there seem to be certain things that all industrialized democracies have in common that push their governments towards a major role in society regardless of ideology (see the box, p. 81). This was well illustrated by Sweden in the late 1970s. In 1976, a non-socialist government replaced the Socialists, who had been in power almost continuously since 1932. This new government had pledged to avoid expanding the role of government, but as Sweden entered a period of economic difficulty and businesses looked as though they might fail, the government felt it had to take over some of them and keep them going to prevent unemployment. Thus, the non-socialist government ended up nationalizing a number of industries, including the country's largest shipbuilding firm.

Industrialized democracies are all subject to similar pressures for an expanded state, but other states of the world are not necessarily subject to the same sorts of pressures.

As we see in the next section, they exhibit considerably more variability in the size of government.

✦ THE ROLE OF GOVERNMENT IN THE THIRD WORLD

The governments that I discussed in the previous section are what we usually call "industrialized democracies"—prosperous states, typically with per capita annual income above $20,000 or so, which also are usually democracies.[2] North America, much of Europe, and certain other states such as Japan, Australia, and New Zealand comprise this set of states. It is also simply called "the West," a term that is a holdover from the Cold War when the "West" was opposed to the Communist "East."

The formerly communist states of Eastern Europe and Central Asia, because of their special shared history, also shared a distinctive pattern of governmental development. Until about 1990 they had hyper-developed governments, but have been shrinking the reach of government since then; they are quite variable as to how far this has progressed, ranging from Estonia with a very liberal regime (in the sense we used the term in Chapter 2) to Belarus, which still has an essentially unreconstructed socialist state apparatus.

However, about two-thirds of the world's population is not found in either group of states. Latin America, Africa, and Asia (except Japan) comprise a set of states that were mostly not involved in the Cold War and acquired the name "Third World" at that time (because they were neither "East" nor "West"). We still generally use this term today. Many of these states are poor, although a number of them have great mineral wealth (Saudi Arabia and other oil-producing states, for example), and others, such as Mexico, Brazil, Singapore, Malaysia, Thailand, and South Korea, have industrialized and become fairly prosperous.

Politically, these states are a grab bag, ranging from still-communist states like Cuba and China to traditional monarchies like Saudi Arabia. Many are democracies, but most of the nondemocracies of the world are also in this region. The poverty of most of these countries constrains how much their governments can develop, as we will see especially in later parts of this chapter when we look at governmental policies. Generally, government operates at a lower level of involvement than in the industrialized democracies, but the size of government ranges widely among these states, as we see in Table 4.1. Note that there is a good deal of variation among these states, from a low of 9 percent in Myanmar to a high of 36 percent in Chad. Also note that none of these states has as full an involvement of government in the economy as the three industrialized democracies in Figure 4.1.

---

[2]The figure of $20,000 is based on the "purchasing power parity" measure of per capita income; this measure attempts to correct for currency exchange rates in order to compare what people in various countries can purchase, compared with residents of the United States. (See the discussion of PPP per capita GDP on p. 82.)

TABLE 4.1

Government's Expenditures as a Percentage of the Gross Domestic Product in Selected Third World States

Country	Government's Percent of Economic Activity
Argentina	26
Bangladesh	15
Chad	36
Costa Rica	20
Egypt	29
Honduras	21
Malaysia	30
Morocco	31
Mozambique	35
Myanmar	9
Peru	18
South Africa	28
Thailand	20

SOURCE: CIA WorldFactbook online (revised June, 2012).

The politics of industrialized democracies involves a rather standard set of pressures from business, interest groups, and the international community, which results in a similar level of governmental activity from one such country to the next. In contrast, politics in the Third World is more variable, less developed, and more fluid. It is thus more difficult to generalize about politics of this region than about the politics of either industrialized democracies or the formerly communist systems.

"How else are we going to pay for the war?"

© Alex Gregory/*The New Yorker Collection*/www.cartoonbank.com

Why Are The World's States Expanding?

Almost all states in the world have expanded in the degree to which they intervene in their people's lives. Why this is so is a challenging puzzle for political scientists. David Cameron ("The Expansion of the Public Economy: A Comparative Analysis," *American Political Science Review* 72 [December 1978]: 1243–61), reviewed five main explanations that have been advanced:

1. As people become more prosperous, they may want more done for them and are willing to pay for it. Therefore, as industrialization makes people more prosperous, the state naturally grows.
2. As governments have become more clever at using "hidden taxes" such as excise taxes and payroll withholding of income taxes, they can get away with taxing people more heavily, and the state grows.
3. Electoral democracy results in a "bidding up" of the state's operations as parties compete to see which can promise more services to the voters.
4. Once governmental bureaucracies are established, they develop internal pressures for expansion. Inevitably, they succeed in slowly ratcheting upward the scope of their operations.
5. As world trade grows and states' economies become more subject to disruption by events in the international economy, their governments are less able to control what is happening in the state. The governments must then grow to compensate for the greater difficulty they find in functioning.

The jury is out, and will stay out for a long time, as to which among these explanations are valid. For examinations of evidence on the subject, see Cameron's article and also David Lowery and William D. Berry, "The Growth of Government in the United States," *American Journal of Political Science* 27 (November 1983): 665–94.

Of the five proposed explanations, note that numbers 1 and 5 are based on the perspective of politics as choice, numbers 2 and 4 are based on the perspective of politics as power, and number 3 is ambiguous.

Ironically, this expansion has coincided with growing challenges to the state (see pp. 67–69).

→ CONSTRAINTS AND CONDITIONS FOR POLICY

Governments do not fashion the policies of the state in a void. They work within constraints of what is possible, and that obviously helps to shape the policies they make. In addition to what is possible, power relationships within the state also help to determine the shape of policy, as those parts of society that hold power will usually shape policies at least in part to benefit themselves. The states' varying ideological traditions also help to guide their policy choices.

There are many constraints that limit possibilities for government. Probably the dominant constraint in what the state can do is how rich or poor it is. We measure this by **gross domestic product,** or GDP: the total amount of all economic transactions in the state. This is the sum of all such things as the value of the food people have produced, the value of mechanics' work on automobiles, or the value of educational activity. The higher the GDP, the greater is the total amount of economic activity in the state. To measure how economically well off the average person is, we divide GDP by the population, to get per capita GDP.

We usually express GDP in dollars. To give a truer comparison of individual well-being, however, economists prefer to use **PPP per capita GDP,** which is per capita GDP adjusted to take into account the fluctuations in value of other currencies relative to the dollar.[3] Instead of making the people of a state look poor or rich because of currency exchange rates, PPP per capita GDP expresses how much of comparable things people in different states can buy. So, when you see that the poor country of Mozambique has PPP per capita GDP of $1100, that means that an average citizen of Mozambique can buy in a year, in Mozambique, approximately what an American could buy with $1100 in the United States. In this book, when I discuss GDP or per capita GDP, I have used the PPP-adjusted figures to give a more accurate picture. These are what I used, for instance, to compare the United States and the European Union in Table 3.1.

You already saw in Table 4.1 that the overall governmental activity of poorer countries is much lower than that of the well-off countries in Figure 4.1, as a result of the GDP constraint. In the sections that follow, you will see that the specific mix of policies pursued by poor countries is also very different than the policy mix in well-off countries.

A second important factor in determining states' policies is whether or not they are democracies.[4] Democracies spread power at least to some limited extent across the full population of a state, rather than restricting power to some segment of the population such as the military, religious leaders, or an ethnic group. As a result, democracies often emphasize policy areas meeting broad needs in the population—education, housing, health. We will see this to some extent in the sections that follow. But more generally, Adam Przeworski and his collaborators demonstrate in a study using all states of the world that after we have taken into account how wealthy the states are, life expectancies tend to be higher in democracies than in dictatorships, and infant mortality is lower. Also, school enrollments are higher in democracies than in dictatorships, for both boys and girls.[5]

A third factor in states' policy decisions is ideology. We saw above that ideological traditions have had something to do with the growth of the overall size of government in states, but they also help to determine the choices governments make within their overall budgets. We will see below, for instance, that the United States, with its liberal traditions, is very willing to spend money for education and scientific research, which are consistent with each individual working to achieve his or her potential. We will also

---

[3]PPP stands for "purchasing power parity"; that is, this adjustment attempts to express per capita GDP in a way that compares purchasing power, i.e., how much people in varying countries can buy as a result of their economic activity.
[4]Democracies and authoritarian systems are dealt with in detail in Chapter 7.
[5]Adam Przeworski, Mike Alvarez, José Antonio Cheibub, and Fernando Limongi, *Democracy and Development: Political Institutions and Material Well-Being in the World, 1950–1990* (New York: Cambridge University Press, 2000), Chapter 5.

see in Chapter 5 that the United States does not make as much effort as many states do to soften economic inequalities in society.

Finally, a variety of other factors may also enter into governments' choices. It makes a difference if some group holds unusual power in the government, for instance. A military government, where officers run the country, usually has a high defense budget, because the officers take care of their own. In the United States, the elderly are a particularly potent political group because they participate more regularly in elections than younger citizens; this may be one factor in the high cost of health care in the United States (seen below in Table 4.6), which is driven especially by the cost of care in the last year or two of one's life.

In addition, the geography of the state may influence its policies. States in dangerous parts of the world, like Israel or South Korea, usually spend more on defense than other states do. A state with abundant oil resources like Saudi Arabia is in one sense blessed, because its GDP will be higher and the government will have greater opportunities than it would otherwise have. However, a resource like oil can also drive out other kinds of economic activity, as everyone focuses just on the one resource; this can create a whole additional set of problems for the government to address.

Shaped by these varied constraints and conditions, governments' policy mixes vary considerably. In the next sections and in Tables 4.2, 4.3, 4.4, 4.5, and 4.6, we will compare governments' activities in several areas. In order to make the comparisons useful, we will follow the same set of states in each of the tables, to see how their differing circumstances and traditions lead them to differing patterns of policy. Here is a thumbnail sketch of each of the states we will include in the comparisons:

- **Bolivia** is a landlocked country in South America, spanning the Andes Mountains and spilling down into the rainforest in the headwaters of the Amazon River. Its per capita GDP of $4800 puts it among the poorer states of the world, and its economy has suffered from an overdependence on mining. It has had a rocky history politically, with many military coups, but has been a democracy since 1985. Currently its government is controlled by a socialist party.

- **France** is a prosperous European democracy, with per capita GDP of $35,000. Control of its government has cycled over recent decades between a moderate socialist party and a moderate conservative party.

- **Israel** is a prosperous Mideastern democracy, with per capita GDP of $31,000. It was established initially by Jews after World War II and the Holocaust, and maintains an avowedly Jewish basis today. It has been governed at various times by moderate socialist parties and by moderate conservative parties. No matter who is in charge, however, its politics is dominated by the security issue of its relationship with its Arab neighbors, especially the Palestinians who were displaced when it was founded.

- **Mozambique** is a poor state, with per capita GDP of $1100, on the southeastern coast of Africa. It was a colony of Portugal until 1975. After independence it was governed by a socialist party, but the country was torn by civil war for many years. In a truce in 1992 all parties agreed to democratic government and a free market economy. The country has been a democracy since then. It changed presidents

84   PART II   THE STATE AND PUBLIC POLICY

through peaceful elections in 2005, but the 2009 election was marked by such a high degree of election fraud that its status as a democracy is now questionable.

- **Myanmar** (formerly Burma) is a former British colony in Southeast Asia. It became independent in 1948, and has been governed by the military since 1962. The military suppressed opposition brutally until recently, but in 2011 they initiated a partial opening to democratic politics. Myanmar is rich in natural resources, but remains undeveloped economically, with GDP per capita of $1300.

- **Singapore** is a small island state in Southeast Asia, a former colony of Great Britain. Since it became independent in 1965 it has been ruled by a single party with close connections to business; it is not a democracy, and opposition figures are harassed, but Singapore allows more freedom of expression and a more open society than in most nondemocracies. It is a very prosperous state, with per capita GDP of $59,900.

- The **United States** is the oldest democracy in the world. It is a prosperous state, with per capita GDP of $48,100. Since World War II it has been a dominant world power, with widespread political and economic interests, and military forces spread around the world. Its politics is dominated by a left-of-center and a right-of-center party, both with liberal roots.

✦ DEFENSE POLICY

Defense is the one area of policy in which governments have almost without exception proceeded by developing and administering programs themselves and have insisted on holding a monopoly with regard to the policy. Governments sometimes tolerate private schools or hospitals, but they do not tolerate private armies!

As Table 4.2 shows, states vary a great deal in the amount they spend on defense. Probably the most important factor driving defense spending is the situation in which a state finds itself. Israel and Singapore are both situated in dangerous parts of the world,

TABLE 4.2

Defense Preparations for Selected States

	Percent of Population in Active Military	Percent of GDP Spent on Defense
Bolivia	0.5	1.9
France	0.4	2.1
Israel	2.4	6.0
Mozambique	0.05	0.6
Myanmar	0.8	4.4
Singapore	1.4	4.6
United States	0.5	4.9

SOURCE: International Institute for Strategic Studies, *The Military Balance 2012* (London: Routledge, 2012).

Planning for Environmental Sustainability in Costa Rica*

Since the early 1980s, Costa Rica has been working hard to transform its consumption patterns to rationalize human uses of natural resources and the environment.

In 1996 the country outlawed leaded petrol and has since cut its lead levels by two-thirds. All vehicles must now pass an annual emissions inspection, new imported cars must have catalytic converters, and industries are required to have systems to treat the contaminants that they produce. Last year the government, responding to citizens' protests, closed the Placer Dome Company's open-pit gold mine because of harm caused to the environment and local inhabitants.

Costa Rica also uses negative incentives, such as higher import taxes on used imported vehicles without catalytic converters and fines for loggers who cut timber illegally. The hundred cleanest companies in Costa Rica are named annually, and the government awards a green seal of quality to gas stations with the best records in preventing air and water pollution and in treating waste water. A red stamp is for those with the worst records.

The government and civil society also apply moral suasion by using ad campaigns to convince people that a healthy environment is a good objective that also contributes to human well-being and is good for tourism. Civil society, responding to a governmental program, has organized thirty-six natural resource vigilance committees nationwide. These groups provide more than 3,000 citizens to serve as voluntary inspectors of natural resource use and compliance with environmental statutes.

In the late 1980s, in one year alone, Costa Rica felled 10 million cubic meters of forest, with an estimated timber value of $422 million. In 1988 the Netherlands purchased part of Costa Rica's external debt at a cost of $5 million and then wrote it off on the condition that Costa Rica spend an equivalent amount in local currency on forestry redevelopment. In 1989 Sweden purchased a further $5.5 million of Costa Rica's debt for a similar purpose. Such debt-for-nature swaps are helpful but need to be pursued on a much broader scale.

Home to about 5 percent of the world's species of flora and fauna, Costa Rica has been a global leader in environmental sustainability, setting aside about 25 percent of the country as conservation or protected areas and arranging debt-for-nature swaps.

*© Human Development Report, 1998 by The United Nations Development Programme (1998) Fig. 5.11.

and we see this reflected in their military spending. The United States is the dominant world power, with far-flung political and economic interests that take it to every part of the globe, and defending such varied interests requires a large defense effort. Furthermore, at the time of the study in Table 4.2 the United States was involved in a war in Afghanistan; a few years before, its defense spending ran about three to four percent of GDP. Mozambique benefits from its location in a quiet part of the world, and as a very poor country it has more important things to do with its resources than spend them on defense. Accordingly, its defense expenditures are the smallest of any state in the table.

Myanmar stands out in the table. Admittedly, it is in the same dangerous part of the world as Singapore, and we might expect it to spend money for defense, but the

4.4 percent of GDP that goes to support its military goes far beyond what would seem reasonable for a very poor country. This is more a matter of those in charge of the government taking care of themselves, than of a state doing what it has to do.[6]

The actual use to which this investment in the military is put varies a great deal from one country to another. The two superpowers, the United States and Russia, invested substantially in nuclear weapons and missiles during the Cold War, because that was the only way they could realistically threaten each other. They have now cut back a great deal because of the end of the Cold War. Beyond this, Russia has always emphasized the development of a large land army, since it had long borders with potential enemies in China and Europe. The United States, with its peaceful borders, has emphasized more the development of its navy and air force, so that it can keep in touch with its allies around the world, head off trouble spots abroad, and address its global interests.

✦ EDUCATION

The most basic service that most governments are expected to offer their people is education. This is a prerequisite of economic development for the country as a whole, and it greatly expands the world of the individuals who are educated. Many nations of the Third World, whose populations were largely illiterate at the time they acquired independence, have had an uphill fight in bringing education to their peoples, but this history over the last fifty years is mostly a success story.

As Table 4.3 shows, most countries invest a substantial effort in this area of policy and our Third World examples have already accomplished a good deal along these lines. Many have had to overcome great difficulties.

TABLE 4.3

Educational Effort for Selected States

	Percent of GDP Spent on Education	Percent of Eligible Young People Enrolled in High School	Adult Literacy Rate (percent)
Bolivia	6.3	68	91
France	5.6	98	c. 100
Israel	5.9	88	c. 100
Mozambique	5.0	16	55
Myanmar	1.3	51	92
Singapore	3.1	NA	95
United States	5.5	89	c. 100

SOURCE: World Bank, World Development Indicators 2012 (http://data.worldbank.org/), accessed July 2, 2012.

---

[6]Note that in this analysis of states' defense expenditures we have partly looked at *choice* (the state responding to conditions that require spending), and partly at *power* (those who wield power within the state using it to get what they want).

One of these, Mozambique, exemplifies the problems that a poor state faces in attempting to educate its people. Mozambique's investment of 5.0 percent of its GDP compares well with other states, but its GDP is so low that even that does not provide a great deal; only 16 percent of children between the ages of fourteen and seventeen were enrolled in school. However, 55 percent of adults can read, a dramatic improvement over earlier years; in 1980, only 27 percent of adults could read. Although only 16 percent of youth in Mozambique are enrolled in high school, 92 percent of children are enrolled in primary school; in 1980 only 36 percent of children were enrolled. The state is doing what it can, despite severely constrained economic resources.

Notice, by the way, that the two nondemocracies in Table 4.2 (Myanmar, which is poor, and Singapore, which is rich) spend lower proportions of their Gross Domestic Product on education than any of the democracies.

→ RESEARCH AND DEVELOPMENT

If states of the Third World must concentrate on spreading basic education throughout their populations, the more highly developed economies of the industrialized democracies depend on continuing technological development to give them a competitive edge in making high-tech goods (computers, electrical machinery, aircraft, etc.) for export, and for increased efficiencies in their own economies. In most of

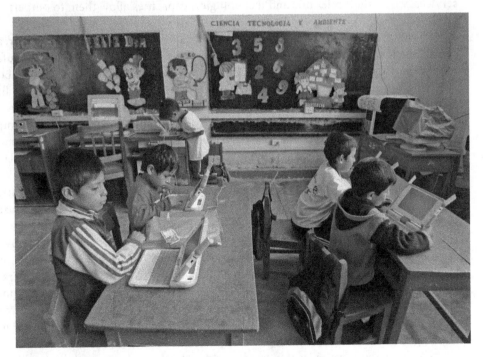

The Peruvian government pursuing educational policy: children at school.
© AP Photo/Martin Mejia

TABLE 4.4

Involvement of Selected States in Research and Development

	Percent of Manufactured Exports High Technology	Researchers in R & D, per Million Population	Government Spending on Research and Development as a Percent of GDP	Net Gain (over expenditure) in License Fees (millions of $)
Bolivia	9	120	0.3	−17
France	25	3,700	2.2	+4,849
Israel	15	NA	4.3	−10
Mozambique	1	15	0.2	−4
Myanmar	NA	18	0.2	NA
Singapore	50	5,834	2.7	−13,991
United States	20	4,673	2.8	+72,133

SOURCE: World Bank. *World Development Indicators 2012* (http://data.worldbank.org), accessed July 2, 2012.

these developed economies, labor costs are too high to allow basic industries such as the manufacture of clothing or of simple plastic goods to compete internationally. Third World states can produce such goods much more cheaply. The special province of the developed economies is in the production of high-tech goods and services, where their scientific and technological capacities allow them to outperform everyone else.

Table 4.4 shows how dependent the industrialized democracies, in particular, are on high-tech industry for their trade with other states. Twenty percent of U.S. manufactured exports were high-tech goods in 2011. In addition, American firms netted about $72 billion through selling licenses for technical processes. This shows up in the fifth column of Table 4.4, "Net Gain (over expenditure) in License Fees." As we see in the table, most poor third world states like Bolivia, Mozambique, and Myanmar are simply not in this game. Prosperous states, however, are heavily involved in the development of technology. They devote considerable resources to it, and they rely on it for a large proportion of their exports.

Net license fees show a state's relationship to technology. The poor countries do not have much of a balance either way, because they have little technical industry that would either pay license fees or generate fees. The United States and France, with established technology industries, reap the benefits of past investments by licensing their technology to companies in other states. Singapore, by contrast, has pushed hard in recent years to develop technologically, supporting large numbers of researchers and spending large sums on research and development. Half of its exports are high-tech products. For now, however, it is still a net consumer of other countries' research, as indicated by the fact that it pays almost $14 billion more in license fees than it generates from its own research.

A fascinating example of a third world state that has successfully established an embryonic high-tech industry is Costa Rica, a relatively poor Central American democracy, with PPP per capita GDP of $11,500. In the mid-1980s, the country cut its tariffs on computers from 133 percent to 10 percent in a successful effort to encourage computer use and literacy. The government assigns every Costa Rican an e-mail address that can be accessed at terminals in all post offices. And by law, expenditures on education must equal at least 6 percent of the gross domestic product.[7] As a result of these and other efforts, technological products have become the largest category of Costa Rica's exports, topping coffee and bananas. Forty percent of Costa Rica's manufacturing exports in 2011 were high-tech products.

In all countries, the technology that makes this sort of industry possible is provided partly by government-sponsored research, partly by research carried on directly by the industries involved, and partly by basic research conducted in universities and other institutions of higher education. We can gain a good idea of the overall level of such activity in a country by observing the number of scientists and engineers in the population. This figure is displayed for our comparison states in the second column of Table 4.4, which gives the number of scientists and engineers engaged in research and development.

✦ HEALTH AND SOCIAL WELFARE

Most modern states have accepted some responsibility for maintaining their people in reasonable health, in adequate housing, with financial security in their old age, and with some security against disability or disaster. Developed economies devote considerable resources to these purposes, while states of the Third World do not do as much. For the people of many poor states, daily life is a series of catastrophes, and it is all they can do to deal with those, much less prepare for future ones. Third World governments must often use any surplus funds they have to develop systems of basic education or to build industrial plants for future economic growth. Finally, as we have already seen, some Third World states are burdened with large military budgets. All these circumstances put such strains on the economies of these states that they usually put social programs on a back burner.

This pattern is evident in Table 4.5, which lists the proportion of national budgets devoted to such items as health, unemployment insurance, pension systems, and housing. The broad pattern is clear: The governments of developed economic systems make a considerable effort to ensure social welfare that poorer governments cannot match. Myanmar spends only 6 percent of GDP on social welfare. Figures are not available for Mozambique, but Madagascar, which is a similarly poor, southeast African state, spends just 8 percent of its GDP on social welfare.

Another notable point in Table 4.5 is that the United States devotes significantly less of its public budget to social programs and health than France. This is a clear reflection of the liberal roots of American ideologies.

What do governments do to promote social welfare? To name a few: Governments may provide child care centers for working parents; psychiatric counseling for emotionally

---

[7]"Who Says the Chips Are Down?" *BusinessWeek,* 10 September 2001, p. 68.

TABLE 4.5

Social Welfare Activity by Selected Governments

	Percent of Governmental Expenditures Devoted to Social Programs, Housing, and Health
Bolivia	27
France	60
Israel	39
Mozambique	NA
Myanmar	6
Singapore	25
United States	45

SOURCE: International Monetary Fund, *Government Finance Statistics Yearbook, 2011* (includes all levels of government, except for Myanmar, which reports only central government expenditures).

troubled people; medical care for their citizens—as the British government does and as the United States does for poor people and for all people over age sixty-five; governments may build residential housing and offer it at inexpensive rates; governments may give grants of money to all families with children to help them with the costs of child rearing (most European governments do this); or governments may provide some sort of minimal national pension for people too old to work. There is quite an array of programs, and countries vary widely in the extent to which they give one or another type of aid.

Table 4.6 presents a more detailed look at one area of social policy—the provision of health care. The table displays the choice governments make of whether to provide a service directly or relegate it to the private sector. The table also compares health care outcomes, showing life expectancy and infant mortality for each country.

In line with what we have seen in other policy areas, general expenditure on health is higher in the richer countries. And we see from the outcomes that this higher expenditure appears to work. Life expectancies are shockingly lower for poor countries like Myanmar and Mozambique. The military government in Myanmar does not make much of an effort, but Mozambique's government dedicates a significant part (4.1 percent) of its GDP to health care. The problem is that the GDP is not very large.

On the other hand, there are fairly large variations in expenditure among the rich countries, and among these countries, greater expenditure does not necessarily translate into better outcomes. The United States spends more on health care than France, for instance, but gets less for it. There are fewer physicians per thousand people in the United States than in France, and life expectancy is lower in the United States than in France. This is generally the case when we compare the United States with other well-off countries. Spending in the United States, as a percent of the GDP, is the highest in the world, but health outcomes lag. In a ranking of overall performance put together by the World Health Organization (WHO), the United States ranks thirty-seventh in the world.

TABLE 4.6

Health Expenditures and Outcomes for Selected States

Country	Government Spending on Health Care, % of GDP	Private Spending on Health, % of GDP	Total Spending on Health Care, % of GDP	Life Expectancy	Physicians per 1,000 People
Bolivia	3.1	1.8	4.9	66	1.2
France	9.0	2.4	11.4	81	3.4
Israel	4.5	3.1	7.6	82	3.6
Mozambique	4.1	1.5	5.6	50	0.03
Myanmar	0.2	1.8	2.0	65	0.5
Singapore	1.6	2.3	3.9	82	1.8
United States	7.9	8.3	16.2	78	2.4

SOURCE: World Bank Group, *World Development Indicators 2012* (http://data.worldbank.org), accessed July 2, 2012.

In 2010 the United States passed the Affordable Care Act (a.k.a. "Obamacare"), an ambitious program to broaden availability of health care not by having government provide the care, but by requiring everyone to buy private insurance. Under the plan the government would pay part of the insurance cost for those with low incomes and would regulate the insurance companies in a number of ways—requiring that they accept anyone regardless of pre-existing conditions, allowing children to stay on their parents' insurance plans until they are 26, barring the companies from dropping anyone because they become sick, eliminating lifetime caps on benefits, and making a number of preventive measures mandatory.

A good source for international comparisons of health outcomes is an OECD report, OECD Health Data 2012, accessible at www.oecd.org/health/health-systems/oecdhealthdata2012.htm.

✦ THE PLACE OF POWER IN POLICY ANALYSIS

It is easy to lapse into an almost pure "choice" perspective in this chapter, because we have been looking at policies, the product of the state. We are thus looking at a variety of choices that states have made, and it is easy to forget the interchanges of power that lie behind the states' decisions. The difference that democracy makes in policy, however, and the impact of a military government like that in Myanmar, offer good reminders that how a government organizes power in the state has much to do with what kind of collective choice it makes.

Good policy analysis will not only assess the objective merits of a policy but also take into account the power constraints under which the policy must work. For instance, any reasonable assessment of U.S. policy in banning the use of marijuana has to take into account factors such as the difficulty of enforcing that law, and the connivance of local governments with marijuana farmers. Once again, we see that even when our subject matter pulls us rather strongly toward one of the poles of power and choice, good analysis requires that we retain both perspectives.

EXAMPLE

The Demographic Challenge

Industrialized countries face a major challenge over the next few decades because of dramatic changes in the age structure of their populations. Over the past half-century, medical advances have meant that people in prosperous countries live longer. At the same time, a number of social and medical changes—the greater involvement of women outside their families, the availability of reliable contraceptive devices—have led to sharply decreased birth rates. As a result, from now through the year 2030 or so, the populations of prosperous countries are going to consist more and more of the aged.

This change has many varied implications for policy, including the question of where support for school expenditures will come from, the possibility that roads may be safer as older drivers are more experienced and pump less testosterone, and many others. However, the most direct and most important challenge posed by the demographic shift is that national pension systems will become very hard to maintain under their present systems of finance.

At present, pension systems in almost all industrialized states are "pay as you go" systems in which those who are engaged in the labor force pay taxes, which the state then passes on to retired people as pensions. Those who are now working expect that when they retire the working population at that time will in turn support them in the same way. The demographic problem, though, means that as time passes there will be more of them, and fewer new workers to support them. The ratio of retired people to those who are working is going to go through the roof. In Europe today there are 35 people of an age to have retired for every 100 people of working age. By 2050, forecasters expect 75 people of an age to have retired for every 100 people of working age. This means that either governments will have to drastically reduce pensions, or workers and their employers will have to pay about triple the taxes that they now pay to fund the pensions. The situation is similar in the United States, though the United States is helped by the fact that it admits large numbers of immigrants each year, almost all of them young. So, the demographic shift in the ratio of pensioners to workers in the United States will be less extreme than that in other industrialized countries.

One solution to the problem could be to shift from "pay as you go" to a "prefunded" system in which workers gradually build retirement accounts through taxes that they and their employers pay into a special fund that invests their money for them. Each worker, when she retires, would then have built up a large pot of money to fund her pension. In other words, her pension would have been prefunded by her earlier taxes and those of her employers, rather than relying on current workers' and employers' taxes. This is happening in many companies' private pension systems, which have shifted from "defined benefit" (a worker gets a pension, funded out of current resources, at a level that has been stated and guaranteed in advance) to "defined contribution" (the worker and company make stated contributions each year the worker is employed, and when the worker retires, he gets whatever the resulting pot of cash yields). Chile has set up its national pension system as a "prefunded" system, and it seems to work well. President George Bush in 2005 proposed a partial change of this sort for the Social Security system in the United States, but his proposals were rejected.

A major problem with shifting from an established "pay as you go" system to a "prefunded" system is that there is a huge bulge that must be funded, because for thirty years or so the government will be paying off the pensions for which it is obligated under the old "pay as you go" system, but the taxes that new workers are paying will be dedicated to prefunding their own future pensions, and cannot be used to support the older retirees. So, how do you pay for the bulge?

 EXAMPLE

Economic Development Compared with "Human Development"

 Economic growth is vital to people's well-being, but we must also take into account things such as how equally the economic benefits are distributed, the state of the environment, or the state of people's health. It is not enough to ask whether the people of a state are prospering; rather, we must ask, how well are they living?

This is hard to assess, because it involves so many diverse things, but the United Nations Development Programme (see Table 4.7) has taken a rough first stab at it in the "human development index."[8] The index combines indicators of gross domestic product per capita, life expectancy, school enrollment, and literacy into a single index; presumably, this measures broad well-being better than gross domestic product alone, and it is interesting to examine how states compare with each other on the two measures.

Qatar, whose people have the world's highest incomes, ranks far lower when life expectancy, school enrollment, and education are added into the equation. The champion at providing a good life given their level of prosperity is Japan, whose people are only the twenty-third richest but rank twelfth on the human development index. A number of other industrialized states also do well, including Germany, Australia, Ireland, and South Korea. The United States does well, with a human development index that ranks fourth in

---

[8]United Nations Development Programme, *Human Development Report,* 2010 (available at http://hdr.undp.org/).

94   PART II   THE STATE AND PUBLIC POLICY

TABLE 4.7

The World's Most Prosperous States, Ranked on Gross Domestic Product per Capita and on the Human Development Index

	PPP Gross Domestic Product per Capita, Worldwide Rank	Human Development Index, Worldwide Rank	Difference in Rankings
Qatar	1	37	−36
Luxembourg	2	25	−23
Singapore	3	26	−23
Norway	4	1	+3
Brunei Darussalam	5	33	−28
United Arab Emirates	6	30	−24
United States	7	4	+3
Switzerland	8	11	−3
Netherlands	9	3	+6
Austria	10	19	−9
Australia	11	2	+9
Kuwait	12	63	−51
Sweden	13	10	+3
Canada	14	6	+8
Denmark	15	16	−1
Ireland	16	7	+9
Finland	17	22	−5
Iceland	18	14	+4
Germany	19	9	+10
Belgium	20	18	+2
Great Britain	21	28	−7
France	22	20	+2
Japan	23	12	+11
South Korea	24	15	+9
Israel	25	17	+8

SOURCE: United Nations Development Programme, *Human Development Report, 2011* (available at http://hdr.undp.org/).

the world. States that have high income based on a restricted product, such as the Arab oil states, tend to do the worst in these comparisons. In particular, many Arab oil producers, such as Qatar, Kuwait, and the United Arab Emirates, have accomplished little despite great resources.

KEY TERMS

gross domestic product
PPP per capita GDP

FURTHER READING

Alstott, Anne L. *No Exit: What Parents Owe Their Children and What Society Owes Parents.* New York: Oxford University Press, 2004.

Blank, Robert H., and Burau, Viola, eds. *Comparative Health Policy.* New York: Palgrave Macmillan, 2004.

Brooks, Arthur C. *Gross National Happiness.* New York: Basic Books, 2008.

Burd-Sharps, Sarah, and Lewis, Kristen. *The Measure of America 2010–2011.* New York: New York University Press, 2011.

Esping-Anderson, Gosta. *The Three Worlds of Welfare Capitalism.* Princeton: Princeton University Press, 1990.

_____. *Why We Need a New Welfare State.* New York: Oxford University Press, 2002.

McKinsey & Co. "How The World's Best-Performing Schools Systems Come Out on Top." Report available at http://www.mckinsey.com/clientservice/ socialsector/resources/pdf/ Worlds_School_Systems_Final.pdf

Mead, Lawrence M. *Government Matters: Welfare Reform in Wisconsin.* Princeton: Princeton University Press, 2004.

Morone, James A., and Jacobs, Lawrence R. *Healthy, Wealthy, and Fair: Health Care and the Good Society.* New York: Oxford University Press, 2005.

Schulz, James H., and Binstock, Robert H. *Aging Nation: The Economics and Politics of Growing Older in America.* Baltimore: Johns Hopkins University Press, 2008.

Scott, James C. *Seeing Like a State: How Certain Schemes to Improve the Human Condition Have Failed.* New Haven, CT: Yale University Press, 1998.

Steinmo, Sven, and Watts, Jon. "It's the Institutions, Stupid! Why Comprehensive National Health Insurance Always Fails in America." *Journal of Health Politics Policy and Law* 20 (1995), pp. 329–72.

CHAPTER 5

ECONOMIC POLICY OF THE STATE[1]

In Chapter 4, we looked at the range of states' policies, but I left one especially important set of policies for separate treatment in this chapter. Economic policy is such a large part of a government's responsibilities and the questions involved in economic policy are sufficiently varied that it deserves treatment on its own. Also, the study of economic policy is intertwined with the broad subfield of *political economy* in political science. This is a part of political science with which you will want to become familiar, and it seemed easiest to present economic policy and political economy together in this chapter.

Certainly, the state of the economy bulks large in our evaluation of a government. In the 2010 election, for instance, the Democratic Party suffered extraordinary losses in both the House and Senate, even though President Barack Obama, a Democrat, was personally well-liked by the electorate. Most analysts ascribed the huge Democratic defeat to the fact that the economy had still not recovered from the 2008–2009 crash; unemployment was still over 9 percent, and the prices of houses had not yet stopped falling. When the economy is performing badly, voters tend to punish whoever is in power. With the economy experiencing a modest recovery in 2012, however, voters reelected Obama—though not by as wide a margin as in 2008.

If nothing else, the centrality of economic policy in a government's responsibilities should be obvious to us from the fact that all of the policies we looked at in Chapter 4 require revenue. For everything else it wants to accomplish—developing military power, educating youth, providing good housing to its people—a government relies on a strong economy to give it the revenues it needs for the policies. Both in its

---

[1]Portions of this chapter are adapted from W. Phillips Shively, ed., *Comparative Governance* (New York: McGraw-Hill, Primis database).

own right as well as instrumentally for the other policies it makes possible, a healthy economy is important to the state.

People's concerns about the economy generally boil down to two broad factors: (1) prosperity and economic growth, that is, the *performance* of the economy; and (2) the *distribution* of economic benefits (how evenly benefits are spread). In the next three sections we will address the most important questions states deal with in making their economic policy, two having to do with performance, and one with distribution. After these sections we will look at some of the conditions that help or hinder governments in dealing with these questions.

❖ ECONOMIC PERFORMANCE 1: GROWTH

Probably the single thing by which governments are most judged is whether the economy of the state grows steadily and rapidly. States certainly vary in how well they provide prosperity and economic growth for their citizens. The map in Figure 5.1 shows the average per capita gross domestic product, or GDP, for the world's states in 2011. (For an explanation of per capita GDP, see p. 82.)

 Baumol's Disease

Political science often uses simple economic analyses to answer tricky questions about politics. (This is part of the subfield "political economy," which I describe on pp. 121–123.) One part of an answer to the question I posed in the chapter on the state, "Why are the world's states growing bigger?" may be provided by an analysis of the economic dilemma of service activities such as the fine arts that William J. Baumol developed in various publications across the 1960s.

His analysis started with the fact that as manufacturing industries become more productive (through more efficient operations, especially the use of new machines that allow a worker to produce more goods in a day), pay scales in manufacturing can increase at a rate greater than inflation.[2] This is great for manufacturing. However, some industries (the so-called "service" sector) produce services that one person does for another. Workers in the service sector cannot as easily increase their productivity, since there are typically no machines to help them produce more service in a day of work. A cellist cannot play more songs in a day. A barber cannot speed up the cutting of hair, or at least not by much. A teacher can only become more efficient by increasing the size of classes—but that usually reduces the quality of the teaching.

As manufacturing workers' pay increased, they would gradually pull away from service workers—if service workers' pay stood still. It does not, though. Over time, as other

Continued

---

[2]"Inflation" is defined on p. 104. Transportation, and distributional industries like retailing, also have a considerable capacity to increase productivity. So, this analysis is not based just on manufacturing alone, although it provides the clearest case.

Baumol's Disease   *Continued*

workers' pay increases, employers in the service sector have to increase their workers' pay similarly to keep them from all moving over into the better paid sectors. Schools have to increase teachers' pay to keep them from quitting and taking jobs in software development, for instance.

As a result, pay in the service sector will increase at a rate greater than inflation, even though the workers in the sector are not producing any more than they have done before. Thus the services that they provide will have to increase in price if they are not to deteriorate in quality (through larger class sizes, for instance). In a sense, there is nothing too awful about this. It just means that everyone in society benefits from the greater efficiency in manufacturing, rather than only those who happened to be lucky enough to work for someone who developed slick new machinery to help them. However, it does lead to the disconcerting fact that, for instance, college tuition will generally rise at a rate greater than overall inflation, as will the costs of hospitalization, symphony concerts, and other labor-intensive services. Economists have coined this "Baumol's disease."

How does this help to answer the question about why states expand? Most of what a state does is to provide labor-intensive services such as education, health care, law enforcement, and safety inspections. As the cost of these services increases, the cost of government will almost inevitably grow at a rate greater than inflation, just in order to keep providing the same set of services. Of course, there are plenty of other things that may be going on as well in the growth of states. It is true that most states have increased their range of services over the past century, but part of the story is that the cost of even constant services has inevitably risen. This is not a story of greedy bureaucrats. It is a story of the gains of sharing productivity with teachers, doctors, and hamburger inspectors.

There are tremendous variations here from one state to another. The average citizen of Luxembourg enjoys $84,700 per year compared with the average citizen of Burundi, with $400 per year. The states of North America and Western Europe are quite prosperous, along with a few east Asian states (Japan, Australia, New Zealand, Singapore, and South Korea), and a few oil-rich Middle Eastern states. With a few exceptions, the states of Africa and central and east Asia are poor. Latin American states, the states of the former Soviet Union, and the states of the Middle East fall in between.

Some of these differences are due to differences in natural resources (Saudi Arabians, who enjoy $24,000 per capita annually, are lucky enough to sit on a lake of oil) or to long and peaceful development as in the case of Canada or the United States. States and their governments, though, do make a difference. In 1972, Ghana and South Korea had roughly the same per capita GDP ($310 and $300, respectively), but by 2011, the per capita GDP of Ghana was only $3,100, while South Korea's had risen to $31,700.[3] Beyond the numbers, what this means is that Ghanaians are still poor,

---

[3]The 1972 figures are straight per capita GDP, because PPP-adjusted figures are not available; the 2011 figures are PPP per capita GDP.

FIGURE 5.1 Per capita gross domestic product of the world's states (PPP), 2005.

SOURCE: © 2013 *The World Bank Group,* All Rights Reserved.

Low-income countries
(less than $4,000)

Lower middle-income
countries ($4,000–$14,000)

Upper middle-income
countries ($14,000–$22,000)

High-income countries
(over $23,000)

while South Koreans have become prosperous—in other words, these numbers really do mean something. However, South Korea is not especially well endowed with natural resources. What happened? The difference between the experiences of the two countries must lie in how they organized themselves and their economies.[4]

One obvious first crack at why countries vary in their growth is that some governments make big mistakes in guiding investment in the economy. Ghana, for instance, like most African states in their first few decades of independence, taxed farmers highly to subsidize food prices for the cities and to pay for ambitious industrial projects. When the industrial projects flopped and at the same time farmers decided not to invest in improving operations on their farms because the government took most of their earnings, the economy was badly hurt.

A lesson that is often drawn from this type of experience is that governments should not try to make fine-tuned economic decisions. Economic decisions, according to this interpretation, require a nimbleness and capacity for handling detailed information that are simply beyond governments. Such decisions are better left to be made separately by individuals in thousands of specific investment decisions. An individual deciding whether to invest money in his or her farm, or perhaps in a nearby factory, can operate more efficiently and will more often choose rightly than the more cumbersome governmental operation. Of course, this leaves out of consideration the reasons why governments may have intervened in the first place—their concern that private market decisions would exacerbate inequalities, for instance, or that they would put investment into projects of which the government does not approve. (I will address the question of government's proper role in economic policy in more detail, pro and con, in Chapter 6.)

Rents and Rent-Seeking

Another reason often advanced for governments to leave economic decisions to free markets is that governments are political arenas and those who are dominant within the government will use their control to extract what economists call **rents**. In this use, *rent* does not mean the fee one pays to live in an apartment. Rather, rents are transfers of money that do not relate to production. If a government uses tax money to build a road or educate children, that is a *productive* transfer of money because the investment (in transportation or in an educated work force) allows the society to produce more. However, if the government uses the general tax money to give its supporters a break on their own taxes, that transfer does not increase society's productivity. It is a *rent*. Other examples of rents would be farm price subsidies, pork-barrel projects, and the creation of unnecessary public jobs for patronage. Governments are in the business of maintaining public support, so if they engage actively in managing the economy, there is certainly a danger that they will gravitate to the economic tool that most easily allows them to buy support—rents.

---

[4]Another possibility would be that United States aid to South Korea after the Korean War helped that country to develop. However, Ghana also attracted a good deal of aid, and South Korea was further handicapped by high military expenditures necessitated by its aggressive neighbor to the north. Probably all of these factors are roughly a wash.

CHAPTER 5   ECONOMIC POLICY OF THE STATE   101

In the case of Ghana, it was because the government's supporters were mostly from the cities that the government taxed the farmers to subsidize cheap food for city dwellers. That is, the government used its power to provide its urban supporters with a rent.

The reason rent-seeking hurts economic growth is that it channels transfers of money into the pockets of the dominant coalition's supporters, rather than into what would be the most efficient economic use of the money. Some degree of rent-seeking occurs in every state. In the United States, for instance, the politically dominant middle class has ensured that the government subsidizes the owners of houses by allowing them to deduct mortgage interest payments on their federal income tax. As a result, there is probably more money spent on housing in the United States (and, therefore, less invested in farms and factories) than makes economic sense. While some degree of rent-seeking occurs everywhere, the extent varies from one state to another. Like Ghana, most of the new states of Africa in the 1960s, 1970s, and 1980s were weak states whose governments could not easily stand up to their own supporters and force consideration of the interests of the unrepresented parts of society. The better organized parts of their societies—urban populations, the military, corrupt officials—made sure they were taken care of, as these states distributed rents with a vengeance. (You see now some of the reason for our consideration of the relative strengths of society and the state on pp. 66–67. When the state is weak relative to society, reliance on rents can flourish.)

Import-Substitution Industrialization

Another policy of the Ghanaian government that probably hurt the economy was the policy of **import-substitution industrialization**. This was a common practice for new, underdeveloped economies in the 1950s, 1960s, and 1970s. To transform their economies to advanced industrial economies, many governments in Latin America, Africa, and Asia tried to encourage the establishment of factories within their own states. They did this by setting high tariffs to discourage imports of manufactured goods from elsewhere. Without competition from producers in other countries, the government thought that new factories would be able to prosper and thus transform the economy. Often, however, the owners of the factories (or their managers, if the factories were owned by the state) simply took advantage of the lack of competition from outside the country to charge high prices for shoddy goods. This did not provide the hoped-for shot in the arm for the economy. Producing overpriced tractors that broke down frequently, for instance, did little to help boost agricultural production. The owners of the protected factories benefited from the policy, but the people as a whole did not get the expanding economy that was supposed to have resulted from this.

The story of Ghana's economy does not end with this catalog of mistakes, however. Coinciding with the reintroduction of democracy in 1992, Ghana's economy began to grow at the healthy rate of 6 percent a year. It is today one of Africa's success stories, both politically and economically. It is still far behind South Korea, however, because of its lost decades of failed economic policies.

The South Korean Experience

The argument so far would seem to be for keeping governments out of economic decisions. Governments, one might argue, are not well suited to the rapid, finely detailed decisions that are required. When they involve themselves in the economy, the argument would go, they are prone to distribute rents unproductively to their supporters.

However, the South Korean side of the South Korea–Ghana comparison suggests another consideration. It is not because the government left it alone that the South Korean economy grew at a wonderful rate. The South Korean state has long intervened directly in business's investment decisions. For many years, for instance, the government controlled which corporations were allowed to borrow money and expand. In addition, in many areas of the economy that it wished to control, the government created large corporate monopolies, which then allowed themselves to be guided by the government in many respects. Finally, the government closed off much international competition by laying down prohibitive tariffs to protect domestic industries. However, instead of aiming at import-substitution industrialization, the government pushed the protected industries to become exporters to other countries. This meant that at least in their export markets, they were still exposed to the discipline of competition with other manufacturers.

If government intervention hurts economic growth, as so many economists say it does, how can it be that South Korea's economy grew rapidly under these conditions? Apparently, the difference between Ghana and South Korea is that South Korea's government was somehow able to intervene in ways that helped the economy rather than hurt it.

First, South Korea had an unusually autonomous state.[5] The population of South Korea is remarkably homogeneous, so there were relatively few societal divisions for the government to balance off. More important, perhaps, the country was faced throughout the period with a strong security threat from North Korea, which had invaded the South once in the 1950s and threatened to do so intermittently thereafter. This threat tended to unite South Koreans and dominated politics so thoroughly that few other conflicts could emerge. All of this gave South Korea's military government a relatively free hand with policy, so that *the government did not have to deal much with rent-seeking.* Its supporters were mostly concerned with national security, and in the name of national security the government could pursue economically rational policies if it chose to do so, rather than diverting resources into subsidies to placate the farmers or pork-barrel projects to placate particular towns or regions. The government left many areas of the economy free to respond flexibly to market forces of supply and demand, even as it controlled certain other strategic parts of the economy tightly.

Some political scientists also credit South Korea's long-established Confucian political culture for the fact that the government did not abuse its power to enrich its followers. The Confucian culture was one that envisioned leaders and followers as being in a natural harmony of mutual obligations, and in this culture leaders were supposed to be modest in their personal demands and fair and farsighted in making policy. This pervades the culture. For example, in a recent study the average CEO compensation in South Korea was 5.6 times as great as the wages of the average manufacturing

---

[5]See the discussion of the *autonomous state,* pp. 65–67.

worker. By way of comparison, the average CEO compensation in the United States was 411 times as great as the average worker's pay.[6]

Finally, South Korea's authoritarian government organized itself in ways that apparently made it more nimble and flexible in economic decisions than is often the case. A good example is the government's response to the oil crisis of 1973, when Mideast oil producers first founded the OPEC cartel of oil producers and oil prices shot up around the world. It took the South Korean government just five months to produce a sophisticated plan to deal with oil prices.[7] By contrast, U.S. President Jimmy Carter proposed a comprehensive energy policy to Congress at about the same time but could not get anything passed. The United States never has adopted a comprehensive energy policy.

This rosy picture of South Korean development could easily leave a misleading impression of perfection. The regime through this period was, after all, an authoritarian military regime. Also, while it is true that the government did a number of things right, and while it is true that it did not have to apply large areas of policy to create rents, still the government made a number of bad investment decisions, and individual government officers often were corrupt. In other words, this picture is not perfect, although it was good enough to bring substantial economic growth to the country. In an analysis based on surveys of businesspeople who were asked how often they had to bribe government officials to do business in various countries, the Transparency International organization ranked South Korea forty-third out of 182 countries in its 2011 Corruption Perception Index—ahead of most Third World countries, which tend to be plagued with governmental corruption, but behind almost all advanced industrial democracies. In addition to the drain of governmental corruption on the economy, the close relationships between governmental officials and the directors of state-sponsored monopolies sometimes led to unwise investments, in which a failing business would be propped up by loans engineered from friendly banks by government officials. These are just warts on the system, albeit important warts. This remained a system that lifted South Korea from deep poverty to become the eleventh largest economy in the world.

However, in 1997, the cumulative effects of such inefficiencies caught up with by the Korean economy. Several banks either went into bankruptcy or proved to be on the verge of bankruptcy, and the South Korean state was forced to seek financial help from the International Monetary Fund—a terrible blow to national pride. This money came with strings attached and led to a large-scale reform of South Korea's banking systems. In 1999, South Korea emerged from the general Asian depression more quickly and more strongly than any of its neighbors. This time the state was again heavily involved, as South Korea reformed radically. When the 2008 worldwide economic crisis hit, South Korea was better placed than most industrialized states. Its economy contracted briefly because many of its export customers had to reduce their purchases, but its financial systems remained reasonably healthy.

---

[6]Sarah Anderson, John Cavanaugh, Chuck Collins, and Eric Benjamin, *Executive Excess 2006*. Published jointly by the Institute for Policy Studies, and United for a Fair Economy.
[7]Dilip K. Das, *Korean Economic Dynamism* (New York: St. Martin's Press, 1992), p. 149.

It is not clear what we should conclude from these two cases about governmental intervention and economic growth. There are a large number of states around the world—not just Ghana, but most African states, the former Soviet Union, and many others—in which governmental intervention has been associated with economic stagnation or even collapse. There are a smaller number where interventionist governments have been associated with strong growth—Japan and smaller Asian countries such as South Korea and Taiwan, but also a country such as France, which has long been noted for its state's strong intervention in the economy. There are several other states, among them Hong Kong and the United States, where noninterventionist governments have presided over prosperity. Finally, many other countries, especially in Latin America, have seen their economies improve markedly when their governments became less interventionist.

Let me offer a speculation, based on these cases: The South Korean case suggests that a crucial factor may be the autonomy of the state apparatus. It is possible that *all* noninterventionist governments, whether or not their state apparatus is autonomous, offer a good possibility for reliable growth, but that interventionist governments are only likely to be successful if they have a good deal of autonomy.[8] According to this thesis, a relatively autonomous, interventionist government would be able to guide successful growth (witness the Korean and French governments). However, less autonomous governments would be subject to so many rent-seeking claims that if they were interventionist the money they might wish to guide into constructive investment would be diverted instead to pay off supporters and cronies with wasteful projects or subsidies. In other words, it is possible that all noninterventionist states can grow reasonably well, but that of interventionist states, only those that are also fairly autonomous can grow well. I do not want to make too much of this argument—free-market systems like that of the United States often have their own sorts of waste—but state autonomy, interacting with interventionist or noninterventionist strategies, may be part of the explanation.

✦ ECONOMIC PERFORMANCE II: CONTROLLING INFLATION AND UNEMPLOYMENT

Another important question about the state and the economy is whether and how the state can control the twin problems of inflation and unemployment.

Inflation

Inflation is a general rise in prices, which means that the currency is worth less than it was previously. Prices of one or another thing will always go up or down, of course, but if prices of most things are rising, that is inflation; a dollar can then no longer buy as much as it could the year before. If everyone could simply adjust to such changes each year, inflation would be no problem. However, inflation hits different people differently.

---

[8]However, both the United States and Great Britain, with relatively noninterventionist governments, did go through years of stagnation in the 1970s.

A person on a fixed income, such as an old person living on a pension, is badly hurt by inflation. Other people may make a great deal of money from it.

Inflation occurs when consumers and governments have a large amount of money to spend, relative to the supply of things they want to buy. This condition, called "excess demand," means that potential purchasers bid against each other for scarce goods; this then drives up the price of the goods. It is important to note that this is a relative relationship: a large amount of money, *relative* to the supply of things. As such, many different factors can shift this relative balance in the direction of inflation:

- A frequent cause is deficit spending by governments. If a government spends more than it takes in taxes, this puts extra money to work without taking a corresponding amount out of private consumption through taxes. In this way, the "money to spend" side of the inflationary balance rises.

- Another possible cause is a shortage in important goods. Bad storms, resulting in a low harvest of grain, can cause inflation by reducing the "supply of things" side of the inflationary balance. A prolonged strike in a major industry such as steel or automobiles can have much the same effect. Similarly, when the major Middle East oil producers cut their production of oil in the 1970s in order to force prices up, this kicked off serious inflation in all other countries of the world. Any of these things can reduce the "supply of things" side of the inflationary balance.

- Monopolies, which allow one company or a group of companies to raise prices without having to worry that their customers will shift to another provider, contribute to inflation.

- Relatedly, trade restrictions between countries can give full or partial monopolies to local providers (since people cannot easily buy from producers in another country) and drive prices up.

Modern economies usually have some inflation, and societies are not badly disturbed by low, regular inflation of less than 5 percent or so a year. When inflation gets higher than that, it has two bad effects: (1) it churns the society up, since some people are hurt by inflation and others make money from it; this accelerates social change and the rise and fall of people's circumstances, creating big winners and big losers in the process. (2) It diverts a good deal of people's energy into figuring out how to circumvent the effects of inflation, rather than how to invest productively.

In many states, at various times inflation has run at high levels. In 1994, for instance, China's inflation rate was 21 percent, Venezuela's was 69 percent, Turkey's was 108 percent, Russia's was 150 percent, and Brazil's was 3,173 percent. That is, prices in Brazil were thirty-one times what they had been the year before! A popular joke in Brazil at the time was that it was cheaper to take a taxi than to ride a bus, because with a bus you had to pay when you got on, while with a taxi you paid at the end of the trip, when the money you gave the driver was worth less than at the beginning of the trip. Levels of inflation like this can cause terrible hardship; this type of inflation destroys everyone's savings as effectively as if every bank in the country had failed. If the money you had saved is worth one thirty-first at the end of the year what it was worth at the beginning of the year, you have effectively lost all of it. One of many stories of personal tragedy in the hyperinflation that struck Germany in the early 1920s (and that many historians think contributed to the rise of Adolph Hitler, because he offered hope of a relief from the misery) is of a retired conductor of the Berlin Philharmonic Orchestra who withdrew his life savings from the bank, bought a subway ticket with the money (all it would buy), rode once around his beloved city, went home, and put a bullet through his head.

A remarkable worldwide development in the late 1990s was that in most countries of the world, inflation dropped a great deal. There were a variety of causes for this. A number of countries reduced their government's budget deficits, which helped to cut inflation. Also, commodities such as oil remained reasonably cheap.[9] Probably the most important reason was that with the end of the Cold War and with various initiatives to make world trade more free and open, companies faced worldwide competition, making it difficult for them to raise prices. Disinflation almost took on a life of its own, sweeping all countries along. Whatever the cause, inflation in the United States was down to 4.1 percent in the fall of 2008, and in Canada to 2.7 percent—both relatively low levels compared with the 1990s. Of the countries that I previously mentioned, many had reduced inflation a good deal: China's inflation rate was down to 6.2 percent, Brazil's to 5.8 percent, Russia's to 14.1 percent, Turkey's to 10.6 percent, and Venezuela's to 30.5 percent. These figures are from just before the 2008–2009 worldwide economic crisis, which forced all inflation levels still lower for a time; for instance, inflation in the United States was just 1.5 percent in early 2013.

✦ UNEMPLOYMENT

Unemployment is a situation in which not enough jobs are available for everyone who wants to work. There is always some amount of unemployment present in any economy as people move from one occupation to another and are temporarily without jobs. Often, however—in fact, most of the time—economies have more unemployment than this minimum base. If a factory closes in a town and unemployed workers do not move away immediately, 20 or 30 percent of available workers in that town may be unemployed. Or throughout a state, economic activity may lessen so that large numbers of people cannot find jobs even if they are prepared to move. In the 2008–2009 worldwide economic crisis economic activity plummeted in most states of the world, and unemployment shot up. The crisis increased unemployment in the United States, for example, from 4.6 percent in 2007 to 9.8 percent in 2010. Even by early 2013 it had only receded to 7.5 percent.

Unemployment hurts society in two ways. First, those who are without work are devastated, because supporting oneself is a basic requirement for social respect in most societies. The inability to find a productive use of one's time robs one of most claims to social standing, so a society with high unemployment is a society with many wasted souls. Second, unemployment is very inefficient. The economy would benefit if everyone who wanted to work productively could do so. There would be more manufactured goods, more food, more available medical care, more of everything.

---

[9]Although, when they began rising again in the 2000s this did *not* especially kick off inflation.

The 2008–2009 economic crash shook the world's financial leaders. Germany's Economy Minister Karl-Theodor zu Guttenberg and Finance Minister Peer Steinbrück contemplate new forecasts of the German gross domestic product, 2009.

© John MacDougall/AFP/Getty Images

To some extent, at least in the short run, controlling unemployment involves a trade-off with controlling inflation. As noted in the preceding section, inflation occurs when goods are in short supply and money is readily available, so that many buyers chase few goods and drive prices up by bidding against each other. Governments' main tool to counteract this is to raise the interest rates that people must pay for loans. (A form of government intervention that even economists like!) As interest rates go up, fewer people borrow money and the amount of money in play declines. Therefore, governments can fairly readily lower inflation by reducing the amount of money available to chase goods.

The problem is that when interest rates go up like this, economic activity declines and, at least in the short term, unemployment rises. Stable, low rates of inflation will eventually allow interest rates to come back down and allow unemployment to drop again—in fact, it will usually drop to a lower level than it had been at before. In the short term, however, fighting inflation by raising interest rates usually cuts back on employment.

Unfortunately, we do not have such clear and simple tools to combat unemployment as we have for inflation. One might think that states could turn interest rates around and lower them to combat unemployment. However, just as the effect of higher interest rates on unemployment was short-term and temporary, so is the effect of lower interest rates. Lowering rates heats up the economy as people borrow more money and spend it, and initially this does produce jobs. Governments often try this, and that is one reason that inflation is no lower around the world than it is. However, this is a temporary effect. The inflation that results from deliberately holding interest rates down in this way causes enough economic dislocation after a while that unemployment goes back up anyway. Now you have managed to create inflation *and* unemployment. This at least is how it works in ordinary times. However, the years after the Great Recession of 2008–2009 were not ordinary. Unemployment was so high during these years that consumers were not able to bid up prices very much, so governments (in the form of their central banks) were able to keep interest rates low for years without stimulating inflation. Interest rates in the United States were held near zero for several years, in an attempt to at least lessen the high unemployment somewhat, and inflation never rose much above 2 percent.

Other state measures to combat unemployment have included creation of jobs through government projects. If governments could be quick at doing this, it would be a very effective tool. They could use otherwise wasted surplus labor for needed investment in roads and schools. The United States did this to a modest extent during the Great Depression under Franklin Roosevelt, and several countries (including the United States) were successful doing this with "stimulus programs" in the 2008–2009 economic crash. However, it is the rare government that can discipline itself to turn job programs on and off quickly as needed. Once a set of jobs is established, a constituency has been created that will now use whatever political power it has in rent-seeking to preserve the jobs as a government subsidy even after the unemployment problem has passed. The reverse is also true: Governments are not only slow to turn off job programs when they are no longer needed; they are also often unable to get a job program started before the emergency for which it was created is almost over. One reason that stimulus spending worked well during the Great Depression and the 2008–2009 crash was that both were long-lasting downturns of several years. Governments did not need to "turn on a dime" to respond to them.

One tool that is always useful for governments is to reduce the "natural" unemployment, which is always present as workers move between jobs or look for new work after local factories have closed, by retraining displaced workers and encouraging them to relocate quickly. Sweden has been particularly successful at this, with large retraining programs and support for workers who relocate to find a job.

Numerous Western European states whose governments are strong and skillful and have tried hard to reduce unemployment but continue to have unemployment levels of close to 10 percent offer evidence that governments find it difficult to reduce unemployment. In "normal times" shortly before the 2008–2009 crash, for instance, unemployment levels in some Western European countries were:

Germany	7.5 percent
France	8.2 percent
Italy	6.7 percent
Spain	12.8 percent

After the crash, in mid 2013 the comparable figures were:

Germany	6.9 percent
France	11.0 percent
Italy	11.5 percent
Spain	26.7 percent

The key to governments' efforts to minimize both unemployment and inflation, as well as sustain economic growth, is to maintain a balance. Low inflation, low unemployment, and high rates of growth are all good things, but each of them is caused by numerous factors. Tools that improve one of these three often make one or both of the others worse. (Raising interest rates to cool down inflation, for instance, will usually slow economic growth and raise unemployment.)

Some strategies, however, improve all three simultaneously. Education, for instance, gives workers more flexible skills so that they are able to adapt more readily as jobs shift; it reduces inflation, by making workers more efficient so that products can be priced more cheaply; and it feeds economic growth. Technological innovation also has a benign effect on all three. It lowers the cost of making things, which lowers inflation; and companies make strong profits because of their lowered costs, so they are able to expand their work forces. This means that unemployment stays low. Some think that the long period of strong growth in the United States starting in the 1990s, combined with low inflation and low unemployment, was the result of technological innovation in the computer industry and the World Wide Web. Technological innovation and good education are two of the best economic tools available to government.

→ Distribution and Economic Inequality

At the outset of this chapter, I noted that not only was the overall performance of the economy important, but also the distribution of goods within the economy. We care not only about how much wealth is generated in the economy but how that wealth is shared among the people of the state. Income inequality is important both as a question of general fairness to individuals and for the effects inequality has on society.

From the standpoint of individuals in society, inequality raises questions of fairness. Is it right for one person to make several hundred times as much as another person? We will address this question in detail in Chapter 6, but it suffices for now to note that to the extent that luck plays a role in your earnings (the family you were born into, the region you live in, the condition of the economy, and the year you entered the labor market), it might well seem fair to smooth out the effects of luck by making incomes more equal than they would otherwise be.

Wide variations in people's incomes also have a number of negative effects on society as a whole. For one thing, it appears that the more widely incomes vary in a country, the less people in that country trust each other and participate politically in their communities.[10] Additionally, it appears that wide income inequality is bad for people's health. Countries with greater income inequality have greater infant mortality, higher rates of obesity, and lower life expectancy than countries with more equal incomes, and the same relationships hold true across the fifty states in the United States. Apparently, the reason for these effects is that inequality creates considerable stress in society; and as is well known, stress is damaging to health in a number of ways.[11]

---

[10]Eric M. Uslaner and Mitchell Brown, "Inequality, Trust, and Civic Engagement," *American Politics Research* (33:6, November 2005), pp. 868–894.

[11]Richard Wilkinson and Kate Pickett, *The Spirit Level: Why Greater Equality Makes Societies Stronger* (New York, Bloomsbury Press: 2009), chapters 6 and 7. Note that the causal connection, while it is certainly plausible, is not firmly established.

"I need some short-term economic stimulus."

© Bernard Schoenbaum/*The New Yorker Collection*/www.cartoonbank.com

Economic inequality varies widely across countries. In Table 5.1 we compare the percentage of all income that goes to the poorest 10 percent of the people in a country, with the percentage that goes to the richest 10 percent. (The greater the difference between the two, the more unequal incomes are in the country.) Here we use the same set of countries for comparison that we used in tables in Chapter 4. Note in the table that the greatest differences between rich and poor are in the poorest states: Bolivia, Mozambique, and Myanmar. This is consistent with the pattern around the world. It is paradoxical, but in the midst of poverty there usually is a small group of people who are quite rich. Modern development—with its widespread education, mobility of populations, and trade unions—alleviates inequality compared to countries with backward economies. So, most poor states have greater income inequality than economically developed states do.

However, rates of prosperity or poverty do not entirely determine a state's level of economic inequality. Government policies can also have an effect. France, Singapore, and Israel all have lower levels of inequality than the United States, though the United States is richer than France or Israel. Some countries stand out with low levels of inequality. Singapore's culture emphasizes community over the individual, and there is

CHAPTER 5   ECONOMIC POLICY OF THE STATE   111

| TABLE 5.1 | | | |

Income Inequality in Selected States

	Percent of Income Earned by Poorest 10% of Population	Percent of Income Earned by Richest 10% of Population	Difference
Bolivia	1	45	44
France	3	25	22
Israel	3	24	21
Mozambique	2	37	35
Myanmar	3	32	29
Singapore	4	23	19
United States	2	30	28

SOURCE: *CIA WorldFactbook*, https://www.cia.gov/library/publications/the-world-factbook/, accessed July 3, 2012.

a surprisingly low level of inequality among individuals in that country, even given that it is a prosperous state. Belarus (not shown in the table), achieves an even lower level of inequality than Singapore, with a difference of eighteen percentage points between the two income groups. Belarus is not as rich as Singapore; its per capita GDP is $14,900. But as a formerly Communist country, still ruled by many of the old Communist functionaries, it continues the traditional Communist effort to equalize incomes.

In broad international comparisons the United States stands out, just as it does in the more limited comparisons of Table 5.1, as a state with a surprising level of inequality given its great overall prosperity. Of 134 states around the world the United States ranks 92nd in equality, which means that only forty-two states have more unequal income distributions than the United States. These are almost all poor states like Bolivia or Mozambique. When compared with other rich, industrialized states, the United States ranks twenty-fourth out of twenty-five.[12]

Governments have two options if they want to create greater equality: (1) special subsidies and aids for the poor and (2) systems of **progressive taxation**. A progressive tax is one that takes a greater percentage of income from a person who is relatively well off and a smaller percentage from one who is not doing so well. Graduated income taxes are designed to be progressive, although they are often filled with loopholes that benefit those who are better off (which makes the tax less progressive). For instance, if an income tax is set up so that a person earning $10,000 a year pays no tax, while a person earning $20,000 a year pays $2,000 (10 percent of that income) and a person earning $50,000 pays $10,000 (20 percent of that income), then the tax is progressive.

Not all taxes are progressive. Many are **regressive** in that they take a higher percentage of poor people's income than they do from those who are better off. The Social

---

[12]CIA WorldFactbook. The comparison was of Gini coefficients, a standard measure of income inequality. Two analyses of income inequality in the United States are Larry M. Bartels, *Unequal Democracy* (Princeton, NJ: Princeton University Press, 2008) and Jacob S. Hacker and Paul Pierson, *Winner-Take-All Politics: How Washington Made the Rich Richer—and Turned Its Back on the Middle Class* (New York: Simon & Schuster, 2010).

Security tax in the United States is an example. In 2013, workers in the United States had to pay 6.2 percent of their income to Social Security, up to a maximum income of $113,700. Any income over that amount was untaxed; thus, a person earning $30,000 a year paid 6.2 percent of that in Social Security taxes, while a person earning $150,000 a year paid $7,049 (that is, 6.2 percent of $113,700) in tax, which was only 4.7 percent of the $150,000 income.

In the United States over recent years, taking all sorts of levies into account, the progressive and regressive taxes have just about canceled one another out, though with mild progressivity, so that people's relative incomes have been just about the same before and after taxes.[13] That is to say, tax policies overall have not changed the distribution of incomes very much.

✦ INDEPENDENT CENTRAL BANKS

In the first four sections of this chapter, we have looked at three general areas in which governments take responsibility for the proper functioning of the economy: growth, inflation and unemployment, and inequality. In doing so, we have looked at a number of the things governments can do to accomplish these things, and we have looked at some of the things that stand in their way. We will conclude the chapter by looking at one major tool: independent central banks, which I will discuss in this section; and at one major impediment: corruption, which I will discuss in the next section.

One institutional tool that many think can help governments make effective economic policy is a relatively independent central bank. A **central bank** is a bank that a government establishes to help handle its transactions; to coordinate the policies of private banks; and above all, to control interest rates either by lending its reserves freely (to lower interest charges by increasing the amount of money in circulation) or by increasing its reserves (to pull money out of circulation and thus raise interest rates). Every modern state has such a bank. In the United States, it is called the Federal Reserve Bank; in Britain, it is the Bank of England; in the European Union, the European Central Bank.

Although the state sets up each of these banks and they are thus public agencies, central banks vary from one state to another in how autonomous they are of the state's political leaders. Some central banks operate independently, while some are controlled. What constitutes "autonomy" may be fairly subtle since the political leaders do, after all, appoint the banks' directors. Britain, for instance, extended greater autonomy to the Bank of England in 1994 simply by starting to publish the minutes of the monthly meeting of the governor of the bank and the chancellor of the Exchequer (similar to the Treasury secretary in the United States). Publishing the minutes made it more difficult

---

[13]Thomas Piketty and Emmanuel Saez, "How Progressive Is the U.S. Federal Tax System? A Historical and International Perspective," *Journal of Economic Perspectives*, 21 (Winter 2007), pp. 3–24. In 2004 the poorest group in the study, the second quintile of the population, had 6.1 percent of national income before taxes, and this rose to 7.2 percent of national income after federal taxes were taken into account; the richest group (the top one-hundredth of one percent) dipped from 3.0 percent of pre-tax national income to 2.5 percent of after-tax national income. Although the taxes were progressive overall, their effect was modest.

for the chancellor to direct the bank to take actions that the bank's governor deemed unwise. This may not look like much, but in the stately world of high finance, it was a major step toward bank independence.[14]

There is always some degree of tension between central banks and the rest of the state's political leaders, and it can sometimes reach dramatic heights. In 2010 President Cristina Kirchner of Argentina tried to fire the director of Argentina's central bank because he was unwilling to release several billion dollars of the bank's reserves for her to use for political purposes. When he refused to leave, she surrounded the bank with police to keep him from entering the building.

Why might it be important for the central bank to be independent of the government's political leaders? Using interest rates to control inflation requires unpopular decisions. In particular, raising interest rates to cut back on economic growth when jobs are expanding rapidly is not a good way to make friends! One chair of the Federal Reserve Bank once said that its job was "to take away the punch bowl when it looks as though people are beginning to enjoy the party." For this reason, political scientists and economists have long thought that a central bank that was closely controlled by political leaders would not work very hard to reduce inflation and that if a state wanted to keep inflation low, it should make its central bank fairly autonomous.

As Figure 5.2 illustrates, states with relatively independent central banks tend to have stronger records on inflation than those whose central banks are more directly run by the government. Germany, with the most independent central bank, averaged about 4 percent inflation from 1972 to 1989, while Spain, Norway, and Belgium, with the least independent banks, averaged inflation of almost 9 percent. It is also the case, not shown on this figure, that when Britain extended more independence to the Bank of England in 1994, that change was followed by an unusually bold increase in interest rates. Thus, there would seem to be something to this.

However, it often happens in political science that although two things coincide, it is not clear which causes which. It might appear obvious from the figure that independent central banks bring lower inflation, but it is at least possible that things are the other way around. It might be that in states where inflation is reasonably low, so that central banks do not have to do the unpopular thing too often, the state's leaders are willing to tolerate more autonomy in their central bank. If the bank has to make people angry fairly often, however, the leaders may act to take control of it and stop it from raising rates so frequently. In other words, it could be that low inflation creates the conditions for independent central banks, rather than the other way around. There is some evidence for this. Javier Ortiz Batalla shows that many Latin American states had established rather autonomous central banks by the late 1920s but that under the pressures of the high inflation of the mid-1930s, most took away that autonomy.[15] In these cases, it looks as though high inflation may have produced central banks that were closely directed by their governments, rather than vice versa.

Thus, there are two possible stories to tell about the picture in Figure 5.2 and some evidence for each. This is often the case in political science because we do not

---

[14] In 1997, the government went even further and gave the Bank of England full, formal independence from the cabinet.
[15] Javier Ortiz Batalla, *Essays on the Early History of Latin American Central Banking*, Ph.D. dissertation in economics, University of California–Los Angeles, 1993.

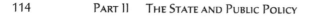

FIGURE 5.2 Inflation and central-bank independence. Annual average inflation rate (percent), 1972–1989.

SOURCES: World Bank, *World Development Indicators 2002*; Alex Cukierman, Steven B. Webb, and Bilin Neyapti, "Measuring the Independence of Central Banks and Its Effect on Policy Outcomes," 6 *World Bank Economic Review* (1992), pp. 353–398.

have the experimenter's luxury of controlling which things will vary and under what conditions. We have to take our coincidences where we find them and interpret them to the best of our ability. That does not mean we must throw up our hands, however. In this example, for instance, while both possibilities are plausible, the first is probably more compelling. There is strong reason to believe that political leaders, if they controlled banks, would allow higher inflation than independent bankers would otherwise have allowed, and thus most people would find it hard to reject that explanation.

On the other hand, the presence of a second potential explanation, with some attendant evidence, makes us keep our eyes open and seek further evidence to help us choose between the two. This is actually a fairly typical example of how political science develops its ideas in all areas.

✦ CORRUPTION

Another political-economic condition that affects the functioning of economies is the degree of **corruption** in the society: that is, the use of public resources for private gain. Our concern is with officials performing their public tasks improperly to receive personal benefits: elected officials selling their votes, police overlooking crimes in return for a bribe, or a housing inspector ignoring an unsafe building in return for a favor.

Frankly, I have never been quite sure where to deal with corruption in this book. It is a factor not only in economic policy, which is the main focus of this chapter, but also relates to politics and policy well beyond economics. If a voter accepts a payoff in exchange for voting a certain way, for instance, that is corruption, even though it is not part of economic policy. On the other hand, corruption usually does involve an exchange of cash or of something with cash value. In that sense, it represents a meeting ground of sorts for politics and the economy. As I will note in this section, the level of corruption in government influences powerfully how the economy functions. So, this chapter seems as reasonable a location as any for the discussion of corruption.

One might first ask, why bother about corruption? It has always been present in human exchange, and there does not seem to be much we can do about it. It may even be the case that corruption occasionally serves good purposes by greasing the skids for commerce. The answer to this is twofold. First, the effects of corruption are horrid, and it is not something society should tolerate. Second, while it does surely exist everywhere, it is worse in some places than in others, so there are clearly things we can do about it.

What does corruption do to the community? Its worst effect may be to produce cynicism, lack of faith, and disregard for the rule of law. Corruption also has direct economic costs. Some of these are obvious and dramatic, such as the billions of dollars the dictator Saddam Hussein extracted from Iraq's economy for himself and his family. More generally, the cost of government services not properly provided and the inflated cost of government programs due to corruption drain economic growth and the benefits we receive from governmental services. It was estimated in 2011 that about one-fifth of the Italian economy evaded taxation, enough to pay down the entire national debt of Italy in eight years.[16] The Turkish minister of energy and natural resources charged in 2003 that because of corruption honest citizens paid 36 percent more tax than they should pay.[17] In Nigeria, one of four police officers exists only on paper, with police

---

[16]Anthony Faiola, "Amid Crisis, Italy Confronts a Culture of Tax Evasion," *The Washington Post*, November 22, 2011. (HYPERLINK "http://www.washingtonpost.com/world/amid-crisis-italy-confronts-a-culture-of-tax-evasion/2011/11/22/gIQAef4JtN_story_1.html" www.washingtonpost.com/world/amid-crisis-italy-confronts-a-culture-of-tax-evasion/2011/11/22/gIQAef4JtN_story_1.html)

[17] Transparency International: Daily Corruption News, July 15, 2003, www.transparency.org.

chiefs collecting the extra pay.[18] A new Internet-based procurement system that Mexico introduced in the late 1990s reduced the Mexican government's purchasing costs by 15 percent, largely by eliminating the personal dealings that breed corruption.[19] In Iraq in 2007, the only way to become enlisted as a recruit for the police force was to pay a $500 bribe.[20] Corruption does not always involve bribes. "Personal gain" may result from cozy relationships between vendors and government purchasing agents in the form of job prospects for the purchasing agents when they leave the government or from the connection between moneyed interests and candidates to whom they made large contributions, or in the form of large campaign contributions to candidates. These may be part of the background on the recurrent miniscandals in government purchasing in the United States, including no-bid contracts in the Iraq War that went to campaign contributors, and favorable treatment in Congressional bills for interest groups and corporations that have contributed to members' campaigns. Although illegal bribes for personal gain appear to be relatively rare in the United States, money clearly distorts policy, in a system that we might term "legal corruption."

A vivid example of how corruption may affect people in their daily lives is health care in Romania. In 2009 one man who broke both legs in a basketball game was taken to a hospital for surgery, but because he did not offer the surgeon a bribe, his work was postponed for a week. It was only after he paid a bribe of $510 that the surgeon would work on him. In another incident, a 63-year-old man died of a heart attack in the waiting room of a hospital when no doctor was willing to treat him; the nurse who was with him thought they refused because he looked poor and unlikely to be able to pay a bribe. "Doctors and patients say the bribery follows a set of unwritten rules. The cost of bribes depends on the treatment, ranging from $127 for a straightforward appendix-removal operation to up to more than $6,370 for brain surgery. The suggested bribery prices are passed on by word of mouth, and are publicized on blogs and websites."[21]

Corruption becomes a culture that spills into all aspects of life. An example of this is parking tickets issued by New York City police to United Nations diplomats. Since they have diplomatic immunity, no states' diplomats to the United Nations may be prosecuted in New York; diplomats can, if they are so inclined, ignore "no parking" signs and throw away any tickets that are issued to them. It turns out that diplomats from states that do not have much corruption are law-abiding even when they do not have to be; it is a habit, a cultural predisposition. For instance, in a study of diplomats and parking tickets in New York, there were no traffic violations by envoys from Sweden, Denmark, Japan, Israel, Norway, or Canada—all states with low levels of corruption. (See the box on p. 117.) Members of the Kuwait mission averaged 246 unpaid tickets each, and diplomats from Chad, Sudan, Pakistan, and Ethiopia also had large numbers of tickets. All of these are states that score high on the corruption scale.[22] Cultures of high or low corruption spilled over to their diplomats' behavior in New York.

---

[18]"A Man and a Morass," *The Economist*, May 28, 2011, p. 26.
[19]"Stopping the Rot in Public Life," *The Economist*, September 16, 2000, p. 41.
[20]Damien Cave, "Nonstop Theft and Bribery Stagger Iraq," *New York Times*, December 2, 2007, p. A14.
[21]Dan Bilefsky, "Medical Care in Romania Comes at an Extra Cost," *New York Times*, March 9, 2009, p. A8.
[22]David Brooks, "The Culture of Nations," *New York Times*, August 13, 2006, section 4, p. 11.

CHAPTER 5   ECONOMIC POLICY OF THE STATE   117

 Corruption, on a Scale of 0 to 10

Transparency International, an international organization dedicated to documenting and tracing levels of governmental corruption, has ranked 183 countries for 2011 by their level of corruption. It combined several polls of businesspeople rating agencies as to how much corruption there is in governments with which they had worked to determine the ranking. A score of 10 means politics is totally clean; 0 means that it is totally corrupt. Here are the scores of 125 states from the study. (Only states with populations over 4,000,000 are included here; the states that I used for comparisons in Chapter 4 are marked in bold.)

New Zealand	9.5	Saudi Arabia	4.4	Tanzania	3.0	Ukraine	2.3
Denmark	9.4	Malaysia	4.3	Algeria	2.9	Central African	
Finland	9.4	Cuba	4.2	Egypt	2.9	Republic	2.2
Sweden	9.3	Turkey	4.2	Senegal	2.9	Côte d'Ivoire	2.2
Singapore	**9.2**	Georgia	4.1	Vietnam	2.9	Kenya	2.2
Norway	9.0	South Africa	4.1	**Bolivia**	**2.8**	Laos	2.2
Netherlands	8.9	Croatia	4.0	Mali	2.8	Nepal	2.2
Australia	8.8	Slovakia	4.0	Bangladesh	2.7	Papua New	
Switzerland	8.8	Ghana	3.9	Ecuador	2.7	Guinea	2.2
Canada	8.7	Italy	3.9	Ethiopia	2.7	Paraguay	2.2
Germany	8.0	Brazil	3.8	Guatemala	2.7	Zimbabwe	2.2
Japan	8.0	Tunisia	3.8	Iran	2.7	Cambodia	2.1
Austria	7.8	China	3.6	Kazakhstan	2.7	Guinea	2.1
Great Britain	7.8	Romania	3.6	**Mozambique**	**2.7**	Kyrgyzstan	2.1
Belgium	7.5	Colombia	3.4	Dominican		Yemen	2.1
Ireland	7.5	El Salvador	3.4	Republic	2.6	Angola	2.0
Chile	7.2	Greece	3.4	Honduras	2.6	Chad	2.0
United States	**7.1**	Morocco	3.4	Philippines	2.6	Democratic Republic	
France	**7.0**	Peru	3.4	Syria	2.6	of the Congo	2.0
Uruguay	7.0	Thailand	3.4	Cameroon	2.5	Libya	2.0
United Arab		Bulgaria	3.3	Eritrea	2.5	Burundi	1.9
Emirates	6.8	Serbia	3.3	Lebanon	2.5	Venezuela	1.9
Spain	6.2	Sri Lanka	3.3	Nicaragua	2.5	Haiti	1.8
Portugal	6.1	Liberia	3.2	Niger	2.5	Iraq	1.8
Taiwan	6.1	Zambia	3.2	Pakistan	2.5	Sudan	1.6
Israel	**5.8**	India	3.1	Sierra Leone	2.5	Turkmenistan	1.6
Poland	5.5	Argentina	3.0	Azerbaijan	2.4	Uzbekistan	1.6
South Korea	5.4	Benin	3.0	Belarus	2.4	Afghanistan	1.5
Rwanda	5.0	Burkina Faso	3.0	Nigeria	2.4	**Myanmar**	**1.5**
Costa Rica	4.8	Indonesia	3.0	Russia	2.4	North Korea	1.0
Hungary	4.6	Madagascar	3.0	Togo	2.4	Somalia	1.0
Jordan	4.5	Malawi	3.0	Uganda	2.4		
Czech Republic	4.4	Mexico	3.0	Tajikistan	2.3		

Prosperous, developed states of North America and Europe tend to have the cleanest records, although Singapore (9.2), Chile (7.2), and Uruguay (7.0) are exceptions showing that non-Western, poorer states are not necessarily corrupt; and Italy (3.9) shows that prosperous, industrialized states are not necessarily clean. The United States does not show up especially well with its score of 7.1, ranking behind a number of other states. Canada looks good with its score of 8.7.

What can we do about corruption? First, corruption is not equally pervasive everywhere, and that should give us some hope. If it varies, there must be reasons that cause it to be greater in one place than another. Unfortunately, a number of these reasons do not offer much leverage. Societies undergoing rapid change often appear susceptible to corruption, partly because norms of behavior are in flux so people do not have stable moral guides for behavior and partly because there are so many opportunities for corruption in a situation of rapid economic change. Two good examples of this today are China and Russia, where corruption has exploded in the shift away from planned economies. This doesn't help us much, though—should we tell societies not to undergo rapid change?

The presence of foreign businesses is also a catalyst for corruption, because they may seem like easy marks and are often better situated financially than local officials, so that what may be a huge bribe to the official may look like a small, normal expense to the foreign business.

Other things that have been found to be associated with corruption are low average incomes, intense factional competition, non-Protestant religious traditions, and a history of colonial rule by some country other than Great Britain.[23]

These are interesting, but none of them are things we can do much about. However, Transparency International has developed a "National Integrity System" that does provide a framework for things a state can do to reduce corruption.[24] Essentially, the National Integrity System prescribes strong watchdog officials, especially in Congress or Parliament, and in an attorney-general and auditor-general; establishment of independent anticorruption agencies; clear and transparent procedures for public procurement; a free and open flow of information to the media; and encouragement of a highly developed civil society.

Many other specific measures can also help. The Foreign Corrupt Practices Act, which bans U.S. multinational corporations from including bribes as part of their operating budgets, has probably helped to reduce corruption in other countries. In an attempt to reduce bribery, Russia in 2001 reduced the number of business activities that require a license (an obvious opportunity for bribery) from 2,000 to just 100. Even a simple change like moving Mexico's border customs posts to the actual border, rather than miles away where it was difficult to oversee the inspectors, helped to reduce corruption.[25] An innovative website, I Paid a Bribe (for India, www.ipaidabribe.com; there are many other "I Paid a Bribe" websites for other countries) asks people around the world to report bribes they have paid; it then publicizes these instances and shames governments into taking action.

---

[23]Wayne Sandholtz and William Koetzle, "Accounting for Corruption: Economic Structure, Democracy, and Trade," *International Studies Quarterly* 44 (2000), pp. 31–50; Daniel Treisman, "The Causes of Corruption: A Cross-National Study," *Journal of Public Economics* 76 (2000), pp. 399–457; Marcia Walecki, "Political Corruption: Democracy's Hidden Disease," *Democracy at Large* 2 (Winter, 2006), pp. 16–19.

[24]The National Integrity System is assessed in a comparative case study of eighteen countries in Alan Doig and Stephanie McIvor, "The National Integrity System: Assessing Corruption and Reform," *Public Administration and Development* 23 (2003), pp. 317–32.

[25]Tina Rosenberg, "The Taint of the Greased Palm," *The New York Times Magazine,* August 10, 2003, pp. 28–33.

✦ OTHER MEASURES AVAILABLE TO GOVERNMENT

A number of policies are available to governments to pursue their general goals of encouraging growth, controlling inflation and unemployment, and shaping the distribution of wealth. We have looked here in some detail at two such policies: maintenance of independent central banks and combating corruption. There are many other things they can do, though. These include:

- Measures to increase the rate at which people in the society save, which thus makes more money available for investment. The main tools for this are various tax breaks to benefit saving and investment.

- Measures to maintain competition among companies, which forces them to keep their prices down or risk losing their customers. The main tool for this is regulation to prevent a single company or a couple of companies from establishing a monopoly in a particular product.

- Measures to increase education, which makes everyone in the society more productive.

- Measures to make it easier for workers to move from one job to another, which reduces unemployment. The main tools for this are retraining programs and unemployment compensation.

- Research and development to develop new technology that will build new businesses or make older ones more productive.

- Measures such as the graduated income tax or social welfare programs to redistribute the fruits of the economy.

In a sense, we have come full circle. I said at the beginning of Chapter 4 that we would set aside political economy and economic policy for separate treatment in this chapter. In looking back at the policies I have bulleted above, however, you should see that many of the policies a state can follow to direct its economy are policies we looked at in their own right in Chapter 4. The truth is that the economy is so bound together with society as a whole that all policies are economic policies and economic policy affects everything else in society as well. For all that, the economy is a particularly critical part of the society. We have only been able to scratch the surface of the concern for political economy in political science or of the variety of questions revolving around economic policy. These concerns will arise repeatedly in succeeding chapters.

✦ GLOBALIZATION: ARE STATES LOSING THEIR ABILITY TO MAKE ECONOMIC POLICY?

We have reviewed in this chapter the range of things states can do to manage their economies. However, the development of a freely moving global economy today calls into question how much room for maneuver governments will actually have in the future. States may see themselves diminished, not by a formal reallocation of their powers but by the growth of actors and processes they cannot control as worldwide economic and social functions begin to operate as a single unit in "globalization."[26] In this case, whole areas of economic policy in which the state might want to act may prove impossible for it to control. The state remains a state; it is just that the range of things the state has the capacity to control may shrink. In effect, the state is not challenged in its formal capacity but is hollowed out by shrinkage in the range of things it can actually do. With the development of a large and fluid world economy, the world's investors and capital markets probably determine each state's economic development so strongly that the state—its government and its central bank—actually has only a rather narrow range of choice in economic policies.[27]

As late as 1970, trade (exports plus imports) was only 8 percent of the U.S. gross national product, but by 2011, it had grown to 25 percent. For smaller countries, trade usually bulks even larger; for Denmark in the same year, the sum of exports and imports was 63 percent of the gross national product, and for Belgium it was 124 percent. The international currency markets each day move \$4 trillion around the world—far more than any state's government or central bank can command.[28]

Under these circumstances, states have begun to find that if their economic policies are too unlike those of their neighbors or look too suspicious to international investors, then capital flees their country and the economy turns down. As a result, all states have found themselves forced into the same relatively narrow range of economic policy alternatives.

The classic example for this is the socialist regime of Francois Mitterrand in France. In 1981, France elected Mitterrand to be its first socialist president since 1958. He immediately began a radical expansionist and redistributive program. Family allowances (cash payments to families with children) were raised by 81 percent over two years. Housing allocations for the poor were raised 25 percent. All workers were given a fifth week of paid vacation. Pensions were increased. As a result of these efforts, unemployment dropped and the economy grew more rapidly than other European economies. Incomes became more equal.

However, the rapid expansion of people's purchasing power led to a surge of imports from other countries. France was soon importing far more than it exported, and the value of its currency dropped. Inflation climbed because this made all imported goods more expensive (each import had to be paid for with more francs). The increase in domestic demand also pushed up inflation.

International investors (and French investors as well), fearful that the francs they were holding would lose value because of the inflation, exchanged their francs for dollars, marks, and yen. No one wanted francs, so their value went even lower. Mitterrand's government was faced with a crisis, and within a year of having taken over as president, he abandoned his program to increase jobs and make incomes more equal. Never again in the twelve additional years that Mitterrand served as president would he move far from the middle of the road in economic policy.

---

[26]See the discussion of "Challenges to the State" in Chapter 3.
[27]This theme is developed especially in Jeffrey A. Frieden, *Debt, Development and Democracy* (Princeton: Princeton University Press, 1991); Sven Steinmo, *Taxation and Democracy* (New Haven: Yale University Press, 1993); and Peter Hall, "The Political Economy of Europe in an Era of Interdependence," in *Continuity and Change in Contemporary Capitalism*, ed. Herbert Kitschelt et al. (New York: Cambridge University Press, 1999).
[28]Estimated for October, 2010. World Trade Organization.

A striking example of the limits to states' control of their economies occurred in the 2008–2009 worldwide financial crisis. Many states around the world—Russia, Germany, and others—at first declared that the crisis was an American problem that would not touch them, only to find themselves forced into drastic economic measures to keep their own economies from collapsing. In the case of Germany, in particular, Chancellor Angela Merkel was forced to support large-scale deficit spending that she had initially strongly opposed on ideological grounds.

A further constraint on many of the world's poorest states—which might otherwise be expected to be rather experimental and innovative with their economic policies, because their current circumstances are so bad—is that they are by now heavily in debt to richer countries and to international banks. The International Monetary Fund (IMF) monitors these states and sets conditions under which the debtholders will be willing to stretch out countries' repayments. The IMF's conditions usually involve cautious economic policies: restraining government spending (especially reducing transfers within the population through subsidies) and raising interest rates to fight inflation. Even though many of these policies will be unpopular, debtor states' governments often feel they must abide by them. The only alternative is to refuse to pay their debts at all, which means no one would lend them anything in the future. That is usually a dead end because these states all need capital if they are to develop their economies.

The overall result of all this has been that the states of the world—from rich, industrial states such as France to poor states such as Côte d'Ivoire—are constrained to follow a more or less uniform set of economic policies, regardless of what their governments might otherwise have wished to do.

These are only the most dramatic instances of the general phenomenon of globalization. As world communications improve and as the world's states come to depend more on each other economically, if we are to understand what happens "within" a state's politics, we must look at least in part to the state's international environment. To paraphrase the British cleric, John Donne: No state is an island, entire of itself.

→ POLITICAL ECONOMY

The economy in its relationship to politics is so important that a whole subfield has opened up in the field of political science to study it. The subfield of **political economy** within political science focuses on how the state and the economy interact. A large part of this subfield involves analysis of economic policy, in which we look at how the state's government influences the economy. That is what we have looked at in this chapter.

However, not only does the state influence the economy; the economy also influences the state, and that is another important part of what we study in political economy. As one example of this, an important set of questions addressed by political economy is, "Why do states exist?" You will recall that in Chapter 3, I raised the question of why states arose in Europe in the sixteenth, seventeenth, and eighteenth centuries. Though I did not label the discussion as such, this came right out of political economy; the question was whether the driving force was the new economic activity of the time that created a *need* for the state to be invented or whether it was the new technology of weapons and communication that *made it possible* to invent the state. In other words, we were looking at how economic developments influenced the development of states.[29]

Beyond asking how the state influences the economy and how the economy influences the state, another way in which political economy functions in political science is to bring the methods of economics to bear on political science questions. Economists have developed a distinctive style of analysis, which centers on a set of shared assumptions—especially, the assumption of "rationality": the assumption that *individuals make their decisions in order to maximize specific goals*. Note that this is a specialized definition of rational. By rational, we do not mean "sensible" or "wise" but merely that actions are directed to achieving a goal or a set of goals and that we can analyze them as strategies to meet those goals. Based on the assumption of rationality, plus (usually) other assumptions designed to address a particular theoretic question, economists then derive mathematically what the consequences of those assumptions should be. We call such theories **rational choice models.** A good example is supply and demand analysis in economics. Based on an assumption that the seller and buyer are trying to maximize the amount of money they retain after a transaction (i.e., that they act "rationally"), plus some assumptions about the information they share, economists predict what price they will agree on under varying circumstances. They can then test such conclusions by observation, to see whether in the real world people act as one would assume they do based on the assumptions one has used. The box on pp. 97–98, "Baumol's Disease," provided another example of this kind of economic reasoning.

This sort of analysis, which the political economy subfield brought into the field of political science, has now become so common that it is often not labeled explicitly as "political economy." You will see numerous examples of it in the chapters to come. Two examples, which you will recognize when you read them, are the question of whether it is rational for people to vote, given the small chance that their single vote will change the outcome of a national election (pp. 243–244; and the question of under what circumstances rational actors will form an organization for common action (i.e., an "interest group"; see Chapter 12). This latter is an application of the general problem of public goods, which I introduced in Chapter 3.

Let me hasten to add that while the "political economy" perspective is widely shared in political science, it does not have domination over the field. One of the good things about political science is that a number of perspectives compete in the field. Not all political scientists would take rationality as a good base assumption for analysis. For instance, another important subfield of political science, **political psychology**, looks at the roles of cognition, emotion, and the framing of questions in people's political decisions; none of these assume rationality.

Also, the questions we ask include normative questions that go behind the question of rationality to ask not "Are people making decisions in order to further specific goals" (our definition of rationality) but rather, "*Which* goals should people be furthering?" So, political economy is an important approach and probably comes closer

---

[29]In a related argument, some political economists argue that for a market economy to operate, the one basic requirement is that property rights be defined and upheld. Since only the state can do this, they argue, that is the reason states exist. See Douglas North, *Institutions, Institutional Change and Economic Performance* (New York: Cambridge University Press, 1990).

than any other to providing the dominant approach in the field of political science—but no approach rules political science entirely.

 ## EXAMPLE

Economic Policy in Germany

From the ruins of World War II, West Germany rose to be one of the world's major economies by the 1970s and 1980s. Since it merged with formerly communist East Germany in 1990, united Germany clearly will eventually be an economic giant, even though the East German economy will require a long time before it is a match for its western counterpart. Germany currently has the fifth-largest gross domestic product in the world, topped only by the United States, China, Japan, and India. As you read this example, note especially how Germany has coped with the problems of a mature economy competing in a global economy.

We can characterize the German political economy by three special things: (1) labor relations and the training of workers that are set up to enhance cooperation and emphasize quality, (2) an economy that has been highly organized through a series of regulations and special government-corporation arrangements known as *Ordnungspolitik* (roughly "policy of structured arrangements" but difficult to translate), and (3) policy that has focused strongly on controlling inflation. We shall look here more specifically at each of these and then look also at a major challenge: maintaining German productivity so that a high-wage, high-benefit labor system can continue in the face of growing international competition. With the stresses of globalization, including competition from nearby low-cost neighbors like Poland, the German economic model came under intense pressure in the early 1990s, but Germany adapted well to the challenge and is now in a strong position economically.

Labor Policy

Relations between labor and management have been set up since the 1950s to emphasize cooperation and the peaceful resolution of conflicts. A German innovation after the war, and an institution that typifies German economic relationships, is the system of **codetermination**. For companies with over two thousand employees, by law half of the members of the board of directors must be representatives of the workers. Therefore, workers are involved, along with shareholders, in the management of each company. In practice, this has led to better pay and benefits, better worker training programs, and increased satisfaction among workers.[30]

---

[30]Jutta Helm, "Codetermination in West Germany: What Difference Has It Made?" *West European Politics* 9 (1986): pp. 637–58.

Codetermination may also have contributed to Germany's very low strike record. Other things that have also probably contributed to this are Germany's pattern of industry-wide, rather than company-specific, negotiations between management and labor, and the pattern, seen throughout German politics, of a reliance on cooperation and negotiation more than on confrontation.

Germany also has an unusual system for worker training, which has helped the country build a highly skilled work force. Over half of young Germans—essentially, all who are not going on to university study—enter an elaborate system of apprenticeships run by industry after they graduate from high school. Over 500,000 companies offer apprenticeship training programs, in everything from hairdressing to computerized manufacture of optical equipment. High school graduates enroll in these programs for a period of three to three and a half years, receiving one or two days a week of formal academic training in school, with the other days spent at the plant. The Siemens Company alone spends $220 million dollars a year, to train 10,000 apprentices in its factories.[31]

German industry is typified by the *Mittelstand* ("middle level"), thousands of family-owned small- and medium-sized manufacturing businesses, many in very technical areas of manufacture. These have made Germany a world leader in the manufacture of machine tools and environmentally-friendly equipment like that for wind power. The demand for German products has been so strong that for the last several years Germany has been the world's leading exporter of manufactured products.

Ordnungspolitik

The German economy is highly regulated. The proper content for manufactured goods is stipulated in law and regulation, as are such things as the working condition of machinery or the hours stores may be open (no stores are allowed to be open on Sundays, for instance, and permissible hours on the other days are set by regional governments). These regulations are often fine-tuned to a degree that seems strange to Americans.

As a result of the net of regulation of *Ordnungspolitik,* combined with a population of knowledgeable consumers who are not tolerant of defects, German industry has become known for consumer products that are finely engineered and of excellent quality but that are not inexpensive. Germany is not a throwaway society.

Anti-Inflation Policy

In fiscal policy (whether the government's budget operates in surplus or in deficit) and in monetary policy (regulation of the supply of money, which helps determine the value of the currency), the German government has always emphasized as its chief goal controlling inflation. This may result partly from the historic experience of ruinous hyperinflation in the 1920s. It probably also results in part from so much decision making in Germany by consensus, with a heavy involvement of the bureaucracy and a resultant lessening of the impact of elected officials. Elected officials have a weakness for inflation. If one spends money this year without raising the necessary funds to pay for

[31]Jack Ewing, "The Apprentice: Germany's Answer to Jobless Youth," *Bloomberg Businessweek Magazine*, October 27, 2009, http://www.businessweek.com/magazine/content/09_42/b4151033735128.htm

purchases—that is, if one runs a deficit—the resulting inflation doesn't kick in until a year or two later. People can then feel artificially good for awhile, and if an election is coming up soon, elected officials have plenty of reason to make people feel artificially good. Therefore, democracies tend to run in deficit and to produce inflation. While the German system certainly is a democratic one, its officials have been hemmed in more than in most countries by a bureaucratic consensus that constrains them against indulging in this way.

Since 2002, monetary policy for all countries using the Euro (a common currency adopted by most members of the EU) has been taken over by a European Central Bank, based in Brussels. Therefore, the German central bank no longer controls interest rates in Germany, and the Germans no longer have that tool available to fight inflation. However, when the European Central Bank was established the Germans insisted that its charter make it lean very strongly toward fighting inflation. Today, Germany, as the largest economy in Europe, has a great deal of influence over the Bank's decisions. Through its influence on the EU and the design of its central bank, in effect, Germany still pursues a strong anti-inflationary policy.

The Challenge of Globalization

Labor peace, a passion for quality, and institutional structures that have provided low inflation—these helped for many years to give Germany enviable economic strength as a state and to give its people a high standard of living. Starting in the early 1990s, however, Germany had to struggle to keep its economy competitive. Its problems were exacerbated by the hugely expensive reunification of East and West Germany at the end of the Cold War. (Even just in direct costs of building infrastructure, the reunification cost the German government about $640 billion in the 1990s; and there were large indirect costs as well.)

Germany's economy is hugely dependent on selling goods to the rest of the world. The very traits that I described approvingly with the terms *labor peace* and *Ordnungspolitik*—the extensive regulatory structures that ensure broad security and benefits for workers and quality of products—proved to be a drawback in the more competitive global world that emerged in the 1990s, but Germany has worked to surmount these problems.

German labor input costs (the cost of wages and benefits per year) had long been higher than its competitors', as Table 5.2 illustrates. This meant that for Germany to sell goods at competitive prices, each German worker had to produce about 15 percent more per hour than a worker in the United States—and had to produce about twenty times as much as a worker in nearby Poland. In other words, German productivity had to be much higher than its competitors'.

Faced with such high costs and finding it difficult to reduce them in Germany's highly regulated economy, many large German firms began to move part of their production abroad to lower-cost labor markets such as the United States (for skilled workers) or Eastern Europe (for less-skilled jobs). This was a major factor contributing to unemployment that ran as high as 10 percent. Note that the problem here was not high pay. If manufacturers can use highly educated workers with technological equipment to produce twenty times as much per hour as their competitors in Poland,

TABLE 5.2	
Labor Cost per Worker in Manufacturing, 1998–2002	
Germany	$33,226
Japan	31,687
USA	28,907
Britain	23,843
Hungary	3,755
Poland	1,714

SOURCE: World Bank, *World Development Indicators 2003*.

then there is no problem paying them twenty times as much. The problem only occurs if they are producing ten times as much but are paid twenty times as much.

Germany responded to this challenge in a number of ways over the next several years, breaking up cozy relationships between banks and the businesses that had borrowed from them, making it possible for employers to take on unemployed workers in what were called "mini-jobs" at reduced pay, and changing unemployment benefits. These were all part of an effort to make industry more competitive. They were painful changes, but as a result, from 2001 to 2008 labor costs in Germany dropped 20 percent relative to countries like Spain and Italy; in 2006 alone, productivity in Germany increased a full 2 percent.[32]

These policies worked. From 2001 to 2008 unemployment dropped from 9.3 percent to 7.5 percent. Today, Germany is the second-largest exporting country in the world, ranked just behind China, and ahead of the United States. Germany also weathered the 2008–2009 crash better than most other European states; unemployment, which rose during the crash as it did in all countries, had dropped back to pre-crash levels by 2011.

 EXAMPLE

Economic Policy in Indonesia

 Indonesia is a vast state in Southeast Asia with 248 million people inhabiting several thousand islands. After the state became free of the Netherlands at the end of World War II, it was ruled by military governments, especially the government of General Suharto, which took power in 1967. Suharto was a clever and capable ruler who, under most conditions, was able to guarantee that his main real opposition was his own eventual mortality rather than any political force. He was brought down only by a regionwide economic crisis that

---

[32]"Back Above the Bar Again," *The Economist*, July 14, 2007, pp. 80–83.

swept over Southeast Asia in 1997. As you read this example, note especially how both politics and the economy are important in allowing a poor state to develop its potential.

The state Suharto took over in 1967 was poor and economically underdeveloped, but it had huge natural resources in oil, metal, and forests. Suharto pursued a policy of development hinging on education of the population, market-centered financial policies, and the use of revenue from the exploitation of natural resources to build economic infrastructure for the future. At the same time, he used the economy for his own political support and the support of his family and cronies, in ways that kept it from developing as well as it could have. By the 1990s, however, Indonesia had clearly turned the corner from a subsistence economy to one that was active and diversified. Early in that decade, for the first time, manufacturing accounted for a greater percentage of the gross national product than agriculture.

When the currency crisis hit Southeast Asia in 1997, at first most observers expected Indonesia to escape any pain. Its financial balances were in fairly good shape, and its currency should have weathered the storm. Indonesia did in the end get caught up in the crisis. However, it was not in as good shape as people had thought—although it was still not in terrible shape—partly because of the general panic in the region and partly because the government and the banks colluded to make the country's debts seem artificially low. In the succeeding economic crash, Suharto was ousted and democracy was established.

Since 1997, Indonesia has experienced rapid changes. Suharto's government collapsed in the face of popular demonstrations in 1998; in the ensuing election after democracy had been established, an enigmatic politician, Abdurrahman Wahid, was elected president. Wahid was the leader of a major Islamic party and had a strong base of support in that movement. However, he frittered away his power in inconsistent decisions, glib jokes where serious statements were required, a revolving door in his cabinet, and general inability to lead. He was impeached in July 2001, nominally for corruption but in reality for incompetence, and was replaced by his vice president (from a rival party), Megawati Sukarnoputri. Sukarnoputri, in turn, lost her position in the election of 2004 to a former general, Susilo Mambang Yudhoyono. By now, Indonesia clearly has a lively democracy, with abundant competing media, and some experience with the peaceful transfer of power through elections.

The economy actually recovered fairly well through this period, but economic progress was retarded by spectacular political and social crises that sapped the country's energy. With regard to the economy, the government moved rapidly in 1998 to seize the failed banks' assets; eventually, the government ended up owning industrial assets worth about one-quarter of Indonesia's GDP. Between 1998 and 2003, it gradually sold these off privately to achieve a new beginning for the economy. The effort to privatize the assets did not go smoothly, however, as old Suharto cronies were often able to buy back large parts of their old commercial empires at bargain prices. There have been some reforms. The Suharto family in particular was ousted from their privileged positions in the economy. While growth in the economy was less than 1 percent in 1999, the growth rate averaged about 4 percent annually over the next three years, and was up to 6.4 percent by 2011.

However, the political system did nothing in the first several years of democracy to help the economy. Indonesia should be doing at least as well as its neighbors—if

Michel Camdessus, director of the I.M.F., watches President Suharto of Indonesia sign a 1998 agreement for fiscal austerity. Mr. Camdessus said later that he just did not know what to do with his arms, but outraged Indonesians thought the picture captured the arrogance of the I.M.F. and their country's subservience to it.
© AP Photo/Muchtar Zakaria

nothing else, it sits on a big lake of oil. Indonesia suffered both from the very long damming up of political conflict under Suharto, which burst out more sharply than in most countries with democratization in 1998, and from its deep ethnic divisions. In the aftermath of the 1997 economic collapse, vast anti-Chinese riots drove much of the entrepreneurial and middle-class Chinese population from the country—a loss Indonesia could not easily afford when it required rebuilding. Immediately, once Indonesia established democracy, the province of East Timor pushed for independence from the rest of the country. It won this, but only after military massacres and destruction that ruined its economy. Regional violence in another part of Indonesia, the Aceh province, caused Exxon in March 2001 to close its giant natural gas plant there, which alone produced about 3 percent of Indonesia's total GDP. The basic problems of Indonesia's economic collapse and recovery were always more political and social than economic.

Since Yudhoyono was elected in 2004, however, there has been a good deal of progress. He has proved to be a popular president, and was re-elected in 2009. Under his rule, Indonesia has begun to make political progress to match its economic progress. With its educated work force and abundant natural resources, Indonesia potentially has much going for it. After the 2004 election the new president pledged economic reforms, with a goal of 6 percent economic growth starting in 2005—a level that is necessary if the many young people now entering the labor market are to be able to find jobs. It took him longer than that to accomplish the goal, but growth was 6.4 percent in 2012. Importantly, Yudhoyono has also managed to reduce greatly the army's influence in politics.

The two biggest problems Indonesia must now address are (1) the corruption and red tape that dog business activity, and (2) the infrastructure of roads, water, and so on that the government neglected during the past several years of crisis. Bribery is rampant and expensive in Indonesia, and red tape slows down business formation. It takes an average of 45 days in Indonesia to complete all the paperwork required to start a company, compared with 6 days in Malaysia and 3 in Singapore.[33] Spending on infrastructure dropped from almost $16 billion in 1996 to $3 billion in 2001; electric power is unreliable, roads are bad, and many Indonesians do not have access to clean water.[34]

Corruption continues to be a major problem. Indonesia ranks 100 out of 182 countries for overall corruption in the Transparency International study described on p. 117; that is, 55 percent of the world's states had less corruption than Indonesia. This represents real progress under Yudhoyono. In 2004 Indonesia ranked far worse in the same study, behind 93 percent of the world's states. President Yudhoyono has taken particular aim at corruption, appointing a tough attorney-general and an independent Corruption Eradication Commission. In 2005, for instance, both the president of the country's largest bank and the head of the national election commission were detained for questioning in corruption cases; and in 2006 the head of the state electricity company, PLN, was arrested. Work on the infrastructure problems is going more slowly, but a stimulus package aimed at ameliorating the 2008–2009 economic slowdown went largely into developing much-needed infrastructure.

---

[33]World Bank, *World Development Indicators 2012* (http://data.worldbank.org), accessed July 6, 2012.
[34]"Time to Deliver," *The Economist,* December 11, 2004, p. 5.

KEY TERMS

rent

import-substitution
   industrialization

inflation

progressive taxation

regressive taxation

central bank

corruption

political economy

rational choice models

political psychology

codetermination

FURTHER READING

Alt, James, and Alesina, Alberto. "Political Economy: An Overview." In *A New Handbook of Political Science,* ed. Robert Goodin and Hans-Dieter Klingemann. New York: Oxford University Press, 1997, pp. 645–74.

APSA Task Force on Inequality and American Democracy. *Inequality and American Democracy.* New York: Russell Sage Foundation, 2004.

Bartels, Larry M. *Unequal Democracy: The Political Economy of the New Gilded Age.* Princeton, NJ: Princeton University Press, 2008.

130   PART II   THE STATE AND PUBLIC POLICY

Fisman, Raymond, and Miguel, Edward. *Economic Gangsters: Corruption, Violence and the Poverty of Nations*. Princeton, NJ: Princeton University Press, 2008.

Iversen, Torben, and Wren, Anne. "Equality, Employment, and Budgetary Restraint: The Trilemma of the Service Economy," *World Politics* 50 (1998), pp. 507–546.

Kohli, Atul. *State-Directed Development: Political Power and Industrialization in the Global Periphery*. New York: Cambridge University Press, 2004.

Morris, Stephen D., and Blake, Charles H. *Corruption & Politics in Latin America*. Boulder, CO: Lynne Riener, 2010.

North, Douglas. *Institutions, Institutional Change and Economic Performance*. New York: Cambridge University Press, 1990.

Ross, Michael L. *The Oil Curse: How Petroleum Wealth Shapes the Development of Nations*. Princeton, NJ: Princeton University Press, 2012.

Sen, Amartya. *Development as Freedom*. New York: Knopf, 1999.

Treisman, Daniel. "What Have We learned About Corruption from 10 Years of Cross-National Research?" *Annual Review of Political Science* 10 (2007), pp. 211–244.

Van de Walle, Nicolas. *African Economies and the Politics of Permanent Crisis, 1979–1999*. New York: Cambridge University Press, 2001.

World Bank. *World Development Report*. Serial. New York: Oxford University Press.

World Economic Forum. *Global Competitiveness Report*. Serial: A detailed analysis of economic and business conditions in all countries of the world, released annually.

CHAPTER 6

WHAT LIES BEHIND POLICY: QUESTIONS OF JUSTICE AND EFFECTIVENESS[1]

In Chapters 4 and 5, we reviewed the varying things that governments do (or do not do) on behalf of their people. In this chapter, we will shift from the "is" to the "ought," as we review the ethical and moral basis of policy making. What are the considerations that lie behind these policies? What things must the leaders and their people think about in considering what the state should do? If you were the leader of a state, what sorts of policies would you opt for?

There seem to be two broad characteristics that almost everyone wants to see in state policies: (1) policies should be "just"—that is, the state should treat people in the way they deserve; and (2) policies should be "effective," producing the greatest good at the least cost. As you might expect, the problem with these criteria is that both are multifaceted and hard to pin down. In addition, even these two broad criteria sometimes come into conflict, because what is most "just" may not be most "effective," and vice versa. Sorting out the various factors that make one policy good and another bad is an art, and people of goodwill may frequently come up with differing conclusions regarding a policy. In this chapter, we shall look at some of the things that make a policy "just" or "effective" and also, perhaps, come to see how complex the final evaluation of a policy must be.

We will begin this chapter by introducing the concept of "justice" and examining what we need to think about to decide whether a policy is just. We will then look at how we might decide whether a policy is effective, and discuss how to choose between having the government make our collective decisions or having the decisions determined by open market processes.

---

[1]Any author of an introductory book owes debts to many people, but in this chapter, a special debt is owed to Charles Anderson, whose splendid book *Statecraft* (New York: Wiley, 1977) pursued similar themes in more detail and with greater elegance than I have done here.

⇥ THE PROBLEM OF JUSTICE[2]

What do we mean by **justice,** by the notion that people should be treated "as they deserve"? Does justice consist of treating everyone equally? Surely not, because we can think of many instances in which treating everyone equally would seem unjust. If you had worked especially hard on a paper but your instructor decided to give everyone in the class the same grade, this would seem unjust. You had worked hard while others sloughed off, yet all got the same reward. *Different members of the class had contributed different amounts, and justice would seem to require that the instructor reward them accordingly.* A rather different consideration appears in the following example: Suppose six people were waiting on a corner on a cold, rainy day, and one of the six was suffering from asthma. Suppose further that a car came along that could take only one additional passenger. Equal treatment would require that the six draw lots to see who should get to go in the car. However, would not justice require that the other five defer to the asthma victim, who was suffering more from the rain than they were? In this case, justice would seem to require that the person whose *needs* were greatest should get special treatment.

Should we then base justice solely on the weight of contributions or solely on need? Neither of these can provide a sufficient basis for justice, though obviously both are part of the picture.

There are many problems with the "weight of contributions." People's contributions are frequently as much a matter of luck as of virtue, and we are often a bit queasy when rewards are based solely on such "lucky" contributions. To continue with the example of grades, what if you worked very hard on your paper but a friend, who was born very intelligent, dashed off a brilliant piece in one evening while drinking beer and received a better grade than you? You would probably have mixed feelings about the justice of the grades. To follow the same line of thought, is it just that a football player, like New Orleans quarterback Drew Brees, should be paid a high salary because his shoulders and back are constructed to help him throw the ball long? Is it just that a worker living in West Virginia should have so few opportunities to find a job as compared with a worker living in Connecticut? Contribution alone, then, cannot provide a sufficient criterion for determining justice. Contribution may often involve elements of luck, so that we are uncertain how much it should be rewarded. Looking only at contributions would also cause us to ignore questions of need; even if four of the six people on the rainy corner had managed to stop a cab (thus contributing more than the other two), we might think it "just" if one of them were excluded to make a place for the asthma victim.

Similar problems arise if we use need alone as a criterion for justice. Like "contribution," "need" is a tricky thing, and we are not always sure that it should be rewarded. If some members of an office staff are having a hard time economically because of bad luck (or bad judgment) in the houses they bought and the debts they've run up, should they receive bigger raises than members of the staff who are not in trouble economically?

---

[2]Those who have used earlier editions of this book may notice that I have departed from my practice of treating justice as a component of a broader concept I called "fairness." That practice was always idiosyncratic, and I have concluded that the confusion it caused far outweighed any benefits. I want to thank A. P. Simonds for finally convincing me to change this section.

Officials in a small town in Pennsylvania notified a Mr. Selby that he would have to tear down a backyard tree house because he had not obtained a permit and the house exceeded the 40-foot height restriction. Mr. Selby ignored the notice, and the following month two police cars, a dump truck, and a powerline truck with a cherry picker returned to the tree house and demolished it. Justice? Of what sort?

Should parents earn better pay because they have children to support? Would this be unjust to single people who are doing the same work as the parents are doing? Again, if need alone were a criterion, this would mean that we would have to ignore contribution. To return finally to the example of grades, how would you feel if the instructor graded the papers solely on her assessment of each student's need for a "positive self-image"?

Justice, then, is a complex issue. It involves a number of things that are often in conflict and need to be balanced—the contributions people have made, their varying needs, and even some further sense that people should not be treated *too* unequally. Not only do these things have to be balanced, but each of them is itself ambiguous and hard to pin down.

This does not mean that justice is an unworkable concept but simply that it is a difficult one. We all have a strong sense for the justice or injustice of certain things, and there is a good deal of agreement among us about these. If this were not so, I could not have expected the previous examples to mean roughly the same thing to each reader. It is when we judge a question of justice differently, though, that we must tackle the problem of working out our disagreement. Different people will weigh contribution, need, and the necessity of equality differently; and they will also disagree on precisely what sort of need or what sort of contribution exists, or on what sorts of things need to be equal. Many would see no injustice in Drew Brees's salary. One could argue that the amount of pleasure he has given millions of people merited this pay, or one could note the limited period during which Brees can play football, since he likely will need to retire in his thirties.

Justice is a complex question, but one on which we can talk productively. By bringing out and examining the differing ways people evaluate contribution, need, and the necessity for equality and by examining the differing weights people place on each, we may at least *clarify* disagreements about the justice of a policy.

→ Other Aspects of Justice: Procedural Justice

The approach I have taken in the section on "The Problem of Justice" falls under the general rubric of **substantive justice**—any conception of justice that emphasizes people receiving what they need and deserve. This is, to me, the central concept of justice. However, the question of justice is sufficiently complex that it goes well beyond the already rich tension between need and contributions that I laid out in that section. Justice is a highly contested concept, a central philosophical problem in all of our consideration of life and humanity. Another conception of justice, less concerned with the fairness of distribution that I emphasized in the "Problem of Justice" section, emphasizes justice as embodied in the *procedures* by which decisions are reached about people. **Procedural justice** is a complex concept. I will raise in this section just some of the sorts of issues that are involved in procedural justice: (1) *whether governmental action is "arbitrary,"* (2) *whether special basic rights are violated, and* (3) *whether special overriding social needs are present.*

Arbitrary Policies and Due Process

Governmental action is **arbitrary** if decisions are made and communicated capriciously, that is, if the people affected by a decision do not know what to expect before the decision is made and do not learn on what grounds it was made. Decisions that single out particular individuals for punishment or reward are arbitrary. For instance, highway patrols sometimes appear to be especially strict in enforcing speed limits and other regulations on drivers of brightly colored sports cars just because of the cars' appearance. (And "racial profiling" is of course an especially abhorrent example of the same problem.) This is arbitrary action. Librarians are acting arbitrarily when they allow people owing fines to escape without paying provided that they are "properly sorry about having been late." In some dictatorships such as Nazi Germany or Idi Amin's Uganda, a person could be killed because someone in the government bore a grudge against him or her. This was the worst sort of arbitrary terror.

The question of arbitrariness is not the same as a question of substantive justice. We might reach a policy that we regard as substantively unjust by means that we admit are not arbitrary. (Many people might regard a prohibitive tax on chocolate to reduce consumption as wrong; but if it were passed constitutionally and applied equally to everyone, it would not be arbitrary.) Arbitrary means could also produce results that we would consider substantively just.[3] Regardless of the substantive justice of the result, however, arbitrariness lessens the justice of a policy.

The notion of **due process** has evolved to help control arbitrary decision making. This is the idea that we must always follow certain standard procedures in making some policies and that if we did not follow those procedures in making a given policy, then the policy should be void. This prevents policy makers from acting arbitrarily, since they want to see their policies stick. To keep from having their policies voided, they stay within the standard set of procedures in making policy.

This sort of standardization involves some costs in that it lessens governmental flexibility. It is not set up for all areas of policy making. Britain, the United States, and Canada especially emphasize due process in criminal trials, because historically those countries have been especially concerned with protecting their citizens from unfair prosecution by the government. In criminal trials in English-speaking countries, due process consists of the following:

1. People may not be accused of crimes unless they could have learned of the existence and meaning of the law before they committed their acts.
2. When people are accused of crimes, they are entitled to know what crimes are charged, they are entitled to know on what evidence the charges are based, and they are entitled to gather and present their own evidence to rebut the charges.
3. Judges must be disinterested, unbiased, and attentive.
4. Once a judgment has been made, some means for later reconsideration must be available.
5. If any of these conditions has been violated in an American, Canadian, or British court except under certain special circumstances, the trial is ruled invalid.[4]

In other areas of policy, such as the setting of regulations, assignment of people to schools, or levying of taxes, there is usually a sense that we should follow the general spirit of due process—that is, policy making should not be arbitrary. However, there are generally not precise and strict rules to safeguard due process, of the sort we find in court proceedings.

Special Basic Rights

Another added factor that enters into considerations of procedural justice is the existence of certain basic rights whose violation is thought to be unjust in and of itself. Such rights have a special status in that only extraordinary circumstances would make it appropriate for policy makers to violate them for anyone. Although almost everyone

---

[3]This often produces uneasiness about legal processes in the United States and other countries with protections against arbitrary criminal investigation. If the police had stopped a sports car and found a bloody ax in the back seat, justice would appear to require investigating the driver for murder. However, the initial search was arbitrary, and a court might dismiss the evidence on the grounds that it had been obtained unfairly. Citizens frequently find it difficult to appreciate these distinctions.

[4]This is of course an idealization of what happens. In fact, American courts, at least, are badly overworked and many shortcuts are tolerated to move the business through. For instance, in plea bargaining, a deal is struck between the accused, the prosecutor, and the judge by which, the accused pleads guilty to a lesser charge, the prosecutor's original charge is withdrawn, and the trial ends. Therefore, many of the theoretical protections listed are avoided.

would think that some such rights exist, it is not always possible to get people to agree on exactly which rights have this status. Three rights that have frequently been held to have the special status are:

1. *The Right to Survive.* It can be argued that because death negates all other rights, we should keep the right not to be killed almost absolute. Opposition to capital punishment is often based on this idea, as is opposition to abortion.
2. *The Right of Free Speech.* It can be argued that because politics depends on the exchange of ideas, policy makers should be especially reluctant to regulate the expression of ideas. Decreasing the flow of ideas decreases politics itself.
3. *The Right to Privacy.* It can be argued that if one's very personality is to exist, there must be some space that one can call one's own, where no one else may peek in, and that governments must if at all possible respect those boundaries. It is for this reason that in British, Canadian, and American law, people may not be compelled to speak about themselves in court and wives or husbands may not be compelled to testify against their spouses.

Few people would hold any of these special rights to be *absolute.* Most people would agree that it would have been good if Hitler had been assassinated in 1942, even those who believe strongly in the right to survive. Almost everyone recognizes that the special right of free speech must have some restrictions, as well; the classic example is that no one should have the right to yell "Fire!" in a crowded theater. Similarly, there must also be some ultimate limits to the right to privacy.

Thus, "special rights" are not absolute. However, to the extent that the idea of special rights is accepted, a society sets aside those rights as having a top priority, so that it would take something unusual for us to compromise them. Under these circumstances, substantive justice, or even due process, might have to be tempered in the interests of one or another special right. As one example of this, many people have opposed the establishment of a central, computerized data file of information about Americans because they are concerned about the potential abuses of people's right to privacy that could result if all official information about a person—military record, tax returns, criminal record, health information, or a record in school—were brought together and made easily accessible. Those opposing the file grant that justice would be better served if such a file existed, because tax fraud and other crimes would be easier to detect, but they think that the right to privacy is more important than these other needs of justice.

Overriding Social Needs

Finally, justice in a broad sense may require that to be just to most of the people, the state must be less just to some people. That is, there may be overriding social needs that enter into considerations of justice. The best example is the military draft. In many countries, young men (and at least in Israel, women) are required to serve a fixed period of time in the military, whether they wish to do so or not. The reasoning behind this is that the people of the state need to have a strong army, but it is difficult to get people to serve in an army of their own free will. Therefore, some people must be compelled to do so for the greater general good. Similarly, affirmative action programs for employment in the United States often require that minorities and women receive a slightly better than even break in hiring decisions (even though an even break would be the "just" decision) to help overcome historic patterns of unjust decisions going the opposite way. The argument is that society will benefit from an integrated work force and that at least modest levels of individual injustice during the transition period are not too great a price to pay.

We see another example of this sort of consideration during wars. When they are at war, most countries subordinate almost everything else to winning the war. Among the subordinated things is a concern for individual justice, due process, and special individual rights. Governments are often given extraordinary powers during wars, and they are not expected to be primarily concerned with justice to individuals. After 9/11, for instance, the United States government was able to take extraordinary steps in its war on terrorism, steps for which it probably never could have gained popular support under more normal circumstances. Sometimes governments do things during war that they later regret. The internment of hundreds of thousands of Japanese Americans in prison camps during World War II, because of their national origin, is a shameful piece of America's past that occurred under the excess and strain of war.

Revolutionary governments often justify suspensions of due process and justice because of the great good that will eventually result from the revolution. Thousands of British sympathizers were driven into Canada at the end of the American Revolution, aristocrats and many others were beheaded during the French Revolution, and millions of farmers were executed or deported to forced-labor camps in the Soviet Union in the 1930s.

Each of these examples—the draft, affirmative action, wartime civil liberties, the needs of a revolution—in fact, any claim to an overriding social need is based on an assumption that ends can justify means. We should not too easily accept *or* too readily reject this assumption. Clearly, there are many means that cannot be justified by many ends. The internment of Japanese Americans by the U.S. government during World War II did nothing to help the American war effort; even if it had helped in small ways, the enormity of the injustice would not have been worth it. That internment was unjustified. Similarly, even if many Soviet citizens had benefited from the Russian Revolution, the immense human suffering during that revolution and the limitation of free speech throughout the existence of the Soviet Union were horribly unjustified.

However, if we should not accept too easily the notion that ends can justify means, neither should we reject it totally. Some social ends, such as secure national borders, may be worth modest degrees of individual injustice. *Some* ends can clearly justify *some* means—as anyone must agree who has ever told a "little white lie."

In the end, then, we see that justice may be a mix of several things: substantive justice (which is itself a mixture: of concerns for contribution, need, and equality); governmental action that is not arbitrary; consideration of special rights; and the possibility of overriding social needs. It is because so many things are involved that people can honestly disagree on whether a policy is just. At the same time, an awareness of what goes into justice can help us to understand and resolve such disagreements.

↦ Effectiveness

We have seen that one question for the policy maker is whether a policy is *just,* both to individuals and to society more broadly. The other basic question is whether the policy is effective. An **effective policy** is *one that gives the state and the people of the state the greatest benefits at the least cost.* The trick in dealing with an effective policy is that often neither the benefits nor the costs of a policy are easy to calculate.

First, many of the effects of a policy are difficult to measure and compare. They bring up the old problem of "apples and oranges" in its severest form. How can we compare the amount of recreational value we gain by building a dam and the value of the protection against flooding that is gained by building it against the cost of pain and inconvenience of those who have to leave their homes to make way for it, the economic loss of farm production on the flooded lands, and the government's cost in constructing it? There is no common unit by which to measure recreational value, protection against flooding, pain and inconvenience, or agricultural loss, and so it is difficult to say whether in this case the gains are greater than the costs.

A second reason the costs and benefits of a policy are not always clear is that policies always have a variety of effects, many of which one cannot anticipate when the policy is set up. We often refer to these as the *unanticipated consequences* of a policy.

As one example of such an unanticipated consequence, consider Germany's public-spirited effort to help slow global warming by relying more on solar energy. The government subsidizes solar energy heavily to encourage its use, but at least in the short run, this actually *reduces* the world's production of energy from the sun! By encouraging the use of solar power generators in Germany through subsidies, the government diverts the world's solar cell production to Germany (where frankly there is not that much sunshine) and away from sunnier, drier climates like Spain's, where the solar cells could be used more effectively.

As another example of unanticipated (and in this case, directly perverse) consequences of a policy, Douglas S. Massey and Kristin E. Espinosa have shown that a series of "get tough" policies against illegal immigration on the United States–Mexican border actually had an effect opposite of what was intended. The U.S. Immigration and Naturalization Service has added extra guards and imposed punishments on employers found to be employing illegal immigrants, and has built a several-hundred mile wall along the border. Massey and Espinosa found that since the border crossing has been made tougher, illegal immigrants who originally would have come to the United States and stayed only for a few months of seasonal labor now stay year-round because they know that it will be hard to get back if they go home. The end result is that the number of illegal immigrants present at any given time is increased, not decreased, by the stepped-up enforcement.[5]

As a third example of the varied effects that a policy may have, consider the Social Security program of the United States. This is a fairly simple program. As of 2013, all employed workers except government employees paid a tax of 6.2 percent of their salary

---

[5]Douglas S. Massey and Kristin E. Espinosa, "What's Driving Mexico–U.S. Migration? A Theoretical, Empirical, and Policy Analysis," *American Journal of Sociology* 102 (January 1997), pp. 939–99.

CHAPTER 6   WHAT LIES BEHIND POLICY: QUESTIONS OF JUSTICE AND EFFECTIVENESS   139

(up to a maximum salary of $113,700), and their employers paid a matching tax of the same amount.[6] From the proceeds of this tax, pensions are paid to people age sixty-six and older who have retired; also, support payments are paid to disabled workers and to children of workers who have died young. The program's direct purpose is to provide a national system of pensions and catastrophe insurance. Among the many *side* effects of the program, some good and some bad, are the following:

1. People with low salaries are taxed relatively more heavily than people with high salaries (see Chapter 5). Therefore, the distribution of incomes in the state is made less equal.

2. Retired people have been made less dependent economically on their families. This has surely been a good thing for them, but it may also have helped to lessen the ties of the extended family, which are already weak in our highly mobile society.

3. The age of retirement has been made more or less standard nationally.

4. The overall production of goods and services has been reduced for the country and all the people are economically somewhat less well-off than they would otherwise be because people are encouraged to retire at age sixty-six rather than at a later age.

5. Conversely, the policy has allowed many who wish to stop working at age sixty-six to do so without being forced by economic need to work beyond that age.

6. The payroll tax on employers takes a higher percentage of the payroll for low-pay employees than for high-pay employees. For example, the employer pays a tax of 6.2 percent of the salary of an employee who earns $30,000 a year but only 4.7 percent of the salary of an employee who earns $150,000 a year ($0.062 \times \$113,700$ is $7,049, which is 4.7 percent of $150,000). Therefore, the policy encourages industries such as the electronics and computer industries, which have highly paid work forces, while it discriminates against industries such as steel and automobile manufacturing, which employ large numbers of workers at lower pay. This encourages the development of clean industries with a great deal of potential for export sales, but it also hurts economically weak areas of traditional industry.

As this example shows, even a fairly simple program like Social Security has many effects beyond those for which it was originally designed. Some of these were not anticipated by the designers, and some have probably not yet even been noticed by scholars. Certainly the previous list does not exhaust all the consequences of the Social Security plan.

As one last example of the unintended consequences of policy, some studies have suggested that stiffer penalties for those caught driving while intoxicated may have led to an increase in hit-and-run accidents, as drunk drivers flee the scene of accidents to avoid the tougher punishment for driving while intoxicated.

Any judgment of the *effectiveness* of a policy must take into account *all* its costs and benefits—so far as we can estimate what these are—not just the *intended* costs

---

[6]An additional 1.45 percent tax on *all* wages, also matched by employers, supports medical care for people over sixty-five years of age.

and benefits. It is often hard to put a price tag on these, as we have seen in the example of Social Security; we are usually comparing apples, oranges, bananas, and grapefruit. Many of the consequences may be difficult to foresee. As a result, it is just as much an art to judge the effectiveness of a policy as to judge its justice. There is nothing terrible in recognizing that policy making is not an exact science; it is simply a good thing to realize that policy choices are neither simple nor direct.

✦ A BASIC QUESTION OF EFFECTIVENESS: AUTHORITY VERSUS THE MARKET

The most basic choice about effective policy is whether we want to rely more on *governmental authority* or on *market mechanisms* to carry it out, and which is better at accomplishing our goals effectively. "Governmental authority" is just what it sounds like. Under governmental authority, policy is made by the government telling people what they may or may not do, how much they may spend on X, or how much the country is to invest in Y. Many policies with which you are familiar are matters of governmental authority. The public school system, in which the government fixes a minimum number of years of education that each child must receive and sets up free public schools to provide that education, is an instance of policy provided by governmental authority. The system of highways and streets, in which the government decides where streets should run and then uses public money to build and maintain them, is another example. So is the nationalized coal industry of China, in which local governments own almost all coal mines and decide how much coal to mine, what sort of equipment to build, how much to pay the miners, and how much the coal will cost.

Under a **market mechanism**, the government leaves such choices as what people are to do or what goods they are to receive, up to the people to choose for themselves, through their exchanges of goods and services with each other. Through the operation of supply and demand, if large numbers of people want G.I. Joe dolls and are willing to pay high prices for them, producers will make more G.I. Joe dolls. If no one wants to pay people well to care for children during the day, there will not be many child care centers. Therefore, collective choices come to be made by millions of individual decisions about proper prices and what objects to purchase. The government depends on the *costs* of action and of goods to restrain people in their choices so that they will end up choosing to do or buy only those things they most want (or can afford). In the coal industry of the United States, which is not nationalized, the choice of how much coal is to be produced is a matter for a number of mine operators to decide on the basis of their operating costs; their decision is strongly affected by the choices of millions of customers as to how much coal they will buy at a given price. The policy decision—how much coal to produce—which in China is made directly by local governments, is made in the United States by the interplay of a large number of individual decisions.

In a modification of the market mechanism, a government may allow the market to settle a policy but may intervene to structure the individual decisions that make up the market choice. Almost every country, for instance, taxes liquor and tobacco products heavily to raise their prices and make it less likely that people will choose to consume such unhealthy substances rather than, say, meat and vegetables. The choice as to what to consume is still the customer's, but the government has taken steps to help determine what that choice will be. By contrast, in banning the consumption of heroin, the U.S. government is relying on governmental authority rather than on a market mechanism to determine the level of consumption of a dangerous substance.

Market mechanisms are not confined to economic transactions. For instance, the way our language develops—what is considered proper grammar, or the coining of new words—may either be regulated by the government or left to the free flow of social interactions. In the United States the language develops by people speaking to each other and imitating each other's usages. It is a very democratic process, in which anyone who is heard by many people exerts an unusual influence over how we all speak. Talk show host and political satirist Jon Stewart influences millions of viewers every day. I as a professor influence perhaps a hundred students a few days a week. Someone else may influence only a small circle of friends.

However, government may also try to shape a language by regulation and intervention. The government of Iceland, for instance, supports an institute for the Icelandic language that actively tries to prevent words entering the language from other languages, developing new official words for new concepts, such as AIDS or computer, as they arise.

Questions of social practice may also be allowed to develop by a market mechanism in day-to-day social interactions, or may be regulated by governments. Who may sleep with whom, religious practice, the use of profanity—all of these have been at one time or another regulated by governments, and all have also often been allowed to emerge from social practice. In Singapore until recently, for instance, it was illegal to chew chewing gum, and in Pakistan it is illegal to insult the prophet Mohammed.

Whether authority or a market mechanism is a better way of making policy is a continual subject of debate. Is it better for the government to nationalize railroads, airlines, and such, and run them in the public interest? Or is it better to leave decisions on scheduling, allocation of investment, and salaries to be worked out by management, workers, and customers through their individual choices? In an energy shortage, should gasoline be rationed (with a set number of gallons allocated per family), or should the price be allowed to shoot up, so that those who do not need gasoline as much as others or who cannot afford it as readily will reduce their driving? Either policy would reduce consumption to meet the short supply, but the two would have different side effects. *Both* types of policy—authority and the market—have considerable disadvantages, as well as advantages.

Problems with Authority-Based Policy

The two main problems with authority as a means of policy are that (1) authority is not good at getting things to the people who need them most or will value them most—that is, it does not *allocate optimally;* and (2) there is a lack of incentives to encourage authority-based policy to use resources as efficiently as they might be used.

Regarding the first of these problems, it stands to reason that if government officials make a choice on behalf of all the people, it is difficult for them to take into account the infinitely varying needs of those people. They might write a thousand exceptions and special conditions into their decision, but it would still be a clumsy instrument for deciding who is to get how much of what. Consider the example of gasoline rationing. If the government states that each family may receive forty-two gallons of gasoline a month, should they not allow rural families more than that because of the long distances they must drive? Then what about an urban resident who must drive to a job twenty miles away? Perhaps the government should allow less gas to those living near a bus line. How about people with weak hearts—should they receive extra gasoline? How about people with small children? People who own a vacation house forty miles out of town? This can go on forever, and even if the government writes terribly complicated rules, there will still be many people who do not receive gasoline in proportion to their desire and need for gasoline. As Lindblom has put it, authority systems have "strong thumbs, no fingers."[7]

The second main problem with policy made by authority is that it often does not lead to a very efficient use of resources.[8] When the government decides how much to

---

[7]Charles Lindblom, *Politics and Markets* (New York: Basic Books, 1977).
[8]However, this is not to say that private decision making does not involve any waste. Expensive wood-paneled executive conference rooms are just one of the possibilities. The point is that overall, the incentives of a market system push toward efficiency even if there are many lapses, while the incentives of an authority system do not.

invest in schools, highways, or coal mining, the government officials responsible do not *personally* gain much of anything from a wise decision or lose much of anything from an unwise one. Under a market arrangement, however, the people making such decisions save money directly from wise decisions and lose money directly from unwise ones. Even with the best intentions in the world, it is natural that, in systems of authority, decision makers may be more careless with resources than they would be under a market system. As an extreme example of the sort of inefficiency that can result, the Soviet Union at one time allowed its farmers to manage small plots themselves and to sell their produce in competitive markets, though most Soviet agricultural products came from large government-managed collective farms. On the private plots, on the average, it took four pounds of feed grain to produce a pound of meat; on the collective farms, it took up to *thirteen* pounds of feed grain to produce a pound of meat.[9]

Problems with the Market

Given these two serious problems, why would anyone ever use authority? Why don't governments leave all decisions to market mechanisms? The reason is that market mechanisms themselves suffer from several serious defects; we shall consider three of them here.[10]

First, as we saw in Chapter 5, wealth and income are distributed unequally in all societies, with some people poor and others better off. When decisions are left to the market, goods and opportunities flow to those who can afford them, and these will not necessarily be the people who need them most. In the section on "Problems with Authority-Based Policy," I wrote that authority systems could not easily sort out varying levels of need in making allocations; market systems are excellent at doing this for two people who have the same amount of money. However, when incomes vary, ability to pay enters along with need in determining what individuals choose, so the allocations will still probably not be the ideal ones. If medical care is allocated by letting the price rise, for instance, poor people who need surgery to avoid being crippled might have to do without, while richer people might be able to afford casual cosmetic surgery. Where a need is especially important, the government may step in to make certain that justice is done in a way that cannot be guaranteed by a market mechanism. This is part of the motivation behind systems of free public education, national health plans (such as the national medical care programs that serve people of all ages in Britain, Canada, and many European states, or Medicare, which serves those over age sixty-five in the United States), and the rationing of food during shortages.

Note that the problem of unequal resources is not confined to the development of economic policies. In the example I used on p. 141 about the development of a language, some people have more resources to influence the language by how they use it than others do, and they gain a disproportionate advantage in shaping the evolution of the language. Jon Stewart, who is heard by millions every day, has much more influence over the language than I as a professor do, and I probably have more influence than many of my students.

---

[9]*The Economist*, 7 February 1981, p. 14.
[10]For a more thorough discussion, see Lindblom, *Politics and Markets*, chap. 6, p. 6.

A row of houses next to a smoking factory. A strong example of "externalities."
© Brian Mitchell/Corbis

A second problem with market mechanisms is that they are not very effective in producing *public goods*. As you recall from Chapter 3, a "public good" is something that benefits all members of the community and that no one can be prevented from using; every member of the community can enjoy the benefits of it whether that person has helped pay for it or not. Some examples of public goods are national defense, medical research, weather forecasting, and public health programs to control the spread of disease. All members of the community benefit from such programs, whether or not they have helped pay for them. Left to the market, such public goods would be very difficult to finance. Each individual could quite sensibly think, "If I don't pay my share, the army will still be there, and I'll get all the benefits of it; why should I pay? I'll let someone else do it!" As a result, no one would pay to finance the army, there would be no army, and all would lose out. Rather than let such paradoxical failures occur, governments often decide not to rely on the voluntary choices of a market mechanism. Instead, they force the people to pay taxes, and they use those taxes to provide the public good that all (or most) desire.

A third problem with market mechanisms is that they do not take into account externalities of individual transactions. An **externality** exists when there are social costs or benefits beyond the individual costs and benefits between two individuals. For example, let us say that a couple contracts with a trash company to dump refuse on their land. For the landowners, the benefit is the money paid by the trash company; the cost is the odor, the sight of the trash, and the portion of their land that the trash occupies. Presumably, the landowners are satisfied with the deal (the benefit outweighs the costs), or there would have been no deal; and presumably the trash company also has greater benefits than costs from the deal. So, the trash company and the landowners are happy, and according to market practices, they will strike the deal. However, there is an externality. All the landowners' neighbors, including a nursing home and a day care center, must also suffer the sight and smell of the trash. They receive no benefits, and so there is a large *social cost* that should be taken into account but does not enter into market calculations. This is the problem of externalities, a problem in which governmental authority is often brought to bear to make certain that the involved parties consider the broader social costs and benefits in transactions, along with the narrower individual costs and benefits of those making the choices. The most obvious externalities are negative ones such as pollution, or the setting up of ugly structures. However, there can also be *positive externalities,* in which there are positive social benefits that would not be taken into account in individual transactions and that government may step in to guarantee. Two examples are the preservation of historic buildings and the requirement that every member of society acquire a basic education. (The notion in the latter case is that society as a whole benefits from literacy above and beyond the benefit any single individual gains from being literate.)

Governmental authority and market mechanisms, then, are two modes for the making of policy. There are problems with each, and so it is hard to argue an absolute case for one as opposed to the other; and personal preferences will play a role. Furthermore, it is clear that certain areas of policy lend themselves better to one mode than to the other. Defense is always provided by governmental authority, not by a market mechanism, probably because it is so difficult to provide public goods through a market mechanism. Art and science seem to flourish best when left to a "marketplace of ideas" rather than conforming to decisions of governmental authority. Many other policy areas—industrial production, health care, and others—seem susceptible to either mode of decision; and we can find examples of both modes from numerous countries.

✦ POWER AND CHOICE

You will of course have realized that I have written this whole chapter from a "choice" perspective. "Why is defense always provided by governmental authority, but art and sciences usually provided by the 'marketplace of ideas'?" was answered, for instance, by stating that a market mechanism cannot effectively produce a public good.

I hope you realize by now that neither power nor choice, alone and in isolation, is likely to account fully for any political phenomenon. Our focus in this chapter has been on justice and effectiveness, which are very important in understanding what happens when policies are chosen, but we know that many other things are going on as well. Power relationships will also have much to do with which policy is chosen. Political leaders may steer a lucrative contract to a friend, or may push for a policy benefiting an ethnic group that is part of their support base. These things happen a *lot.*

Once again, we recall that both the power perspective and the choice perspective are usually necessary, to obtain a full picture of political outcomes.

✣ THE NEED TO ACT, EVEN UNDER UNCERTAINTY

In this chapter we have introduced the twin goals of justice and effectiveness as ways of assessing which policy we should pursue; we have looked particularly at whether (and under what circumstances) it is better to have the government or open markets determine our collective choices. All of the concepts involved turned out to be complex, and often in conflict with each other.

At this point, you might think the message of this chapter is that policy making is awfully complicated. This is understandable. We have seen that the question of justice is complex, and that reckoning efficiency is similarly tricky—that it is difficult to count accurately the costs and benefits of a policy to choose the one that gives the greatest benefits at the least cost.

Unfortunately, a description of the complexity of policy decisions could lead some people to give up in discouragement. If it is difficult to decide what policy is most just and most efficient, why bother to try? Carried too far, an appreciation of complexity can be paralyzing.

We must always carry on a difficult balancing act between recognizing that our decisions are fallible and therefore require continual reexamination, and the ability to act decisively on our best judgment at any given time. The fact that analysis is complex does not mean that "anything goes" or that one opinion is always as good as another. These questions are important enough to justify hardheaded analysis. It is the duty of those who recognize the complexity of decisions to hold themselves always ready to act despite knowing that their choices might be wrong. Otherwise, the only people to act would be those who did not understand the complexity of policy choices, and the world would be ruled by simpletons.

EXAMPLE

Political Choice

Here are four examples of policy questions that have concerned governmental decision makers. In each instance, the policy issue is stated; this is followed by some of the questions that those making a decision on the issue must consider:

1. ***The Problem of Need-Based Scholarships.*** Most systems for providing college scholarships are based on some definition of financial need, with scholarships generally awarded only to those students who most need financial help to attend school.

   Is need, rather than academic ability, the best basis on which to choose those students who are to be encouraged to attend college?

   - Which way of choosing who gets aid is the more just?
   - Which is the more efficient? Is the overall educational level of society increased more by giving financial aid to bright students or to needy students? Presumably, the aid offers more leverage to needy students, because they all need the money

to attend college, whereas many of the bright students would attend college in any case. However, is a smaller number of bright students the more important addition?

Assuming we wish to use need as a basis, how do we determine "need"?

- Is need a function of parents' income? What, then, do we do about children of wealthy parents who are living independently of them and get no aid from them? Should they be punished for their parents' wealth? If they are given aid, won't all students, to get aid, claim to be independent of their parents?

- Is need solely a matter of family income, or shouldn't we take a family's financial obligations into account? Doesn't it make more sense to give aid to someone whose parents must put eight children through school than to someone from a family of four with the same income? In a possibly parallel situation, should a family that carries big mortgages on two large homes get preference because they don't have much money left to spend on college? (Many scholarship systems do count mortgage payments as contributing to need.) Does doing this merely reward imprudence? Is there a difference between the case of the eight children and the case of the large mortgages?

- How should parents who are not married but are living together and supporting their children jointly be counted? Most systems allow just one of the parents to be counted as the "supporter," and if the one who earns less is so designated, the family will show up as more "needy" than most people would consider them to be. Is this fair to married couples? Does it discourage marriage? If it is not allowed, how can one address the problem of separated couples where one of the parents does not pay a fair share of support? In this case, the single responsible parent and children would appear as *less* needy than they really are. Whichever way you decide to define need in the case of unmarried parents, how can you police the system?

2. ***The Problem of Water Pollution.*** Most states have laws to limit the pollutants that can be dumped into the water.

- How do we decide which pollutants to ban? Should we ban primarily those that are dangerous to human health? Those, such as phosphates or DDT, that have especially bad effects on fish, birds, and mammals? Those that discolor the water? Those that stink?

- Who is to bear the cost of cleaning up the water?

- Is it better to use a flat ban on pollution or to charge people and corporations a stiff fee for polluting? (This is an example of the choice between government authority and market mechanisms.) The main argument against the latter is that it puts the government in the position of saying that pollution is acceptable (or at least legal) as long as one can pay the fee. The main argument in favor of this is that it adds flexibility to the law. Cleaning up pollution always carries costs and may lead to plant closings, higher prices for consumers, and other socially undesirable consequences. The fee system would allow some continued pollution where the cost of cleaning up would be prohibitive. Where the cost is not so high, people would choose to clean up rather than pay the fee. Therefore, the system would become more efficient but at the expense of losing some of the moral and symbolic vigor of the law. Which is the better course?

3. ***Children as an Externality.*** A society needs to raise children to replace its members who die, or the society would disappear over a couple of generations. One could, therefore, think of the production of children as a positive externality. Those who do not have children benefit from the child-rearing labors of those who do; they enjoy a society of varied ages in which to live as they grow older, and a labor force of younger people is available to support them in their retirement. Should all then share in the economic costs of raising the children? In the United States, the cost of educating children is borne collectively through the system of public education, but most other costs of raising children are treated as private costs of the parents. In about half the world's states, however, the full society assumes some of the responsibility for all costs of child rearing by giving direct grants to families with children. These grants are often pegged to the median income of workers in the country: the government might give 10 percent of the country's median income to any family with two children, for example.

- Should such aid go to all families with children or only to poor families? Public education goes to all families, but should this be treated the same?
- How would it change society to define child rearing as a collective effort, rather than the parents' private efforts?
- Would this be a good way to address such problems as malnutrition, child abuse, and poor education?
- In a sense, this would mean the government was paying people to have children. Is this a wise policy in a period of worldwide population growth?

4. ***The Problem of Gender-Based Pension Payments.*** Almost all insurance companies have varying insurance rates for low- and high-risk categories of people. Many companies give lower insurance rates to students who maintain a B average, for instance, on the assumption that those students drive better (or less often) than others and therefore will have fewer accidents. Similarly, young drivers carry higher rates for auto insurance, nonsmokers have lower rates for life insurance with many companies, and almost all companies give lower life insurance rates to women because women live longer than men. In the same spirit, many insurance-based pension plans pay women who retire at age seventy a lower monthly pension than men who retire at that age because, since women have a longer life expectancy, the companies can reasonably expect to make payments to the women for a greater length of time.

- Is it just that a woman who has worked as hard as a man should not enjoy as comfortable a retirement as the man?
- On the other hand, if payments are made equal, a man who has worked just as hard as a woman can expect to draw out a smaller total amount of retirement income before he dies. Is this just?

CHAPTER 6   WHAT LIES BEHIND POLICY: QUESTIONS OF JUSTICE AND EFFECTIVENESS   149

- If the system changes to give equal payments, will men reinvest their retirement savings in other ways that allow them to draw out their retirement income in whatever way they wish? This could result in an insurance-based scheme with only female clients, thus defeating the purpose of the change.
- Why should gender be singled out as a basis for this distinction? People who live in Iowa live longer, on the average, than people from Rhode Island. If we're to be consistent, shouldn't Iowans draw a smaller pension than Rhode Islanders? How about people who exercise regularly, people who don't smoke, or slender people?

KEY TERMS

justice   arbitrary action   market mechanism
substantive justice   due process   externality
procedural justice   effective policy

FURTHER READING

Adler, Matthew D., and Posner, Eric A. *Cost-Benefit Analysis: Economic, Philosophical, and Legal Perspectives.* Chicago: University of Chicago Press, 2001.

Anderson, Charles. *Statecraft.* New York: Wiley, 1977, especially chaps. 1–6.

Hardin, Garret. "The Tragedy of the Commons." *Science* 162 (13 December 1968), pp. 1243–48 (the original statement on the problem of producing public goods through voluntary contributions).

Hochschild, Jennifer. *What's Fair? American Beliefs about Distributive Justice.* Cambridge: Harvard University Press, 1981.

Lindblom, Charles. *The Market System: What It Is, How It Works, and What to Make of It.* New Haven, CT: Yale University Press, 2001.

Olsaretti, Serena, ed. *Desert and Justice.* New York: Oxford University Press, 2003.

Ostrom, Elinor. *Governing the Commons: The Evolution of Institutions for Collective Action.* Cambridge: Cambridge University Press, 1991.

Scott, James C. *Seeing Like a State: How Certain Schemes to Improve the Human Condition Have Failed.* New Haven, CT: Yale University Press, 1998.

The Citizen and the Regime

PART III

The Citizen and the Regime

CHAPTER 7

Democracies and Authoritarian Systems

In Part II, we looked at the state and at questions that go into the setting of state policies. Now we have reached a point in the text at which we will begin to look inside the state. How does "the state"—which comprises many different people—choose a particular set of policies? What goes on within a state that determines the policies it will pursue? The state is not a simple decision-making mechanism, and its complex organizational structure strongly influences the processes of political choice. In the next two parts— Chapters 7 through 8 and 9 through 17—we will look at those internal structures.

In this chapter, we will examine two broad types of regime: democracies and authoritarian systems. A **regime** is the general form of government of a state, including its constitution and rules of government. A regime generally continues beyond the terms of individual officeholders. The United States, for instance, has had a democratic regime for better than two centuries, across many presidents and lawmakers. A state, in turn, is in principle more enduring than a regime. For instance, a state may shift between different regimes, as Nigeria has moved back and forth between democracies and military governments. Thus a state is more lasting than a regime, which in turn is more lasting than individual officeholders.

❖ Democracy

A **democracy** is a regime in which all fully qualified citizens vote at regular intervals to choose, from among alternative candidates, the people who will be in charge of setting the state's policies. Democracy is "government of the people"; therefore, there is also a sense that the full population of citizens will be actively engaged between elections in debate over alternative policies and in the work of setting the policies. How fully engaged they are varies across democracies, and whether they are sufficiently engaged has long been a matter of debate. Examples of this debate include proposals for refer- endums, workplace democracy, and citizen caucuses, all of which are intended to give citizens more detailed involvement in policy-making than is possible just in voting for alternative leaders.

As we look at the states of the world that we characterize as democracies, we must remember that although the full population of citizens has more access to the power of government in democracies than in authoritarian systems, there is really no pure de- mocracy, in the sense of a state in which every citizen has equal access to governmental power. The vote is important, but there are also other resources that give some citizens more access than others, as we will see in succeeding chapters—money, armed force (the military, in some states), education, and others. Democracies vary in how equal the access to government is for ordinary citizens.

At the bottom range of democracies, we even find a broad gray area of **authori- tarian democracies** where we are not sure whether there is enough democracy in the system to really merit the name. Examples include Russia, where the Constitution gives the executive immense power and President Vladimir Putin has built on this by intimi- dating opponents and cowing or seizing almost all of the press, and the African state of Zimbabwe, where President Robert Mugabe has won continued electoral victories in large part by campaigns of intimidation, assault, and beatings of opposition support- ers. The term "authoritarian democracies" indicate that these states are at the margin between the two regimes.

"Democracy" then, is actually a range of things rather than a single thing. But as we will see, there is a real difference between democracies (even if they constitute a range of things) and authoritarian systems. Democracy does make a difference.

Most of you are familiar with democratic government from your own experience. However, although most of the world's states have been democracies at one time or an- other since the 1960s, only a relatively small number of the world's states are stable de- mocracies. Democracy requires an implicit agreement by the conflicting groups in a state to accept the possibility that they will lose out in the making of policy. In effect, it requires an agreement among labor unions, corporations, farm groups, environmentalists, vege- tarians, motorcycle enthusiasts, and all other groups to take their chances on the outcome of a process of policy making in which the population as a whole gets the deciding voice. Each group accepts that it must abide by the end result and hopes that it will be able to get enough of what it wants out of the process. This is the "democratic bargain."

When we look at it in this way, it is easy to see why democracy might be fragile. All that is needed to make a democracy collapse is for one or more important groups to reject the results of the democratic bargain and to have access to enough power to over- throw the system. Many parts of the world are beset by problems of overpopulation, ethnic and religious conflict, poverty, and chancy positions in world trade—problems so fierce that it becomes difficult for powerful groups to face policy defeats philosophi- cally. The stakes are just too high, and military forces or popular movements usually lie close at hand, willing and able to overthrow the system.

As one might suspect, under these circumstances only a small number of the world's states are stable democracies. Of the 104 states that were independent as of 1960, only 29 have had an uninterrupted record of electoral democratic government over the time since then.[1] Most of these are prosperous industrialized states whose people can more easily afford to compromise on the "democratic bargain." However, some poor states such as India, Jamaica, Malta, Botswana, and Costa Rica have also had steady histories of democratic government.

✦ THE COMING AND GOING OF DEMOCRACY

The world's imagination was seized in 1989 when the Iron Curtain and the Berlin Wall fell, and most of the communist states of Eastern Europe suddenly threw off their old systems and established democracies. The drama of the failed coup in the Soviet Union in 1991 and the victory of the pro-democratic forces there had people glued to their television sets. These dramatic changes were only part of a larger move toward democracy that covered two decades and ranged across many parts of the world.

Southern Europe saw three shifts from right-wing dictatorships to democracy in the late 1970s: in Greece, Portugal, and Spain. A bit later, a wave of democratization swept Latin America, as several states reestablished democracies after periods of military (mostly right-wing) dictatorship: Ecuador and Peru in 1978, Bolivia in 1982, Argentina in 1983, Uruguay in 1984, Brazil in 1985, and Chile in 1989.

Finally in 1989 and 1990, along with the wave of democratization in the formerly communist states of Eastern Europe (East Germany, which has since merged with former West Germany; Poland; Czechoslovakia; Hungary; Bulgaria; Romania; and Yugoslavia), several states scattered around the world moved to democracy: Algeria over the period 1989–1991; Haiti in 1990; South Korea in 1987; Nepal in 1990; Nicaragua in 1990; Pakistan in 1988; the Philippines in 1986; and South Africa in 1994.

This was not a story of uniformly forward progress. After establishing democracy in Algeria, the military was afraid that the fundamentalist Islam party would be victorious, and it abruptly banned elections in 1992. In Haiti, the military ousted newly elected President Jean-Bertrand Aristide in a 1991 coup; he was only reinstated in 1994 after strong pressure from the United States and the temporary occupation of Haiti by U.S. troops. The military overthrew the democratically elected government in Pakistan in 1999 and installed their commanding general in power. Democracy is tenuous in most parts of the former Soviet Union. And the new elections in Africa include only a few in which a government has actually been replaced; often, the old dictators have managed to prevail under the new democratic rules, sometimes through ruthless violence. Although there have been many such backslidings and failures, still overall, there was a clear movement toward more democracy over a period of about twenty years.

The shifts of the 1980s and early 1990s occurred in regional waves, but they were all part of a larger wave of democratization, often called simply the **Third Wave** of democratization.[2] Movements to democracy have generally occurred in three worldwide waves. The first wave of democratization came in the wake of World War I, as Germany

[1] Adam Przeworski et al., *Democracy and Development* (New York: Cambridge University Press, 2000), appendix 1.2.
[2] Samuel P. Huntington, *The Third Wave: Democratization in the Late Twentieth Century* (Norman: University of Oklahoma Press, 1991).

154   PART III   THE CITIZEN AND THE REGIME

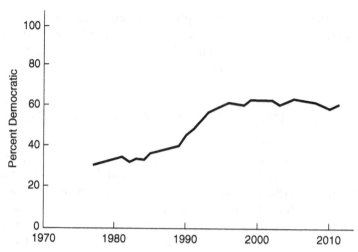

FIGURE 7.1   Percent of the world's states democratic, 1977–2011.

SOURCE: Freedom House, *Freedom in the World*, various editions.

became a democracy in 1918 and new democracies emerged in Eastern Europe. At about the same time, a number of Latin American states also established democratic regimes. Many of the democracies established at this time, however, failed either under the economic pressures of the Great Depression or in the violence of World War II. A second wave of democratization occurred after World War II, as countries such as Germany and Italy reestablished democracy and large numbers of former European colonies in the Third World achieved independence. Again, while many of those democracies survived, many also fell to military coups.

The third wave started in the late 1970s with the successful reintroduction of democracy to Spain and Portugal. During the third wave, democracies rose from 31 percent of the world's states in 1977, to 61 or 62 percent in the mid-1990s. As you see in Figure 7.1, the increase was actually steepest towards the end of this period, from about 1989 to 1995. The growth of democracy during these two decades is dramatic, but it is perhaps just as notable that since the mid-1990s there has been essentially no net growth in the number of democracies. Political scientist Larry Diamond has dubbed this period, starting with the coup in Pakistan in 1999 that overturned the country's democratic government, the "democratic recession."[3]

It is clear that movement to democracy is not a one-way street. We experienced a wave of democratization in the last few decades of the twentieth century, but at other periods during that century there were waves of dictatorship. The 1920s were such a period, as Germany, Italy, Spain, and various Eastern European states overthrew democracy; and in the 1950s and 1960s, a wave of dictatorship spread over South America and Africa. Democracy is fragile, even though it has many strengths, including especially the greater dignity it confers on all citizens and its relatively strong protection against

---

[3]Larry Diamond, *The Spirit of Democracy* (New York: Times Books, 2008) chapter 3.

arbitrary treatment by governments. In the wake of the democratization of the former Soviet Union a number of commentators crowed prematurely about the triumph of democracy. There was even a very widely read essay with the rather silly title, "The End of History?" which argued that the question of democracy was now permanently answered and the ideological conflicts ushered in by the nineteenth century were dead.[4] However, history does not stop. We are likely to see movements both to democracy and to authoritarianism over the coming decades. Most recently, the 2010 "Arab spring" saw attempts to establish democracy in Tunisia, Libya, Egypt, Yemen, and Bahrain.

➜ POSSIBLE EXPLANATIONS

What brought about the push for democracy at this point in history? Three possible reasons are: fatigue of some authoritarian regimes; international pressures; and people's desire for security against arbitrary abuse.

In a few cases, authoritarian systems became "tired" and lost popular support. In Spain and Portugal, long-term dictators died, and their regimes had already lost steam long before their deaths. In Argentina, the military government lost a war with Britain. Most dramatically, the exhaustion of the Soviet Union at maintaining its control of Eastern Europe was a critical element in the wave of democratization in that region in 1989, and the corruption and senility of its Communist Party led to the victory of democracy in the Soviet Union. The exhaustion of the old system was evident in a botched coup attempted by the communists in the Soviet Union in 1991. The old party could not muster enough imagination and organization to take advantage of what was actually a good opportunity to reestablish its rule.

Also, in many cases at this time there was international pressure on non-democratic regimes to change, orchestrated by activist networks from around the world. Spain, Portugal, and Greece came under pressure from their neighbors to become democratic, and the carrot of membership in the European Union was offered to them implicitly if they established democratic systems.[5] South Africans were under international trade and investment sanctions for several years to force them to give democratic rights to their black majority, and those sanctions helped lead to democratic government in 1994. Although pressure for democracy in China has been repulsed since the Tiananmen Square massacre in 1989, concern for international reactions has slightly softened the suppression of democratic movements there. Nicaragua's government held free elections under quasi-military pressure from the United States, which promoted a civil war in the country to force a change in regime.

Probably more important than either international pressures or the weakness of the old regimes, however, were the remaining two factors: a desire for human rights and security against abuse and, especially in the communist states of Eastern Europe, economic failure. A desire for security and dignity must have been high among the reasons for democratization in South America, where many of the military regimes had been brutally oppressive. In Argentina and Chile, thousands of people disappeared during the dictatorships and are

---

[4]Francis Fukuyama, "The End of History?" *National Interest* 16 (Summer 1989), pp. 3–19.
[5]See Chapter 3 for a discussion of the European Union.

156   PART III   THE CITIZEN AND THE REGIME

presumed to have been tortured and killed. In the Philippines, the murder of an opposition leader sparked the move for democracy. In East Germany, after the overthrow of the communist regime, it was learned that the secret police had maintained files on 6 million people, out of a total population of 16 million, and had employed hundreds of thousands of informants. In the formation of most democracies, a yearning for dignity and security has always played a large part. This was true in the establishment of the first democracies in Europe and North America in the nineteenth century, and it is true today.

These are some of the factors that we think led to the widespread shift to democracy over the last forty years. Concentrating on the sources of democratization, as we have done here, does carry the risk that we can come to see the coming of democracy, and the continuation of democracy, as natural and normal. They are not. As we noted above, for example, a new democracy may often establish itself lacking a broad base of support that would allow it to survive. A shift to democracy may even bring with it some side effects that actually make democracy *more* difficult to sustain. Democracy's openness often unleashes regional nationalist pressures that had been held in check by more oppressive regimes. Unless the state is strong and lucky, it may be pulled apart. Alternatively, the danger to the state may then prompt an antidemocratic reaction from the military, and we may end up back at dictatorship. As Iraq enters into independence after the U.S. occupation, for instance, both of these potential outcomes are dangers for its new democratic government.

⤳ WHAT DID WE LEARN FROM THE THIRD WAVE?

The challenge of explaining the Third Wave has helped to further a fairly substantial shift in the whole field of comparative politics. Explaining *distinct* and *specific events* as compared with analyzing ongoing stable situations leads us to emphasize individuals' choices, and especially the choices of individual leaders and popular movements. Stable situations are often appropriately analyzed by looking at stable, broad background factors such as the constitution, the balance of groups' power, broad economic structures, and the historical background of the state. However, a specific event that occurs at a given point in time is usually not determined in a precise way by such factors. So to analyze such an event, we must look more specifically at the particular actors involved—at their strategic situations and their decisions.[6] We call this approach **agent-centric explanation;** that is, it puts individuals' choices ("agency") at the forefront, rather than social or economic structures. The great interest attracted by the wave(s) of democratization at the end of the twentieth century helped to shift the study of comparative politics somewhat in this direction. In the terms I used in Chapter 1, it increased the "interpretive" aspect of comparative politics. (See p. 19.)

1. ***The Importance of "Pacts."*** An early work that formed the basis for much further analysis of the Third Wave was a broad review by O'Donnell and Schmitter of what were then the most recent cases of democratization, primarily in Latin America and southern Europe.[7] This study did not so much develop a theory as note and comment on similarities across cases.

   One important conclusion the authors reached was that it may be important for successful democratization that the democratizers form **pacts** with those whom they are ousting to ensure a smooth transition and to lay a good base of support for the future democracy. Such pacts might include, for instance, amnesty from prosecution for crimes committed under the dictatorship; symbolic affirmation of the old regime, as in the maintenance of a powerless or weak monarch; or guarantees of funding for the army. "Pacts" figured importantly in Spain and the Latin American states.

   As always in looking at democratization, however, there are few universal truths. In the wave of democratization across Eastern Europe in 1989, which occurred after the study by O'Donnell and his coauthors, pacts were not nearly so important. Unlike southern Europe, this was not a case of ousting a military associated with powerful domestic forces, which had to be dealt with gingerly. Rather, the ousted force was primarily the Soviet army, and broad nationalist sentiment coincided with the democratic thrust. Therefore, the new democratic leaders in Eastern Europe did not need to bargain very much with their discredited predecessors. Also, broad-based social movements were much more at the forefront of these moves to democracy than had been the

---

[6]For an opposed view, see Nancy Bermeo, "Myths of Moderation: Confrontation and Conflict During Democratic Transitions," *Comparative Politics* 29 (April 1997), pp. 305–22.

[7]Guillermo O'Donnell and Philippe C. Schmitter, *Transitions from Authoritarian Rule: Tentative Conclusions about Uncertain Democracies* (Baltimore: Johns Hopkins University Press, 1986).

158   PART III   THE CITIZEN AND THE REGIME

Jubilant protesters in Cairo celebrate the overthrow of President Mubarak of Egypt.
© AP Photo/Emilio Morenatti

case in southern Europe, and the members of these movements had little tolerance for generous pacts with the old regime.

2. ***Sudden Changes.*** Many of the recent shifts to democracy have taken observers by surprise. No one predicted in 1988, for instance, that by the end of 1989, many Eastern European states would be democracies, and in the fall of 2010, no one predicted that a year later dictators would have been toppled in Tunisia, Egypt, and Libya.

One scholar has provided a good explanation for why these shifts might be sudden and difficult to predict.[8]

Under an authoritarian regime, there are few rewards and many punishments for anyone coming out in favor of democracy. However, this is a function of how likely it is that democracy will be established. If democratization in the end succeeds, there will be many rewards and no punishments for those who had come out in favor of it. The key factor is that the net rewards of coming out may tip suddenly as the probability of success shifts over from less than even to greater than even. Figure 7.2 depicts this graphically. As the probability of success rises from zero to 0.2, 0.3, or 0.4, the net rewards for favoring democracy do not increase much. In fact, regimes may crack down more on opponents as their situation becomes slightly less secure. Suddenly, however, a tipping point is reached at which time the danger in favoring democracy appears to decrease. People find that when they demonstrate in the street, there are thousands of other people there, too many for the government to take on. Almost overnight, favoring

---

[8] Adam Przeworski, "Some Problems in the Study of Transition to Democracy," in Guillermo O'Donnell, Philippe C. Schmitter, and Laurence Whitehead, eds., *Transitions from Authoritarian Rule: Comparative Perspectives* (Baltimore: Johns Hopkins University Press, 1986).

FIGURE 7.2 Probable reward for coming out in favor of democracy, as probability increases that democracy will in fact be established.

democracy can shift from being a dangerous activity, restricted to the hard core, to an easy activity that may carry future rewards.[9]

3. ***Economic Crisis or Not?*** Stephen Haggard and Robert Kaufman have pointed out that a transition to democracy occurs differently if it comes in response to an economic crisis in the state than if it occurs under good economic conditions.[10] Some examples of **crisis transitions** are the 1989–1991 Eastern European transitions and most of the Latin American transitions. On the other hand, a number of East Asian transitions, such as those in Thailand and Korea, occurred in the presence of prosperity, as did transitions in Spain, Turkey, and Chile.

When an economic crisis spurs a transition, the ruling authoritarian government often has little credibility and cannot influence the path of the transition much at all. Pacts are less important in such transitions, and the military are less likely to retain any influence in the new regime. In Turkey and Thailand, with their "noncrisis" transitions, the resulting democracies had to constantly look over their shoulders to see how the military viewed any decisions. When Turkey formed a pro-Islamic cabinet in 1997, for instance, the military forced it to dissolve after several months because they thought it would weaken the secular, Western-oriented doctrines that they supported.[11]

---

[9]I do not mean here that the process is automatic from this point on. China is an example of where this point had been reached in 1989; thousands were flocking to the democratic banner, but the government responded with the Tiananmen Square massacre, thus moving the probability of success back to a lower level. Similarly, in Iran in 2009 huge pro-democracy demonstrations were effectively repressed by a brutal government crackdown.

[10]Stephen Haggard and Robert Kaufman, *The Political Economy of Democratic Transitions* (Princeton: Princeton University Press, 1995).

[11]Later, however, the military did acquiesce in 2003 in the formation of a moderately Islamic cabinet.

160   PART III   THE CITIZEN AND THE REGIME

Politics is also likely to be more open after crisis-driven transitions, with fewer restrictions on broad participation by a full range of parties and interest groups. As a result, the politics that follow are likely to be marked by greater representation of the political left, and to be more tumultuous, than the politics that follow a noncrisis transition.

Several Websites that deal with democratization and sustainable democracy are:

National Endowment for Democracy: **http://www.ned.org**

International Institute for Democracy and Electoral Assistance (International IDEA): **http://www.idea.int/**

United Nations Development Programme: Democratic

Governance: **http://www.undp.org/governance**

Network Institute for Global Democratization: **http://www.nigd.org/**

Comparative Democratization Project, Stanford University: **http://democracy.stanford.edu**

✦ WHY ARE PROSPEROUS COUNTRIES LIKELY TO BE DEMOCRACIES?

One of the most regular and predictable things in the comparative study of politics is that prosperous countries are much more likely to be democracies than poor countries. We noted noble exceptions above, such as India and Costa Rica, but there are really not all that many exceptions. The median per capita income (PPP) of democracies in 2011 was $12,350, of nondemocracies, $3,350.[12] There is nothing natural or inevitable about this. Poor people want dignity and security from abuse as much as rich people. Why is it that they are less likely to enjoy democratic government?

One explanation, of course, could be that democracies are better at fostering economic growth than nondemocracies, and so countries that are democracies become more prosperous over time than nondemocracies. I do not think this is true, though. I will give my reasons in more detail at the end of this chapter, but for the moment it may be enough to note that democratic India did not grow more rapidly over the last fifty years than Communist China, although both started at about the same level of poverty.

At any rate, if you will allow me for now to stipulate that the economies of democracies do not grow more rapidly than the economies of nondemocracies, then there must be something about prosperity that makes a state more likely to be a democracy. What could be the reason for this? Rather than look at ways prosperity might cause states to become democracies, it is probably more fruitful to realize that states become democracies for all sorts of reasons having little to do with economic prosperity—the collapse of Soviet military power in Eastern Europe in 1989, the breakup of colonial empires in Africa and Asia in the 1950s and 1960s, international pressure on South Africa in 1990, the United States' overthrow of Saddam Hussein in Iraq in 2003—and look instead at whether, once a state has for whatever reasons become a democracy, prosperity has anything to do with the chances that it will *remain* a democracy.[13]

---

[12]Calculated from CIA WorldFactbook, www.cia.gov (July 23, 2012); democratic/not from Freedom House, *Freedom in the World 2012*. Only those states are included for which 2011 per capita GDP was available.

[13]This idea is developed in Adam Przeworski and Fernando Limongi, "Modernization Theories and Facts," *World Politics* 49 (1997), pp. 155–83.

CHAPTER 7   DEMOCRACIES AND AUTHORITARIAN SYSTEMS   161

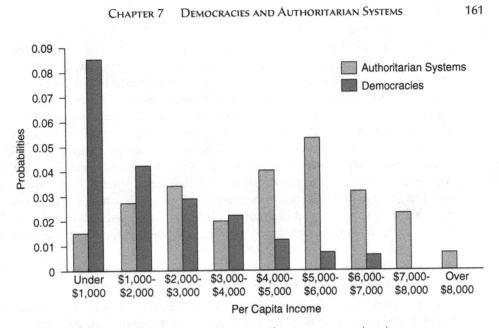

FIGURE 7.3 Probabilities of overthrow in democracies and authoritarian systems.

SOURCE: Based on Adam Przeworski, "Political Regimes and Economic Development," in Richard Sisson and Edward Mansfield, eds., *The Evolution of Political Knowledge* (Columbus: The Ohio State University Press, 2004), Table 1.

Figure 7.3 shows a very clear relationship, in which the probability that democracies are overturned marches steadily lower with each increment of prosperity.[14] At per capita annual income under $1,000 (in purchasing power parity dollars), the probability that a democracy would have been overthrown in any given year from 1951 to 1999 was over .08; the probabilities decrease steadily, until they are approximately zero at per capita annual income over $7,000. By contrast, the probability that an authoritarian system would have been overthrown and replaced with democracy is pretty much unrelated to the prosperity of the country; these probabilities wander throughout the figure.[15]

It appears that this holds the key to our question: why are prosperous countries more likely to be democracies? States may become democracies for all sorts of reasons, but once they have become a democracy, if they are prosperous they are much more likely to remain one than if they are poor. The same is not true of authoritarian systems. Whether they are overthrown in any given year does not seem to have much to do with whether they are prosperous or poor.

What is it about democracy that might make its survival peculiarly dependent on prosperity? Remember that at the beginning of this chapter I wrote about the "democratic bargain," an agreement by which all groups in society agree to abide by the results of an election and await their chance at power in the future. In order for this to happen, the losers must feel reasonably secure for the present while they wait to take power at some

---

[14]W. Phillips Shively, "The Asymmetry of Democratization and Democratic Breakdown (Or Is It Authoritarianization and Authoritarian Breakdown?): Przeworski's 'Political Regimes and Economic Development,'" in Richard Sisson and Edward Mansfield, eds., *The Evolution of Political Knowledge* (Columbus: The Ohio State University Press, 2004).
[15]For a critique of some aspects of this interpretation, see Carles Boix and Susan Stokes, "Endogenous Democratization," *World Politics* 55 (2003), pp. 517–549, and Ben Ansell and David Samuels, "Inequality and Democratization: A Contrarian Approach," *Comparative Political Studies* 43 (2010), pp. 1543–1574.

point in the future. This must surely be easier to do in a society with ample resources. If a drop of one-fourth in your income means that you must sell the cow, this will probably mean more to you and your children than a one-fourth drop in income means to an average West European, although obviously both are harsh events. Since disaster is always closer to citizens of a poor country, it is likely that those citizens, more than the citizens of richer countries, would try to make their system provide predictable outcomes. That is, when under stress, poorer countries should be more apt to shed the unpredictable future of democratic power-sharing. However, it is not just the poorest people in those countries who will seek the certainties of an authoritarian system. It will usually be a powerful group in the state, such as the military, a large ethnic group, or a business coalition, that seeks to tie things down rather than leave things open in the democratic bargain, often because they fear the poor. In an impoverished country, everyone is on edge.

✦ Democracy and Freedom

Many people think of democracy and individual freedom as almost synonymous. Certainly, it is apparent that democracy and individual freedom must have some sort of connection. After all, democracy and a variety of individual freedoms derived originally from the same basic principles of liberalism.[16] For purely practical reasons, democracy requires at least minimal levels of freedom of speech and freedom of association if the public bargaining that is the essence of democracy is to proceed at all.

However, a variety of other freedoms—such as freedom of religion, free markets (see the next section, on "Democracy and Capitalism"), freedom to travel where you will, or freedom to consume alcohol—are *not* necessary and inevitable companions of democracy, although we may find in practice that they usually go together.

A good example showing that freedom and democracy do not necessarily imply each other is Hong Kong, which as a British colony until 1997 never had democratic government but which had an open society with many liberal freedoms such as a free press, freedom of religion, and freedom of speech and association. The United States furnishes examples from its history in which, although we are a democracy, we have seen the level of freedoms rise and fall. The internment of Japanese-Americans during the Second World War, the system of legal racial segregation in many parts of the country through the first two-thirds of the twentieth century, the McCarthy period in which freedom of expression was limited—all help to demonstrate that there is not an automatic correspondence between democracy and freedom. Perhaps the most dramatic demonstration that freedom and democracy do not automatically coincide is that for the first half-century of its democratic history, the United States continued a brutal, institutionalized system of slavery.

Journalist and author Fareed Zakaria has presented an interesting argument along these lines, arguing first (as I have done above) that democracy and liberal freedoms do not always or necessarily imply one another, but then drawing the further argument that under some circumstances a less fully developed democracy may actually be more conducive to freedom than "all-out" democracy.[17] He points out that several countries

---

[16]As we saw in Chapter 2.
[17]Fareed Zakaria, *The Future of Freedom: Illiberal Democracy at Home and Abroad* (New York: W.W. Norton, 2003).

in Southeast Asia have gradually developed liberal freedoms *before* establishing electoral democracy (Singapore, for instance, which has very clean government, enjoys a much more open discussion of politics than in the past, but is still an essentially undemocratic government; Taiwan, which only instituted electoral democracy in the 1990s, but had a very open society well before that; and South Korea, which similarly instituted electoral democracy only in the 1990s). He also notes that some states that opened up electoral democracy rapidly in a sudden transition from an authoritarian system—Russia is one of his prime examples—only succeeded in creating a playground for shady characters and powerful economic interests.

The question of how and whether democracy and individual freedom are linked arises especially as authoritarian systems move to democracy because in some countries authoritarian systems have gradually become more liberal and open, often with no shift to democracy for some years. Democracy has then come—or not come—only as a last step. Thus, it has been necessary, in analyzing the process of democratization, to separate the two processes. It appears that democratization may work best where it has been preceded by slow liberalization, which has provided time for opposition leadership to form, for organizations of representation to be established, and for working relationships to be established between the old regime and the forces for change. For example, in Brazil the military regime in 1974 began a process of *abertura*, or "opening," under which discussion became more open, local governments became more independent, and political parties could form. It was not until 1985 that Brazil established democracy.[18]

On the other hand, countries often do not have the luxury of a gradual prior liberalization. If democracy comes quickly, as it did in the fall of Soviet-backed regimes in Eastern Europe in 1989 or in the Arab Spring in 2011, democracy and liberalization (if it comes) must come at the same time.

✦ DEMOCRACY AND CAPITALISM

Another pairing that often seems natural to people is democracy and free-market capitalism. Partly this may be because the most prominent democracy in the world, the United States, is also the most prominent capitalist, free-market economy in the world, but to some extent the two also have a rough natural affinity. Both are based on the aggregation of individual choices as a way to make collective decisions, and both reflect the basic liberal value of making individuals responsible for their choices.[19] Of course, the same ideology, classical liberalism, originally backed both democracy and free-market capitalism. So, these two have much in common, and it is no surprise that most democracies of the world have market-based economies.

However, there have been plenty of non-democratic states in the past that used market mechanisms for their economy.[20] Hong Kong, again, is a good example. It operates with an open market economy yet has never had fully democratic government, either under Britain or now as part of China. Many dictatorships and military governments in

---

[18]For a discussion of why military regimes might choose to yield up power in this way, see pp. 168–169.
[19]See Charles Lindblom, *Politics and Markets* (New York: Basic Books, 1977), chap. 12.
[20]See Chapter 6 for a discussion of "market mechanisms."

Africa rule states that essentially have market economies. Nazi Germany operated with a market economy. China, even as it has been putting down the movement for democracy since 1989, has allowed a rapid evolution of its economy away from communist planning and toward market mechanisms.

Therefore, there is no automatic connection between democracy and capitalism, and the Eastern European states could in principle have made a shift away from communist economies without moving to democracy. Very likely, however, their rejection of the past and their desire for change and integration with the West were such that it seemed natural to become "Western" in politics as well as in economy. A radical change in the economy would have been very difficult without a thorough change of leaders; therefore, a basic governmental change of *some* sort was probably necessary, whether or not it was a move to democracy.

✦ AUTHORITARIAN SYSTEMS

I noted at the beginning of this chapter that democracy is a fragile thing: of the 104 states that had been independent since 1960, only 29 have had an uninterrupted record of electoral democratic government during that time. Authoritarian government has its own fragilities, however. Of those same 104 states, only 13 had an uninterrupted authoritarian system across the same period of time. In the sections that follow, we will (1) look at some of the major forms of authoritarian government and (2) explore the sources of their fragility and success.

An **authoritarian system** is any state in which those who hold power in the government are not formally responsible in their exercise of power to the broad citizenry of the state. In other words, it is a state that is not a democracy. The authoritarian alternatives to democracy are by no means of one piece. Consider this sampling:

- **The Union of Soviet Socialist Republics (1917–1991)** From the Russian Revolution (1917) until a couple of years before the breakup of the union in 1991, power in the Soviet state was lodged clearly with the Communist Party. It was self-sustaining, recruiting new young members who could progress through it to build careers. Although Stalin's rise to power in the 1930s was bloody, after Stalin the party saw five peaceful, orderly transitions of leadership. As far as we know, the party made decisions collectively from within, with strong leadership by the party head and a great deal of influence from such groups as the army. Ordinary people did not have a great deal of personal freedom, but—compared with the bloody past—laws were at least predictable and dealings with the governmental apparatus were usually orderly.

- **Myanmar (formerly known as Burma)** Myanmar became independent from Great Britain in 1948. It has been ruled by the military since 1962. In 1990 the military allowed elections, but when the pro-democracy party won overwhelmingly they refused to yield power, and imprisoned the leader of the party, Aung San Suu Kyi. Pro-democracy movements have periodically challenged the military junta, most notably a series of demonstrations led by Buddhist monks in 2007, which the government suppressed brutally. In 2010 the military staged an election in which their favored party won over 70 percent of the seats in parliament, but many observers judged that election invalid. Since the election, however, the government has initiated modest steps towards liberalization, freeing Aung San Suu Kyi from house arrest, allowing her party to hold a small number of seats in the parliament, and legalizing labor unions. It remains to be seen whether this is the beginning of a general liberalization, or a temporary shift.

- **Saudi Arabia** Saudi Arabia has been an absolute monarchy since early in the twentieth century, with power lodged in the Saud family. This is a large, extended family that provides not only the king but also most of the council of ministers and other high government officials. It appears that while the king figures importantly in the making of decisions, this is a genuinely collegial effort in which the council of ministers (including the king) discusses issues and decides on policies. Members of the Saud family are conservative in religious matters and enforce strict Muslim standards of behavior, although they have been enthusiastic about economic modernization. Even the turmoil of the two Gulf Wars left this system essentially unchanged.

- **Democratic Republic of the Congo (formerly known as Zaire)** Zaire became independent from Belgium in 1960 and immediately plunged into a civil war fomented by Belgian mining interests. After a chaotic period of civil war, coups, assassinations, and attempts to establish democracy, Colonel Joseph-Désiré Mobutu seized power in 1965, with strong support from the United States. Mobutu established a one-party state and remained in power from then until 1997, as president and, at various times, chair of the single party and head of the armed forces. Charges of massive corruption and widespread abuses of human rights characterized his rule, but Mobutu proved adept at maintaining his rule despite unrest by giving ground at critical moments and retaking it when the opportunity arose. From about 1982, an organized opposition operated, based mainly abroad but sometimes openly, when circumstances permitted, in Zaire. In the 1990s, Mobutu fended off strong opposition pressure and student riots, while the country sank more deeply into social and economic disorganization. In 1997, a rebel group led by Laurent-Désiré Kabila, a long-time opponent of Mobutu from the eastern region of Zaire, finally defeated Mobutu's forces. Mobutu fled, and Kabila renamed the country and established himself as president. His regime was marked by the same sort of oppression as Mobutu's reign, but he was never able to establish full control of the country. He was assassinated in 2001 and succeeded by his son, Joseph Kabila, who has initiated a democratic constitution and was elected president in 2006. However, Joseph Kabila still does not have full control of the country. The civil wars continue, fomented by Congo's neighbors, and have almost broken the country into a set of independent regions. More people have died in these wars in Congo than in any other conflict since World War II.

These examples are roughly representative of authoritarian systems. First, they are quite varied politically. They range from conservative Saudi Arabia to the bureaucratic Soviet Union to the personal dictatorship of Zaire. Second, many of the authoritarian systems are not organized stably. The Soviet Union disintegrated in 1991. Some of its parts have moved toward democracy, but often a shaky democracy; others are authoritarian systems, masked by sham democracy. Mobutu did not ultimately retain power in Zaire,

Are Regime Changes Contagious?

Both democratization and military coups tend to cluster at certain times and in certain regions. Suddenly a rash of coups will break out in a region such as Latin America or southern Africa, for instance, and then coups will once again decrease. Statistical tests have shown that this is not coincidental. Coup makers apparently watch each other's successes, and if they have seen a number of their neighbors succeed, they are likely to have fewer qualms about undertaking a coup themselves. Furthermore, if a number of coups have recently occurred in the neighborhood, this lessens the problems of legitimacy. If coups are a frequent thing in the region, initiating a coup will not seem as flagrantly illegitimate as if yours were the only army doing it. Beyond considerations in any one state, then, coups appear to involve broad, wavelike regional processes.*

Similarly, democratization occurs in waves at different times, in different parts of the world. Most Eastern European states shifted to democracy between 1989 and 1991, for instance, and in 2010 a popular uprising in Tunisia sparked the Arab Spring of pro-democracy demonstrations in many other North African and Mideastern states, including the successful movement to oust the repressive regime of Mubarak in Egypt. There is evidence that movements for democracy in one area are often influenced by movements in another.**

*A good example of statistical analysis to measure these processes is Richard P.Y. Li and William R. Thompson. "The 'Coup Contagion' Hypothesis," *Journal of Conflict Resolution* 19 (March 1975), pp. 63–88.

** See, for instance, Douglas Anglin, "Southern African Responses to Eastern European Developments," *Journal of Modern African Studies* 28 (no. 3, 1990), pp. 431–56

but his successor was as much an authoritarian as he was. Saudi Arabia, on the other hand, appears to have a relatively stable system.

→ MILITARY GOVERNMENT

The most dramatic alternative to democratic government is **military government**, in which a group of officers use their troops to take over the governmental apparatus and run it themselves. This is called a **coup,** from the French *coup d'état* (strike at the state). For instance, in 2012 dissident soldiers from the north of Mali took over the presidential palace in a coup and seized the government.

Only a handful of the world's states are under military government. We might have expected that military governments would be quite common. After all, the military in any state control more armed power than anyone else. If they choose, as a group, to oust the existing government—or even if only a part of the military choose to do so and the rest decide to sit it out—there is no one who can stop them. Civilian governments must depend for their safety on the military's satisfaction, on their disunity, or on their reluctance to take over the government. While each of these protective shields is evident in many military groups, it must not be unusual that all three would from time to time fail and that the military would break out in a coup. This is particularly likely in a

CHAPTER 7   DEMOCRACIES AND AUTHORITARIAN SYSTEMS   167

"Good news. The 'Times' has upgraded us from a 'junta' to a military government."

© Joseph Mirachi/*The New Yorker Collection*/www.cartoonbank.com

new state, where a tradition of civilian government has not had time to take hold. It is not surprising that military coups occur with some frequency around the world.

In a few states, coups have become so routine that they have almost been institutionalized as the normal method of governmental change. In such cases, other political forces become involved informally, much as they would under other arrangements. One or another military faction may seek out key groups such as labor unions as potential allies, and—even though they do not themselves bear arms—their weight is felt.[21]

In Bolivia, for instance, factions of the armed forces in the past regularly depended on other political groups when they were attempting a coup.[22] In 1978, the army, aided by left-wing allies in the unions and political parties, overthrew a right-wing government. After an attempt at an election in 1979, a right-wing coup was tried, but it failed because its leaders were not able to get the support of Congress. In 1982, yet another military group was forced out of office by a general strike led by the unions. In a bizarre way, coups under these circumstances become a system that draws a fairly wide range of people into the political process. Usually, however, they are more isolated events.

Military governments vary greatly in their political role. In Myanmar, the military have ruled without interruption since they took power in 1962; theirs was until recently a very repressive regime, with no dissent tolerated. In Nigeria, a series of military

[21]Martin C. Needler, "Political Development and Military Intervention in Latin America," *American Political Science Review* 60 (September 1966), pp. 616–26.

[22]Bolivia experienced military coups regularly—almost annually—until 1985. Since 1985, Bolivia has had a democratic regime.

governments ruled from 1966 to 1978 and again from 1983 to 1999. During much of that time, except for the corrupt and vicious rule of General Sani Abacha from 1993 to 1998, there was considerable civilian support for the military regimes. In Turkey, the military have taken over the government three times since World War II—in 1960, 1971, and 1980—each time when Turkey's democratic government was verging on chaos. The Turkish takeovers were at the time broadly supported and were followed by a return to democracy after stability was restored.

Military governments also vary widely in the one thing in which we might have expected that they would be similar: their political direction. They are not all of the political right or of any other direction, even though the usual stereotype is of the right-wing officers' coup. Some coups are clearly of the right or the left, but many are not identifiable as either. Their political direction depends on which group of officers leads the coup. There are many officers of the left in most countries, as well as of the right, especially if recruitment is not limited to the upper class.

These two aspects of coups—that they sometimes become incorporated in the broader political process and that they have no clear political complexion, of the left or of the right—have made political scientists a bit cautious in assessing them. In a study of Venezuelans' views of democracy and military coups, David J. Myers and Robert E. O'Connor found that Venezuelans considered occasional coups part of the normal political process but distinguished sharply between coups and military dictatorships:

> . . . self-professed democratic Venezuelans perceive no incompatibility between endorsing democracy and supporting an occasional coup to rectify problem situations. Approving military intervention differs from favoring long-term military dictatorship. We find no evidence of the latter but widespread support of the former. Many respondents seemed to view coups as a device equivalent to a parliamentary vote of no confidence. It is indeed a serious action but is consistent with their understanding of democratic rules.[23]

✦ Why Aren't There More Military Governments?

Good or bad, though, it is still surprising that the military does not govern more countries. There are not as many coups as we might expect, and most military governments stay in power only a few years. This may be partly because most states take pains to imbue their military officers with inhibitions against political intervention. Adolf Hitler required officers to swear oaths of personal allegiance to him, for instance; and in the training of its officers, the U.S. government ensures in many ways that they will understand their proper role to be nonpolitical.

However, more important than such inhibitions are a series of significant problems which military governments face—problems that make officers reluctant to take

---

[23]David J. Myers and Robert E. O'Connor, "Support for Coups in Democratic Political Culture: A Venezuelan Exploration," *Comparative Politics* 30 (January 1998), p. 206. Since 1998 Venezuela has been an authoritarian democracy under President Hugo Chavez until his death in 2013, and then under his successors.

CHAPTER 7   DEMOCRACIES AND AUTHORITARIAN SYSTEMS   169

and hold power. A uniquely serious problem for them is that of legitimacy (see pages 15–17). Legitimacy is a widespread belief among the people of a state that a particular form of government is appropriate, and that its officials are therefore entitled to rule. We can see why this might pose special problems for a military government. A military government takes power through no regular process but simply seizes it, so how can it claim that no other group should similarly displace it? A democratic government is legitimized by the electoral process that produced it; a monarchy is legitimized by the rules of succession on which it is based; a communist government is legitimized by Lenin's theory that the Communist Party must lead the revolution. However, no process of selection legitimizes the military government. Those who live by the sword shall die by the sword, they say, and a military government must always be concerned to justify its existence. To this end, many military governments add civilians to their governing apparatus or set future dates for a return to democracy. Others try to rally the people through wars and appeals to nationalism.

Another problem of most military governments is that while their leaders *may* be skilled politically, there is little in the profession for which they have been trained that makes this especially likely. Military organization is usually marked by a fairly orderly passage of commands from higher officers to lower officers, without a great deal of argument in between. We should not exaggerate this orderliness, but many military officers are clearly frustrated by the jabber of daily political requests and arguments with which they must deal once they have taken over the power of the state.

Yet another problem for military governments is the problem of succession. How does the system provide for transfer of power from one leader to another, either on the first leader's death or because it appears to be time for a change? Democracies accomplish this through regular elections. Monarchies accomplish it by the designation of a child or other relative to be the monarch's successor. However, in military governments there is no clear institutional basis for arranging the transfer of power.

Finally, many military governments are fairly shaky alliances, united primarily by their opposition to the regime they have displaced and likely to fall apart as new issues arise that may divide their members.

As a result of these problems, purely military governments are actually rather fragile. Unless they set up the institutions to transform themselves into one-party states (see the next section), there is a good chance that they will eventually yield to the establishment of democracy. If a military regime is internally divided or has problems generally in governing and if enough of the key figures concerned feel that the uncertainty of the outcome of democratic choice is preferable to the certainty of any other particular group being in control, the stage is set to introduce democracy—or reintroduce it, as the case may be.[24] In the last two decades of the past century, for example, twenty-two states switched at least for a time from purely military government to democracy.[25]

---

[24]For an expansion of this argument, see Adam Przeworski, "Some Problems in the Study of the Transition to Democracy," in Guillermo O'Donnell, Philippe C. Schmitter, and Laurence Whitehead, eds., *Transitions from Authoritarian Rule: Prospects for Democracy* (Baltimore: Johns Hopkins University Press, 1986), pp. 47–63.
[25]Argentina, Bangladesh, Bolivia, Brazil, Burkina Faso, Burundi, Chile, Ecuador, Fiji, Ghana, Honduras, Nigeria, Pakistan, Panama, Paraguay, Peru, the Philippines, Portugal, South Korea, Thailand, Turkey, and Uruguay.

✣ One-Party States

Most authoritarian systems are not straight military governments but **one-party states**. The one-party state is distinguished by the fact that the government is based on and supports a political party, and that this is the only party allowed in the state. One-party arrangements have often had their origins in military coups. For example, in Libya, Colonel Muammar Khadaffi seized power in a coup in 1969 and established the Arab-Socialist Union as the sole political party; its general congress, chaired by Khadaffi, was in effect the chief governing body of the state. Other one-party arrangements have originated in national independence movements, which were then institutionalized as the single party. In Tanzania, for example, Julius Nyerere led the movement for independence, and his independence movement, the Tanganyika Africa National Union, won seventy of the seventy-one seats in the first election to the National Assembly. Four years later, a constitution was written that established it as the state's sole party. A number of one-party states originated in socialist revolutions, either indigenous, as in the cases of Cuba, China, and the U.S.S.R., or imposed by the U.S.S.R., as in the cases of (pre-1989) East Germany, Czechoslovakia, and other Eastern European states.

What distinguishes these states from other authoritarian systems, especially from straightforward military governments, is the existence of a reasonably large national political party that bolsters the government and provides an institutional basis for it. Compared with military rule, the one-party state offers a more stable and responsive form of government. The military government is necessarily limited by the field of vision of the officers who hold power. There is little provision for dealing with broad factional conflict or for the intrusion of diverse opinions. The government itself came into existence by irregular means; therefore, there is no regular set of arrangements to provide for the replacement of old leaders by new. These are things that the single political party may provide.

A national party is likely to embrace at least a reasonable range of the social groups in a state—labor leaders, industrialists, intellectuals, and military leaders. Not all of these may be equally happy with the party; however, they have little choice but to cooperate with it if asked. The party, on its side, needs to involve them if only to keep tabs on potential troublemakers. As a result, the single party as an organization is usually able to have a broad feel for opinion in the countryside. It provides institutional links between the government and the population.

Second, the party can provide an arena in which varied political positions can develop into factions. In this way, new conflicts may develop within an existing system rather than arising outside it and posing a threat to it.

Finally, the single party may provide a set of arrangements by which a nation can accomplish a transition of leadership. An example of this capacity was the fairly easy transition from Konstantin Chernenko to Mikhail Gorbachev in the Soviet Union after Chernenko's death in 1985. During Chernenko's illness, there had been some process at work by which the Communist party leadership decided who would take over from him.

The one-party state must be distinguished from a democracy with a dominant-party system.[26] A few democracies have party systems in which a single party has dominated government over a long period. Italy is a good example: From 1945 to 1994, without a break, the Christian Democratic Party received the largest vote of any party at each election, and except for a couple of years, it dominated all coalition cabinets during that period. (It finally fell from grace in 1993 as a result of its leaders' involvement in massive scandals.) What distinguished Italy from the one-party states during this period is that other parties were able to organize and did so. It was also universally recognized that those other parties would gain office if enough people voted for them—and this did finally happen in 1994.

To summarize our treatment of one-party systems, this is the most frequent form of authoritarian government. It may originate in all sorts of ways—military coups, movements for national independence, socialist revolutions, and many others. Distinctively, the one-party state has one (and only one) political party that the government fosters. This party adds to the government's capacities and helps to make these regimes more stable than straight military governments.

✦ MONARCHIES AND THEOCRACIES

There are two other significant forms of authoritarianism in the world:

- **Monarchies** are systems in which the power to rule is inherited through descent in a family. Most monarchies of the world are in the Mideast, and are often relatively underdeveloped states not much touched by modernity. Monarchies would not figure importantly in our study of politics today, except that several of them sit on huge reserves of oil. That is a good way to attract people's attention. Some examples of oil-rich monarchies in the Mideast are Saudi Arabia, Qatar, and Kuwait.

  Do not confuse monarchies with "constitutional monarchies" like Great Britain, Spain, or Sweden where a hereditary monarch exists as part of a democracy. Constitutional monarchs play a purely symbolic and ceremonial role. (I will discuss these further in Chapter 14.)

- A **theocracy** is a state ruled by a set of religious leaders, who derive their power from their positions in the religion. Its legitimacy comes from the shared faith of the citizens. Iran is the most prominent theocracy today. Vatican City, a tiny sovereign territory ruled by the Pope, is another example, if a minor one.

  There is no particular set of principles we can lay out for how a theocracy is ruled, because power in the state is simply a function of how power is acquired and exercised within the religion. Some religions, like the Catholic Church, are strictly hierarchical, with a single clear leader at the top. In contrast, Islam in all of its forms is very loosely

---

[26]Dominant party systems will be discussed in detail in Chapter 11, pp. 263–266.

172   PART III   THE CITIZEN AND THE REGIME

organized, and power is a function of how widely respected a religious scholar is. At any given time there are usually many diverse leaders within an Islamic group.

Theocracies are few today, but popular movements in many Islamic states are pushing for the establishment of theocracies in their state.

✦ DEMOCRACY VERSUS AUTHORITARIANISM: MATERIAL CONSIDERATIONS

It may seem odd to ask the question, which is better—democracy or an authoritarian system? People all over the world have "voted" often for democracy through popular movements, revolutions, and "with their feet" through emigration. The basic appeal of democracy is surely the individual dignity it confers, at least implicitly, on each citizen, and the partial protection its rule of law offers against arbitrary actions by the government. However, there have often been arguments about other good things in life as well, and whether they were easier to achieve under democracy or under an authoritarian system. Some have argued, for instance, that economic growth is easier for a poor country to achieve if it is not burdened by the debates of democracy, but can instead focus its efforts under authoritarian leadership.

In this section, drawing on the research of Adam Przeworski, Michael E. Alvarez, José Cheibub, and Fernando Limongi, I will look both at the question of how democracies

Muammar Khadaffi, former leader of Libya: originally, leader of a military coup; later, head of the single party.
© Bettmann/Corbis

TABLE 7.1

Life Expectancy under Authoritarianism and Democracy

Per Capita Income, $	Life Expectancy, Democracies	Life Expectancy, Authoritarian Systems	Difference
0–1,000	47.2	46.4	0.8
1,001–2,000	56.3	52.2	4.1
2,001–3,000	63.6	59.2	4.4
3,001–4,000	67.3	64.2	3.1
4,001–5,000	70.2	65.0	5.2
5,001–6,000	71.3	68.6	2.7
6,001+	73.2	67.6	5.6

SOURCE: Copyright © 2000 Adam Przeworski, Michael E. Alvarez, Jose Antonio Cheibub and Fernando Limongi. Reprinted with the permission of Cambridge University Press.

compare with authoritarian systems in economic growth, and in the overall quality of life as measured by life expectancies.[27] In both of these comparisons, democracy looks good, so the more material aspects of life give the same answer as the basic values cited above—democracy trumps authoritarianism.

First, with regard to economic development, Przeworski and others show through careful measures both of democracy and of economic development that the average performance of democracies over four decades was about the same as that of authoritarian systems. States with both sorts of regime grew at about a 4 percent annual rate. However, these averages conceal a major difference between authoritarian systems and democracies. Although on the average both regime types were equal, the range of possible outcomes for authoritarian systems was wildly greater than for democracies. All of the states whose economies grew at an annual rate of 7 percent or more were authoritarian systems—but so were almost all of the states whose economies grew at a rate of less than 1 percent annually. With democracies, given that economic policy represents some sort of a negotiated bargain among the economic interests of society, you get results that are all in the same, moderately positive ballpark. With authoritarian systems, since the government is free to put all of its eggs in one basket, you can get results ranging from miracles to disasters.

With regard to general well being, consider Table 7.1, which shows the life expectancy of people in authoritarian systems and democracies, for states at varying levels of prosperity.[28] The main thing determining life expectancy is how well-off the state is, but at each level of per capita income those living in democracies can expect to live significantly longer than those in authoritarian systems (as much as 5.6 years longer, for the most prosperous states).

---

[27]Adam Przeworski, Michael E. Alvarez, José Antonio Cheibub, and Fernando Limongi, *Democracy and Development: Political Institutions and Well-Being in the World, 1950–1990* (New York: Cambridge University Press, 2000).
[28]Ibid., p. 230.

174   PART III   THE CITIZEN AND THE REGIME

I conclude this look at the material differences between democracy and authoritarianism with the triumphal note of Przeworski and his colleagues: "Thus, we did not find a shred of evidence that democracy need be sacrificed on the altar of development."[29]

✦ "POWER AND CHOICE" AGAIN

To return to the theme of our text, authoritarian systems—especially the military governments—might appear to embody a rather pure strain of politics as power. After all, when political control depends on who has the guns it is hard to deny that power is at work. On the other hand, it is a common mistake to think of authoritarian systems simply as raw examples of power at work.

One-party governments often see themselves as pursuing communal objectives and develop organizational mechanisms for bringing a wide spectrum of opinion to bear on the government's decisions. Even military governments usually portray themselves as heeding the country's call, and there is often broad support among the people for a military coup. We shall deal with governments such as these more wisely if we remember that the picture is not black or white but that politics in these states—as in democracies—consists of power and choice.

EXAMPLE

Egypt in the Arab Spring

In 2011 demonstrations to overthrow authoritarian regimes broke out all across the Mideast, in what has come to be called the "Arab Spring." Perhaps the most notable of these was the Egyptian revolution. Lying in the northeast corner of Africa, Egypt has a population of 84,000,000 and a political history that stretches back 3,000 years to the pharaohs. For sixty years Egypt had been a one-party state ruled by the National Democratic Party. President Hosni Mubarak, leader of the party, had ruled since 1981 after members of the Muslim Brotherhood, an Islamic political movement, assassinated his predecessor.

The National Democratic Party had maintained a one-party state, banning the Muslim Brotherhood and other potential opposition parties from significant political action. It was flexible, however, and tried to avoid cracking down completely. Thus it allowed a certain number of Muslim Brotherhood members and others into the Parliament—but never enough to bring the governing party below a two-thirds majority. The regime endured by appealing to nationalism, by providing favored people with jobs and subsidies that kept them loyal to the regime, and by maintaining a large and repressive police force. It bought off many potential disruptors, imprisoned others, and encouraged resignation and apathy among most of the population.

---

[29]Ibid., p. 271.

CHAPTER 7   DEMOCRACIES AND AUTHORITARIAN SYSTEMS   175

By 2010, however, political conditions in the country were becoming difficult. Mubarak was getting old, and had worked for some years on a scheme to let his son Gamal succeed him as president in 2011. Gamal was surrounded by a group of cronies who had become rich through their association with him. Many viewed him and his group as a center of corruption and bribery. As part of the plan to set up Gamal in power, the National Democratic Party eliminated even the usual token representation of opposition groups in the 2010 parliamentary elections. They took 97 percent of the seats, leaving other groups angry.

At the same time, young Egyptians were frustrated by unemployment after the world-wide crash of 2008. Paradoxically, unemployment was highest among young Egyptians with advanced education, producing an incendiary group of young people with many skills, but no way to advance themselves. Throughout 2010 a number of movements of young people formed through Facebook groups, including the April 6 Movement (named for a textile workers' strike on that date), and "We are all Khaled Said," established in honor of a young man beaten to death by the police. The latter of these gained more than one million supporters.[30]

The first uprising of the Arab Spring took place in Tunisia, where peaceful demonstrations led to the establishment of democracy in January 2011. This first success of Arab democratization coincided with a large demonstration called by youth activists for Tahrir Square in Cairo on January 25, to protest against police brutality. The demonstrations were nonviolent, but the next day police killed a number of demonstrators. On January 28, a Friday (traditionally a day for protests after Friday prayers at the mosques), massive protests began. These culminated in a march estimated by the press at 2 million people on January 31. The demonstrations remained peaceful, but by early February, attacks by Mubarak supporters—some riding camels with whips through the crowded demonstrations—heightened tensions.

The military played a key role in these events. Unlike the hated police, the military had not been much associated with the regime's repression. They were professional, and saw their role as semi-independent of the regime. On the other hand, they had many economic ties with the regime through special subsidies and business deals.[31] So it was not clear how they would stand when the regime was attacked. In the end they opted for neutrality, sending tanks into the demonstration areas to keep both sides apart and prevent violence, but not initially coming down on either side.

Mubarak periodically made concessions to the demonstrators—at various times firing his cabinet, promising that he would not run again for president, turning over some of his powers to his vice president, and even having his son resign as a leader of the National Democratic Party. These were always too little, too late, however—the demonstrators wanted Mubarak himself ousted. Finally, on February 11 the Supreme Council of Egyptian Armed Forces announced that Mubarak was stepping down and that they would rule.

The military ruled Egypt for the next sixteen months, during which they promulgated a constitution, oversaw parliamentary elections, and set up presidential elections. Mubarak was tried and sentenced to life imprisonment. The period was marked by many disputes

---

[30]Dina Shehata, "The Fall of the Pharaoh: How Hosni Mubarak's Reign Came to an End," *Foreign Affairs* 90 (May/June 2011), p. 28.
[31]Eva Bellin, "Reconsidering the Robustness of Authoritarianism in the Middle East: Lessons from the Arab Spring," *Comparative Politics* 44 (January 2012), p. 134.

between the former Tahrir Square demonstrators and the military. The demonstrators, who were only loosely organized, found themselves ill-equipped to compete with more traditional groups like the Muslim Brotherhood. They argued for a delay in elections until they could organize themselves better, but they never were able to form an effective party.

The presidential election was held on June 24, 2012, and Muhammad Morsi, a member of the Muslim League, was elected. It was thought that the military would hold Morsi in close check once he was elected, and indeed they had written into the constitution a number of guarantees for their continued power. However, Morsi ousted most of the leaders of the Supreme Council of the Armed Forces six weeks after the election and established full control of the government. It is striking that the Muslim Brotherhood, which did not lead the democratization movement and was rather reluctant to take part in it, in the end benefited the most from it. It is still not certain how the party will participate in a democratic system, however.

The prospects for any new democracy are always chancy, and Egypt faces many problems. Its population is growing rapidly and needs a growing economy to accommodate its young people. There are deep divisions in the society, both in economic class and in religion. On the other hand Egypt's democracy does have a number of things going for it. Its population is well-educated, and it has a number of people with political experience to help provide leadership. Most importantly, it has a culture of community and trust. This was demonstrated especially when, as police authority was collapsing during the demonstrations, neighborhoods all over Cairo spontaneously formed volunteer policing organizations that successfully maintained order.[32]

 EXAMPLE

Authoritarian Drift in Venezuela?

Venezuela has been an electoral democracy since the 1950s. From the 1950s until the late 1990s it was dominated by two political parties, both tied to the upper middle class, who maintained their support by a good deal of pork-barrel spending and corruption. This system was upended in the late 1990s by Hugo Chavez, an army officer who became president in 1998 by running against both parties.

In reading this example, note the possibilities for authoritarian suppression of dissent even in a functioning democracy, and also the resources that opposition can use to counteract the suppression. There is a continuing tension in Venezuela between democracy and the strong class-based concerns of Chavez and his followers.

---

[32] Lisa Anderson, "Demystifying the Arab Spring: Parsing the Differences Between Tunisia, Egypt, and Libya," *Foreign Affairs* 90 (May/June 2011), p. 6.

In 1992 Hugo Chavez had attempted to carry out a military coup against the government, accusing them of corruption and of disregarding the needs of the poor and of indigenous peoples. The coup failed, but the government allowed him to broadcast his surrender nationally. His fiery speech, in which he said his movement had failed "for now" instantly made him a national figure. After he was released from jail in 1994 he became active politically. He was elected president in 1998, in a campaign that attacked both major parties and their corruption and promised a new, revolutionary program for the country. He won 56 percent of the vote, mostly from the poor and the lower middle class.

Chavez was an engaging, sometimes crude figure. His rambling Sunday morning show on state television, Aló Presidente, was energetic and unpredictable. His rule had been marked by new initiatives to help the poor, by the rise of new political elites aligned with him, and by rising conflict with the middle and upper classes. He was reelected in 2000, 2006, and 2012 by healthy margins, but also had to survive a coup attempt in 2002 that almost succeeded because of broad support for the coup from the middle class. He survived a referendum to remove him from office in 2004, winning with 58 percent of the vote, but he narrowly lost a referendum in 2007 in which he proposed sweeping changes to the constitution. In 2009 he won a referendum to abolish the two-term limit for the presidency; this allowed him to run again in 2012.

His aggressive programs had stimulated the growth of a new liberally oriented opposition, based on the middle class. Especially in the 2007 referendum, a new sort of opposition emerged, led by university students. Between the revitalized middle class opposition and declining support among the poor, his strength had diminished in recent years. In the 2010 National Assembly elections, his party and its communist allies received slightly less of the vote than the opposition parties did. Gerrymandered districts (with distorted boundaries designed to help his party) allowed Chavez to retain control of the Assembly, but his majority was then too small to change the constitution or to vote him the power to rule by decree, which he had often done in the past.

Chavez always had an ambivalent attitude towards democracy. Between his release from jail in 1994 and his election as president in 1998, he and his followers debated whether it was better to seek power by military revolution or by democratic election. In office, he had conducted and abided by free and fair elections. However, he had tried to use a number of devices similar to those of authoritarian leaders like Putin of Russia to secure uncontested power within a democratic framework. In 2006, for instance, Chavez decreed that no licenses would be allowed for television stations that promoted "fascism" and coups. Among other results of that decree, the most popular radio/television station in Caracas was closed. In the 2012 election Chavez's regulatory commission ruled that his opponent was limited to three minutes of television exposure each day, but all television channels were required to interrupt their regular programming whenever Chavez wanted to speak.

He had also harassed the opposition parties in a number of ways. Before regional elections in 2006, for instance, 260 candidates (almost all from the opposition) were barred from running. When Antonio Ledezma, an opposition figure, was elected mayor of Caracas in 2008, Chavez supporters occupied his offices and the national government took away most of the functions of mayor, transferring them to a federal official appointed by Chavez. After an opposition figure was elected governor of the western state of Zulia, Chavez cut the state's budget by one-third.[33]

After the opposition parties did well in the National Assembly elections of 2011, Chavez and his supporters took advantage of their control of the lame-duck Assembly (before the new members were sworn in) to pass new rules drastically weakening the Assembly. The lame-duck members passed a law allowing Chavez to rule by decree for the following eighteen months, and they passed new rules that restrict the meetings of the Assembly to only a few days each month and ban any television channels but those the government runs from broadcasting Assembly debates. The last of these provisions allowed the President to gag any debates that are embarrassing to him.

In these and other ways, Chavez has tightened his control of government, but Venezuela is still a democracy. Unlike Putin's Russia, there is strong support among the public for democratic government and it would be difficult to establish the sort of authoritarian control that Putin has achieved. However, Venezuelan politics entered a new and dangerous phase when Chavez died of cancer in March of 2013, shortly after having been reelected. In the election to replace him his Vice President, Nicolás Maduro, won by a margin of just 1.5%, far less than Chavez's margin a few months before. The opposition challenged the vote and asked for a recount, but the government refused the recount. Without Chavez at the helm, his movement appears gravely weakened. The economy is in very bad shape, Venezuelan society is split down the middle, and Maduro's supporters have moved to silence dissent even more. There has been talk of intervention by the army. In the aftermath of Chavez's death, Venezuela's politics seems on a knife's edge.

At www.freedomhouse.org you can find annual evaluations of the state of democracy and individual freedoms in Venezuela and all other states of the world, published by Freedom House.

 # EXAMPLE

Theocracy in Iran[34]

Iran has a government that is a blend of democracy and theocracy, but with the theocratic aspect clearly dominant. The present system emerged in 1979 from a revolution to overthrow the unpopular emperor of Iran, Shah Mahammed Reza.

Iran's system is one in which there is a democratically elected parliament, the Majles, and an elected president. The elections are freely contested, but are managed indirectly by the clerics, who can veto any candidates they choose. Despite their managed character, the elections

---

[33]"Feeling the Heat," *The Economist*, May 15, 2010, p. 30.
[34]I owe a debt in this section to Mohsen M. Milani, "Iran," in *Comparative Governance*, Primis database.

are lively events, and have in the past sometimes put into power reformers who wanted to gradually ease the Islamic character of Iranian life. Currently, conservative Islamic forces dominate the Majles, after most reformist candidates were barred from the 2008 Majles election by the Council of Guardians (representing the clergy). After the presidential election of 2009, the Council of Guardians declared that the incumbent president, Mahmoud Ahmadinejad, had been reelected by a large margin. The reformist candidates charged that the vote had been rigged, however, and there followed weeks of nonviolent protest, with massive street demonstrations by reformers, who were met by crude violence from militias loyal to the government. Even after the streets were finally cleared by the militias, reformers took to the rooftops, with thousands chanting "God is great! Death to the dictator!" after sunset each night. After several weeks of these protests, the government succeeded in suppressing the movement by brutal police interventions and mass arrests. Iran is quiet today, but no one believes that the underlying tensions and the desire for democracy have disappeared.

Existing alongside the democratic structure, but much more powerful than the democratic structure, is a somewhat loosely organized theocratic governing body. The heart of this is the Supreme Leader, a figure who emerges by informal, consensual selection from among the learned elders of the faith in Iran. Once selected, the Supreme Leader rules for life. The first Supreme Leader was Ayatollah Khomeini, who had led the revolution against the Shah. At his death in 1989 he was succeeded by Ayatollah Ali Khameini, who rules today.[35]

The Supreme Leader has immense powers, and there are no checks on how he exercises them:

- He is commander-in-chief of the armed forces.
- He sets overall policy for Iran, and can annul acts of the president and Majles.
- He controls immensely rich foundations, which hold all of the wealth seized from the monarchy when it was overthrown.
- He appoints the Friday prayer leaders of the mosques, and controls the Shi'i seminaries.
- He appoints the heads of the radio and television networks.

The Supreme Leader is aided in his control of the democratic side of things by the Council of Guardians, who examine the compatibility of all laws on legislation with Islamic law and the Islamic Constitution of Iran. They can annul any law. They also review the credentials of all candidates for the Majles and the presidency, and can eliminate any candidates they choose. Half of the members of the Council of Guardians are appointed by the Supreme Leader; the other half are judges whom the Majles choose from a list prepared by the judicial branch of government.

In short, the Supreme Leader is indeed supreme. This does not mean, in practice, that he rules arbitrarily or by whim. He is chosen in the first place because he represents in his views something of a consensus of the clerical establishment, and Shi'i Islam is a very open, free-wheeling structure with much room for dissent. The Supreme Leader rules from within an establishment in which individuals continually raise many

---

[35]"Ayatollah" signifies a religious leader with a significant following. Shi'i Islam, the dominant form of Islam in Iran, does not have a single leader; rather, various ayatollahs build sets of followers.

viewpoints, and in a country where public opinion is a force to be reckoned with. If nothing else, the Islamic state always has to deal with the possibilities of passive resistance by the public, and it has to be careful not to get totally out of step.

For instance, state censors prevent almost all Western films and music from entering the country—yet a large black market exists in which, at least in the cities, Iranians can get almost any sort of entertainment they want. This is tacitly tolerated by the theocratic state.

Like all authoritarian systems, we see that the Iranian theocracy is neither absolute nor unchallenged. The peculiar mix of democracy and theocracy in Iran, however, is probably unstable in the long run. If the Supreme Leader receives guidance from God, what does it matter whether 51 percent of the voters agree with him? Alternatively, if the people of Iran are to rule, what place is there for a Supreme Leader? Iran has suffered from a decades-long crisis of legitimacy. In the end, a basic question is, "What use [is] a Supreme Leader in a democracy, and what use [are] elections in a theocracy?"[36]

The 2009 presidential election, and the violent crackdown on reform that followed, may have finally put Iranian politics at a tipping point from which this basic instability will now be resolved. It appears that a new fault-line may have appeared, with Ahmadinejad and Ayatollah Khameini allied with the huge Revolutionary Guards apparatus, but opposed both by reformers and by a surprising number of conservative clerics who disapproved of the crackdown. Severe economic dislocations due to sanctions led by the United States also began to stress the system in 2012, and these have added still more uncertainty to the situation. Both because of the inherently unstable design of its government and because of its contentious role in international politics, Iran could be on the verge of major change. But it is really not clear what path Iran will follow. There are many possibilities in the current situation—democracy, a military-based dictatorship, a religious renewal, or other possibilities that are still unforeseen.

---

[36]Laura Secor, "Whose Iran?" *New York Times Magazine*, January 28, 2007, p. 53.

KEY TERMS

regime	pacts	one-party state
democracy	crisis transitions	monarchy
authoritarian democracy	authoritarian system	theocracy
Third Wave	military government	
agent-centric explanation	coup	

FURTHER READING

Boix, Carles. *Democracy and Redistribution.* New York: Cambridge University Press, 2003.

Brooker, Paul. *Non-Democratic Regimes: Theory, Government, and Politics.* New York: St. Martin's Press, 2000.

Brown, Nathan J., ed. *The Dynamics of Democratization: Dictatorship, Development, and Diffusion.* Baltimore: Johns Hopkins Press, 2011.

Gandhi, Jennifer. *Political Institutions Under Dictatorship.* New York: Cambridge University Press, 2008.

Haggard, Stephan, and Kaufman, Robert R. "Inequality and Regime Change: Democratic Transitions and the Stability of Democratic Rule." *American Political Science Review* 106 (August, 2012), pp. 495–516.

Maravall, José Maria. "The Myth of the Authoritarian Advantage." *Journal of Democracy* 5 (1994), pp. 17–31.

Munck, Gerardo L. *Measuring Democracy.* Baltimore, MD: John Hopkins University Press, 2009.

Przeworski, Adam. *Sustainable Democracy.* Cambridge: Cambridge University Press, 1995.

_____, Alvarez, Mike, Cheibub, José Antonio, and Limongi, Fernando. *Democracy and Development: Political Institutions and Material Well-Being in the World, 1950–1990.* New York: Cambridge University Press, 2000.

Roeder, Philip G. *Red Sunset: The Failure of Soviet Politics.* Princeton: Princeton University Press, 1993.

Schmitter, Philippe, and Karl, Terry. "What Democracy Is . . . and Is Not." *Journal of Democracy* 2 (1991), pp. 75–88.

Skidmore, Thomas E. *The Politics of Military Rule in Brazil, 1964–1984.* Oxford: Oxford University Press, 1988.

Wedeen, Lisa. *Ambiguities of Domination: Politics, Rhetoric and Symbols in Contemporary Syria.* Chicago: University of Chicago Press, 1999.

CHAPTER 8

POLITICAL CULTURE AND POLITICAL SOCIALIZATION

The **political culture** of a society consists of all attitudes and beliefs held communally by a people, which form the basis for their political behavior. We have borrowed the term from anthropology, in which the term *culture* (a people's whole interrelated set of beliefs and ways of thinking) forms a central organizing concept.

It is clear that political culture varies a good deal from one state to another and that it is responsible for major differences in how politics is conducted. We can often detect differences in culture by looking at popular behaviors and sayings. For instance, we sense that the Japanese put a greater emphasis on consensus than do Americans and value conflict less than Americans, when we compare two popular sayings:

> The nail that sticks out will get pounded down. (Japan)

and

> The squeaky wheel gets the grease. (United States)

Basic differences such as those reflected in these sayings must surely have something to do with the fact that compared with the United States, political decisions in Japan are more likely to be made on the basis of unanimous consent rather than by a vote (with one side losing). Individualistic assertion and challenges are less highly valued in Japan than in the United States.

Political culture is important, but it is difficult to evaluate concretely. It almost seems that such a big concept resists precision and invites fuzzy generalization. There is always a temptation to lapse into stereotyping of peoples: lockstep, obedient, efficient Germans; unflappable British; breezy, pragmatic Americans; hot-blooded Latins. However, even with these difficulties, political culture is too important to ignore. A work that demonstrates the potential importance of cultural analysis is *Culture Shift*

CHAPTER 8   POLITICAL CULTURE AND POLITICAL SOCIALIZATION   183

in Advanced Industrial Society by Ronald Inglehart.[1] Inglehart argues that prosperous, industrial societies are undergoing a shift in culture in which concerns for security are being replaced by concerns for self-expression, and he uses this shift to account for broad generational changes occurring across Europe.

One striking characteristic of political cultures is that they usually change slowly. A good example of this is provided by Alexis de Tocqueville in *Democracy in America*.[2] De Tocqueville visited the United States in the early nineteenth century to examine the workings of U.S. democracy, but his description of the American approach to politics is still recognizable—the emphasis on individuality and freedom, reliance on local politics and voluntary organizations, the restlessness and desire for progress. This despite that the America he saw was an almost totally agricultural society, without modern means of communication and without the quasi-imperial world role that the United States has adopted since the Second World War, and despite that since his study, American society has absorbed many waves of immigrants who initially came to America with very different cultures. Our state and society have changed immensely since he wrote his book, but the underlying culture has remained recognizably the same.

The role of political culture in political science theory is somewhat like the role of history. Essentially, political science theory is a search for levers that might at least potentially help us to change society. This is why almost all political science theory is causal (see the methodological appendix). If we understand causal relationships, they allow us to predict that a change in A (something under our control) will cause a change in B (the thing we wish to change); in this way, they offer us at least a potential lever for change. Thus, we are interested in the sources of political parties' influence because that knowledge can at least potentially help us to make parties more influential or less influential. Similarly, we look at the roles of political institutions, the effects of regulating campaign finance, the impacts of different systems of organizing health care, because understanding these things can offer us tools that might help us to effect change.

History and political culture play a slightly different role in our theories; they do not themselves offer levers, because we cannot easily change them. History is beyond our manipulation, and a culture is very difficult to change. It is in this sense that Hernando de Soto, a community activist, once said:

Culture is interesting to read about, but what does one do with it?[3]

History and culture are important, however, as the *context* within which any levers will succeed or fail. They may not be things we can control, but the effects of all the things we *can* control will vary depending on the history and culture of the society within which we try to use them. For instance, we can expect political parties to operate differently and to have different effects in Japan than they do in the United States.

We must understand the effects of the historical and cultural context if we are to understand properly how any of our levers will work. A common mistake is to export

[1]Ronald Inglehart, *Culture Shift in Advanced Industrial Society* (Princeton, NJ: Princeton University Press, 1990).
[2]Alexis de Tocqueville, *Democracy in America* (New York: Knopf, 1980).
[3]Matthew Miller, "The Poor Man's Capitalist," *New York Times Magazine*, 1 July 2001, p. 47.

184   PART III   THE CITIZEN AND THE REGIME

TABLE 8.1

The Role of the Citizen

	United States	Britain	Germany	Italy	Mexico
Should be active in the community	51%	39%	22%	10%	26%
Expect they could do something about an unjust national regulation	75%	62%	38%	28%	38%

SOURCE: Adapted from Almond and Verba, pp. 171 and 185.

an institution from Western democracies to a new democracy and assume it will work there as we would expect. The difficulty of establishing democracy in Iraq between 2003 and 2011 was due in part to American leaders' failure to understand the political culture of the various parts of that country and the burden of history there.

✦ ANALYZING POLITICAL CULTURES

Since political culture includes all attitudes and beliefs that are relevant to politics, if one is to analyze political cultures it is necessary to focus on some particular group of beliefs. Obviously, different analysts may focus on very different things in studying political culture. Two issues that scholars have focused on frequently are: (1) how citizens view the state and their obligations as citizens, and (2) citizens' values, and what they see as important issues of policy.

Citizens' Roles: The Civic Culture

One of the first modern studies of political culture focused on the first of these issues.[4] In the early 1960s, Gabriel Almond and Sidney Verba studied how citizens viewed their role in affecting government policy, which they thought was key to democracy. They found wide variations in this among the five states they studied, as we see in Table 8.1.

At the time of the survey, both Germany and Italy had only had democratic governments for fifteen years, and were only that long removed from their defeat in World War II. Mexico had a much more primitive economy than it does today. Table 8.1 shows two examples of the sort of questions Almond and Verba examined; in both examples the United States and Britain stood out from the other three states in the extent to which people felt and acted like engaged, responsible citizens of a democracy.

---

[4]Gabriel A. Almond and Sidney Verba, *The Civic Culture: Political Attitudes and Democracy in Five Nations* (Princeton, NJ: Princeton University Press, 1963).

TABLE 8.2

The Civic Culture Revisited, 1990

	Percent who believe they could do something about an unjust law	Percent who had ever signed a petition
United States	57	70
Britain	40	75
Germany	28	55
Italy	35	42
Mexico	42	31

SOURCE: World Values Survey, 1990 wave.

Thirty years later, in 1990, related questions were asked in a new set of surveys administered by the World Values Survey.[5] The questions asked are not exactly the same as those asked by Almond and Verba in 1959, but they are comparable. We see in Table 8.2 that although the differences between the countries remain roughly as they were earlier, they had softened as Italy and Germany gained three decades of experience with democracy and peace, and Mexico became a more modern economy.

We will see at the end of the chapter more detail on how Germany's political culture evolved after its defeat in World War II.

Values: Ronald Inglehart

Ronald Inglehart has focused not so much on citizens' roles as on what they value in society, and especially on how citizens' values evolve as states become more prosperous and more highly developed economically.[6] He has concluded that values can be most usefully arrayed along two dimensions:

- *Traditional vs. secular/rational.* Societies that are very traditional value religion highly, tend to emphasize deference to authority, value the family as a core social structure, and reject divorce, abortion, euthanasia, and suicide. Secular/rational societies are the opposite.

- *Survival vs. self-expression.* Societies that are very poor emphasize especially security and survival; they emphasize economic security, freedom from crime, and other types of personal security that are often lacking under conditions of poverty. At the other end of the dimension, which Inglehart believes is only likely to emerge once basic economic needs have been met, people emphasize values associated with what he calls "postmaterialism"—environmental protection, freedom of speech and artistic expression, political participation, and tolerance of diversity.

---

[5]World Values Survey, http://www.worldvaluessurvey.org/, 1990 wave.
[6]See especially Ronald Inglehart, *Modernization and Postmodernization* (Princeton, NJ: Princeton University Press, 1997) and Ronald Inglehart and Wayne Baker, "Modernization, Cultural Change and the Persistence of Traditional Values," *American Sociological Review* 65 (February 2000), pp. 19–51.

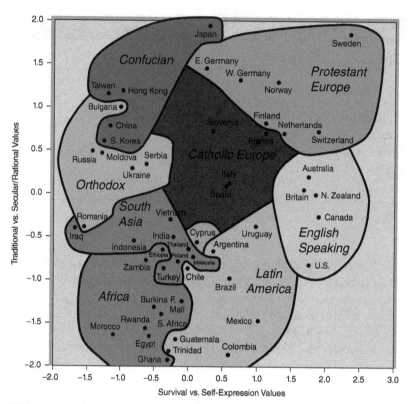

FIGURE 8.1   States are placed on this graph according to where they fall on Inglehart's two dimensions; clusters of states that share a common culture are indicated.

SOURCE: Ronald Inglehart and Christian Welzel, "Changing Mass Priorities: The Link Between Modernization and Democracy," *Perspectives on Politics* 8 (June 2010), p. 554.

Inglehart has mapped many states of the world onto the graph in Figure 8.1, the "Inglehart–Welzel Values Map." Each state is placed on the graph according to where it falls on the traditional vs. secular/rational dimension and the survival vs. self-expression dimension, and groups of similarly located states are then indicated as clusters.[7] For instance, the United States and other English-speaking states are located at the far right of the map, indicating that self-expression is a strong value in their societies (perhaps because liberalism has historically been a strong ideology in Britain and other English-speaking states; see Chapter 2). However, they fall at about the middle vertically, indicating that religion and traditional values are moderately important in their societies. By contrast, "Protestant Europe" states like Sweden or Switzerland are also located at the far right of the map, showing that self-expression is as important in their societies as in the English-speaking states, but they are located higher on the map than the English-speaking states, indicating that religion and traditional values are less important for them.

---

[7]For more detail, go to the World Values Survey website: http://www.worldvaluessurvey.org/ and click on "The WVS Cultural Map of the World."

CHAPTER 8   POLITICAL CULTURE AND POLITICAL SOCIALIZATION   187

You can work with much of the data Inglehart and his colleagues use at the website of the World Values Survey: http://www.worldvaluessurvey.org/. Click on "online data analysis," then choose either "WVS2005 Codebook" for the 2005 study, or "Integrated Questionnaire of the 1981–2002 Aggregated Values Surveys" for earlier studies; then choose the country or countries you want and the variable(s) you want to look at.

✦ RELIGION AND POLITICAL CULTURE

A religion is an encompassing set of ideas about our creation, our relationship to a creator, and ethical and moral imperatives that flow from that relationship. For some, religion may have very little to do with politics—the ethical and moral imperatives of a religion may all have to do with personal faith and one's private life. For others, religion may have a great deal to do with politics. To the extent that a religion is political, it becomes a facet of the political culture. When that is the case, the emotional strength of religious beliefs is such that they become a particularly important part of the political culture.

Religion in the early twenty-first century appears to be increasingly important in politics. In the United States religious issues such as abortion, homosexuals' rights, and teaching the theory of evolution in schools occupy much of the public debate. Around the world religious or at least partially religious conflicts such as al Qaeda's attacks on the United States and its allies have increased in number and intensity.

Ironically, this increase in religious political activity comes at a time when, at least in North America and Europe, religious belief and participation in religious services have been declining or standing still. If religion and its practice are in some decline, at least in North America and Europe, how is it that it seems to play an increasingly prominent role in politics? A number of things, coming together, may have caused this. First, the decline in organized conflict about class issues as socialist parties have splintered and lost support may have simply created a vacuum that religion could fill. Also, new forms of communication such as television and the Internet may have made it easier for those outside the usual political elite to organize effectively and bring their issues into the body politic. After all, religious issues in politics are not all that new (witness the prohibition movement in the United States in the early twentieth century); the new thing is that religious leaders can easily reach a million people at a time. Finally, the increasingly broad and graphic portrayal of sexual matters in a secular world is simply abhorrent to many believers. Religious politics may be a pushback.

Outside the United States, the most dramatic manifestation of religion's increased role in politics is the rise of political Islam. Most versions of Islam are rather nonpolitical, playing down the role of the state; people should be governed not so much by governments as by God. However, various groups within Islam have developed political agendas in the last few decades and, like the politically religious in the United States, have used modern technology and communications skillfully to pursue their goals. Their appeal has been heightened by Muslims' discomfort with the sex culture of a secular society and by Arab feelings of disrespect and exploitation by the West. The Islamic state in Iran, Islamists in other countries like Pakistan, and extreme groups like al Qaeda all attest to the growing importance of political Islam. Samuel Huntington's *The Clash of Civilizations and the Remaking of World Order* argues that with the decline of class politics in the

188   PART III   THE CITIZEN AND THE REGIME

TABLE 8.3

Values of Americans and Iranians

	USA	Iran
I. Democracy and Religion:		
Agree: It is important to live in a democracy	88%	82%
Agree: Religious leaders should not influence how people vote	61%	60%
II. Social Values:		
Agree: Homosexuality is never justified	32%	82%
Agree: Abortion is never justified	26%	61%
Agree: University is more important for a boy than for a girl	8%	56%

SOURCE: World Values Survey, fifth wave. www.worldvaluessurvey.org

twenty-first century world politics will be driven by clashes between different "civiliza-tions" with differing sets of values—especially a clash between Islam and Christianity.[8] Interestingly, however, despite all of the flash-points of the unresolved Israeli-Palestinian conflict, the American occupation of Iraq, and tensions between (Islamic) producers of oil and (often Christian) consumers, differences in values between Islamic populations and, say, those in the United States are less than we might have expected.

Table 8.3 compares the values of people in the United States and people in Iran, a Muslim country. As you see in the table, on issues such as support for democracy and the role religion should play in public life, the two peoples are not very different.[9] On social issues such as homosexuality and abortion there are sharp differences, but these hardly seem the stuff of a "clash of civilizations."

✦ POLITICAL SOCIALIZATION

People acquire their values and assumptions about politics in a process called **political socialization**—the learning of political values and factual assumptions about politics.[10] In principle, this can occur at any age and under any circumstances, but it tends to be concentrated at certain points of our lives.

The importance of political socialization is evident, if nothing else, in that without it, any political culture would disappear after one generation. Children and other new citizens learn all of the cultural underpinnings of politics, and many other

---

[8]Samuel P. Huntington, *The Clash of Civilizations and the Remaking of World Order* (New York: Simon & Schuster, 1996).
[9]Even in Iraq as it was moving toward a sectarian civil war, a survey conducted in December 2004 found that six times as many Iraqis thought democracy was good for Iraq as thought it was bad. Mark Tessler, Mansoor Moaddel, and Ronald Inglehart, "What Do Iraqis Want?" *Journal of Democracy* 17 (January 2006), p. 41.
[10] Three good general reviews of political socialization are Richard G. Niemi and Mary A. Hepburn, "The Rebirth of Political Socialization," *Perspectives on Political Science* 24 (Winter 1995), pp. 7–16; David O. Sears and Sheri Levy, "Childhood and Political Development," in David O. Sears, Leonie Huddy, and Robert Jervis, eds. *The Oxford Handbook of Political Psychology* (New York: Oxford University Press, 2003), pp. 69–109; and Virginia Sapiro, "Not Your Parents' Political Socialization," *Annual Review of Political Science 2004* (Palo Alto, CA: Annual Reviews, Inc.), pp. 1–23.

TABLE 8.4

Development of Political Orientations among Swedish Youth

Age	Percent Undecided as to Best Party
11–12	73
13–15	66
16–18	55
19–21	47
22–24	32
25–27	35

SOURCE: Adapted with the permission of The Free Press, a Division of Simon & Schuster Adult Publishing Group, from *Political Socialization: A Study in the Psychology of Political Behavior* by Herbert H. Hyman. Copyright © 1959 by *The Free Press.* Copyright renewed © 1987 by Helen Hyman. All rights reserved.

more transient values, through political socialization. It is political socialization that allowed the United States to absorb millions of Irish, Italians, Russians, Poles, Chinese, Vietnamese, and so many other peoples and yet maintain political continuity.

Like most learning, political socialization apparently comes most easily and fully in childhood, and diminishes as we grow older. However, we do not pick up much explicit and detailed information about politics before the teen years. Children learn in their families many basic social attitudes, such as trust in people and attitudes toward authority, which will be important in shaping their later response to politics. However, most children acquire only rather primitive ideas about what government is and how politics works. We primarily learn these things in adolescence and early adulthood and continue to learn them to some extent throughout adult life. For example, Table 8.4 shows the percentage of Swedish youths of varying ages who were undecided as to which political party was the best. Among eleven- to twelve-year-olds, 73 percent did not have a preference among the parties. This indecision declined to 35 percent by early adulthood. (I realize that these findings come from quite an old study, but I have not found a more recent study that gets at this; enumerating attitudes of young people as they age has rather gone out of style. I believe most political scientists would expect that similar relationships are not much different today.)

One of the concerns of political scientists studying socialization is to assess the varying roles of different **agents of socialization.** We must learn about politics *from* someone, and the various sources of learning are what we call the agents of socialization. Different agents operate in different ways and affect different areas of our values and assumptions about politics. We learn about politics from many different agents, but a few particularly important ones are our families, schools, and peer groups.

In order to have a strong impact on socialization, an agent must meet two conditions:

- the agent must be *credible,* and
- the agent must be seen as *relevant* to politics.

As you will see in our review below, agents frequently have one of these characteristics but not both, and this limits their impact as agents of socialization.

From our parents we acquire a number of social values that will apply to politics as they do to other aspects of our lives. Also, some think that we gain expectations about how politics should occur in the state by extension from the way that families conduct politics (the making of family decisions by the use of power); an authoritarian family may prepare one for an authoritarian state and a democratic family for a democratic state.[11] More specific political values and assumptions do not develop as much through the family as we might suppose, since we tend to acquire them during adolescence—a period when most children are trying to establish an independent identity. Just at the time at which they would be relevant to an emerging interest in politics, parents become somewhat less credible as guides. Make no mistake, though; they are still potent agents of socialization.

Schools are of particular interest as agents of political socialization because they are the agent that the state controls and through which the leaders of the state can attempt to mold the citizenry. In all states, there is some degree of guided socialization through the schools. Schools in the United States try to develop informed, patriotic citizens directly through civics classes and salutes to the flag and indirectly through class materials in history, literature, and other courses. Some states such as Cuba, China, and Nazi Germany have used the schools vigorously and directly to attempt to remake their citizens. In general, however, governments have had relatively little success in doing this. The Nazis failed notably, for example, in their attempts to produce the "new German man."

One group of schools that do seem to have been successful at socializing young people and shaping their political beliefs are the *madrassas,* Koranic schools supported across the Mideast by Saudi Arabia. The success of the *madrassas* may stem from the fact that unlike most government-sponsored socialization efforts in schools, which have attempted to move children away from their parents' belief systems, the *madrassas* seek to exaggerate parents' Islamic beliefs rather than to oppose them, and then add political direction to those beliefs. Thus they do not end up in conflict with families.

Peer groups are extremely influential in developing adolescents' tastes and their view of the world, but they vary considerably in their political impact. In most friendship groups of adolescents, politics does not figure importantly in the attention of the group. Normally, the group will influence its members' choices in clothes or social behavior strongly but will not affect their political identity very much. In other words, although teenage friends may be extremely credible, they usually have little relevance to politics. A major exception to this is provided, however, when youths who are already somewhat involved in politics gravitate together as a friendship group; when this happens, the group may have a profound impact on the political development of all its members.

From our discussion of schools as socializing agents, one would probably conclude that governments do not have much of an impact on political culture, even if

_____

[11]This is a controversial position; many scholars think it oversimplifies a complex process of the development of values. A good presentation of the position is Harry Eckstein and Ted Robert Gurr, *Patterns of Authority* (New York: Wiley, 1975).

they try. One instance, however, in which governments were able to affect political culture rather strongly is offered by the cultures of East and West Germany at the time they were united in 1991. After the Second World War, Germany was divided into two states, the Federal Republic of Germany (West) and the German Democratic Republic (East). The two states were aligned with opposite sides in the Cold War, and although they had shared a common history and culture leading up to the defeat in 1945, for the next forty-five years, they were separated by international events. From 1960 on, any travel between the two was made impossible by the infamous Berlin Wall.

When scholars began to study the culture of newly united Germany after 1991, they found many sharp contrasts between the cultures of West Germans and of East Germans. For instance, 31 percent of West Germans but only 11 percent of those from the East prided themselves on the democratic institutions of Germany.[12] 81 percent of easterners but only 44 percent of westerners agreed with the statement "Socialism is basically a good idea that was only badly carried out."[13]

Why was Germany an exception? One factor is probably just the long time that the two governments had at their disposal; they had from 1945 to 1991 to work on the cultures of their states. Also, at least after 1960, the two populations were forcibly isolated from each other. Anthropologists have even found that villages a few miles apart but separated by the Wall developed over that period of time recognizably different accents and dialects of German. Finally, as I describe in the example on Germany in this chapter, the culture of defeated Germany was in many ways a shattered remnant and was probably easier than most cultures to reshape. Whatever the explanation, Germany provides an example demonstrating that major cultural shaping is not impossible—although it may take an unusual constellation of advantageous circumstances for it to occur.

✦ MEDIA AS AGENTS OF POLITICAL SOCIALIZATION

News media (newspapers, radio and television, the Internet, and social networks) are an obvious possible agent of political socialization. For many years, political scientists' view of media was that they did not greatly affect people's views on politics. Newspapers' endorsements of candidates had little or no effect on voters, and the media that people watched or read did not seem to affect their attitudes. In the terms that we used in the last section, media were seen as *relevant* to politics, but viewers and readers had their guard up and did not find them *credible* as political guides.

In recent years, however, this appears to be changing. For instance, a study of beliefs about the Iraq War found that of those who relied mainly on print media for their news, about 17 percent believed (mistakenly) that weapons of mass destruction (WMD) had been found in Iraq after American forces had deposed Saddam Hussein's government in 2003. Of those who relied primarily on CNN or the established national television networks—NBC, ABC, and CBS—about 20 percent believed WMD had been

---

[12]David P. Conradt, "Political Culture in Unified Germany: Will the Bonn Republic Survive and Thrive in Berlin?" *German Studies Review* 21 (1998), p. 92.
[13]David P. Conradt, *The German Polity*, 7th ed. (New York: Longman, 2001), p. 85.

found. Of those who relied primarily on the Fox network for their news, about 33 percent shared this belief.[14] It apparently made a difference whether people watched Fox or one of the other networks, or followed the print media.

The reason for this change may be that parts of the media have shifted from the predominant model of the twentieth century—a model that was consciously nonpartisan and prized objectivity—to a newer model that is overtly partisan and more argumentative. Ironically, it appears that there was more resistance to guidance from the older, more objective media than there is to guidance from the newer forms.

The norm of journalistic nonpartisanship and objectivity developed especially after the Second World War in the United States. For most of the second half of the twentieth century, just three television networks and newspapers provided the national news, and most cities were served by just a single newspaper, literally the "only game in town." Since there were so few outlets, each sought as wide a market of readers or viewers as possible. It was important to offend as few readers or viewers as possible, and a journalistic ethic of nonpartisanship and objectivity helped to accomplish this.

People's choice among media has exploded since then. Today a wide range of cable television networks compete with the traditional Big Three; syndicated talk radio shows span the nation, so radio has joined national news markets; many blogs compete for readers' attention on the Internet; and news flies across YouTube and social networks. With so many choices competing, it makes sense for many of them to become niche locations, appealing primarily to a group of people who are predisposed to agree with them and to find their arguments and evidence persuasive.[15] Conservatives watch Fox news programs, liberals watch MSNBC.[16] Such outlets, more focused and with a self-selected audience, seem able to move people in a way that the older media did not.

Worldwide, media are both expanding and diversifying. While newspapers are in decline in the United States and Western Europe, elsewhere they are expanding. Newspaper circulation grew by 40 percent in India, for instance, in just four years from 2005 to 2009.[17] Everywhere, new and more diverse television channels have expanded the range of available options. A particularly important development is *Al Jazeera*, an Arabic news network founded in Qatar, which has transformed news coverage in the Mideast with 24-hour coverage that provides vivid images of events and allows viewers to hear dissenting viewpoints. Also, citizen journalists using blogs and social networks speed news videos around the world. For instance, the 10 most popular clips of Japan's 2011 tsunami received a total of over 135 million views worldwide; and the half-hour long KONY video produced by the non-profit Invisible Children drew 112 million views in just six days.[18]

---

[14] Stephen Kull, Clay Ramsay, and Evan Lewis, "Misperceptions, the Media, and the Iraq War," *Political Science Quarterly,* 118 (Winter, 2003–2004), pp. 569–598. Cited in Gary C. Jacobson, *A Divider Not a Uniter: George W. Bush and the American People* (New York: Pearson Longman, 2007), p. 251.

[15] Bruce A. Williams and Michael X. Delli Carpini, *After Broadcast News* (New York: Cambridge University Press, 2011), especially chapter 3.

[16] Pew Research Center for the People & the Press, "In Changing News Landscape, Even Television is Vulnerable," report released September 27, 2012.

[17] "Special Report: The News Industry," *The Economist,* July 9, 2011, p. 4.

[18] Jane Sasseen, "The Video Revolution," a report of the Center for International Media Assistance, August 28, 2012. The KONY video was controversial, and stimulated a number of reports rebutting many of its claims.

These more focused, specialized media seem able to reach audiences that are very ready to be convinced by them.

✦ POLITICAL CULTURE AND THE "DEMOCRATIC CITIZEN"

Authority, through the legitimacy on which it is based, depends on the relation between the government and its citizens. (See the discussion of authority and legitimacy in Chapter 1.) Modern democracy poses a particularly interesting problem in authority and legitimacy. A democracy is a state in which fully qualified citizens vote at regular intervals to choose, among alternative candidates, the people who will be in charge of developing the state's policies. It is in one sense an odd sort of state, because the government has power over the citizens (it makes the laws), but the citizens also have power over the government (they can vote it out of office). What sort of relationship between state and citizens is best in a democracy?

The one most special thing about the relationship between a democratic state and its citizens is that democracy requires citizens who will do more than obey and follow the government. In our previous discussion, it was more or less sufficient, for authority to exist, that the people regard the actions of the government as legitimate. This would ensure obedience to the laws.

Some non-democratic states go a step further and try to generate *enthusiastic* support for the government. Hitler—through his pageantry, his rallies, and his network of youth organizations, and sports clubs—tried to generate enthusiastic support for Nazism that would help him to build a powerful German military force more rapidly. The Soviet Union and other communist countries always tried to build enthusiastic support through rallies, discussion groups, parades, and strenuous campaigning, even when their elections were restricted to a single party.

Democracy goes yet a step further than this. In a democracy, we hope not only that people will obey the laws and be enthusiastic citizens but that they will also and at the same time be *critical* citizens. Democratic citizens are expected to walk a difficult line—supporting enthusiastically the authority of their government leaders but, at the same time, being critical enough of those leaders that they might readily vote them out of office at the next election. This requires a complex and sophisticated view of politics. It is not easy to be a citizen of a democracy.

What sort of political culture would we hope to see in a democracy? What sorts of attitudes and behaviors should characterize the "democratic citizen"?

1. *Tolerance.* If varied groups are to present their opinions, it is necessary that people have a reasonable tolerance for diversity. If people could be prevented from setting forth unpopular ideas, then the democracy would not function well. Therefore, citizens must be at least minimally tolerant of different races, different social behaviors, different religions, and political beliefs that may depart sharply from their own. At the very least, most citizens in a democracy must be willing to allow these various groups to present their cases freely. If they are not, then there is a danger that the democracy will not allow the voters a full range of options from which to choose.

2. *Active Participation.* Democracy requires that citizens do more than just obey the laws the government lays down. Authority in a democracy is a two-way street; therefore, the citizens must take concrete political actions to exercise their authority over the government. At the very least, they should vote in elections. Better yet, they should maintain frequent contact with the government by, for instance, writing to their representatives or serving on citizen committees. If the citizens do not do this, a state simply cannot be a democracy. Its government will have authority over its citizens, *but not vice versa.*

3. *High Level of Interest and Information.* It is not enough that citizens participate actively. If they do not know what is happening, they can be as active as they wish but they will have little effect on what the government does. Action based on no interest or understanding would be aimless, and one person's act would tend to cancel another's. If the citizens' active participation is to be constructive, democracy requires also that those citizens be well informed.

4. *Varying Support for the State, the Regime, and the Government.* Finally, while the three characteristics noted are required in order for the people to maintain authority over the government, democracy requires also that the government maintain authority over the people. This is difficult, since the people are required to remain skeptical about the holders of government positions and must stand ready to vote them out of office if that is necessary. What is necessary, if this balancing trick is to work, is that citizens (1) identify with and support the state (without this there is real danger of things falling apart); (2) retain an abstract support for the regime (the ongoing set of rules and procedures that place certain individuals into positions in the government; see discussion of "regime" on p. 151); but (3) remain skeptical about the particular individuals currently holding those positions.

✦ HOW WELL DO CITIZENS MEET THESE REQUIREMENTS?

As you see, it takes work to be a citizen in a democracy. How well do the citizens of modern democracies measure up? In particular, how do citizens of the United States measure up?

1. *Tolerance.* The citizens of most democracies will readily agree with abstract statements guaranteeing minorities the right to express their opinions freely. However, concrete applications of this principle may be another matter. For instance, people often think that even conventional political participation should be banned for those who they think are wrong or dangerous. In a study in the United States, people were asked to name the political group they liked the least. (For instance, one might ask them to choose among skinheads, militant gays, born-again Christians, secular humanists, the American Civil Liberties Union, or the Ku Klux Klan.) They were then asked several questions about what rights that group should have to participate in politics. Only 27 percent thought that members of the group they disliked should be allowed to serve

TABLE 8.5

Percentage of Americans Engaging in Seven Different Acts of Political Participation

Type of Political Participation	Percent
Voted in the most recent presidential election	70
Contacted a government official within the past year	34
Made a campaign contribution for the most recent election	24
Worked informally with others in the community to deal with some community issue or problem within the past year	17
Worked in a campaign for the most recent election	8
Attended a protest, march, or demonstration within the past two years	6
Served in a voluntary capacity on a local governing board or attended meetings of such a board on a regular basis within the past two years	3

SOURCE: Reprinted by permission of the publisher from *Voice and Equality: Civic Voluntarism In American Politics* by Sidney Verba, Kay Lehman Schlozman, and Henry E. Brady, p. 72, Cambridge, Mass.: Harvard University Press, Copyright © 1995 by the President and Fellows of Harvard College.

as president if elected, only 18 percent thought that members of the group should be allowed to teach in the public schools, and only 32 percent thought that the group should not be outlawed. A related study in Israel showed that Israelis were even less tolerant in these ways than Americans.[19]

2. Active Participation. At the very least, citizens in a democracy should vote regularly in elections. As we shall see in Chapter 10, even this we cannot take for granted. However, it is also necessary, if the democracy is to function well, that good numbers of citizens go beyond voting to involve themselves in more demanding tasks such as writing or phoning officials, organizing neighborhood groups, or working in political campaigns.

Table 8.5 presents the results of a survey of the American public in which people were asked whether they participated in a variety of ways. In looking at this table, you must bear in mind that people usually tell pollsters that they are more active than they truly are; actual turnout in that presidential election was 50.2 percent in the year of the survey, for instance, although 70 percent of the people polled said that they had voted. Still, the figures give a rough idea of the relative frequency with which people participated in these various ways.

Do the people depicted here participate a lot or a little? Political science is often the science of the half-filled glass. (Is it half full, or is it half empty?) Against a standard of what a democracy *should* be, these citizens fall short. Only 17 percent of them (or fewer, if some were exaggerating) had worked with others to solve a local problem. On the other hand, against a standard of what we might feel we could realistically expect, these

[19]John L. Sullivan, Pat Walsh, Michal Shamir, David G. Barnum, and James L. Gibson, "Why Politicians Are More Tolerant: Selective Recruitment and Socialization Among Political Elites in Britain, Israel, New Zealand and the United States," *British Journal of Political Science 23* (January 1993), p. 60.

"Is it OK to discriminate against bigots?"
© John Jonik/ *The New Yorker Collection*/www.cartoonbank.com

figures show considerable activity. To turn the earlier sentence around, fully 17 percent of the people polled had worked with others to solve a local problem in that year.

Table 8.6 presents similar information comparatively across several democracies. The states in the table range from developed democracies like the United States, France, and Canada, through poorer democracies like Mexico, India, and Ghana. In the case of Ghana the democratic system was just a few years old in 2007, when the survey was taken. Interestingly, the less demanding, more individualistic acts of signing a petition or joining a boycott are much more common in the developed democracies. The somewhat more demanding, collective act of demonstrating varies less by how well-off the countries are.

3. *High Level of Interest and Information.* Of course, people who regularly turn out and vote in elections might know little or nothing about the candidates among whom they were choosing; in that case, they would contribute little to the working

TABLE 8.6

Percentage That Have Ever Engaged in a Variety of Actions More Demanding Than Voting, for Selected Countries

Country	USA	Canada	France	Mexico	India	Ghana
Signed a petition	70	73	67	21	29	4
Joined a boycott	20	24	14	3	15	2
Attended a lawful demonstration	15	26	38	16	19	9

SOURCE: World Values Survey, fifth wave. www.worldvaluessurvey.org, January 2009.

of democracy. How interested are citizens of democracies in what goes on politically and how accurately informed are they? Voters in the United States are rather interested in politics, according to most studies. For instance, a poll of Americans in 2008 showed that 26 percent said they followed what was going on in government and public affairs most of the time, 37 percent said they followed it some of the time, 25 percent now and then, and 12 percent hardly at all.[20]

However, most people will exaggerate to a stranger how much they do something as virtuous as following public affairs. In actuality, how well informed are these virtuous-sounding people? Not very. Only 29 percent of a national survey of American adults can name their representative in Congress, and only 30 percent can name both of the senators from their state.[21]

In a study of the 2000 presidential election, Thomas E. Patterson asked citizens to identify where George W. Bush or Al Gore stood on each of twelve issue questions that had figured prominently in the campaign (see Table 8.7). Looking just at the key issue for each candidate, he found that only a narrow majority of citizens were able to identify correctly the candidate's position.

So, on their signature issues, the candidates had only gotten through correctly to about half of the electorate. On the average, across all twelve issue areas, only 38 percent identified a candidate's position correctly, while 16 percent identified it wrongly, and 46 percent said they did not know the candidate's position.

4. Support for the State. You will recall that what is needed here is a general abstract support for the state and for the regime (the state's constitution and rules of government), which can coexist with skepticism about the qualities of individual officeholders. Many democracies seem to be fairly successful at commanding this type of respect from their people.

A 1959 survey asked Americans, "Generally speaking, what are the things about this country that you are most proud of?" They could mention anything they wished, such as religious values, the wealth of the country, landscape, or culture. Over

TABLE 8.7

Percentage Accurately Stating Candidate's Position on His Key Issue

	Correct Answer (yes)	Incorrect Answer (no)	Don't Know
Gore: favor free prescription drugs for the elderly?	58%	8%	36%
Bush: favor large cut in income taxes?	52%	11%	37%

SOURCE: From *The Vanishing Voter* by Thomas E. Patterson. © 2003 by Alfred P. Knopf, a division of Random House Inc. Used by permission.

---

[20]National Election Studies, the ANES Guide to Public Opinion and Electoral Behavior, www.electionstudies.org/nesguide.
[21]Michael X. Delli Carpini and Scott Keeter, *What Americans Know About Politics and Why It Matters* (New Haven: Yale University Press, 1995).

60 percent of the things mentioned were aspects of government and politics.[22] At about the same time, a 1958 survey revealed that 73 percent of those polled said that they trusted the government in Washington to do what was right either "most of the time" or "just about always."[23] As we shall see later in this chapter, there has since then been an erosion of this sort of generalized confidence and support of their government by the American people. The point is that the American people maintained such support at a time when, in the same study, Americans felt considerable skepticism about the *people* running the government. In 1958, 24 percent thought that "quite a lot" of the people running the government were crooked; 37 percent said that the people running the government did not usually know what they were doing; and 85 percent said that the people in government wasted "some" or "a lot" of the money they paid in taxes. At about this time also, the American electorate repudiated their Republican president Dwight Eisenhower by giving the Democrats a landslide victory in the 1958 congressional election.

This balance between support for state institutions and skepticism about officials is hard to maintain, and many shaky democracies are rarely able to achieve it. As we shall see in examples later, one democracy, West Germany, had to build it up over a twenty-year period, while another, the United States, has to some extent lost it.

✦ SOCIAL CAPITAL

Robert Putnam and his coauthors, in a study of what makes democratic government effective in Italy, concluded that the necessary ingredient is what they called **social capital:** intricate webs of voluntary involvement in organizations that bind people together and give them the political resources and the necessary mutual trust to make any cooperative form of government work. Democracy is the quintessentially cooperative government form. Examples of the interwoven organizations they addressed were people's involvement in trade unions, community choirs, PTAs, birdwatching clubs, professional organizations, social service organizations to help the needy, the American Legion, churches, and book clubs. In parts of Italy where people were involved in rich networks of such participation, democratic government worked well; in parts where people were not so involved, democratic government did not work well.

"Social capital" might seem slightly out of place in this chapter, because it is not an attitude or a set of attitudes. Rather, it is a pattern of community interaction that *produces* desirable attitudes of efficacy and trust, and that gives people practical experience in persuasion and collective action so that they can function well in a democracy. Social capital appears vital to an understanding of democratic citizenship, however, and that is why I have included it here.

The United States has long been a society with high voluntary participation in community organizations, although there is a debate whether that high level of

---

[22]Gabriel Almond and Sidney Verba, *The Civic Culture* (Boston: Little, Brown, 1965), p. 102.
[23]University of Michigan, Center for Political Studies, 1958 National Election Study. Data made available by the Inter-University Consortium for Political and Social Research.

CHAPTER 8   POLITICAL CULTURE AND POLITICAL SOCIALIZATION   199

participation is diminishing.[24] Putnam argues that Americans are turning inward and individualistic. He points out, for instance, that while bowling alley use is up in the United States, bowling league membership is down; more Americans are "bowling alone." Whether or not voluntarism and participation in civic organizations have declined in the United States, though, they still appear to be relatively high compared with other countries. A set of surveys in the early 1990s found that 49 percent of Americans had done volunteer work in the preceding twelve months compared with 13 percent of Germans and 19 percent of French respondents.[25] The high rate of Americans volunteering continues today, and has increased by about one-fourth from 1989 to 2007.[26]

The Saguaro Seminar, originally set up by Putnam to promote social capital, maintains a website describing its activities and providing analysis of social capital at: http://www.hks.harvard.edu/programs/saguaro.

❋ EXAMPLE

Building Authority and Legitimacy in West Germany after World War II[27]

After the defeat of Germany in 1945, the Germans as a people were demoralized politically. They had bought a dream of greatness from Adolf Hitler, but he had brought them defeat and international disgrace. They were hated throughout Europe, their country had been cut up on the map, and their industries and farms were in ruins. Germans who were fifty years old in 1945 could not be blamed if, having been dazzled by politics, they now withdrew from it. They had grown up under the Kaiser's monarchy and had seen it overthrown in disgrace at the end of World War I, when they were in their early twenties. They had then lived through fifteen years of a chaotic attempt at democracy, which never really established its authority and legitimacy with the people and ended in Hitler's dictatorship. They were thirty-eight years old when Hitler came to power; in the next twelve years, they saw Germany approach world conquest and then come close to total destruction. They could be pardoned if they were shy of politics after all of this.

---

[24]For a pessimistic view, see Robert Putnam, "Bowling Alone: America's Declining Social Capital," *Journal of Democracy* (January 1995); "The Strange Disappearance of Civic America," *American Prospect* (Winter 1996): pp. 34–48; and *Bowling Alone* (New York: Simon & Schuster, 2000). For an opposing view, see the June/July 1996 issue of *Public Perspective:* Everett C. Ladd, "The Data Just Don't Show Erosion of America's 'Social Capital,'" *Public Perspective* (7 June/July 1996), p. 1; and associated reports, pp. 7–47.

[25]Helmut K. Anheier, Lester M. Salamon, and Edith Archambault, "Participating Citizens: U.S.–Europe Comparisons in Volunteer Action," *Public Perspective* 5 (March–April 1994), p. 17.

[26]Corporation for National and Community Service. Volunteering in America. Accessible at www.volunteeringinamerica.gov/newprofile.cfm (accessed February, 2009).

[27]West Germany and East Germany were reunified as Germany in 1991.

TABLE 8.8

Attitudes toward the Past, 1951–1970

Q.: When in this century do you think Germany has been best off?

	Year of Survey			
	1951 (Percent)	1959 (Percent)	1963 (Percent)	1970 (Percent)
Federal Republic (present)	2	42	62	81
Under Hitler before the war (1933–1939)	42	18	10	5
Under the Kaiser, before World War I	45	28	16	5

SOURCE: From *Changing German Political Culture, The Civic Culture Revisited*, edited by Gabriel Almond and Sidney Verba, 1980, 1989, pp. 226. Copyright © 1989. Reprinted by permission.

In many ways, West Germany after 1945 gave political scientists much the same opportunity to observe an evolutionary development as a new volcanic island rising from the sea offers to biologists. When a new island is formed, biologists get a rare chance to observe which animals are the first to appear on it and see how long it takes a diverse flora and fauna to be established. Similarly, political scientists get few chances to see attitudes toward politics establish themselves among a people who initially have essentially no attitudes. West Germany after the war approximated such a case.

For many years, political observers asked themselves whether democratic behavior and attitudes could possibly develop among Germans. Some said that the people who had put Hitler into office could not develop into democrats. Others thought that if Germany was lucky enough to have a period of peace and economic stability, democracy would be able to establish itself. No one could hazard a guess as to how long the process would take.

As we can see in Tables 8.8, 8.9, and 8.10, the optimists were correct; in fact, the development of democratic support occurred steadily and fairly rapidly. As we see in Table 8.8, during the first twenty years the democratic regime established itself as the best arrangement Germany had known—better than Hitler's dictatorship or the Kaiser's monarchy.

It was not simply that the country was economically well off. The political institutions of democracy became more popular during this period. In 1959, in the survey on which the Almond and Verba study was based (see page 184), Germans were asked what they were proud of about their country. Only 7 percent pointed to Germany's political institutions. In 1978, the question was repeated in a survey. By that time, 31 percent of the things mentioned were aspects of government and politics. By 1988, the figure had grown to 51 percent.[28]

Support for democracy in the abstract also grew across the first two decades. In 1953, only a bit over 55 percent of the Germans stated in the abstract that democracy

---

[28]David Conradt, *The German Polity*, 5th ed. (New York: Longmann, 1993), p. 55.

CHAPTER 8   POLITICAL CULTURE AND POLITICAL SOCIALIZATION   201

TABLE 8.9

Trust and Hostility among Germans, 1948–1976

a. Percent "trusting most people"

1948	1959	1967	1973	1976
9%	19%	26%	32%	39%

b. Percent thinking more people are evil minded than well-intentioned

1949	1951	1953	1971	1976
46%	43%	34%	17%	16%

SOURCE: From *Changing German Political Culture, The Civic Culture Revisited,* edited by Gabriel Almond and Sidney Verba, 1980, 1989, pp. 226. Copyright © 1989. Reprinted by permission.

TABLE 8.10

Frequency of Political Discussion, 1953–1972

	1953 (Percent)	1959 (Percent)	1961 (Percent)	1965 (Percent)	1969 (Percent)	1972 (Percent)
Daily	9	11	10	10	37	50
Occasionally	29	50	51	66	40	34
Never	63	39	39	25	23	16

SOURCE: Reprinted by permission of the publisher from *Germany Transformed: Political Culture and the New Politics* by Kendall L. Baker, R. J. Dalton, and K. Hildebrandt, Cambridge, Mass.: Harvard University Press. Copyright © 1981 by the President and Fellows of Harvard College.

---

was the best form of government.[29] By 1976, 90 percent answered yes to the same question.[30]

The sort of social relations among people that are required if a loose system of authority (such as democracy) is to work was also developing. In a society where people are hostile and suspicious of each other, democracy cannot work well. As we see in Table 8.9, trust grew steadily and social hostility decreased during this time.

Finally, it is necessary that the people begin to be active and interested citizens. As we see in Table 8.10, this also developed steadily.

West Germany did not necessarily become an ideal democracy, but it is interesting to see that there were established, over a couple of decades, patterns of behavior and support similar to those of such democracies as the United States or Great Britain. No one would have predicted this with any confidence in 1950, and it was an eye-opener for political scientists.

---

[29]Kendall Baker, Russell Dalton, and Kai Hildebrandt, *Germany Transformed* (Cambridge: Harvard University Press, 1981), p. 24.
[30]David Conradt, "Changing German Political Culture," in Gabriel Almond and Sidney Verba, eds., *The Civic Culture Revisited* (Boston: Little, Brown, 1980), p. 234.

 EXAMPLE

Declining Democratic Legitimacy in the United States

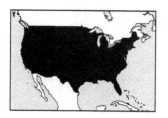 The story of the past half century in the United States has been in some respects the opposite of what we have seen in Germany. Since about the mid-1960s, there has been a puzzling decline in people's confidence in officials and in the political system. Table 8.11 shows a drop from the 1950s and 1960s in the percentage of Americans thinking that one can trust the government to do what is right most or all of the time; and an increase in the percentage thinking that the government is run for the benefit of a few big interests and that many people running the government are crooked. The steadiness of the trend across various events and various presidents makes it look as though it were not a response to particular disappointments, but political scientists are frankly at a loss to say just what *did* cause the decline.[31]

Interestingly, while this drop in trust and legitimacy was occurring, Americans remained an attentive and reasonably active citizenry. As you can see in Figure 8.2, while turnout in elections dipped a bit in the 1970s and 1980s, it is essentially unchanged over the past half-century, with 59 percent of the electorate voting in the 1956 presidential election and 62 percent in 2008.

The number of people performing the more substantial act of writing to members of Congress has risen steadily, from 6 percent in 1958 to 36 percent in 1992.[32]

The percentage who state that they follow what is going on in government and public affairs some or most of the time has not changed: 63 percent said that they did so in 1960 and 64 percent in 2008.[33]

The decline in Americans' trust in government has many varied effects, but surely a combination of a still attentive citizenry who have lost some of their faith in government must be alarming. It does not bode well for a continuation of stable, constructive democracy, and it is important that we find out the causes of the change. The person who does so will have made an important contribution to our understanding of democracy.[34]

---

[31]Arthur Miller and Jack Citrin presented an interesting interchange concerning the possible causes of the decline in "Political Issues and Trust in Government 1964–70," *American Political Science Review* 68 (September 1974), pp. 951–1001; see also Arthur H. Miller and Stephen A. Borrelli, "Confidence in Government During the 1980s," *American Politics Quarterly* 19 (April 1991), pp. 147–73; and Burns Roper, "Democracy in America: How Are We Doing?" *Public Perspective* 5 (March–April 1994), pp. 3–5.

[32]*Public Perspective* (June–July 1996), p. 12.

[33]University of Michigan, Center for Political Studies, National Election Studies. Data made available by the Inter-University Consortium for Political and Social Research.

[34]Part of the explanation may lie in the fact that something similar appears to have been happening in most of the world's mature democracies over the same period. See Susan J. Pharr and Robert Putnam, eds., *Disaffected Democracies: What's Troubling the Trilateral Countries?* (Princeton: Princeton University Press, 2000).

CHAPTER 8   POLITICAL CULTURE AND POLITICAL SOCIALIZATION   203

TABLE 8.11

Decline of Confidence, 1958–2008

	1958	1964	1968	1972	1976	1980	1984	1988	1992	1996	2000	2004	2008
Percent trusting the government to do what is right	73	76	61	53	33	25	44	40	29	33	44	50	31
Percent thinking the government is run for a few big interests	—	29	40	53	66	70	55	64	75	70	61	56	70
Percent thinking government people are crooked	24	29	25	36	42	47	32	40*	46*	44*	36*	35*	52*

*Slightly different question wording after 1988: "quite a few" crooked.

SOURCE: University of Michigan, Center for Political Studies, National Elections Studies. Data made available by the Inter-University Consortium for Political and Social Research.

FIGURE 8.2   Percentage of voting-age population voting, United States.

SOURCE: U.S. Bureau of the Census, *Statistical Abstract of the United States.*

KEY TERMS

political culture   agents of socialization
political socialization   social capital

FURTHER READING

Chu, Yun-Han, Diamond, Larry, Nathan, Andrew J., and Shin, Doh Chull. *How East Asians View Democracy.* New York: Columbia University Press, 2008.

Cohen, Mitchell. *Why the French Don't Like Headscarves: Islam, the State, and Public Space.* Princeton, NJ: Princeton University Press, 2006.

Dalton, Russell J. *Citizen Politics: Public Opinion and Political Parties in Advanced Industrial Democracies.* Washington, DC: CQ Press, 2008.

Gibson, James L., and Gouws, Amand. *Overcoming Intolerance in South Africa: Experiments in Democratic Persuasion.* New York: Cambridge University Press, 2002.

Harris-Lacewell, Melissa Victoria. *Barbershops, Bibles, and BET: Everyday Talk and Black Political Thought.* Princeton: Princeton University Press, 2004.

Hibbing, John R., and Theiss-Morse, Elizabeth, eds. *What Is It About Government That Americans Dislike?* New York: Cambridge University Press, 2001.

Hooghe, Marc, and Stolle, Dietlind, eds. *Generating Social Capital: Civil Society and Institutions in Comparative Perspective.* New York: Palgrave Macmillan, 2003.

Huntington, Samuel P. *The Clash of Civilizations and the Remaking of World Order.* New York: Simon & Schuster, 1996.

Inglehart, Ronald. *Culture Shift in Advanced Industrial Society.* Princeton: Princeton University Press, 1990.

———. *Modernization and Postmodernization.* Princeton, NJ: Princeton University Press, 1997.

Marcus, George E., Sullivan, John L., Theiss-Morse, Elizabeth, and Wood, Sandra L. *With Malice Towards Some: How People Make Civil Liberties Judgments.* New York: Cambridge University Press, 1995.

Norris, Pippa. *Democratic Deficit: Critical Citizens Revisited.* New York: Cambridge University Press, 2011.

———, and Inglehart, Ronald. *Sacred and Secular: Religion and Politics Worldwide,* 2nd ed. New York: Cambridge University Press, 2011.

Pharr, Susan J., and Putnam, Robert D. *Disaffected Democracies: What's Troubling the Trilateral Countries?* Princeton, NJ: Princeton University Press, 2000.

Putnam, Robert D. *Bowling Alone.* New York: Simon & Schuster, 2000.

———. *Making Democracy Work: Civic Traditions in Modern Italy.* Princeton, NJ: Princeton University Press, 1994.

Sears, David O., Huddy, Leonie, and Jervis, Robert, eds. *Oxford Handbook of Political Psychology.* New York: Oxford University Press, 2003.

Sniderman, Paul. and Hagendoorn, Luke. *When Ways of Life Collide.* Princeton, NJ: Princeton University Press, 2007.

Verba, Sidney, Schlozman, Kay Lehman, and Brady, Henry E. *Voice and Equality: Civic Voluntarism in American Politics.* Cambridge: Harvard University Press, 1995.

The Apparatus of Governance

PART IV

The Apparatus of Governance

CHAPTER 9

CONSTITUTIONS AND THE DESIGN OF GOVERNMENT

Every state—in fact, every political organization, club, or other group—has a **constitution**, or set of rules by which power is distributed among the members. No group of people engaged in politics could exist without rules of this kind.

We speak of such an encompassing set of rules as a "constitution with a small c," meaning the generally understood rules, both formal and informal, by which power is distributed in any political group—rules that have come to be accepted over time. These rules may be either formally laid down in statutes and other documents or informally understood.

Most organizations and states have as a part of their constitution a formal set of central rules that outline the basic ways in which they conduct their affairs. The Constitution of the United States (note the capital C) is such a document, as are Canada's Constitution Act of 1982, the Basic Law of Germany, and the Constitution of the Netherlands. Typically, such a document tells who is to carry out the major functions of politics (proposing, deciding on, and implementing laws), how the people holding those positions are to be chosen, who is to be in charge during an emergency, what their powers are, and by what procedures the constitution itself may be changed. Often there is also a section, such as the Bill of Rights in the U.S. Constitution, that sets out certain basic rights of the citizen or basic aims of the state. Thus, a constitution may state that citizens are guaranteed the right of freedom of speech (U.S.A.) or that the state guarantees full employment (France) or that the state is socialist (China).

Before the United States was ever founded as a state, the American Indian Iroquois Confederation had an elaborate constitution, maintained in an oral tradition. It takes several days for elders to recite the constitution, which specifies a veto right for each member nation but dominance for the Mohawk nation in making new initiatives; the establishment of a ruling council and procedures for selecting confederation leaders; special elevation for those excelling at war; and provisions for relations with other nations not in the confederation.[1] The Constitution of the Iroquois Nations is available at www.constitution.org/cons/iroquois.htm.

No state can put all the rules governing the distribution of power into its formal constitution: Much must always be left to informal arrangements or to other documents. In the United States, the Constitution lays out a basic structure for politics. However, the "constitution with a small c" includes more than just the Constitution. It includes the understanding that the U.S. Supreme Court may overturn an act of Congress—a rule not written into the Constitution but only developed later under the strong Chief Justice John Marshall. Furthermore, it includes the tradition that presidents take a leading role in the making of foreign policy. It includes the bylaws of both houses of Congress, it includes rules in some states limiting the number of terms members of the legislature may serve, and much else besides. All these things are rules governing the distribution of power, which are not part of the Constitution but are part of our constitution.

There is often some disparity between the formal rules of the Constitution and actual political power. In the United States, a reading of the Constitution would lead one to think that the members of the electoral college have great power, because they are elected to meet and select a president; in fact, however, the practice and expectation have developed that the members of the electoral college ratify the vote of the citizens of their states, so that in practice, they have essentially no political power. (This expectation is another part of our constitution with a small c.) As another example of the frequent disparity between formal political power and actual power, consider that no constitutions in Europe or North America mention the great political power of newspapers, television networks, or blogs other than in passing.

A website with the constitutions of many countries is http://www.servat.unibe.ch/icl

✦ VARIATIONS IN FORMALITY

Constitutions vary as to how much is set out formally in a central document and how much has gradually developed outside of it. Older constitutions put less into a central document; newer ones, more. Two of the oldest political bodies in the world, Great Britain and the Catholic Church, have no central written constitution. Rather, the rules of politics for each are embodied in a variety of documents, traditions, and accepted practices. Each has a constitution (with a small c); people are aware of it and cite it frequently in British or church politics, but when they do they are not referring to a single document.

The United States is a relatively old state, and the original U.S. Constitution was approximately forty-three hundred words long; twenty-nine hundred words have since been added in amendments. Germany is a new state, and its Basic Law, written in 1949, is approximately 19,700 words long; this includes numerous amendments. France's most recent constitution, adopted in 1958 and amended only slightly since, is about

---

[1]Donald S. Lutz, "The Iroquois Confederation Constitution: An Analysis," *Publius* 28 (1998): pp. 99–127.

ninety-one hundred words long. Perhaps constitutions that have been written in more recent years are longer because their writers are aware of the greater size and importance of the state and have taken greater pains to protect the state's power from difficulties that might arise. A large part of Germany's Basic Law is devoted to who is to govern during emergencies, though this is admittedly unusual. The one thing that is true of recent constitutions is that they tend to be specific and complicated.

✦ THE VIRTUE OF VAGUENESS

Such specificity is by no means always an advantage. Napoleon once said that a constitution should be short and obscure. If rules are stated specifically, it becomes difficult to adapt a constitution to unforeseen or changing circumstances. Just as French generals in the period from 1919 to 1933 devised a marvelous fortification (the Maginot line) that would have served well for the trench warfare of World War I but was useless against the changed strategies of World War II, writers of constitutions often include in their design solutions to the problems with which they have become familiar. If these solutions are precise and inflexible, they are likely to produce new problems. Republican lawmakers in the United States were upset that Franklin Delano Roosevelt (a Democrat) had served more than the customary two terms as president. After his death, they wrote a stern amendment into the Constitution, limiting presidents to two terms of service. A few years later, they were faced with Dwight Eisenhower, a popular Republican candidate whom they would have loved to nominate for a third term but who was constitutionally barred from running again.

Similarly, the writers of the Basic Law of Germany were preoccupied, after the war, with the fact that Hitler had been able to take over the democratic government of Germany peacefully and at least quasi-legally in 1933 and transform it into a dictatorship. In dozens of ways, they tried to make their new constitution "Hitler-proof." One of the many devices they added was a restriction on the ability of the parliament to unseat the chancellor and his cabinet. This power of parliament was hemmed about by numerous conditions, which led to an unpleasant comic opera when in 1972, Willy Brandt's socialist-led government had lost so much support in the parliament that it could not even pass the national budget. Brandt and his cabinet wished to step down and call for a new election, since, under the circumstances, they could not govern effectively. However, for six months no one could think of a way by which this could be arranged under Germany's complicated constitutional provisions, without the embarrassment of the socialists formally voting themselves out of office (which they were not willing to do). The authors' precise and detailed constitutional tinkering with the Basic Law, designed to "win the last war," led to unforeseen difficulties in governing Germany.

Another example of misplaced specificity in writing constitutions comes from a regional political science association in the United States. This group publishes a scholarly journal, and the editor changes every three years. At one time, it was suggested that the term of the editor might be lengthened to four years, since it cost the association several thousand dollars each time they changed the editor and the journal's operations had to move from one campus to another. This was not a big issue, but everyone agreed that the change would be a good idea because it would save some money and inconvenience. On looking at the association's constitution, however, members found that they could not make the change easily. This document, instead of sensibly stating that the editor should serve a term "to be determined by the association's council," plainly said that "the editor shall serve a term of three years. . . ." An amendment to the constitution, tedious and difficult to arrange, would have been required to change the editor's term; therefore, the association dropped the idea. One would think that the political scientists who wrote this document would have known better!

→ OTHER PRINCIPLES OF CONSTITUTIONAL DESIGN

Let us assume that you are in a position to help design or amend a state's constitution. Are there any additional principles that might help guide you? Beyond the general principle that you should not try to be too specific, a few additional rules of thumb you might consider are as follows: (1) The constitution should preferably not break drastically with long-standing traditions of government, (2) the constitution should be relatively easy to change, and (3) "incentive compatibility" should be built in as much as possible, so that the holders of power will find it personally advantageous to do what society as a whole needs from them. Let us consider each of these in some detail.

The Importance of Long-Standing Traditions

If a set of rules is to work, it must not be too far out of line with what most people in the state wish to do. One famous instance of a rule that did not work because it deviated too far from the people's wishes was the prohibition of liquor in the United States in the 1920s. In 1919, the country passed a constitutional amendment forbidding the possession or consumption of alcoholic beverages in the United States. While many people supported this amendment (else it would not have passed), many opposed it. People openly disobeyed the law, and criminals like Al Capone flourished from the illegal traffic in liquor. Eventually, the state gave up, and in 1933, the country amended the Constitution again to make alcoholic beverages legal.

It is not enough, either, to set up rules that the people are willing to obey only reluctantly; we need something more than bare acquiescence. As we saw in Chapter 8, it is important that a state have a reservoir of goodwill and positive support from its people to carry it over the occasional rough times. A good constitution will be not only one that people are willing to obey but also one that comes close enough to their preconceptions that they will be able to identify enthusiastically with the system. Many historians think it is unfortunate that when Germany lost World War I, the monarchy to which its people were accustomed was destroyed. The 1919 democratic constitution did not provide for the sort of personal, emotional attachment that the monarch always had. Instead, the first president of the new system was a quiet man, the son of a lowly saddle maker, with no dash or glamour. Hitler was later able to exploit the people's hunger for an exciting focus of patriotic devotion. It might have been better if the 1919 constitution could have made a less dramatic break with the past by including a powerless but handsomely dressed monarch. This would not by itself have solved all of Germany's problems, but it might have helped.

This is not to say that a constitution can never depart from what the people expect. Many revolutionary states have imposed new systems of government and society that deliberately set out to transform their people's expectations. (China in 1949, for example, or Kemal Atatürk's remaking of Turkey between 1919 and 1924.) Revolutionary change is always hard on people, however, and such states have had to keep tight control of things, causing much human suffering, to ensure the state's stability. There is inevitably a price to pay in instituting rules for which the people are not prepared. In some instances, however, the price might be worth paying.

The Importance of Amendability

If a new constitution must come reasonably close to reflecting the people's expectations, it must also be open to revision or amendment in response to changing needs. It is always a temptation, when writing a formal document, to "protect" it by making it difficult to change.

For example, the Founding Fathers made the U.S. Constitution difficult to change. As a result, in the more than two hundred years that it has been in force, only seventeen amendments beyond the original Bill of Rights have been added. Such inflexibility could have been dangerous, because the conditions of U.S. politics obviously have changed immensely over more than two centuries. Fortunately, a new device for adaptation appeared when the Supreme Court took onto itself the power to interpret the Constitution with a certain amount of discretion. The Constitution was sufficiently "obscure," in Napoleon's sense, that the Court could adapt it with reasonable ease to changed circumstances. In 1954, for instance, the Court ruled that in light of modern sociological theory, "separate but equal" schools for blacks and whites could not be taken to provide the equal protection under the laws that the Constitution guarantees. The Court ruled in this way despite that in earlier decisions, without the benefit of such theory, it had ruled that segregated school systems were constitutional.[2] Allowing nine judges who are appointed for life the discretion to adapt the Constitution may not be the best or the most democratic way to proceed, but it has at least provided a flexibility that the authors of the Constitution were not wise enough to build in.

In many states, provisions for adapting the constitution are much simpler. Often, a simple majority in the parliament is sufficient.

The Importance of Incentive Compatibility

In any political system, it is important that people in positions of power have personal incentives to do what society as a whole needs from them. That is, holders of power should find that they are personally rewarded when they do what society needs done and personally punished when they do not; this is **incentive compatibility.**

We may safely assume that when people find that what is good for them personally conflicts with what is good for the state, they will usually choose what is good

---

[2]*Brown v. Board of Education,* 347 U.S. 483 (1954).

for themselves. This is not necessarily because they are selfish. It is easy for the individual to conclude that the damage to the state will be tiny compared with the benefit to him or her because the state and the individual are so different in size. As a result, people can usually make the "selfish" choice without feeling that they are doing much damage to the state. If a little cheating on my income tax can save me $300, what does that matter to a national budget of billions upon billions of dollars?

The problem, of course, is that if large numbers of people find themselves in a similar position, the result can be serious. Precisely this problem occurs in constitutions. The constitution—the set of rules determining who has what kinds of political power—places individuals in positions in which they will make choices that society needs. We expect presidents and members of a congress or parliament to make laws for the state. We expect public health officials to watch out for epidemics, judges to settle legal disputes fairly, police officers to keep order, and members of town councils to set rules within their towns.

It is not enough to say what a person is to do in one of these positions, however. If costs and benefits are not set up to encourage officials to act in the intended manner, there is a good chance that they will act in ways that suit their personal interests rather than those of society.

For instance, the U.S. Congress was set up to make rules for the country as a whole. However, members of Congress are rewarded or punished not by the country as a whole but by the voters of their districts. It is a well-known problem of American democracy that if the two conflict, members of Congress will frequently pursue the needs of their districts rather than those of the country as a whole. If the United States had stronger political parties, which could develop national programs and punish members of the Congress who did not support their party's program, then the personal incentives to members of the Congress would be different, and we might expect to see them support national interests even when these conflicted with their own districts' interests. As we will see in Chapter 11, many of the world's states do have political parties of this sort, and there we find that members of the parliament are less prone to place local needs over national ones. In the United States, however, which has relatively weak parties, this source of incentive incompatibility poses a serious problem.

We could draw other examples to show the importance of designing incentive structures to reward people for doing what the constitution intends them to do rather than for something else. This is necessary not because holders of public office are especially greedy or cynical or selfish. Rather, like the income tax cheater, they are faced with differences in scale such that important things for them personally (security in their jobs, advancement) are balanced against almost trivial losses to the state.

- What does it really matter if I vote for an inefficient project for my district? It is tiny compared with the overall budget.

- Is it really that important to the United States that my office, the transcribing division of the Southwest Regional Advisory Branch of the Weedgit Marketing and Regulatory Board, functions at top form?

As with the problem of tax evasion, the problem here is that from the point of view of the single official, little damage is done to the state; but because there are

"THE HECK WITH THE CONSTITUTION—
I'M GOING TO SHOUT 'FIRE'."

(In 1919 Supreme Court Justice Oliver Wendell Holmes wrote in a famous decision that illustrates the flexibility necessary to constitutional interpretation: "...protection of free speech would not protect a man falsely shouting 'Fire' in a theater and causing a panic.")

thousands of officials like this, their combined impact may be grave. We can expect most of these individuals to do what they are actually rewarded for doing, not necessarily what they are meant to do. Therefore, we must try to design our constitution so that rewards follow for what officials are meant to do.

⇥ CONSTITUTION-WRITING

In normal times, constitutions usually continue without much discussion. So the principles of constitution-writing that we discussed in the section above do not often come up in day-to-day business. They *do* come up, however, at the formation of a new state, or during a crisis or turning point for an existing state.

The actual writing of a constitution for a new or transformed state is a messy business, in which the competing claims of different groups in the population have to be balanced with sufficient care that all of them (or almost all) will buy into the new procedures for allocating power. If some groups fear other groups and think that power going to those groups will mean oppression or obliteration for themselves, then striking the balance may take political skills of a very high order.

A famous example of this is the creation of the U.S. Senate in 1789, to give small states a platform to defend themselves against larger states. Another example is the partial independence of provinces from the central government written into Canada's two Constitution Acts, in order to protect various geographic minorities. Scholars have suggested that where deeply divided ethnic groups fear each other, formal division of power between the groups should be written into constitutions.[3] For instance, in Lebanon, the president must always be a Maronite Christian, the prime minister a Sunni Moslem, and the speaker of the assembly a Shiite Moslem.

A good current example of the difficulty of writing constitutions is the constitution for the state of Iraq. Iraq comprises three large ethnic/religious groups which have historically been very suspicious of each other: Kurds in the North, Sunni Arabs in the central part of the country, and Shiite Arabs in the South. All are Moslems, but the Kurds are ethnically different from the Arabs, and the Sunni and Shiite Arabs represent the two main forms of Islam. Of the three groups the Shiites are the largest in Iraq, making up a majority of the population.

The Sunnis, who make up only 20 percent of the population, had historically dominated Iraq (including under Saddam Hussein, who was a Sunni). Even after the American overthrow of Hussein in 2003, they were not reconciled to their loss of control and wanted to keep Iraq tightly unified, looking ahead to what they hoped would be a restoration of their dominant position. The Kurds, on the other hand, wanted to have the right to secede. Finally, the Shiites wanted the country more-or-less held together so that with their majority they would have the possibility of controlling it, but they also wanted some autonomy for themselves in the South in case that failed. Add to all this that a civil war between the Sunnis and Shiites was developing over the period when the constitution was being written and implemented, and you can see the difficulties!

A constitution was finally drafted in the fall of 2005, and barely passed in a referendum. In order to reassure the Sunni and Kurd minorities, the rule had been set that if three of the country's eighteen provinces rejected the draft constitution in the referendum by votes of more than two-thirds, it would not go into effect. Two heavily Sunni provinces rejected the draft by votes of over 90 percent, but a third, in which there was a sizable Kurdish minority, rejected it by only 55 percent. All fifteen Kurdish and Shiite provinces supported the constitution strongly in their votes, so it went into effect, on October 15, 2005.

The major provisions of the constitution are:

- The state is a "federal" system (i.e., decentralized; see the explanation of federalism in the next section), with provinces having a great deal of autonomy. Provinces are also allowed to unite among themselves into "super-regions," which would have similar autonomy. This includes the right of super-regions to maintain a regional guard, their own armed militia.

- The question of how to divide oil revenues is a contentious issue because the Sunni region has no oil and wants to share the revenue. This question was ducked in the writing of the constitution, and was passed on to the parliament to take care of as a

---

[3]Arend Lijphart, *Democracy in Plural Societies: A Comparative Exploration* (New Haven: Yale University Press, 1977); see also his *Power-Sharing in South Africa* (Berkeley: Institute of International Studies, University of California, 1985).

regular law. Finally, in February 2007 the various factions were able to work out a compromise law governing oil revenues.

- The state was given a muted religious character. This was a very contentious issue, and the end result was a compromise: the constitution states, "Islam is a basic source of law," and the Supreme Court (which can overturn acts of the government) is a mix of legal specialists and religious scholars.

- There is an extensive set of provisions for individual rights.

- A democratically elected parliament vests the executive powers of government in a prime minister and cabinet. The office of president is a largely ceremonial figure. (This is a "parliamentary" system; I discuss parliamentary systems in detail in Chapter 14.)

- At least one-fourth of the members of the parliament must be women.

✦ THE GEOGRAPHIC CONCENTRATION OF POWER

In later chapters, we will look at a variety of questions on one aspect or another of constitutional design, such as how states should choose officials, how they should pass laws, and what the best ways are to administer policies. However, one general question of constitutional design deserves treatment in this chapter.

That is the question of how much political power should be concentrated in the central government and how much should be distributed among the governments of cities, of "states" (as in the United "States"), or of regions. Some constitutions place almost all political power in the central government, with little independent decision making left to localities or regions. Others create a relatively weak central government, with many political decisions made at lower levels. A variety of arrangements that fall between the two are possible.

What makes this a particularly important question is that all over the world, hot conflicts frequently rage between central governments and local groups. This is the single greatest cause of political conflict—a more incendiary one, for instance, than the perennial conflict between haves and have-nots or any of the newer conflicts such as those associated with feminism, religion, or protection of the environment. In Spain, separatists have for years waged an intermittent campaign of terror on behalf of their claims for a separate Basque state or at least for a greater degree of local independence in making political decisions. Since 1982, Canada has been involved in a divisive constitutional crisis over the relationship between Quebec and the rest of the country. In Britain, a Scottish nationalist party has regularly received a significant vote in British parliamentary elections with its claim for independence for Scotland and has been rewarded by the establishment of a separate Scottish Parliament; in 2014 Scots will vote in an election to decide whether they should leave Great Britain and become independent. India is divided into many districts speaking different languages; these districts operate fairly independently of the central government, and disputes over language policies and job preferences for those speaking different languages are always hot political items. Until 1991, the Soviet Union consisted of fifteen governmental units called "republics" (one of which was Russia); many of these had their own languages, and there were frequent conflicts among them. In the end, the union had to be dismantled, with each of the republics declaring independence. In another part of the world, many parts of Africa have had intense center-region conflicts; Nigeria, Ethiopia, the Sudan, and Zaire have witnessed civil wars between the central government and one or more regions that wished to break away. In the Mideast, Kurdish regions of Turkey, Syria, Iraq, and Iran have been a source of political tension for those countries for many years. As one last example, remember that the one time that politics in the United States has heated up to the level of civil war was 1861, in a dispute between the central government and a region of the country.

✦ "FEDERAL" AND "UNITARY" STATES

The question of central versus local control is thus a hot item of politics; how is it dealt with constitutionally? There is a formal distinction between states that are unitary and those that are federal. We shall look first at the formal distinction (a characteristic of constitutions with a capital C) and then consider less formally (and more realistically) the division of power between central governments and their local or regional units.

A **unitary state** is one in which no other governmental body but the central government has any areas of policy that are exclusively under its control. In a unitary state, the central government may potentially overrule local and regional political bodies in any political decision they make. In a **federal state,** by contrast, local governmental authorities of some sort are set up by the Constitution (usually for regions of the state, as in the "states" of the United States or the "republics" of the Soviet Union), and these authorities are given certain political decisions over which they have a legal monopoly of control.[4] In a federation, then—a federal state—two governments control the same group of people but with regard to different political questions.

Germany is an example of a federation. The regional governments, called Länder, have total control of education, television, and radio; the central government has total control of defense, diplomacy, the postal service, railroads and air transport, and copyrights; the central government and Länder share responsibility for all other areas of policy.[5]

A federal system has often been the result of a compromise by which reluctant members were induced to join in a state; this is how the United States was originally formed, for instance. Federal systems usually exist where there was some difficulty in uniting the state or where the state is so large or so culturally diverse that there might be problems holding it together. Small states are less likely to be federal systems than large ones because problems like these are more likely to have cropped up in large states with diverse populations.

As of 2012, a total of twenty-one states were federal systems, while 174 were unitary. From this it might appear that the question of federalism is unimportant, because so few states are federal systems. However, the federal states tend to be the larger ones. Although these twenty-one states represent only 11 percent of the world's states, they contain 39 percent of the world's people and cover 50 percent of the world's land area. Figure 9.1 indicates the twenty-one states that are federal.

[4]William Riker, *Federalism: Origin, Operation, Significance* (Boston: Little, Brown, 1964), chap. 1.
[5]In what is coming to be called "layered sovereignty," the central government of Germany in turn yields total control of certain policies—especially currency, monetary policy, and agricultural policy—to the European Union, of which it is itself just one geographic unit. Thus German sovereignty is exercised in three layers, although it ultimately resides in the German state.

FIGURE 9.1 Federal systems (shaded areas) of the world.

⇥ The Distinction Between "Unitary" and "Centralized" States

A formal definition like those I used in the "'Federal' and 'Unitary' States" section usually requires an understanding of informal arrangements to supplement it. I stated that in a federal system, separate governmental units coexist on the same territory, each with its own constitutionally set areas of policy. In a unitary system, by contrast, the central government has the authority to make all policies, although it may deputize other governmental structures to act on its behalf. From this, we can see that in at least a formal sense, political power is more centralized (concentrated more on a central authority) in unitary systems than in federal ones.

However, politics is filled with surprises, and there are many informal arrangements that modify the centralizing tendency of the unitary state and the opposite tendency of the federal state. First, actual control of money counts at least as much in politics as the formal authority to make decisions. "Who pays the piper, calls the tune," as they say. Table 9.1 shows the percentage of governmental revenues collected and controlled by central, regional, or local governments in a variety of federal and unitary systems. While the central government usually controls much more of the money in unitary systems than in federal systems, there is considerable variation within each category and some overlap across the two. Sweden's central government, with a unitary system, draws only 64 percent of governmental revenues, less than the 91 percent drawn by Malaysia's central government, the most centralized of the federal systems displayed here. Clearly, if we look at the control of cash, there is variation in degrees

TABLE 9.1

Percentage of Revenue Collected by Different Levels of Government

	Central Government	"State," Regional, and/or Local Governments
Federal Systems		
Malaysia	91	9
Germany	65	35
Argentina	62	38
United States	54	46
Switzerland	51	49
Canada	46	54
Unitary Systems		
Chile	95	5
Israel	93	7
Great Britain	91	9
France	85	15
Sweden	64	36

SOURCE: International Monetary Fund, *Government Finance Statistics Yearbook 2010*, Table W3.

of government centralization that goes beyond the constitutional distinction between "federal" and "unitary."

In other ways, less easily measured than revenues, states vary in their degree of centralization. France and Britain, for example, look fairly similar on Table 9.1. Both are unitary states, and the central government of France draws 85 percent of revenues while the central government of Great Britain draws 91 percent. However, how states use authority and revenues is as important as whether they use them. In Britain, the central government has traditionally kept only a loose control over local governments' actions and expenditures. For instance, in the last few years Great Britain has given its regions of Scotland and Wales extensive control over spending within their borders, even though all the revenue is technically revenue of the central government.

In France, on the other hand, power was for centuries lodged firmly in Paris. A minister of education in the late nineteenth century is said to have demonstrated this to a visitor, when, checking his watch, he looked up and said, "My friend, at this moment every third-grade pupil in France is reciting 'The Blue Bird.'" Power in France was quite centralized for many years; there was a time when for almost any major decision—whether to build a new town hall or school, for instance—cities had to gain the approval of the government in Paris. In 1981 President François Mitterrand instituted a number of decentralizing reforms, devolving many functions on new regional and departmental councils, but the system remains, on balance, centralized.[6]

To summarize, the degree of centralization in politics is greatly influenced by the formal constitutional choice between federalism and a unitary arrangement, but it is also strongly affected by all sorts of less formal arrangements.

✦ HOW MUCH CENTRALIZATION IS GOOD?

Any country has to strike some balance between centralized and decentralized politics. With totally decentralized politics, the state would cease to exist; it would break up into many small independent states. Even short of this, strong decentralization might lead to uncoordinated policies and confusion. Strong centralization, on the other hand, especially in a state that is large or geographically varied, could make for inflexible and insensitive government.

How much centralization is good will vary from state to state and with the circumstances the state faces. Large and diverse states find it necessary to be less centralized than other states in order to meet varying local needs flexibly. If a given state is faced with an emergency, as in time of war, it may feel that it must pull all power together centrally so that it will be able to concentrate its resources on the single goal of meeting the emergency. (Most decentralized systems do give their central governments extraordinary temporary power during war.) There is no single level of centralization of politics that one can necessarily prescribe for all states at all times.

The industrialized states of the world have shown signs of converging toward a fairly similar degree of centralization. Apparently, the circumstances in which these

---

[6]See Vivien A. Schmidt, *Democratizing France: The Political and Administrative History of Decentralization* (New York: Cambridge University Press, 1991).

states find themselves are sufficiently similar that a common level of centralization has seemed appropriate to the leaders of each.

For instance, super-centralized France moved over the latter half of the twentieth century to decrease the centralization of power. The Mitterrand reforms of 1981 sharply decreased the powers of the "prefects," civil servants who were formerly responsible for keeping Paris in control of what local governments were doing. On the other side of the coin, in the decentralized United States, the last fifty years—despite recurrent attempts to reverse the trend—have been marked by an extension of power by the central government over the states and localities. This has often been accomplished by aid grants from the central government to the state or local government that carry with them some control over how they can spend the money. As one example of this, the central government now has the power to order school districts to supply certain services to handicapped students. This would have been out of the question fifty years ago.

We cannot give a simple answer to the question of how much centralization of government is good. Around the world, however, complex industrialized states are indicating by their own choices that they are most comfortable with a considerable but limited degree of centralization. The main exceptions are states such as Belgium and Canada, where deep ethnic conflicts have boiled up to threaten the state, and a radical decentralization may be the best solution.

✦ CONSTITUTIONS AND GUARANTEES OF RIGHTS

As I noted earlier in the chapter, constitutions may include things beyond the distribution of power among institutions. One thing that almost all constitutions include is some enumeration of basic individual rights. These can be just as important as a clear set of rules assigning and governing power. They can establish the role of citizens in the state, just as other provisions establish the role of government; and, they can provide protection for individuals against abuse.

For instance, the Bill of Rights (the first ten amendments to the U.S. Constitution) guarantees United States citizens' freedom of speech, freedom of religion, freedom of association, and other basic rights. As another example, the Danish Basic Law guarantees to all citizens that they "shall not in any manner whatever be deprived of their liberty because of their political or religious convictions or because of their descent." More specifically, it protects them against unreasonable searches, against being held in jail without being charged with a crime, and against having their property expropriated. It also guarantees them free and equal access to trade; the right to a job or, if unemployed, to public assistance; the right to free education through elementary school; the right to free speech; and the right of free association.

Most constitutions include some set of guarantees like this, but not all do. For instance, the Australian Constitution does not.[7] Australia has left the protection of individuals' rights up to the judiciary, through the body of precedents they develop. The Australian example demonstrates that although it is often good and useful to guarantee rights in a constitution, there may be other ways to achieve protection for individuals as well.

---

[7]There have been several recent proposals to add a Bill of Rights to Australia's constitution, but so far none have succeeded.

In contrast, there is no other way to lay out the rules by which power is assigned among institutions and exercised by them. Only a constitution can do this.

→ "CONSTITUTIONALISM" AND THE RULE OF LAW

Constitutions are a tool to build the **rule of law**, that is, an assurance that actions of the government are based on general principles that it applies equally to all people. Under the rule of law, governmental actions are not arbitrary, and are not based on personal connections or payoffs.[8]

Constitutions, by laying out rules about power and its exercise, provide the platform for a rule of law. We have seen in the preceding section that guarantees of individual rights may contribute to this, but it is also true of the structural elements of the constitution, which assign power to various parts of government.

However, another factor—beyond the rules of the constitution—is also critical to the rule of law. **Constitutionalism** consists of faithful adherence to the letter and spirit of the constitution: Given that each state has a constitution, how faithful is a state to its constitution? That is, how fully do the states' leaders honor the rules of politics in the state? "Constitutionalism" is the doctrine that states should be faithful to their constitutions because the rules provided in the constitution are all that can protect the citizens from arbitrary decisions by powerful people. There is also a notion in "constitutionalism" that constitutions should be designed fairly, rather than to give undue advantage to one particular group.

Constitutionalism is especially strong in Britain and its former colonies, like the United States, Canada, Australia, and New Zealand. In the United States, for example, the Supreme Court, rather insulated from political pressure, has the power to overturn any act of government if it finds that the act is unconstitutional. The Court has been particularly active in guarding the Bill of Rights. Britain has only had a supreme court since 2009; before that, it relied for centuries on a long tradition of impartial obedience to the rules of politics and to the protection of individuals from arbitrary official action. Even in these five countries, however, constitutionalism is only relatively strong. It is not, and probably can never be, an absolute. Especially in times of national emergency, the governments of these countries have sometimes felt that it was necessary to temporarily suspend rights that they would ordinarily honor. Great Britain, for instance, held no elections for the duration of World War II, even though an election had been due in 1940; Churchill and the other party leaders thought that an election would be an unnecessary distraction during wartime, and they were critical of the United States for going ahead and holding its presidential election in 1944. Similarly, President Roosevelt ordered the internment of most Japanese-Americans during the war on the grounds that they were security risks. The president would never have had the power to do this in peacetime.

A country in which traditions of constitutionalism are slightly weaker is France. While individual rights are secure there, leaders' faithfulness to the rules of politics

---

[8]For "arbitrary" actions, see p. 134.

is more fragile than in the United States, Canada, or Britain. Over the last century, France has had four constitutions, and it has had a total of nine systems for holding elections. In particular, the government often has manipulated the election laws to benefit the party in power. Also, parties when they have been in power have in the past manipulated news reports on public television and radio to enhance their election chances, and French embassies abroad have in the past tried to manipulate absentee voting to help the party in power. Finally, aside from these cynical manipulations of the rules of electoral politics, three times in the twentieth century French military leaders gave up on democratic rules altogether and tried to seize power; twice they were successful.

If France is a bit weak in its constitutionalism, though, many states are far weaker. Many of the world's people live in systems that give them only small protections against arbitrary power. In China from 1966 to 1976, over a million people were killed in the Cultural Revolution, which the state's leader, Mao Tse-tung, initiated to restore the Communist Party to its original revolutionary zeal. China showed a similar disregard for individuals in the 1989 suppression of the student movement at Tiananmen Square. In the late 1970s under a right-wing military regime, several thousand Argentinians "disappeared" when they were seized by the state police; they were never tried and were not seen again. The government of Sudan unleashed rape and murder on its citizens in Darfur province between 2003 and 2010.

EXAMPLE

Constitutional Government in Great Britain

Great Britain is an unusual example of constitutional government in that it has no written constitution—no single document that claims to set out the central principles of the organization of power.

What does the British constitution consist of? Some of it is made up of statute, or acts that Parliament has passed; the Parliament has the power, by a simple majority vote, to change any aspect of the British constitution. Much of the rest of the constitution consists of court precedent, decisions that judges have made in cases of constitutional significance. Some important parts consist of practice—behavior that has arisen in the day-to-day conduct of government and is not written down anywhere. In all of this, Parliament is ultimately supreme, because a new statute passed by it would override decisions by any court and would, of course, override any practices that had grown up. In the absence of contrary action by the Parliament, however, court decisions or

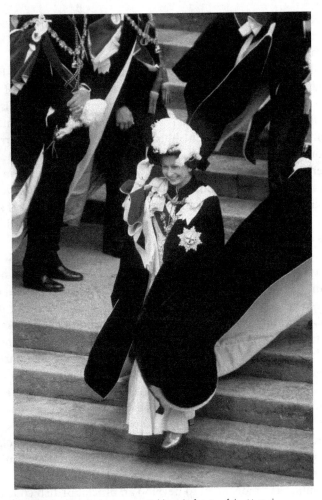

Queen Elizabeth II, the ceremonial head of state of the United Kingdom.
© Tim Graham/Getty Images

practices stand. Much of the British constitution consists exactly of this: practices and court precedent that the Parliament has not chosen to change by statute.

The Magna Carta is one of the earliest parts of the British constitution. In 1215, an unpopular king (John) was forced by rebellious barons to sign this document limiting the king's authority over them in a number of ways. This document was later read into statute in 1295. Other important statutes have settled the system for determining who succeeds to the crown when a king or queen dies (Act of Settlement of 1701) and have laid out the powers of the two houses of Parliament (Parliament Acts of 1911 and 1949). Many smaller matters are also dealt with in statutes.

Court precedents have also contributed importantly to the constitution. For instance, a long series of precedents from court cases over the centuries have largely determined the powers of the queen. The definitions of individual rights—which in the United States are written into the Constitution as the Bill of Rights—evolved over centuries of court decisions in Britain.

Finally, and this is perhaps the most puzzling thing to non-British readers, important parts of the constitution are not written in any document whatever but exist in practice. They are "what one does." For instance, the prime minister and cabinet are probably the most powerful single part of the process of government in Britain. The cabinet initiates all but a few of the bills which Parliament considers each year, and the cabinet controls closely what happens in the Parliament. (You will see more about this in Chapter 14.) However, nowhere in any statute or in the decision of any court is the cabinet set up or its powers defined. The only law that mentions the cabinet is one setting the salaries of cabinet ministers and providing them with staff support.[9] The rules governing the cabinet's behavior and defining its powers have arisen in practice and remain as unwritten understandings.

One might ask how a constitution like this is enforced. How do we ensure that people play by the rules if not all of the rules are even written down? For instance, the prime minister is dominant within the cabinet and can ask members to resign or to exchange posts. This is a matter of practice. What would happen if a prime minister fired a cabinet minister, but the cabinet minister did not leave? As another example, an important aspect of the British constitution is that a British monarch will always sign into law a bill passed by the Parliament. Without the signature, the bill does not become a law, and in principle, the monarch has a right to veto acts of Parliament. In practice, however, this is not done. (What would happen if a monarch were to try to exercise the right? The answer, probably, is a constitutional crisis in which the monarchy would be eliminated.)

"Ancient and unwritten," by the way, does not mean unchanging. Over the past few decades there has been a great deal of constitutional ferment in Britain. The state's entry into the European Union was itself a major constitutional change, and it in turn stimulated a movement to develop an official British code of individual legal rights (like the United States' Bill of Rights) to allow British law to function more easily with the European Court. On another front, when Tony Blair became prime minister in 1997, he undertook several major constitutional revisions. In its first couple of years, his cabinet moved through the Parliament seventeen constitutional bills, including bills to establish quasi-federal autonomy for Scotland and Wales, a bill to incorporate the European Convention on Human Rights into English law, a bill to remove most hereditary peers from the House of Lords, and establishment of a Supreme Court.

For good or bad, an "unwritten" constitution is not something a state can decide to start at any time. It must be received from the past, and so it is unlikely that a state could deliberately imitate Britain and set up an unwritten constitution! However, we may draw the lesson from Britain that it is well to leave some aspects of our constitution to custom, if that is practical, rather than trying to write everything down.

---

[9]Ministers of the Crown Act, 1975.

EXAMPLE

Constitution-Writing in South Africa

From 1948 to 1993 the Republic of South Africa was dominated by its white minority, even though they comprised only about 10 percent of the population. The state was nominally a democracy, and did have electoral democracy for whites. The government ruled that its black majority were not citizens, however, and segregated them into racially defined "homelands," sometimes forcibly removing them from the places they lived to accomplish the racial segregation. Schools, health care and other services were segregated by race. This system of racial segregation and denial of citizenship to blacks was called *apartheid.*

The African National Congress (ANC), led by Nelson Mandela, fought this system by strikes, boycotts, and bombings. The white government responded harshly, with armed confrontations and arrests. Mandela himself was arrested, and imprisoned for twenty-seven years. In the 1980s and 1990s, however, it became increasingly obvious that South Africa could not sustain the system of *apartheid.* The economy was sluggish, and needed the active participation of the 90 percent of its population who were not white. The state's security efforts were expensive. And international anti-*apartheid* boycotts, in which businesses and consumers did not invest in South Africa or buy its products, were growing. Starting in 1990 the white government, led by the National Party, began to negotiate with Mandela how to dismantle *apartheid* and move to full democracy.

For three years, from 1990 to 1993, the main political forces in the country negotiated over how they would carry out the transition to democracy. The main participants in the negotiations were the ANC, the National Party, the Inkatha Freedom Party (representing the Zulu tribe) and a white right-wing party, the Freedom Alliance. The National Party and the ANC were the main protagonists. The National Party especially wanted to guarantee power to all ethnic minorities (including itself, of course, but also including the Zulus), by a requirement that all government institutions would have guaranteed membership for all groups, and that each group would be able to veto any proposed policies. The ANC, however, wanted a democratically elected constitutional convention (which it expected to be able to dominate) to write a straightforwardly democratic constitution with no special guarantees for ethnic groups.

The period from 1990 to 1993 was marked by protracted negotiations, and a good deal of violence. Finally, all parties agreed on an interim constitution in 1993. Under the interim constitution, there would be a democratic election in 1994, with full black participation. The new parliament would then write a final Constitution. However, the interim constitution provided that the final Constitution must honor several principles:

- a democratic government with universal adult voting rights and regular elections
- a multi-party system

- a strong, independent Constitutional Court
- a strong Bill of Rights that guaranteed individual freedoms, including the right to hold property
- a federal system, with nine provinces having constitutionally guaranteed powers

On any question that arose as the new parliament was writing the final Constitution, the Constitutional Court would have the right to rule that what they were considering violated these basic principles and could not become part of the Constitution.

This interim constitution cleverly compromised the conflicting desires of the National Party and the ANC. The National Party could be satisfied that a major part of the constitution-writing was completed and set in place before the election that the ANC wanted, and the ANC could be satisfied that a democratically elected body, rather than the existing institutions would write the final Constitution. While the establishment of a federal system gave some protection to regional ethnic interests, as the National Party wished, it avoided the guaranteed ethnic representation in parliament that the ANC opposed.

The ANC won a clear majority in the ensuing election, with 252 of the 400 seats, so it was able to dominate the discussions in the Constitutional Assembly. The National Party was in a weak position in most of its disputes with the ANC, because the interim constitution had stated that if the writers of the new Constitution could not agree by a two-thirds majority, the Constitution would be put to the people to vote on directly in a referendum. The three issues the National Party felt most strongly about—the right to property, the right of ethnic minorities to have special schools attuned to their own culture, and the right of employers to lock out employees in labor disputes—were all ones on which the ANC position was very popular. If the National Party failed to support the final draft of the Constitution, it knew it would face a campaign in which it was likely to lose on every issue.[10] Accordingly, though the Inkatha Freedom Party walked out of the deliberations and refused to vote for the final Constitution, the National Party supported it and it was enacted in October, 1996.

The property clause was probably the key issue in the negotiations. All had agreed in 1993 that property rights should be included in the Bill of Rights, but the ANC was also concerned that the right to property should not stand in the way of land reform to return large areas of land that had been taken from blacks by the government during the *apartheid* period. In the end, the negotiators resolved the debate by leaving the issue largely unresolved, so that future governments and courts could work out what to do. They retained the property clause in the Constitution, but added a separate clause granting the state a limited exemption from the property clause in order to achieve land and water reform to redress past racial discrimination.

The final Constitution includes perhaps the world's most comprehensive list of guaranteed individual rights, along with a federal system and many watchdog agencies to protect the rights of cultural and other minorities (a Commission for the Promotion and Protection of the Rights of Cultural, Religious and Linguistic Communities, a Commission for Gender Equality, a South African Human Rights Commission, and others). The experience of South Africa in writing its Constitution exemplifies the sort

---

[10]Heinz Klug, *The Constitution of South Africa: A Contextual Analysis* (Oxford: Hart Publishing Ltd., 2010), p. 53.

of negotiation and delicate compromise that a state needs when a deeply divided society designs a framework for government.

KEY TERMS

constitution   unitary state   rule of law
incentive compatibility   federal state   constitutionalism

FURTHER READING

"Constitutions and Constitutionalism." In *International Encyclopedia of the Social Sciences.*

Erk, Jan. "Does Federalism Really Matter?" *Comparative Politics* 39 (2006), pp. 103–120.

Ferejohn, John, Rakove, Jack N., and Riley, Jonathan. *Constitutional Culture and Democratic Rule.* New York: Cambridge University Press, 2001.

Grindle, Merilee S. *Going Local: Decentralization, Democratization, and the Promise of Good Governance.* Princeton, NJ: Princeton University Press, 2007.

Horowitz, Donald G. *A Democratic South Africa? Constitutional Engineering in a Divided Society.* Berkeley: University of California Press, 1991.

Lijphart, Arend. *Power-Sharing in South Africa.* Berkeley: University of California Press, 1985.

McHugh, James T., ed. *Comparative Constitutional Traditions.* New York: Peter Lang, 2002.

Reynolds, Andrew. *The Architecture of Democracy: Constitutional Design, Conflict Management, and Democracy.* New York: Oxford University Press, 2002.

Sunstein, Cass R. *Designing Democracy: What Constitutions Do.* New York: Oxford University Press, 2001.

CHAPTER 10

ELECTIONS

In the long swing of history, elections with broad mass participation are rather new. Such elections originated with democratic government, which means that they came along at the end of the eighteenth century and the beginning of the nineteenth. Today elections are widespread around the world, even though a number of the world's states are not democracies. Even many non-democratic states, such as Syria, hold them regularly. Why are elections so in vogue?

Part of the answer, of course, is that *democracy* is a word that purrs with respectability. Even states that are not democratic wish to appear democratic, and holding elections is one of the easiest ways to display some of the forms of democracy even if the state is not democratic.

A second reason is that elections can serve more purposes for the state than just the democratic one of allowing the mass of people to help in the selection of leaders and policies. Elections were invented to make democracy possible; but once invented, they turned out to have further uses. This is an interesting aspect of political institutions that we shall encounter frequently in later chapters. We may devise institutions to serve a particular purpose, but once they are in existence, they may be adaptable to a variety of purposes.

In this case, the thing that recommends elections to the leaders of authoritarian states is that they can serve two main purposes: not only (1) the purely democratic purpose of allowing the mass of people to have some direct say in the *choice of leaders and policies,* but also (2) the universal purpose of *allowing the state to mobilize its people and to build up their support for the state by acting out support and participating in the process of government.*

✦ ELECTIONS AS A MEANS OF BUILDING SUPPORT

Let us consider the second of these first. Many authoritarian systems around the world hold elections, and often invest quite a lot of effort and money to ensure a large turnout. In modern times, such states as Azerbaijan, Guatemala, Egypt, Syria, Algeria, North

Korea, Paraguay, Belarus, Cuba, Côte d'Ivoire, Singapore, and many others have staged elaborate elections of which the outcome was never in doubt. And, they have accomplished electoral turnout in these non-contests that are equal to or better than the turnout in United States presidential elections: Azerbaijan, 75 percent in the 2008 election; Belarus, 91 percent in 2010; Singapore, 93 percent in 2011.

In the Soviet Union (before it dissolved in 1991) intense efforts by the Communist Party ensured a 99 percent turnout:

> The network of agitators is fully activated during the ten days preceding the election. Agitators must visit each voter in the precinct, explaining the virtues and qualifications of the sole candidate. The mass media publicize the biography of each candidate to the larger soviets and urge a resounding vote of confidence for the regime. The candidate spends no money campaigning but holds meetings with voters. . . . Refusal to vote is regarded as an unpatriotic act. Even the sick are expected to vote and ballot boxes are brought to the bedsides of hospital patients. Voting occurs on ships that are at sea on election day, as long as there are at least twenty-five voters aboard; the votes are added to those cast in the ship's home port. Passengers on long-distance trains vote in special precincts while in transit.[1]

The elections took up a great deal of time and were very expensive. Over 2 million candidates were elected each time—better than one out of every hundred adults—and they invested a great deal of time and energy in the campaign. Millions more were engaged in activities such as agitation, and serving on electoral commissions. It was an expensive business, and yet, the single candidate of the Communist Party was going to win each seat. Why did they go to all of this effort?

The most reasonable guess is that the main purpose of elections in the Soviet Union was to renew the people's enthusiasm and support for the regime. Elections provided a recurring opportunity for the newspapers to pour out praise for the leaders of the state and for citizens, through their actions, to feel that they were a part of it. As behavioral therapists know, a good way to ingrain a particular point of view in a person's consciousness is to have the person act it out. This would be reason enough for the Soviet Union to have put its population "through their paces" at regular intervals.

While we do not normally think of elections in democracies as functioning to build support for the system, research indicates that elections serve this purpose in democracies as well as in authoritarian systems. A study of presidential elections in America highlighted this quite well.[2] At the 1968 and 1972 presidential elections, a sample of American adults were asked before and after the election whether they agreed or disagreed with the statement "People like me don't have any say about what the government does." Before the 1968 election most people, whether or not they ended up voting in the election, agreed with the statement, as Table 10.1 shows. The electorate in 1968 was quite disillusioned and had lost a great deal of its faith in the nation's leaders. Conflict over civil rights and American involvement in the Vietnam War had soured people on politics, and the American public had seen the Democratic nominating convention in Chicago torn apart by demonstrations

---

[1] John S. Reshetar, Jr., *The Soviet Polity*, 2nd ed. (New York: Harper & Row, 1978), p. 196.
[2] Benjamin Ginsberg, *The Consequences of Consent: Elections, Citizen Control, and Popular Acquiescence* (Reading, MA: Addison-Wesley, 1982), pp. 166–170.

TABLE 10.1

Percentage Agreeing That Ordinary People Have Little Say in Government

	Voters	1968 Nonvoters	Total
Before the election	71	83	74
After the election	37	58	42
Change	−34	−25	−32
	Voters	1972 Nonvoters	Total
Before the election	34	58	40
After the election	29	54	36
Change	−5	−4	−4

SOURCE: Recalculated from Benjamin Ginsberg, *The Consequences of Consent: Elections, Citizen Control, and Popular Acquiescence* (Reading, MA: Addison-Wesley, 1982), pp. 167 and 170.

and by the reaction of the police to the demonstrations. Of those who voted in that election, 71 percent initially agreed that ordinary people do not have any say in government, as did 83 percent of those who ended up not voting. Over the campaign and the election, this outlook changed considerably. After the election, only 37 percent of those who had voted agreed with the cynical view of government, for a drop of 34 percentage points. Among those who did not vote but who experienced the period of campaigning and election, the figure also dropped, but by somewhat less: 25 percentage points.

The circumstances in 1972 were different, but there again the election apparently served to reassure the public about the political system. The pre-election public in 1972, in contrast to that of 1968, was not turned off to politics. The incumbent Nixon administration was popular (Nixon would get 61 percent of the vote), and the Vietnam trauma had passed. Only 34 percent of those who would eventually vote, and 58 percent of those who would not, initially agreed with the cynical view of government. The campaign was not one to inspire confidence in the system. It was marked by the forced withdrawal of Thomas Eagleton as the Democrats' vice-presidential nominee because it became known that he had a history of mental illness; by a great deal of personal vituperation between the candidates; and by rumors of corruption and "dirty tricks" that would later produce the painful Watergate scandal.

In spite of this, the campaign period and election of 1972 produced small moves toward greater support of the system, even among an electorate who were already rather supportive before the election. After the election, 5 percent fewer voters and 4 percent fewer nonvoters agreed with the cynical view.

The figures in Table 10.1 were based on the National Election Studies (hereafter NES) surveys for 1968 and 1972.[3] The only other United States election for which a

---

[3]National Election Studies, Center for Political Studies, University of Michigan.

Difficulties of Elections in a New Democracy

All new democracies find the actual conduct of elections difficult at first, especially if they are poor and lack a good infrastructure for communication. Papua New Guinea's election in 2002 offers a particularly horrific example, complicated by poor internal communications in an impoverished country, ethnic warfare in its highland region, and continued tensions coming from its war of independence from Australia. The story, however, is as much one of great hope at the efforts made by local democrats and their international partners to establish democracy in a country that faces great problems.

Voting in the 2002 election started on June 15, 2002, and polls were supposed to close on June 29. (The two-week duration was required by the difficulty of people reaching the polling places on a single day.) The polling was so marred by gangs intimidating officials and voters, by tampering with ballots, and by arson at polling places that the voting was extended for another month, to July 29. Even then, election results could only be declared for 80 of the 109 seats; the rest, all in the southern highlands, were decided in a supplemental election in June 2003.

After the election, Transparency International (an international anti-corruption organization; see p. 117) worked with the government to change the electoral system to limited preferential voting, in which not only voters' first choices count, but also their second and third choices. The intent was to make vote-buying and bribery difficult; since all votes count in the end, there are too many people to bribe easily. The new system was introduced for the 2007 election.

The press releases of the Papua New Guinea Electoral Commission in its early years of 2002 and 2003 provided a fascinating and moving picture of good people dealing with politics in the raw. The commission complained of attacks by thugs, of police inaction, of bribery, and of obstruction by local officials. The language was blunt and vivid. Yet what remains at least for me is a strong sense of the faith and dedication of these officials, working under the worst of circumstances, to establish democracy and the rule of law.

similar analysis is possible from NES data is 1996. For that election, Wendy M. Rahn, John Brehm, and Neil Carlson found exactly the same process as we saw for the earlier elections in Table 10.1.[4]

Still further evidence for the effect comes from a study of Canadian elections in the 1980s. For all Canadians (not distinguishing between those who voted and those who did not vote), regard for Parliament, on a scale of 0 to 100, rose from an average of 53 before the 1988 election to 59 after the election. A dozen similar comparisons worked in the same way.[5]

---

[4]Wendy M. Rahn, John Brehm, and Neil Carlson, "National Elections as Institutions for Generating Social Capital," in Theda Skocpol and Morris P. Fiorina, eds., *Civic Engagement in American Democracy* (Washington, DC: Brookings Institution, 1999), pp. 111–62. Simply looking at the overall result for voters and nonvoters combined, they found that from before the election to after the election, Americans reduced their agreement with the cynical position by 8.4 percentage points. Additionally, in a careful multivariate analysis of the sources of this change, they found that whether or not a person had voted in the election added significantly to the effect.

[5]Allan Kornberg and Harold C. Clarke, *Citizens and Community* (New York: Cambridge University Press, 1992), pp. 187–191.

From all of this, it appears that such renewal of support for the system is a widespread attribute of elections. In Chapter 8, we examined the state's need to maintain sufficient support among its citizens so that its authority would continue undiminished. For democracies and authoritarian systems alike, elections apparently furnish a potent tool to help ensure this popular base of support. At regular intervals, people's acceptance of the system is reinforced as the citizens act out their identification with the state and its leaders.

⇥ Elections as a Means of Selecting Leaders and Policies

In democracies, however, elections are meant to do more than just bolster support for the regime. They are the means by which leaders and (sometimes) actual policies are chosen by the people. For this to be the case, an election must involve a choice between candidates or a decision on a particular policy. Even in some states that are not democratic at the level of national government, elections are allowed to function in this way at least at the local level.

In democracies, the choice of political leaders at all levels is made by competitive elections. In addition, some democracies provide for the **referendum**, a device by which the voters choose directly through their ballots whether a particular proposal will become law. Authoritarian systems sometimes use controlled referendums to exhibit and stimulate support in the same way as other elections. I discuss the referendum in the "Referendums" section of this chapter.

⇥ Electoral Systems

If we are to use elections to choose political leaders, there must be some rule for translating people's votes into a particular selection of leaders. This is not as simple a matter as one might think. For instance, one might state simply that the candidate who gets the most votes will win the election and take office. What of the people who voted for a losing candidate: Should their votes count for nothing? What if there were a dozen candidates and the one who got the greatest number of votes had only about 20 percent of the vote: Would we want that person to take office? There is no single obvious way to translate the votes cast by the electorate into the people who will take office. States need to design rules determining which people win office as a result of any particular result in the voting; we call these rules the **electoral system** of the state.

Rulers of states can, if they wish, write many detailed differences into their electoral systems. At one or another time and place, for instance, a party has been required to win at least 5 percent of the vote to obtain a seat in the legislature, owners of businesses have been given double votes to increase their weight in the electoral choice, some seats in a legislature have been reserved for members of one or another race, and votes have been counted separately and weighed differently for rich people and poor people. The possibilities are limited only by the imagination of those in charge of the state.

However, almost all democracies use two broad types of electoral system: **single-member-district plurality systems** and **proportional representation systems**. For convenience, I will refer to them from this point on by their initials, SMDP and PR.

SMDP and PR Systems

In the SMDP system, the state is divided into a set of districts, usually having roughly equal populations. One representative is elected from each district to be a member of the legislative body of the state, and whoever gets a plurality of the votes wins the seat. (A *plurality* is the largest number of votes cast for any candidate; if there are many candidates running, the plurality may be less than a majority of votes cast.) Hence the name: A *single member* is elected from each *district* by a *plurality* of votes.

This arrangement is familiar to U.S. and Canadian students, because both countries use versions of the SMDP system. In Canada, the members of Parliament are elected by the SMDP system. In the United States, members of the House of Representatives are elected by an SMDP system and members of the Senate by a variant of SMDP. (There are two senators from each state of the United States, but they are elected in separate years by a plurality so that, in effect, the senatorial electoral system is SMDP.)

Britain is an SMDP system, and indeed these systems tend to be limited, worldwide, to Britain and its former colonies such as the United States, Canada, and India.

Most electoral democracies of the world use versions of proportional representation (PR). PR is simple. Although democracies use various formulas and methods to calculate the proportional result, the basic principle of PR is that political parties' representation in the legislative body is set roughly proportional to their strength in the electorate. That is, if the Fundamentalist Neopejorative Party received 18 percent of the votes cast in the election, it would obtain roughly 18 percent of the seats in the legislative body; if it received 30 percent of the votes, it would obtain roughly 30 percent of the seats.

The simplest form of PR is "list PR." In list PR the state is divided into a relatively small number of large districts, each of which sends a large-ish number of members to the parliament. There may even be only one "district," the entire state itself. (The Netherlands and Israel do this, for instance.) However, most states set up a number of districts in order to ensure that all regions receive their fair share of representation. Argentina, for instance, is divided into 24 districts that elect 257 representatives, for an average of about 11 representatives per district.

Before the election each party prepares a ranked list of candidates for each district (hence the name, "list PR") and registers that list with the election commission. After the election the commission determines the number of seats each party should have, based on its proportion of the vote, and counts down the ranked list from the top, awarding places to that number of candidates. If the Socialist Party gets 40 percent of the vote in a district with fifteen members, for instance, the commission will award six seats (40 percent of the 15) to the Socialists; the first six names on their list will then become members of the parliament.

The proportional outcome seems reasonable, but PR was invented precisely because SMDP does *not* give a proportional result. Instead, SMDP generally favors large parties and hurts small ones. This is because a small party, if its voters are spread evenly

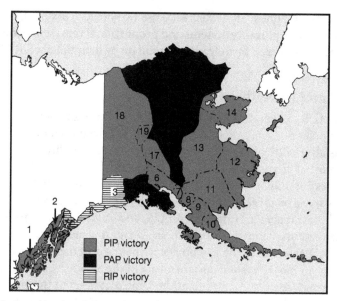

FIGURE 10.1   Aksala: A hypothetical SMDP result.

geographically, will have only a small number of voters in each district and may not have enough in any one district to achieve a plurality and win there. Figure 10.1 illustrates this. The hypothetical country of Aksala is divided into twenty districts, each having 50,000 voters. In its most recent election, the Prudential Improvidence Party (PIP) polled 450,000 votes, or 45 percent of the total; the Protection of Artifacts Party (PAP) polled 350,000 votes, or 35 percent of the total; and the Revolutionary Inaction Party (RIP) came in third with a still substantial poll of 200,000, or 20 percent of the votes. As you can see from the map, the PIP won fourteen seats with its 450,000 votes, the PAP won five seats with its 350,000 votes, and the poor RIP obtained only one seat for its 200,000 votes. That is, 45 percent of the vote received 70 percent of the seats, 35 percent of the vote received just 25 percent of the seats, and 20 percent of the vote received only 5 percent of the seats.

How is it that RIP did so badly, getting just one out of the twenty seats for its one-fifth of the votes? As we see in Table 10.2, RIP's votes were spread around so that it received, for example, 25 percent in one district, 13 percent in another, 29 percent in another, and 3 percent in another. Only in district number 3 did RIP's 42 percent share of the vote top the shares of both PIP and PAP, so that it won.

This is a fairly typical result of SMDP. Although the example is fictional, it was not deliberately constructed to produce this result beyond stating the initial condition that the three parties were of those sizes and had a fairly even distribution of their voters across the country. Most real life examples of SMDP fit the same pattern. In the British election of 2010, for instance, the Liberal Democrats (the third-largest party in the country) polled 23 percent of the votes but won only 9 percent of the seats in the House of Commons.

In their early elections, most European states used electoral systems similar to SMDP. It was at the urging of small or new parties that felt unfairly discriminated

TABLE 10.2

Percent of the Vote for the RIP, by District

District	Vote	Percent
1	12,500	25%
2	13,500	27
3	21,000	42
4	14,000	28
5	13,000	26
6	11,000	22
7	5,000	10
8	6,500	13
9	8,500	17
10	10,500	21
11	12,000	24
12	9,500	19
13	9,500	19
14	3,100	6
15	1,500	3
16	2,300	5
17	14,600	29
18	2,000	4
19	14,300	29
20	15,700	31

against that most states changed to PR systems in the early part of the twentieth century. Why, you may ask, do any states retain SMDP as an electoral system when it is so unfair? The reason is that there is a practical benefit to the distortion in favor of large parties, which many observers think may compensate for the unfairness to smaller parties. Small parties are disadvantaged by SMDP; therefore, there is a tendency for them to disappear or to merge over time. As a result, SMDP electoral systems tend to encourage the emergence of two large parties rather than a variety of smaller parties.[6] With only one major exception—Canada—SMDP systems have only two major parties, which may make it easier to govern the state. And with only occasional exceptions, PR systems have more than two major parties. This may make it difficult to govern the state, but only if parties have difficulty cooperating; while in some notable cases multiparty government has been associated with instability, most PR/multiparty

---

[6]The standard statement on the effects of electoral systems is Maurice Duverger, *Political Parties* (New York: Wiley, 1954). See also Douglas Rae, *The Political Consequences of Electoral Laws,* rev. ed. (New Haven: Yale University Press, 1971); Rein Taagepera and Matthew S. Shugart, *Seats and Votes: The Effects and Determinants of Electoral Systems* (New Haven: Yale University Press, 1989); Gary Cox, *Making Votes Count: Strategic Coordination in the World's Electoral Systems* (New York: Cambridge University Press, 1997).

governments function smoothly. (We will discuss the relative merits of having two parties in Chapter 11—there are arguments on both sides!)

The trade-off between the two systems is one of fairness to minorities and small parties, on the one hand, versus simplifying the party system by weeding out small parties, on the other. Three other issues that may enter into a choice between the two electoral systems are:

- Many voters may feel that their vote is wasted under SMDP. Under SMDP, voters who are in the minority in their district (a Republican in San Francisco, a Conservative in Quebec City, or a Democrat in suburban Salt Lake City) may feel that there is no sense in voting, because their candidates cannot win.

- Since PR usually produces a system of more than two parties, the voter is likely to have a wider range of choices under PR and find a party that is a close fit to her values.

- SMDP provides legislators with a tie to a particular locality, with a particular set of constituents; most PR systems do not make this kind of connection.[7] Under PR voters vote for a party list, not a single candidate, so there is no one person they can think of as "my member of Congress."

Two Conditions for the SMDP Bias

The bias of SMDP in favor of large parties is a function of two conditions: *First, if a small party has most of its strength concentrated in just a few districts, it may not be hurt by the SMDP system*, because it may have enough strength in those few districts to win there. Consider if a Southwestern Autonomy Party had appeared in Aksala and had polled 60,000 votes spread across just the four southwestern districts. Depending on how its votes were spread among the four districts, it might well have won in one or two of them. (It would have averaged 30 percent of the vote across the four districts, and the rest of the vote would have been spread among three parties.)

Again, there are plenty of real life examples of this exception to the rule of SMDP bias. One is the Plaid Cymru, a Welsh nationalist party, which in the British election of May 2010 polled only 0.6 percent of the vote nationally but, by concentrating that vote in Wales, won three of the 650 seats in the House of Commons, for 0.5 percent of the seats. (Remember that in that same election the Liberal Democrats, with their strength spread more evenly across the country, got 23 percent of the vote, but only 9 percent, of the seats.)

Another good example is Canada, which, as I noted, is the major exception to the rule that SMDP electoral systems tend to limit a country to two major parties. Four major parties are active in Canadian politics, but each of them has a distinct regional base, so there is little selective pressure on them from the SMDP system.

---

[7]A variant of PR, which was first invented by Germany in the early 1950s, elects half of the representatives from single-member districts, but then tops off those members (who, as one would expect, overrepresent the larger parties) with an additional and equal number of seats distributed among the parties in such a way that the overall membership of the parliament is made proportional. This provides each district in the country with an identifiable member who is "their" member in the parliament, while arranging that the overall distribution of seats is proportional, so that small parties are not disadvantaged. This blend of the two systems has proved very popular in new democracies since the 1990s.

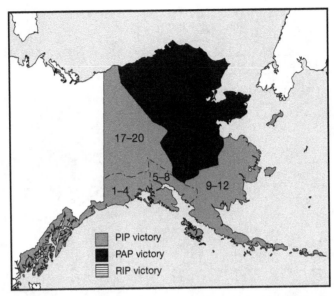

FIGURE 10.2   A hypothetical election by SMDP, with Aksala divided into only five districts.

Second, the smaller the number of districts, the more likely it is that small parties will be hurt by SMDP. If the state is divided into a small number of large districts, there is less chance that a small party will happen to have enough votes to win in a particular district.

This is illustrated in Figure 10.2, in which the districts of Aksala from Figure 10.1 have been grouped by fours, so that there are five larger districts. Under this arrangement, the largest party (PIP) expands its share of the seats from 70 to 80 percent, the PAP drops from 25 to 20 percent, and the "small" RIP (with 20 percent of the vote) disappears.

To carry this to an extreme, if there were only one seat in the legislative body, the whole country would be one single-member district, with a plurality winning. In this case, the ultimate distortion would occur, with the PIP candidate winning 100 percent of the "seats" (i.e., the one seat), even though PIP had gained only 45 percent of the total vote.

This last extreme possibility sounds silly, but it actually does happen in the real world, and is important. If a state has a president who is popularly elected by all the voters, the election functions, in effect, as a legislative election with one seat under SMDP. (Many democracies do not have an elected president, but some do—the United States, France, Mexico, and others. I discuss presidential government at length in Chapter 15.) Where there is a presidency, small parties are driven out of contention, and there is strong pressure for the system to evolve into one with two large parties. An example of this is France, which in 1962 shifted to a popularly elected presidency. After that shift, small parties gradually declined. Today French politics is dominated by two main parties—the Union for a Popular Movement (right of center) and the

2	GENERAL ELECTION STATE OF IDAHO	Jefferson County, Idaho, November 04, 2009

CANDIDATES FOR UNITED STATES OFFICES

UNITED STATES SENATOR VOTE FOR ONE	Larry LaRocco (Dem) →
	Kent A. Marmon (Lib) →
	Pro-Life (A person, formerly known as Marvin Richardson (Ind) →
	Rex Rammell (Ind) →
	Jim Risch (Rep) →

CANDIDATES FOR UNITED STATES OFFICES SECOND CONGRESSIONAL DISTRICT

| U.S. HOUSE OF REPRESENTATIVES Second District VOTE FOR ONE | Deborah Holmes (Dem) |
| | Mike Simpson (Rep) |

TO CONTINUE VOTING TURN TO NEXT PAGE

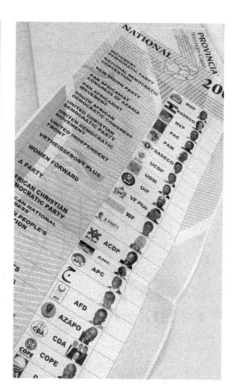

Ballots from Jefferson County, Idaho (left) and South Africa (right). The Idaho ballot illustrates an SMDP system, the South African ballot a PR. Note that in the SMDP election the voter chooses one from a list of candidates, while in the PR election the voter chooses one from a list of parties.

SOURCES: Reprinted with permission of the Independent Electoral Commission (IEC) of South Africa. We do not make any representations or warranties, implied or otherwise, that the use at your own risk and we will not be liable for any and all damages whatsoever.

Socialists (left of center)—plus a third party off on its own dimension of opposition to immigrants. The conclusion is unavoidable that the institution of the presidency forced France's quarrelsome parties to coalesce into something like a two-party system.

To summarize the point of this section dealing with electoral systems: The SMDP system tends to drive out small parties and ultimately to produce an arrangement consisting of two large parties. This effect is less strong if the parties have geographic concentrations of voters and may disappear altogether, as in the case of Canada, if all parties' strengths are concentrated by region. The effect is heightened by reducing the number of districts and is especially strong when the state is a single district, as in presidential elections.

✦ REFERENDUMS

Many democracies restrict their citizens' involvement in the affairs of state to a vote that expresses their choice among potential political leaders. The state's policies are then set by the elected leaders, without any direct input from the voters. A number of democracies, however, allow voters under some circumstances to choose directly, in an election, whether the state should follow a given policy. We call such an electoral choice a referendum. The United States does not have any provision for national referendums, but many localities and states do provide for them. California is particularly noted for their use, as in the Proposition 71 referendum in 2004, in which the state's voters established a large trust fund to sponsor stem-cell research, or the Proposition 8 referendum in 2008, which amended the state's constitution to ban same-sex marriage. Outside the United States, a few democracies provide for the regular use of national referendums. France and Switzerland are two examples, the latter relying on them rather heavily.

Beyond these few instances, many democracies that would not accept the regular use of referendums do use them on rare occasions for decisions of great gravity, where it is felt that all the people should be involved in the decision. Spain, for instance, when it initiated its new democratic Constitution in 1978, held a referendum so that the people could ratify the Constitution. Similarly, when the powers of the European Union expanded in a new constitution in 2005, Spain, France and the Netherlands held referendums to allow their people to decide whether to approve it. (Spain voted yes, but defeats in France and the Netherlands killed the draft constitution.)

Why are democracies so reluctant to give "power to the people" by using the referendum to make laws? The main objection is that a proposed law cannot receive the sort of careful consideration and detailed examination in an election campaign that it would receive in a legislature or parliament. Voters typically do not have the time or resources to inform themselves about the intricacies of a bill. In a sense, this is "what they hire politicians for." Especially when many bills are voted on in a single campaign—as in California, where twenty or more may appear on a single ballot—only one or two will have been widely discussed among the voters. The other bills may be decided by chance factors such as how enticingly they are worded or where they appear on the ballot, or by the small number of people who may stand to gain from them in special ways and therefore take a special interest in them.

✦ ELECTORAL PARTICIPATION

Let us shift from elections and electoral systems to examine how voters act in elections. We shall confine our attention to voters in democratic elections.

It is evident that not all of those who are entitled to vote, do vote. In the 2012 American presidential election, for instance, only 58 percent of those who were eligible to vote did so; in most elections for local office, the turnout is even less than this.

There is great variation from one place to another, and among different sorts of people in any one place, as to how active people are in elections. At roughly the same time that 58 percent of eligible Americans voted in the 2012 presidential election. The following percentages of the eligible electorate voted in a variety of European elections: Great Britain, 61 percent; Netherlands, 71 percent; Germany, 65 percent; Sweden, 85 percent; Switzerland, 40 percent. European democracies usually exhibit higher levels of electoral participation than the United States, but there are certainly some countries that are lower. Within the United States, electoral turnout varies a good deal as well.

TABLE 10.3

Who is Likely or Unlikely to Vote?

Groups Unusually High in Participation	Groups Unusually Low in Participation
Suburban residents	Young people
Well-educated people	Poor people
Well-off people	Women (except in Europe and North America)
Farmers (U.S.A.)	Ethnic minorities (U.S.A.)
Old people	

Hawaii had the lowest turnout among the fifty states in 2012, with only 44 percent; Minnesota had the highest, with 75 percent.

A website with worldwide data on turnout in elections is International IDEA: http://www.idea.int/.

Beyond geographic variation, certain types of people seem especially likely to vote. Table 10.3 lists various types of people who seem especially likely or especially unlikely to vote. Notice from the table that especially in the United States, where low participation is found both among ethnic minorities and those with low income, participation is highest among those who are more privileged in society. As we see in Figure 10.3, voter turnout among African Americans is nearly as high as that among whites, but turnout among Asians and Hispanics is far lower, leaving them less represented in elections than the other groups.

In 2012 a civic campaign called Ya Es Hora ("Now is the Time") brought together Hispanic civic groups and the Univision television network to saturate Hispanics with

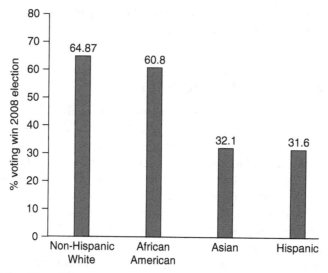

FIGURE 10.3   Voter turnout among major American ethnic groups.

SOURCES: U.S. Census Bureau, http://www.census.gov/hhes/www/socdemo/voting/publications/p20/2008/index.html, various tables.

FIGURE 10.4   Voting and volunteerism in the American states.

Each dot represents a different state. The unusual state with 43 percent volunteerism (the highest in the country), but a relatively low 33 percent voter turnout, is Utah. The strong emphasis on voluntary service in the Mormon church may account for this anomaly.

SOURCES: United States Census Bureau, Statistical Abstract of the United States; Corporation for National and Community Service, Volunteering in America (http://www.volunteeringinamerica.gov[VAC1], accessed March 27, 2009).

the message that they should vote. It appeared to produce a solid upturn in Hispanic turnout relative to 2008.

What is it that leads some people to vote more regularly than others? Partly it seems to be a matter of cultural traditions. The high electoral turnout in Minnesota, for instance, seems likely to be a result of the tradition of constructive citizenship that was strong among the Scandinavian immigrants who comprised a large part of Minnesota's early population.

Social capital seems to be another factor leading to higher voter turnout (see the discussion of social capital, pp. 198–199). Figure 10.4 shows the relationship between voter turnout in the states and the rate of volunteering for community programs. Each dot represents a different state, and where it falls on the graph depends on its combination of volunteerism rates and voter turnout. As you see, there is a strong relationship between voluntarism and turnout. States in which people frequently volunteer to serve the community tend to be the states in which people vote in large numbers. A culture of community participation appears to be a major factor in voter turnout.

Partly, however, turnout is a function of practical, almost mundane questions about how elections are organized—whether as in the United States polling day is on a working day rather than on a Sunday, for instance, or whether registration to vote is cumbersome or easy. (In most countries, the local authorities automatically register voters, and this requires no specific action by the citizens registered.) A number of countries even make failing to vote a minor crime punishable by a small fine. This increases participation substantially, and it reduces disparities in participation among groups in society, since nearly everyone votes.

Also, it is partly a function of the difficulty of making political decisions. This may help explain why well-educated people are more likely to vote than people with less education; those with less education presumably find politics more puzzling and confusing than those who are better educated. This problem surely helps to explain why voter turnout is low in referendums, which demand more from a voter than choosing a party or a candidate.

Finally, it is partly a function of the political circumstances under which the election is held. A close election stimulates greater turnout than one that promises to be a walkaway for one side. National elections, because of the great stakes of war and peace that are involved, get a higher turnout than they probably deserve as compared with local elections. Blue-collar workers in Europe participate more faithfully than those in the United States partly because unions in Europe are more active than American unions in mobilizing their voters.

That some social groups are more likely to vote than others makes a real difference in what views are brought to bear on the election—and therefore on the views to which elected officials will pay attention. In the United States, young, poor, ethnic citizens are less likely to vote than older, better-off, white citizens, and the impact on the views officials must consider is dramatic. In September 1998, the New York Times ran a poll in which it distinguished those citizens most likely to vote in the next election.[8] (Such citizens said they definitely expected to vote in the 1998 election, they were paying considerable attention to the campaign, and they had voted in both 1994 and 1996.) How did registered voters as a whole compare with those who were really likely to vote?

Of registered voters as a whole:

- 44 percent favored the Democrats, 39 percent the Republicans.
- 66 percent approved of President Bill Clinton's performance in office.
- Only 29 percent thought that Clinton should be impeached.

Of registered voters who appeared most likely to actually vote:

- 41 percent favored the Democrats, 53 percent the Republicans.
- 48 percent approved of President Bill Clinton's performance in office.
- 50 percent thought Clinton should be impeached.

Since elected officials only need to worry about what voters want, and can ignore those who do not vote, it was the latter group that called the shots.

---

[8]"Likeliest Voters Favor Republicans," *New York Times*, 25 September 1998, p. A18.

What Is the Best Level of Participation?

A major argument among political scientists in the 1960s and 1970s turned on this question: Is more participation always better, or is there some optimal level of participation that is lower than 100 percent? Among others suggesting that more was not always better, Gabriel Almond and Sidney Verba expressed the opinion, in *The Civic Culture* (Boston: Little, Brown, 1965), that the ideal citizen participated up to a point but then sat back and trusted government officials to take things from there. This guaranteed an attentive citizenry, but one that would also give its government trust and support. Seymour M. Lipset also fueled the distrust of excessive participation by his finding, in *Political Man* (Garden City, NY: Doubleday, 1960), that the high turnout in the German elections of 1932 and 1933 had had a great deal to do with Adolf Hitler's victories.

Of the several responses, that of E. E. Schattschneider—*The Semisovereign People* (New York: Holt, Rinehart and Winston, 1960)—suggested that nonparticipants were like a time bomb waiting to disrupt the system. They were not building patterns of support for the existing system by participating; therefore, they could cause dangerous results, if they suddenly flooded in as the German voters for Hitler did. Schattschneider concluded that we should try to get everyone to participate as much as possible. Carole Pateman, in *Participation and Democratic Theory* (Cambridge: Cambridge University Press, 1970), drew an argument straight from classical liberal theory. A main purpose of participation was to help people improve themselves by exercising their judgment and by informing themselves on what was happening. Whether or not instability results, more participation is in and of itself a good thing; the more there is, the better.

This question is alive today, and very relevant to the spate of laws passed in states of the United States in 2011 and 2012 that made voting more difficult. More than twenty states changed their election procedures in ways that were likely to reduce participation, mostly by requiring picture identification to vote, or by shortening the period for early voting. Though partisan motivations were pretty clearly involved (all of the changes were made by Republican legislatures and governors, and would affect especially groups who usually vote for Democratic candidates), much of the debate concerning the changes revolved around whether it was necessary to restrict participation in order to ensure the quality of votes.[9]

✦ EFFECTS OF CHOICE AND INFORMATION ON TURNOUT

Sometimes factors that determine political behavior work in unexpected ways. This can be especially notable when combinations of factors interact with each other.

I noted earlier (p. 234) that we think citizens should be more likely to vote in PR systems than in SMDP systems, because the multiple parties that typically result from PR offer a wider range of choices. This is, roughly, true. However, it interacts in an odd and perverse way with how well informed voters are about politics. Once we see this, it is not so clear which electoral system produces "better" participation.

[9]"For instance, George F. Will argued in a column in *The Washington Post* on December 19, 2012, that nonvoting is a voluntary act and that making registration difficult improves the caliber of the electorate by screening out less motivated voters (George F. Will, "Mountain out of a Molehill," www.washingtonpost.com/opinions).

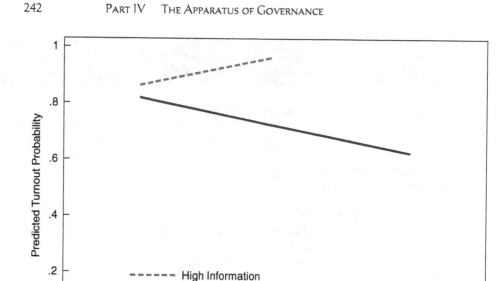

FIGURE 10.5   Turnout by number of parties, for well-informed and less-informed voters.

Adapted from Karen Long Jusko and W. Phillips Shively, "Applying a Two-Step Strategy to the Analysis of Cross-National Public Opinion Data," *Political Analysis* 13 (2005), pp. 327–344, Figure 3.

Figure 10.5 presents the results of a statistical analysis, conducted across 25 countries, of how frequently well-informed and less-informed citizens vote, in the presence of party systems that give them varying ranges of choice.

As you see in the figure, the analysis shows that as the number of parties increases, participation increases for well-informed voters (the dashed line), just as we would expect, but look at the less-informed voters! The solid line representing their participation decreases as the line moves across the graph to larger numbers of parties. Apparently, for the less-informed the greater difficulty of choosing among larger numbers of parties affects them more greatly than the fact that they now have more options available, and so they drop out in discouragement.

The perverse effect of this is that PR, the electoral system that is supposedly designed to get better participation, produces an electorate that is increasingly less representative of the full public. As the well-informed flock to vote and the less-informed quit in discouragement, the end result is an electorate considerably more skewed to the well-informed. Now, you might think that is great: what's wrong with a country dominated by the well-informed? However, the well-informed tend to be those parts of society that have been able to benefit from education. The poor, ethnic minorities, older generations (depending on the country) are likely to cluster among the less-informed. Which is the fairer system?

As you see, it is at least an open question whether the broader choice likely associated with PR systems really improves participation.

➜ THE PARADOX OF VOTING

We might also flip the question of participation around, and instead of asking "Why doesn't everyone vote?" ask, "Why are all these people voting?" Looked at in one way, it can appear irrational to take the trouble to vote. Seeing how unlikely it would be for a single vote to decide a U.S. presidential election, one might consider it hardly worthwhile to spend a half hour and 99 cents worth of gasoline to get to the polling place. (The odds must be less than one in a trillion that the other 80 million voters would split exactly evenly, so that one vote could decide the outcome.) As a character in Skinner's *Walden Two* remarks to his friend,

> "How is the people's will ascertained? In an election. But what a travesty! In a small committee meeting, or even a town hall, I can see some point in voting, especially on a yes-or-no question. But fifty million voters choosing a president—that's quite another thing."
>
> "I can't see that the number of voters changes the principle," said Castle.
>
> "The chance that one man's vote will decide the issue in a national election is less than the chance that he will be killed on his way to the polls. We pay no attention to chances of that magnitude in our daily affairs. We should call a man a fool who bought a sweepstakes ticket with similar odds against him."[10]

This is what we call the **paradox of voting**.[11] It is paradoxical because, if we consider things from this perspective, *no one who is sensible should vote*. If the outcome of the election is nearly certain to be the same whether you vote or not, why should you take the time and go to the expense? To put it in the concrete terms alluded to in the quotation from Skinner, over the years more people are hit by trucks and killed on the way to the polls than change the results of national elections by their single votes. On the average and over the long run, from this point of view voting looks like a dangerous and unproductive act.

Paradoxes have solutions, and we can try two possible solutions for this one. First, the paradox obviously holds only for voters taken one at a time. If a large group of voters chose to sit out an election, it is quite possible that their absence could change the outcome, as we saw earlier in our example from the *New York Times* poll. Most politicians spend more time and effort in their campaigns in trying to ensure that the right people get to the polls than in trying to change the minds of people who are planning to vote for their opponents.[12] Politicians certainly recognize the importance of turnout rates in determining elections. Therefore, the paradox of participation is a paradox

---

[10]B. F. Skinner, *Walden Two* (New York: Macmillan, 1948), pp. 220–221. A study has shown that on average 24 more people have died in car crashes on presidential election days than on other October and November days, going as far back as 1976, so there seems to be something to the quotation. (D. A. Redelmeier and R. J. Tibshirani, "Driving Fatalities on US Presidential Election Days," *Journal of the American Medical Association*, October 1, 2008, pp. 1518–1520.)

[11]William H. Riker and Peter C. Ordeshook, *An Introduction to Positive Political Theory* (Englewood Cliffs, NJ: Prentice-Hall, 1973), pp. 45–68, esp. pp. 57–58.

[12]However, see W. Phillips Shively, "From Differential Abstention to Conversion: A Change in Electoral Change, 1864–1988," *American Journal of Political Science 36* (May 1992), pp. 309–30.

only for voters taken individually. This might resolve the problem for us—except that a voter's decision whether to vote *is* taken individually. That is, groups do not decide whether to vote, *voters* decide whether to vote. So the paradox remains.

A second way of addressing the paradox is to note that it looks at voting solely as an act to provide benefits to the individual voting. The paradox arises only if we think that people vote solely because of their wish to exercise their own power in making the government's policies. While it is true that this is the democratic justification for holding elections, we must realize that it casts voting as essentially a *selfish* act in which voters participate only to increase their own political power. However, we saw in Figure 10.4 that voting appears to be associated with a culture of community service, which suggests that at least in part, voters are turning out for something more than what they can individually gain from the election. They are voting out of a desire to do their duty, out of a love of country, and often because of a good deal of social pressure from those around them. In other words, voting for them may be more of a communal act than an individual one.

This would certainly help to explain what is otherwise unexplainable—that millions of people vote in elections even though we can easily demonstrate that voting is of no benefit to them as individuals. This seems an attractive resolution to the paradox partly because it elevates our discussion of voting above selfish calculations of individual costs and benefits. Love of community and country is a noble sentiment, and if electoral participation is based partly on it, all the better for elections.

→ THE BASES OF INDIVIDUALS' ELECTORAL CHOICES

For whatever reason, great numbers of people vote in elections. How do they choose which party or candidate to vote for? Any number of things may serve as the basis for voting choice in one country or another.

We can distinguish usefully between short-term factors and long-term factors in voting choice. Short-term factors are things about a particular election that may lead a person to vote one way or another. The state of the economy usually operates in this way, for instance. If times are bad, a number of people will vote against whoever is in office as a way of showing their unhappiness, and in good times they will reward the party in office. Michael S. Lewis-Beck and Tom W. Rice have estimated that for a drop of 2 percent in national income the president's party would lose four seats in the U.S. House of Representatives in a mid-year election or twenty seats in a presidential election year.[13] François Gélineau and Éric Bélanger, reviewing Canadian elections from 1953 to 2000, estimated that an increase in the unemployment rate of 1 percent led to a drop of 1.3 percent in the vote for candidates of the governing party, while an increase of 1 percent in the rate of inflation led to a drop of 0.4 percent in the vote. Candidates in provincial elections were also punished and rewarded for the performance of the national economy when their party was in power nationally, even though they themselves had nothing to do with national economic policy.[14]

Other short-term factors may include the particular appeal (or lack of same) of a candidate. This particularly appears to be the case in the United States and Canada, where

---

[13]Michael S. Lewis-Beck and Tom W. Rice, *Forecasting Elections* (Washington, DC: Congressional Quarterly Press, 1992).
[14]François Gélineau and Éric Bélanger, "Electoral Accountability in a Federal System," Publius: *The Journal of Federalism* 35(2005), pp. 407–424.

"HOW BINDING ARE CAMPAIGN PROMISES MADE ONLY IN PRIMARIES?"

© Copyright ScienceCartoonsPlus.com

the personalities of possible presidents and prime ministers sway a large number of voters. In most European countries, on the other hand, the voters have often seemed to weigh primarily the various political parties as whole organizations, with less emphasis on the personal characteristics of a party's leading candidate. As we will see in Chapter 11, political parties in the United States and Canada are weak organizations compared with those in most countries; as a result, individual candidates in American or Canadian elections carry more personal weight. In countries with strong parties, the focus of the electorate is more on the parties, and individual candidates do not count for as much.[15]

A particular candidacy, the state of the economy, an international crisis—such short-term factors can be potent in deciding an election. However, most elections most of the time are determined largely by things that do not change much or that change only gradually.

One such long-term factor is the identification of some people with a particular political party. We all know some older person who says he or she has been a Democrat

---

[15]Over recent decades this difference has been diminishing, however, as electorates everywhere shift more to an emphasis on candidates. For instance, in the 2002 election in Germany, an initial 10 percent advantage in the polls for the Christian Democratic Party dwindled over the course of the campaign to a virtual tie in the election, due almost solely to the bland personality of its candidate, Angela Merkel. Despite these shifts, however, the United States and Canada still stand out in this regard.

TABLE 10.4

Social Bases of Support for the Social Democratic Party of West Germany, 1953–1972

	1953	1972	2005
Percent voting socialist of:			
Working class	58	70	40
New middle class			39
Old middle class	28	53	17
Those who never attend church	63	74	40
Those who occasionally attend church	48	61	37
Those who frequently attend church	17	28	23

SOURCE: Calculated from *Germany Transformed: Political Culture and the New Politics*, by Kendall Baker, Russell Dalton, and Kai Hildebrandt, Cambridge: Harvard University Press, Copyright © 1981, by the President and Fellows of Harvard College, and from Russell Dalton, *Citizen Politics*, 5th edition Washington DC, CQ Press, 2008. The "new middle class" comprises primarily salaried white-collar employees and civil servants, while the "old middle class" comprises traditional parts of the middle class such as self-employed professionals, managers, and shopkeepers.

(or a Republican or a Conservative or a Liberal or a Labour voter or whatever) "since I was a kid." To such a voter, a particular candidacy or the state of the economy makes less difference than to other voters. Most of the time, this person is going to vote by party no matter what is happening. Political scientists call this sort of continuing tie **party identification**.[16] It adds a good deal of stability and predictability over time to election results. We will discuss party identification in more detail in Chapter 11, but for now it is enough to note that party identification, as a stable learned attitude, is a result of the process of political socialization that I presented in Chapter 8. In particular, party identification is to a significant extent learned from one's parents.

Another long-term factor that adds stability over time is the commitment of various social groups to one or another party. As we see in Table 10.4, for the last fifty years the working class and the less religious have been a fairly stable base of support for the Social Democratic Party of Germany. (Of course, the flip side of this is that the middle class and the religious have been fairly stable in *not* supporting the party.) The fortunes of the party have gone up and down from one election to another, but at every election—and many more elections could have been displayed, all showing the same thing—the working class have been more supportive than the middle class, and the nonreligious more supportive than those who attend church.

In other countries and at other times, the following social differences have functioned importantly as bases for voting distinctions:

- *Region.* The "solid Democratic South" of the United States from the 1870s to the 1960s is an example, or the regional basis of all Canadian parties.

---

[16]Angus Campbell, Philip Converse, Warren E. Miller, and Donald Stokes, *The American Voter* (New York: Wiley, 1960), chaps. 6 and 7.

- *Language.* The Swedish People's Party of Finland is an example.
- *Farming.* Many countries have had agrarian parties; Norway and Sweden are two examples.
- *Country of origin.* Mexican-Americans in the United States tend to be Democrats, for instance, while Cuban-Americans tend to be Republicans.
- *Race.* Blacks tend strongly to vote Democratic in the United States; the politics of Guyana has been almost totally determined by conflicts between blacks and East Indians.
- *Gender.* Women in many countries favor conservative parties, although this may be an indirect effect of religion rather than a direct effect of differences between men and women; by contrast, a "gender gap" has opened in the United States and several European countries, with men voting more conservatively than women.
- *Age.* In 2005, only 26 percent of Germans aged eighteen to twenty-five voted for the Christian-Democratic party, while 43 percent of those over 60 did so.[17] In the 2008 election in California, a majority of voters under 65 voted against the Proposition 8 ban on same-sex marriages, but a 67 percent positive vote by voters over 65 carried it.[18]

A website with electoral maps for the United States going back into the mid-nineteenth century is Dave Leip's Atlas of U.S. Presidential Elections: http://www.uselectionatlas. org. You can see how various parts of the country voted from one election to another; note in examining these maps how stable the regional distribution of the vote is from one election to another.

 EXAMPLE

Proportional Representation Elections in Israel

The Knesset (Israel's parliament, with 120 seats) is elected every four years by an unusually simple and direct form of proportional representation. Parties submit lists of candidates (in ranked order) to the electoral commission. Any party that receives 2.0 percent or more of the vote nationally gets at least one seat in the Knesset, and each party's number of seats is proportional to how

---

[17]Doreen Namislo and Karina Schorn, "Wählerverhalten bei der Bundestagswahl 2005 nach Geschlecht und Alter." Statistisches Bundesamt Deutschland, accessible at www.destatis.de.
[18]Patrick J. Egan and Kenneth Sherrill, "California's Proposition 8: What Happened, and What Does the Future Hold?" Report commissioned by the Evelyn & Walter Haas, Jr. Fund, accessible at www.haasjr.org.

large a percentage of the vote it received. In the 2013 election there were 32 lists on the ballot.

Voters cast their vote for a list. Candidates on the list enter the Knesset according to their rank in the list; for instance, the Shas Party qualified for eleven seats in the Knesset in 2013, so the first eleven names on the list became Knesset members. If a seat is vacated before the next election, the next person on the list steps in.

Where candidates rank on their party's list is obviously important. Parties put their key leaders at the top of their lists, to ensure that they are elected, but beyond that, groups and factions compete to get their people placed high. Who does the placing varies by party. Of the two traditionally largest parties, Labour uses a primary election to determine the internal placement of its candidates on its list; in the Likud Party, the "center" (a gathering of one thousand to three thousand leaders of the party, broadly representative of its constituent parts) does the ordering.

Larger parties receive a small boost from the way votes that had been cast for parties failing to meet the 2 percent threshold are reassigned. The bottom line, though, is that the Israeli system of PR is unusually straightforward and faithful to proportionality. As a result, many parties usually get into the Knesset.

In 2013, the results were:

	Votes (%)	Seats
Likud (nationalist)	23.3	31
Yesh Atid (a new party in 2013)	14.3	19
Labor (left of center)	11.4	15
The Jewish Home	9.1	12
Shas (ultra-orthodox)	8.8	11
United Torah Judaism	5.2	7
Hatnuah	5.0	6
Meretz (left-oriented)	4.6	6
United Arab List	3.7	4
Hadash	3.0	4
Balad	2.6	3
Kadima	2.1	2
Otzma LeYisrael	1.8	0
Total for 19 other parties	5.3	0

Such a diverse party system—twelve different parties in the Knesset!—could produce unstable government, since it might prove difficult to combine enough different parties to make up a working majority in the parliament (especially when, as in Israel, they are deeply divided on policies). This has not usually proved the case in Israel, possibly because the country's constant exposure to external danger has forced the parties to cooperate in spite of their inclinations. However, one major result of the dispersion of the parties is evident. It has usually been impossible to form a governing majority without including at least one of the small religious parties; this has given them a good deal of leverage, by which they have commanded patronage and policy concessions way out of proportion to their electoral strength.

EXAMPLE

Elections in Nigeria

Nigeria has had elected democratic government for only twenty-three of its fifty-two years of independence—from 1960 to 1966, from 1979 to 1983, and again starting in 1999. Obviously, Nigeria's democracy is fragile; elections there illustrate well the difficulties of conducting an election in a large, new state whose diverse ethnic elements are still only weakly united.

Even aside from the military's propensity to throw out the results, electoral politics is difficult for any country like Nigeria. First, it tends to bring out sectarian conflicts between ethnic groups and regions of different religions, which always threaten to tear the state apart. Nigeria fought a bloody regional civil war from 1966 to 1969 in which over a million people died, and thousands have died at various times in Christian-Moslem riots. Violence between ethnic groups is also common.

Nigeria is a large, spread-out country. During an election, it must manage 120,000 polling places, some of them in remote areas. This logistical challenge is multiplied by political and social disorganization that make it even more difficult to conduct a fair election. In the 2007 presidential election, for instance, the Independent National Electoral Commission (INEC) barred the main opposition candidate from running because he was on an administration list of officials deemed too corrupt to run. The Nigerian courts reinstated him to candidacy just days before the election, and the INEC then had to print 65,000,000 new ballots and get them to polling places around the country in just fifteen hours. The ballots could not be serially numbered to prevent fraud, and they arrived too late for voting at all in many places. The legitimacy of the hastily prepared election was further marred by an error-filled registry of voters and allegations of ballot-stuffing.

In the end, that election came off with an estimated 58 percent turnout. The two major defeated candidates refused to accept the election results as fair, and the chief EU observer of the elections, Max van den Berg, criticized the elections as "far short" of basic international standards. "The process cannot be considered to be credible."[19] Estimates of the number killed in election violence ranged from 65 to 200.

In 2011, the country took great care to do a better job than in 2007. The INEC was put in new hands, and carried out an ambitious reworking of the registration of voters, with fingerprints and photographs to help prevent fraudulent voting. At the request of the INEC, the election was delayed from January to April to allow it more time to perfect the registration of voters and train administrators.

The incumbent, Goodluck Jonathan, won with 59 percent of the vote. Turnout, at 53 percent, was down a bit from 2007. However, the election was hailed as generally clean

---

[19]"Nigeria Election 'Worst Ever Seen,'" *The Sydney Morning Herald*, April 24, 2007, http://www.smh.com.au/news/world/nigeria-election-worst-ever-seen/2007/04/24/1177180600209.html

and fair—in fact, the best election held yet in Nigeria. Pre-election violence was at least as bad as in 2007, with numerous bombings and shootings, but there were few indications of fraud or manipulation. The biggest problem associated with the election stemmed from the fact that Jonathan is from the South and the North felt that it was its turn to have a president, under informal rules to rotate the office by region. In the days following the election there was widespread violence in the North, with mobs seeking out activists of Jonathan's party and burning police stations and residences.

With all its difficulties, Nigeria now has peacefully transferred power to three different presidents since the reestablishment of democracy in 1999.

KEY TERMS

referendum
electoral system
single-member-district plurality electoral system
proportional representation electoral system
paradox of voting
party identification

FURTHER READING

Abramson, Paul R., Aldrich, John H., and Rohde, David W. *Change and Continuity in the 2008 and 2010 Elections.* Washington, DC: CQ Press, 2011.

Bowler, Shaun, Donovan, Todd, and Tolbert, Caroline J., eds. *Citizens as Legislators: Direct Democracy in the United States.* Columbus: Ohio State University Press, 1998.

Dalton, Russell J. *Citizen Politics: Public Opinion and Political Parties in Advanced Industrial Democracies,* 6th ed. Washington, DC: CQ Press, 2013.

Diamond, Larry, and Plattner, Marc, eds. *Electoral Systems and Democracy.* Baltimore: Johns Hopkins University Press, 2006.

Flanigan, William H., and Zingale, Nancy H. *Political Behavior of the American Electorate.* 12th ed. Washington, DC: CQ Press, 2009.

Herrnson, Paul S. *Congressional Elections: Campaigning at Home and in Washington.* Washington, DC: CQ Press, 2008.

Lindberg, Staffan I. *Democracy and Elections in Africa.* Baltimore: Johns Hopkins University Press, 2006.

Lutz, George, and Marsh, Michael, eds. *Electoral Studies* 26 (3, September 2007) is a special issue devoted to the consequences of low turnout.

Nelson, Michael, ed. *The Elections of 2008.* Washington, DC: CQ Press, 2009.

Patterson, Thomas E. *The Vanishing Voter.* New York: Alfred A. Knopf, 2003.

Romer, Daniel, Kenski, Kate, Waldman, Paul, Adasiewicz, Christopher, and Jamieson, Kathleen Hall. *Capturing Campaign Dynamics: The National Annenberg Election Survey.* New York: Oxford University Press, 2003.

Shugart, Matthew Soberg, and Wattenberg, Martin P. *Mixed-Member Electoral Systems: The Best of Both Worlds?* New York: Oxford University Press, 2001.

CHAPTER 11

PARTIES: A LINKING AND LEADING MECHANISM IN POLITICS

In preceding chapters, I have talked a good deal about political parties. The political party crops up in all aspects of politics. It is an invention that first developed in the nineteenth century in response to the new phenomenon of elections involving large numbers of voters. Politicians developed the political party at that time as a device to help themselves and like-minded friends get elected, but the party proved to have many other uses as well and went on to become a ubiquitous feature of modern politics. I shall explore this theme in later sections, but first, questions of definition.

✦ THE POLITICAL PARTY

*A **political party** is a group of officials or would-be officials who are linked with a sizable group of citizens into an organization; a chief object of this organization is to ensure that its officials attain power or are maintained in power.*

The latter part of this definition distinguishes the political party from the "interest group," which I will discuss in Chapter 12. In most countries, there are many interest groups such as the American Medical Association, the American Dairy Farmers' Organization, the Natural Gas Supply Association, or Friends of the Earth—groups of people with a common interest who band together to try by way of lobbying, campaign contributions, and other tactics to ensure that the government's policies will be in tune with their wishes. Interest groups are distinguished from political parties in that they try to influence which policies the government follows without actually taking power or setting policies themselves; parties, on the other hand, have as their central purpose the acquisition of power and the direction of policy.

There is nothing about the definition that says political parties are restricted to democracies and to electoral activity. Revolutionary parties may be organized not to win elections but to seize control of the government by force. Parties like the Nazi Party of Germany in the 1930s, the Communist Party in China, or the Ba'ath Party in Syria today (and in Iraq until Saddam Hussein's overthrow in 2003) may oversee the machinery of a non-democratic state.

Finally, a party joins people together in a formally organized structure. U.S. political parties surely fall at an extreme in the looseness of their organization, but in most countries, the parties are clearly delineated, with formal membership that sets those who are in the party apart from the rest. For instance, the Conservative Party of Britain has about 300,000 dues-paying members. The Communist Party of China has about 80 million members, who must pass a probationary and training period, generally taking more than a year and a half, before they are accepted for full membership.

The party's nature as a structure, tying together a large group of officials and citizens, provides an avenue by which one part may control or communicate with another. It is this that has made it such a versatile tool of modern politics. We will explore this topic in more detail in the sections that follow.

✦ Origins of the Modern Party

Although the party has turned out to be useful for a variety of tasks that require control or communication, it was first invented for a more limited and self-serving purpose. Long before the coming of electoral democracy, the state had had a varied structure of public officials such as mayors, members of parliament, and ministers for defense. Before democracy arrived, people attained these offices in a variety of ways: by being born into them, by buying the office (much as we might today purchase a fried-chicken franchise), by bribery, or by appointment.

With the introduction of democracy, however, many of these positions were filled by election. This was different from the old ways of choosing officials in one important respect: In the old ways, the person who wished to have the office dealt with a single king or perhaps with a few people whom he could bribe; but now, under democracy, the would-be official had to seek the votes of a thousand or more people—too many to bribe.

It did not take long for politicians in the new democracies to see that some sort of club or organization that bound them together with large numbers of voters would help them to mobilize voters, in order to attain and hold office. Furthermore, large national clubs binding together a whole set of officials with voters throughout the country could function more effectively than a local club built around a single official. With a nationwide organization, voters were not lost to the club as they moved from one place to another; a popular official could go from place to place, helping to convince the voters to choose the organization's other candidates; and there would be enough money to hire professional staff who could help with the job of organizing thousands of voters. Thus, the political party was born.

The first modern electoral democracy was the United States of America, and it was here that the first parties developed. By the 1820s, there were well-organized parties, and the Democratic Party, which can trace its roots back to that time, is the oldest political party in the world.

In Britain, 1867 was the first year in which there was a reasonably widespread extension of the vote. As of that year, 10 percent of the population was entitled to vote, and the establishment of organized political parties followed over the next couple of decades. The possibility that an expanded suffrage would lead to the development of political parties was one of the arguments which some members of Parliament raised against expanding the suffrage in 1867:

> with a widely enlarged suffrage the candidate would find himself less and less able to come face to face with his constituency, and would be compelled in consequence . . . to rely more and more on the aid of the election agent, and, as in America, of that of committees and canvassers whose mouthpiece and delegate he would have to make himself.[1]

Similarly, all over Europe, whenever a reasonably large and varied electorate was established with the coming of democracy, the political party appeared.

Like elections themselves, political parties have been widely copied and are found in many countries that are not electoral democracies. For instance, the National Democratic Party governed in Egypt for over thirty years as a one-party state until massive pro-democracy demonstrations toppled it in 2011. China is governed by the Communist Party, Zimbabwe by the Zimbabwe African National Union–Patriotic Front, and Syria by the Ba'ath Party, which also governed Iraq until the fall of Saddam Hussein. We could note many more examples, for many regimes that do not require parties to win elections have found that the modern political party—with the links it creates between masses of people and a set of political leaders—is useful to them. One of the wonders of modern politics is that this invention, originally devised in order to help some office-holders keep their jobs, has proved adaptable to all sorts of other purposes. The political party has become a "miracle glue" of sorts for politics. Whenever one group of people wishes to control another group or even just keep in contact with them, the party has turned out to be a useful tool.

Let us look at some of the ways in which the political party operates. Parties provide the following: a basis for the mobilization of masses of citizens; a means of recruiting and socializing political leaders; structured political identity at the mass and elite levels; and a method of control within a government structure. We shall look at each of these in turn.

✦ POLITICAL PARTIES AND THE MOBILIZATION OF THE MASSES

I argued in Chapter 10 that one of the main effects of holding elections was to involve the masses of ordinary citizens in acting out their support for the state and, by so doing, strengthen that support. For this to happen, millions of voters must be stimulated to go out and take the trouble to vote. Governments cannot easily entice people to the polls, so how to reap this particular advantage of elections poses a bit of a problem. The problem is particularly great where only one slate of candidates is allowed, so that there is

---

[1]M. Ostrogorski, *Democracy and the Organization of Political Parties*, vol. 1 (Garden City, N.Y.: Doubleday, 1964), p. 78.

no suspense whatever about the outcome of the election. How can a government mobilize the voters to get out and vote under these circumstances? A political party is a good instrument with which to stir up the electorate and get them to the polls. It is controlled by its leaders, who are at the same time the rulers of the state; and it may have a membership that extends down into every village, so it is strategically placed to turn out large numbers of people.

In the United States, political parties make great efforts to get out the vote. They do this not to bolster support for the regime, although that is a side effect, but to help themselves win elections. In Singapore, which is not a democracy, the People's Action Party (which holds 81 of the 87 seats in Parliament) has no such motive for stirring up the electorate; however, its leaders are anxious to generate a good show of support, and so the party does much the same things as American parties do at election time.

Aside from elections, political parties may serve to **mobilize** the people for special purposes or to meet crises. When President Anwar Sadat of Egypt was assassinated in 1981 and was succeeded by Vice President Hosni Mubarak, over a million people joined a demonstration in Cairo to show their support for Mubarak. The demonstration was partly organized by the government apparatus itself but also, in large part, by the ruling National Democratic Party. When the regime of Charles de Gaulle was threatened in France by a general strike in 1969, the turning point at which his opponents were defeated came when his Union of Democrats for the Republic Party organized a massive demonstration in

A powerful image of mobilization: Greece's New Democracy Party stages a rally.
© Evi Zoupanos/ZUMA Press/Corbis

Paris for which over 100,000 supporters were bused in from the countryside. When Syria came under intense international pressure in 2005 to withdraw its troops from the neighboring state of Lebanon, its allies in the Lebanese Hizbollah Party mobilized a demonstration of 500,000 supporters (Lebanon has only 3.7 million people!) to support Syria's role there.

A party may also mobilize masses of people against a regime. Many of today's political parties in Third World states—the Congress Party in India, for example, or the National Front for Liberation in Algeria—were initially organized to carry out a campaign to overthrow a colonial ruler such as Britain or France. The African National Congress led the successful decades-long fight to end the discriminatory system of *apartheid* by which whites in South Africa subjugated the black majority. When German armies occupied much of Europe during World War II, it was the churches and the political parties that provided the basis for a resistance movement because they were the only structures binding together large and widespread groups of people in ways that made coordinated resistance possible. Today, the most important focus of opposition to many regimes lies with political parties.

→ POLITICAL PARTIES AND THE RECRUITMENT AND SOCIALIZATION OF LEADERS

Another use to which parties have lent themselves, beyond what they were originally designed for, is the recruitment and socialization of leaders. Somebody has to do this in any society, and where there are political parties, they are an obvious choice for the task. What other organization could better seek out promising young people, give them experience at relatively small jobs, and gradually move those who do well to more important jobs, while imbuing them with the values that the political leadership wishes to encourage?

In Britain, for instance, an ambitious young woman who was interested in entering politics might work for a while at lesser tasks for one of the major parties, such as the Conservative Party. Before too long, if she were interested in standing for Parliament, she might be nominated from a district. To get the nomination, she would have to convince the local selection committee of the Conservative Party in that district that she was their best nominee. As a beginner, she would probably be selected in a hopeless district, where no Conservative had much of a chance; but once she had proved that she could campaign well in one or two lost causes, she might get the nomination from a decent district, win, and enter the House. In the House, the party would continue to mold and guide her. If she were the sort that party leaders like—witty in debate, hard working, and above all a faithful party voter—she might advance into positions of real responsibility, such as party spokesperson on defense or on health. Eventually, she might aim so high as to be prime minister. To be selected for this position, she would have to win an internal election at which all the Conservative members of the House of Commons vote to narrow the choice of nominees to two of their members; the 300,000 enrolled members of the party then vote by mail ballot to choose which of the two will be party leader. Throughout this career, her advancement would have been primarily due to her support from her party organization. She would have risen to the top only because she was the sort of person her party wanted and because, in each position she held, she would have learned from the rest of the party how to behave in the ways they preferred. This is essentially the only route to a political career in Great Britain, and it is controlled at all points by the party.

In the United States, too, parties are important as devices for the recruitment and socialization of leaders. However, parties in the United States are weaker organizationally than those in Britain, and so they do not hold the same monopoly in this regard that British parties do. Most political leaders have worked their way into place through the apparatus of either the Democratic or Republican Party, starting at fairly lowly positions. However, primary elections at which a candidate can appeal directly to the voters for nomination, rather than relying on party leaders, can also allow a popular celebrity such as the actor Arnold Schwarzenegger to enter directly into politics at a high level. (The existence of primary elections, which take the selection of candidates out of the hands of party leaders, is often considered the single most important cause of American parties' organizational weakness.) Furthermore, people who have distinguished themselves at some other career are often appointed to a president's cabinet directly without any prior political career and thus without any screening by a party. When John Kennedy appointed his brother Robert as attorney general, when George W. Bush appointed Stanford professor Condoleezza Rice to be national security adviser, or when Barack Obama appointed economist Timothy Geithner to be secretary of the treasury, no party experience was involved.

In a one-party state such as China, the single party may serve as the major avenue to any sort of political advancement. The Chinese Communist Party actually restricts its membership to keep out opportunists who would join to advance themselves. By strict entrance requirements and by purges, the party tries to limit itself to a membership comprising about 5 percent of the population. Party leaders have good cause to be concerned about the problem of opportunism. There is ample reason for ambitious young people to seek membership no matter what their political beliefs because all important public officials and most leaders of institutions, such as universities, are required to be Communists.

→ POLITICAL PARTIES AS A SOURCE OF POLITICAL IDENTITY

Another unforeseen effect of political parties was the extent to which parties, once one was associated with them, became an important part of one's identity. Party is probably not the first thing a person would mention when asked "What are you?" A more likely reply would be "I am a Presbyterian," "I am a woman," "I am a student," or "I am a Canadian." Along the way, if you keep prompting, you may well be given the name of the political party with which that person feels associated. As we saw in Chapter 10, we call this source of identity **party identification.**[2] For those who become quite active, the political party may become a vital and central personal concern. What would

---

[2]The concept of "party identification" was first developed fully in Angus Campbell et al., *The American Voter* (New York: Wiley, 1960), chaps. 6 and 7. For a review, see Richard Johnston, "Party Identification: Unmoved Mover or Sum of Preferences?" *Annual Review of Political Science*, vol. 9 (2006): pp. 329–351.

"WHAT I DON'T UNDERSTAND IS HOW, IN A FEW YEARS, WE'LL BECOME CONSERVATIVE REPUBLICANS."

Nancy Pelosi have been without the Democratic Party? What would Angela Merkel of Germany have been without the Christian Democratic Party, or Xi Jinping of China without the Communist Party?

One important thing about party as a source of identity is that it can provide continuity in a political world that is otherwise quite fluid. Candidates come and go, wars start and end, political issues arise and fade and are replaced by others, but parties may go on across many lifetimes. The two major parties of the United States are over a century old; the Communist Party of the Soviet Union was over seventy years old at the time of its collapse; Britain's Conservative Party is over a century old, and its Labour Party is almost ninety years old.

By furnishing individuals and politically active people with a lasting political identity, the party can give them a source of political community throughout their lives. Parties may provide an even longer-range continuity in politics than that of a single lifetime if party connections are passed on from parents to children or if local party organizations continue their activity across generations. The state of Tennessee provides an ironic instance of the way in which parties can create this sort of continuity. At the time of the Civil War the state was divided as to whether or not to secede. In Figure 11.1a we can see which counties were most strongly opposed to secession, as indicated by the vote for John Bell, the Constitutional Union candidate in 1860.

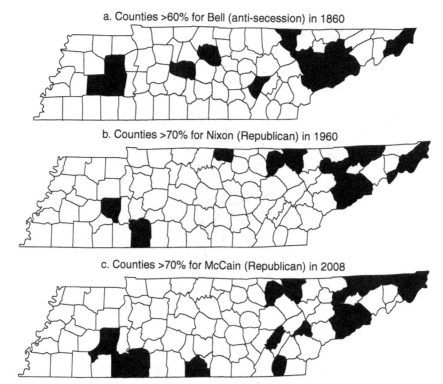

FIGURE 11.1 Continuity of Republican strength in Tennessee, 1860–2008.

Two areas of opposition stand out: eastern Tennessee, and a pocket of opposition in the west. After the War, opposition to secession translated into support for the Republican Party, which had held the Union together. This made sense at the time, but the pattern continued to hold in election after election, long after the issues of the Civil War had receded into the depths of history. In the second map in the figure the areas in which Republican Richard Nixon ran most strongly in 1960 are approximately the same areas in which secession was opposed in 1860. The pattern still holds today, 150 years after the War. The third map in the figure shows the areas in which Republican John McCain ran most strongly in 2008; again we see the same two main areas of strength.[3] To follow Tennessee from election to election since 1860, you can access an interesting animated series of electoral maps for the United States at http://geoelections.free.fr/USA/thema/18562004_ANIM.htm.

Although this is a French website, it is not too hard to figure out even if you do not know the language. On the map counties carried by the Republican Party are blue, with high percentages in dark blue; yellow/brown represents the Democratic vote; and green and red represent "other parties." You can readily follow the stability of the Republicans in eastern Tennessee visually across elections, along with other areas of partisan

---

[3]Of the 16 counties most opposed to secession in 1860, 8 were among Nixon's strongest counties in 1960, and 9 were among McCain's strongest counties in 2008.

stability such as a Republican patch in the hill country of Texas, or a Democratic area in northern Minnesota.

➔ POLITICAL PARTIES AS A CHANNEL OF CONTROL

A final unforeseen effect of political parties was to provide some political leaders with a new channel through which to exert control over other leaders. This has been an important factor in modern politics.

Remember that a party is an organization that binds a sizable group of political leaders together with a sizable number of ordinary citizens. It is the only sort of organization that regularly does this. It spreads so widely within the set of political leaders and out into the mass of people that it offers an excellent channel for power through which political leaders can control the actions either of other political leaders or of the citizens.

As a channel for controlling other political leaders, the party is important in all sorts of states. The leaders of a party have many punishments and rewards at their disposal such as nomination for various offices, and support in passing favored legislation. Perhaps the greatest carrot or stick most of the time is the chance to advance to more powerful positions within the party. Leaders use these inducements deliberately, for example, to force obedience on lesser party figures in legislative votes, or campaign activity. Sam Rayburn, who was for many years the leader of the Democratic Party in the U.S. House of Representatives, used to caution new members, "To get along, go along." That is, to advance within the House hierarchy, obey orders. In the British House of Commons, the party organizations expect such pure obedience in voting that the life of ordinary members is in some ways rather dull, because they are almost always just following orders in how they vote.

As we shall see in Chapter 14, this channel of control is crucial in making the parliamentary governments of Western Europe and other parts of the world work. However, party functions as a channel for power in all sorts of other systems as well. In one-party states, the party may provide a means by which the apparatus of the state, especially in touchy areas such as the armed forces, is kept under the control of the party leaders. As much as possible, only party members were allowed to serve as high-ranking officers in the armies of the communist countries, for instance, and their standing in the party strongly affected their advancement.

Parties may also serve as a channel for power by which the leaders of the state control the mass of citizens. This is more common in authoritarian states than in democracies, where direct control of citizens is supposed to be the exception rather than the rule. For example, one particular problem for authoritarian systems is the control of intellectual activity, which might pose a threat to the leaders of the state if it proceeded freely. By placing party members in leadership positions in writers' organizations, universities, professional associations, and the media, the leaders of the state can help to ensure their control over what the citizenry thinks and says. This has particularly been the practice in communist systems, although military dictatorships, the fascist regimes of the 1930s, and other authoritarian regimes have attempted it as well.

☩ PARTY ORGANIZATION

Political parties in the United States are unusual in their organizational structure because they are loose and informal. Any other organization in the country—a savings bank, a birders' club, a church—has some sort of formal membership, for which one applies and in return receives a membership card. Political parties in the United States do not require this of their "members"; in fact, it is often difficult for people to be sure whether or not they are members of a party. Political scientists have some difficulty specifying just what group of people they are describing when they speak of the "Republican Party." Do they mean only the elected Republican officials in Congress and elsewhere? Do they mean the people who run the party's offices? Do they mean just the people who work for Republicans in election campaigns? Do they mean those who are registered as Republicans (even if they regularly vote Democratic)? Do they mean those who sympathize with the Republicans? There is no formal organization defining those who "belong" and those who do not, so anyone is free to define the set as desired.[4]

In other states, however, parties are set up in a more normal way as formal organizations. If one wishes to be a member of the party one applies for membership, pays some sort of dues, and is formally enrolled with a membership card. As explicit, well-defined organizations, these parties have organizational structure.

The Conservative Party of Great Britain offers a fairly typical example of organizational structure. As we see in Figure 11.2, the party consists of several parts. The key position is occupied by the leader of the party, who is a Conservative member of the House of Commons, elected in a two-step process in which the other Conservative members of the House first narrow the choice to two candidates, and then party

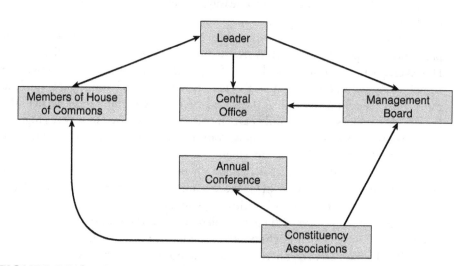

FIGURE 11.2 Organizational structure of Great Britain's Conservative Party.

---

[4]For a more detailed analysis of this problem, see Marjorie Randon Hershey, *Party Politics in America*, 14th ed. (New York: Longman, 2011), chap. 1.

members around the country vote to choose one of the two. If the Conservative Party is in power, the leader serves as prime minister for Britain.[5]

One-way arrows (indicating power) go out from the leader to all other units with which the leader interacts except the members of the House. With regard to the latter, power is a two-way street—the members may unseat the leader, and this occurred several times in the twentieth century; but the leader directs the business of the Conservative Party in the House.

Other parts of the party serve as a supporting structure for the leader and the party's members in the House. There are about 300,000 dues-paying party members around the country organized into constituency associations by parliamentary district. These determine local party policy—including the important question of who will be the party's candidate from that district—but they have little influence otherwise in national party policies. Their only influence in this regard is to send delegates to the party's annual conference, from which, as Figure 11.2 illustrates, no arrows of power go anywhere. Issues are discussed at the conference and resolutions passed. These are not binding on anyone; however, the party's leaders may treat them as important symptoms of discontent that must be taken seriously. Members also participate in the choice of a leader, but only after candidates have been narrowed to two by the Conservative members of the House of Commons.

The Central Office is a large and well-financed party bureaucracy that hires regional and local party agents, conducts research on policy, and publishes propaganda. The Central Office is closely controlled by the leader, who directly appoints most of its top officials.

The Management Committee of the party is a group with representation from among members of parliament, members from the constituency associations, and professional staff. The party's leader appoints a majority of its members, but some are elected by the constituency associations. The management board oversees the party's day-to-day operations.

Thus, the Conservative Party has a complex structure, dominated by the members of the House of Commons through their leader. Other parts of the structure are important to the members of the House as a support group, but except for the important power over nominations held by local constituency associations, they have little power over the party's policies. This is not to say that the outside structure is unimportant; if nothing else, membership dues are a major source of party finance. The party's website, http://www.conservatives.com/, provides a sense of how the party operates, and of its organizational structure.

Most parties outside the United States have organizational structures more or less similar to this. They may vary in the degree of power given to the outside structure. (The Labour Party of Britain, for instance, gives more real power to its annual conference than does the Conservative Party.) The parties may vary in how tightly they exercise control. In communist parties, "lower" units in power generally have to toe the line much more precisely than in noncommunist parties; this allows the leader to direct party policies more completely and more efficiently than leaders of other parties.

---

[5]I discuss this arrangement in more detail in Chapter 14.

⇢ PARTY FINANCE

Parties obtain the money with which to finance their activities from a variety of sources. In the United States, parties do not have a monopoly on political finance, since candidates raise it directly from individual contributors and organized interest groups. Since a reform in 2003, and the Citizens United constitutional decision by the Supreme Court in 2010, independent groups loosely aligned with candidates, but not under their direct control, have also played a major role in campaigns.[6] Parties still are able to generate enough resources from individual contributors, often solicited over the Internet, to function actively; but they do not dominate campaign finance. A good source for information about campaign contributions by various groups is the Center for Responsive Politics, at www.opensecrets.org. Another good source is the Federal Election Commission, at www.fec.gov.

Outside of the United States, parties generally raise the money and determine its use themselves.[7] The money may come from many sources:

- *Public finance:* Most states pay a portion of their parties' campaign expenses from public funds. It is always difficult to decide how much money to give to which parties. Established parties benefit disproportionately, since a new party, with no prior electoral success as a claim to funds, is on its own. Most importantly, however, state support for campaigns lessens parties' dependence on other sources, such as those below—some of which distort the policy process by tilting it toward those who have provided the money.

- *Individual membership dues:* These may provide a good deal of income to a party, especially one with a large membership.

- *Bribes and kickbacks:* Especially where a single party is associated with a dictatorship, the closeness of the party to government allows it to organize corruption on its own behalf. In 1993, the Liberal Democratic Party of Japan, which had ruled without interruption for so long that it closely approximated one-party government, became embroiled in a huge scandal involving kickbacks of millions of dollars from construction contractors.

- *Interest-group donations:* Business and labor groups, and a few others, may subsidize favored parties heavily.

- *Profits from business enterprise:* Many parties own their own newspapers, banks, and other service firms, which they operate for the benefit of their members. Usually these cost money rather than make it, but some may be profitable.

- *Subsidies from foreign countries:* The United States, Venezuela, Libya, China, Israel, France, Japan, and other states have, at times, subsidized parties in other countries to further their own policies.

---

[6]*Citizens United v. Federal Election Commission* 558 U.S. 50(2010).
[7]Two reviews of party finance in various countries are Robert Williams, ed., *Party Finance and Political Corruption* (New York: Palgrave Macmillan, 2000) and Eduardo Posada-Carbó and Carlos Malamud, eds., *The Financing of Politics: Latin American and European Perspectives* (Washington, DC: Brookings, 2005). A fine reference is Reginald Austin and Maja Tjernström, eds., *Handbook on the Funding of Political Parties and Election Campaigns* (Stockholm, Sweden: International IDEA, 2003). It is accessible, along with an associated, current database, at http://www.idea.int/parties/finance/.

→ Political Party Systems

So far I have addressed questions such as what a political party does and how it is structured. All these questions have involved a single political party, looked at by itself. Another important set of questions revolves around the pattern which political parties form in a state. We speak of a **party system** as the set of all parties. Political scientists distinguish such systems primarily by the number and relative size of the parties.[8]

A **one-party system** is one in which the government permits only a single political party. Tanzania, Syria, many other new states of the Third World, communist states like China or Cuba, and the right-wing dictatorships of Nazi Germany or Franco's Spain are examples of the one-party system. In such systems, the government and the party are closely identified, because the government enforces the rule that other parties are not allowed to be active. The party may closely control the governmental apparatus, as was the case in communist states, or those in charge of the government may have simply created the party. The party in a one-party system concentrates heavily on the tasks of mobilization, communication, and control. It cannot serve well as an alternative source of political ideas because it is so closely tied to those who are already running the state.

A **dominant-party system** is similar to the one-party system in that a single party holds power all the time, but it differs from the one-party system in that other political parties are allowed to function openly and with reasonable effectiveness; after a generation or so most eventually break the dominant party's monopoly of power.[9]

A good example of a dominant-party system is that of Mexico. This system broke down in 2000 and looks unlikely to reestablish itself, but it provides a good illustration of the system. For seventy years a single party, the Party of the Institutionalized Revolution (PRI), won every presidential election, usually with 60 to 70 percent of the vote. Those attuned to Mexican politics well understood that serious politics occurred only within the PRI. Because of this party's long dominance of politics, the whole governmental structure from the civil service on up had developed intimate ties to it, and the party had an identification with the system (which it dominated) of the sort that we observe also in one-party states. Thus, the PRI was concerned about raising electoral turnout not because it thought it would be more likely to win a high-turnout election—it would win in any case—but because the system that it dominated needed high electoral participation to build citizen support for the regime. In many ways, then, a dominant-party system is like a one-party system.

However, the fact that other parties are tolerated in the system does lead to important differences. For one thing, the existence of alternative parties provides a base for criticism of the government and guarantees that there will be more open debate about politics than in a one-party system. Alternative points of view must inevitably be openly present in a dominant-party system. The largest opposition party in Mexico, for instance,

[8]For good discussions of each of the party systems examined here, see Maurice Duverger, *Political Parties* (New York: Wiley, 1954). See also Giovanni Sartori, *Parties and Party Systems* (Cambridge, England: Cambridge University Press, 1964).
[9]See Alan Arian and Samuel Barnes, "The Dominant Party System: A Neglected Model of Democratic Stability," *Journal of Politics* 36 (August 1974), pp. 592–614. Also Ariel Levite and Sidney Tarrow, "Legitimation of Excluded Parties in Dominant Party Systems: A Comparison of Israel and Italy," *Comparative Politics* 15 (April 1983), pp. 295–327.

Michels' "Iron Law of Oligarchy"

In *Political Parties* (first published in 1915), Robert Michels argues that a political party can never be faithful to the program and constituency for which it was originally founded. For the party to vie successfully for power, he wrote, it is necessary that it be organized through a specialized division of labor in which certain people become full-time leaders. Once this has happened, however, the leadership group inevitably develops a set of values and perspectives that is different from the original aims of the party. The leaders deal daily with the enemy, sitting with them in parliament, bargaining with them; the party may develop its own stake in the status quo (many European parties, for instance, own banks, newspapers, and other business enterprises) that makes its leaders cautious about rocking the boat; and finally, it is in the leaders' interests for the party to grow as large as possible, and the easiest way to effect this is to moderate the party's positions so as to bring in new groups that had previously not been willing to support it. In short, a political party is caught in a dilemma: It may refuse to develop central leadership, in which case it will probably not attain power; or it may develop central leadership, but at the cost of losing its soul.

Political Parties was perhaps the most influential social scientific work of the twentieth century. Michels' theme has been picked up time and again to explain why parties disappoint their followers. It was popular among Eastern European critics of their communist regimes. It provided the theme of George Orwell's novel *Animal Farm*. The Green parties of several Western European states (radical environmental protection parties) have taken it to heart, with the West German Greens, at least in their early years, rotating their leadership at short intervals so that they would not develop a "leadership class."

Whether one regrets Michels' conclusion depends to some extent on whether one likes radical parties. However you feel about the question, though, two factors put it in a slightly different light:

1. All the factors that Michels sees at work (contact with the enemy, development of a stake in society, etc.) are things that occur over time. If a movement is successful quickly, we might expect to see Michels not apply. The Bolshevik seizure of power in Russia in 1917 and the Nazi seizure of power in Germany from 1930 to 1933 are two such cases, and both parties followed their original programs fairly closely. On the other hand, large communist parties attempted unsuccessfully across the second half of the twentieth century to gain power in France and Italy, and both moderated their positions considerably; in fact, the Italian party dropped the title "communist" in 1991. This suggests that for the opponents of a radical movement, "buying time" is not a trivial strategy but can systematically help to change the movement.

2. Even if Michels is right, all is not lost from the radical standpoint. It may be true that every radical party gradually becomes more moderate, yet we might also see party systems in which, over long periods of time, there were always radical parties present, because new parties would replace older parties. This apparent paradox depends on whether we look at things from the viewpoint of the individual party or of the party system. A similar paradox exists with regard to our own lives. Everyone is constantly growing older and, à la Michels, "youth is impossible to maintain." This is true for each individual, but it is not true for society because new young persons are continually being born to replace their elders. Similarly, if a party system is very open to new parties, young radical parties may always be ready at hand.

was for many years the National Action Party, a party of the middle class that had been opposed to the PRI's emphasis on labor and the poor. In 1982, for the first time, a group of socialist parties to the left of the PRI also figured significantly in a presidential election, gaining about 10 percent of the vote. In the 1988 election, the candidate of the Left almost beat the PRI candidate—and would have beaten him, most observers believe, but for fraudulent counting of the votes. The 1994 election was more genuinely competitive—and the PRI did not win automatically. In the 1997 election, the PRI lost control of the lower house of Congress and lost the powerful mayoralty of Mexico City. Finally, in 2000, Vicente Fox of the National Action Party won the presidency, the first non-PRI figure to hold the post since the constitution was written. Thus the domination of the PRI eventually broke down. This pattern of long-term dominance eventually giving way to true competition is typical of dominant party systems.

A frequent pattern associated with dominant-party systems in Third World states is for the independence movement and its leaders to form a political party once they have achieved independence. They will have been united in the movement for independence, and so it is easy for them to come together in a single party. Furthermore, the problems facing a new state are so awesome that its leaders often agree that it would be better if the state were spared internal disagreement for some time. However, once the dominant party that results from this has ruled for a few decades, it may begin to lose its dominance. Corruption may set in with a group of entrenched officials; the state, now better established, can more easily afford internal disagreements; and the issues of independence fade while new issues that may divide the old ruling group arise. This is part of what happened in Mexico; governmental corruption was one of the most important issues in the 1997 and 2000 elections.

In addition to Mexico, India and Israel provide two other examples of this pattern. For three decades after attaining independence in 1947, the Congress Party, which originated in Mohandas K. Gandhi's independence movement, dominated India's politics. Elections during this period were sure to provide a Congress majority in Parliament, and important political maneuvers occurred solely within the Congress Party. In 1977, however, Congress slipped below 50 percent of the vote and a coalition of many small, opposed parties came into power. Since then, Congress has held power much of the time, but its dominance has not been ensured in the way it was in the decades after independence.

After the state of Israel was established in 1948, the Labour Party (formed by the mainly European leaders of the Zionist movement) held nearly unchallenged power until 1977. It was a great surprise to everyone when, in that year, a coalition of opposition parties called Likud, led by Menachem Begin, defeated Labour at the polls. In this case, the usual problems of a party that had been in power too long were magnified by demographic change. In the 1950s and 1960s, there had been massive immigration into Israel of Jews from other parts of the Mideast, and by 1977, the country was split about evenly between voters of European origin and those of non-European origin. The almost exclusively European-led Labour Party had drifted badly out of touch with about half of the electorate.

A new example of a dominant party system is now developing in South Africa. In 1990 South Africa ended *apartheid*, the period of undemocratic, exclusive white domination, after a long struggle led by the African National Congress Party. In the first four elections of the new democracy, the African National Congress has received over 60 percent of the vote each time. Meanwhile, parties opposed to the African National Congress have been quite fragmented; the next-largest party in 2009 got only 17 percent of the vote, to the ANC's 66 percent.

The point of these examples is that, while a dominant-party system is similar in important ways to a one-party system, the availability of other active parties does guarantee that there will be fairly open discussion and debate, and it also provides for possible long-term flexibility and eventual adjustment to the system.

A third type is the **two-party system**. In a two-party system no one party can count on always holding power, but only two parties can normally expect to have a chance at doing so. The two major parties together will typically receive over 90 percent of the votes cast, but neither party will very often receive more than 55 or 60 percent of the vote. A prime example is the U.S. party system, in which only the Republican and Democratic parties are normally serious contenders for power. A two-party system does not necessarily have only two parties; a dozen or so parties run regularly in U.S. presidential elections, including the Libertarians and the Socialist Workers' Party. But only the two major parties generally have any real expectation of winning. Other examples of two-party or nearly two-party systems are those of Great Britain and Australia.

In contrast to a dominant-party system, a two-party system offers more regular variety and choices in policies and candidates. At the same time, a single party usually wins an election cleanly and is able to govern by itself without forming a coalition with other parties. Thus, two-party systems are typified by a certain amount of choice combined with fairly stable and straightforward governance.

The final type of party system that we will discuss here is the **multiparty system**. This system consists of more than two major parties. A good example is Norway, whose Parliament, after the election of 2009, consisted of representatives from the following parties:

Labour Party	64 seats
Progress Party (anti-tax)	41 seats
Conservative Party	30 seats
Left Socialists	11 seats
Centre Party (environmentalist, agrarian)	11 seats
Christian People's Party	10 seats
Liberal Party	2 seats

There are 169 seats, so 85 are required to control a majority vote in the parliament. Since no one party had enough seats to rule on its own, after the election the Labour Party, the Left Socialists, and the Centre Party, with 86 seats, formed a coalition to govern. The leader of the Labour party, Jens Stoltenberg, was named prime minister, since Labour was the largest member of the coalition.

Most democratic systems are multiparty systems. The one factor that seems strongly to determine whether a given state will have a two-party or a multiparty system is its electoral system. If a state uses a form of single-member district plurality electoral system, it will almost surely have a two-party system. If it uses a proportional representation system, it will almost surely have a multiparty system. The reason for this should be clear from the discussion in Chapter 10. Under a plurality system, large parties have such an advantage that small parties are driven out, until only two major parties are left.

Compared with a two-party system, a multiparty system offers the voter a wider range of choice. Not only are there more choices, but the parties are able to be more distinctive than they could be in a two-party system. In a two-party system, because a party must command half or more of all votes cast in the election to succeed, there is great pressure on both parties to appeal simultaneously to many different groups. A party may not stake out a clear appeal to farmers, for instance, because it might alienate its supporters in the cities; it cannot appeal clearly to the East because it might lose votes in the West. Such parties are apt to present a pretty fuzzy picture to the electorate. Parties in a multiparty system do not have this problem. The formation of a coalition is likely in any case; therefore, a party does not have to be huge to get some share of the power. In the Norwegian example, the Labour Party represents the special interests of the labor unions, fishing crews, and various other groups; it is a bit bland. The Conservative Party represents especially the urban middle class, who want taxes kept down and do not want moralistic constraints imposed by the state. The Christian People's Party represents devout Lutheranism and favors prohibition of liquor, religious instruction in the schools, and a ban on abortion. The Centre Party has a special concern for farmers but as these have declined in numbers it has also taken up special concerns of white-collar workers and the environment. The Left Socialists have a variety of programs but have been most noted for their opposition to Norwegian membership in NATO and protection of the environment. The Progress Party is a right-wing party sharply opposed to the welfare state and to immigration. What a "smorgasbord," compared with any existing two-party system! The voter simply has a greater range of choice in multiparty systems than in two-party systems.

However, there is a balancing advantage to the two-party system. Most of the time, multiparty systems require a coalition government to operate smoothly; therefore, a government cannot be set up unless two or more parties agree to cooperate by forming a coalition. Now this may be fine. Sweden, Norway, Finland, Germany, and other countries have been ruled by stable coalitions of one sort or another through most of their postwar history. If the need for a coalition coincides with a great deal of animosity among the political parties, however, there may be trouble. Under this combination of circumstances, it may be difficult to assemble a coalition of parties; or if one is formed, it may be torn apart by mutual mistrust before it has lasted very long. A prime example of this problem is Italy, governed by sixty-three different coalitions since 1945, many of them short-lived.[10] In 2011 Belgium went without a cabinet for over seven months when no set of parties could cooperate enough to establish a coalition.

---

[10]To address this problem, Italy changed its electoral system at the end of the century from proportional representation to a mostly single-member-district electoral system, and the 2001 election produced, for the first time, a cabinet with a stable majority of support in the parliament. (However, in 2005 the government changed the system back to a variant of a PR system, because it thought it would be more likely to win under PR than under SMDP.)

✦ POWER AND CHOICE

The disjunction between politics as choice and politics as power has led to some distortion in our view of political parties in a democracy. We have viewed the party much as what Michels wishes it could be—an instrument that expresses politically the unified choice of its members. We have viewed parties as unitary actors and have thought of them, from the standpoint of their members, predominantly in terms of choice. We have not thought of a party as consisting of various groups that may be at odds with each other and that exercise power over one another.

More often than not, a chief function of a party is to serve as a conduit by which one part may exercise power over other parts. It is this that has made the party almost as important to nondemocracies as to democracies, and we have seen that this conduit for power is also an important function of democratic parties.

Our emphasis on the party as a vehicle for expressing choice has often helped make us insensitive to its importance as a channel for the use of power. Once again, power and choice are necessary to a full understanding of politics.

EXAMPLE

The Communist Party of China

For thousands of years, China was a powerful empire, the premier force in eastern Asia. However, throughout the nineteenth century and the first half of the twentieth century, it was weak and corrupt, dominated by European powers that carved it up into spheres of influence.

During World War II the country was occupied brutally by Japan, but in the aftermath of the war, and following a further civil war, China became unified again, this time under the Communist Party, led by Mao Tse-tung. The Party established a one-party socialist state, which Mao led until his death in 1976.

Under Mao the Party saw itself as the leader of a socialist revolution and therefore would not tolerate any other political organizations, which it worried would get in the way of the revolution. It established a society in which there was very little private property. People's lives revolved around their factory or their collective farm, which provided them with housing, health care, old-age care, and care for their children.

After Mao's death a new leader, Deng Xiaoping, turned the economic direction of China on its head, shifting the country instead to a largely capitalist economy, with individually owned farms, private property, and considerable scope for entrepreneurs. Just as the Party had guided the socialist revolution, it guided this shift away from socialism as well, arguing that China needed to rapidly develop economically in order to take its rightful place in the world. It continued to ban all other political organizations, presumably because it needed clear and unified leadership to accomplish the changes that would bring rapid economic growth.

In effect, the Party first led a socialist revolution, and would allow no opposition because it required clear leadership. It then led a nationalist revolution with an emphasis on capitalism, but would still not allow opposition.

This is not to say there is no dissent or conflict under the Communist Party's rule. China has always been a big, sprawling, rather loosely organized country, and the Party simply cannot control people's lives tightly. The Party has tolerated vocal individual dissent, as long as it does not crystallize into a broader organization opposed to the Party. For the last couple of decades, for instance, there has been a lively tradition of "wall posters" on which individuals could write scathing criticism of governmental policies. More recently, a large and lively community of bloggers has developed in China. However, when the Party thinks that a group has organized formally in a way that might pose a potential threat, it comes down hard. Obviously, no other political parties are allowed, but even cultural and religious organizations like the Falun Gong sect are repressed strenuously.

Although no other organizations are allowed to maintain themselves, there are many spontaneous, unorganized demonstrations around the country that the Party worries about, but cannot really control. (I will discuss "social movements" of this sort in Chapter 13.) In 2006, there were an estimated 23,000 riots or protests in rural areas, mostly over land seizures, increases in fees, or local government corruption. One of these was a protest of 20,000 people in Hunan province against a doubling of bus fares, which was put down brutally by 1,500 police. Scores of people were injured, and one student was beaten to death.[11]

The Party rules as the sole political organization, but it rules over a rather loosely organized state. How does it maintain its central control? The Communist Party of China is a huge organization, with 80 million members. It actually has to take pains to keep itself relatively small, and has a goal of never exceeding 5 percent of the population; in 2009 20 million Chinese applied for membership in the Party, but only 2 million were admitted.[12] In order to become a member one must pass a one-year probationary period. Members are expected to implement the directives of Party leaders.

With such a large number of picked members, the Party can insert itself into all of the points of power of the state. Most judges are Party members, for instance, and subject to its discipline. Most high-ranking military officers are Party members. The Party organizes itself in committees parallel to all of the organs of the state, to keep control of them.

The Party is organized hierarchically. The top national leadership of the Party is lodged with the Politburo, a group of twenty-four officials, who in turn actually are led by their Standing Committee, a subgroup of nine members who constitute the real leaders of the state as well as the Party. (Two members of the Politburo Standing Committee, for instance, are the president and vice president of China.) Parallel

---

[11]"Rural Unrest in China," *Economic Intelligence Reports*, March 15, 2007, www.economist.com.
[12]"China's Communist Party Members Near 78 mln," Xinhua news agency, June 28, 2010. Accessed at http://news.xinhuanet.com/english2010.

270   PART IV   THE APPARATUS OF GOVERNANCE

to the Politburo is the Party's Central Military Commission, which coordinates military affairs. Below the Politburo, in descending order of scope, are provincial Party committees, prefecture Party committees, county Party committees, township Party committees, and village Party committees—all set up to coordinate with and control their respective governmental units.

The Party's control of the state apparatus is thus fairly close; however, this does not result in a lockstep, totalitarian society, partly because the Party is itself not monolithic. The same looseness that characterizes China itself also shows up in the Party. Factional conflict guarantees fairly lively political debate behind the scenes.

For instance, Party leaders introduced a new bill to define and protect private property in 2006 in the normally docile National People's Congress, but there was so much uproar about it from the left wing of the Party, who had not given up on the spirit of Mao's revolution, that it had to be pulled. It was passed the next year, in 2007, but only after the Party had taken the unusual step of banning all press coverage and pressuring universities to keep some prominent critics quiet.

 EXAMPLE

Canada's Political Parties

Canada's party system is unusual in that it has several major parties, despite having a single-member-district plurality (SMDP) electoral system.[13] Currently there are five significant parties in Canada, with shares of the vote in the 2011 election varying from 4 percent to 40 percent. These five parties are:

- The *Liberal Party*, for most of the postwar period the largest party in Canada; but as we see in Table 11.1, it recently dropped from its usual dominant position to get just 19 percent of the vote and 34 seats in the House of Commons in 2011. It had been in power for a number of years when it became embroiled in a scandal before the 2006 election over the use of national funds to put some of its supporters on the payroll of firms hired by the government. It is a broad party without a particularly clear set of programs or principles, but has generally favored holding the Canadian state together as a loose federation (i.e., not having Quebec secede to become an independent state), and has been opposed to religiously based social policies such as banning same-sex marriages. Regionally, its core strength has always been in the huge central province of Ontario (which elects about one-third of all seats in the House of Commons), plus significant strength in the other very large province, Quebec. In 2011, however, the Conservative Party beat it badly in Ontario, while the New Democratic Party did very well in Quebec.
- The *Conservative Party of Canada*. This was traditionally the second-largest party of Canada, but was almost destroyed when it lost badly in the 1993 election and limped badly thereafter.

---

[13] See the discussion of SMDP systems in Chapter 10, pp. 231–236.

TABLE 11.1

The Canadian Election of 2011

	Votes (%)	Seats
Conservative Party	39.6	166
New Democratic Party	30.6	103
Liberal Party	18.9	34
Bloc Québécois	6.0	4
Green Party	3.9	1
Other parties	0.6	0

However, one of the agents of its destruction at that time, a new "Reform Party" which arose as a fairly conservative antiparty party in 1993, merged with the remnants of the old Conservative Party just before the 2004 election, and their newly recreated Conservative Party of Canada received 30 percent of the vote and 99 seats in that election. Over the next few elections their leader, Stephen Harper, who had engineered the reunification of conservative parties in 2004, led the party through ever-larger successes to a resounding victory in 2011. Like the Liberal Party, the Conservative Party does not have a very clear set of programs, except that most of its members support religiously based social positions such as banning same-sex marriage and abolishing abortion. The Conservative Party is strongest in western Canada, where its largest share of the vote generally comes from the Prairie Provinces of Manitoba, Saskatchewan, and Alberta.

- *Bloc Québécois.* This is a regional party, operating only in Quebec, and its program is primarily just one of autonomy or independence for Quebec. From 1993, when it was founded, through the 2008 election, it held most of Quebec's seats. However, it collapsed in 2011, dropping to just 6 percent of the vote and 4 seats. The Bloc's main strength now lies in its control of the provincial government in Quebec.

- The *New Democratic Party* is a socialist party with origins in prairie populism, but also with considerable support from organized labor. It had traditionally been the fourth party in the House, but vaulted to second place in 2011, increasing its share of the vote to 31 percent from 18 percent in 2008. It is more generally spread nationally in its support than the other parties, which usually hurts it in the SMDP electoral system.

- The *Green Party* is fairly new to Canada. It drew just 4 percent of the vote in 2011, winning one seat. It espouses a "green" environmentalist program.

The explanation for one of the mysteries about Canadian parties—how a multiparty system survives the SMDP electoral system—may be evident from the descriptions above. Of the four main parties, three have distinctive regional bases of support, and as we saw in Chapter 10 (see especially p. 234), small parties with regionally concentrated support do not suffer diminution from SMDP in the same way as those with geographically broad support.

One puzzle left unexplained, however, is why the (rather) broadly based New Democratic Party did not disappear over earlier decades under this electoral system. (Before 2011, it had never done better than 18 percent of the vote.) The answer may be that it is the one large party with a truly distinctive set of positions on economic and foreign policy questions. The Bloc Québécois focuses primarily just on the Quebec question, and the other two parties are large, inclusive "umbrella" parties that until recently did not have programs that were very distinct from each other, and now differ only on rather narrow "social" issues. They woo the electorate primarily with local "pork barrel" projects rather than ideological programs.

Canadian voters are considerably more volatile than those in most other North American or European democracies, as evidenced most recently by the huge shifts in 2011.[14] Parties have fairly often come and gone over the past few decades—a "Social Credit" party based in western Canada regularly garnered from 5 to 10 percent of votes in the 1960s and 1970s, but then petered out; both the Reform Party (now gone by merger) and the Bloc Québécois popped up in 1993. Additionally, turnover in Canada's House of Commons is considerably greater than in U.S. House of Representatives elections or British House of Commons elections. Since 1935 turnover in the Canadian House has averaged about 30 percent, reaching 75 percent in the unusual election of 1993.[15]

It may be that the nonprogrammatic, patronage/pork basis of Canadian parties helps the electorate to behave in such a volatile way. Party identification in Canada is about as high as in most industrialized countries, but Canadians seem to view their parties as electoral tools rather than electoral homes. This also shows up in quite varying patterns of votes for the same party in provincial as compared to national elections. A voter may identify with one party for national purposes, but another one for provincial purposes.

Whatever the cause of the volatility, it may be salutary for the quality of democracy in Canada. Other democracies might benefit from active accountability of the Canadian sort.

---

[14]Bakvis, Herman, "Canada," in *Comparative Governance*, Primis database.
[15]Ibid., footnote 9.

KEY TERMS

political party	party system	two-party system
mobilization	one-party system	multiparty system
party identification	dominant-party system	

FURTHER READING

Aldrich, John. *Why Parties? The Origin and Transformation of Party Politics in America.* Chicago: University of Chicago Press, 1995.

Cohen, Marty, Karol, David, Noel, Hans, and Zaller, John. *The Party Decides: Presidential Nominations Before and After Reform.* Chicago: University of Chicago Press, 2008.

Dalton, Russell J., Farrell, David M., and McAllister, Ian. *Political Parties and Democratic Linkage: How Parties Organize Democracy.* New York: Oxford University Press, 2011.

Duverger, Maurice. *Political Parties.* London: Methuen, 1954.

Hale, Henry E. *Why Not Parties in Russia?* New York: Cambridge University Press, 2005.

Hershey, Marjorie Randon. *Party Politics in America.* 15th ed. New York: Longman, 2012.

McCormick, Richard L., ed. *Political Parties and the Modern State.* New Brunswick, NJ: Rutgers University Press, 1984.

Panebianco, Angelo. *Political Parties: Organization and Power.* New York: Cambridge University Press, 1988.

Scheiner, Ethan. *Democracy Without Competition in Japan: Opposition Failure in a One-Party Dominant State.* New York: Cambridge University Press, 2005.

Stokes, Susan C. "Political Parties and Democracy." *Annual Review of Political Science* 2 (1999): pp. 243–67.

Webb, Paul, Farrell, David, and Holliday, Ian, eds. *Political Parties in Advanced Industrial Democracies.* New York: Oxford University Press, 2002.

CHAPTER 12

STRUCTURED CONFLICT:
INTEREST GROUPS AND POLITICS

In Chapter 11, we distinguished the political party from the interest group. A party is concerned with the process of leadership selection and the organization of government, while an interest group is concerned primarily with trying to affect what those in power do. *The **interest group** is an organized group of citizens, whose central political goal is to ensure that the state follows certain policies.*

All sorts of organized groups may function as interest groups. Some are organized solely to lobby governmental officials on behalf of one or another cause. The Sierra Club, a U.S. organization that lobbies for the preservation of wilderness areas, is an example of such an organization. Other groups may be organized primarily for other purposes but take on lobbying and other ways of influencing policy as an important task. Examples of such groups are labor unions, primarily organized to bargain with an employer but also usually active politically. Still others focus on other goals but give some attention to politics. An example would be a university, whose first concern is to educate students and conduct research but which is likely to maintain one or two people to lobby the government on bills that concern it. A number of interest "groups" are individual corporations that lobby the government for a contract or a regulatory decision.

There are many interest groups in a modern state, so many that it is hard to form a precise idea of their numbers. Table 12.1 presents a reasonably good census of interest groups in Germany in the mid-1990s. Note how many of these are economic interest groups (industrial organizations, trade unions, and professional organizations); this is fairly typical of industrialized countries. However, noneconomic groups have been growing relative to economic groups; this is also fairly typical, at least for Western European and North American countries. In a comparable census of interest groups in Germany twenty years earlier in 1974, 79 percent of all groups were economic groups.

TABLE 12.1

German Interest Groups, 1994, by Type

Category	Number of Organizations	
Economic	65%	
Corporate groups		41%
Unions		5%
Professions		15%
Other		3%
General	35%	
Ideological		3%
Social help		16%
Cultural		11%
Recreation, sports		2%
Environmental		3%

SOURCE: Martin Sebaldt, *Organisierter Pluralismus* (Opladen, Germany: Westdeutscher Verlag GmbH, 1997), pp. 79–82.

We can see from Table 12.1 that by 1994, this figure had dropped to 65 percent. The major gainers over the twenty years were cultural, recreational, and environmental groups.

No one knows exactly how many different interest groups a large and diverse country such as the United States has, but there must be many thousands.[1] In 1997, statistics indicated that an estimated thirty-five hundred to four thousand interest groups lobbied the German government in Bonn.[2] The 1996 directory of pressure groups lobbying the European Union offices counted over seventeen hundred groups, about 80 percent of which were corporate or trade associations; the other 20 percent consisted of unions and humanitarian and religious groups.[3]

Interest groups are not confined to democracies or open societies. All states have interest groups. Some do not permit a wide diversity of formally organized, politically active groups to exist, since this would seem threatening to their governments. However, even in such states, organizations set up for other purposes—the army, universities, natural history clubs, scientific associations, sports clubs, factories—exert political influence to help mold government policies.

---

[1] One estimate is that there were approximately 24,000 national interest groups active in the United States in 1995. Beyond this, there were many local interest groups that were not active in Washington. Martin Sebaldt, *Transformation der Verbändedemokratie: Die Modernisierung des Systems Organisierter Interresen in den USA* (Wiesbaden, Germany: Westdeutscher Verlag, 2001), p. 48. In 2007 there were 14,868 registered lobbyists in Washington, DC, up from 10,693 in 1998 (Center for Responsive Politics, www.opensecrets.org, accessed August 2012). 2007 is the last year for which an accurate number is available. The number of registered lobbyists dropped after that year, but only because of new regulations that were instituted in that year; many lobbyists avoided registering so as not to come under the new egulations. In 2011, 12,654 lobbyists were registered, compared with over 14,000 in 2007, but no one believes there were actually fewer lobbyists in 2011 than in 2007.

[2] Thomas Saalfeld, "Germany: From Dictatorship to Parliamentary Democracy," *Parliamentary Affairs* 50 (July 1997), p. 386.

[3] Alan Butt Philip and Oliver Gray, eds., *Directory of Pressure Groups in the EU* (London: Cartermill, 1996).

The liquor and restaurant lobbies appear to have been feeding Congress's habit.

A 1998 Herblock Cartoon, © The Herb Block Foundation.

→ Interest Groups and Representation

Interest groups are probably the main vehicle in most states for representing public opinion and bringing it to bear in an organized (and therefore effective) way on the governmental authorities. Political parties cannot do this very well, because they are involved in trying to acquire governmental power for themselves. This quest for power forces parties to incorporate many compromises in their programs in order to appeal to the broadest spectrum. If the state is a democracy, this may take the form of an attempt to appeal to a wide range of voters; if the state is not a democracy, it may mean trying to have such a broad appeal that neither the army, the air force, the navy, urban workers, the church, nor any other major group will try to overthrow them. Whatever the case, a political party, by virtue of its most basic goal, cannot serve to articulate and represent any one group's wishes. It has a different task: to blend various wishes into a larger coalition. The party seeks to make differences fuzzy, but an interest group is free to present its group's wishes clearly and precisely. The task of representing the people's desires, then, falls primarily on the interest group. How well do interest groups do this?

Interest groups usually accomplish this fairly well; otherwise, they would not be the workhorses of political advocacy that they are. However, there are four important barriers that keep interest groups from functioning as well in this area as we might wish:

1. *Many interests do not become fully organized as interest groups, because of the problem of public goods and free riders.* As explained in the box "The Logic of Collective Action," interest groups are another instance of the problem of public goods, which we introduced in Chapter 3 in connection with the state (see the discussion, pp. 55–57). As you recall from that chapter, a public good is something which, if produced, cannot possibly be denied to anyone in the affected group. We saw, for instance, that certain actions of the state, like providing national defense, are public goods for the citizens of the state. In the case of interest groups, the fruits of their political activity are a public good for their members and potential members. If the group succeeds in getting a new law passed, it cannot make that law apply only to the members who have joined and contributed to the interest group. The law will apply to all citizens, whether or not they helped to pass it.

   This means that the potential members of the group may be inclined to save their dues money and not join the group, because they can enjoy the benefits of the group's activity whether they have joined or not. They will be **free riders.** What is rational for the individual may be bad for the group, however, because if most potential members choose to be free riders the group may never form at all or may be small and weak. In the end everyone in the group, free riders and members alike, will suffer.

   Some groups find it easier than others to overcome the free rider problem. (See the box for a discussion of some of the ways they can do this.) In particular, the group may offer **selective benefits**—benefits that *can* be withheld from anyone who does not join the group. For instance, the National Automobile Dealers Association (NADA) in the United States is a powerful lobbying group that helps to shape national regulation of retail car sales. Anything it can accomplish in the area of regulation is a public good for its potential members, so they could be very tempted to be free riders. However, besides its lobbying work the NADA offers its members advice and information on laws and regulations, develops research data on the industry which it distributes to members, runs training programs for dealers and their staff, provides employee benefits plans for dealers, and offers discounts on PCs and other IT equipment. All of these added benefits can be restricted just to members, so many potential members who might otherwise decide to be free riders with regard to the organization's lobbying efforts choose to join in order to receive the selective benefits. As a result, 91 percent of United States new-vehicle dealers are members of NADA.

   Not all groups are in a position to offer such attractive selective benefits, however, so some groups are weakly organized while others are strong.

2. *Aside from the problem of free riders, there are other factors that mean not all interests will be equally well organized.* Groups whose members have enough leisure to be active in politics are likely to enlist more of their potential clientele than other groups. Similarly, we see high enrollment among interests whose members are concentrated in particular localities, rather than spread out; have a

TABLE 12.2

Percentage of Eligible Employees in the United States Who Are Enrolled in Labor Organizations, by Industry, 2011

Type of Industry	
Agriculture	1
Mining	7
Construction	14
Manufacturing	11
Transportation and public utilities	21
Leisure and hospitality	3
Finance, insurance, real estate	2
Government	37

SOURCE: U.S. Bureau of Labor Statistics, *Union Membership*, Press Release January 27, 2012, Table 3.

basic economic stake in the outcome of politics; or are well educated. Table 12.2, for example, lists enrollment percentages for labor organizations in several different occupational groups.

Perhaps the most universal and significant break between groups that are readily organized and those that are difficult to organize is represented by "producer" interests and "consumer" interests. A producer interest is any group of people involved in producing something. For any product, there may be a few producer interests: a corporation, a trade union, one or more professional organizations. Examples of producer interests are Microsoft Corporation, the AFL-CIO, the American Medical Association, and the National Farmers' Union—any economic entity made up of those who produce something. A consumer interest is a group of people consuming a product. Examples would include the National Association of Homebuyers and the American Automobile Association; it is harder to come up with examples of consumer groups, however, because most groups of people who share in consuming a product are not formally organized.

To take one example, every family in the United States pays about $40 more for food each year because of import restrictions on sugar that the powerful American Sugar Alliance of sugar growers defends.[4] The higher cost of sugar shows up not only in candies and soft drinks, but feeds through to the cost of many other sorts of food, such as mayonnaise and bread. That is a significant added expense for a family, but it is not sufficiently large that they would give up evenings and weekends to organize against it.

---

[4]Calculated from O. Gokcekus, J. Knowles, and E. Tower, "Sweetening the Pot: How American-Sugar Buys Protection," in Devashish Mitra and Arvind Panagariaya, eds., *The Political Economy of Trade, Aid and Foreign Investment Policies* (Amsterdam: Elsevier, 2004), p. 178. (calculated for a family of four in 1998)

Migrant farm workers, Imperial Valley, California. Moving frequently, working long hours, lacking education and political skills, such workers find it difficult to organize themselves for political action. Note in Table 12.2 that only 1 percent of agricultural workers are in labor organizations.

© Peter Menzel/Stock Boston

However, that money accumulates across the country to $3.9 billion, which is concentrated on sugar cane growers in Florida, Louisiana, and Hawaii; beet sugar growers in a few states in the northern plains; and a few sugar processing plants. The money is enough to make a difference of 10 or 20 percent—or more—in the profits of the companies and the earnings of their workers, and that is something for which people *will* give up evenings and weekends. Washington is saturated with letters, campaign contributions, and lobbying visits from the affected companies and their workers—but hears very little from the people who bear the extra costs. While the producers are strongly organized to support the restrictions, there is very little organized opposition to them.

The bias of interest group activity toward producer groups pervades a wide range of policies—from regulations on telecommunications, finance, and other areas to product safety and the prices that consumers pay. The difference between producers and consumers holds in many other countries, not just in the United States. In a survey of German interest groups, for instance, 61 percent of all interest groups were corporate groups, unions, or professional associations. Only 3 percent were "other" economic groups, mostly consumer groups.[5]

As a result of these and other disparities, some interest groups can speak strongly and confidently as representatives of their interest, and they are listened to with respect.

---

[5]Martin Sebaldt, *Organisierter Pluralismus* (Opladen, Germany: Westdeutscher Verlag GmbH, 1997), pp. 79–82.

Other interest groups, which formally represent only a small percentage of their potential clientele, must speak with a more muted voice. The overall system of interest groups, as a result, does not represent all interests equally well. Those that are easy to organize bulk larger in the system, and their voices are heard more loudly than they deserve to be on the basis of their numbers.

3. *Also, some groups command a disproportionate voice in the interest-group system because they have special advantages.* Consider the following examples:

   - In almost all Western countries, business groups have influence beyond what one would expect based on the size of their memberships. They gain added influence for several reasons: they have a great deal of money to spend on politics; they have a good deal of expertise in advertising and organization, which they can use to political benefit; and the well-being of the country is so closely tied to their own well-being that others must listen to them with respect.
   - In many states whose governments are shaky, large landowners or corporations as a group gain exaggerated political influence because of their ties to the army, which may be expected to intervene politically on their behalf.
   - In Israel over past decades, rather small groups of fundamentalist Jewish sects have wielded influence out of proportion to their numbers because the Likud and Labour parties have been so evenly matched in elections that the small religious parties have held the balance of power.
   - In almost all countries with much coastline, the fishing industry has had disproportionate influence because its members are concentrated in what are often key locations politically and because they are willing to go to great lengths to protect their livelihood and their traditional way of life. (It is for this reason, for instance, that it has been so difficult for other countries to get Japan to stop the hunting of whales, even though only a few thousand members of Japan's huge labor force are involved in the whaling industry.)

Such examples are numerous. Partly because not all interests are equally well organized and because some have special advantages such as these, the sum total of interest-group representation may give quite a distorted picture of the interests in a country.

4. *Finally, most interest groups lack structures to ensure that leaders will be closely responsive to the members' wishes.* The leaders of an interest group are usually able to build a base of support within the group's administrative structure and among its members, which makes it difficult to unseat them. Even where the group's members elect the leader periodically—as is true of most labor unions, for instance—an "inside" group usually dominates the election, so that the same person is elected year after year.[6] Many interest groups—such as universities, armies, and corporations—are not even set up to allow periodic elections.

---

[6]Seymour Martin Lipset, Martin A. Trow, and James S. Coleman explored an exception to this rule in *Union Democracy* (Garden City, N.Y.: Doubleday, 1962). Another, more recent example was the running battle during the 1990s between the reform and the traditional factions in the Teamsters union.

TABLE 12.3

Percentage of Members Who Would Stay in the Association If It Did Not Lobby at All

Minnesota Farm Bureau	77
Minnesota Farmers' Union	63
Minnesota Retail Federation	57
Minnesota-Dakotas Hardware Association	70
Printing Industries of the Twin Cities	94

SOURCE: From *The Organization of Interests* by Terry M. Moe, The University of Chicago Press, 1980. Copyright © 1980 The University of Chicago Press. Reprinted with permission.

The internal structure of interest groups is not very democratic; therefore, there is a real danger that their leaders may gradually drift away from the ordinary members and follow their own political line. Democratic accountability to the membership could prevent this, but in its absence, there is little to keep it from happening.

We might expect that the free market would provide a control over this. That is, if the leaders drifted too far from the ordinary members, the latter would be able to "vote with their feet" and join a competing group. For example, there are many different conservation societies, and so we might expect that if some members of, say, Friends of the Earth did not like their leaders' positions, they would drop their membership and join some other group, such as the National Wildlife Association.

The trouble with this solution is that the situation with regard to conservation groups is rather atypical. Often, a group's political positions are not major factors determining an individual's continued membership in the group, since group leaders rely heavily on selective benefits—above and beyond their political activity—to keep members in the group and prevent them from becoming free riders. This is especially true of economic interest groups. For most union members, the important thing is how skillful their union is in negotiating a good contract with their employer. Another important consideration is the package of extra benefits the union can provide, such as low-cost group insurance, educational and entertainment programs, and low-cost package vacations. For many members, the union's political activity is a weak runner-up among the things that matter to them.[7]

A survey of several business and agricultural associations asked members whether they would stay in their association if it stopped its political activity altogether but continued to offer them the other benefits they enjoyed. Table 12.3 shows that a majority of each group said that the association's other benefits (i.e., their selective benefits) were important enough to them that they would continue their membership even if the group did nothing in politics.

If the selective benefits available through an organization are sufficiently attractive, they can provide the organization's leaders with a great deal of leeway in their

---

[7]Mancur Olson, *The Logic of Collective Action* (Cambridge: Harvard University Press, 1965).

The Logic of Collective Action

One of the more interesting works of abstract theory in the social sciences is Mancur Olson's *The Logic of Collective Action* (Cambridge: Harvard University Press, 1965). This was one of the earliest works to develop the general problem of public goods (you will recall from Chapter 3 that a public good is one that no member of the group can be prevented from enjoying). However, it was developed particularly to account for when interest groups organize or do not organize. Olson notes that organized groups will be plagued by the problem of public goods. Even if a business owner does not join the local chamber of commerce, for example, he or she will still benefit from its lobbying activities with the government. To Olson, this means that the potential members of the group will be inclined to be free riders.

Olson notes four possibilities that help to explain how one might be able to organize groups in spite of the problem of collective goods:

1. If a group is sufficiently small, it may be easier to organize. Each member's contribution is then not trivially small, and so all potential members can see that there will be less of the public good available if they withhold their contribution to the group.
2. The group may offer selective benefits, such as life insurance programs or travel packages, that they can withhold from those who do not enter the group.
3. The group may be able to coerce members to join whether they wish to or not. The closed shop is an example of this in labor relations. In "neocorporatist" systems (see pp. 294–296), the government may require that the group form so that it can help to carry out the government's policies.
4. If one member of the group bulks large relative to the others, then that member may see that the public good would be impossible to attain without its participation. Therefore, that member may join and carry things forward even though smaller members who do not join get a free ride. The largest department store in town, for instance, can hardly avoid joining the chamber of commerce. For a slightly different "group," this helps to explain why the United States figures so importantly in the NATO alliance and provides its smaller allies with a partially free ride.

Note that of the four possibilities, the first, second, and fourth are concerned only with politics as choice. The third, which I drew from a later chapter of Olson's book because it actually does not appear in his core chapter, takes into account that decisions in politics are made through the use of power. This emphasis on choice rather than on power in politics is typical of models based on economic theory (like Olson's).

choice of political positions. Leaders of labor unions, for instance, have been able to take political positions varying from rather conservative Republican (the Teamsters union in the United States, at various times) to communist (many French and Italian unions).[8]

---

[8]An added factor that may hold members in groups and that certainly operates in the case of many labor unions is coercion. "Union shop" contracts often require that a worker must be a member of the union to hold a job.

For all of these reasons, the overall result of lobbying and other political activity on the part of a state's interest-group leaders may be unrepresentative of the overall wishes of the population.

As a few examples of how the interest-group system may distort public opinion, consider the following:

- In Israel, in deference to small orthodox groups, the national airline El Al does not fly on the Sabbath even though it is expensive to have the planes sit idle and most Israelis would prefer to have Sabbath flights.[9]

- In the United States, a majority of those sampled in public opinion polls have at most times since polling began favored tighter regulation of handguns. However, the National Rifle Association has effectively blocked such laws in most localities.

- In countries with state-run television networks, programming is almost always more "educational" (and dull) than the people would prefer. Leaders of cultural associations are in part responsible for this.

✦ TYPES OF INTEREST GROUPS

Three major types of interest groups are **sectoral interest groups, institutional interest groups,** and **promotional interest groups**:

1. Sectoral Groups. Sectoral groups are those that represent a sector of the economy— a corporation, a union, an association of members of a profession, or, less frequently, a consumer group. Examples include the National Manufacturers' Association, Ford Motor Company, the National Farmers' Union, the AFL-CIO, and the American Automobile Association. Since these are groups associated with the economy, they often combine great financial resources with fairly narrow concerns. An industrial organization might find, for instance, that the issue making the greatest difference to its members' earnings is an obscure and highly technical rule about depreciation rates, a rule that falls below most other groups' radar. With its resources, the organization can vigorously pursue changing that rule. Needless to say, sectoral groups are usually effective. They also dominate most interest-group systems. We saw in Table 12.1 that 65 percent of Germany's interest groups are "economic" (sectoral).

2. Institutional Groups. Institutional groups are set up primarily for purposes other than political activity and would certainly exist even if they did not deal with politics; they become politically active only to defend their own interests in the state's policy decisions. Examples of this sort of group would include an army, set up to defend the state, that may become active—even dominant—in the politics of the state to help the defense budget and further the common interests of its members; a public university, set up to educate students and conduct research, that may hire lobbyists to procure a

---

[9]In 2004, the Israeli government transferred El Al to private owners—in part to get it out of politics and to allow it to stop losing money because of shutting down for one day each week. In 2006 the airline did begin to schedule Sabbath flights, but after a boycott by ultra-orthodox Israelis, the airline backed down and promised not to fly on the Sabbath.

2013 MacNelly Archive

larger annual budget from the government; or the Red Cross, set up to help people in emergencies, that lobbies actively for national emergency help grants.

3. Promotional Groups. Promotional groups organize around an idea or a point of view—to support an ethnic group, a foreign policy position, religious values, a position on the environment, a recreational activity, or whatever. These are the groups we commonly think of first when we hear the words "interest group."

Around the world, promotional interest groups have increased in recent decades. We noted in connection with Table 12.1 that the fastest-growing categories of interest groups in Germany from 1974 to 1994 were the cultural, recreational, and environmental groups. In Britain, the Royal Society for the Protection of Birds has more members than the three major political parties combined, with membership in 2010 of over one million people. Amnesty International, an organization that campaigns against political oppression, has 360,000 members.[10] Fathers4Justice, a deliberately disruptive "guerrilla" interest group promoting fathers' rights (in 2004 they pelted the prime minister with purple flour bombs), has 6,500 members.

Promotional interest groups appear to be especially important in the politics of the United States, compared with most other states of the world. This is probably because (1) United States parties are weaker and less unified on policy than most other states' parties and thus are not well equipped to lead in a debate over ideas; and (2) the two-party system does not provide room for small, specialized parties such as Israel's religious parties, able to directly seek a portion of the governmental power through participation in coalitions.

---

[10]360,000 members in the United States; worldwide, Amnesty International has approximately 3 million members.

Instead, those seeking to pursue a policy goal in the United States must usually operate indirectly through an interest group to influence those who have attained power.

Some examples of powerful promotional interest groups in the United States are the National Rifle Association, MoveOn.org, National Right to Life, the Sierra Club, the NAACP, and Focus on the Family. The National Rifle Association has about 4.3 million members, more than one out of every one hundred Americans.

In contrast to the promotional groups, sectoral groups probably vary less in their role from one state to another. The economy is such a central part of any modern society that sectoral interest groups have a natural entrée to government everywhere. Therefore, their presence and their activities are probably less variable than is true of promotional interest groups. Nearly every state has a politically active manufacturers' association, for instance, but promotion of feminist goals varies widely from one state to another. Some states such as the United States and Sweden have active feminist groups—although in Sweden, this interest is channeled somewhat more through political parties—while in others such as Japan, there is almost no feminist presence.

✦ TACTICS OF INTEREST GROUPS

The tactics an interest group will use are determined by the sources of its power and by the opportunities that the political system offers for the use of power. An interest group with many members but little money will concentrate on tactics that take advantage of numbers rather than money, while a group with few members but plenty of money will follow different tactics. We may expect groups that have similar sources of power but find themselves faced with different sorts of political structures to follow different tactics. In their political activity, U.S. labor unions, for instance, emphasize electoral activity and campaign contributions to public officials. For Solidarity, the labor union that transformed the politics of Poland in the 1970s and 1980s in spite of suppression by the communist government, these focuses of political activity were not available, and so it concentrated instead on sit-ins and mass demonstrations.

Let us look specifically at several tactics available to interest groups in a democracy. What leads a group to choose one or more of these?

1. **Lobbying.** When representatives of the group meet with officials regarding a law or regulation, this is **lobbying.** In the United States, lobbyists experienced in Washington decision making can help a group affect national decisions. Lobbying firms often employ former members of Congress, cabinet officials, or Congressional staffers to help present their positions to Congress and the administration. These former players know how to frame arguments in a way that will influence government officials; they know how decisions are made; and they are often intimately familiar with the details of the particular policies in which they specialized. While both former members of Congress and cabinet officials can help to arrange contact with current officials, whom they knew when they served, former staffers may have more thorough knowledge of policies and procedures than former officials.

The public's picture of lobbying generally involves a lobbyist persuading a member of Congress to do what the member otherwise would not do—often because of a large campaign contribution from the lobbyist's group. Certainly, contributions are a factor in lobbying, but the reality of lobbying is more subtle than that picture. Most of the time lobbyists approach legislators who already agree with them or are likely to do so. They are less likely to approach a Congress member whom they already know to be opposed to the group, since for many reasons the odds of changing that member's mind are usually low.[11] Perhaps the member has long-standing, close ties to the other side, or perhaps the member represents a district that would be hurt by the lobbyist's proposal. The member may also have a strong, well-known ideological position that is inconsistent with the proposal. For whatever reason the lobbyist is likely to avoid that member, and approach members who are already likely to favor the proposal.

If lobbyists are not typically trying to persuade a member of Congress, what do they talk about when they meet? To a large extent, lobbyists view the member as a potential ally on their proposal. In their visit they extend an invitation to collaborate on the proposal. They draw on their own technical expertise and present the member with in-depth policy analyses and sound arguments to use in debate. Sometimes, they will even offer the member special studies that show the impact their proposal would have on a particular group (hog farmers, auto dealers, or perhaps all of the people in the member's district). Lobbyists may assist in crafting legislative language for a bill. They may report to the member how other members feel about the issue, and recommend which officials they've identified as key people with whom they can bargain. They can offer a headcount of how many members are already committed on either side of the proposal. All of these strategies help a member who is already inclined to support the group, and thus increase the group's chances of success.

Members of Congress are generalists, while lobbyists are specialists, so the relationship between them is mutually beneficial. On top of the many varied demands on the Congress members' time, they also have to deal with a wide range of bills. Lobbyists do not face the same demands on their time, because they work on one policy area, mastering it in depth. Therefore, lobbyists can offer members of Congress detailed policy information and valuable political advice on an issue, which members simply do not have time enough to gather for themselves.[12]

Politico.com, an excellent online political news source, has a dedicated page on lobbying activities at http://www.politico.com/lobbying/. Even lobbyists have an interest group! Visit the home page of the American League of Lobbyists at http://www. alldc.org/

2. Outside Lobbying. One tactic that groups use to supplement their lobbying is "outside" lobbying, in which an interest group uses its members to help its lobbyists influence a bill. Obviously, for this tactic to be effective, the group needs a large membership that is committed enough to write, send emails, phone, or come to Washington for a "lobbying

---

[11] Marie Hojnacki and David C. Kimball, "Organized Interests and the Decision of Whom to Lobby in Congress," *American Political Science Review* 92:4 (December, 1998), pp. 775–790; Richard L. Hall and Alan V. Deardorff, "Lobbying as Legislative Subsidy," *American Political Science Review* 100:1 (February, 2006), pp. 69–84.
[12] Richard L. Hall and Alan V. Deardorff, *op. cit.*

day" with their members of Congress. Groups like the NRA or Planned Parenthood can rely on members and supporters to help in their efforts, and these activities can be very effective. As one congressional staff member described his boss's vote to repeal catastrophic health insurance a year after having voted in favor of it:

> It was a no-brainer. He got over five thousand letters for the repeal of the insurance, and literally eight letters in favor of the current insurance. He didn't have much choice really. He had to vote for repeal.[13]

A barrage of letters, phone calls, or emails is a way for the interest group to flex its muscle and demonstrate that it can mobilize large groups of people. The politician or official has to believe that a group member committed enough to go to the trouble of writing a letter or traveling to Washington might also vote as the group advises, so the member typically takes the group seriously.

3. Control of Information and Expertise. Sometimes the members of an interest group control specialized information that is important to the government—even information that the government may need if it is to control the group. Doctors, for example, are the only people with the necessary expertise to judge the quality of medical treatment. Scientists are the only ones sufficiently skilled technically to judge a variety of scientific questions. Oil corporations know more about the oil business than anyone else. In all these cases, a government that wishes to make policy relating to an interest group must depend on the members of the group for the necessary information and expertise. This gives the group a great deal of power, because the resulting interpretation of things is likely to be slanted a good deal toward the group's prejudices. It does not require that anyone operate dishonestly. Everyone always has a certain slant on things, and if the members of an interest group are the only ones giving the government analysis and interpretation, their slant will inevitably enter the picture.

This tactic requires that relevant information and technical skills be scarce. Labor unions, religious groups, or hobby organizations cannot make good use of the tactic, because the skills and information they have are widely available. A dramatic example of power based on the control of information appeared in lawsuits and investigations in 2006, where it was revealed that the United States Department of the Interior had no independent source of information on how much oil companies were drilling on public lands. It had to rely on the companies to tell the government how much they were drilling.

4. Electoral Activity. Electoral activity is especially suitable for groups with a large number of members who are at least moderately committed. Such a group may raise money from among its members to contribute to candidates, provide campaign workers to candidates, and deliver its own members' votes for candidates—all in an effort to ensure that people favorably disposed to the group end up in office. If the members of the group are not sufficiently committed to it to choose their vote on the basis of its recommendations, this tactic is of little use; an automobile club, for instance, would

---

[13]Ken Kollman, *Outside Lobbying: Public Opinion and Interest Group Strategies* (Princeton, NJ: Princeton University Press, 1998), p. 5.

not be able to deliver its members' votes. Groups that have used this tactic success-fully include labor unions, large religious organizations, and ethnic groups. Some other special organizations such as the National Rifle Association in the United States or the wine growers of France have also been successful in this way.

5. Use of Economic Power. An interest group of economic importance to the state may influence the state by threatening to disrupt its economic contribution. Strategi-cally placed unions, such as those of railroad or postal workers, have often been able to enlist the government's help by threatening a strike that would be catastrophically dis-ruptive to the state. Businesses often threaten communities by telling them that if they don't give them tax advantages or other considerations, they will move their operations elsewhere. Professional sports franchises have been particularly skillful at this kind of threat, forcing communities to provide them with subsidies and build stadiums to house them. The civil rights movement of the 1960s in the United States gained great impetus when an unknown preacher named Martin Luther King, Jr. organized a boy-cott of the city bus system of Montgomery, Alabama, to force the city to allow blacks to sit anywhere they wished on the buses. Similarly, economic boycotts of white businesses were an effective tool for blacks in South Africa in the late 1980s. At some times, as in Czechoslovakia in 1989 or Bolivia in 2005, a general strike in which all unions stop working at the same time has been used to try to force the whole government out of office.

This tactic requires that a large economic stake be maneuverable. That is, the group must be able to turn on or turn off a large enough part of the economy to threaten dire results. This can be accomplished either by a single large corporation, for which it is usually fairly easy, or by a large number of people who, though they are not indi-vidually that important to the economy, are willing to coordinate economic disruption (a strike or boycott) so that their combined impact is important.

6. Contributions. Another, considerably cheaper, way by which groups can use eco-nomic power is in contributions to political candidates. Here the group does not use its economic strength to produce the threat of disruption but rather to buy access to political leaders, and it is sometimes astonishing how cheaply they can buy influence in this way. Contributions in the hundreds of thousands of dollars may net a corpora-tion or trade group a special provision in a bill that is worth many millions of dollars to it. Ballooning expenditures on political campaigns in the United States have made political leaders more dependent on interests that can provide money. Around the world, states vary considerably with regard to the importance of interest groups' money for campaigns, depending on election laws and on custom. In most European states, campaign expenditures are regulated and do not bulk as large as they do in the United States. Japan, on the other hand, is another state where the appetite of parties for cam-paign finance is insatiable.

The Center for Responsive Politics is a research group that tracks money in U.S. politics and its effect on elections and public policy. It has a searchable database of organizations (like the Sierra Club), lobbying firms, and individual lobbyists (http://www.opensecrets.org/lobby/). You can also find the top spenders and top lobbying firms.

7. Public Information Campaigns. A group that does not necessarily have a large mass base but does have substantial access to the media may try to change policy by the most indirect of means—by changing the minds of the entire population in the hope that this will influence government policy. Institutional interest groups frequently use this tactic, because many other tactics are barred to them. The U.S. Air Force, for instance, helps to encourage movies that put the Air Force in a good light. Government agencies in all states use "public service advertisements" which provide information such as health advice and moral admonition to keep themselves in the public eye while they also accomplish indirectly a secondary goal of the advertisements: to build public support for the agency.

This tactic is also useful for an interest group with enough money to buy advertising time, especially if other tactics do not look promising. A famous success in the early 1990s was a series of ads sponsored by insurance companies in which "Harry and Louise" sat at their kitchen table and talked about why President Bill Clinton's proposed health plan would harm their health care. The ads were widely credited with turning public opinion against Clinton's proposals. You can see the "Harry and Louise" ads, with commentary from CSPAN, at http://www.youtube.com/watch?v=CwOX2P4s-Iw.

In the United States in the 1990s, this technique was further refined as interest groups learned to target public opinion in the districts of members of Congress who were seen as swing votes on important bills. In 2009, labor unions and business groups targeted select states and congressional districts with television advertisements arguing for and against a proposed bill to make it possible to unionize workplaces without a campaign and secret-ballot election. They chose states and districts where they thought Senators or members might be led to change their vote if public opinion shifted.

8. Litigation. In litigation an interest group attempts to affect policy by working within the court system. The historic reversal of segregated schooling in the United States began in this way when, in 1954, the National Association for the Advancement of Colored People (NAACP) sponsored a constitutional test of segregation in the courts. A black student, with the help of the NAACP, sued her school board to force it to admit her to the white school, and she won.[14]

Through court cases, an interest group may hope to change the interpretation of a law or, in some countries, even get it thrown out as unconstitutional. Also, court procedures can be so slow and expensive that the mere threat of tying a governmental agency up in court may get the agency to compromise.

However, litigation is a strategy based on weakness. For a group to be successful at litigation, it must depend on the way the law was initially written—something over which it has little control if litigation is its main tactic. It must depend on finding a sympathetic court, which is also rather chancy. The great appeal of litigation is that it does not require large numbers (all one has to have is a lawyer) or enormous economic power. Therefore, it appeals particularly to small weak groups. Groups that have depended fairly heavily on litigation in the United States include environmentalists,

[14] *Brown v. Board of Education*, 347 U.S. 483(1954).

the handicapped, and groups favoring abortion rights. These are relatively weak groups that have often been on the defensive.[15]

9. Demonstrations, Protests, and Boycotts. Interest groups occasionally use tactics that are outside the political process, such as demonstrations, protests, and boycotts. These tactics are highly visible and are meant to help sway broad public opinion. They can be very effective under some circumstances—the Civil Rights Movement in the 1960s was built on demonstrations, marches, and boycotts—but they often do not have much effect. They can be most effective when a group strikes a sympathetic chord with the public that might have been difficult to tap except by showing the determination of its members. Civil rights demonstrations and Gay Pride parades have both been successful in this way. Antiwar demonstrations can be effective if a war is broadly unpopular, but they usually do not have much effect if there is not a broad underlying uneasiness about the war.

In general, groups emphasize demonstrations and protests if they have a devoted membership and broad support in the population, but lack other resources. Most well-organized interest groups that have significant resources do not use demonstrations and protests as a tactic. For social movements, which we examine in the next chapter, demonstrations are a major tactic, since they lack the resources for most other sorts of activity.

10. Coalition Formation. A frequent tactic of interest groups is to form a coalition with other groups that are on the same side of an issue. Members of a coalition pool their resources and help each other. Almost every major bill involves coalitions of groups on both sides of the bill. Occasionally coalitions can create strange bedfellows. Some conservative evangelical Christian groups worked with labor unions and immigrant groups in the United States in 2010 to try to pass a bill making it easier for illegal immigrants to become citizens.[16] The evangelical groups would not usually be on the same side of the issues as liberal groups, but they were drawn into the coalition by their concern for Hispanic church members and by Christian doctrine.

One notable type of coalition involves bringing together a group with ample financial and lobbying resources, but lacking public sympathy, with another group that has fewer financial resources but greater public sympathy.[17] Ethanol producers such as Archer Daniels Midland have often worked with environmental and clean air groups, for instance, to support bills mandating that a certain proportion of gasoline be ethanol-based. In another example, telecommunications companies pushed in the early 2000s for a bill to eliminate the 3 percent excise tax on telecommunications. While they paid all the expenses of the lobbying campaign, they asked a number of citizen and consumer groups (whose members would benefit from the reduction in the price of

---

[15]See, for example, Susan M. Olson, *Clients and Lawyers: Securing the Rights of Disabled Persons* (Westport, CT: Greenwood Press, 1984). In 1989, the abortion rights movement strengthened a good deal in a popular reaction to an unfavorable court decision, and with its increased strength, it began to shift its attention from litigation to electoral activity.

[16]Laurie Goodstein, "Obama Wins Unlikely Allies in Immigration," *The New York Times*, July 19, 2010, p. A1.

[17]Complementary coalitions of this type are often called "Baptist-bootlegger" coalitions, from local coalitions that often supported laws banning the sale of alcoholic beverages in states and counties after the repeal of national prohibition in 1933. Churches, such as the Baptists, supported banning liquor for religious reasons, while bootleggers quietly provided them with money to support their campaigns, because the bootleggers could continue making large profits as long as it was illegal for others to sell liquor in stores.

telecommunications) to sign letters with them and show up with them at press conferences. In particular, they recruited Mexican-American groups, because Mexican Americans make a large number of long-distance calls. It was a strong coalition—the citizen groups put a human face on the issue for the coalition, while the telecommunications companies paid the bills.[18]

11. Violence. An interest group may also try to dramatize its case by violent or disruptive activity, or it may try by violence and disruption to convince the leaders of the state that they will pay a high price in turmoil by not yielding to the group's demands. The Boston Tea party, in which American colonists destroyed a shipload of tea from Great Britain as a protest against import duties, was an early example of political violence by a group.

Violence, however, has grave drawbacks as a technique, because it is likely to cost the group what public sympathy it has and to call forth strenuous efforts at control by the authorities. It may work well, though, when one region is united in its opposition to the rest of a state and wishes to separate from it or at least to change its legal relationship to the government. A separatist group under these conditions can launch violent attacks on the rest of the state without losing the sympathy of the only "public" that counts for them, the people in their part of the state. The violence is likely to bring down harsher regulation and police activity in their region, which will serve to further strengthen local support for the separatist cause. Many separatist movements—the Irish Republican Army in Britain, the Basque separatists in Spain, Moslem separatists in the Philippines—have used this tactic with success. By the same logic, international terrorist groups like al Qaeda, who attack people of other nationalities or religions on behalf of their own group, may find a sympathetic home among their own people, whom they do not attack. (For more on terrorism, see Chapter 18, pp. 404–405.)

✦ THE CHOICE OF TACTICS

The descriptions of various tactics above have emphasized that interest groups choose tactics that fit the resources they have. A group with money but without a large membership base, for instance, will emphasize lobbying, campaign contributions, and public information campaigns. Another group with less money but more members may emphasize electoral activity and "outside" lobbying.

The history of the civil rights movement in the United States provides varied examples of how circumstances determine strategy. In the 1940s and 1950s, the movement for civil rights for blacks was relatively weak. The majority of blacks were still barred from voting in the South; blacks were poor and did not have a great deal of money to contribute; and the movement did not have many white allies, either in public office or outside it. The chief civil rights organization at this time was the NAACP, and its chief tactic was litigation. It achieved several important successes in court, among other things overturning segregated schooling in the South and outlawing the exclusion of black voters from primary elections.

---

[18]Frank R. Baumgartner, Jeffrey M. Berry, Marie Hojnacki, David C. Kimball, and Beth L. Leech, *Lobbying and Policy Change: Who Wins, Who Loses, and Why* (Chicago: University of Chicago Press, 2009), p. 205.

With the increase in support for civil rights in the 1960s, and partly as a result of the earlier successes, more money and resources became available to the movement. Blacks had become bolder politically; many more blacks were willing to march in demonstrations to help draw attention to their cause, and they began to acquire significant white allies. At this time new, rival organizations using different tactics appeared. The Congress on Racial Equality (CORE) and Martin Luther King Jr.'s Southern Christian Leadership Conference (SCLC) were two new organizations that emphasized the use of economic power, nonviolent demonstrations, and the provocation of segregationists into violence. (Note the clever twist on the use of violence as a tactic—here white officials were goaded into violence so that they would lose public sympathy.) Massive demonstrations were held, requiring large numbers of dedicated black and white participants. Violence of their own was never a part of these leaders' strategy; but the provocation of white violence was useful, and the civil rights leaders used black urban riots of 1965–68, which occurred spontaneously, as evidence for their claims that blacks had to be treated more fairly.

At this time, electoral activity was not especially emphasized because during the 1960s many southern blacks could not vote or were just acquiring the vote and, at the same time, demonstrations and disruption were proving to be such powerful tools. By the 1970s and 1980s, however, demonstrations began to be less effective. The public was more used to them and therefore less impressed by them, and police and public officials had learned not to respond in the picturesquely violent ways that demonstrators had once counted on. At the same time, the electoral importance of blacks had grown. The black percentage of the electorate in many northern cities had reached a point at which blacks could often determine the outcome of mayoral and other elections. In the South, thanks to the gains of the 1960s, most blacks were free to vote and could determine many elections. In the 1970s and 1980s, accordingly, the activity of black civil rights groups shifted to emphasize more their importance in elections.

We can see in this evolution of the tactics of the civil rights movement a good illustration of our general principle that interest groups will pick those tactics that best fit the group's resources and the political opportunities offered by those resources.

→ PATTERNS OF ORGANIZED INTEREST-GROUP ACTIVITY

In all of our discussions of interest groups, we have talked about them primarily from the point of view of the individual group. However, we must also look at the pattern of all group activity in a state. In looking at political parties, we found that the overall pattern formed by the system of parties was important to the state's politics; similarly, we will see that the overall pattern of interest-group activity is also important. Interest-group systems vary in (at least) two important ways.

1. Degree of Organization. In some countries, people are heavily organized by groups; in others, they are not heavily organized at all. Most states of the Third World are only weakly organized. Institutional interest groups such as the church and the army bulk much larger in the politics of these states than they would otherwise, because interest groups of other sorts are weak.

Among industrialized states, there is also a good deal of variation. In authoritarian states such as China, the formation of groups is suppressed, and here again institutional interest groups gain in importance by default. Even among open societies, there is a good deal of variation. The Scandinavian countries are probably more thoroughly organized than any others in the world. For example, 69 percent of Danish workers are members of trade unions, compared with 26 percent for Great Britain and 11 percent for the United States.[19] The percentage of people belonging to political organizations is about twice as high in Norway as in the United States.[20]

2. Degree of Direct, Formal Involvement of Interest Groups in Government and Administration. We saw earlier in this chapter that government officials must often depend on interest groups for information and expertise. Ways in which governments may tap into this vary from casual arrangements, in which officials occasionally call up interest-group representatives or look up a figure in the group's publication, to quite formal arrangements in which interest-group representatives may sit on administrative committees of the government. Under the latter arrangement, which is fairly common in northern Europe, it may be hard to draw the line between interest groups and government.

We can identify two important types of interest-group systems by variations on these two dimensions. These are pluralism and neocorporatism. They are important concepts for understanding how interest groups operate in democratic systems.[21]

✦ PLURALISM

Pluralism is an idealized system in which all interests organize and compete freely and no one group is able to dominate. The government is open to pressure from the interest groups, and politics consists largely of the competition among these interest groups to see that the government adopts the policies they favor.[22] In terms of our two dimensions listed in the section on "Patterns of Organized Interest-Group Activity," the ideal of pluralism is high on the scale of "organization" and low on "direct involvement of interest groups in government"; that is, interest groups are well organized but are quite distinct from the government. There is, however, no state that is truly "pluralist"; the term is an abstraction. The United States approaches the type more closely than most and is often used as a chief example of pluralism at work, but even the United States falls far short of the full organization of all groups that is envisioned in pluralism.

Those who favor a pluralist system of politics point out that with numerous groups operating, there is a good deal of spontaneity. It is relatively easy for new ideas to appear from the grass roots, and there is a good deal of flexibility. Furthermore, because the government is simultaneously influenced by many competing groups, negotiation

[19]OECD. StatsExtracts, http://stats.oecd.org/index.aspx?DatasetCode=UN_DEN (accessed May 31, 2013).
[20]Robert B. Kvavik, *Interest Groups in Norwegian Politics* (Oslo: Universitetsforlaget, 1976), p. 46; a dated source, but the difference is probably about the same today.
[21]Here, as in our discussion of interest-group tactics in this chapter, we will focus our attention on democracies.
[22]The chief source is David Truman, *The Governmental Process* (New York: Knopf, 1951). See also "Pluralism" in *The International Encyclopedia of the Social Sciences.*

and compromise should be the order of the day. Politics should typically be pragmatic and nonradical.

Pluralist writers see pluralism as an ideal way to reach the common ground of society. The various interests in society pull in their varying directions, and the government responds to their pressure by ending up at a kind of equilibrium point where the pressures balance. With a minimum of distortion, the government reaches the most desired mix of policy.

However, in any real state—as distinct from the idealized abstraction—the set of interest groups cannot represent the people of the state very well, because not all interests are equally able to "organize and compete freely." I discussed this at the beginning of this chapter in the section "Interest Groups and Representation." Therefore a pluralist system might have the advantages cited by those who favor it, yet it would still have serious drawbacks because policies based on "pluralist" deliberations could be expected to slant systematically in favor of those groups that can operate effectively and against those that cannot.

�� NEOCORPORATISM

Neocorporatism is another abstraction. It takes its name from a system popular in the early twentieth century called *corporatism,* in which instead of individuals being represented by right of being citizens, as in liberal democracy, *functions* of society were to be represented in governmental decisions. The basis of corporatism was the idea that the various functional parts of society (business, labor, agriculture, universities, etc.) were all vital and must be taken into account, much like the parts of the body (hence the word's root in *corpus,* Latin for *body*). Like the parts of the body, the various functional units should not be in conflict with each other (how can the heart fight the liver, for instance?). This notion of representation came up in various settings at that time, including the left wing of the Labour Party in Britain, but was most noteworthy in its adoption by Mussolini's fascist dictatorship in Italy. The latter, of course, left it with a strong and unpleasant odor. Neocorporatism consists of corporatist-like practices that have appeared in a number of countries since the fall of Mussolini: they have often arisen more or less spontaneously in well-established democracies like Sweden, but in their non-democratic form, they have also sometimes been imposed from above, as in Brazil's military dictatorship in the 1970s.

It is a system in which all interests are organized and the government deals directly with all affected interests at all stages in the making and administration of policy. Unlike pluralism, under neocorporatism the government does not merely respond to the interest groups' pressure but actively involves the groups in the job of governing.[23] In terms of our two dimensions listed in the "Patterns of Organized Interest-Group Activity" section, neocorporatism is high both on the scales of "organization" and "direct involvement of interest groups." It is also higher than pluralism on the "organization" scale; the practice of involving interest groups in government generally stimulates an especially high degree of participation in interest groups, just because the stakes of interest groups' activity become higher.

---

[23]A good presentation of the model is Martin O. Heisler and Robert B. Kvavik, "Patterns of European Politics: The 'European Polity' Model," in Martin O. Heisler, ed., *Politics in Europe* (New York: David McKay, 1974), pp. 27–90.

Not only does the government draw interest groups into the governmental process in neocorporatism, but parts of the government may also act rather like interest groups. This is not so much a matter of "institutional interest groups" lobbying for their own perquisites and budgets as it is active engagement in political debate on behalf of certain policies: Parts of the bureaucratic apparatus may take on a greater role of representing popular constituencies and initiating policy demands than is common under pluralism. They are in effect "self-starters" who try to mobilize popular support for their positions. An example is the founding of the European Common Market in 1956; the campaign for unification was spearheaded not by party leaders but by civil servants. From both sides, then, the boundary between government and interest groups becomes fuzzier in a neocorporatist system.

Unlike what we saw in the case of pluralism, some states do follow the neocorporatist model fairly closely. This is especially true of the Scandinavian countries. For instance, in Denmark:

- The government is constitutionally required to send copies of any bill it is drafting to affected interest groups and to solicit their responses at all stages of the legislative process.

- The drafting of most bills is shaped by discussions in a special commission set up to consider the bill. Civil servants and representatives of all affected interest groups sit on such a commission.

- Once the bill is passed, its administration will often be turned over to the affected group. For instance, the government's unemployment compensation program is administered not by a governmental agency, but by the trade unions.

- Policies are set in a spirit of cooperation and compromise. There is a reluctance to push any affected group to the wall.

Those who admire neocorporatism point to the cooperative attitude brought forth by such a system. For such a system to work, there *must* be a cooperative spirit, and putting the system in place may therefore help to call forth the required cooperation.

Also, neocorporatism eases the problem of unequal organization of groups, which flaws pluralism. Groups must be well organized to take part in governing; therefore, it becomes more important that they organize their members, and they tend to do so. Indeed, the government sometimes writes a law in such a way that its administration requires the creation of a group that does not yet exist; when this situation has arisen, the government has organized the group![24]

On the other hand, the neocorporatist system is a fragile one, because it depends so much on cooperation and on everyone's willingness to avoid rocking the boat. Neocorporatism sets up an officially sanctioned set of actors in the system, each with rights to a piece of the pie; therefore, no group can go for the jugular of another without endangering the whole system.

---

[24]This illustrates what is probably the most basic difference between the pluralist and neocorporatist models. Pluralism assumes that the state apparatus responds to the system of interest groups. Neocorporatism assumes that the state has a good deal of autonomy; to some extent, it creates the system of interest groups and determines how it operates.

This suggests a second important problem in neocorporatism. It defines a set of groups with claims on the state and routinizes the process by which the state consults with them. As a result, the neocorporatist system tends to petrify the existing line of conflict as of the time it was established. In effect, the government "licenses" an existing set of interest groups. We can expect that lines of conflict will change over time, as old conflicts fade and new ones arise. It is difficult for the neocorporatist system, with its intricate organizational structure of established and "entitled" interest groups, to adjust to such change. As an example of this problem, one of the more difficult challenges faced by Danish politics in the 2000s has been to find a way of providing political expression to the new concern over immigration and a multicultural society.

In this section, we have considered what one might call "cooperative" neocorporatism of the sort typified by politics in the Scandinavian states. Neocorporatism of this sort arises from the desires of the government and the interests to develop consensus and minimize conflict in policy making. Another form of neocorporatism, usually called "state neocorporatism," occurred especially in Latin America (Brazil in the 1970s and Perón's Argentina in the 1950s). This system is imposed on the interests by the state to keep them under its control. Although both types of government are "corporatist" in that the government deals directly with groups, the nature of politics is very different in the two types.

✦ Pluralism and Neocorporatism: Power and Choice

Of "power and choice," pluralist writers certainly emphasize a "choice" perspective. They view the public choice—policy—as a balanced outcome of the different pressures of organized interests, almost like a physical equilibrium, and they treat the government rather as an unexamined "black box." Pluralists tend to play down power relations within the government, and especially the difference in power of various interest groups.

One might expect that the main alternative abstraction, neocorporatism, would take an opposed side of this great divide, but oddly it, too, embodies more of a "choice" than a "power" perspective—at least in the cooperative form we have looked at here. (Where one analyzes corporatism as a tool by which authoritarian governments construct their control of society, the emphasis is more on a "power" perspective.) In its cooperative form, neocorporatism is a system in which, as in pluralism, the interests of society come together in a rather natural way to produce their most-preferred mix of policies. The main difference between the two abstractions is in the role accorded government in the process: Under pluralism, the government is a passive receiver of pressures from interests; under neocorporatism, it is a stimulator and shaper of those pressures, and the government blends with the system of interest groups. In both abstractions, the production of policy is portrayed as the natural outcome of a process designed to produce public choices. An interesting exercise would be to design an alternative abstraction of interest-group activities in democracies that is based more on a "power" perspective.

EXAMPLE

Interest Groups in France

France has a system that probably falls somewhere between the pluralist and neocorporatist models of politics. It also shows interesting peculiarities of its own, especially in a certain looseness and unpredictability of structure. French interest groups are rather fragmented, and compared with groups in other states they are relatively more likely to engage in provocative violence.

These characteristics are often attributed to two aspects of French political culture: (1) the French tradition of a strong state, relating directly to the population, which leads to disdain and disapproval of intermediary organizations such as interest groups; and (2) a second French tradition that romanticizes direct political action, "taking politics to the streets."[25]

French interest groups have fairly low enrollments from their potential members. Labor unions enroll only 8 percent of their potential membership, and other sorts of groups have similarly low enrollments.

Furthermore, the organized groups are deeply divided. Frequently, several different organizations compete for the same membership, which in other countries would be united behind a single organization. The few workers who are in unions, for instance, are divided among five separate unions: the CGT (a communist union with 30 percent of the total union strength), the CFDT (an independent-minded, socialist union with 26 percent), Force Ouvrier (a reformist union independent of parties with 16 percent), the CGC (a union of managers, engineers, and technicians with 8 percent), and the Catholic Confederation (with 9 percent); independent unions account for the rest.[26]

Promotional interest groups, such as environmental groups, veterans' groups, and feminist groups, are mostly local in their organization rather than national, which means that there are thousands of them, but that they have little clout in national politics.

French politics at all levels is punctuated by sporadic, intense activity against a background of cynical disengagement, and this holds as true of interest groups as it does of other aspects of politics. The line between interest groups and social movements is even harder to draw in France than in other countries (see "social movements," Chapter 13). The weakly organized interest groups of France flare up from time to time into what we really should think of as social movements. Large street demonstrations (and occasionally more dramatic barricades, kidnappings, etc.) are not an uncommon tactic of some groups, including unions, farmers' organizations, and public employees.

---

[25]Andrew Appleton, "France: Party-Group Relations in the Shadow of the State," in Clive S. Thomas, ed., *Political Parties and Interest Groups* (Boulder, CO: Lynne Rienner, 2001), p. 48.
[26]Ministry of the Economy, INSEE, *Annuaire Statistique de la France, 2011,* http://www.insee.fr/fr/themes/detail. asp?ref=id=asftravail

298   Part IV   The Apparatus of Governance

In their relations with the government, French interest groups are in some instances bound to the government by formal ties of intimacy of the sort we associate with neocorporatism. More often, interest groups and government maintain the sort of distance we expect under pluralism. The agricultural sector comes closest to the neocorporatist model. One group, the Federation Nationale des Syndicats d'Exploitants Agricoles (FNSEA), which includes about 70 percent of all farmers, has become something like the "official" agricultural group for the government. The FNSEA dominates French agricultural politics, and performs a number of administrative duties, including most of the educational and training tasks that are carried out in other countries by agricultural extension agents. In most areas, the government recognizes the FNSEA as the coordinating representative of farming interests.[27] The presence of strong representation for agriculture in an otherwise often fragmented interest-group system is reflected in a history of very strong programs of price supports and subsidies for farmers.

Like everything else in French politics, the growing importance of European Union policies has hugely reshaped the activities of interest groups. Interest groups have responded to this in two ways: by establishing lobbying activities directly at the EU Commission in Brussels, and by lobbying the French government to protect their interests in EU decisions. Sectoral groups have actually been rather slow to respond to the growth of EU policy making and have reacted to it for the most part defensively. Promotional interest groups, however, have found that the EU offers them new and better opportunities than they have formerly found at home. After being routinely brushed aside in Paris, groups such as antihunting organizations have found that they can combine with similarly minded groups from other EU member states to accomplish much of what they want through Union policies, rather than try to accomplish them through political action at home.[28]

�҉ EXAMPLE

Attenuated Interest Groups in Bangladesh

What would politics be like in a country without interest groups? Without interest groups, policy makers might never see the need for policy changes; and they might never learn how proposed changes would affect different groups of citizens. Interest groups are an important part of the political process that is largely absent in many poor countries such as Bangladesh.

Bangladesh is a small, poor, densely populated country in South Asia that adjoins India. Per capita GDP is just $1,700, and a population of 158 million

---

[27] Adam D. Sheingate, *The Rise of the Agricultural Welfare State: Institutions and Interest Group Power in the United States, France, and Japan* (Princeton: Princeton University Press, 2001), pp. 192–93. For a dissenting view, see Pepper D. Culpepper, "Organizational Competition and the Neo-Corporatist Fallacy in French Agriculture," *West European Politics* 16 (July 1993), pp. 295–315.
[28] Emiliano Grossman and Sabine Saurugger, "Challenging French Interest Groups: The State, Europe and the International Political System," *French Politics* 2 (2004), p. 205.

people (about half the population of the United States) is squeezed into a land mass about the size of Iowa. Only about half of adult Bangladeshis can read and write. Since Bangladesh gained its independence in 1971, the army and two major political parties have dominated its politics: the Awami League and the Bangladesh Nationalist Party. Control of the government has gone back and forth between the two parties, with intervals in which the army has seized control and governed by itself. The two parties devote most of their energy to settling old grudges and historical grievances, or to creating disadvantages for the other party through constitutional change.

To deal with government or economic problems, especially in rural regions, Bangladeshis rely primarily on a patron who provides them with emergency help when needed and intercedes with the government on their behalf. In return, they offer their patron loyalty and support. Such a system is called **clientelism.** The population consists of innumerable clientelistic networks of this sort, some based on one or another of the parties, some based on families or alliances of families, and some based on rural villages and their leaders.

Rural Bangladeshis' reliance on local clientelistic networks makes it difficult to form national interest groups around a shared idea or occupation. As a result, existing interest groups are found almost entirely among the one-quarter of the Bangladeshi population that live in large cities. These interest groups comprise mostly the urban governing elites, who agitate to protect their own interests in government. The three strongest organized interests in all of Bangladesh are the Bangladesh Civil Service (Administration) Cadre Association, which represents highly ranked civil servants in the capital; the Bangladesh Supreme Court Bar Association, representing lawyers who work with the Supreme Court; and the army.[29] Aside from these, there are organizations representing businesses of Dhaka, the capital city; a variety of unions for workers in the cities; and foreign aid organizations that lobby the government. Many other possible interests are left unrepresented. For instance, there is not a well-organized interest group for agriculture, even though Bangladesh is a predominantly agricultural country.

What does this mean for the country? Politics has for decades involved a struggle for power and advantage between the parties, with relatively little concern for initiatives to improve people's lives. The political elite live in a world of their own, where the problems of the people of the country rarely intrude. For instance, in June 2009, when a hurricane killed 200 people in southwestern Bangladesh and left hundreds of thousands homeless, the prime minister did not visit the site nor did the government do much to help those who were affected. With no political organizations representing the rural populations of southwestern Bangladesh, the government felt free to ignore the problem.

To the extent that people's problems are addressed, they tend to have been addressed outside the realm of government and policy. For instance, the well-known cooperative program that makes micro-loans to village women is run not by the government, but by a private charitable foundation.

---

[29]Abdul Maleque, *Pressure Groups: Dynamics of Bangladesh Politics* (Dhaka, Bangladesh: Academic Press and Publishers Library, 2007), pp. 359–362.

KEY TERMS

interest group	institutional interest group	pluralism
selective benefit	promotional interest group	neocorporatism
free rider	lobbying	clientelism
sectoral interest group		

FURTHER READING

Baumgartner, Frank, and Leech, Beth. *Basic Interests: The Importance of Groups in Politics and Political Science.* Princeton: Princeton University Press, 1998.

——, Berry, Jeff, Hojnacki, Marie, Leech, Beth, and Kimball, David. *Lobbying and Policy Change: Who Wins, Who Loses, and Why.* Chicago: University of Chicago Press, 2009.

Berry, Jeffrey M., and Wilcox, Clyde. *The Interest Group Society.* 5th ed. New York: Longman, 2009.

Christiansen, Peter Mark, and Rommetvedt, Hilmar. "From Corporatism to Lobbyism? Parliaments, Executives, and Organized Interests in Denmark and Norway." *Scandinavian Political Studies* 22 (1999), pp. 195–220.

Cigler, Allan J., and Loomis, Burdett A., eds. *Interest Group Politics.* 8th ed. Washington, DC: CQ Press, 2011.

Greenwood, Justin. *Interest Representation in the European Union.* New York: Palgrave Macmillan, 2003.

Levine, Bertram J. *The Art of Lobbying.* Washington, DC: CQ Press, 2008.

Loomis, Burdett A., Francia, Peter L., and Strolovitch, Dara Z., eds. *Guide to Interest Groups and Lobbying in the United States.* Washington, DC: CQ Press, 2011.

Olson, Mancur. *The Logic of Collective Action.* Cambridge: Harvard University Press, 1965.

Sheingate, Adam. *The Rise of the Agricultural Welfare State: Institutions and Interest Group Power in the United States, France, and Japan.* Princeton: Princeton University Press, 2001.

Thomas, Clive S., ed. *Political Parties and Interest Groups.* Boulder, CO: Lynn Rienner, 2001.

CHAPTER 13

SOCIAL MOVEMENTS AND CONTENTIOUS POLITICS

The last two chapters dealt with two formally organized, institutionalized ways that citizens and interests enter into the political process: political parties and interest groups. However, there has always been a more flexible, less formal way that broad groups of citizens have engaged in politics. "Grassroots," often ephemeral, organization of people has taken many forms, from sudden riots, to petition drives, to well developed but still fairly informal organizations that may persist for as long as a few decades. Such efforts have often had major political impacts. In England in the eighteenth century an underground pro-democracy movement gathered millions of signatures in just a few months on a petition urging the king to establish a democratic constitution; the effort failed at the time, but as is often the case, its goal was realized a century later. When the Jewish foreign minister of Germany, Walter Rathenau, was assassinated in 1922, over a million Berliners took to the streets within hours in a demonstration supporting the new democratic government. India achieved independence from Britain in 1947 through the efforts of Mahatma Gandhi's massive civil disobedience movement, in which millions of Indians passively disobeyed the British administration. The civil rights movement of the 1960s in the United States was pursued partly by established interest groups like the NAACP, but much more by informal organizations like Martin Luther King's boycott of the Montgomery, Alabama bus system. Much of the Islamic fundamentalist presence in countries of the Mideast, Africa, and Asia is based on loosely organized movements following various religious leaders. In 2003, massive protests against a proposed natural gas pipeline (and implicitly, against globalization) forced the president of Bolivia to resign. In 2008, tens of thousands of South Koreans, facing police barricades, filled the streets of central Seoul and succeeded in blocking a proposal to allow Koreans to import beef raised in the United States. In 2011 spontaneous street demonstrations ousted the authoritarian presidents of Tunisia and Egypt. Probably the most momentous accomplishment of

Demonstrators against a new pipeline for natural gas crowd the streets of La Paz, Bolivia. After weeks of such demonstrations, with eighty deaths, the president of Bolivia had to step down.
© Aizar Raldes/AFP/Getty Images

such grassroots movements in the last century was the wave of democratization in the formerly Communist states of Eastern Europe.[1]

However, not all such efforts have been on as large a scale as these. Often a local issue will ignite a sudden, fairly specific protest. In Minneapolis, Minnesota, for instance, an energetic movement tried several years ago to stop the extension of Route 55 through a grove of bur oaks which Native Americans hold sacred. In the end the movement failed, but only after it had tied up local politics (and the highway construction) for months. Its bumper stickers "Go Oaks! Stop 55!" were everywhere.

Such informal movements are called **social movements.** They are spawned by "contentious politics"—confrontations between ordinary people and governing or economic elites. A social movement is an informal collective movement of people, loosely coordinated in their actions and using flexible tactics, with some sort of leadership group to give its actions coherence. A truly leaderless group, such as spontaneous looters after a storm, is not a social movement. A social movement, even though it is very informally organized, has purpose and direction, and so some sort of leadership is necessary to focus the efforts of the group.

Social movements often draw their energy from civil society, and in general, where there is a vibrant civil society, social movements are very active. You will recall from p. 66 that civil society consists of all organizations that are not directly or indirectly

---

[1]See Chapter 7; in Czechoslovakia, for instance, in November of 1989 hundreds of thousands of protesters gathered each Sunday in Wenceslas Square in Prague, ringing bells to call for democratic government. The demonstrations increased in size each week, culminating in a mass demonstration of 750,000 people in Letna Park on November 25 and a general strike, called on November 27. On November 29 the Communist government capitulated to the pro-democracy forces.

part of the government, are not families, and are not set up for economic activity. Since social movements require a leadership catalyst and some sort of network for communication, we can readily see why abundant religious organizations, hobby groups, and professional associations could help social movements to form and operate. For instance, African-American churches were key sources of leadership and support for the civil rights movement in the United States in the 1960s.

The one major exception to this rule is that in some states where alternative organization is actively repressed, so that there is only "one game in town"—the government game—the repressed desire for an outlet for opposition to government policies can emerge in very ad hoc social protests, even without the help of a strong civil society. China, where the Communist Party maintains a monopoly on organized political expression, is a prime example of this; you will recall the discussion of the Chinese Communist Party and ad hoc rural unrest on p. 269.

Social movements have driven more and more of politics in recent years. Just in one issue of the *New York Times,* on April 25, 2011 the front section included the following stories:

- Syria's brutal repression of peaceful demonstrators
- a defiant pray-in by Jewish settlers at Joseph's tomb, in Palestinian territory
- Muslim/Christian riots over the election in Nigeria
- an insurrection by Berbers in western Libya
- protests by truck drivers in Shanghai, China
- protests against the president of Yemen
- an illegal Easter service held in a public square in Beijing
- thousands demonstrating for reform in Morocco
- a demonstration outside St. Patrick's Cathedral in New York during Easter services to protest homophobia

Nine stories in just one day, showing the power of social movements to drive politics everywhere from New York to the mountains of western Libya.

✦ WHY NOW?

Why have social movements blossomed in the twentieth and twenty-first centuries? They have always been around (the mobs of Rome were an important political force). However, as the newspaper topics above indicate, they are far more widespread and influential today than in earlier times. At least one reason for their explosive development in the last several decades may be that social movements depend heavily on rapid and easy communication—how else can one mobilize people readily? Technical advances in communication have always gone hand in hand with social movement politics. The French Revolution could probably not have occurred without the invention of printing. More recently, communist governments in the 1970s and 1980s drastically limited access to new tools of communication in a vain attempt to keep the lid on social change. In 1989, for instance, the government still had not allowed Romania's nuclear power plant to buy a photocopier! The twentieth century saw the greatest advances in communications in human history. At the beginning of the century people communicated by letter, by telegraph, and by newspapers; at its end, they were communicating by cell phones, texting, social networks, television, and the Internet. Recognizing the importance of such technology, during the massive demonstrations in Egypt in 2011 the government closed down all cell phone and Internet service for the country, in a desperate effort to halt the demonstrations. It may be these recent advances in electronic communication, together with the democratic doctrine that ordinary people should share in the making of governmental policies, that have led to the explosive growth of social movements in the last decades.

Two additional possibilities are: (1) Social movements may have burgeoned because of the rise of "post-material" political issues such as the environment, women's rights, and ethnic relations that are not so easily handled by the political parties and interest-group systems that developed out of the older class and ideological conflicts associated with industrialization. Or, (2) it also may be that a general decline in the centrality of political parties to politics, as evidenced by declining memberships in parties over the last few decades and increasing volatility of party-voting by the electorate, has opened up opportunities for new, more flexible organizations.

The explanations above attempt to account for the increased presence of social movements as a whole. However, political scientists studying social movements have also developed a wide variety of more specific explanations for the rise of particular social movements. Doug McAdam, John D. McCarthy, and Mayer N. Zald group these explanations into three types: political opportunities, mobilizing structures, and framing processes.[2]

- **"Political opportunity structures."** Aspects of the broader political system may offer a social movement advantages. These include the presence of potential allies in the government or opposition, international organizations that are sympathetic to them, and a breakdown in confidence in an incumbent leader.

- **"Mobilizing structures."** Various characteristics of the movement itself may account for its success, or lack of success. One reason that the indigenous people's movement of Chiapas Province in Mexico has been more successful than most indigenous movements, for example, appears to be that it has some members who have been especially adept at communication in the Internet age. (I discuss the Chiapas movement—"Zapatistas"—in more detail in the next section.)

- **"Framing processes"** (i.e., how issues are presented and framed). In order to form a social movement a group must both feel a grievance and have some hope that by collective action they can redress the grievance. What changed between the 1950s in the United States, for example, when there was essentially no feminist movement,

---

[2]Doug McAdam, John D. McCarthy, and Mayer N. Zald, *Comparative Perspectives on Social Movements* (New York: Cambridge University Press, 1996), especially pp. 3–20.

and the 1970s? The major change appears to have been a growing sense among many women that they shared common interests and that there was something they could do to further those interests by collective action; certainly, the opportunities in the system had not changed much, nor had the political skills and other organizational attributes of American women.

Having categorized the types of explanation, McAdam and his coauthors conclude that we normally need all three types of explanation to account for any given social movement and how well it succeeds; the types of explanation are complementary, not competing.

Whatever the causes, loose and informal political movements are increasingly active in the twenty-first century, and have become adept at marshalling ephemeral international coalitions that are very difficult for states to handle. From the anti-globalization movement to al Qaeda, from transnational environmental movements to local groups protesting noise from an airport, social movements are engaged in every part of international and domestic politics.

➢ SOCIAL MOVEMENTS AS A PUBLIC GOODS PROBLEM

Social movements provide an interesting example of our old friend, the problem of public goods. (See p. 55.) Dennis Chong, in his excellent book on the United States civil rights movement, develops the concept of "public-spirited collective action": large-scale political action driven by broad public goals such as civil rights, protection of the environment, or women's rights.[3] These are all public goods, in that if a group achieves them, they cannot parcel them out just to some people and deny them to others. Thus the dread problem of free riders appears: since all citizens will reap the fruits of the effort, whether or not they have contributed to it, why should I stick my neck out and participate?

As Chong points out, social movements enjoy some advantages in overcoming free ridership, in that the movement itself can be an enjoyable social group, with value in and of itself to the individual. Also, social movements usually involve goals that evoke strong emotions; potential supporters may well feel so strongly about the goal that they do not require much of a personal incentive to participate.

Chong also identifies another factor, beyond the problem of public goods, that is critical to maintaining participation—the ultimate probability of the movement's success. If participants do not feel that they have a reasonable chance to succeed, it is hard for them to keep participating. In this case, social movements rapidly dwindle to a small, irrelevant group of demonstrators huddled on a street corner under a couple of signs.

Accordingly, Chong says, an important dynamic of social movements is that the movement's leaders will actively talk up their chances of success; and conversely, the government (or corporation, or whatever the movement is opposing) will try to convince everyone that it will hold out forever. This is a very recognizable aspect of unions'

---

[3]Dennis Chong, *Collective Action and the Civil Rights Movement* (Chicago: University of Chicago Press, 1991).

306   PART IV   THE APPARATUS OF GOVERNANCE

strikes against companies, and Chong shows that it was also the usual story in civil rights demonstrations against governments in the south in the 1960s.

✦ ADVANTAGES (AND DISADVANTAGES) OF INFORMAL ORGANIZATION

It is the loose organization of social movements that sets them apart from both parties and interest groups. You will recall that parties were distinguished from interest groups in that parties seek to control who sits in the government, while interest groups seek to influence one or more policies of the government. Social movements may seek either of these goals. A social movement may seek to oust a leader of a country and replace him or her with someone else, as in the case of the "Orange Revolution" movement that forced President Viktor Yanukovich out of power in Ukraine in 2004, or the general strike organized in Venezuela in 2003 in an attempt to oust President Hugo Chavez. A social movement also may seek to change a specific government policy, as in the Montgomery bus boycott that achieved the right of African Americans to sit anywhere they wish in buses in Montgomery, or the attempt to stop the extension of Highway 55 in Minneapolis. The thing that always typifies social movements is not their goal, but the way they are organized (loosely) and conducted (flexibly). This is illustrated in the charting of parties, interest groups, and social movements in Figure 13.1.

Social movements vary in how loosely they are organized. At their more organized end they may be difficult to distinguish from traditional interest groups. A Canadian group, the Castle-Crown Wilderness Coalition, while it was the subject of a study titled "New Social Movements and the Environmental Policy Process," actually operates more like a very grassroots, volunteer-based interest group—it negotiates with government

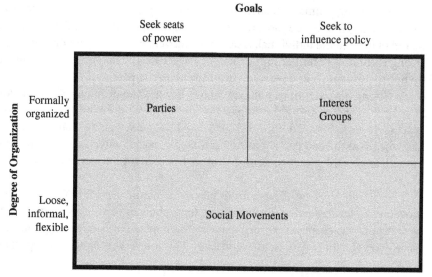

FIGURE 13.1   Parties, interest groups, and social movements.

agencies, it does not engage in "direct action," and it is not particularly flamboyant in its media relations.[4] At the other end of the spectrum of loose organization, a series of demonstrations in 2005 by retired Russians protesting proposed cuts in their subsidies appears to have been almost entirely spontaneous, with no organizational structure and no obvious leadership. Thousands of desperate elderly people simply appeared at street corners and started spontaneous actions to protest the cuts; they were very effective in changing the Putin government's policies.

Informal, loose organization carries with it two important disadvantages. First, because by definition the movement does not have a well-organized and established staff and structure, it is difficult for it to amass many of the sorts of resources to which political leaders respond. Social movements typically do not have much money. They also do not typically have specialized expertise that governments will want to tap. Additionally, they do not have ongoing staffs capable of handling long-term, tedious organizational jobs like amassing voter databases and getting voters to the polls.

Second, because social movements usually are ephemeral, counting their organizational lives not in decades but in months or years, policy makers often know that they can outlast them. A corporation, trade union, or church will be around for a politician's entire career, but social movements come together and disband fairly easily. A politician may feel able to wait them out.

However, social movements' informality also gives them some distinct advantages: First, because they do not have an entrenched staff and old, established members to whom they must defer, they can be very nimble in defining and framing their issues. They can shift quickly if tactical necessity arises. A group of rubber gatherers of Acre province in Brazil, for instance, were able to frame their movement variously as a movement for indigenous people's rights, as an environmental movement, or as a labor movement, depending on whom they were dealing with. All of these framings were true, but the point is that since the rubber gatherers had only the most informal of organizations they were not bound by an organization's self-definition and the set of people an organization gathers around it. They could bob and weave, and this gave them real advantages.[5]

In another example of flexible framing, the question of female circumcision did not really take off until a campaign initiated by a group of women's and human rights organizations reformulated the issue as one of "female genital mutilation," which sounded more horrible and less voluntary than "circumcision."[6]

Al Qaeda is not exactly what we usually think of as a social movement, because it is a secretive group of terrorists rather than an open, broad movement. Other than its use of terror as a strategy, however, it is actually fairly typical of social movements. Osama Bin Laden was adept at using the media, and the group uses its loose organization

[4]Lorna Stefanick, "New Social Movements and the Environmental Policy Process: The Case of Alberta's Castle Wilderness Area," in Joanna Everitt and Brenda O'Neill, *Citizen Politics: Research and Theory in Canadian Political Behaviour* (New York: Oxford University Press, 2002), pp. 426–38; the activities of the Castle-Crown Wilderness Coalition can be reviewed on their Website, http://www.ccwc.ab.ca.
[5]Margaret E. Keck, "Social Equity and Environmental Politics in Brazil: Lessons from the Rubber Tappers of Acre," *Comparative Politics* 27 (July 1995), pp. 409–24.
[6]Margaret E. Keck and Kathryn Sikkink, *Activists Beyond Borders: Advocacy Networks in International Politics* (Ithaca, New York: Cornell University Press, 1998), p. 20.

masterfully as a way of evading interventions by governments. Like other social movements, al Qaeda has also proved to be flexible in framing its goals: at its start it was formed to get American troops out of Saudi Arabia, and explicitly did not involve itself in the Israeli-Palestinian conflict; but after the Iraq war, it saw opportunities in linking its goals to the generalized anti-Americanism of the Arab "street" and moved to accomplish this by taking up the Palestinian cause.

Of course, social movements are not the only political groups that can re-frame issues creatively. Americans for Tax Reform, a well-established and thoroughly organized interest group—i.e., no social movement—brilliantly recast the estate tax in the 1990s as the "death tax," and succeeded in getting it repealed in 2002. The point, though, is that social movements are more nimble than well-organized groups in making these shifts. They make a virtue out of their weakness by relying on the flexibility they gain from not having resources and organization.

Second, the lack of resources and organization also allows social movements to change tactics quickly and be very opportunistic. Indigenous peoples, who started out appealing to labor groups and human rights groups for help, quickly realized that they should shift more to environmentalists and anti-globalization groups. Social movements can also capitalize quickly on opportunities when they arise. Underground pro-democracy movements in the Soviet Union responded quickly when disagreements among the Communist leadership made Mikhail Gorbachev available to them as an ally.

Third, social movements have the ability to form networks beyond the boundaries of their state. More formal organizations tend to be inward looking, and do not often form effective partnerships with similar organizations in other states. The Chamber of Commerce of the United States, for instance, does not get together in concerted action with the Chamber of Commerce of Canada, and pro-life organizations in the United States do not form partnerships with Christian-Democratic parties in Europe that also oppose abortion. However, social movements often draw on similar movements in other states for support. Margaret Keck and Kathryn Sikkink describe what they call the "boomerang pattern," in which a social movement that its own government blocks from accomplishing its goals asks a similar movement in another country to persuade its government to pressure the first government to yield to the social movement within its borders.[7] For instance, a human rights group working for release of a political prisoner in Zimbabwe might enlist human rights groups in Britain to lobby the British government to pressure the government of Zimbabwe to release the prisoner.

Because they are nimble, and because communication and the flow of information are so important in their own mobilization, social movements are often adept at communication and at using information effectively. A good example is the Zapatista movement of indigenous communities in the Chiapas province of Mexico. The movement has been engaged in sporadic conflict with the Mexican government, but has been able to transcend its role as a disaffected region by creative use of the Internet and other venues of communication. They developed a romantic, dramatic figure as leader,

---

[7] Ibid., p. 13.

Subcomandante Marcos, the charismatic leader of the Zapatista movement, addresses reporters at the outset of a 1,900 mile protest drive and march from Chiapas to Mexico City.

© Arturo Fuentes/AFP/Getty Images

Subcomandante Marcos, who appears frequently in Mexico City and elsewhere, giving speeches and reading poems about the movement. You can easily access their Internet presence from http://www.actlab.utexas.edu/~zapatistas/, a server in the United States, indicating once again the frequent reliance of social movements on international ties. They have been able to draw widespread support from around the world.

Most of the examples of social movements that I have described in this section are of the left, but the right also has its social movements. In the United States, skinheads, militias, white power groups, and various kinds of tax protest groups flourish in exactly the same kind of nimble informal organization as social movements of the left. Like movements of the left, they are heavily represented on the Internet, and also have developed effective networks of private discussion groups. Like other social groups, they also utilize international ties.[8]

More recently, and less far to the right than these groups, the Tea Party movement arose in the United States in 2009 and 2010 as a disparate group whose core beliefs appear to be: a distrust of elected officials and a desire to remove most of them from office; a belief that the constitutional order of the country has been undermined by extra-constitutional actions of government; and a desire to lessen the impact of government in people's lives—especially by lowering taxes. Most of the participants in its rallies are people who were not previously very active politically. It is a loosely organized, strongly anti-elite movement of people who feel themselves to be scorned by political and media elites, and respond in kind.

[8]The Fall 2001 issue of the Southern Poverty Law Center's *Intelligence Report* has several articles describing U.S. right-wing social movements' strategic partnerships with groups outside the United States.

EXAMPLE

The Battle of Seattle[9]

The "Battle of Seattle" is a classic example of political action by social movements, including elements common to many social movement events: loose coordination (though there definitely was some coordination); varied elements of the movement, with varied goals; dramatic flair and unpredictability; and an eventual shift of focus from the issues at hand to the police reaction.

In 1999 the World Trade Organization (WTO) scheduled its biennial Ministerial Conference in Seattle. The WTO is an organization of many industrialized states that regulates trading rules among the states. The Ministerial Conference is its top level of governance, at which the finance ministers of the states come together to make all major decisions for the organization. Its meeting in Seattle provided a focus for anti-globalization, labor, and environmentalist groups that were opposed to prevailing international rules for trade and economic development.

Months before the meeting, Mike Dolan, an official of Ralph Nader's Public Citizen organization, moved to Seattle to coordinate protests against the WTO and to help organize logistical support for demonstrators. Dolan worked closely with the AFL-CIO, which was planning demonstrations and a protest march, and he maintained close ties with environmental groups like the Sierra Club. In general, Dolan and the groups he worked with favored a large, peaceful march to oppose free trade.

Other groups, however, were basically opposed to the capitalist system, and wanted to initiate street theater and disruption. A loose alliance of anarchists, former Greenpeace activists, and anti-capitalist groups formed the Direct Action Network (DAN) to pursue these tactics. Labor organizers and the DAN had cool relations with each other and did not cooperate directly, but Dolan kept some contact with the DAN, even helping to pay the rent for a warehouse where they housed their members.

November 30, the day of the demonstrations, saw a confusing series of events. The labor march in the afternoon attracted between 25,000 and 50,000 participants, the largest group who had ever gathered to oppose free trade. But in the morning DAN activists blockaded major intersections around the convention center, preventing most delegates from reaching the meeting. Other DAN street actions included street theater (including activists dressed in green turtle costumes), teach-ins, and marches by students and Third World citizens. The Seattle police were cut off in two groups, one around the convention center, and another outside the lines of demonstrators who could not reach their fellow-officers inside. The situation was further complicated around noon when a group

---

[9]Many of the details here, especially concerning the relations between labor and more radical activists, are drawn from Margaret Levi and Gillian Murphy, "Coalitions of Contention: The Case of the WTO Protests in Seattle", *Political Studies* volume 54 (2006), pp. 651–670. The article includes a very interesting analysis of how coalitions form between groups.

of black-clad anarchists began a planned attack on several businesses, smashing windows and pushing dumpsters into intersections.

The police were overwhelmed by the numbers of demonstrators and the disorganized, varied nature of the events with which they had to deal. In some confrontations with demonstrators they used tear gas, pepper spray, and rubber bullets. The protests, and sporadic confrontations with police, continued into the night, and the next day the city declared a curfew in the downtown area, banning demonstrations in the business district. Several hundred people were arrested that day for violations of the curfew and ban.

There were surprisingly few injuries during these events, but the police were criticized for their inability to react quickly enough to the rapidly escalating disorder, and many criticized the city for the scale of arrests. The reaction of the police and the city managed to do what activist leaders had not been able to do before November 30—it brought labor and the more radical activists together in a common cause. After the events of November 30 the radical activists needed labor's legal and financial help, and labor leaders were angry enough about the police and city response that they welcomed the radicals warmly.

What were the outcomes of the Battle of Seattle? Locally, the police chief lost his job, and the mayor of Seattle was defeated in the next election, although it is unclear whether this was because of the "Battle." Nationally and internationally, "anti-globalization" became a more frequently used slogan than it had been earlier. WTO meetings since 1999 have seen large demonstrations, though nothing as large and disruptive as the events in Seattle.

In 2007 Stuart Townsend produced a movie, "Battle in Seattle," loosely based on the 1999 events.

✳ EXAMPLE

The "Orange Revolution" in Ukraine

Ukraine is a large state southwest of Russia, part of the Soviet Union until 1991. It established electoral democracy in 1991, but corrupt governments dominated by former Communist officials manipulated the democracy. At the time of the presidential election on November 21, 2004, the old guard was still firmly in control.

The election campaign was very dirty. The establishment candidate was Viktor Yanukovich, an unsavory official who had once been convicted of robbery and assault and who had close ties to corrupt businessmen. During the campaign the reform leader, another Viktor (Viktor Yushchenko) was poisoned and nearly died. He had to cease campaigning for a month to recover, and his face is still horribly scarred. The reform opposition was harassed in many ways, and barred from almost all television channels.

Students living in university housing were told by university officials that if their districts voted for the challenger, they would be evicted from their dorms in the middle of winter. When election day came, at polling sites in several areas where support for Yushchenko was high monitors discovered that pens had been filled with disappearing ink so that ballots would appear blank after they were cast.[10]

The election was clearly going to be close. Although the reform movement was strong in western and central Ukraine where most of the population are ethnic Ukrainians, the old guard was popular in eastern Ukraine, where in many provinces a majority of the population is ethnic Russian. The Russians favored the old Communist leaders because they felt they would keep closer ties between Ukraine and Russia than the reformers would. On election night, nonpartisan exit polls showed the reformer Yushchenko had won by 52 percent over Yanukovich's 43 percent. However, after a mysterious delay of several hours in which a number of eastern districts revised their original reports of turnout upward to incredible figures, the official result was reported to be Yanukovich 49 percent, Yushchenko 47 percent.

Yushchenko's supporters, in a fairly spontaneous movement, descended on the capital, Kiev, and set up a huge camp in Independence Square, with tens of thousands of demonstrators all wearing Yushchenko's trademark orange colors. There was some organization to the movement; a side effect of the old government barring Yushchenko from the television meant that he had been forced to go from town to town speaking directly to voters, and this had allowed him to build up a large, loose network of supporters. However, it was hardly what we would call an organized party.

For seventeen days the demonstration grew in Independence Square, and the campers vowed to stay until a new election was called. The capital was shut down. During this time two important sets of forces were engaged in the standoff and played key roles in the outcome.

First, the demonstration and the crisis of the regime attracted intervention from outside Ukraine. President Putin of Russia intervened strongly for dismissal of the demonstrators and the establishment of Yanukovich as president. At the same time the European Union, and especially Poland and Lithuania, intervened on behalf of Yushchenko. The Soros Foundation and other international organizations sent money and advisors to help the demonstration.

Second, and most surprisingly, a major faction of the Ukrainian secret police were concerned enough at the prospect of bloodshed and chaos that they intervened vigorously behind the scenes to protect the demonstrators. On November 28, the government ordered ten thousand troops to attack the demonstration in Kiev, but officials of the secret police hurried to Independence Square to warn the demonstrators, while others warned the government that if their forces attacked the demonstrators, forces from the army and the secret police would attack the attackers. The crisis was defused.[11]

After two and a half weeks the government gave in and a new election took place, at which Yushchenko was decisively elected president.

---

[10]Adrian Karatnycky, "Ukraine's Orange Revolution," *Foreign Affairs* 84 (March–April 2005), pp. 35–52.
[11]C. J. Chivers, "How Ukraine's Top Spies Changed the Nation's Path," *New York Times*, January 17, 2005, p. A1.

The importance of outside factors in the Orange Revolution is quite a common pattern in social movements, which usually succeed only when they can also find some outside sources of power and energy to complement their own. The revolution probably would have failed but for the support of the secret police and some of the army. Also, it might have failed if the EU, Poland, Lithuania, and international organizations had not intervened, but none of this is to minimize or trivialize the accomplishment of the courageous demonstrators of Independence Square. They probably would not have succeeded without the help of the secret police, the EU, and others, but if they had not first put their bodies on the line, nothing at all would have happened.

Afterword: This was the "Orange Revolution," and it was glorious. Sadly, however, not all revolutions turn out well. Remember—the loose organization that is in many ways a virtue of social movements does not particularly prepare them for organizing day-to-day government. After the election, Yushchenko took up the office of president and Yulia Tymoshenko, who had helped lead the revolution, became prime minister and leader of Yushchenko's supporters in the Parliament. It did not take long, however, before Yushchenko and Tymoshenko clashed over a mix of largely personal squabbles. The resulting paralysis of government discredited the new regime, and in the 2006 parliamentary election, Yushchenko's old rival Yanukovich took over control of the parliament. Yanukovich went on to be elected President in 2010, so he is firmly back in control. There have been ominous signs that a repressive, authoritarian quasi-democracy is returning. Opposition leaders, even including Tymoshenko, have been imprisoned.

KEY TERMS

social movement
mobilizing structures

political opportunity structures
framing processes

FURTHER READING

Barker, Colin, Johnson, Alan, and Lavalette, Michael, eds. *Leadership and Social Movements.* Manchester, UK: Manchester University Press, 2001.

Della Porta, Donatella, and Diani, Mario. *Social Movements: An Introduction,* 2nd ed. Oxford, UK: Blackwell, 2006.

Goodwin, Jeff, and Jasper, James M., eds. *Rethinking Social Movements: Structure, Meaning, and Emotion.* Lanham, MD: Rowman & Littlefield, 2004.

McAdam, Doug, McCarthy, John, and Zald, Mayer, eds. *Comparative Perspectives on Social Movements: Political Opportunities, Mobilizing Structures, and Cultural Framings.* New York, Cambridge University Press, 1996.

O'Brien, Kevin J., and Li, Lianjiang. *Rightful Resistance in Rural China.* New York: Cambridge University Press, 2006.

Scott, James C. *Weapons of the Weak: Everyday Forms of Peasant Resistance.* New Haven: Yale University Press, 1985.

Tarrow, Sidney, McAdam, Doug, and Tilly, Charles. *Dynamics of Contention.* New York: Cambridge University Press, 2001.

Tilly, Charles. *Contentious Performances.* New York: Cambridge University Press, 2008.

CHAPTER 14

NATIONAL DECISION-MAKING INSTITUTIONS: PARLIAMENTARY GOVERNMENT

In this chapter and Chapter 15, we will examine formal arrangements for governing democracies. This chapter will deal with parliamentary government, while Chapter 15 will deal with presidential government. **Parliamentary government** is conceptually the simpler of the two and is the form found in about half of all democracies. As you can see from the map in Figure 14.1, most European states are parliamentary systems, as are a number of African and Asian states. Parliamentary government will seem unusual to many American readers, however, since the United States is one of the democracies that operates with a presidential system.

In **presidential government,** the executive and legislature are selected in separate elections. (This is true even if the elections are held at the same time; in the United States, for instance, the President and members of the Congress are elected on the same day but voters choose them separately, on separate parts of the ballot.) In a parliamentary system, the only vote a citizen casts is for members of the parliament. The parliament then sets up the executive.

The basic principles of a pure parliamentary system are as follows:

1. The citizens of the state elect a parliament of representatives. It normally consists of one hundred to several hundred representatives. The parliament is the only elected body in the state. Bills passed by the parliament are the law, and no one can overrule them.

2. The state's executive power (managing the bureaucracy, conducting relations with other states, etc.) is lodged with a **cabinet** of women and men who are selected by the parliament to conduct the state's affairs. Most or all members of the cabinet are usually members of the parliament who take on executive responsibilities while still

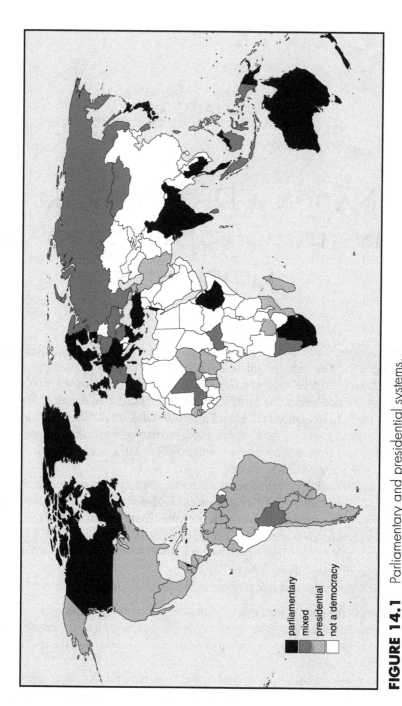

FIGURE 14.1   Parliamentary and presidential systems.

SOURCE: John Gerring, Strom C. Thacker, and Carola Moreno, "Are Parliamentary Systems Better?" (unpublished paper, October 6, 2005) table 1.

maintaining their seats in the parliament. Even the cabinet's leader (variously called "prime minister," "premier," "chancellor," etc.) continues to sit in the parliament.

3.   The cabinet retains executive power only as long as it has the "confidence" of the parliament; that is, only as long as it can command a majority of the votes. At any time, a majority vote in the parliament may unseat a cabinet and cause a new set of people to be selected as a cabinet.[1] We refer to this as the "government falling." If parliament does not actually take a vote to unseat the cabinet but the cabinet finds that it is unable to assemble majorities to pass its important bills, it is expected that the cabinet will resign.

4.   Just as the parliament holds the cabinet in jeopardy, the leader of the cabinet usually has the right to have the parliament disbanded, forcing a new election that will lead to a new distribution of power.[2]

This, in short, is parliamentary government. We will examine some finer points and some variations, but these four principles are basic. It is a simpler form than presidential government because, at least in its pure form, it does not allow for any separation of powers. The parliament and the cabinet (which operates only by the support of the parliament) hold all the state's governmental political power. The cabinet runs the operations of government, and takes the lead in developing proposals to be put into law by the parliament. Rather than acting as opposition forces like those in a presidential system such as the United States, the executive and legislative institutions are joined at the hip. The bottom line is that in a parliamentary system, with this simple concentration of power, political decisions should in principle be made clearly and directly with a minimum of delay. The cabinet and the parliament should at least most of the time be in agreement on important issues—if they were not, presumably the cabinet would fall. In most systems no court or any other body can block their will.

✦ Head of State

How, exactly, does all of this work? First of all, every parliamentary system has a separate, almost purely symbolic figure, called the **head of state.** In some countries (for instance, Great Britain, Denmark, Spain, the Netherlands), the head of state is a **constitutional monarch**—a monarch who carries out ceremonial functions but has little or no real political power.[3] In other states (Germany and Italy, for example), an official called "president" fills this role. Such states are not presidential systems, in which a president directs the politics of the state; we will deal with presidential systems in Chapter 15. Rather, such presidents conduct only the state's ceremonial functions.

The head of state is the state's ceremonial and symbolic leader. It is the head of state who dedicates hospitals and welcomes dignitaries. In most parliamentary systems

---

[1]In May 2005, for example, the Conservative Party introduced a motion of no confidence in the Canadian House of Commons, seeking to take advantage of a scandal plaguing the Liberal-led cabinet. They wanted to force an early election, which they expected they could win. The motion failed by just a single vote, after the Liberal prime minister lured a Conservative member to vote against the motion by giving her a cabinet position.

[2]In 2011, Irish Prime Minister Brian Cowen, faced with disintegrating support within his own party for austerity measures he believed were necessary, resigned his position and dissolved the parliament, which led to a new election.

[3]This is why we did not include countries like Spain or Great Britain under "monarchies" among autocratic systems in Chapter 7. Their monarchs are not the rulers of their states.

there is a further sense that in a time of great emergency and breakdown of the state, the head of state (who otherwise has little power) would assume great emergency power to pull the state through. For instance, when Germany suddenly occupied Norway during the Second World War it was the king, not the cabinet, who rallied the Norwegians to resist, and set up a government in exile.

In normal times, however, the main political function of a head of state in a parliamentary system is to ask one of the parties' leaders in the parliament to form a cabinet. Even in this, the head of state normally has little choice in the matter of whom to ask; most parliamentary systems have rules the head of state must follow, such as the rule that the leader of the largest party is the one who has the right to form a cabinet.

✦ HEAD OF GOVERNMENT

In addition to the head of state, a parliamentary system is led by a cabinet and its leader (variously called "prime minister," "premier," or "chancellor"), who serves as the **head of government.** The head of government and the cabinet carry out the executive functions of overseeing the bureaucracy, conducting military and diplomatic affairs, and taking the initiative on developing the budget and major policies. The head of government directs the state's business, but does not carry the symbolic weight that attaches to the head of state.

In a presidential system, the functions of head of state and head of government are combined in one person, the president. Barack Obama is the symbolic leader of the United States; for instance, it was his speech that people looked to for consolation after a shooter tried to assassinate Congresswoman Gabrielle Giffords in Tucson, Arizona, in 2011. But he also is the head of government, conducting diplomacy, directing the military, overseeing the bureaucracy, and proposing the budget and major policy initiatives.

Cabinets are formed in parliamentary systems in a straightforward manner. If one party has a majority of seats in the parliament, the party's leader becomes the "prime minister," "chancellor," or "premier," and appoints other members from the party to oversee different parts of policy, such as a foreign minister, a minister of defense, a health minister, or an agriculture minister.

If no one party holds a majority of the seats, then two or more parties, who together hold a majority of seats in the parliament, must form a **coalition** to lead the parliament. In forming a coalition, they will divide cabinet positions among themselves (for example, party A gets to name the premier, the minister of economics, the foreign minister, and the minister for agriculture; party B gets to name the minister for defense and the minister for industry). In the parliament, they agree that they will always cast their combined parties' votes on behalf of legislation proposed by the cabinet.

A cabinet always has to be constituted after an election. However, if for any number of reasons a cabinet has to be replaced at a time when elections are not due, that can happen readily without a new election. If the members of a coalition cease to agree about governing together, for instance, the cabinet may "fall" in the sense that it no longer commands a majority of votes in the parliament, and it must assemble a new coalition. In that case, the head of state will ask a leader of another party to negotiate a new coalition.

Less dramatically, after the Labour Party of Great Britain won a majority of seats in the House of Commons in the 2005 election, Prime Minister Tony Blair promised

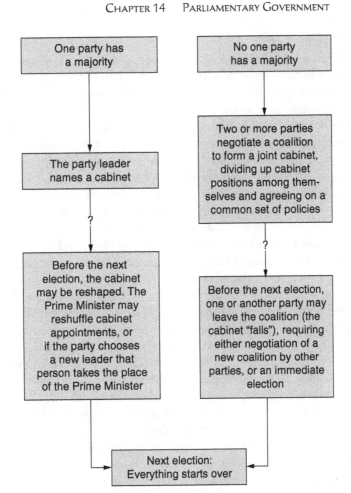

FIGURE 14.2   The process of cabinet formation.

that he would not stay in office the full time until the next election, but would step down by 2007. He had served a long time, and his personal popularity was compromised by his support for the Iraq War. When he stepped down, the process was simple. A new election was not necessary; rather, the Labour Party selected a new leader—Gordon Brown—to be the prime minister, and Brown stepped into the role.

Figure 14.2 summarizes the process of cabinet formation.

→ CABINET CONTROL

If parliamentary government is to function smoothly, the cabinet must be able to control what transpires in the parliament. If a cabinet could be voted out casually because the mood of the parliament had changed, no one would find that a satisfactory situation; government would be far too unstable. Particularly if the cabinet is based on a coalition of parties, the basis for bargaining on the cabinet's makeup is the number of votes each party can deliver. If the cabinet were not able to count regularly on the votes of one or another of the parties, the rest of the coalition would feel cheated and the coalition would not last long. As it happens, this was a large part of the problem for many years in Italy; the Christian Democratic Party was an important part of almost every coalition from 1945 to 1994, but the party was fragmented internally and was never able to guarantee its parliamentary support very well.

On the basis of this reasoning, we might expect to see, in the many smoothly functioning parliamentary systems, that the cabinets dominate their parliaments. And this is indeed the case. The usual situation is that the cabinet proposes legislation and Members of Parliament (MPs) debate it in the parliament; after all, it is only there that the opposition parties have their innings. Aside from the addition of minor amendments, however, there is rarely any question that the parliament will pass the legislation. In effect, the parliament is a rubber stamp for the cabinet.

It is ironic that a body that the parliament elects and that can be brought down at any time by it—a body that is, in effect, created by the parliament—can turn around and control what the parliament does. It is readily understandable that this should be the case, however. Recall that the cabinet members are top leaders of their parties. They are skillful politicians, and they have every reason to find ways to control what happens in the parliament to protect the power they enjoy as cabinet members.

In Chapter 11, we saw that a side effect of political parties was that they bind a number of people together in a single organization and provide a channel by which some of those people can control others. It is by this channel that cabinets control their parliaments. Cabinet members participate in parliamentary debates; they vote in parliament; but most important, they are leaders or powerful members of their party organizations in the parliament. For the other members, the party provides the avenue for advancement in the parliament. Debate time, committee assignments, the chance of a cabinet post someday—these are controlled for MPs by their party. Those who do not cooperate with their party's leaders do not advance. It is by this source of discipline, in their capacity as party leaders, that the cabinet members are able to impose their will on the parliament.

✦ WHAT DOES A PARLIAMENT DO?

The governmental role of a parliament, because it is so controlled by the cabinet, is difficult for students from the United States to appreciate. With regard to the passage of legislation, most parliaments are rubber stamps. In the 2009–2010 session, for instance, the British House of Commons approved every single bill that the cabinet submitted to it.[4] Britain's cabinet also tightly controls amendments to bills. From 1967 to 1971, the cabinet proposed 1,772 amendments to various bills; of these, 1,770 were approved. By contrast, other members of the House proposed 4,198 amendments during the same period, but only 210 of these passed.[5]

It is apparent that whatever parliaments do, deciding what legislation is to become law is not chief among them. In the unified governmental arrangement of a

---

[4]A good review of how a law is passed in the British Parliament is the House of Commons' "Brief Guide to Making Laws," at http://www.parliament.uk/documents/commons-information-office/Brief-Guides/Making-Laws.pdf
[5]Richard Rose, "Still the Era of Party Government," *Parliamentary Affairs* 36 (Summer 1983), pp. 284–85.

parliamentary system, the executive and legislative parts of government must work together to make legislation; and because over the years cabinets have learned to protect themselves by controlling their parliaments, it is generally accepted that cabinets call the tune in designing laws.

Is parliament then a useless appendage? No, because it still serves a number of purposes that are similar to those of the U.S. Congress, and one further purpose that is peculiar to parliamentary systems:

Public debate. First, a parliament furnishes a forum for the public debate of bills. The opposition parties have a chance, before a bill passes into law, to present their position on it and to stimulate public discussion. Often, bills do evolve under pressure of public opinion stimulated by parliamentary debate.

Scrutiny. Second, a parliament is a place where a bill that the cabinet wants to enact into law is submitted to detailed scrutiny both by the cabinet's friends and by its enemies. It may be that a number of small problems may be uncovered in a complicated bill, problems that the cabinet is happy enough to have brought to its attention. In the British example, almost all of the 1,772 amendments introduced by the cabinet were amendments to its *own bills*, because the House of Commons considers almost no legislation except legislation submitted by the cabinet. Most of those amendments were cabinet responses to problems that were discovered in the course of the parliament's consideration of their bills.

Oversight of policy. Third, a parliament is one of the few parts of the governmental apparatus that has an interest in keeping a critical eye on how the cabinet is administering public policy. The opposition parties are especially eager participants in this, for obvious reasons, but there is also a tradition that the cabinet must report regularly to the parliament how it is managing the affairs of the state. This sort of accounting takes many forms. In most parliamentary systems, there is some sort of annual speech made to the parliament describing in broad outlines the state of the nation and the cabinet's plans for the coming year, and this speech leads to a significant debate on the cabinet's overall program. In addition, many parliaments use a device called **question time,** in which various cabinet members appear regularly to answer questions from other members of the parliament about the way they are running their ministry. The answers they give may spark lively debates. You can view videos of the prime minister's question time in the British House of Commons at http://www.c-span.org/series/Prime-Ministers-Questions/. Click on a recent Question Time; then click on "video link."

This third function of parliaments—watching what the executive part of the government does—is not met as well in parliamentary as in presidential systems. The reason is that committees are not strong in parliaments, as we will see in the next section. Committees in a legislature have the potential to provide a powerful site for overseeing the executive. They are groups of legislators who specialize in a particular area of policy and who may become expert in it over the years. If they have a good professional staff, they may be able to match the offices of the executive in expertise and in the ability to handle evidence. If the committee can hold hearings and subpoena witnesses, it can provide a strong investigative force. However, committees in parliamentary systems are usually weak, and so the oversight function devolves primarily on individual MPs who are not much of a match for the experts of the executive office. In presidential systems like

"Delegate" and "Trustee" Models of Representation

An enduring debate in political science centers on what role representatives should assume vis-à-vis their constituents. In the **delegate model,** they should regard themselves as speaking for the constituents and should cast each vote as they think the constituents would wish it to be cast. The **trustee model** assumes that representatives learn more about an issue than any of their constituents could possibly know and have been chosen on the basis of their superior judgment; we would then expect that on at least some occasions they would vote differently than their constituents would wish them to vote.

Edmund Burke put the case for the trustee model beautifully in a speech to the electors of Bristol on November 3, 1774, after they had chosen him to represent them:

Certainly, gentlemen, it ought to be the happiness and glory of a representative, to live in the strictest union, the closest correspondence, and the most unreserved communication with his constituents. Their wishes ought to have great weight with him; their opinion high respect; their business unremitted attention. It is his duty to sacrifice his repose, his pleasures, his satisfactions, to theirs; and, above all, ever, and in all cases, to prefer their interest to his own. But, his unbiased opinion, his mature judgment, his enlightened conscience, he ought not to sacrifice to you, to any man, or to any set of men living. These he does not derive from your pleasure; no, nor from the law and the constitution. They are a trust from Providence, for the abuse of which he is deeply answerable. Your representative owes you, not his industry only, but his judgment; and he betrays, instead of serving you, if he sacrifices it to your opinion.

My worthy colleague says, his will ought to be subservient to yours. If that be all, the thing is innocent. If government were a matter of will upon any side, yours, without question, ought to be superior. But government and legislation are matters of reason and judgment, and not of inclination; and, what sort of reason is that, in which the determination precedes the discussion; in which one set of men deliberate, and another decide; and where those who form the conclusion are perhaps three hundred miles distant from those who hear the arguments?

To deliver an opinion, is the right of all men; that of constituents is a weighty and respectable opinion, which a representative ought always to rejoice to hear; and which he ought always most seriously to consider. But authoritative instructions; mandates issued, which the member is bound blindly and implicitly to obey, to vote and to argue for, though contrary to the clearest conviction of his judgment and conscience; these are things utterly unknown to the laws of this land, and which arise from a fundamental mistake of the whole order and tenor of our constitution.

SOURCE: Works of Edmund Burke (Boston, 1839: Charles C. Little and James Brown), vol. 2, p. 12.

that of the United States, in contrast, congressional committees can at their best operate as tough and knowledgeable watchdogs. (At their worst, of course, they can be tough, cranky, and perverse watchdogs—to some extent, this depends on one's point of view.)

From the discussion up to this point, it might seem that a parliament is a poor fish. It has little control over legislation except inasmuch as the cabinet can be persuaded to amend its own bills, and it is not as powerful in oversight of the executive as legislatures elsewhere. The one thing we have noted that it does well is to conduct public debate of bills. All this looks meager as compared, say, with the Congress of the United States.

Source of the executive. However, there is another function of parliaments that is peculiar to parliamentary systems. The fourth function of a parliament in a parliamentary system is to provide a pool of trained people for service in the executive and a setting in which they operate while serving in the executive; a legislature like the U.S. Congress does not do this. In most parliamentary systems, nearly all cabinet members and other political appointments in the executive are MPs. In Britain in 2012, 101 members of the House of Commons were serving in such positions as prime minister, minister for defense, first lord of the admiralty, other cabinet positions, or lesser executive positions such as parliamentary undersecretary to the minister for defense. These were members from the Conservative and Liberal-Democratic Parties, since the cabinet was based on a coalition of those two parties, and so at the same time, something like another hundred members of the Labour Party were hoping for electoral success that would give their party control of parliament and put them into executive positions. At any given time, therefore, about one-third of the members of the House of Commons either hold executive positions or are waiting for them; and of course, most of the rest are hoping to eventually be in this position.

The members of the political executive in a parliamentary system are men and women whom other members of their party have selected for executive tasks, and that selection is based largely on how well they have performed in debate and other tasks in the House. They are selected after some years of service in the House, which, like any organization, imposes norms of behavior on its members and in many subtle ways changes their behavior and the manner in which they react to things. Once they are in executive positions, these people are still sitting members of the House and take part in its daily business such as debate and voting on bills. Even while they hold executive office, they rub shoulders daily with their colleagues in the House.

Thus, an important task of parliament in a parliamentary system is to produce those who will hold executive office, train them in the ways of politics, select them, and then serve as the site from which they conduct the executive functions. In a presidential system, the legislative part of government exercises its strength in opposing the executive; but in a parliamentary system, it exercises its strength *through* the executive.

⤳ PARLIAMENTARY COMMITTEES

Committees of the U.S. House of Representatives and Senate are well known as independent, bristly bodies that presidents, civil servants, and even other members of the Congress defy only at their own risk. The State Department quivered in the 1950s when the House Un-American Affairs Committee investigated some of its younger personnel. Most bills that are introduced in the U.S. Congress are killed by a committee that refuses to vote them out with a recommendation, or else they die through delay in committees. This may even be true of bills originating in the presidential office. In one study, about one of every

Debate in the Canadian House of Commons.
© CP Images

thirteen presidential nominations for court justice, cabinet membership, or other office failed because a committee in the U.S. Senate refused to act on the nomination.[6]

Such independent bodies within a parliament would greatly weaken the central unity of parliament with the executive, because as independent sources of power, the committees would make it more difficult for the executive leaders to control what happened in the parliament. For a parliamentary system to work well, power must as much as possible be lodged with party leaders and no one else.

For this reason, parliamentary **committees** are generally a good deal weaker and less assertive than those in the U.S. Congress. All parliaments must have committees, of course. If hundreds of bills are submitted to a parliament in a year, the work of scrutinizing those bills carefully must be divided among the membership in some way or other; there is simply not time for each member to carefully scrutinize all bills that come down in a year. But care is taken that the committees do not operate too independently in doing their work.

As an extreme example of this, consider committees in the British House of Commons. Where the U.S. Congress uses "standing committees"—such as the Committee on Foreign Affairs, with a set group of members who serve for years and may become expert in the areas of policy that they cover—the British set up an ad hoc committee for each bill as it comes in. The members of this committee are not people who regularly work together; they have been put together to consider this bill. They have not had years

---

[6] Jon R. Bond, Richard Fleisher, and Glen S. Krutz, "Malign Neglect: Evidence that Delay Has Become the Primary Method of Defeating Presidential Appointments," *Congress & the Presidency* 36 (Issue #3, 2009), pp. 226–243, table 1.

of specialized experience in a particular area of policy. They cannot subpoena witnesses and do not hold open hearings on their bill. They have no permanent staff. As one might imagine, although they read the proposed bill carefully, discuss its implications, and propose changes to the cabinet, their ability to transform legislation and put their own independent stamp on it is quite limited. The cabinet need not fear that a committee in the House of Commons will stop or mangle its bill.

Other parliamentary systems are not so extreme. It is more convenient to use standing committees, so that a new group does not have to be constituted for each bill. Even the British have set up limited standing committees for the House of Commons (to oversee the executive and bureaucracy, not to review proposed bills). In smoothly working parliamentary systems, however, even standing committees still do not operate with the independence of the committees in the U.S. Congress.

✦ UPPER HOUSES

Since the basic principle of parliamentary government is to unify power so that it can be exercised smoothly, the existence of two legislative bodies would pose an obvious problem. In a presidential system like that of the United States, it is not infrequently the case that different parties control the two houses of Congress. (After the 2012 election, for instance, the Republican Party had a majority in the House of Representatives while the Democratic Party had a majority in the Senate.) If both houses' consent were required for a bill to pass in a parliamentary system, the cabinet's ability to dominate the legislative process would be greatly reduced.

Accordingly, although most parliamentary systems have two houses of parliament, the upper house usually has little political power. In all parliamentary systems, for instance, the cabinet is responsible only to the lower house; that is, a majority of members in the lower house can oust a cabinet, but that is not true of a majority in the upper house. Also, the ability of the upper house to reject legislation is usually limited. The House of Lords is the upper house of Britain's parliament, for instance, but it only has the power to delay a bill for one year if it disagrees with it.[7] If the House of Lords votes a bill down, the House of Commons can pass the bill a year later and it will become law even without the Lords' assent.

✦ ADVANTAGES AND DISADVANTAGES OF PARLIAMENTARY GOVERNMENT

Parliamentary government has two special advantages and two disadvantages:

Advantages

1. The government can respond directly to changed circumstances because power is unified. For example, parliamentary systems were more successful than more

---

[7]If the bill is a "money" bill dealing with taxes or expenditures, the Lords can only delay it for a month.

fragmented systems such as the United States at developing national energy policies in response to the shortages of oil in the 1970s. In a parliamentary system, all it takes to make a law is a majority of the votes in the parliament, and so it is straightforward for the party or parties in power to develop a policy and write it into law. In more fragmented systems such as that of the United States, many barriers are raised that can slow down or halt the passage of a law. The president may veto the law, the Supreme Court may rule it unconstitutional, or states may have proper jurisdiction over it.

2. A second advantage to a parliamentary system is that the lines of responsibility for policy making are clear. Elections should mean more, because voters can know exactly whom to blame for their current situation: the party or parties in power. Parties can be held to their election promises once they are in office, because there is nothing to prevent them from accomplishing in office what they had said they would do. In a more fragmented system such as that of the United States, this is not so. There are so many independent centers of power that we cannot blame an unhappy policy on any one of them. For example, the president can say that Congress did it, or Congress can point to the Supreme Court. President Harry Truman was famous for his desk-top slogan, "The buck stops here"; but in 1948, he campaigned across the country charging that the "do-nothing 80th Congress," controlled by the Republican Party, was to blame for his not having accomplished his goals as president. Elections can mean more with regard to public policy in a parliamentary system than in a more fragmented system because once election results are in, the party or parties that have won control of the parliament have no excuse for not enacting the policies they had promised.

Disadvantages

1. In a parliamentary system, there are few protections for a minority that feels it is being wronged. In a presidential system, a minority may hope that even if it has lost its fight in the legislature, it may retrieve things with the president or in the courts. As a result, the support of a bare majority is usually not enough to enact a law.

    We may view this as either an advantage or a disadvantage. It is the flip side of the advantage I noted previously, that in a parliamentary system policy making is straightforward. Although this is in general a good thing, it is clear that there must be some times when we would wish that the government had been slowed down and had been prevented from taking hasty action or action that did not have fairly broad support. A parliamentary system, because of its efficiency, does not necessarily do this.

2. A second disadvantage to the parliamentary system is that it may produce unstable government. If no single party holds a majority of seats, as I have noted above, a coalition of parties must form a cabinet. This is fine if the coalition partners are in general agreement on most issues. But any coalition is strictly a marriage of convenience. If the parties in it disagree on enough things, it may be hard to keep

them together and cooperating for very long. A socialist party may pull out because the coalition has not been able to agree on a program to stimulate employment, or a Hindu party may pull out over a question of religious policy. At that point, the government "falls," and parliament must negotiate a new coalition.

If this happens only occasionally, it is no problem. Political change must come from time to time. But in a parliamentary system, it sometimes happens that the numerical strength of the parties and their relationships with each other are such that it is always difficult to find a coalition that will keep together. This may lead to a paralyzing succession of governmental breakups, in which governmental control is so unstable that people lose confidence in the whole process. Germany suffered from this problem from 1918 until 1933, when Hitler overthrew the weakened democracy. France suffered from it until 1958, when the military intervened and imposed a presidential system. Italy has suffered from it chronically since 1945; in sixty-seven years (as of 2013), Italians have had sixty-two governments.[8] On the other hand, most parliamentary systems have not had this problem. The Scandinavian countries, the Low Countries, postwar Germany, and others have had long histories of stable government by coalitions.

→ LET'S MAKE SURE I HAVEN'T MADE THIS SOUND TOO SIMPLE

So far in this chapter I have described a "pure case" of parliamentarism, which is probably not met with exactly in any country of the world, although Great Britain comes close. You may have noticed that in describing parliamentary government, I hedged many of my statements with qualifiers like "usually" and "generally." I am a little concerned that you may have drawn the impression that lawmaking in a parliamentary system is easy for the cabinet, that it can just shoehorn bills through. Compared with most presidential systems (which we will look at in the next chapter), lawmaking in parliamentary systems is more straightforward. But it is not automatic, and it does not come without conflict or debate.

Actually, many parliamentary systems have incorporated various rules or institutions that soften the cabinet's or parliament's monopoly on power. For instance, Germany, Canada, India, and some other parliamentary systems are federal states; this means that important areas of policy are taken out of the hands of the cabinet and parliament. Also, Germany and some other parliamentary systems tolerate fairly strong and independent committees in parliament, which obviously lessens the cabinet's domination of the parliament. Finally, a number of parliamentary systems—Austria and Germany are two examples—have courts that can overrule an act of parliament.

---

[8]To address this problem, Italy changed its electoral system from proportional representation to a mostly single-member-district electoral system in 1999, and the 2001 election produced, for the first time, a cabinet with a stable majority of support in the Chamber of Deputies. (Not content with a good thing, though, in 2006 Premier Berlusconi forced through a return to PR, but with a bonus for large coalitions of parties. He thought his party would do better under PR, but despite the maneuver his party and its allies lost their majority.)

In these and other ways, most parliamentary systems incorporate a few exceptions to the basic principles that I listed at the opening of this chapter. Overall, however, even with these exceptions, the principles I have laid out hold, and those systems still have relatively more straightforward lawmaking than presidential systems.

The Inter-Parliamentary Union maintains a website with links to the parliaments of many countries: http://www.ipu.org.

✧ "CONSENSUS" PARLIAMENTARISM

The most notable exception to "pure case" parliamentarism is a variant called **consensus parliamentarism** that we find in a number of northern European states. Germany, Austria, the Scandinavian states, the Netherlands, and Belgium—roughly those states that have neocorporatist interest representation (see Chapter 12, pp. 294–296)—have parliamentary systems in which the distinction between government and opposition is more muted than in the "pure" sort of parliamentary system that I have sketched above. These states comprise a very important exception, obviously covering much real estate and making up a major part of the world economy.

Consistent with the thrust toward consensus in neocorporatist interest representation, the emphasis in these states is on forming a consensus among all parties in parliament, whether they are in the cabinet or in the opposition. Therefore, the cabinet does not run things so single-handedly, but negotiates and compromises at many points.

How does such cooperation work? First, as we saw when we looked at neocorporatism in Chapter 12, significant parts of the political process are removed from parliament (where the cabinet could control things) and are given to royal commissions or similar consultative committees, in which all interested parties are brought together. Then, once the process enters the parliament, the cabinet does not exert ruthless control over outcomes. Typically, for instance, parliaments in these states have fairly strong committees—and most importantly, the cabinet does not maintain control over the direction of the committees. Committee chairmanships are allocated to all of the parties in the parliament, whether they are in the cabinet or not, proportionally to how many members they have in the house. As a result, important policies tend to be developed over a longish period of negotiation, involving all parties.

Since in such a system it does not matter so hugely whether a party is in the cabinet or not, it is not uncommon to see a **minority cabinet,** one based on a coalition holding less than 50 percent of the votes in the parliament. Often, a party will decide that it would just as soon not be in the cabinet at that point in time, possibly for tactical reasons; and so it will promise not to vote for motions of no confidence even though it is not in the cabinet. This allows a smaller coalition of parties, which could not otherwise survive as a cabinet, to serve at its pleasure.

There are clearly some advantages to consensus parliamentarism. One important advantage is that policy remains more consistent over changes in the party makeup of cabinets. When a Labour-led coalition replaced a Conservative-led coalition in Norway in 2005, for instance, there was some change in emphasis, but no really dramatic change in policy—for the simple reason that Labour had been in on the making of these policies all along.

The main disadvantage of consensus parliamentarism is that it loses the clean accountability that I earlier noted as one of the advantages of pure parliamentarism. In "pure" parliamentarism of the British sort we always know which party is responsible for government policy. Elections can function effectively to enforce accountability, as voters look over the government's record and decide whether to "throw the rascals out." Under consensus parliamentarism it is harder to do this. In a sense, all of the parties are equally "rascals" (or not), since they have all been involved in the making of the policies.

How did consensus parliamentarism come about? These are all states with proportional representation electoral systems, which means that they have multiparty systems, and this in turn means that they must have coalition governments. Some have argued that it is this need for coalition that has led habits of cooperation to develop, and that it is therefore the proportional representation electoral system that lies at the heart of consensus parliamentarism.[9] However, many multiparty-based parliaments elsewhere—Canada, India, Italy, Spain, Greece, and others—have not developed the same sort of consensus and cooperation between government and opposition. It appears more likely that the political culture of northern Europe provides hospitable ground for such cooperation, which shows up both in neocorporatism and in consensus parliamentarism.

The contrast between consensus parliamentarism and "pure" parliamentarism may offer another instance of the distinction between power and choice. Certainly, the exercise of power is direct and uncompromising in "pure" parliamentarism, while in consensus parliamentarism one has a sense of governing parties yielding some of the power advantages they might otherwise enjoy, in order to help reach more stable solutions to collective choices.

✦ PARLIAMENTS IN AUTHORITARIAN SYSTEMS

Many states that are not parliamentary systems as described still have a parliamentary body. We saw in Chapter 10 that many non-democratic systems have found it useful to hold elections for a variety of reasons. Similarly, many of them find it useful to have a parliament. All a parliament is, after all, is a set of people who are designated to represent other groups of people, usually with some sort of geographic focus to the represented groups. It is not necessary that the parliament be able to operate independently or that it have discretion over laws. It can still do a number of useful things.

China's National People's Congress, for instance, is expected to—and does—ratify all laws that are submitted to it by the cabinet. It is not an elected body. Rather, its members are selected by municipal and provincial congresses, whose members are also not elected. The single legal party, the Communist Party, controls selection at all levels, and the Party makes sure that not many mavericks get into the Congress.

The Congress is not intended as a body to control the making of laws, or in any other way to control China's politics. It is obvious just from its size of about three thousand members, and from the fact that it meets only once annually for two weeks (which

---

[9]Arend Lijphart, *Patterns of Democracy: Government Forms and Performance in Thirty-Six Countries* (New Haven: Yale University Press, 1999); G. Bingham Powell, Jr., *Elections as Instruments of Democracy: Majoritarian and Proportional Visions* (New Haven: Yale University Press, 2000).

"TODAY THE PRIME MINISTER SIGNED TWO TREATIES, HELPED INCREASE OUR STEEL PRODUCTION, NARROWLY AVERTED WAR, AND SUGGESTED YOU BOTH SIGN UP AT SUNNYVALE RETIREMENT VILLAGE."

was reduced to 9 days for the 2009 session, in order to avoid discussions of that year's economic crisis), that it is not meant to do demanding work. About 70 percent of its members are government officials, and are not about to kick up dust. The meetings of the Congress consist of listening to speeches, voting to approve bills submitted by the government (which always pass), and appointing officials (who are always approved).[10]

Is this institution purely a decoration, then? The National People's Congress does not make law, but it does serve other useful purposes. Many of the members, especially those who are not government officials, submit bills of their own; these are not expected to pass, but they provide an occasion for debate, which helps the cabinet and the rest of the Party establishment sense the concerns of people outside Beijing. Each year, over a thousand such proposals are submitted.[11]

The Congress, like the Party itself, serves as a useful conduit for popular feeling. In a governmental system that permits neither a fully free press nor the formation of

---

[10]The national People's Congress did refuse in 2006 to ratify a new law explicitly protecting private property, which left-wing factions of the Party were very uncomfortable with. It was pushed through in 2007, however. See p. 270. In 2012, 8 percent of delegates abstained or voted against a new set of procedures for police interrogation of suspects. But such shows of independence are rare.

[11]"In China's Congress, A New Sense of Responsiveness," *New York Times*, March 8, 2005, p. A8.

organizations that might serve as rival foci of power, the government needs ways to obtain feedback and keep in touch with sentiments in the population; the Congress provides one way of maintaining contact. Since 1998 the government has begun to publish some of its bills before it submits them to the Congress for ratification and has allowed public comment on them. Usually these comments are ignored, but sometimes adjustments are made to the proposed laws, based on public reaction.[12]

Congress also serves as a symbol of a unified nation. Three thousand delegates drawn broadly from across the country serve as a fine platform from which to lay down both symbolic and real statements about national purpose. The formality of enacting a law or appointing an official adds legal finality to a process that primarily has occurred within the Party.

 ## EXAMPLE

Parliamentary Government in India

The general constitutional arrangement chosen for the new state of India in 1947 was largely drawn from the British parliamentary model, but a few devices were also borrowed from the United States. As is the case with any new state, including the United States in the early nineteenth century, India provides an interesting example of the evolution of governmental structure through custom and practice. It took the first four decades of politics in India to straighten out the relative power of the various parts of the government.

In the general outline of its constitution, India has a parliament consisting of two houses: The lower house is the Lok Sabha, or Council of the People, and the upper house is the Council of the States. A powerful prime minister and cabinet are responsible to the Lok Sabha, and a rather weak president oversees the whole structure. Thus far, India is a fairly standard parliamentary system, but it departs from common practice in two ways: (1) It is a federal system, with state governments that have a good deal of programmatic discretion, and (2) it has a powerful Supreme Court that can overturn actions of the rest of the government.

India faced grave problems on independence. Its people are relatively poor, with an average annual income per person of $3,700. This places the country among the bottom one-third of the world's states. At the same time, India's population of 1 billion people makes it the second largest state in the world and an important power on the international stage. India is deeply divided internally along ethnic and religious lines, with three major religions (Hindu, Sikh, and Muslim) and over fifteen major languages.

---

[12]Andrew Batson and Jason Dean, "Communists Move to Adapt Their Rule to a Richer China," *Wall Street Journal*, October 17, 2007, p. A1.

Until 1947, India was a colony of Great Britain. The pacifist leader Mohandas K. Gandhi and his Congress Party led a prolonged movement for independence, which succeeded in 1947. The Congress Party dominated early elections in the young democracy, and it was only after 1990 that real competition among parties developed as Congress lost its role as the dominant party.

Against this background, let us look at the development of India's governmental institutions and particularly the Lok Sabha. One important issue that had to be worked out in practice over the early decades of independence was the power of the president, who is elected by an electoral college consisting of the members of both houses of Parliament plus the members of the state legislatures. Thus, it is conceivable that a president could be of a different party than the party that controlled the Lok Sabha and cabinet. The written constitution initially gave the president broad powers, so it might have happened that a strong, independent presidency would have evolved in India.

The dominance of the Congress Party in the early years ensured that this did not happen, however. Congress controlled both houses of Parliament and most state governments; and so a series of electoral colleges dominated by the Congress Party selected the early presidents. The prime ministers, who led Congress, made certain that weak and unaggressive people who would be willing to do what the prime minister told them to do were put into the presidency. Thus, the presidency developed into an office much like that of the queen in Great Britain. In a formal sense, all of the powers enumerated are the president's, but the president will exercise them only on the advice of the prime minister. This was formalized in an amendment to the Constitution in 1976, stating that the president "shall" act in accordance with the advice of the cabinet and prime minister.

A second important question that had to be settled during this period was the relative power of Parliament and its cabinet vis-à-vis the Supreme Court. This question came to a point of crisis in 1967, when the Supreme Court ruled that an earlier amendment under which government land reforms were administered was unconstitutional because it violated the fundamental rights guaranteed elsewhere in the Constitution.[13] (Among other things, the fundamental rights include a right against the expropriation of property.) Therefore, the government could not constitutionally carry out land reform programs of the sort it wanted, and there was no way in which the Constitution could be amended that would allow it to do so. In effect, the court ruled that the fundamental rights constituted a special part of the Constitution that was above all parliamentary action.

As one might expect, this ruling caused considerable uproar. Over the next few years, the court held to its position that the fundamental rights occupied a special place in the Constitution and struck down various acts of Parliament in their name. A crisis was finally reached in 1971, when Prime Minister Indira Gandhi, frustrated at her inability to pass her reform programs, asked the president to dissolve the Lok Sabha and call for new elections. The single theme of this election was the question of parliamentary supremacy over the court. When her Congress Party swept to victory with 352 of the 518 seats in the Lok Sabha, the prime minister had a popular mandate

---

[13]Under the Indian Constitution, Parliament is responsible for initiating amendments to the Constitution. Many sorts of amendments can be passed by a simple majority in both houses, while certain sensitive areas require a two-thirds majority in both houses. Ratification by half the states is then necessary for the amendment to become law.

to establish Parliament as supreme. Parliament amended the Constitution with this simple addition:

> Notwithstanding anything in this constitution, Parliament may, in exercise of its constituent power, amend by way of addition, variation or repeal, any provision of this Constitution in accordance with the procedure laid down in this Article.

The next year this amendment was challenged in the Supreme Court. After the longest series of arguments ever heard there, the court gave in and sustained Parliament's right to amend any part of the Constitution.

Between these two developments—the establishment of the supremacy of Parliament and its cabinet first over the president and then over the Supreme Court—a basically parliamentary framework similar to that of Britain's was ensured.

To focus more specifically on the Parliament of India and how it operates, let us first note that the upper house, the Council of States, has less power than the lower house, as is typical of parliamentary systems. The members of the Council of States are not directly elected by voters, which would give them more prestige and legitimacy, but rather are chosen by the state legislatures and are sent to the Council of States to represent their states. Most bills do require the Council of States' assent to become law, but there is an important limitation on this power: money bills, including the annual budget and all tax laws, do not require its assent. Finally, the most important of all limitations on the power of the Council of States is that, as in all parliamentary systems, the prime minister and cabinet are responsible only to the lower house.

The Lok Sabha plays a role much like that of the House of Commons in Britain. It has full powers to pass or deny legislation, and the cabinet depends on it for its power. However, because of party discipline, the cabinet controls the Lok Sabha and its members do not feel individually all that powerful. In 2008, for instance, fifty-one of the fifty-two bills introduced by the cabinet were passed; none of the thirty-six bills introduced by individual members were passed.[14]

Aside from the usual informal cabinet domination of Parliament via party discipline, the Indian Constitution also gives the cabinet some formal powers that allow it further to dominate the parliament. The most important of these is the power to rule by decree when Parliament is not sitting. This was originally intended to allow for small matters that might need immediate attention when Parliament was not in session, but cabinets have come to use it as a device for taking measures they are not sure they could pass through Parliament. Such actions as wage freezes, excise taxes, and rules to control smuggling have become law in this way, sometimes just days before or after Parliament was in session.

Still, the Lok Sabha functions importantly as a place for debate and one where the opposition can regularly scrutinize cabinet activities. "Question time" has been borrowed from the British and has taken on a vigorous life in India. During the first hour of each parliamentary day, members of the cabinet are questioned by members of the house and their answers debated. In 2008, 152 questions were debated in this way out of 919 that had been submitted.[15]

---

[14]Lok Sabha Secretariat, *The Fourteenth Lok Sabha, 2004–2009: A Study* (New Delhi, Lok Sabha Secretariat, 2010), pp. 173–174.
[15]Ibid., pp. 154, 155.

In discussion of important, controversial bills, the Lok Sabha can become quite unruly. Perhaps the most extreme example in recent years was debate of the cabinet's bill for nuclear cooperation with the United States:

> India's legislators have a habit of unruliness: unsurprisingly, perhaps, when many— including over 100 currently—face criminal charges. But a special chaos prevailed during this debate. There was almost constant barracking and chanting; stray backbenchers raged inaudibly amid the din, for the television cameras and unknown reasons. Partly they were playing to the media gallery: some consider their constituents to be more impressed by strong words than sense. But it also reflected an ill-tempered display of horse trading, floor crossing, and, the opposition alleged, vote buying by the government.
>
> Prison cells were opened to allow five pro-government parliamentarians out to vote. The government also renamed the main airport in the northern state of Uttar Pradesh after the father of an important fence-sitter: the leader of a small party, Ajit Singh (who, in the event, voted against the government). But ten opposition members, including four from the main opposition Bharatiya Janata Party (BJP), voted with it. Perhaps anticipating this, three BJP members staged an unprecedented protest in Parliament. Shortly before the vote, they interrupted an angry Communist in mid-flow, by displaying wads of rupees to the packed chamber. They said this was the first installment of a 90 m-rupee ($2.1 m) bribe given to them by the government's camp; and that they could prove it.[16]

The Lok Sabha has had the usual rocky road of an institution with a new constitution that is being "broken in," but the parliamentary system of which it is a part seems to have established itself reasonably well in India.

---

[16]"A Tarnished Triumph," *The Economist*, July 26, 2008, p. 48.

✳ EXAMPLE

Parliamentary Government in Germany

Germany has a parliamentary system of the "consensus" sort, but with an emphasis on dividing power at numerous points so that negotiation is unavoidable. (This contrasts with a system like that of Sweden or Norway, which does not have so many possible places that a policy can be vetoed, but emphasizes more engendering cooperation by pulling policy out of parliament altogether, through the use of royal commissions.) The system was first set up in West Germany and has been extended, since German unification in 1990, to the eastern portion of the state as well. When the system was first established in 1949, the disaster of Hitler's rule was still vivid in everyone's mind. The occupying forces from France, Britain, and the United States were anxious to prevent the rise of another dictator, as were the Germans who wrote the new Constitution with them. Accordingly, power was deliberately fragmented, so that it would be hard for any one person to seize it all. The resulting system of "checks and balances" may seem natural to American readers, but it is unusual in parliamentary government, even of the consensus sort.

Parliament is not wholly supreme in Germany, as it would be in a "pure" parliamentary system and as it nearly is in India. First, Germany, like India, is a federal system, so there are many areas of governmental activity that are not controlled by the national government. And compared with India, the national government has not devised as many ways to control what the state governments do. Furthermore, there is an active system of judicial review in Germany, with one of the most accessible Supreme Courts in the world.[17] Among other things, the court has, for example, barred national administrations from outlawing the Communist Party and from establishing a national television network, and has determined the shape of Germany's laws on abortion. Federalism and the system of judicial review were new constitutional devices for Germany in 1949, inserted into the Constitution to diffuse and limit the exercise of power.

Another limitation on the power of the Bundestag (the lower house) and its cabinet is that Germany's parliament has a powerful upper house that may bar the lower house from many actions. We have seen that the House of Lords in Britain and the Council of States in India have limited power to block bills. However, the upper house of the German parliament, the Bundesrat, does have the power to block bills of many kinds.

The Bundesrat was strengthened in the Constitution to protect the powers of the newly established states. Its members are not directly elected but are appointed by the governments of the states. Under the Constitution, its consent is required for constitutional amendments and for any law that affects the administrative, tax, or territorial interests of the states. Such bills require the support of a majority in the Bundesrat to become law. An amendment to the constitution in 2006 reduced the number of bills deemed to fit this requirement to a bit over one-third of all bills. On all other bills, the lower house may override a Bundesrat veto.

As a result of these provisions, the lower house and its cabinet often do not have the free play to make policy that should theoretically be theirs in a parliamentary system. Whole areas of policy, such as education, are under the control of the states. Also, the cabinet and lower house may find that what they wish to do is ruled unconstitutional by the Supreme Court. Finally, if the Bundesrat is controlled by a different party than the lower house, the cabinet may find that it continually has to compromise with the opposition to pass bills. From 1991 to 2012, the governing coalition in the Bundestag only had a majority in the Bundesrat in seven of the twenty-two years.

The system generally produces compromise, but it can sometimes produce gridlock. A good example was the government's failure in July 1997 to pass a major tax reform. The Christian Democratic–controlled cabinet passed in the Bundestag a program to reduce high-end income taxes. This was defeated in the Social Democratic–controlled Bundesrat. The Social Democrats then passed in the Bundesrat their own counterproposal, to reduce labor costs in return for increased taxes and social benefits; this plan in turn was defeated in the Bundestag. End result—no change.

---

[17] Any German citizen may bring a case directly to the Supreme Court by simple petition; this does not even require a lawyer.

336   PART IV   THE APPARATUS OF GOVERNANCE

The lower house is set up along the familiar lines of parliamentary government. The cabinet is responsible only to the lower house, as is standard parliamentary practice, and so the lower house controls who sits in the executive. In its turn, the cabinet uses its control of party organization to ensure strict party voting in support of its bills. In fact, usually the members of the Bundestag do not vote individually; party leaders cast each party's total vote for or against a bill, and there is no roll call of individual members.

Even within the lower house, however, there are more checks and balances than we find in a pure parliamentary system. While party leaders expect total support for their parties' positions, ordinary members have more influence over what those positions will be than is the case in Britain.

First, the parties meet regularly as caucuses to determine their positions on bills. Policies are debated extensively within the party caucus, and the parties have full committee structures within the caucus, parallel to the committees of the Bundestag itself, to give careful and skilled scrutiny to each proposed bill. Thus the position the party will take on a bill is not dictated to ordinary members by the party leaders so strongly as it is in Britain—but once the party position is set, all members must vote for it unanimously.

Second, unlike the British House of Commons, there are about two dozen specialized standing committees with professional staffs. The committees scrutinize bills before they go to the full house, and the committee may amend the bills heavily.

The end result of all this is that German parliamentarism does not provide simple lines of responsibility. Even a defeat of the cabinet on a major bill in the lower house does not necessarily lead to the fall of the cabinet, because the Constitution provides for the ouster of a cabinet only under carefully specified conditions.[18]

The electorate cannot necessarily hold the ruling parties responsible for the state of public policy, because the policy may actually not have been the ruling parties' choice. It may have been forced on them by the Bundesrat or the Supreme Court, or it might be policy of the "states" rather than of the central government. German parliamentarism, while it retains the general form and most of the flexibility of parliamentarism, lacks the usual advantage of a clean line of responsibility.

[18]The only way a cabinet can be brought down is for the opposition to propose a motion of no confidence, including a statement of who the new chancellor would be; the motion requires a majority to pass. The cabinet is not required to resign if one of its major bills fails to pass.

KEY TERMS

parliamentary government	constitutional monarch	committees of parliament
presidential government	coalition	consensus
cabinet	question time	parliamentarism
head of state	delegate model	minority cabinet
head of government	trustee model	

Further Reading

Cox, Gary W. *The Efficient Secret.* New York: Cambridge University Press, 1987.

Dodd, Lawrence C., and Oppenheimer, Bruce I. *Congress Reconsidered,* 10th ed. Washington, DC: CQ Press, 2013.

Fish, M. Steven, and Kroenig, Matthew. *The Handbook of National Legislatures: A Global Survey.* New York: Cambridge University Press, 2009.

Lijphart, Arend. *Patterns of Democracy: Government Forms and Performance in Thirty-Six Countries.* New Haven: Yale University Press, 1999.

Loewenberg, Gerhard, Squire, Peverill, and Kiewit, D. Roderick, eds. *Legislatures: Comparative Perspectives on Representative Assemblies.* Ann Arbor: University of Michigan Press, 2002.

Pitkin, Hanna Fenichel. *The Concept of Representation.* Berkeley: University of California Press, 1967.

Poguntke, Thomas, and Webb, Paul. *The Presidentialization of Politics: A Comparative Study of Modern Democracies.* New York: Oxford University Press, 2004.

Sawer, Marian, Tremblay, Manon, and Trimble, Linda. *Representing Women in Parliament: A Comparative Study.* Oxford, UK: Routledge, 2006.

Strøm, Kaare, Müller, Wolfgang C., and Bergman, Torbjørn. *Delegation and Accountability in Parliamentary Democracies.* New York: Oxford University Press, 2004.

Parliamentary Affairs and *Legislative Studies Quarterly* are useful specialized journals relevant to this chapter.

CHAPTER 15

NATIONAL DECISION-MAKING INSTITUTIONS: PRESIDENTIAL GOVERNMENT

Presidential government is a democratic system in which the legislature and the executive exist independently and are elected independently of each other. Both parts of the governmental apparatus are responsible for the making and carrying out of law; but they are independent, so it often happens that they compete and find themselves in conflict. The executive and the legislature are not forced into the kind of cooperation that tends to be ensured in a parliamentary system, where the two depend closely on one another.

As you noted from the map in Figure 14.1 of the previous chapter, there are a large number of presidential systems in the world. The United States is probably the best known, but most Latin American states are also presidential systems, including large and important states like Mexico and Brazil. Most of the democracies in Africa are presidential systems, as are some Asian democracies. A number of Eastern European states—including the hugely important country of Russia—are presidential systems.

In a presidential system the president is elected by all of the voters in the state; the campaign offers a choice among individual candidates, although they are often nominees of political parties. Once the president has been elected, he or she chooses a cabinet of other figures to administer various parts of the government—for instance, a secretary of defense, a secretary of health, and others. The president and the president's cabinet operate much more independently of the legislative wing of government (usually called the Congress, or Assembly) than is the case in a parliamentary system. The president is not chosen by the Congress, and cannot be ousted by Congress except under extraordinary circumstances. (For instance, in the United States the Congress may impeach the President and if they convict him, remove him from office, but *only* for "treason, bribery, or other high crimes and misdemeanors.") Cabinet members may need to be confirmed by the Congress (in the United States, they must be confirmed by the Senate), but once confirmed they operate independently of the Congress. Their boss is the president.

Members of the legislative branch are chosen in a separate election, although their election may occur at the same time as the president's. They operate independently of the president. In a parliamentary system, the cabinet organizes the business of the legislature, but in a presidential system the members of the legislative branch organize their own agenda and their own work. How do they do this? The U.S. Congress provides a good example.

The U.S. Congress consists of two equal houses, the House of Representatives and the Senate. Each house is governed by leaders elected by the party that has a majority in the house and by strong, independent committees whose chairs are appointed from among members of the majority party. Seniority—the length of time one has served in the house—is an important factor in deciding who will chair committees. For instance in 2013, the Democratic Party had a majority in the Senate; the majority leader of the Senate was Democrat Harry Reid of Nevada. The Republicans had a majority in the House of Representatives, and the speaker of the House was Republican John Boehner of Ohio. These leaders exercised considerable influence over the business of their two houses, partly through their ability to persuade and partly through formal powers, such as the power to influence appointments to committees, to assign bills to committees, and to preside over debate.

However, the leaders cannot dominate their houses. A committee must first consider any bill before the house votes on it, and these committees operate independently and put their own considerable mark on bills that they bring to the full house. Power in each of the houses is so diffused—among leaders, committees, and the minority party—that no single person can control what happens in either one.

In most presidential systems each bill must be introduced by a member of the Congress, though presidents and their cabinets often initiate a bill indirectly by asking a member of the president's party to introduce the bill. The leaders of the Congress control how the bill is considered: which committee will consider it, how it may be amended, and when it will come up for a vote. If Congress passes a bill it goes on to the president, who has the power in most presidential systems—as in the United States—to either sign the bill into law or to veto it.

✦ POLITICAL PARTIES AND PRESIDENTIAL GOVERNMENT

Just as the political party provides a glue that allows the parliament and its cabinet to function in intimate cooperation, in a presidential system the political party may operate to soften the natural competition between independent executives and legislatures. In the United States, for example, the president, as head of one of the two great parties, is always guaranteed a large number of friends in the Congress. The system does not force the sort of unity on the president and his party's members of Congress that we would see in a parliamentary system, but still the bond of party allows for a good deal of coordination and cooperation. We noted in the preceding section that the President often will ask a member of his party to introduce a bill he wants Congress to consider.

However, note two things about presidential-legislative cooperation via party ties:

1. Parties are often more loosely unified in presidential systems than in parliamentary systems. In parliamentary systems, the premier and cabinet hold over the heads of ordinary members of parliament the threat that they may not advance into executive office if they do not cooperate with the leadership. In a presidential system, the president has little control over the careers and advancement of members of the legislature and cannot force unity on them. Even when the president's party has a majority of the seats in the legislature, the president will usually not be able to control what happens in the legislature as closely as most cabinets can control their parliaments in parliamentary systems.

2. There is no guarantee that the party that holds the presidency will also control the legislature. The two parts of the governmental apparatus are elected independently, so it may well happen that one party will have prevailed in the presidential election and another in elections for the legislature. For instance, after the 2012 election the Democratic Party held the presidency and controlled the Senate, but the Republicans controlled the House of Representatives. When there is divided control such as this, cooperation between the two branches of government is even more fragile.

In some multiparty, presidential systems (Brazil is an example), presidents negotiate formal coalitions of parties to support their program, awarding cabinet posts to their leaders. This may help to lessen the possibility of gridlock. However, even in Brazil the continued existence of the cabinet does not depend on its ability to pass its program, as it would in a parliamentary system. The president is independently elected and will continue in office no matter what happens to his bills. Not "joined at the hip" as in a parliamentary system, presidents and their congressional supporters, even those in a legislative coalition, have a much looser relationship than a cabinet and its supporters in a parliamentary system. Under these circumstances, parties provide a weaker attachment than they do in parliamentary systems.

The weak party link is heightened by the fact that voting in Congress is less a party affair than it would be in a parliament. As we have seen, in a parliamentary system regular failure by members to support their party's position would lead to collapse of the cabinet; for this reason, among others, members usually vote tightly along party lines. In a presidential system this incentive for discipline is lacking, so members of Congress choose their votes more individually. Although congressional parties in the United States are more united than they used to be, only about three-quarters of all conflictual bills passed by the House of Representatives are "party votes" even in the modest sense that over half the Democrats voted on one side and over half the Republicans on the other.[1]

---

[1]Richard Fleisher, Jon R. Bond, and John E. Owens, "A Reassessment of Party Voting in the US House." 2007. Paper presented at the Annual Meeting of the Midwest Political Science Association, Chicago, Illinois, April 12–15. "Conflictual" votes are those that were supported by fewer than 90 percent of the members of Congress—i.e., bills on which there was any significant disagreement among members.

CHAPTER 15   PRESIDENTIAL GOVERNMENT   341

A president has to straddle a range of supporters in Congress.

Copyright © Gene Basset. Reprinted with permission.

➜ PRESIDENTIAL LEADERSHIP

In a presidential system there is a much greater focus on one person—the president—than there is in a parliamentary system.

First, a president is clearly the most prominent political figure in the state, and is the source of most policy initiatives. Presidents have a personal mandate from the voters, and are therefore able to take more direct personal charge of policy than the cabinet can in a parliamentary system. A parliamentary cabinet owes its position to its parties' members in the parliament, and it must operate with them as a team. The president, on the other hand, is the only public official personally elected by the voters of the entire nation. This personal mandate focuses attention on the president, who is accordingly thrust into a position of policy leadership. In the United States the President's State of the Union message is the most closely watched event in the Congressional year. In that speech the President lays out his or her major policy initiatives for the year. In the making of laws, the legislative branch in a presidential system usually puts itself in a passive stance, waiting to respond to proposals that the president is expected to put forward.

The president, as head of state, also serves as the moral leader and symbol for the nation. At times of national emergency, it is the President people look to for guidance and comfort. Three days after the 9/11/2001 terrorist attack on the World Trade Center, President George W. Bush's speech at ground zero expressed the nation's grief in a way no one else could have done. Bush also used his position in later speeches to help Americans view 9/11 not as an attack by Muslims, but as an attack by terrorists, repeatedly urging that America was not at war with Muslims. When Congresswoman

Gabrielle Giffords was shot in an assassination attempt that horrified and gripped the nation in 2011, it was President Barack Obama's speech that expressed the nation's feelings and provided comfort.

You can view President Bush's ground zero speech at:

www.americanrhetoric.com/speeches/gwbush911groundzerobullhorn.htm.

President Obama's speech after the Gifford shooting is available at:

http://www.americanrhetoric.com/speeches/barackobama/barackobamatucson-memorial.htm

Unlike the cabinet in a parliamentary system, a presidential cabinet does not usually consist of party notables whose appointments are obligatory.[2] Rather, presidents appoint a group of cabinet officials who will be beholden to them personally for the appointment. In the United States these officials often come from positions in which they have had little political exposure: Over the last several decades, presidential cabinets have included college professors, lawyers, auto company executives, military officers, school superintendents, a president's brother, and other relatively nonpolitical figures. In general, prominent political figures are not included, and this helps to focus attention directly on the president, who dominates the executive branch.

In most presidential systems, the president is constitutionally designated as the commander-in-chief of the state's armed forces and is personally charged with the responsibility to direct the affairs of the state, semi-dictatorially if necessary, in the event of war or emergency. The president is also given personal responsibility for the direction of foreign policy.

A presidential system, then, provides for a coherent and unified policy leadership that may be lacking in a parliamentary cabinet, especially if that cabinet is formed of a coalition of parties, and most especially if the state suffers from cabinet instability.

→ PRESIDENTIAL AND PARLIAMENTARY SYSTEMS COMPARED

What difference does it make whether a state is a parliamentary or a presidential system? Some differences include the following (I will expand on each of these in the next several sections):

- Responsibility for policy is more difficult to identify in a presidential system.
- Comprehensive policy is more difficult to accomplish in a presidential system than in a parliamentary system.
- Recruitment of executive leaders differs in the two systems.
- There are special problems for review and control of the executive in a presidential system.
- The political process is less flexible in presidential systems than in parliamentary systems, because of presidents' fixed terms.

---

[2] As I noted earlier, countries like Brazil are the exceptions to this.

- The symbolic and political aspects of the executive are unified in a presidential system but split in a parliamentary system.
- Constitutional review of some sort seems to be more necessary in a presidential system, as is true in general of divided systems of power.

→ RESPONSIBILITY FOR POLICY

Although a presidential system provides a clear focus for leadership, ironically, it blurs the final responsibility for policies. In a presidential system, no one part of the governmental apparatus can be held responsible for any particular policy or any particular lack of policy. If the president proposes a new energy tax and the tax is defeated in Congress, who is responsible for the lack of tax reform? Is the Congress obstinate? Should the president have proposed a tax that would have been more apt to pass? Should the president have lobbied harder for the bill? It might also happen that the bill would pass, but with amendments that changed it substantially. Is it now the president's bill? Congress's? No one's?

This hazy attribution of responsibility leads to two important weaknesses. First, when voters cannot pin the responsibility for policies on any particular official, their electoral choices become less significant. Should a voter who was upset at high unemployment in the United States in 2012 have voted Republican? That would have been a vote against the party of President Barack Obama, who should perhaps have been held responsible for the unemployment. But what if the Republican-controlled House of Representatives was at fault, as Obama claimed? Faced with a choice like this, the bewildered voter must vote on less policy-related criteria, such as a candidate's personality or personal favors that an incumbent candidate has been able to do while in office. Eventually, elections come to function less as vehicles by which voters can affect the making of policy.[3]

A second weakness of presidential government caused by its blurring of responsibility is that when public officials do not have clear responsibility for a policy, they may literally begin to behave irresponsibly. If Congress is not directly held responsible for producing a balanced budget, it is easy for members of Congress to vote simultaneously to cut taxes (which will look good to their constituents) and to build highways (which will also look good). "Through the fault of no one in particular," the government may spend more than it raises in taxes.

Campaign platforms of U.S. parties provide another example of the chronic irresponsibility of presidential systems. Because a party's president cannot be blamed for failing to enact into law the party's promises—after all, Congress might not cooperate—it becomes easy for the parties to promise in their campaign platforms whatever they think the voters would like to hear, or whatever ideological activists in the party demand. With power as fragmented as it is in a presidential system, the

---

[3]A large body of literature has long urged that the United States should try to accomplish "responsible party government" similar to that of Britain. The argument has been that U.S. parties should become more tightly disciplined, not that the constitutional division of power should be changed. A good example is E. E. Schattschneider, *Party Government* (New York: Holt, Rinehart and Winston, 1942).

parties will never lack for an alibi if the voters should take them to task for not delivering on their promises.

PRESIDENTIAL SYSTEMS AND COMPREHENSIVE POLICY

It is more difficult to make comprehensive policies in a presidential system than in a parliamentary one. Policies are more likely to be patched together of varied compromises or perhaps not put together at all. The United States is one of the few democracies that lack a national energy policy, though this has not been for want of trying. Presidents have proposed energy policies to Congress but have never been able to reach agreement on anything recognizable as a policy.

It is not enough that a mere majority of the people want something done, because a bill can be blocked at the many points in a fragmented system; considerably more than a majority is required if all the defensive positions provided by a fragmented system are to be overrun. Universal background checks for buying guns, prayer in the schools, and the equal rights amendment are examples of policies that a majority of the U.S. population probably wants but that have been impossible to enact into law.

If you are suspicious of majorities, as many of the authors of the U.S. Constitution were, this may be a good effect of the fragmentation of power. However, there is no denying that it makes the government slow to respond to change.

RECRUITMENT OF EXECUTIVE LEADERS

There is a significant difference between the sorts of leaders who emerge in parliamentary and presidential systems. In a parliamentary system, all or almost all the leaders in the executive have emerged from careers in parliament; they continue to serve in the parliament while they hold executive office. This means that they will have had fairly similar lives before they entered the executive. For a decade or two, their jobs will have consisted of crafting the wording of bills and serving the voters in their constituency. They will have had a long period of exposure to the wide range of issues facing the state in areas such as diplomacy, tax policy, education, and defense.

The similarity of these executive officers is made greater by the fact that they are mostly selected from among MPs on the basis of a common set of criteria. Members who move up to executive office are those who do a good job as MPs: They debate well, they keep their noses to the grindstone, they vote with the party.

Recruitment in a parliamentary system has the virtue that officials are chosen by those who know them and their work (their fellow MPs) during a career that has made them familiar with most of the issues they will have to face. It has the disadvantage that there is not much variety among the types of people chosen, they have had little experience in managing things (legislators spend most of their time responding to initiatives of others), and there are few "mavericks" or adventurers included.

In a presidential system, recruitment into executive office is fairly independent of the legislative parts of government. While a president may have started off with a legislative career, this is by no means necessary. Consider the last eleven presidents of the United States:

President	Background
Dwight D. Eisenhower	Army general
John F. Kennedy	Senator
Lyndon B. Johnson	Senator
Richard M. Nixon	Senator; vice president
Gerald Ford	Member of Congress
Jimmy Carter	Farmer; governor of Georgia
Ronald Reagan	Film actor; governor of California
George H.W. Bush	Appointee to various foreign policy positions; vice president
William Clinton	Governor of Arkansas
George W. Bush	Governor of Texas
Barack Obama	Senator

More than half of these men had established themselves with the public by something other than service in one of the houses of Congress.

Furthermore, the recruitment of other officials to staff the executive does not draw heavily on Congress in the United States, or in most other presidential systems. Only a few members of recent U.S. presidents' cabinets have been drawn from careers in the Senate or House; four of the fifteen members of Barack Obama's initial cabinet, for instance, had served in Congress. Many of the most distinctive and interesting cabinet members have been drawn from careers that were far from Congress, careers that gave them interesting points of view of their own. Some examples are Henry Kissinger, secretary of state under Nixon and Ford, a political science professor; Donna Shalala, secretary of health and human services under Clinton, chancellor of the University of Wisconsin; Colin Powell, secretary of state under George W. Bush, Army general; Timothy Geithner, secretary of the treasury under Barack Obama, president of the Federal Reserve Board of New York; and Steven Chu, secretary of energy under Barack Obama, Nobel Prize-winning physics professor.

The way presidents and their cabinet secretaries are selected has the advantage of bringing varied talents and backgrounds to the task of executive leadership. Through the introduction of new blood, problems may be seen in a new light. New points of view and the zeal of amateurs may be brought into policy making at a high level, as in Jimmy Carter's campaigns on behalf of human rights.

On the other hand, selection is often haphazard, because it is not done by those who have worked directly with the candidates; candidates may have had little previous experience in important areas (Carter, Reagan, Clinton, and George W. Bush, for instance, had no experience with foreign policy before they became president); and inappropriate choices are more likely than in a parliamentary system.[4]

In short, in a parliamentary system you know much more what you are getting than in a presidential system. For better or for worse, executive officials will not surprise you in a parliamentary system—but they will not disappoint you, either.

---

[4]An argument for the desirability of recruitment in the parliamentary mode is made in Harold W. Chase, Robert Holt, and John Turner, *American Government in Comparative Perspective* (New York: Franklin Watts, 1980), chap. 2.

346   PART IV   THE APPARATUS OF GOVERNANCE

→ REVIEW AND CONTROL OF THE EXECUTIVE

Most organizations have some sort of plural board to which the executive leader is responsible and reports regularly. The president of a business corporation must report regularly to a board of directors, the president of a university reports to the board of trustees of the university, and a superintendent of schools reports to a school board.

In a parliamentary system, the parliament serves this purpose. The prime minister and cabinet regularly report to the parliament on the conduct of their business, answer questions, and engage in give and take with members. There is regular and frequent contact between the cabinet and the parliament regarding the conduct of government.[5]

In a presidential system, however, the members of the executive operate in relative isolation. The media looks over their shoulders constantly, of course, and there is occasionally contact between them and the legislature regarding a particular bill or investigation. However, there is no broader body to which the president or other members of the executive regularly report.

This isolation of the presidency often leads to an inward-looking presidential office, with "inside" staff persons accused by those on the outside of arrogance and insensitivity. The presidential office is often characterized as a "bubble."

---

[5]For further comparison along these lines, see William S. Livingston, "Britain and America: The Institutionalization of Accountability," *Journal of Politics* 38 (November 1976), pp. 870–94.

✦ FLEXIBILITY OF THE POLITICAL PROCESS

Parliamentary systems are able to adjust readily to changing circumstances. If a parliamentary leader loses support after a couple of years, or if new political issues arise that rearrange the political landscape, it is not very complicated for the system to adjust. The existing cabinet can be ousted if some of the parties that originally supported it withdraw their support, or if the current leader is discredited, and then a new cabinet can be negotiated—with a new leader, or arranged along different political lines, or whatever is needed to accommodate the changed circumstances. A presidential system, however, exists unchanged for a fixed term of years, until the next presidential election. The president cannot easily be ousted if circumstances change. A particularly difficult problem is posed if the president becomes very ill, in which case there is always a good deal of uncertainty about who has the power to declare the president incompetent to govern and replace him or her with someone else. And if the president dies, in many presidential systems this means that a vice president will succeed to supreme power—someone typically who would never otherwise have attained the leadership of the state, and who may be quite inappropriate for the job.[6]

✦ THE SPLIT EXECUTIVE OF PARLIAMENTARY SYSTEMS

As I noted in Chapter 14 (see pp. 317–319), the executive is split in parliamentary systems into the prime minister and cabinet who are responsible for political and administrative leadership, and a head of state who is responsible for the symbolic leadership of the state. In a presidential system, these functions are united in a single person—the president.

In Britain, the prime minister and cabinet are responsible for political and administrative leadership, but it is the queen who carries on the ceremonies and personifies the state. It is she who opens new hospitals and bridges; it is her health and that of her family that the media subjects to ghoulish scrutiny; it is she at whose death the nation will go into deep mourning. Like the president of the United States, she is greeted by a special song when she enters a room, and crowds press in on her wherever she goes. The prime minister remains a more mundane figure, one who goes about the daily business of governing but does not personally represent the state.

It is clear why the two kinds of executive function are united in one person in a presidential system. The executive is weakened in a presidential system because its legislature is not under its control; for strong leadership to be available to the state, almost everything that can be done to strengthen the president's hand must be done. One such thing, an important one, is to give presidents an aura of majesty that they can use to bolster their political power. More than one member of Congress has gone into the White House and walked out shaken, muttering, "When the president of the United States asks you to vote in the country's interest, what can you do?"

In a parliamentary system, there is no need to add to the power of the cabinet in this way, because the cabinet is capable of providing effective leadership without it. If it

---

[6]Juan Linz, "The Perils of Presidentialism," in Arend Lijphart, ed., *Parliamentary Versus Presidential Government* (New York: Oxford University Press, 1992).

is not necessary to combine the two faces of the executive in a single office, as is done in presidential systems, there are some obvious advantages to separating them.[7]

First, the symbolic representation of the state in a person appears to fill a deep need of a modern people. The devotion people feel for those who personify their state is real. Consider the following examples. At John F. Kennedy's assassination in 1963, many Americans felt what they later reported as an almost religious experience; some people felt his wounds as stigmata, just as some devout Christians feel Christ's wounds on the cross. In Britain, the most disturbing political event of the twentieth century, with the sole exception of the two world wars, occurred when Prince Edward VIII left the throne to marry a divorced American. Norwegians credit King Haakon VII with having almost singlehandedly kept the government from surrendering to Germany in 1941, taking his family into exile and making it possible for Norwegians to fight on in the Resistance. Finally, consider the heart-wrenching difficulty with which Americans faced what would have been a fairly simple task if they had not revered the presidency so much—the ouster of Richard M. Nixon in 1974 when he had been implicated in petty crimes.

If modern people need a person on whom to focus their reverence for the state, it is better if this is someone who has little involvement in day-to-day politics. The queen of Britain, the king of Sweden, the emperor of Japan, the president of Germany (not a president as I have used the term in this chapter, but an almost purely ceremonial head of state)—these people have almost no political power and are not involved in routine decision making. This allows them to serve as unblemished objects of national affection. Presidents of the United States, in contrast, must excite mixed feelings among the many people who find themselves in political disagreement with them. On the one hand, these people want to revere the president, but on the other hand, they find themselves faced with a political leader whose policies they may despise. Conservative Republicans were in many ways deprived of an object for national reverence by the presidency of Barack Obama, as were Democrats during the presidency of George W. Bush.

Thus, one problem of blending the political executive and the symbolic executive in a single office is that the symbolic function cannot be performed as well when it is located in an office that is inevitably involved in controversy.

The flip side of this problem is that political leadership does not operate as cleanly when reverence for the state gets mixed up with it. A president of the United States gains unfair political advantage from serving as the symbol of the state. Franklin Roosevelt, Lyndon Johnson, Richard Nixon, and Ronald Reagan were adept at taking positions that had questionable public support, appearing on radio or television with the sober attention that a president can command, and selling that endangered program to the public. After all, this man is the president of the United States! Whom can we trust more than him?

We may welcome this as a way to cut through the confusion of the divided powers of a presidential system, but it is still unfortunate that, on any public issue at

---

[7]Note that my interpretation here is based on choice rather than power. I have been trying to explain why the two kinds of executive function are united in presidential systems but not in parliamentary systems, and my explanation has rested on the claim that the needs of society will have led systems to sort out in this way. In other words, since the collective choice of unified executive power is better for presidential systems, that is what will be chosen; since unified executive power is not needed in parliamentary systems, it will not occur there. A power interpretation might have been given instead, based perhaps on the greater opportunities a president has to aggrandize all executive power to herself.

a given time, only one side is able to take advantage of this reverential response. In a parliamentary system, the cabinet and the opposition operate on more even terms in seeking public support for their political positions.[8]

✦ WHY AREN'T ALL DEMOCRACIES PARLIAMENTARY SYSTEMS?

Let us review for a moment what we have looked at in the last section. We examined several points on which presidential government and parliamentary government differ:

- Difficulty of locating responsibility for policies.
- Difficulty of making comprehensive policy.
- A different pattern of recruitment for executive leaders.
- Special problems for review and control.
- The inflexibility of fixed terms in presidential systems, and the need for a vice-president.
- A merger of the symbolic and political aspects of the executive in a single person.

While not every one of these differences showed the presidential system to disadvantage, most did. You have probably been left with the impression that parliamentary systems are better than presidential ones. The parliamentary system is a simpler, more direct, and usually more efficient way of making public choices. Why, then, aren't all democracies parliamentary systems?

The main reason lies in the very faithfulness with which a parliamentary system translates political divisions into the policy-making machinery. Policy is set and administered in a parliamentary system by a party or a cooperative coalition of parties that controls a majority of the votes in the parliament. This makes for straightforward policy making if a stable majority is possible in the parliament. If the country is divided into numerous parties that are intensely hostile to each other, however, it may be impossible to find a large enough number of members of parliament who can work together cooperatively as a governing coalition. It may be that no working majority is available.

Under these circumstances, a parliamentary system may limp along with an unstable government, as Italy has since 1945, or the country may prefer to use a presidential system because it is more stable than what parliamentarism could provide.

France after World War II was plagued by parliamentary instability similar to that of Italy. The Communists could not cooperate with any of the other parties, Catholic parties had trouble cooperating with Socialists, and many other parties had irreconcilable conflicts. In 1958, the regime collapsed through a revolt by French settlers in Algeria. The military terminated the Fourth Republic and asked Charles de Gaulle to design a new system; his new constitution replaced parliamentary government with a **hybrid presidential system**—a mixture of parliamentary and presidential government, leaning heavily toward the latter. (See the detailed French example pp. 356–358.)

---

[8]You may find related arguments in Edward Shils and Michael Young, "The Meaning of the Coronation," *Sociological Review* 1 (December 1953), pp. 63–81; and in Lewis Lipsitz, "If, as Verba Says, the State Functions as a Religion, What Are We to Do Then to Save Our Souls?" *American Political Science Review* 52 (June 1968), pp. 527–35; see also William E. Scheuerman, "American Kingship? Monarchical Origins of Modern Presidentialism," *Polity* 37 (2005), pp. 24–53.

Presidential Leadership

The presidency offers us a particularly good chance to study a vital aspect of politics that political science neglects—leadership. Certainly, few things are more important to politics than the qualities that produce effective political leadership, but leadership is a difficult thing to pin down for analysis. Most political figures—members of Congress, prime ministers, cabinet officials—operate within such constraints of power that their main accomplishments come through bargaining and deal-making or through coalitions where their role is blended with that of others. It is often hard to pull out of a particular political outcome the contribution of any one person's leadership.

The American presidency, however, offers us an office whose leadership is available for examination every day in almost all political questions that face the country. Further, it is exceedingly well documented, with huge libraries of the papers of all postwar presidents. Various scholars have taken this opportunity to study leadership by studying the presidency—notably Richard E. Neustadt, who analyzed presidents' political strategies in *Presidential Power and the Modern Presidents* (New York: Free Press, 1991), and James David Barber, who analyzed presidents' emotional security and its effect on how productively they could provide leadership in *The Presidential Character* (Englewood Cliffs, NJ: Prentice-Hall, 1977). A superbly broad view of presidential leadership, based on decades of observation and reflection, is Fred I. Greenstein's *The Presidential Difference: Leadership Style from FDR to George W. Bush* (Princeton: Princeton University Press, 2nd ed., 2004).

Greenstein views leadership as a function of six qualities, which could probably never all be perfected in any one person; for him, each of our modern presidents has represented a mix of strengths and weaknesses on these six qualities:

- *Proficiency as a public communicator*
- *Organizational capacity*—the ability to choose good advisors and to use them in such a way that they did not just parrot back his desired opinion but helped him to work through policy choices in a thoughtful way.
- *Political skill*—the ability to get other people to do what he wanted.
- *Vision*—having an overarching goal and the ability to see how specific policies would help bring about that goal.
- *Cognitive style*—the ability to process the torrent of advice and information the president receives on every issue. In other words, the ability to understand the policies he was pushing for.
- *Emotional intelligence*—"the ability to manage his emotions and turn them to constructive purposes, rather than being dominated by them and allowing them to diminish his leadership."[9]

Greenstein does not rank these six characteristics (and resists in his book playing the cheap and easy game of ranking the presidents), but it appears that for him, the most critical qualities are proficiency as a public communicator and emotional intelligence. Cognitive style appears to rank surprisingly low among the criteria for success. As Greenstein points out, two presidents whom he regards as weak in cognitive capacity—Truman, because he relied too much on oversimplified analogies drawn from his readings of popular history, and Reagan because he just didn't care about details—were two presidents who had a major impact on the country.

[9]Fred I. Greenstein, *The Presidential Difference: Leadership Style from FDR to George W. Bush* (Princeton: Princeton University Press, 2004), p. 6. Both Greenstein and I, by the way, use the exclusively male pronoun here to describe an office that until now has always been held by men. This almost certainly will not be the case for much longer.

In much of the Third World, too, democracies have often found that they must provide a more stable base for executive leadership than is possible under parliamentarism, even if this means fragmenting and complicating public decision-making processes. Many Latin American democracies, under the influence of the United States, used presidential systems from the start; Mexico and Costa Rica are good examples. Many African and Asian democracies—faced with the political stresses of poverty, modernization, and ethnic diversity—have had to modify what started out as parliamentary systems. Nigeria, for example, abandoned parliamentarism when it reestablished a democratic government in 1975 and set up a system with an independent presidency rather like that of the United States.[10]

Perhaps the message of this chapter, in the end, is that a parliamentary system is the best form of democracy if a country is sufficiently unified to cooperate in parliamentary politics.

✦ DEMOCRACY AND THE QUESTION OF ACCOUNTABILITY

In this chapter and in Chapter 14 we have looked at national policy-making institutions. In a democracy, these institutions—the parliament or congress, and the president (if there is one)—are representative institutions: they are elected by the citizens of the state in order to represent them in setting the policies of the state. An important question for democracies is how such institutions can be made accountable to the citizens. **Accountability** of a democratic government is the extent to which citizens can hold members of the government responsible by rewarding them when they do what the citizens want and punishing them when they do not.[11] Accountability is central to democracy, but as we will see it is not easy to accomplish.

The problem with accountability is that legislators and executives are engaged full-time in massive, detailed and technical work that is beyond the capacity of citizens to follow closely, even with the help of the press and reporters. For instance, the *Federal Register*, in which new regulations of the national government are published, comprised 77,186 pages just for the year 2012. Not even a member of the United States Congress can possibly read all of the bills on which she votes.

Thus, it is difficult for citizens to hold government officials accountable for their actions, for the simple reason that it is difficult for citizens to follow all of the actions of officials. Edmund Burke alluded to this problem in his argument (see box, p. 322) that his constituents should think of him as a "trustee" rather than a "delegate" whom they should reward or punish for his votes. Since they could not adequately follow the details of the issues on which he was voting, they should rather judge him by his general character, and vote for him if they trusted him to make choices on their behalf. They should not try to hold him accountable, because it was not possible for them to do so in a satisfactory way.

This is a genuine problem, because government officials have so much more control of information about what they have been doing than ordinary citizens have. Officials can manipulate the information that reaches citizens to create the picture

---

[10]This, in turn, succumbed to a military coup in 1983, but an elected presidency was reestablished in 1999.
[11]An excellent set of essays on the problem of accountability in democracies is Adam Przeworski, Susan C. Stokes, and Bernard Manin, *Democracy, Accountability, and Representation* (New York: Cambridge University Press, 1999).

they want citizens to see, whether or not it is accurate. For instance, it is possible for members of Congress to simultaneously satisfy both the broad citizenry and narrow interests; they can vote the way the citizens want on a few highly publicized bills, and vote to satisfy the narrow interest on hundreds of amendments and procedural votes that the interest groups focus on keenly, but that do not rise to the attention of the general public.[12] In this and other ways, officials can control, to a considerable extent, the picture the public gets of how they are doing their jobs.

The problem described here is an instance of a more general problem in politics and economics called the **principal-agent problem**. This problem can arise when one party (the "principal") delegates powers to another (the "agent") to use on the principal's behalf. A principal-agent problem then exists if (1) the agent has interests that differ from the principal's (i.e., there is a situation of incentive incompatibility—see the discussion of incentive incompatibility on pp. 209–211), and further, (2) the agent is able to control information so that the principal has difficulty finding out whether the agent is truly serving the principal's interests rather than his or her own. The principal-agent problem arises in many situations: when managers of a company are supposed to be serving the interests of shareholders but may be tempted instead to engineer large raises for themselves; when civil servants may benefit from using up their entire budget by the end of the fiscal year whether the spending is needed or not; and in the case of Congress, when members may benefit from serving the needs of narrow interests, even when doing so does not serve the needs of most of their constituents.

In any principal-agent problem, the solution lies in finding ways to either align the interests of the agent with those of the principal, or to find ways for the principal to overcome the difficulty of following what the agent is doing. In the case of democratic accountability, most of the solutions that are available involve the latter strategy— finding ways for voters to overcome the problem of following what the agent is doing. Three possible solutions are transparency and active reporting; focusing on parties as teams rather than on individual officials; and "retrospective voting."

- **Transparency and active reporting.** Reporters, unlike citizens, can work full-time at trying to understand what is happening in the government. Well-researched reports that distill information for the public can be very helpful, and these provide most of the information citizens receive about officials' actions. There are limitations to the utility of this solution, however, since the process is too vast even for reporters to comprehend fully. Additionally, reporters—like the public they serve—are to some extent at the mercy of the officials' control of the information.

  Beyond the work of the press, various groups and special interests study the voting records of members of Congress and develop measures of their tendency across votes. For instance, Project Vote Smart (www.votesmart.org) gathers key votes of public officials from the president down to members of state legislatures, and reports them by issue area. It also publishes important speeches by the officials, and gives various interest groups' ratings of the officials' voting records (scores from Planned Parenthood, National Association of Wheat Farmers, Americans for Tax

---

[12]Murray Edelman, *The Symbolic Uses of Politics* (Champaign, IL: University of Illinois Press, 1964).

Reform, etc.). For Senator John Cornyn, for instance, in 2012 the website listed ratings from 218 different interest groups. This information can be very helpful to citizens.

- **Focusing on parties as teams.** If parties are tightly disciplined and usually operate in unison, rather than as holding companies of individual officials, the citizens' task of holding government accountable becomes easier. The press and the public can then track what a few political parties are doing, rather than what hundreds of individual officials are doing. Under a system of "responsible party government" (see footnote 3, p. 343), a party publishes regularly a program of what it will enact if it achieves power and then, when in power, votes in such a disciplined way that it is able to enact any bill it wants. Under these circumstances, it should be possible for voters to expect a party to do what it has promised and to hold it responsible if it does not do so. "Responsible party government" is an ideal not fully achievable anywhere. It is easier to approximate in parliamentary systems than in presidential systems, because the unified powers of a parliamentary system make it more difficult to shift and evade responsibility for policies than under the divided powers of a presidential system. (See p. 343.) Limiting the focus to a few disciplined parties rather than to a larger number of individual officials does not eliminate the problem of accountability, but it does make it a good deal easier.

  In the United States, citizens focus partly on what individual officials do and partly on what members of a party do together. Voting for members of Congress, for instance, is partly a matter of the member's party designation, but also partly a matter of votes that are cast for the member as an individual. Voters' use of parties as a summary indication of what their representatives have been doing helps them, to some extent, to solve the problem of information.

- **Retrospective voting.** In **retrospective voting,** voters look back at the years an official has been in office and vote to reelect the official if their lives and the lives of those around them have gone well over those years; if not, they vote to oust the official. This allows them to skirt the problem of information. When voting retrospectively, citizens do not need to know specifically what officials have been doing (information that officials can control), but need only to know whether their own lives are going well (information that they control).

  In 1980, when Ronald Reagan was challenging the incumbent president, Jimmy Carter, he famously asked voters, "Are you better off than you were four years ago?" He suggested they vote for him if they were not. Carter lost the election. In the 2008 U.S. election, with the economy doing very badly, voters rejected the Republican Party's presidential candidate, but also punished Republicans right down to the level of state legislative candidates. In 2010, with the economy still going badly, they turned around and voted strongly against the Democrats, who had then been in charge for two years.

  Retrospective voting solves rather neatly the problem of accessing information by changing the question from "What are officials doing?" (which is difficult for citizens to assess) to "How is my life going?" (which is easy for citizens to assess). It is a blunt instrument, however. Officials may be held responsible for circumstances that they cannot really control. It is arguably the case, for instance, that the long-awaited bursting of an economic bubble in 2008 was something that had been developing

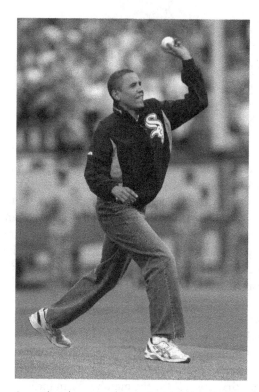

A president does many things—President Barack
Obama throws out the ceremonial first pitch.
© Jamie Squire/Getty Images

for twenty years, and was not exclusively the responsibility of George W. Bush and
the Republicans. However, they were the ones in office at the time, and they were
punished for it. Similarly, in 2010 Democrats were in their turn punished because
the country was still in recession, even though the economic downturn had probably
been so deep that no one could have turned it around in just two years.

Christopher H. Achen and Larry M. Bartels argue in a serious, sometimes
amusing, paper, "Blind Retrospection: Electoral Responses to Drought, Flu, and
Shark Attacks," that voters often punish incumbents if bad things happen, whether
or not the government could actually have done anything about them. Achen and
Bartels investigate droughts and other such adverse events, including voter reaction
to a rash of deadly shark attacks on the southern New Jersey coast in July 1916.
Resort business was badly hurt, and people's incomes suffered in those New Jersey
counties. In the presidential election that November, support for President
Woodrow Wilson, who was running for reelection, was about 3 percent lower in
the coastal counties than would otherwise have been expected. The president could
not have prevented the shark attacks, but he was punished at the polls for them.

None of these three solutions is perfect, though all help. The basic problem remains that
it is not possible for voters to control all of the information that is necessary for them

to hold officials fully accountable. We know that there is considerable accountability, if only because elected officials seem to be concerned about how voters are responding to them, but accountability is spotty and is almost surely dominated by those voters who are organized into interest groups.

✦ A NOTE ON INSTITUTIONS AND POWER

Having looked at formal governmental arrangements in this chapter and in Chapter 14, I should note an important principle of constitutions that is well illustrated by the development of some of the governmental institutions we have examined.

We saw in Chapter 9 that written constitutions are not static but change and develop as they are put to use. One predictable way in which constitutions evolve is this: *If power is given constitutionally to a body that lacks the resources to exercise it, informal mechanisms usually develop that lead to the de facto loss of that power even though the formality of power remains.*

One excellent example of this principle at work is the domination of parliaments by their cabinets. Parliaments are vested with supreme authority in the constitutions of parliamentary systems, but a parliament is too large and diverse a group to actually take charge of governmental policy by itself. Over the years, cabinets have developed ways to bully parliaments through the informal mechanism of the disciplined political party. This has shifted actual power from the parliament to its cabinet, which allows policy to be made coherently; but the parliaments remain formally supreme. Political parties are rarely even mentioned in the written constitutions of democracies, but they are an important part of living constitutions.

A second example is provided by the Bundesrat, the upper house of the German parliament, which I described in Chapter 14. The Bundesrat, you will recall, was established in the Constitution to protect the independence of the new "states" from the central government. If Germany was to be a federal system, it was reasoned, the states needed a lever in the central government to allow them a veto over actions that would take away their rights. Therefore, the Bundesrat was established. It consists of representatives from the state governments and must give its consent to any action affecting their tax, administrative, or territorial interests.

Ironically, setting up the Bundesrat and giving it these powers has made it, and the states that appoint its members, sufficiently important to national political leaders that they try to control what goes on in state politics and have undermined the independence of state leaders in important ways. Elections for state governments often turn on a national issue rather than on those of the state. Central government leaders campaign hard in the state, not for local figures or for the local party but on national political questions. Once a state election is over, national leaders often put pressure on local leaders to form a particular sort of coalition in the state parliament solely because of the effect the nature of the local coalition will have on the state's votes in the Bundesrat. The existence of the Bundesrat has arguably had an effect just the opposite of what the framers of Germany's Constitution intended. The states' prerogatives would have probably been protected adequately by the Supreme Court if the Bundesrat had never been established, and local political leaders would have been free to operate more independently of national leaders.

In these examples, actual power relationships—the living constitution—have fit themselves to the power of groups in ways quite different from what those who designed the formal document intended. Such mismatches between reality and formal rules usually result from a failure to appreciate fully the "power" in "power and choice." If one thinks of politics primarily as a question of working out proper choices for the state, it will seem that an appropriate set of procedures should do that, and good politics will follow from good written procedures. This ignores the necessities and possibilities of power and can lead to surprises for those who write rules.

✳ EXAMPLE

Presidential Hybrid in France

After World War II, France established a fairly standard parliamentary system. It was immobilized, however, by the hostility of various parties to each other and by weak discipline within many of them, which made it difficult for coalitions to form and hold together. The average life of a cabinet was about six months, and because ministers did not stay in place long enough to establish full control of their offices, France was governed by its bureaucracy rather than by its elected leadership.[13] There was a sense of drift, and when in 1958 tensions associated with Algeria's war for independence were added to the mix, things fell apart. With some involvement by the military, the existing government stepped down and Charles de Gaulle, the hero of World War II, was brought in to set up a new system.

De Gaulle and his advisers designed a new type of democracy with elements of presidential and parliamentary government in which, however, the presidential elements have gradually come to dominate. As first designed, the system consisted of a cabinet responsible to the National Assembly (the lower house of parliament) and of a rather powerful but nonpolitical president. The president, indirectly elected by an assembly of parliament and of mayors, was, in turn, to designate the premier and to preside over the affairs of government, especially foreign affairs and defense policy. The president could bring issues before the French electorate in the form of a referendum and could, if necessary, declare a state of emergency and take over power for up to six months at a time. The president could not veto acts of parliament.

It was not certain just what the president's role would be under this constitution. The key question was whether the French president would act as a primarily symbolic figure, performing these functions only on the advice of the cabinet, or would realize

---

[13]Ironically, the bureaucracy governed France rather well. During this period, France pioneered in establishing the European Economic Community, and its per capita income grew at a rate of 3.5 percent annually in real terms throughout the 1950s.

the full potential of the office's powers. De Gaulle served as the first president under the new system from 1958 to 1969, and he strengthened the power of the president in many ways. Most importantly:

- He had the Constitution changed so that the president was directly elected. The president has since then carried great prestige as the only official elected by all the people of France.
- He established the principle that a president could dismiss a premier at will. The Constitution states that the president "designates" the premier but says nothing about dismissal. In 1962, de Gaulle asked his first premier, Michel Debre, to resign, and Debre did so. From that point on, another important element of presidential power had been established.

Today, as long as the same party simultaneously holds the presidency and controls the parliament, the premier and cabinet function as agents of the president, conducting much of the day-to-day business of the state and representing the president in relations with the parliament.

The new Constitution included a large number of constraints on the independence of the parliament, intended to prevent the immobility that had characterized French government before 1958. Numerous rules allow the cabinet directly to manage the passage of a bill through the parliament. Among other things, the cabinet, not the parliamentary leaders, sets the calendar and determines under what circumstances bills can be amended. Also, the independence and power of parliamentary committees were decreased by the simple device of limiting their number to six. This ensured that they would be large bodies (the average size of committees is over a hundred members) covering broad areas of policy and that they would never again be able to develop into tight-knit groups of specialists.

By laying down these rules, the new French Constitution brought about executive supremacy of the sort that in most parliamentary systems is achieved informally through the political party. Constitutional design was used to ensure executive supremacy because parties had failed to establish the necessary discipline. One could argue that the informal device is better because it is more flexible, but the constitutional devices appear to have worked well in France.

These rules established executive domination over the parliament, and—as things have developed in France—"executive" usually means the president. However, an oddity of the French hybrid of parliamentary and presidential systems is that, because the president governs through a cabinet that can be turned out of office at will by the National Assembly, it is crucial whether the same party controls the presidency and the National Assembly. If the president's party has a majority (or close to it) in the National Assembly, things work smoothly in the way I have described previously; the president names a cabinet, and the party's majority in the National Assembly supports it. This has been the situation for all but ten of the fifty-five years since the establishment of the Fifth Republic.

However, if the president's party does not control the National Assembly, there is a possibility of deadlock. It is at least theoretically possible that the president could name cabinet upon cabinet that would be voted down by the National Assembly as quickly as they were named. The president could not rule under these circumstances.

Split control of the presidency and National Assembly has occurred three times. In 1985, conservatives won a majority in the National Assembly, and President François Mitterrand, a socialist, had to appoint Jacques Chirac, a Gaullist, to the premiership.

No one knew how this would work; but it turned out that when the premier and the president are of different parties, more of the executive power rests with the premier than with the president, although both are then powerful. Mitterrand chose the ministers for defense and foreign affairs, while Chirac chose the rest; legislative initiatives lay wholly with Chirac and his cabinet, although Mitterrand limited Chirac's ability to promulgate decrees; and at international conferences both Mitterrand and Chirac represented France, dividing allotted speaking time between them (!).

This period of split control, dubbed "cohabitation" by the French, lasted only three years, until the next election. There have been two more intervals of cohabitation since then, and by now, the French have worked out good precedents and traditions to handle cohabitation. They appear to like having the president and the cabinet be of different parties.

Nonetheless, this is still a constitutional oddity. In all sorts of ways, the constitution of France (constitution with a small *c*) changes abruptly when different parties come to control the National Assembly and the presidency. It is almost as if France has two constitutions, which switch on and off like lights.

The current president of France is François Hollande, elected in 2012. His Socialist Party holds a majority in the parliament, so the constitutional light switch is set to "on" for the president.

 ## EXAMPLE

Presidential Government in Mexico

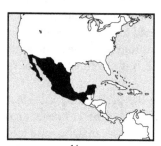

The presidency of Mexico offers a fascinating example of a political institution in transition. The Mexican presidential system arose out of a decade and a half of chaos, from 1910 to 1925. In a swirling tumult of banditry, revolutionary battles, and civil war, approximately a million Mexicans starved or were killed. The period of violence ended in the establishment of the dominant Party of the Institutionalized Revolution (PRI), which we examined in Chapter 11.[14] By the 1930s, the rule of the party had centered on a strong presidency, and that regime has continued.

Under the system as it arose at that time and as it lasted until well into the 1990s, the president dominated Mexican politics. Although the Constitution provided for an independent Congress and Supreme Court much like those of the United States, neither of these bodies operated independently of the president. Mexico was a dominant party system (see pp. 263–266), with the PRI controlling almost all offices, and until 1988, all but a handful of members of Congress were from the PRI.

A president in office had great power. What saved the system from an unbearable concentration of power was the firm tradition that presidents must step down after a

---

[14]Actually, initially the party called itself the Mexican Revolutionary Party; it restructured itself and changed its name to the PRI in 1946.

single six-year term. For six years, a single person ruled, but then the party (influenced strongly by the incumbent president) chose another person to serve the next six years.[15] It was at this point that the system showed some flexibility over the years. The outgoing president based his decision on a combination of negotiations among party leaders, consultations with the PRI's three "sectors," interest-group pressures, and consideration of the popular mood.[16] Therefore, when the mood was to the left, a president emerged from the left; corrupt presidents were often succeeded by reformers.

Such concentration of power, even if it was temporary, encouraged corruption, which has been a chronic problem of Mexican politics. Mexico under the PRI appeared to go through alternate waves of corruption and reform. Although presidential corruption was obviously costly and broad, some speculated cynically that it had the hidden virtue of making possible the regular six-year transition in power. If it were not for the illicit wealth on which they could retire, so this reasoning went, some officials would have devised a way of subverting the six-year rule so that they could stay in office!

During the period of reform from 1982 to 2000, however, a series of three reform PRI presidents oversaw the gradual opening of the political and economic system that culminated in the PRI's final loss of power in the 2000 election. The last of these, Lopez Zedillo, was especially active in reform and in opening up the political system. In the congressional elections of 1997, the PRI lost control of the lower house of Congress, although it kept control of the Senate. This had enormous implications for the all-powerful Mexican presidency, since without control of the Congress, President Zedillo was unable to continue the one-man show that had always been the Mexican presidency. Fortunately, he was already oriented toward reform of the system. He had been trying to open up the party and take control away from the "dinosaurs"; for instance, he had encouraged his attorney general to fire all twenty-three hundred officers in the corrupt narcotics investigation agency, rehiring only six hundred who were judged reliable. With the PRI's loss of dominance in the Congress, Zedillo appeared almost to welcome his party's losses as a chance to establish more reasonable working relations with the Congress. He was patient with the inevitable growing pains of a new opposition who had never before held real power, and while he lost on several significant issues—elimination of his huge secret "President's discretionary fund"; establishment of a new fund that he opposed, which sent several hundred million dollars of federal money back to towns and cities with no strings attached; and a cut in the value-added tax—he was able to get his budget through the opposition-controlled Congress in essentially the form he had requested.

In 2000, the transformation was completed by the ousting of PRI from the presidency with the election of Vicente Fox, the candidate of the PAN party. Since then, Mexico has had a presidential system marked by somewhat messy "checks and balances." Fox's party did not have a majority in the Congress, and he often failed to get his proposals passed—inconvenient for Fox, but probably healthy for Mexican democracy. In a frustrating judgment of his administration, Mexico's voters cut his PAN

---

[15]Again, with increasing competition from opposition parties, the party's nomination will never again confer the office as automatically as it did through and including the 1988 election. In all elections since then, the outcome was open and competitive; the PRI candidate lost in the 2000 election.

[16]Rubio F. Luis, "The Presidential Nomination Process," in George W. Grayson, ed., *Prospects for Democracy in Mexico* (New Brunswick, NJ: Transaction Publishers, 1990), p. 76.

party's representation in Congress from 207 to 155 in elections in July 2003. In 2006 they elected as Fox's successor yet another PAN president, Felipe Calderón, but the party still fell short of a majority in both houses of Congress. In 2012 a PRI candidate, Enrique Peña Nieto, was elected, but the PRI did not gain a majority in the Chamber of Deputies. Mexico is now clearly a competitive democracy.

The immense changes in the working of Mexican government over just twenty years illustrate how closely the formal governmental structures of politics interact with informal structures such as parties, interest groups, and the media. The written Constitution of Mexico did not change from the 1980s to 2000, but Mexico's governmental institutions changed immeasurably. They changed because the way in which parties structured political conflict changed.

Key Terms

presidential government	accountability	retrospective voting
hybrid presidential system	principal-agent problem	

Further Reading

Cheibub, José Antonio. *Presidentialism, Parliamentarism, and Democracy*. New York: Cambridge University Press, 2007.

Edwards, George C., III, and Wayne, Stephen. *Presidential Leadership*, 8th ed. Florence, KY: Wadsworth Cengage, 2010.

Gerring, John, Thacker, Strom, and Morena, Carola. "Are Parliamentary Systems Better?" *Comparative Political Studies* 42 (2009), pp. 327-359.

Greenstein, Fred I. *The Presidential Difference: Leadership Style from FDR to George W. Bush*. Princeton: Princeton University Press, 2004.

Lijphart, Arend., ed. *Parliamentary Versus Presidential Government*. New York: Oxford University Press, 1992.

Linz, Juan J., and Valenzuela, Arturo, eds. *The Failure of Presidential Democracy*. Baltimore: Johns Hopkins University Press, 1994.

Mainwaring, Scott, and Shugart, Matthew Soberg, eds. *Presidentialism and Democracy in Latin America*. New York: Cambridge University Press, 1997.

Neustadt, Richard E. *Presidential Power and the Modern Presidents*. New York: Free Press, 1991.

Pika, Joseph A., and Maltese, John Anthony. *The Politics of the Presidency*, 8th ed. Washington, DC: CQ Press, 2012.

"Presidential and Parliamentary Democracies: Which Works Best?" Special Conference Issue, *Political Science Quarterly* 109 (no. 3, 1994).

Przeworski, Adam, Stokes, Susan C., and Manin, Bernard, eds. *Democracy, Accountability, and Representation*. New York: Cambridge University Press, 1999.

Shugart, Matthew Soberg, and Carey, John M. *Presidents and Assemblies: Constitutional Design and Electoral Dynamics*. New York: Cambridge University Press, 1992.

CHAPTER 16

BUREAUCRACY AND THE PUBLIC SECTOR

In the last few chapters, we reviewed the structure of governments. However, a great deal goes into policy making beyond what government leaders do. The government may establish by law that the speed limit on highways is fifty-five miles per hour, but what this means in detail is determined by thousands of traffic patrol officers across the country. It is they who decide whether they ticket if you drive fifty-six miles per hour or whether there is a "zone of grace" so that they ticket you only for speeds of sixty miles per hour or above. It is they who decide whether a woman with a bleeding wound in her arm is in bad enough shape that she is justified in speeding to the hospital at seventy-five miles per hour. It is they who decide whether to treat a well-dressed man in a dark blue sedan differently from a young person in blue jeans who is driving a bright yellow car, warning the one and ticketing the other.

The local police officer, the public health inspector, the teacher in a public school, also high level managers like the president of a state university or an assistant secretary of defense—these are as much a part of the policy-making machinery as the legislator, judge, or U.S. president. For most citizens, it is these people—and not the legislator, judge, or president—who embody the state and its policies. People receive the policies of the state from police officers, immigration officials, IRS agents, schoolteachers, agricultural extension agents, and members of fire departments, not from the nation's president or members of Congress.

Any state, if its operations are at all complex, must have a large number of people like this—people who are not directly involved in politics in the sense that they share in making major decisions but who are involved in the construction and implementation of the policies that carry out those decisions. These are collectively called the **public administration** of the state. A modern state has a large number of people in its public administration. Figure 16.1 charts the growth of the public administration of the United States since 1950.

361

362   PART IV   THE APPARATUS OF GOVERNANCE

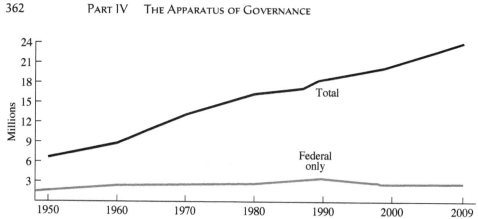

FIGURE 16.1 Total number of civilian public employees (combined local, state, and federal) in the United States, 1950–2009.

SOURCE: U.S. Bureau of the Census, *Statistical Abstract of the United States.*

The number of public employees in the United States climbed from 6.4 million in 1950 to over 22 million in 2009, almost wholly from increases at the state and local levels. (Federal civilian employment increased over this period only by about 1.2 million.) Public employment climbed not only in absolute numbers but also as a proportion of the total civilian labor force. In 1950, 11 percent of employed civilians were public employees; by 2009, this had risen to 15 percent. In other words, by 2009, better than one out of seven employed persons was a member of the U.S. public administration.

This actually understates the growth of government operations by a good deal. Federal operations grew by much more than the growth in federal employment shown in the chart. What happened is that the federal government has tended over the years to expand its operations by contracting out jobs to private research firms and service providers not directly in the government.

✦ PUBLIC ADMINISTRATION AS A POLITICAL PROBLEM

That such a large number of people are involved in policy making poses something of a problem for the state. Public administrators as a group have significant governmental power, yet they are too numerous and individually too unimportant to be controlled effectively. Therefore, *a significant part of the governmental power of any state is of necessity not under close political control.*

Examples of the governmental discretion of administrators are numerous. American police officers have a good deal of discretion, for instance, in whom they stop to search for weapons or illegal substances; investigations of the New Jersey state police in 1999 revealed "racial profiling"—identifying possible suspects based on certain physical characteristics—for stop-and-search actions that are probably widespread around the country. As another example, consider IRS agents in the United States who audit taxpayers' returns. Inevitably, given the complexity of our tax laws, interpretation of the

CHAPTER 16   BUREAUCRACY AND THE PUBLIC SECTOR   363

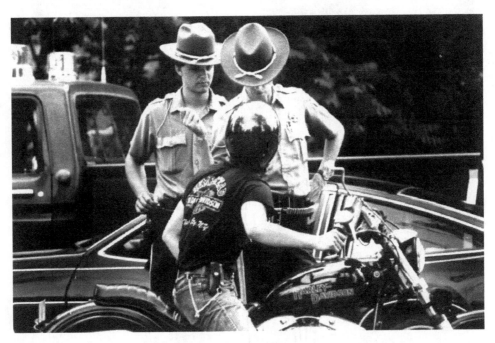

The state meets a citizen, Woodstock, New York.

© Mark Antman/Stock Boston

laws will vary from one agent to the next. As a result, the outcome of a tax audit depends at least to some extent on which agent handles it. Finally, consider that the teachers of America determine, by their individual actions, the grading system that has such important ultimate effects on students' careers.

These and other examples show that even rather minor administrators make a good deal of governmental policy. The politically responsive part of government (elected officials, party leaders, military juntas, courts, or whatever) must be concerned to make certain that, at least in broad outline, they control the policies implemented by administrators. This control is not easy to design, however. An early study in this area illustrates the problem. In 1948, the U.S. Supreme Court ruled that it was unconstitutional for school districts to schedule certain hours during the day in which religious groups would come to school and provide classes in religion for those students who desired it. (Students who did not wish to have religious instruction were sent to study hall.) The Court ruled that this practice violated the constitutional separation of church and state. Nearly ten years later, in a survey of Pennsylvania school superintendents, one-tenth of those responding stated that their school districts continued this practice, even though it was unconstitutional. The survey also ascertained that the superintendents understood the Court decision fully; they were acting not out of ignorance but deliberately.[1]

---

[1]Frank J. Sorauf, "*Zorach v. Clausen:* The Impact of a Supreme Court Decision," *American Political Review* 53 (September 1959), pp. 777–91.

364   PART IV   THE APPARATUS OF GOVERNANCE

✦ CHARACTERISTICS OF GOOD PUBLIC ADMINISTRATION

The way in which we organize our public administration should aim to help us maximize some desirable traits. Among these are the following:

1. *Honest, accurate translation of political leaders' decisions into more specifically designed policies:* The principal-agent problem (see p. 352) clearly applies to public administration, where political leaders hire a large force of administrators to put in place policies that implement the leaders' decisions. The problem here is to ensure that public administrators actually do what political leaders intended.

2. *Flexibility in dealing with special cases at the point of delivery:* While administrators should be obedient to directions from above, they should not be slavishly obedient. If a police officer pulls a driver over for speeding and discovers that the driver is trying to whisk a child with a gaping wound to the hospital, we do not want the officer to write a ticket.

3. *However, this flexibility should not be used arbitrarily:* "Arbitrary" action is action that we take capriciously, without regard to the important circumstances of a case. Stopping and searching blacks because of their race is an arbitrary act, for example. Another example would be to allow some students to take a makeup examination but to deny the makeup opportunity to others who had had the same excuse.

4. *Feedback of expert advice; active imagination and assertive inquiry on the part of administrators:* We hope that administrators, since they know more about their areas of work than anyone else, will not hang back from sharing their expertise with the public and their political leaders.

5. *Efficiency:* We hope that all this can be accomplished without costing too much.

All of these are desirable traits. However, since some of them are to a certain extent mutually contradictory, we cannot simultaneously meet all of them fully. For instance, there is some tension between item 1 (honest, accurate translation) and item 2 (expecting administrators to follow their own judgment). Item 3 is difficult because one person's capriciousness is another person's courageous judgment. Item 4 (feedback of expert advice) assumes an independent-minded set of administrators who may fit oddly item (1): honest, accurate translation.

It follows that there is no one best way to organize public administration; various modes of organization will emphasize one or another of these good things. Therefore, under varying circumstances, we may prefer varying modes.

➔ "BUREAUCRACY": A REFORM OF THE NINETEENTH CENTURY

Bureaucracy is one way to organize the public administration, one that has become fairly standard, at least as an ideal, throughout the world. We often use the word bureaucracy in common language to mean the public administration, usually with a connotation of distaste. However, social scientists have a precise meaning for it: a particular mode of administrative organization that was developed as a reform in the nineteenth century and spread widely to be the most generally used mode today.

Let us first set the stage of the eighteenth and early nineteenth centuries to show how bureaucracy developed as a reform of the systems then in place. At that time, in Europe and North America, positions in the public administration were treated as pieces of property, to be exchanged among people. In the United States, this took the form of the infamous "spoils system," in which administrative jobs were treated as commodities with which victorious candidates rewarded their party's workers. When the presidency changed hands, for instance, all post office managers in the country were fired and new people from the victorious party were put in their place. The same thing happened with state highway and surveyor jobs when one party replaced another in a state capital; so also with fire and police jobs when city hall changed hands.

In Europe, positions in the public administration were individually bought and sold more or less as investments. A wealthy family wishing to establish a son in a comfortable life would buy him a position in the customs service, an officer's commission in the army, or some similar position.

Such loose arrangements produced inefficient service, and there was little control over the quality of officials. In the United States, for example, some post office managers could not read. For most officials, getting the job in the first place was the only trick (what they did once they were there did not bear consequences for them), so controlling officials' actions was difficult.

366   PART IV   THE APPARATUS OF GOVERNANCE

In the nineteenth century, there arose a new reform method of organizing public administration, one that social scientists call "bureaucracy."[2] Under a system of bureaucracy:

1. Members of the public administration are appointed and promoted on the basis of their qualifications for the job they are to do.
2. Special requirements of training or experience are set for the position.
3. Administrative procedures are standardized, so that relatively little is left to individual officials' biases or passions.
4. Clear lines of command are established, in which an order from a high official goes to a lower official, who then passes the order on to the next level, until it reaches the point of operation. We call this arrangement a **hierarchical command structure.**
5. Finally, public administrators are shielded from day-to-day political pressure, usually with a system of tenure.

This new, cleaner, and more efficient way of organizing the public administration was first used in appointments for procurement officers with the French and Prussian armies in the eighteenth and early nineteenth centuries. It demonstrated its usefulness in this area and spread rapidly. In the United States, the coming of the bureaucratic mode was embodied in the move for civil service reform at the beginning of the twentieth century, which eventually took most administrative positions out of party control and based them on competitive civil service exams. By World War II, some form or another of bureaucracy was the usual method of organizing public administration throughout Europe and North America. As new states attained their independence, they also adopted some form of bureaucracy. It is today the usual mode of administrative organization throughout the world, although there are many variations on its themes.

✦ BUREAUCRACY VERSUS FLEXIBILITY

As I noted previously, there is no ideal way to organize administration. Of the various things that may be desirable in public administration, bureaucracy is particularly strong in addressing the principal-agent problem, and in preventing arbitrary behavior. Believe it or not, it is also rather efficient. (The public mind has to some extent identified bureaucracy as wasteful because the public has high expectations for how cheaply one might expect administration to be done. The administrative costs of public agencies are not that different from those of private businesses.)

However, the standardization and clarity of command that accomplish these good things mean that bureaucracy cannot easily provide for local flexibility. Also, although the requirements for training and for decisions based on merit produce well-qualified officials, the system of standardization does not encourage independent-mindedness on their part, and so bureaucracy does not especially tend to produce helpful expert advice to political leaders. Administrators under most versions of bureaucracy tend to hold their advice until someone asks for it.

---

[2]For the definitive statement, see Max Weber, "Bureaucracy," in H. H. Gerth and C. Wright Mills, *From Max Weber* (New York: Oxford University Press, 1958), pp. 196–244.

This means that the bureaucratic form of organization will fit some administrative needs better than others. Where standardization and obedience are especially important, bureaucratic organization fits well. Where independence and flexible judgment are especially important, it does not. Military service is one area in which standardization and obedience are important, because if a general is conducting a wheeling motion on a battlefield, everything could be lost if one battalion wheeled in the wrong direction. The bureaucratic model fits military operations well, and indeed the military—with its clean lines of command and its tendency to "do things by the book"—exemplifies the bureaucratic model. On the other hand, public enterprises in which obedience is less important than individuality are not as well served by bureaucratic organization. A university or college is such a place: The object is to put a gifted individual in the lab or in front of a class and let that person do creative things.

It follows that bureaucracy is a better form of organization for some areas of the public administration than for others, depending on the relative needs for smooth obedience and individualistic judgment. To a considerable extent, these differences are reflected in the organization of various agencies; almost universally the armed forces are the most bureaucratically organized agencies in any state's public administration, and universities tend to be rather decentralized.

However, there is often a tilt toward bureaucracy, with most operations organized more bureaucratically than would really be necessary. Most public administrators appear to incline toward standardization and away from individual initiative, a natural result of the human desire for safety and security. An official working within standardized procedures, unlike one who is supposed to make independent choices, cannot be blamed for the results. Procedures shelter bureaucracies, so bureaucracies foster procedures. Impressionistic evidence for this, at least, is that there are apparently no armed forces in the world set up in anything but a straightforward bureaucratic mode; whereas universities, which would not require bureaucratic organization and would almost surely benefit by its absence, are nonetheless often hemmed in by tight rules.[3]

☩ THE PROBLEM OF PROTECTED INCOMPETENCE

Another common problem of bureaucratic organization stems from a combination of two factors: (1) the difficulty in public administration, as compared with private business, of evaluating how well a person has performed a job; and (2) the requirement in a bureaucracy that administrators be shielded from direct political pressure, usually by a system of tenure.

In private business, a standard yardstick is available to evaluate how well a person has performed in a job. If profits have increased in that person's sector, or if sales have been high—if the person has made money for the company—then the job has been done well. You and your boss know whether or not you have sold a million dollars of insurance this year, but how do we evaluate the performance of public administrators? There is no notion of "profit" in the operations of a public school, the army, or a state's highway department.

[3]For example, in some European universities, there are official limits on the number of pages that students may be required to read. In Norway in 1983, the limit for a political science course was six hundred pages, total, across a fifteen-week semester.

A professor is supposed to teach well, but there is no dollar figure that can tell us how well the professor has taught. A highway superintendent is supposed to maintain the roads well, but there is no simple dollar figure that can tell us how well they have been maintained.

Combine this with the fact that political intervention against members of the bureaucracy is difficult and unlikely, and you have a situation in which incompetent administrators will rarely be removed from their positions. Few unambiguous standards of their performance are available, and—in the absence of clear-cut evidence—superiors will be reluctant to take action for fear that they will be accused of favoritism or political interference.

As a result, although bureaucracies do not especially attract incompetent people—and although, by their entrance requirements, they select unusually competent people—those incompetents who do get in are probably less likely to be removed than they would be in private businesses.

→ ADJUSTMENTS TO BUREAUCRACY

Although bureaucracy is only one way to organize the public administration, it is the dominant mode of organization across the world, as we have seen. It is so dominant that the word bureaucracy has become almost a synonym for public administration, in much the way that *Kleenex* has come to be synonymous with facial tissues.

As a term loosely signifying public administration, *bureaucracy* has a number of unpleasant connotations. People think of bureaucrats as lazy, arrogant, inflexible, shortsighted—and too numerous. Partly this is because it is impossible to construct an ultimate, best form of organization for the public administration; as we have seen, the various characteristics we would wish to see in a good public administration are to some extent mutually contradictory. Partly it derives from real weaknesses of bureaucracy.

In various parts of the world, adjustments have evolved or have been invented that can soften bureaucracy when it is excessively "bureaucratic." Among these are the office of ombudsman, provisions for opening government files for inspection, informal interference in the bureaucracy by political leaders, and pressure from public opinion.

1. *The office of ombudsman* is a Swedish invention. An **ombudsman** is a government official whose primary duty is to seek out citizens' complaints of abuse by public administrators and to negotiate changes in the offending practices. Many other countries have copied the ombudsman idea. The United States has not used it much at the national level; but Hawaii, Florida, and other states have established ombudsman offices, and nationally the Internal Revenue Service has an Office of the Taxpayer Advocate that operates as an ombudsman. Many nongovernmental institutions have also found it an attractive idea. Some universities have established ombudsman offices for their students or faculty, for instance, and many newspapers have established a readers' ombudsman.

2. *Freedom of information laws* have been passed in many countries, and the United States was a pioneer in this direction. Under such laws, individuals are guaranteed the right to examine most kinds of "internal" governmental documents, including dossiers that may have been gathered on them personally. The intent of the laws is to allow citizens to find out what procedures administrators are following in

processes that are of interest to them; more specifically, it allows citizens to check and correct any information the government has gathered about them.

3. ***"Interference" in administration by political leaders*** may act as a safety valve to help correct abuses. You will recall that in the bureaucratic mode of organization, administrators are shielded from much direct intervention by political leaders. This was intended to avoid the excesses of a spoils system.

   However, it does not compromise the bureaucratic model greatly if political leaders take advantage of their potential power over administrative budgets to seize bureaucrats' attention and get them to deal with a constituent's problem. In the United States, in particular, this has become a major part of the job of a member of Congress and has developed into an important corrective for bureaucratic inflexibility. It is well understood that if you are having trouble getting a passport or your Social Security check has been held up, you should call your member of Congress for help. In 2012, for instance, the office of Representative Steve Chabot (first congressional district, Ohio) assisted over seven hundred constituents with a wide variety of concerns. The most common problems involved the Social Security Administration and the Veterans Administration.[4] In effect, members of Congress serve the ombudsman role in the United States.

4. ***Pressure from public opinion*** can help to correct bureaucratic sluggishness and abuse. Administrators are ultimately dependent on political processes for their offices' budgets, and so they must be attentive to public opinion. Also, because they are human, they want to be liked and admired for what they do. Public criticism hurts them and will usually lead to improvements where there have been problems. Agricultural agencies, welfare services, research agencies, the postal service—all are worried by stories in the media about shortcomings in their operations and keep in reasonably close touch with their "clients," the groups most affected by their policies.

   Even in authoritarian systems, where civil servants often have broad opportunities for abusive actions, public opinion can function as a corrective. In China, for instance, a county in Hubei province ordered county employees to buy thousands of packs of the province's brand of cigarettes, but reversed the order after weeks of ridicule on national blogs. A village in another province required unmarried women to pass a chastity test before they could receive compensation for expropriated farmland, until they were overruled by higher officials responding to publicity.[5]

→ SOCIAL REPRESENTATIVENESS OF PUBLIC ADMINISTRATION

Members of the public administration are not under direct political control, and adjustments such as those I have described can go only so far. Therefore, there has been recurrent concern over how socially representative top bureaucratic decision makers are; that is, they should not be too different from the population as a whole in such things

---

[4]Ron Lieber, "When to Call Your Elected Representatives for Help," *The New York Times*, October 20, 2012, p. B1.
[5]Sharon LaFraniere, "Salute All Cars, Kids. It's a Law," *The New York Times*, October 26, 2009, p. A1.

370   Part IV   The Apparatus of Governance

  Immigration Agencies as an Example

Perhaps the best evidence that public opinion serves as an important corrective to bureaucracy may be found by looking at an agency that is not under much direct pressure from public opinion. In democracies all over the world, immigration agencies are relatively free from pressures of public opinion because their "client group"—those who wish to enter the country as immigrants—cannot vote in elections and usually lack powerful friends. It is almost universally true that these offices are less responsive to their clients and more inclined to make arbitrary judgments than other government agencies:

- *Item:* When Bulgarian soprano Alexandrina Pendatchanska was asked by the Pittsburgh Opera to sing the lead role in Handel's *Julius Caesar*, the U.S. Bureau for Citizenship and Immigration Services (BCIS) spelled her name wrong on the visa allowing her entry to the country. When the mistake was discovered, the BCIS told her that her application would have to go back to square one, which would take another six months—long beyond the date of the performance. Even though it was their mistake and not hers, she lost the job and was replaced by another singer.[6]

- *Item:* In 2008 an Italian who flew to the United States to visit his girlfriend was abruptly seized at Dulles airport and was neither allowed to return to Italy nor to proceed to his girlfriend's house. Instead he was taken in shackles to a rural Virginia jail where he was locked up without charges for ten days while his girlfriend and her parents tried to get him released. In his fear and confusion, he asked his girlfriend whether Virginia had the death penalty.[7]

- *Item:* When the Norwegian government in 1980 decided to reduce the number of work permits it would grant to foreigners by 50 percent, the Norwegian Immigration Service also reduced the staff to deal with those requests by 50 percent. It ignored the fact that although it was going to say yes only half as often, just as many people would be asking. It was not long before the office had such a backlog that applicants were required to wait nine months to a year for an answer.

- *Item:* In 1997, the U.S. Congress empowered BCIS border agents, after a brief examination and with no procedure for appeal, to turn back foreign citizens at the border and bar them from crossing the border for five years. In the first seven months of the new rule, twenty-three thousand people were barred, and in several incidents, it was clear that these were, for example, foreign citizens trying to visit family members in the United States, or Canadians working for United States–based firms.[8]

- *Item:* In 2001, the BCIS, which was at that time taking more than two months to process applications for temporary work visas, offered a special expedited service that would take only fifteen days—for a fee of one thousand dollars!

[6] *Minneapolis Star Tribune,* February 28, 2004, p. B4.

[7] Nina Bernstein, "Italian's Detention Illustrates Dangers Foreign Visitors Face," *The New York Times,* May 14, 2008, p. A13.

[8] *The New York Times,* November 14, 1997, p. 1.

as class background, race, or gender. There has been some controversy over this. On the one hand, advocates of **representative bureaucracy** urge that if administrators are not politically responsible, we should at least do all we can to ensure that they will look at things in the same ways that the common people would. On the other hand, skeptics have responded that we should not want "common people" in positions of uncommon importance and that we should not expect top public administrators to be any more socially representative than the leaders of corporations, universities, or other large institutions.[9]

Whatever our feelings on this, certainly many governments have made efforts to ensure that top public administrators will be reasonably representative. After World War II, many European countries (France, for example) attempted to increase the proportion of their officials who were from the working class. They did this by changing their entrance procedures and providing for internal promotions from less important administrative posts. These efforts have worked. In the late 1970s, 96 percent of France's senior administrative officials were from the upper class. By 1997 only 46 percent of senior civil servants came from the upper class, with 35 percent from the middle class and 17 percent from the working class.[10]

In recent years, a similar concern in most countries has been to increase the representation of women and minorities in the bureaucracy. The United States has long tried by affirmative action programs to increase numbers of minority and women officials. By the mid-1990s women comprised 45 percent of senior civil servants in the Netherlands and 23 percent of senior civil servants in Sweden.[11]

EXAMPLE

The French Bureaucracy

The "ordinary" bureaucracies of industrialized states do not vary greatly from one country to another. Mail carriers, teachers, and agricultural extension agents are organized and do their jobs in fairly similar ways around the industrialized world. However, there is considerable variation in how the **higher civil service**—managers, diplomats, and specialists—are organized and work. In this realm, the French are quite distinctive; theirs is arguably the best civil service in the world.

In this section, we shall address almost solely the higher civil service. First, however, I should note one

[9]See discussions in Samuel Krislov, *Representative Bureaucracy* (Englewood Cliffs, NJ: Prentice-Hall, 1974); Kenneth John Meier, "Representative Bureaucracy: An Empirical Analysis," *American Political Science Review* 69 (June 1975), pp. 526–42; Sally Coleman Selden, *The Promise of Representative Bureaucracy* (London: M. E. Sharpe, 1997); and Kenneth J. Meier, Robert D. Winkle, and J. L. Polinard, "Representative Bureaucracy and Distributional Equity: Addressing the Hard Question," *Journal of Politics* 61 (November 1999), pp. 1025–39.

[10]Calculated from Joel D. Aberbach, Robert D. Putnam, and Bert A. Rockman, *Bureaucrats and Politicians in Western Democracies* (Cambridge: Harvard University Press, 1981), table 3.3, and Luc Roban, "The Civil Service in France," in Edward C. Page and Vincent Wright, *Bureaucratic Elites in Western European States* (New York: Oxford University Press, 1999), calculated from figures 4.1 and 4.4.

[11]Ibid., essays by Marleen Brans and Annie Hondeghem ("The Senior Civil Service in Belgium," p. 138) and Jon Pierre and Peter Ehn ("Senior Civil Servants in Sweden," p. 258).

thing that is unusual about the "ordinary" French civil service: It is relatively large, perhaps due in part to the French state's high level of regulatory activity. There are approximately 6 million full-time local and national civil servants in France, including the military. They make up about 25 percent of the labor force, compared with 13 percent in Germany and Britain.[12]

The higher civil service of France consists of about four to six thousand highly trained persons. Most of these work within one of the ministries (defense, health, etc.), but at any given time, over a thousand of them are working in more independent ways, either as staff advisers to the premier or ministers or in relatively autonomous administrative bodies, which I shall describe. Furthermore, a certain number of them are at any time on loan to businesses, universities, or local government.

One of the things that distinguishes the French higher civil service is the training and ability of its members, which leads also to a high degree of self-confidence and pride. There are two main routes of entry into the higher civil service. If one wishes to be a specialist, such as a scientist or statistician, one usually receives a university education from one of the "great" technical schools, such as the Polytechnic or the School of Agronomy, followed by more specialized training at an institution such as the School of Mines or School of Statistics and Economic Administration. If one wishes to be a generalist, after university one enters the famous National School of Administration (the ENA). One of the most difficult schools in the world to enter, the ENA gives its graduates a general training in administration and in the social sciences. Whether from one of the "great schools" or the ENA, higher civil servants in France are noted for their verbal skill and for a tendency to abstraction and mathematical reasoning. They are pragmatic rather than ideological and usually emphasize economics over politics. Many French presidents and premiers have been alumni of the ENA.

The second thing that sets French higher civil servants apart is the tradition of "detached service," whereby they may leave the national civil service for periods of time, either on personal leave or on loan by the national government, to work in business, local government, or the universities or to hold elective office. In the 1970s, for example, about one-fourth of the members of the parliament were civil servants on leave from their administrative posts, and in 1984, there were twenty-five national civil servants on loan to the city of Paris.

Under these circumstances, the French have developed a more politicized civil service than that of most countries, one that lives on the frontier between "politics" and administration.[13] For instance, one set of high national officials in France are the **prefects,** who oversee the operations of local and regional government. Prefects coordinate the operations of all state agencies, including the police, for a city or region. They also oversee the operations of the elected city or regional governments, holding them to account if they question the legality of their operations. Inevitably, these are sensitive political positions. Such politicization appears to have added vigor to the higher civil service and has allowed French civil servants to lead aggressively in the development of such new

---

[12]"France's Public Sector—They Love It," *The Economist*, 26 May 2001, p. 50.
[13]This also fits the more general culture of the French and other continental Europeans. English is the only European language that distinguishes between politics and policy; in French, both are called *politique*.

CHAPTER 16   BUREAUCRACY AND THE PUBLIC SECTOR   373

political thrusts as the campaign for a tunnel under the English Channel, the adoption of the value-added tax, and the formation of the Common Market.

I stated previously that the French higher civil service is "arguably" the best in the world. The other side of the "argument" is raised by those who see the civil service as too insulated from the rest of the population, too haughty, and overly given to technical fixes:

> Instead of a homogenous administration equally open to everyone, one sees established an aristocracy of a few thousand young men produced through privileged channels; the isolation of their education easily persuades them that they are destined to retain among themselves (and for themselves) the administration of the state, and above all its best jobs. Less and less are they touched by doubts; the assurance of their elders and their own success convinces them that it is enough to advance confidently under cover of their technique to make obstacles disappear. The sharing of a certain exoticism of language or of modern administrative techniques or of economics; the sense of making up a kind of network between the bosses and dauphins of the great public and private businesses; the exhilaration, still hardly acknowledged, of feeling in their hands such means of action, and such docile underlings; all these make up the psychology of a senior civil servant, young and ardent, certainly devoted to what he considers the public good, but more inclined to define it himself, or to let it be defined by the boss, than to listen on this subject to the aspiration of the country.[14]

 EXAMPLE

Bureaucratic Cultures in Europe and Africa

The bureaucratic model of public administration may work out very differently, depending on the culture of the civil servants—their collective attitudes on the best ways to make decisions, for instance, or the importance of remaining flexible. Many states in Africa, Asia, and Latin America are thought to have especially "bureaucratic" civil servants, who are not very flexible, emphasize the hierarchical nature of authority, and follow written rules whether or not they fit a situation well. John C. Munene, Shalom H. Schwartz, and Peter B. Smith have compared ways in which European and African civil service managers make decisions, and the results are rather dramatic.[15]

---

[14]"Le Regime des 'Jeunes Messieurs,'" *Courrier de la Republique*, November 1965, quoted in Anthony Sampson, *The New Europeans* (London: Hodder and Stoughton, 1968), p. 345.
[15]John C. Munene, Shalom H. Schwartz, and Peter B. Smith, "Development in Sub-Saharan Africa: Cultural Influences and Managers' Decision Behaviour," *Public Administration and Development* 20 (2000), pp. 339–51.

TABLE 16.1

Managers Ranked by Country (Out of 44) in How Frequently They Would Rely on a Given Source

| Nations | Unbureaucratic | | | Bureaucratic | |
	Rely on Own Experience	Follow Unwritten Rules	Consult Subordinates	Consult Boss	Follow Formal Rules
Europe:					
Finland	3	11	3	34	44
France	17	4	8	18	38
Germany	7	37	4	23	41
Netherlands	5	19	2	43	40
Sweden	16	33	7	41	14
Africa:					
Kenya	34	38	34	8	4
Nigeria	44	32	20	42	8
S. Africa	31	29	42	11	10
Tanzania	NA	42	16	26	13
Uganda	38	34	40	20	3
Zimbabwe	29	31	34	5	2

SOURCE: Adapted from John C. Munene, Shalom H. Schwartz, and Peter B. Smith, "Development in Sub-Saharan Africa: Cultural Influences and Managers' Decision Behaviour," *Public Administration and Development* 20 (2000), p. 347.

In a study of forty-four countries, managers were asked what sources they would turn to for guidance in making a variety of common decisions, such as whether or not to order a new piece of equipment or how to introduce new work rules into a department. The study asked, among some other options, how often managers would rely on their own experience, would rely on unwritten rules, or would consult the people working under them (all of which would be "unbureaucratic") or would rely on formal rules or consult their boss ("bureaucratic"). Table 16.1 compares European and African managers, with a 1 indicating that managers of that country were the most likely to engage in the activity, and a 44 indicating that they were the least likely of managers in any of the countries to engage in it.

As we see here, the African managers are distinctly more "bureaucratic" than the Europeans. All five European countries, for instance, rank among the top ten countries in the extent to which they would consult the people working under them when they made a decision—a distinctly "unbureaucratic" thing to do. The six African countries all rank high in following formal rules, that is, "going by the book."

One could bemoan the bureaucratic culture of Africa as one that will make progress difficult in these mostly very poor countries, but that is probably not very fruitful; as we have noted elsewhere, culture is usually difficult to change. So, if we hope for progress in these countries, bemoaning the bureaucratic culture is not going to get us very far. Munene and his coauthors note that one implication of their findings is that those seeking change in African countries must learn the culture they are working with among officials, and find ways to work with that culture. Though it is not like the European culture, it is certainly not a bad one—the emphasis on hierarchical organization and the tendency to avoid individual responsibility probably fit with a general African culture that emphasizes embeddedness in groups and family, in contrast to individualistic Western culture.

Often, however, international organizations or foreign aid donors approach African government agencies assuming that the agencies must operate just like Western agencies, and then spend much time and energy being frustrated. Studies like this one can help donors understand better how to work within the cultural expectations of local officials.

KEY TERMS

public administration	bureaucracy	prefect
ombudsman	representative	hierarchical command
higher civil service	bureaucracy	structure

FURTHER READING

Crozier, Michel. *The Bureaucratic Phenomenon.* Chicago: University of Chicago Press, 1987.

Lewis, David E. *The Politics of Presidential Appointments: Political Control and Bureaucratic Performance.* Princeton, NJ: Princeton University Press, 2008.

Naff, Katherine C. *To Look Like America.* Boulder, CO: Westview Press, 2001.

Page, Edward C., and Wright, Vincent. *Bureaucratic Elites in Western European States.* New York: Oxford University Press, 1999.

Peters, B. Guy. *Politics of Bureaucracy: An Introduction to Comparative Public Administration,* 6th ed. Oxford, UK: Routledge, 2006.

Wilson, James Q. *Bureaucracy: What Government Agencies Do and Why They Do It.* New York: Basic Books, 1989.

CHAPTER 17

LAW AND THE COURTS

The **law** is a collection of rules laid down by the government, binding all members of the state, including members of the government itself. The law does two things: (1) It sets society's norms and rules for behavior; for instance, it may state that one may not steal another's property, that one may not expose oneself indecently, or that religious practice other than the state religion is illegal. (2) It sets the rules by which individuals in the state must relate to each other such as rules governing divorce procedures, or rules for the honoring of contracts.

The rules making up the "law" may reside in the state's constitution, may be statutes passed by the state's legislature, or may be decrees announced by the state's executive officers such as the president, military junta, or dictator. They may also, in some states, develop out of decisions of courts.

Courts are an odd part of the government in that they have the responsibility for interpreting all parts of the law and adjudicating—when various parts of the law are in conflict—which part takes precedence. Their oddity lies in that they are part of the government but must judge fairly among citizens of the state, including those in the government. Thus, while courts are part of the government, they must be to some extent independent of it. This independence has developed so far in some states that the courts are able to share independently in creating the law.

The tension implicit in being part of the government but at the same time independent of the government, and how this tension is resolved, are important aspects of the world's major legal systems, which we shall examine. **Legal systems** are general, organized sets of legal principles that form the basis of law and adjudication in states. They organize legal practice for states in a way somewhat parallel to the role ideologies play in organizing the thought processes of individuals. (See Chapter 2.)

✦ ANGLO-SAXON CASE LAW

The legal system that is most familiar to Americans and Canadians is Anglo-Saxon **case law**. This is the system that developed in England during the late Middle Ages and early modern period and spread to such former British colonies as the United States, Canada, India, and Nigeria. We often call it "common law," though we more often apply that term to the specific body of English law that developed over centuries of case experience.

The system of case law views courts as largely independent of the state's government, so independent that in the cases they decide they share to some extent in the making of the law, because those cases serve as precedents for future decisions. This is why we call the system "case law."

The heart of the system is a belief that the law is something that exists partially independent of the government. From this there follow several important aspects of case law:

- The task of judges is to find proper law, and the law evolves over time with a certain degree of flexibility. Thus, the U.S. Supreme Court in its landmark *Brown v. Board of Education* decision took note of changing sociological evidence to decide that segregated schools (which were previously legal) were against the law.[1]

- Training of judges and lawyers proceeds in special schools, separate from the rest of the university; their training—largely by other lawyers—emphasizes clarity of thought and expression, and skills at searching out and applying precedents.

- The role of the judge is to be a neutral arbiter, ruling on behalf of the law after listening fairly passively to opposing arguments by the lawyers.

- Especially where the government brings charges against an individual (a criminal case), the law protects the individual against the disproportionate power of the government. The burden of proof lies with the government (the defendant is "innocent until proven guilty"), and a whole series of protections hold: For example, an individual may not be held more than twenty-four hours without a charge (right of **habeas corpus**), and spouses may not be forced to testify against each other.

I do not mean to suggest that in case law systems judges manufacture the law. The courts base their decision not only on precedents but also on statutes passed by the government, including (in the case of the United States) the Constitution. If the government changes the law by statute, the courts follow its directions, and so the government is the final authority on the law. If the United States government were to amend the Constitution to make racially segregated schools constitutional, for instance, *Brown v. Board of Education* would be annulled. However, in the absence of government action, and by filling in the details of government statutes, the courts work with the government to make the law. For instance, when a tax code revision is passed in the United States, commentators will note that we need to wait for two or three years of court cases to know exactly what the new law means. In a case law system, then, courts operate largely independently of the rest of the government, although statutes and the constitution have the final word.

---

[1] *Brown v. Board of Education*, 347 U.S. 484 (1954).

✦ CONTINENTAL EUROPEAN CODE LAW

Case law developed in England out of local customs and was popular especially with the same emerging commercial elites who would help to develop the ideology of liberalism.[2] With its emphasis on the law as something existing at some remove from the government and on the law's capacity to restrain illegal governmental action, case law has a clear affinity with liberalism's desire for limited government.

On the continent of Europe, forces for the limitation of governmental power were never as strong as in England, probably because the establishment and maintenance of the continental states were usually more difficult than the establishment of a secure state in England, protected as it was by the English Channel. Where the state was difficult to establish and fragile to maintain, governments may have felt that they needed to keep everything under direct control. The legal tradition on the continent has been to rely on variants of the Roman system of law, which involved a detailed code of law produced and interpreted by the government. The law, in this tradition, is an expression of governmental policy. Napoleon, when he was building his French Empire in the early nineteenth century, gave this tradition added life by encoding existing French law in the Code Napoleon; he later imposed similar codes in many of the European states that he conquered. In one way or another, **code law** eventually dominated across the continent.

From the basic principle that the law is an instrument of the government rather than something that exists semi-independently of the government, there follow several notable characteristics of code law:

- It is not based nearly as much as case law on the accumulation of precedents. While code law judges of course try to keep in step with each other, lest the law degenerate into chaos, they rely more on the statute or code as an authority—not on previous judges' decisions. They do not "make the law" as case law judges do.

- The training of code law lawyers and judges, accordingly, is more general, not as specialized as what one finds in case law systems. Code law views legal officials primarily as just another kind of civil servant, so they are trained in the general university rather than in a separate school by special professors of law.

- The distinction between law as a tool of the state (code law) and law as something above the state (case law) is most marked in criminal cases, where the state itself (in the person of the prosecutor) is a party to the case. Under most code law systems, in a criminal case the judge is not a neutral arbiter of the arguments between the prosecution and defense; rather, as a servant of the state, the judge enters directly into argument, questioning witnesses and even, in some systems, directing the police investigation of the crime. The judge's role is not to pass judgment on the state's case but rather, as a servant of the state, to try actively on behalf of the state to learn the truth in the case. There is no presumption of innocence, as in case law; there is no presumption at all. The state, through the court, simply tries to find out what happened. Finally, in most code law systems, there do not exist the elaborate structures of protection for the accused that we see under case law such as

---

[2]See Chapter 2.

Emile Durkheim's Theory of Law

Law is the set of rules that bind a society together, and so theorists of society have often looked to law as the critical point for analyzing society. Emile Durkheim, a great nineteenth century French sociologist, analyzed law in his work *The Division of Labor in Society* to address the question, "How do societies hold themselves together?" He saw law as functioning in varying ways at different stages of societal development to provide the mechanism for maintaining the society intact. In analyzing the role of law, he had much to say about why law develops as it does.

He first asked the question, "Why would people be moved to stay together as a society?" As an answer, he pointed to two bases for staying together: "mechanical solidarity," or the similarity among people of the same society that makes them feel akin to each other and comfortable with each other, and different from people not in that society; and "organic solidarity," the benefits of economic cooperation by which, for instance, a group of people with varying specialized skills are able by cooperating to build an automobile—something no one of them could possibly have done alone.

These two reasons for staying together as a society, however, operate under a natural tension. To build the kind of division of labor that yields large returns of organic solidarity, it is necessary for people to be different from each other. One person must be a designer, another a capable machinist. This must diminish the similarity that builds mechanical solidarity. Therefore, as society comes to rely more on organic solidarity, it must rely less on mechanical solidarity.

What does this imply for law? Durkheim points out that the two kinds of solidarity require different things of the law. Mechanical solidarity, based on people feeling similar to each other, requires law that makes people behave like each other and—when this similarity is broken—law that gives dramatic, public punishment. This reemphasizes the rules and reassures the public that the break has been compensated. Laws will prescribe things such as sexual practice, dietary practice, religion, and dress; and punishment will be revengeful and memorable such as stoning to death, hanging, confinement in the stocks, and electrocution.

Organic solidarity, based on cooperation, needs law that ensures and regulates that cooperation such as law enforcing the fulfillment of contracts, or law regulating ownership of property. Where a law has been broken, monetary compensation is necessary, or enforcement of a contract, rather than societal retribution.

The development of law in modern societies—as improved technology makes the payoffs of cooperation ever greater, and we appear to rely increasingly on "organic" rather than "mechanical" solidarity—does seem to bear Durkheim out. Punishments for crimes have become less dramatic and emphasize rehabilitation more than revenge. Public hangings were common in criminal cases in the United States in the nineteenth century, for instance, but are not used today. The vast body of contract law is a relatively "recent" addition of the last few centuries.

Durkheim is squarely on the "choice" side of "power and choice." He emphasizes legal structures arising to suit the needs of individuals making up society, not because someone imposes them. The question Durkheim poses at the beginning is based on the idea that people choose to be in a society, that the existence of society is based not on the use of power but on an accumulation of individual choices.

right of habeas corpus, right against self-incrimination, and right against spouse's testimony. The task of the court is not to "prove guilt beyond any reasonable doubt"; rather, it is to decide what is most probably true in the case.

To an American raised on "innocent until proven guilty," this may seem strange.

The original code law systems were European. As new states were established in other parts of the world, unless they were former British colonies, they adopted some form of code law. When a revolutionary government or a new state based on an independence movement has needed to make an abrupt break with the past, it has seemed more straightforward to design a code of law directly, rather than build one gradually through an accretion of judicial decisions.

✦ THE BLENDING OF CASE LAW AND CODE LAW

The differences between case law and code law are mostly differences of degree. For instance, case law is not "made by judges"; statute is also an important part of the law, and the state can always change "judge-made" law by passing a new law or amending the constitution. In code law, similarly, judges do not totally ignore precedent. They cannot decide a case by looking at the code and ignoring what other judges are doing, or things would become quite chaotic; nobody would know what the law was, because different judges might decide similar cases quite differently.

Therefore, the distinction between these two types is a matter of degree. Still, matters of degree can matter a great deal, as we have seen in comparing how the two systems handle criminal cases.

In recent years, we find that even these distinctions between the systems are becoming less clear, as code law systems adopt some aspects of case law, and vice versa. For instance, in the general spirit of "constitutionalism," protections of individuals against abuse by the state have become popular even in many code law systems.[3] In 1959, France established for the first time the right of habeas corpus. In the mid-1990s, Italy changed its practice of putting judges in charge of the police investigation of a crime, and in 1999, the French parliament passed a bill to establish the presumption that an accused person is innocent until proven guilty.

Furthermore, most industrialized states with complex governmental structures have found it necessary to establish some sort of avenue for individuals to sue the state; if the state was supposed to pay you a pension through the social security system but did not, for example, you need some way to force it to honor its obligation. In standard code law systems, this was difficult because the law was a tool of the state and could not stand judge over it. Furthermore, faced with the complex governmental regulations of the twentieth century, government agencies often find themselves operating in quasi-judicial roles. An antitrust office, for instance, must rule on whether a proposed merger of companies will restrict trade unduly. Such decisions require "judicial" procedures within an administrative agency.

---

[3]For a discussion of "constitutionalism," see Chapter 9.

To handle questions like these, a wholly separate system of administrative courts has developed in many states, and these make law by precedent. In France, the administrative court system has a caseload larger than that of the regular courts, and its law is developed on a case basis.

Therefore, many code law systems are evolving to look more like case law systems. The opposite process has not been as marked, but some case law systems are becoming more like code law in certain ways. Legislatures and parliaments in some case law systems have begun to write codes in various areas to which judges are bound. For instance, many states in the United States have set up codes of uniform sentencing guidelines that set narrow ranges within which a judge may set the sentence of a person convicted of any particular crime. Also, in Great Britain—where case law started—after long debate, the European Convention on Human Rights was incorporated into English law in 2000, in effect inserting a code of human rights into the English legal system.

The historic differences in how legal systems originated in Europe may be receding far enough that the differences they produced are overridden by the great similarity of conditions across modern industrialized states. These states need the strong coherence that code law can provide, but at the same time, their governmental operations are so large and complex that individuals feel a need for some protection against abuse by government. It may be that under these circumstances, a blend of code and case law is most appropriate.

Notice, by the way, that my account of the convergence of case law and code systems in the above paragraph is based on a choice perspective, rather than a power perspective. In my account, the needs of contemporary states account for the evolution of the legal systems.

✦ RELIGIOUS LAW: THE SHARIA

All states of the world have some version of case law or code law, often referred to as "Western law," introduced by the European powers or borrowed from them. A number of other legal systems survive partially, however. The most enduring are various forms of religious law; and of these, the most important is the **Sharia**—Islamic law—which makes up part of the legal system of such Islamic states as Morocco, Tunisia, Indonesia, Egypt, Syria, Jordan, Iraq, Mauritania, Yemen, Iran, Afghanistan, and Pakistan. Even in Western states where Islam is a minority religion, like Britain and Germany, Islamic courts supplement the regular courts.[4]

No state is governed exclusively by the Sharia, and this is true of other traditional legal systems in use; rather, where it is used, it supplements and blends with Western law. For instance, the code systems of Egypt and Syria instruct judges to fill any gaps in the code according to principles of Islamic law. Many states, like Indonesia and Pakistan, have essentially Western law but use Sharia for some aspects of marriage and family law. Even in a primarily non-Muslim state like Germany, Jordanian couples (for instance) are married or divorced according to Sharia principles. Militant Islamic movements in many parts of the world are currently pushing for the expansion of

---

[4]Elaine Sciolino, "Britain Grapples with Role for Islamic Justice," *The New York Times*, November 19, 2008, p. A1.

Defendant facing the judges of a Sharia Islamic court, Nigeria.
© Fred Noy/AFP/Getty Images

Sharia law, however. This has led to clashes between militant Islam and more secular parts of Islamic society, and to conflict as well in states like Nigeria where a variety of religions live together.

The two states that use the Sharia most extensively are Iran and Saudi Arabia, and it comes close to being the dominant form of law in these two countries. In both countries, between 2000 and 2010 there were scores of amputations for thievery, and several individuals were stoned to death, mostly for sexual transgressions. In other states the role of Sharia is more minor. In Jordan, for instance, the only role of Sharia is to provide separate courts for divorce proceedings for Christians and Muslims (in the Islamic courts the testimony of two women is held equivalent to the testimony of one man; in Christian courts the two are equal).[5] Even in countries like Iran or Saudi Arabia, harsh punishments like amputation and stoning are now becoming unusual and controversial; but the Sharia continues to clash with modern sensibilities in the role it prescribes for women.

The two broad divisions of Islam differ in how they define the body of Islamic law. Shia Islam, which is dominant in Iran and eastern Iraq, and is present in patches of Moslem populations elsewhere, holds that the true Sharia consists only of the Qur'an and the traditions and sayings of Prophet Mohammed. Sunni Islam, which is dominant in the rest of the Moslem world, sees the Sharia as broader and somewhat more flexible. In addition to the Qur'an and the traditions and sayings of Prophet Mohammed, it includes in the law both *ijma* (consensus), the discussions of Mohammed's friends, and also *qiyas* (to establish and obtain a decision), arguments by analogy from these sources. Analogies, especially, offer some room for flexibility.

---

[5]"A World of Ways to Say 'Islamic Law,'" *The New York Times*, March 13, 2005, sec. 4, p. 4.

Beyond this basic division, Sharia in many regions incorporates local customs as well as the basic, shared principles. So, Sharia is not one single set of Islamic laws, but we must consider it as it exists in any particular region.

Although the parts of Sharia that deal with sexual morality and that prescribe harsh punishments like amputation are jarring, the underlying principles of Sharia are rather attractive. Sharia centers on obligations—to God and to other people—rather than on rights or entitlements. It is based on central Islamic principles of justice, good deeds, equality, and human brotherhood, as these were applied in the first few centuries after Mohammad to specific questions of behavior. The law was set by the tenth century A.D.; many elements that seem odd in modern society made sense for the medieval society in which they developed, but they have not changed since. What seem to us unbearably harsh punishments, such as cutting off a hand for thievery, were common and perhaps enlightened in the tenth century; certainly, they did not differ from European practice of that time.

Unfortunately, because Islamic law is based on divine inspiration, it is not easily adapted by judges. It is not totally inflexible, however. New circumstances can be adjudicated by analogy to older cases, and complex evasions can be worked out that honor the letter, if not the spirit, of the old laws. For instance, the Sharia bars charging interest on loans, because loans should be given out of a generous heart; but various evasions are used to get around this, such as giving a valuable gift in return for the "gift" of a loan, or treating the borrower and lender as partners in an enterprise, who share its profits.[6] The application of Sharia in Nigeria, reflecting the basic generosity at the heart of Islam, has begun to emphasize recycling, aid to beggars, and education for girls in a mixture of traditional Islamic education and math and reading.[7] At its heart, however, a God-given law cannot be as flexible as human law.

It is perhaps the flexibility of Western systems that has led them to be so widely used. Modern commercial transactions, especially, require rules such as the enforcement of contracts that most traditional legal systems never envisioned. Where traditional law is used, it is always combined with many elements of Western law.

→ COURTS

Courts are organized in sometimes rather complicated ways to take care of the variety of questions that come before them. The one common element to all courts is that they are organized to be somewhat removed from other sources of political power. This is necessary if the courts are to be independent and able to give fair decisions no matter who is involved in a case.

Judges and other court officials in most of Europe are professional civil servants and are protected by the traditions of the bureaucratic model from political pressure.[8]

---

[6]In recent years, with the growing wealth and growing financial sophistication of a number of Islamic countries, special Sharia-compliant financial products have begun to be significant in international finance. In particular, *sukuk* (a bond-like instrument) issues of $1 billion or more have become common. This is still a small part of international finance, but it is growing.
[7]Lydia Polgreen, "Nigeria Turns from Harsher Side of Islamic Law," *The New York Times*, December 11, 2007, p. A1.
[8]For the "bureaucratic model," see Chapter 16.

384   PART IV   THE APPARATUS OF GOVERNANCE

"I WAS IN JAPAN FOR A WHILE. VERY BORING.
NOBODY SUES ANYBODY THERE."

In the United States, federal judges are appointed by the president with approval of
the Senate, but the appointments are lifetime appointments so that no judge can be
threatened with expulsion for having made an unpopular decision. Judges for state and
local courts are elected in many states, but those elections are usually set for long terms
in office and are often formally nonpartisan, to insulate the judges from the ordinary
give-and-take of politics.

Where constitutionalism is less well established, however, the judiciary may have
little independence. In Paraguay under Stroessner's military government, for example,
the courts were subordinate to the military, and the president's office directed judicial
decisions in all cases involving political prisoners.[9]

Courts are often organized separately to handle different kinds of law, especially:

- **Criminal law** involves a charge that a person has disobeyed a law prescribing
  proper conduct. In such cases, the state (through a prosecutor, district attorney,
  etc.) is the party that brings the case, and the person charged is the "defendant."
  The outcome of a criminal case is either acquittal of the defendant or punishment
  such as imprisonment or a fine.

- **Civil law** regulates relations between people. Civil cases may include disputes about
  the meaning of a contract, suits for damages in cases of injury, and questions of mutual
  responsibility in marriage or divorce. The outcome of a civil case is some decision by
  the court as to mutual responsibilities such as how much money is to be paid in child
  support, or how a contract is to be met. Civil cases involve private disputes rather than
  the breaking of a law that affects the broad public, so civil cases are conducted between
  individuals, without state involvement as a party to the case.

---

[9]George Thomas Kurian, *Encyclopedia of the Third World* (New York: Facts on File, 1987), p. 1572.

It is possible in civil law not only to receive compensation for something that has happened in the past but to prevent a person from doing something in the future that will harm you or force them to do something that you wish. To do this, the court declares an injunction that the person should (or should not) do the thing required. An example would be an injunction against a neighbor draining a marsh that you share; the injunction might be necessary if the marsh, once drained, could never be the same again biologically, so that undoing the damage after the fact would not be possible.

- **Constitutional law** involves disputes about the nature of the political process and about whether laws are consistent with the constitution.

Aside from being organized by substance, courts may also be organized by jurisdiction:

- *Lower courts* handle disputes directly.

- *Appeals courts* handle disputes about whether lower courts have decided cases properly.

- *Constitutional courts* exercise judicial review (see section below).

- *Juvenile courts* handle criminal cases involving defendants who are not yet adults. Using separate courts allows for more flexible, private proceedings for defendants who are not yet fully responsible for their actions.

- *"State" courts* (federal systems only) handle cases under the separate "state" laws in a federal system.

- *Religious courts* are used in a state such as Iran, where religious law coexists with Western law.

- Many others.

→ JUDICIAL REVIEW

Judicial review is an aspect of law and the courts that has a special impact on national politics and the making of policy. In general, courts apply and implement the laws as passed by the legislative and executive institutions of the state. However, in many states, special constitutional courts are empowered to judge whether those laws, and other actions of the legislature and executive, are properly within those institutions' powers under the state's constitution. In other words, constitutional courts have the power to overrule other government institutions if they judge that their actions violate the constitution. We call this power to overrule actions of other parts of the government on constitutional grounds **judicial review.**

Today, 158 of the world's 195 states provide for some form of judicial review.[10] Obviously it is possible for a state to function without judicial review, since 37 of them do so. If there is no system of judicial review, whatever the governmental institutions do or provide for in law is subject only to their own understanding of what is constitutional.

---

[10]Tom Ginsburg, "The Global Spread of Constitutional Review," in Keith E. Whittington, R. Daniel Kelemen, and Gregory Caldeira, eds., *The Oxford Handbook of Law and Politics* (New York: Oxford University Press, 2008), p. 82.

This does not mean, however, that "anything goes." A number of states with strong traditions of constitutionalism function in this way, including stable democracies like the Netherlands. (See discussion of "constitutionalism," pp. 219–220.) Until the middle of the twentieth century most states did not provide for judicial review.

States have adopted judicial review for two main reasons. The first, and most obvious, is that where power is divided—either between different parts of the government as in a presidential system, or between the central government and regional governments as in a federal system—there has to be some provision for a referee to settle disputes about whether one part of the system has encroached on the powers of the other part.

In a presidential system, for instance, where the president has part of the power and a legislature has another part, how do we resolve the kind of dispute that must inevitably occur when the legislature says to the president, "You've just done something that's supposed to be left up to us"—or vice versa? The solution is to have some third institution that is empowered to serve as a referee. The situation in a federal system is similar. A referee is necessary in both situations of shared power, and this has almost always meant establishing a system of judicial review.

Notice that of the states in Table 17.1 that are either presidential or federal systems—in other words, those states above the dashed line—only one of the nine states does not have a system of judicial review. Of the parliamentary, unitary states below the dashed line, three of ten states do not have judicial review. The special need for judicial review in systems where power is shared is evident in this table.

This leads us to the second main reason why states adopt judicial review. The table poses a question for us: Even without divided, shared governmental power, two-thirds of the states below the dashed line have provisions for judicial review. What led them to do this? The reason appears to be that judicial review became popular around the world in the second half of the twentieth century as a way to protect individuals from the arbitrary use of state power, even when it was not required for its referee function. That is, individuals viewed judicial review as a tool of constitutionalism, in which a relatively nonpolitical court can help to place limits on the government's authority. This especially helps to explain the popularity of judicial review in Germany after the Nazi dictatorship, although the federal system there probably would have required it in any case. More to the point, it also helps to explain the institution of judicial review in Italy immediately following Mussolini's fascist dictatorship in 1945.

Constitutional courts—the courts that conduct judicial review—vary around the world as to how they operate. The Constitutional Council of France serves as a referee for the other units of government; the only way a government can bring a case to the Council is by a request from the president, the prime minister, either house of the parliament, or a lower court to rule on the constitutionality of a law, either before or after it is passed. In Germany, the Constitutional Court may be accessed in a variety of ways: Any high national official, and any *Land* (regional government) may ask the Court to rule on the constitutionality of a law, either before or after it is passed; either party to a case in a lower court, if it has lost in that case, can appeal the decision to the Constitutional Court, asking it to rule that the law on which the decision was based is unconstitutional; and most remarkably, any citizen can request a decision from the Court on whether a law is constitutional, without going through lower courts.

TABLE 17.1

Constitutional Review and Shared Powers: Western Europe and North America

	Constitutional Review?
Presidential or Hybrid Systems	
France	Yes
Mexico	Yes
U.S.A.	Yes
Parliamentary Systems (Federal)	
Austria	Yes
Belgium	Yes
Canada	Yes
Germany	Yes
Spain	Yes
Switzerland	No
Parliamentary Systems (Unitary)	
Denmark	Yes
Great Britain	Yes
Iceland	Yes
Ireland	Yes
Italy	Yes
Luxembourg	No
Netherlands	No
Norway	Yes
Portugal	Yes
Sweden	No

In the United States, the Supreme Court functions solely as the highest appeal court of the state. It is not possible, as it is in France or Germany, for a legislative leader to request a ruling in advance on whether a proposed law would be constitutional, and it is certainly not possible for an ordinary citizen to request a ruling on a law. The only way that a case can reach the Supreme Court is after it has been ruled on in a lower federal court of appeals. A law's constitutionality cannot be tested in the Supreme Court until the law has been passed by Congress and the president, and then challenged in cases in lower federal courts. If a person has lost a case in a federal appeals court, that person can present the case as an appeal to the Supreme Court, arguing on the question of whether the law is constitutional. The Court does not accept all cases that are submitted to it, but if it does so, the Justices of the Court will consider whether the law is consistent with the Constitution and (in our case law system) with all earlier Supreme Court interpretations of what the Constitution means.

For instance, in 2008 a conservative group, Citizens United, tried to run a documentary film, *Hillary: The Movie* on television during the presidential primary of that year. The documentary was very critical of candidate Hillary Clinton, and the Federal Election Commission barred running it under provisions of federal campaign laws that prohibited corporations from sponsoring political ads within 30 days of a primary election. Citizens United sued the Commission in the U.S. District Court for the District of Columbia, but lost its case there. It appealed to the Supreme Court, which accepted the case and in 2010 issued its decision in *Citizens United vs. Federal Election Commission*. On a vote of 5 to 4, the nine Justices ruled that the original federal law on campaigns unconstitutionally barred corporations from certain kinds of political activity. The majority on the Court argued that corporations are in effect individuals, and are entitled to the protections of individual free speech embodied in the first amendment of the Constitution. The decision had wide-ranging effects, since it meant that corporations could fund political advertising directly out of their operating budgets.

Oyez, at http://www.oyez.org/, is a website that allows you to listen to arguments in cases before the United States Supreme Court.

For all that it is popular as a protection of individual rights (and that it is a necessity, as a referee among various parts of the government if power is divided and shared), judicial review fits oddly with democracy. In judicial review, a set of judges who are presumably not accountable to the citizenry are given power over the decisions of the state. In the United States, for example, over the last two centuries, the Supreme Court has established that it has the right to annul acts of presidents and laws passed by Congress whenever it deems either body to have exceeded its proper powers. Although there is occasional grumbling about the Court and its power, it is striking how readily this essentially undemocratic arrangement is tolerated. Think of it! Nine people who are appointed by the president and the Senate and thereafter serve for the rest of their lives without ever being subject to popular election—these nine people wield huge power in our otherwise democratic system. The only explanation for Americans' ready toleration of this is their recognition that the fragmentation of power requires something like this to make their system work. That, and the recognition that even democratic governments can be arbitrary and unreasonable, and that courts can provide a partial protection against this.

✳ Example

The Law in China

Chinese law is shaped by China's Confucian tradition and by the needs of the state's leaders. For thousands of years, until the end of the nineteenth century, China was dominated by Confucian thought. In the Confucian view of the world, society was meant to be in harmony. This harmony was thought to be maintained by leaders' continual demonstration of virtue, which instilled a sense of virtue into the rest of the people; and it was maintained also by complex networks of rites and mutual obligations based on the family and clan.

Problems were supposed to be worked out among disputants, perhaps with the help of a local person of superior rank, in a way that was conciliatory and that left everyone in agreement. No one was to lose; no one was to lose face. There were lawyers and law in China then, but they were to be appealed to as a last resort. The truth is, Confucian China did not like law and disapproved of it. Legal proceedings were made so unpleasant that most Chinese would go to any lengths to avoid them; and avoiding them was easier because the alternative of mediation and conciliation was urged on the disputants by their families and communities with a good deal of social pressure. Proceedings were deliberately made difficult and dangerous by Confucian rulers to discourage use of the law. The seventeenth-century emperor K'ang Hsi is quoted as saying:

> Lawsuits would tend to increase to a frightful amount, if people were not afraid of the tribunals, and if they felt confident of always finding in them ready and perfect justice. As man is apt to delude himself concerning his own interests, contests would then be interminable, and the half of the Empire would not suffice to settle the lawsuits of the other half. I desire, therefore, that those who have recourse to the tribunals should be treated without any pity, and in such a manner that they shall be disgusted with law, and tremble to appear before a magistrate.[11]

When the communists gained power in China after World War II, they continued the tradition of minimizing use of the law and legal procedures. While continuing that general tradition, however, they transformed it from the Confucian system to their own brand of informal rule. The old aristocratic leadership and old networks of obligation and ancestral rites were replaced by factory committees, neighborhood committees, and party officials. However, the basic principle remained: disputes were resolved by conciliation and mediation processes with a great deal of social pressure on the disputants to reach a mutually acceptable solution.

From 1949 until 1976, the government passed little legislation, preferring to govern less formally through enunciation of doctrines by party leaders. Courts and the legal process were rarely used. In 1981, on the eve of Deng Xiaoping's opening of the system, there were only five thousand lawyers for a Chinese population of approximately 1 billion, compared with half a million lawyers for a U.S. population a quarter the size of China's.[12]

With the death of Mao Tse-tung in 1976, a power struggle developed between Mao's supporters, who had pushed society in a radical left direction during the 1966–76 Cultural Revolution, and more centrist leaders such as Deng Xiaoping, who had been victims of the Cultural Revolution. Deng and his supporters prevailed, and among the changes they introduced was a much greater reliance on law and legal proceedings than what had gone before. The body of statutes was expanded dramatically, with codes of law for many areas previously not ruled by law, including industrial safety, environmental protection, and patents. Criminal law, marriage law, and many areas of civil law were expanded. The legal profession grew

---

[11]Cited in René David and John E. C. Brierly, *Major Legal Systems in the World Today*, 3d ed. (London: Steven, 1985), p. 520n.
[12]Xinhua General Overseas News Service, Item 1009065, 9 October 1990.

dramatically as well, with a tenfold increase by 1990. Especially in criminal law, changes were dramatic, with procedures set up rather along the lines of European code law.

These changes were probably made for two reasons:

1. *To establish a "rule of law"*: The informal procedures of Confucian China, once the Confucian structure of society had been destroyed, left the way open for purely arbitrary power. Deng and his friends had suffered grievously from informal, arbitrary proceedings during the Cultural Revolution—Deng, for instance, was sentenced to hard labor, and his son was permanently crippled when his back was broken during interrogation—and they wanted to set up somewhat greater protections for the individual.

2. *To handle the problem of economic disputes*: Deng wished to liberalize the Chinese economy, introducing large elements of market choice. Before 1976, there was little civil law in China. There was practically no individual property under communism, so there were few private disputes except for matters such as marriage that could be handled reasonably in conciliation by local bodies. With the development of a partial market economy, however, there would be long-distance disputes between suppliers and customers, and partners, and these could not be handled locally. Also, economic exchanges required precise, dependable rules—not informal social processes—for resolution. With the use of market mechanisms, civil law was necessary, and this could not easily be provided without building a more formal legal structure.

Economic development proved Deng right; by 2004, 4,300,000 civil cases were heard in Chinese courts annually, mostly involving disputes between businesses.[13]

Individuals have also begun to sue government agencies in increasing numbers, but the outcomes are chancy. In one well-known case, three women who were forced to retire at age fifty-four by the China National Fisheries Group, even though Personnel Ministry regulations set the retirement age at sixty, sued and won in two different courts. However, the courts have no power of enforcement, and the fisheries group simply ignored the judgments. On the other hand, in 1996, a restaurateur who had been jailed for fifteen days on charges that he had put opium in his hot pots successfully sued the police for false arrest. Overall, Professor Minxin Pei estimates that by the late 1990s, 39 percent of such suits were bringing at least partial victory for the person bringing the suit.[14]

Just how Chinese law will develop depends on how the Communist Party will maintain its monopoly of political power. The Party is caught in a dilemma with regard to the rule of law. On the one hand, the Party's leaders recognize that they need an effective legal system in order for China to realize its potential economically. On the other hand, they do not want an independent source of political power to develop in the state. Judges are required to clear their decisions with trial committees, which the Party appoints and controls. Additionally, lawyers who refuse to be warned off by the Party from taking on controversial cases (such as defense of Christian churches or the Falun Gong sect, or of poor people protesting governmental expropriation of their property) may lose their license to practice law. However, since the Party also needs to modernize economic relations, it actually allows many challenges to occur. The situation remains in flux.

---

[13]Joseph Kahn, "Legal Gadfly Bites Hard, and the Party Slaps Him," *The New York Times,* December 13, 2005, p. A1.
[14]Elisabeth Rosenthal, "A Day in Court, and Sometimes Justices, for Chinese," *The New York Times,* April 27, 1998, p. A1.

EXAMPLE

The European Court of Justice

As you saw in the example at the end of Chapter 3, the European Union is an organization of twenty-seven European states attempting to merge their markets and economies. The Union has an elaborate governing structure, although the members remain independent, sovereign states.

One of the governing structures is a court, the European Court of Justice. Observing this court provides us with a fascinating case of how a court may develop a body of law in "new ground"—twenty-seven independent states that are bound together to form a common market. The court consists of twenty-seven justices, one from each member state, who are appointed by the unanimous consent of the member states. A justice serves a term of six years and is sworn to act on behalf of the Union.

The treaties on which the European Union is based established the Court of Justice, but they did not spell out clearly the court's jurisdiction or powers. Much like John Marshall's Supreme Court in the early days of the United States, the Court of Justice has made its place in the order of things through a series of decisions, in effect defining its powers by what it has been able to get away with. It has moved cautiously, but steadily, to make its law supreme within the European Union.

In an important early decision, the court ruled that the Rome Treaty set up a new order for the members, which was not governed by international law; in effect, the court established that the European Union would have an internal system of law. The key question was whether a member state could retaliate in kind if it was injured by another member violating the Rome Treaty. Under international law, this would be permitted; and so if the Rome Treaty were simply a treaty among sovereign states, a member could do this. The court ruled, however, that one member could not retaliate against another but must instead seek relief through the Union's institutions. It thereby transformed the Treaty of Rome from a treaty into a constitution.

In a later decision, the Court of Justice expanded the right to bring cases from member states to include also individuals and corporations in those states. Therefore, citizens of states in the Union could bring cases against their own governments. Most cases in the court have involved trade regulations because the Union is, after all, primarily an organization to enforce free trade within its borders. However, the most dramatic development of law by the Court of Justice has been in the area of individual rights.

The Treaty of Rome did not specify many rights for individuals. It was a document intended to set up a free market, and most of the few rights that are mentioned in it are economic, such as the right to free movement of capital, the right to bargain collectively, and the right of women to earn pay equal to that of men. The court, however, has gradually developed across several dozen cases a set of rights based on "the constitutional traditions common to the Member States" and on other treaties that member states may have signed, such as the European Convention on Human Rights—even though the court is nowhere directly empowered to enforce those treaties. In these decisions, the Court has overruled laws of member states, and some of the decisions have gone deeply into what would be the independent responsibilities of states: British schools have been directed to stop using corporal punishment, the Dutch army has had to change its disciplinary procedures, German courts have had to provide access to lawyers before a suspect is charged with a crime.

Because so little was written into the Treaty of Rome along these lines, the Court of Justice has proceeded by building a body of case law. As is usually true where case law develops, the court has been tolerated in this because it was seen as a constructive force in the development of the Union and because the alternative—states retaliating against each other for trade violations, for instance—could bring chaos.

KEY TERMS

law	habeas corpus	civil law
courts	code law	constitutional law
legal systems	Sharia	judicial review
case law	criminal law	

FURTHER READING

Abraham, Henry J. *The Judicial Process: An Introductory Analysis of the Courts of the United States, England, and France.* New York: Oxford University Press, 1998.

Baum, Lawrence. *Judges and Their Audiences: A Perspective on Judicial Behavior.* Princeton, NJ: Princeton University Press, 2006.

_____. *The Supreme Court,* 11th ed. Washington, DC: CQ Press, 2011.

David, René, and Brierley, John E. C. *Major Legal Systems in the World Today.* 3rd ed. London: Steven, 1985.

Gibson, James L., and Caldeira, Gregory A. "The Legal Cultures of Europe." *Law and Society Review* 30 (1996), pp. 55–85.

Ginsburg, Tom. *Judicial Review in New Democracies.* New York: Cambridge University Press, 2003.

Kagan, Robert. *Adversarial Legalism: The American Way of Law.* Cambridge, MA: Harvard University Press, 2005.

Whittington, Keith E., Kelemen, R. Daniel, and Caldeira, Gregory A. *The Oxford Handbook of Law and Politics.* New York: Oxford University Press, 2008.

International Politics

PART V

International Politics

CHAPTER 18

GLOBAL POLITICS: POLITICS AMONG STATES (AND OTHERS)

In the preceding chapters, we looked at the manner in which politics—the use of power to make collective choices for a group of people—is carried on within a state. However, states also carry on politics among themselves. For instance, they sign trade agreements setting up special arrangements for the exchange of goods between firms in two or more countries, or a number of states may agree to coordinate their military activities, as in the NATO alliance. States set up regular exchanges of scientific information. They draw up agreements in which groups of states commit themselves to such things as a promise not to test nuclear weapons in the open air. States draw up treaties to protect wildlife that migrate across state borders. They fight and settle wars. Each of these events makes a collective choice for a group of two or more states, and so these are examples of politics—the use of power to make collective choices—for a group of states, rather than within one state.[1] We commonly call politics of this sort **international politics** or **global politics**. The two terms mean approximately the same thing, except that "global politics" emphasizes by connotation that more than just states are involved in the politics. The states are central participants, but international social movements, multinational corporations, and other nongovernmental actors are involved as well.

How is global politics like that which we have been looking at so far in this book, and how is it different? In its main outlines, politics among states is a good deal like politics within states. Both address the same sorts of policy questions such as regulation of potentially harmful behavior, aid programs for the weak, and guarantees of standard weights and measures. Like politics within states, politics among states is marked by the use of force and by appeals to the common good, that is, by power and choice. Both types

---

[1]Recall the definition of politics in Chapter 1: making of common decisions for a group through the use of power. Here the "group" is a group of states.

of politics reach political decisions—decisions on behalf of groups. However, in important ways international politics differs from politics within a state. The most important difference is that there is no single central authority to provide an ultimate settlement of a dispute among states. Also, political figures are more likely to follow overtly selfish ("selfish," that is, on behalf of their states' interests) strategies in politics among states. Finally, political interchange does not proceed as easily in politics among states as it does in politics within a state. Let us look at each of these points.

✦ THE ABSENCE OF CENTRAL AUTHORITY

As a state carries out politics, the various antagonists are subject to a central government that has the authority to settle a question firmly. If environmentalists square off in conflict with a mining company, both sides know that ultimately their dispute will be resolved by some higher authority that has the power to make them accept that decision, even if they do not agree with it. In the United States, that authority would be Congress, the president, or perhaps the Supreme Court; in Britain, it would be the Parliament; in Saudi Arabia, it would be the king. Within any state, there is some central authority, more powerful than any single political force, which can enforce decisions on any question. The only exception to this would be a state involved in a civil war, which is precisely a situation in which there is no clearly established central authority.

In politics conducted among states, however, there is no central position of authority. Therefore, states that become involved in disputes must ultimately settle the disputes themselves, whether by negotiations or through war. Other states may give helpful advice and exert pressure on the disputants, but there is no central body of any sort that can impose a settlement.

The **United Nations** would be a potential body of authority. It is an organization of 193 states, almost all of the states of the world, which accepts responsibility for many of the things a government would do within a state. That is, it is concerned to preserve law and order by preventing violent solutions to disputes (wars); it promotes health programs, education, and research; it tries to see that poorer states are helped.

While the United Nations tries to do the things a government does, it cannot do them the way a government would do them. It has no army or police force of its own to enforce its decisions. Rather, it must depend on voluntary help from its member states. Few states are going to send their soldiers voluntarily into a place where they are not wanted—and risk war with the people on whom they are enforcing the United Nations' decision; therefore, this has effectively meant that the UN can almost never send in a police force unless the disputants agree voluntarily to accept it. (The First Gulf War in 1991, in which a United Nations force drawn from a number of countries and led by the United States ousted Iraq from Kuwait after Iraq had invaded that country, was the first exception to this rule in decades.)

Despite these limitations, the UN has frequently been able to play a helpful role when the nations involved in a dispute want to bring in a neutral group to police their negotiated settlement. For instance, United Nations forces successfully enforced the peace agreement that established the new state of East Timor when it seceded from Indonesia. From 2002 to 2005 the UN peacekeeping mission guarded East Timor while it established its capacity to be a self-sufficient state. This is a far cry from the real policing power that would give the United Nations the authority to force a decision on the parties in dispute, but it has helped on a number of occasions to reduce international violence. (I discuss the United Nations in more detail in an example at the end of this chapter.)

Another potentially ultimate authority in the system of states is the **International Court of Justice,** headquartered in the Netherlands. The court is a branch of the United Nations, but the body of "international law" over which it decides goes back far beyond the United Nations, which was founded only in 1945. From its founding to 2012, the Court has dealt with 152 cases, but again, any solution laid down by the court sticks only if the parties of the dispute voluntarily abide by the court's ruling. In 2004, for instance, the court ruled that Israel's construction of a security barrier, crossing areas of the West Bank of Jordan that were occupied militarily by Israel, violated international law. However, when Israel refused to admit that the court had jurisdiction, the court could do little. Most cases that come to the court are not of this sort but are cases in which those involved have agreed in advance to accept the court's decision, whatever it may be. In these circumstances, the court can serve as a useful tool for resolving disputes. Overall, however, it cannot play the role a government would play.

Developments in the late 1990s may produce new strands of international law in which heads of state (or at least former heads of state) can receive punishment for crimes committed by their states. (I will discuss this in detail below, on p. 411.) The enforcing agents in these cases would be other states, bolstered by broad consensus among the people of the world, rather than a formal international authority. Even if this process continues, however, we will still be a long way from holding sitting rulers of powerful states—in contrast to disgraced former rulers of weak states—accountable for their states' actions.

With no ultimate governmental authority in the world, politics among states is in many ways what we might expect politics within a state to be if that state had no government. States that are large and strong are able to bully smaller states, and they usually get what they want. Small states must attach themselves to stronger states, through alliances, for protection. In effect, gangs of states join together for mutual protection just as, in a state without government (anarchy), people would form gangs.

↦ FIDUCIARY POLITICAL ROLES AND INTERNATIONAL MORALITY

Before we consider the second special aspect of international politics, we must define a new concept—the **fiduciary role** in politics.[2] Someone acts in a fiduciary role if that person operates as an agent on behalf of another person's interest. A real estate agent acts in a fiduciary role on behalf of a person who wishes to sell a house, a lawyer acts in a fiduciary role for a client.

---

[2]William H. Riker presents the concept of fiduciary role in much the way it is used here in *A Theory of Political Coalitions* (New Haven: Yale University Press, 1962), pp. 24–27.

The important thing about fiduciary roles for our purposes is that a person acting in a fiduciary role stands in a peculiar moral position. Let us assume that the fiduciary agent is personally upright and moral and that among the agent's "upright" traits is a strong sense of duty toward the person whose interests he or she is representing. Now let us suppose that the agent is caught in circumstances in which doing the thing that is personally moral will hurt the interests of the person who is represented. Consider the lawyer, for instance, who may need to browbeat a timid witness to defend a client. What is the right thing to do? We hope such a lawyer would never browbeat a timid person on her own behalf, but is it right for her to impose her personal scruples on the client's case and thereby injure the client's interests? We recognize that a different moral situation exists when people do something on behalf of others than when they do it to help themselves. We feel differently about a woman who shoplifts caviar than we do about a mother, in dire straits, who steals food for her children.

How does all this relate to international politics? It is important to international politics because here, more than in the politics within a state, almost all decisions are made by those who see themselves as acting in fiduciary roles, on behalf of the people in the state they represent. In politics as it occurs within a state, political figures act to some extent as fiduciary agents (members of Congress, for instance, represent their constituents); but they are largely personal decision makers who represent no clear single interest. Leaders of states, however, work on behalf of a single clear "client," the people of that state. It is well understood that a state's leader owes first duty in international politics to the state and its interests, and that anything or anyone else in the world for whom the leader feels affection must run a distant second. We expect Barack Obama to serve the interests of the United States, Prime Minister David Cameron to serve the interests of Great Britain, and President Dilma Rouseff to serve the interests of Brazil.

This gives a different and colder moral tone to international politics than we find in politics within states. We expect leaders of states to be more cold-blooded in international politics than they would be domestically. What is regarded as personal virtue in domestic affairs may be seen as perverse and harmful in international politics.

Leaders of states have often been forgiven for official acts that, if done for personal gain, would have blackened their names forever. Harry Truman, for instance, killed thousands of Japanese civilians when he ordered atomic bombs dropped on Hiroshima and Nagasaki, and Winston Churchill launched devastating firebomb attacks on German cities. However, they were judged at least partly in light of their official positions. Nationalism further reinforces the view of leaders as filling fiduciary roles, as it can lead us to see other peoples as less human, less deserving of justice and mercy, than our own. This makes the leaders and populations of states more comfortable than they might otherwise be with their states' amoral behavior.

I should not overstate this case, however, because the political actions of states are not solely based on calculations of cold rationality. Emotions play a role, and some of these may be generous. For instance, U.S. support for Great Britain in World War II was based on more than rational considerations, although there were elements of rationality involved. U.S. support of Israel over the last few decades has certainly involved something beyond rationality. In its broad outlines, however, we can distinguish international politics from politics within states by its relatively greater tone of "selfish" calculation.

↬ Impediments to International Communication

A third major difference between international politics and politics within states is that communication between leaders is more cumbersome and more vulnerable to misunderstanding than communication within any one state. Within a state, the various political leaders speak the same language. More important, they "speak the same language" in that they know each other fairly well, have a common fund of experiences and stories, and share the same culture.

In international politics, the people involved must often use interpreters to converse, which makes the proceedings more formal and slow, and leaves a good deal of room for misunderstanding. The problem of interpretation can lead to amusing moments, as when President Jimmy Carter's statement that he was happy to be in Poland was translated as "I lust for Poland."

More serious yet are deep cultural and religious differences, and the frequent lack of shared assumptions and motivations, which may lead to a failure of communication between states. After World War I, U.S. diplomacy was deeply flawed by President Woodrow Wilson's inability to understand the motives of the United States' allies, Britain, France, and Italy. The leaders of Britain and France in the 1930s responded to Hitler in what was probably an inappropriately gentle way because they did not understand what he wanted to do. Most recently, the United States and North Korea have had continual trouble dealing with one another appropriately because they have approached their mutual interchanges with very different historical and political assumptions.

↬ Power and International Politics

Under these circumstances—with most decisions made by reciprocal bargaining or through conflict, with a relatively naked rationality operating and with severe difficulties of communication—international politics is a rough game. More simply and directly than in politics within a state, the raw power of the participants determines the outcomes. On what is this power based?

Military Power

First and foremost, a state's *military power* determines its overall power in international politics. Military power is hard to assess, because different states emphasize different types of arms. Israel does not have much of a navy, but it has an excellent small army and air force. How do we compare it with Great Britain, which has an excellent small navy? How does nuclear capacity figure in our calculations? Beyond this problem of comparing apples and oranges, there are imponderable questions such as toughness, morale, and battle readiness that must be considered. Israel's armed forces are stronger than their small size would suggest, because of their spirit and their level of training and because they have had frequent combat experience; they are "tried and true."

Finally, any armed force will fight better when defending its home soil. A smaller and weaker army may be able to defend itself successfully against a stronger army under some circumstances. A good example of this is the tough resistance that Argentina was

TABLE 18.1

Eleven Major Military Powers

	Defense Expenditure (billions of dollars)	Persons in Uniform	Air Force and Missile Forces	Nuclear Weapons
United States	739	1,569,000	443,156	Yes
China	90	2,285,000	441,000	Yes
Great Britain	63	174,000	45,920	Yes
France	59	239,000	50,169	Yes
Japan	58	247,746	56,923	No
Russia	53	956,000	237,000	Yes
Germany	44	251,465	46,792	No
India	37	1,155,000	134,000	Yes
South Korea	29	655,000	65,000	No
Israel	15	176,500	34,000	Yes
North Korea	2	1,190,000	110,000	Yes

SOURCE: International Institute for Strategic Studies, *The Military Balance, 2012* (Oxford, UK: Routledge, 2012).

able to maintain in 1982 against the more imposing and experienced British armed forces in the Falkland Islands war, although Argentina eventually lost. An even better example is the defeat dealt to large and powerful U.S. forces by North Vietnam in the early 1970s. Table 18.1 displays a few aspects of the military strength of eleven states that are probably among the strongest military powers in the world.

Soft Power

The United States found in the first years of the twenty-first century, however, that the Bush administration's reliance simply on military power was not very effective. As the United States became more and more isolated in the world, it became clear that multinational cooperation, appeals to shared ideas, personal links between elites, willingness to consult with others—a whole set of things often referred to as "soft power"—were at least as important.[3] Military might alone will carry you only so far.

Soft power consists of a state's reputation as a constructive member of the world community, and as an example that other states wish to emulate. How can states build soft power? They can build it by sponsoring exchanges between citizens, maintaining libraries in other countries, and in all sorts of other ways fostering other countries' familiarity with their culture. They can build it by sharing ideas, and by listening to other countries as well as espousing their own views. States can build it by popular entertainment like movies that they export. They can also build it by knowing other countries' languages and addressing people in their own language. Soft power helps states *persuade* others, in contrast to military power, which helps them to *coerce* others.

---

[3]Joseph S. Nye, *Soft Power: The Means to Success in World Politics* (New York: Public Affairs Press, 2005).

Economic Power

Even if it is not militarily powerful, a state may figure importantly in international politics if it controls something of economic importance. Saudi Arabia has only a small military force, for instance, but it has often been able to get other states to do what it wishes because they depend on it for their oil imports. Germany's army is reasonably effective, but it is constitutionally limited to defense or to multilateral action, and so cannot realistically be used as a threat to make other states do what it wishes. Greater leverage for Germany comes because it has had the strongest, most stable economy in Europe. In 2010 when small European countries like Greece and Ireland suffered financial crises and had to be bailed out by the rest of Europe, Germany's dominant economy meant that it was the biggest contributor to rescue packages for those countries, and could dictate the terms of the rescue.

Economic position may also fail to provide a political tool, however, as is illustrated by the various attempts of the United States in the 1970s to use threats of economic punishment to get the Soviet Union to do what it wanted. The United States could not credibly threaten the Soviet Union militarily (a war between the two superpowers would be so destructive that no one would dare to start it); therefore, the United States at various times tried to use its economic muscle to influence the Soviets. When the Soviet Union invaded Afghanistan, the United States canceled its grain exports to the Soviets, promising to start them up again if the Soviets changed their policy. Similarly, in the 1970s, the United States tried through economic sanctions to convince Soviet and Polish leaders to liberalize the regime in Poland. These efforts did not work because the United States was not important enough economically to the Soviet bloc countries, whose economies were rather self-contained, to force them to back down on policies that were important to them. I discuss economic sanctions as a tool of international politics in more detail in the next section, "The Process of International Politics."

Leadership

Finally, skilled leadership may make a difference in the weight a state carries in international politics. Charles de Gaulle, by skillful diplomacy and a flair for public relations, was able to make France the leading state of Western Europe in the late 1960s and 1970s. Woodrow Wilson's leadership probably diminished the influence of the United States at the end of World War I. Hitler and Mussolini led their states into disastrous, overreaching wars of conquest.

✦ THE PROCESS OF INTERNATIONAL POLITICS

If power is the basic tool of international politics, how exactly does it work? What do the leaders of states, of international organizations, and of nongovernmental organizations do as they make collective choices in international politics?

Diplomacy and Other Nonmilitary Measures

Although ultimately the military power of states remains in the background of most major international decisions, the vast majority of things that happen in international politics do not directly invoke military power. Thousands of small decisions are made

every day—small-scale trade decisions, issuing of amnesty to refugees, visits of scholarly delegations—and these do not involve the full power of a state. Also, many large
and important actions take place without any military involvement: the formation and
expansion of the European Union, for instance, or the international agreement to ban
the use of land mines (see box, p. 411).

The process of reaching international decisions in such ways is called **diplomacy**.
States maintain a formal diplomatic apparatus for conducting politics with other states.
The United States, for instance, employs over two thousand Foreign Service officers to
conduct its diplomacy; in addition, a number of ambassadors and high-ranking officials
in the State Department are directly appointed by the president from outside the professional ranks of Foreign Service officers.

States deal with small-scale transactions, such as handling visitors' problems or
promoting local business deals, through a system of **consulates**. These are local offices
to represent a state in major cities of another state. Germany, for instance, operates ten
consulates in major cities in the United States. Consuls, who are in charge of the consulates, do not represent their governments in major international negotiations; their job
is to maintain a ceremonial presence locally for the state (U.S. consuls host a Thanks-
giving dinner each year for local notables in their city, for instance) and to take care of
the myriad of small problems and decisions that come up from day to day.

Ambassadors are the officials charged by their state to conduct high-level politics
with the state to which they are posted. A state appoints only a single ambassador to another
state, and that person will be based in the capital city. Ambassadors, or even higher officials
from the foreign ministry, will represent the state in negotiations over major agreements.

Another major function of ambassadors and the rest of the diplomatic corps is to
gather information about the state to which they are posted—commercial information,
political information, and military information. They do this openly, by reading the
press and talking to the state's leaders and citizens. These efforts are often supplemented
by spying operations (the United States' Central Intelligence Agency, for instance) that
mix open and clandestine information gathering.

It is in diplomacy, rather than military action, that most activity by IGOs and
NGOs takes place. The box on p. 411 describes one such set of activities by nongovernmental actors. Other examples would be the active lobbying of the European Community governing structures by international interest groups such as the Cereal Producers'
Association, or the initiatives of Amnesty International to obtain better treatment of
political prisoners in numerous states by publicizing the cases and bringing international
public opinion to bear on those states. The one exception to the "nonmilitary" nature of
nongovernmental actors is international terrorism, in which non-state groups seek to
meet their international goals by independent violent action such as bombings or kidnappings. (See the discussion of terrorism, pp. 404–405.)

That diplomacy does not directly involve military action does not mean that it is
purely cooperative. The use of power in diplomacy, like the use of power in any other
sort of politics, may run the full range from persuasion to coercion. In persuasion, diplomats try to convince another state that it is in that state's interest to do what the first
state wants. A good example might be trade negotiations, in which one state might try to
convince another that open trade in a certain commodity would benefit both. Relations
between states such as Canada and the United States consist primarily of persuasion.

Further along the coercion continuum, diplomats of a state might argue with leaders of another state that if the state does not open its markets, the first state might choose to shift its trade elsewhere.

Furthest along the continuum, short of military action, would be a threat by diplomats of the possibility of military action. United States diplomats have sometimes cautioned various other states that if they did not do what the United States was asking, the United States might attack them. This is still diplomacy, not military activity; but it certainly is not warm and fuzzy. As Will Rogers is supposed to have said, "Diplomacy is the art of saying 'nice doggy' while looking around for a rock to smash it with."

Economic Sanctions

A form of nonmilitary coercion that the United States often uses, even in dealing with friends, is the imposition of **economic sanctions.** Imposition of an economic sanction consists of a state or group of states deliberately withholding normal economic relations to punish another state. For instance, the United Nations has asked its members to withhold most trade from Iran in an attempt to force it to stop developing its nuclear capabilities. So far, the effort has been unsuccessful, although by early 2013 it was beginning to bring real economic pain to Iran.

An economic sanction is certainly direct coercion, although it involves no military activity. It is the analogue, in international relations, of a strike or consumer boycott in domestic politics. In a few important instances, economic sanctions have been successful. For instance, the United Nations' boycott of trade with Iraq in the 1990s kept Iraq involved for several years in a grudging process of disarmament and inspections. The most successful use of economic sanctions historically was the international boycott of investment in South Africa that led to the fall of that country's undemocratic, white-dominated government.

The key to success in economic sanctions is that one must be able to close the spigot completely. In the Iraq and South Africa cases, nearly all states of the world cooperated in the boycotts, so Iraq and South Africa had no alternative sources of supply. In the case of Iran, sanctions were for a long time limited by the reluctance of China and Russia to participate fully in closing down trade.

The United States has often been tempted to pursue unilateral economic boycotts of other states because all by itself it is such a large economic force in the world. These have almost never been successful, yet we keep trying. At various times, we have withheld trade from Cuba, Iran, the Soviet Union, Vietnam, China, and numerous other countries. At the same time, "states" and cities of the United States, pursuing their own *mini* foreign policies, have enforced economic sanctions on such states as Pakistan, Switzerland, and Indonesia. Inevitably, the target country has bought from Germany, France, or some other supplier the things we were unwilling to sell it. The United States can inflict pain and inconvenience on a target, but rarely enough to make it buckle. We must also remember that economic sanctions hurt the sanctioner as well. Economists estimate that in 1995, the United States lost $20 billion of exports, at a cost of 250,000 jobs, to enforce its trade sanctions.[4] Additionally, sanctions have not added to the world's love for us.

---

[4]Cited by Paul Magnusson, *BusinessWeek*, November 17, 1997, p. 115.

402   PART V   INTERNATIONAL POLITICS

It is easy to understand why a state, especially a genuinely major economic force such as the United States, might turn to economic sanctions. No one wants to use military force if it can be avoided. Economic sanctions can give people the feeling of doing something, whether or not they have any effect; but they rarely succeed, unless they are universally enforced.

War

States conduct the vast majority of international transactions peacefully, through diplomacy. However, war is a real part of international politics as well. Many important international political outcomes, such as the freeing of Kuwait after its invasion by Iraq in 1990, the unification of South Vietnam and North Vietnam in 1975, and the occupation of Kosovo by the United States and its allies in 1999, have resulted directly from military action. Even when diplomats negotiate peaceably, their states' power—that is their capacity to wage war or their capacity to manipulate economic outcomes—always lies beneath the negotiations.

War is also not a sometime thing in international politics. Even though most international politics does not involve war directly, there is almost always some warfare going on, somewhere. Since 1939, there has not been a single day that war was not waged somewhere in the world.

Because war is so damaging to so many people, political scientists have long wrestled with the question of why wars occur. The causes of war appear to be complex:

- *Nationalism* probably is not a major determinant of whether war occurs, because wars were already a common tool of political leaders long before the modern era

A son mourns a father lost in Syrian conflict.
© AP Photo/Rodrigo Abd

in which nationalism blossomed. If nationalism is not a cause of war, however, it certainly has added to the brutality of war, along with its companion, racism (the other great popular emotion of the modern era). Atrocities come naturally if you think of your enemy as less human than yourself.

- *Transitions* seem to breed war. Change breeds uncertainty in which leaders may imagine either great threats or great opportunities for conquest and expansion. Change also may create unstable state boundaries. One example of change that bred numerous wars was the establishment of new states throughout the Third World after World War II, as former colonies attained national independence. As I noted (p. 58), many of these new states had arbitrary boundaries, which might throw together historically hostile peoples. Numerous civil wars followed the establishment of these new states. Another period of danger is the break-up of empires, when a former hegemon that has kept order in a region loses its capacity to hold things together. The break-up of the Turkish Empire after World War I is an example. The break-up of the Soviet Union and its system of satellite states in Eastern Europe after 1989 involved dangers of this sort as well.

- *Misperceptions by leaders,* either of their risks or of their opportunities, may spark wars (which might suggest that we should applaud effective spying rather than disapprove of it! It helps to prevent leaders from misreading their situation). All of the states that joined initially in the bloody combat of World War I thought they and their allies were so strong that they would win the war in a matter of weeks. They could not have been more wrong. Similarly, Saddam Hussein of Iraq badly miscalculated when he invaded Iran in 1980. He thought that Iran's new Islamic government would be weak and that he could seize territory by invading the country. Due to his miscalculation, Iraq became bogged down in an eight-year war that killed over a million young men.

- *Rich, powerful* states do not seem to make war with each other very often. They have too much to lose in war, and each has too much capacity to damage the other. Similarly, desperately poor states tend not to engage in war at all, because they do not have the capacity to win a war. Most wars involve in-between states that are poor but not destitute; or they may involve a conflict between a powerful state and an in-between state.

- *The most fascinating* regularity that political scientists have explored is the almost universal observation that democracies do not wage war with other democracies, the so-called **democratic peace.** There has never been a case in which two well-established democracies have gone to war, although there have been "gray area" cases in which a democracy warred with a marginally democratic state. Political scientists debate whether this regularity is due to mere coincidence or really means something, but those who argue that it does mean something note that it could be caused by popular aversion to warfare. In this interpretation, it is ordinary people who bear the costs of war, not leaders. In a democracy, unlike an autocratic system, the people can hold leaders accountable for an unpopular policy, so leaders will try to avoid involvement in war. Therefore, if two state leaders involved in a conflict are democratically accountable to their people, it may be that they will try to resolve the conflict by some means other than war.

The causes of war are multiple and complex. (I have not even gone into the further complication that wars seem to cycle over time with some periods having large numbers of wars and other periods being relatively peaceful.) However, the costs of war are so terrible that working through the complexities to our best understanding of war is one of the most important projects of political science.

Terrorism

Terrorism is perhaps the signature political phenomenon of the twenty-first century. This is true not because of political goals that terrorism has accomplished—most terrorist movements have not accomplished their goals—but because of the intense focus terrorism has drawn to itself. Every government in the world is concerned with it.

Terrorism is a phenomenon that I could have placed almost anywhere in this book. (You will recall from Chapter 5 that I had the same problem with corruption.) Terrorism is a tactic, and thus may apply to any political arena. It can be part of domestic politics, as in the hideously successful terrorism by which the Ku Klux Klan robbed newly enfranchised African Americans of their vote in the southern United States in the late nineteenth century. It can be used in civil wars within states, as in the terrorism engineered by the government of Sudan against the population in the secessionist province of Darfur. It also can be part of international politics, as in al Qaeda's attack on the United States on September 11, 2001. Either governments or non-state actors can initiate terrorism, but it is usually a tactic of the latter—if only because governments usually have other, more promising strategies available to them.

I have chosen to discuss terrorism in this chapter rather than elsewhere in the book because international relations scholars have studied terrorism more than other political scientists. Most materials available on terrorism deal with its international aspects, civil wars, or failed states.

Terrorism is the use of violent acts against civilians in order to accomplish political goals. Terrorists attempt to accomplish their goals by gaining publicity for their cause, disrupting normal government and infrastructure, and inflicting fear. Terrorism is usually designed to be dramatic and fearsome, including torture, maiming, rape, and indiscriminate bombing.

Conditions under which groups are especially likely to use terrorism are:

- *Better, alternative tactics are not available.* Terror is a tactic of strategic weakness. It is effective at keeping an issue to the fore, but it is difficult for terrorism to actually bring about a desired solution. If other, more promising tactics are available it is not likely that terrorism will arise.

- *The object of the attack can be portrayed as "the other."* Other ethnic groups or religions, an occupying military force, another country—these can be seen by the terrorists' base of support as alien or "other," and so violence against them will not upset the terrorists' supporters as much as attacks against their own group. Terrorists are usually careful to avoid attacking their own people, because they will quickly lose public support if they do so.

- *The object of attack is widely seen as lacking legitimacy.* It is relatively easy to sustain support of the base group for attacks against an illegitimate central government, a military occupying force, or an ethnic group against whom ancient grievances can be remembered (or invented). In the Bosnian civil war, for instance, Serbs justified atrocities against Moslems by harking back to battles fought five centuries before; this does not necessarily mean that the old grievances were what set off the civil war, but rather that they were brought up as justifications for the atrocities.

- *The government institutes harsh counterterrorism measures after it has been attacked.* Because we usually find terrorists living among the group on whose behalf they started the campaign, harsh counterattacks almost inevitably will injure innocent bystanders and fuel anger that morphs into greater support for the terrorists. For instance, Israel started harsh counterterrorist reprisals against Hamas and Islamic Jihad in the autumn of 2000, including tearing down many Palestinians' houses and assassinating leaders of the groups. Before the Israeli response, no more than a third of Palestinians supported suicide bombings against Israel; but in the months following the response, support for suicide bombing shot up.[5]

- *Paradoxically, though, democracies are easier to attack than autocracies because there are limits to what they can or will do in response.* It is possible to put down terrorism, or at least limit it, if you are willing to be brutal in ways that are probably impossible for democracies. There was little or no terrorism in Saddam Hussein's Iraq, because he was willing to torture and kill opponents on a large scale and drain the marshes across a huge part of the country to deny them hiding places.

Terrorism is especially effective at bringing an issue forward, particularly an intractable issue that might otherwise lie ignored. Even a relatively small group of people, without great financial resources, can keep a grievance in the news for years if they are willing to resort to dramatic, violent acts. Groups like the Catholics of Northern Ireland, the Palestinians, the Tamil separatists in Sri Lanka, the Basque independence movement in Spain, and Islamic fundamentalists in various Moslem states have been able to keep their demands on the agenda for years or decades. The problem for terrorists is that while they can keep an issue open, their tactic does not help lead them to a satisfactory solution. In fact, by heightening tensions and building mutual grievances, the tactic almost always makes a solution more difficult to reach.

Nonetheless, terrorism is a pervasive part of modern politics, especially of international politics. There are many frustrated causes in the world, with no obvious outlets for solution. A tactic that takes relatively low resources (although intense commitment) may engage enough supporters to keep a conflict open for many years.

→ THE EVOLUTION OF THE INTERNATIONAL SYSTEM SINCE WORLD WAR II

From the seventeenth century until the twentieth, most of the world's wealth and military power were concentrated in Europe, and various European states used that power to subjugate large populations around the world and form them into colonial empires.

---

[5]Mia Bloom, *Dying to Kill: The Allure of Suicide Terror* (New York: Columbia University Press, 2005).

By the early twentieth century, European dominance was weakening, especially because of the increasing power of the United States and Japan. The Europeans then hastened their slide from power by squandering their wealth and slaughtering their youth in World Wars I and II. Although other powers such as the United States and Japan were eventually involved in these wars and they have been called "world wars," almost all of the fighting and destruction centered in Europe. The European states emerged from World War II in 1945 exhausted, with only enough strength left to reconstruct their own states internally.

Two major changes in international politics resulted from this exhaustion of Europe: (1) Two new superpowers—the Soviet Union and the United States—arose to fill the power vacuum, and (2) the European states' empires threw off European rule, because the Europeans no longer had the power to hold them in subjugation.

The rise of the Soviet Union and the United States to dominate world politics created quite a different kind of system than what had gone before. When Europe dominated world politics, a number of substantial powers were involved in the system because Europe was so fragmented. Britain, France, Germany, Italy, and to some extent the Soviet Union, Japan, and the United States could figure in alliances. Many varying combinations of states in alliance were possible, and patterns of alliance shifted as states jockeyed for position. In the world after 1945, however, and especially from 1945 to about 1960, the system of politics consisted of a bipolar rivalry between the United States and the Soviet Union.

The two superpowers had been allies in the war against Hitler and initially set out into their domination of the world with pledges to cooperate in building a new, peaceful political order. However, they differed deeply in political philosophy, and they had conflicting political and economic goals. The Soviet Union used its dominating military force in the region to bring most of Eastern Europe under its control for economic advantage and to insulate itself militarily and politically from Western European states such as Germany and France (which had frequently attacked it earlier in the century). By 1946, Winston Churchill had coined the phrase "Iron Curtain" in his famous speech at Westminster College, Missouri:

> From Stettin in the Baltic to Trieste in the Adriatic, an iron curtain has descended across the continent. Behind that line lie all the capitals of the ancient states of Central and Eastern Europe. Warsaw, Berlin, Prague, Vienna, Budapest, Belgrade, Bucharest and Sofia, all these famous cities and populations around them lie in what I must call the Soviet sphere, and all are subject in one form or another not only to Soviet influence but to a very high and, in many cases, increasing measure of control from Moscow.[6]

In 1947, President Harry S. Truman announced that the United States was sending economic aid to the embattled anticommunist government of Greece, and the Cold War began.

The period of rivalry between the Soviet Union and the United States from 1945 on into the 1960s (and periodically until 1989) is called the "Cold War" because while at times it involved intense animosity, it never developed into full-scale "hot" warfare. Various skirmishes were fought—the Soviet blockade of West Berlin in 1948, war between

---

[6]Randolph S. Churchill, ed., *The Sinews of Peace: Post-War Speeches by Winston S. Churchill* (London: Cassell, 1948), p. 100.

the United States and the Soviet client state of North Korea in 1950—but there was never direct fighting between the two superpowers. There is a clear reason for this. Not only was the international system turned into a bipolar system after 1945, but the two superpowers of that system were armed with a new kind of weapon that made a war between them essentially unwinnable. Nuclear weapons are so destructive that in an all-out nuclear war, either combatant would be able to ruin the other.[7] As a result, the bipolar system that followed World War II was marked by a frustrated rivalry in which the two superpowers chewed on their animosity toward each other but were not able to do much about it.

The other main result of Europe's exhaustion after World War II was the breakup of the old colonial empires. One hundred of today's 195 states were colonies of European states at the outbreak of World War II. In other words, there are more than twice as many states in the world now as there were in 1941. These new states, together with some older states such as China, Thailand, Egypt, and the states of Latin America, comprise the Third World.

The growth in numbers and importance of the Third World states changed the international system markedly. The Third World commands many of the world's natural resources and comprises about three-fourths of its population. However, it does not command anything close to a proportional share of wealth or military power. Most of the states of the Third World are individually weak, although some such as India and Brazil have developed into moderately important powers, and China has become a major power. As a group, they account for so much of the world that they cannot and should not be ignored. Many Third World states, as they grow in wealth and military strength, have a great potential as future powers; China, in particular, is likely to rival the United States in size and importance within a few decades, and India also has that potential.

✦ THE WORLD SINCE THE COLD WAR

As of the mid-1970s, then, we could have described the world as a fairly stable system of states dominated by two main conflicts—a military standoff in the Cold War animosity between the Soviet bloc and the bloc led by the United States, and an economic and political "north-south" tension between the Third World and the industrialized states of both blocs. Over the next three decades, however, five major developments changed this system into the more fluid, more complicated, but less tense one we face today:

1. *Steadily the set of actors involved in international politics expanded and became more varied.* At the beginning of this period, international politics were conducted pretty much by the states of the world plus the United Nations and its agencies.

---

[7]A revisionist literature has questioned whether nuclear weapons prevent war. This literature points out that in the 1920s, many people thought that the existence of poison gas, in combination with the development of modern air forces, had made all-out war unwinnable. Any power, even if it were going down in defeat, could launch such deathly attacks with gas canisters that the winner of the war would be destroyed. Therefore, it was agreed, no one would dare wage war against a power that had poison gas weapons. As it turned out, full-scale war was waged in World War II, but without gas. The participating powers had chemical weapons, but none used them for fear of retaliation in kind. The revisionist literature argues that all-out conventional warfare could similarly occur today without the use of nuclear weapons. See, for example, John Ellis van Courtland Moon, "Chemical Weapons and Deterrence: The World War II Experience," *International Security* 8 (Spring 1984), pp. 3–35.

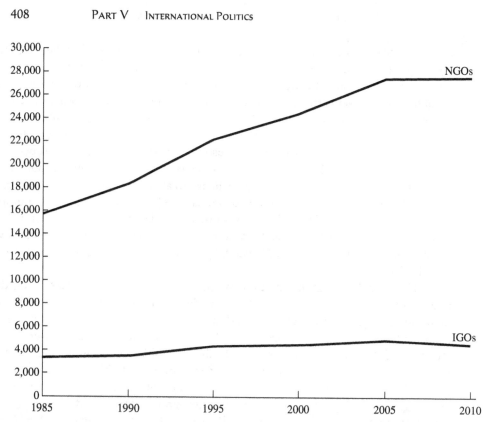

FIGURE 18.1   Growth of non-state participants: NGOs and IGOs.

SOURCE: Union of International Associations, *Yearbook of International Organizations 2010/2011* (Brussels: DeGruyter Saur, 2010), vol. 5, figure 2.9. All types of international organizations in the figure are included except inactive or dissolved organizations; no figures from before 1985 are used here, because the definitions of organizations changed frequently in earlier years, and are only stable from 1985 on.

Starting in the 1970s and 1980s, however, the number of non-state participants in international politics began to grow explosively—growth that continues, as we see in Figure 18.1.

Two types of non-state participant developed over this time: **nongovernmental international organizations (NGOs)**, and **intergovernmental organizations (IGOs)**. NGOs are organizations that governments did not establish, and that operate independently of any government. Not all of them are actively engaged in international politics. The International Political Science Association, for instance, exists mainly to promote communication among scholars, although it will occasionally act to promote or defend academic freedom in various parts of the world. Many others, however—Amnesty International, the Pugwash Conferences on Science and World Affairs, the Union of National Radio and Television Organizations of Africa, the International Federation of Journalists, GreenPeace, to name only a few—are politically active in all sorts of ways.

IGOs are organizations founded by treaties among governments, but which operate with an independent governing structure and staff so that they are not under the direct control of any particular government. They include the United Nations, various arms of the UN such as UNICEF (the United Nations International Children's Fund), international financial structures such as the Bank for International Settlements, other specialized international coordinating organizations such as the International Whaling Commission and the World Trade Organization, and regional groups such as the Asian & Pacific Coconut Community. These organizations play a different role than NGOs. Usually they administer and implement international agreements among states—but as we saw in Chapter 16, those who implement a decision often put their own stamp on it. Compared with NGOs, these organizations usually operate with legal authority under treaties to make decisions. Where NGOs play more the role of gadflies or watchdogs in international politics, IGOs operate with authority of their own, removing a number of international decisions from the individual states.

In addition to formal organizations, other kinds of new actors have joined the scene. Many corporations are so large and their operations spread across so many states' boundaries that they bargain directly with the states almost as equals. Terrorist groups, too, have become significant actors in international politics. The terrorist attack on the United States on September 11, 2001, reshaped the whole role of the United States in the world. Non-state actors have become major factors in international politics. I provide another example of how important non-state actors have become in international politics in the box, "Banning Land Mines."

A useful website to review international organizations is the Union of International Associations, with the online Yearbook of International Organizations, plus many links: http://www.uia.org.

2. *The interdependence of the world's states grew enormously*. One way this has shown up is in the dependence of states' economies on their trade with each other. For the United States, for instance, trade as a proportion of economic activity was fairly stable through the 1950s and 1960s, but it became an increasingly significant part of the United States economy in the 1970s and 1980s. Figure 18.2 shows that it doubled as

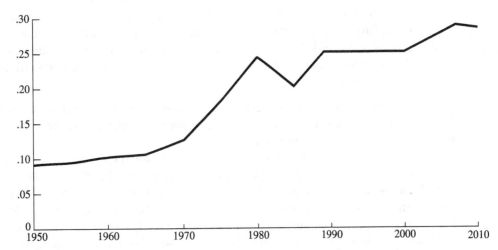

FIGURE 18.2   Trade in goods and services (exports plus imports) as a proportion of U.S. gross domestic product.

SOURCE: U.S. Bureau of the Census, *Statistical Abstract of the United States,* various years.

a proportion of the United States' gross national product between 1970 and 1980. Not only did international trade play a larger role in states' economies, but because many of a state's largest corporations were spread across numerous countries, states' economies depended more on what was happening in other states than was the case in the first half of the twentieth century.

Environmental policy is another area in which interdependence has increased explosively. As the world becomes more industrialized, the environmental impact of what we do is less a matter of concern only for the polluting state. The depletion of the ozone layer and the increase in carbon dioxide in the atmosphere that causes global warming affect all states' populations. These and other problems are the ultimate "externality," and as we saw earlier (p. 144), any externality forces a search for collective decisions. The Kyoto Accords to reduce global warming, signed by 178 states in 2001 (but not by the United States), are a good example of the environmental collective choice that externalities from the industrial economy increasingly require.

Finally, partly through the expansion of worldwide communications such as Cable News Network and Al Jazeera network, and partly because the people of the world are more literate and better educated than in the past, we seem more aware of what happens in other states than we used to be. What once would have been claimed to be "internal affairs" of sovereign states—apartheid in South Africa, human rights abuses in many other states—are now part of international politics.

It is a cliché, but still a good one, that the world is becoming a smaller place.

3. *The bipolar system of rivalry between the Soviet Union and the United States disappeared.* This had already been happening, fairly slowly, for about twenty years as the U.S.S.R. and the U.S.A. gradually lost their monopolies of economic and military power to such upstarts (communist and noncommunist) as Japan, China, Germany, and France. The system of rivalry finally ended rather suddenly with the economic exhaustion of the Soviet Union about 1989 and its internal collapse in 1991.

The results of this shift were momentous. The very way we defined the system of states—West, East, "Third World"—had been based on the old rivalry. Defense establishments suddenly found themselves searching for a new *raison d'etre*. Client states, such as Cuba or Indonesia's Suharto regime, found themselves abandoned by their superpower partners.

4. *Starting roughly in the mid-1980s, a large number of states around the world shifted their economies more in the direction of open markets; as a result of this, the states of the world became somewhat more alike.* Partly this shift resulted from the collapse of formerly communist systems. Partly it resulted from the formation of new trade alliances and the necessity of meshing the economies of once heavily regulated states with the more open economies of their new partners; Mexico's economy moved to a more open condition after formation of the NAFTA partnership with the United States, for instance. Finally, a number of economies in Africa (early 1990s) and East Asia (after 1997) were forced by the International Monetary Fund to become more open following financial collapses.

Politically, too, the states of the world grew more similar to one another. There are fewer authoritarian regimes today than there were in the 1970s. Governments have

Banning Land Mines

In September 1997, nearly one hundred states signed an international treaty in which they agreed not to use land mines, and to destroy any they had already laid down. Land mines are a weapon that is especially dangerous for civilians. After a war is over, they usually remain hidden in the ground for years, so most of the victims they claim are farmers plowing fields or children at play.

The ban was not engineered by the states that signed it. Rather, it is a prime example of the growing influence of non-state actors in international politics. In 1990, a coalition of the Vietnam Veterans of America (United States), Human Rights Watch (United States), Physicians for Human Rights (United States), Medico International (Germany), Handicap International (France), and the Mines Advisory Group (Britain) began to work for an international ban. They waged a vivid public relations campaign featuring the late Princess Diana of Britain comforting land mine victims in Bosnia and Angola, and importantly they gained a key ally among the world's states in Canada, whose foreign minister took on the ban as a personal cause. In 1995, the International Red Cross joined in with a large ad campaign—the first time that this prestigious organization had ever joined a controversial cause. Canada called a special conference of states in 1996 to discuss a general ban, and from there, the process moved swiftly.

become more interested in open trade relations than they were when their economies were treated as fortresses. The technocrats who run most states' economic policies "speak the same language" and often were educated at the same American universities; therefore, negotiations for cooperative economic policy have become somewhat easier.

5. *In the late 1990s, a body of international law began to develop that has the potential to impose enforceable law on the leaders of states and thus on the states themselves.* A number of treaties had been in effect since the Second World War that brought the actions of states under international jurisdiction, but no one had tried seriously to enforce them. For instance, most of the states of the world had signed a convention against genocide in 1948, but no state leaders had ever been brought to justice for violating the treaty. In the late 1990s, however, human rights organizations and their supporters in governmental posts successfully began to use treaties like this one to bring former heads of state to judgment for their actions. The first instance of this was the arrest of former President Augusto Pinochet of Chile, who had presided over a military dictatorship marked by the use of torture and kidnappings. After the return of democracy to Chile, Pinochet had lived in peaceful retirement as a result of the pacts by which democracy had been restored; but when he traveled to Britain in 1998, a Spanish judge asked for his extradition to Spain so that he could be tried for crimes against international law. Although heads of state traditionally had not been held personally liable for their actions as leaders of their state, the British Law Lords (the highest court in Britain) ruled in an important precedent that Pinochet was indeed liable as president for violations of the International Torture Convention, which Chile had signed. Note that the

International Torture Conventions treaty, under which Pinochet was tried, is one of the few international treaties that includes international jurisdiction—that is, it allows any country to punish violators of the treaty.

In a second important case, Serbia in 2001 surrendered its former president, Slobodan Milosevic, to NATO to be tried by the United Nations War Crimes Tribunal in the Netherlands for crimes associated with the deportation of hundreds of thousands of ethnic Albanians from the Serbian province of Kosovo. Unlike the trial of Pinochet, which was decided on very narrow grounds (the Law Lords ruled that Pinochet could be tried only for violations of the International Torture Conventions and then only for tortures committed after 1988, when Chile had signed the convention), the UN court worked with a broad case law based on the Nuremberg trials of Nazi war criminals and the general development of international law since those trials, including the Torture Convention and the International Convention on Genocide.

Finally, the **International Criminal Court** was established in 2003, based in the Netherlands—able to try any individuals, including heads of state and other government officials, for a broad range of crimes, including genocide, "crimes against humanity," war crimes, and the crime of aggression. As of 2013 the treaty establishing the Court has been signed by 122 countries, and even the United States has begun to support it and see its value, although it is not a member and it had earlier been worried that its officials might be charged with international crimes and have to deal with the court. In 2012 the Court tried Charles Taylor, former president of Liberia, and sentenced him to 50 years in prison for atrocities committed during the civil war in Sierra Leone.

PEACE COMES TO BOSNIA

The internationally maintained peace in Bosnia's civil war felt a lot like war. A cartoonist's view . . .

We are still only beginning to work out the implications of these changes in the international system. There are many dangers inherent in some of the changes. There are likely to be more "small wars," for instance, as the superpowers no longer feel a need to keep a lid on boundary disputes around the world; and while these may be "small" wars, we have seen in Bosnia, Somalia, Kosovo, Rwanda, and Darfur that they can be dirty and cruel. However, the new, fluid system also offers rich opportunities. Before those opportunities can be realized, however, we will have to see what norms and rules emerge to govern states' intervention in other states in this new world that is emerging.

Some of the pieces that will add up to what the new international system looks like are:

- The rapid rise of China, India, and Brazil, especially China, to the status of major powers, both economically and militarily. The rise of new powers is always stressful for a region, as it shakes old connections and patterned relationships.

- Increasing Islamic militancy, exacerbated both by the unpopularity of undemocratic governments in many Islamic states, and by American foreign policy over the last decade with regard to the Palestinian question and to Iraq.

- The negative reaction to globalization, which may turn many states inward rather than outward in their policy focus.

- The growing crisis of resource sustainability and global warming, which puts added strain on all states, but might also bring about greater cooperation.

- The 2008–2009 economic crisis, which showed how interconnected financial institutions are around the word, and demonstrated the need to work out better systems to regulate them.

Each of these probably embodies as many promises and opportunities as it does hazards and danger. But finding the opportunities and avoiding the dangers is going to call for skilled leadership, and some luck.

✦ POWER AND CHOICE IN INTERNATIONAL POLITICS

It is easy to see the "power" side of international politics, but with no central authority to define common goals for the international system, it is not so easy to see that international politics may also involve "choice." Some theorists think that the international system can work toward certain common goals, however, even in the absence of a coordinating authority.

Regime theory, for instance, sees international politics as transcending the power relationships of states. A "regime" is:

(a set of) principles, norms, rules, and decision-making procedures around which actors' expectations converge in a given issue-area.[8]

---

[8]Stephen D. Krasner, ed., *International Regimes* (Ithaca, NY: Cornell University Press, 1983), p. 1; see also Andreas Hasenclever, Peter Mayer, and Volker Rittberger, *Theories of International Regimes* (New York: Cambridge University Press, 1997).

In other words, above and beyond the power relationships of states and other international actors, there may emerge a set of values and principles in the international community that modifies members' behavior. States may be moved by a shared vision of the common good, not just by narrow interpretations of their individual interests. Since the Second World War, for instance, a basic assumption of the international order, embodied in institutions such as the International Monetary Fund, has been that trade should expand so that all economies may operate more efficiently. This "regime" has not been uncontested; leaders of the Third World have argued that the regime should instead emphasize redistribution of wealth, rather than taking the existing disparities between rich countries and poor countries as a given and striving only for maximal exchange and overall efficiency of the world economy. The point is, though, that there has been a set of values with a power of its own that has affected how states act above and beyond the power relationships of those involved.

Other regimes have been identified in areas such as human rights, justice, and protection of the environment.[9]

Proponents of regime theory see it as a way to address common problems in a more hopeful way than my bleak description of the "fiduciary role" might lead us to expect. However, critics argue that regimes are froth on the international system, that they are no more than expressions of the power relationships of those involved—that the international regime on trade, for instance, has been what it was because that suited Western and especially United States' interests.

At this point, regime theory is important for us because it suggests that, even in the anarchy of international politics, we may interpret politics as more than just the exercise of power. As I have tried to show throughout this book, a proper understanding of politics requires that we remain simultaneously aware of its two sides. With some of the changes that I have described in this chapter, the bleak picture of traditional international politics may have acquired some cooperative highlights. The growth of interdependence and the entry of more non-state actors (which softens somewhat the starkness of the fiduciary role) may make international politics in the future a more balanced mix of "power" and "choice."

 EXAMPLE

An International Failure: Rwanda

 Rwanda is a small, landlocked state in central Africa, about the size of Massachusetts. It is an agricultural country with significant exports of coffee and tea, and with milk production and grain for local consumption. The country is one of the most densely populated in Africa, with over seven hundred people per square mile— a population density slightly greater than that of Massachusetts.

---

[9]See, for instance, Helmut Breitmeier, Oran R. Young, and Michael Zurn, *Analyzing International Environmental Regimes* (Cambridge, MA: MIT Press, 2007).

Before Rwanda came into contact with Europeans at the end of the nineteenth century, it was already a fairly well-developed state ruled by a king. The population was ethnically divided between two tribes. The Tutsis were a tribe of cattle herders and warriors. They controlled politics (the king and most warriors were Tutsi), even though they were numerically a distinct minority. The much larger Hutu tribe were land-based farmers, raising crops rather than grazing cattle on the open range. As of the 1956 census, 16 percent of Rwandans were Tutsi, and 83 percent Hutu.

The "tribal" distinction was to some extent physical, with Tutsis taller and longer-faced, but there had been a good deal of intermarriage over the years, and this had blended such physical differences significantly. The operating distinction was in part also an economic one between haves and have-nots. A Hutu could become a Tutsi if he acquired large numbers of cattle, and a Tutsi could become so impoverished that he sank to being a Hutu.

After Rwanda became independent in 1962, there were periodic outbursts of ethnic violence, and throughout the 1980s, about 250,000 mainly Tutsi refugees lived outside Rwanda in neighboring countries. In the early 1990s, a Tutsi-led rebel force based in these refugee groups began to have significant success against the Hutu-led government, and by 1993, they occupied much of the northern part of the country. The government and the rebels reached a peace accord that called for democratic, multiparty elections, but it was a fragile peace. It was especially ominous that the (now predominantly Hutu) army refused to honor some of the peace directives from the government, even though the government was nominally in charge of the army.

On April 6, 1994, newly elected President Juvénal Habyarimana, a Hutu who had been actively promoting reconciliation, was assassinated when the plane in which he and the president of neighboring Burundi were passengers was shot down over Rwanda's capital. Immediately, a well-organized campaign of assassinations and massacres began in which Habyarimana's allies (including the prime minister and the president of the Constitutional Court) were murdered, along with other Hutus who favored reconciliation, educated Tutsis, and a number of United Nations personnel. Over the following several weeks, an organized campaign to kill all the country's Tutsis was carried out, in which an estimated five hundred thousand Tutsis—half the total population and including many children—died. The killings were brutal. Some of the tall Tutsis had their feet chopped off "to bring them down to our size."

Meanwhile, the rebel Tutsi force continued to gain ground on the government, although it was too late to save many Tutsis from murder. By July, they effectively controlled the country. Now millions of Hutus fled the country, to live as refugees in neighboring Zaire. They were kept there by rumors their leaders spread of Tutsi vengeance, even though there was remarkably little evidence of any revenge by the new Tutsi-led government.

A chilling history! Yet the United States and other Western countries did not pay much attention to it, except for brief expressions of horror at moments when the violence periodically erupted at its worst. Rwanda was not of great economic importance, lacked natural resources such as oil, and was not strategically located with regard to shipping lanes or to international conflicts. The West had never paid much attention to Rwanda, and its response even to the 1994 genocide was half-hearted. The French, who had had a continuing relationship with the Hutu government, and consistently had the largest Western military presence in the area, did little to protect the Tutsis. Britain offered fifty unarmored trucks to aid in helping prevent the slaughter.

The United States was not bathed in glory, either. American diplomats as a matter of stated policy denied the term genocide in reference to Rwanda until late in the killings, by which time over a third of Tutsis had been killed. In the end, little was done, and order settled on the deathly country without much help from anyone.

After the victory of the Tutsi rebels, a massive exodus of Hutus began. For the next two years, about one-fourth of the population of Rwanda lived in squalid refugee camps on its border, mainly in neighboring Zaire. They were Hutus, afraid to return home because they believed they would be attacked by Tutsi hard-liners in the army. In the meantime, they were often terrorized by the Zairean army—which wanted to force them back to Rwanda to ease the burden of caring for them—and by their own defeated Hutu army, which was trying to prepare a new invasion of Rwanda. The United Nations tried to be helpful by offering humanitarian aid, building camp shelters, and sending observers to check on conditions in Rwanda's prisons. There was little more the United Nations could do. The situation was in the end "resolved" by the descent of Zaire into a chaotic civil war in which thousands of the Hutus, innocent bystanders in Zaire's internal conflict, were killed. The remaining Hutus fled back to Rwanda. They were initially repatriated with relatively little violence. However, the basic ethnic conflict between Tutsis and Hutus remains unresolved.

Perhaps the most effective response to date has been that of the International Criminal Tribunal for Rwanda, established by the United Nations in 1994 to try individuals

Bodies float at the bottom of a waterfall after a massacre of Hutu refugees in Rwanda.
© AP Photo

accused of participation in the Rwanda genocide. As of 2010, the Tribunal had convicted 31 persons of participation in the genocide, including Jean Kambanda, the interim Prime Minister. You can examine the Tribunal's work at its website, http://www.unictr.org/.

I titled this "An International Failure," but this may have been unfair. Perhaps there was little the rest of the world could do about the ethnic poison in Rwanda. However, much of the poison was created by the rest of the world during the colonial period. It just does not feel right to throw up our hands at a problem like this, and history does repeat itself. The massacres and genocide in Darfur between 2003 and 2010—unimpeded by any serious international attempt to stop the killing—seemed almost to be a rerun of the events in Rwanda.

✳ EXAMPLE

The United Nations

The United Nations was established by the victorious Allies at the end of World War II as an organization to help maintain world peace. It was to do this partly by imposing sanctions against those who broke the peace and partly through programs to remove what were thought to be the causes of war—poverty, suffering, and ignorance. Today, the United Nations has 193 members, nearly all of the world's states.

The decision-making structure of the United Nations was established by the victorious powers to make them the core of the organization and the guardians of peace. All members of the United Nations are represented in a General Assembly, each with one vote, which is democratic, although it does give undue voting power to tiny countries. However, the victorious Allies added to this General Assembly another body, the Security Council. This body must also agree to any significant action of the United Nations, and each of the World War II victors (the United States, France, Britain, Russia, and China) was made a permanent member of the Security Council. Not only were the victors made permanent members of the Security Council, but each was given an individual veto over its decisions. Thus, each of these five permanent members was given the right to veto any significant actions of the UN. Ten other states rotate on and off the council for terms of two years each.

The executive leader of the United Nations is the Secretary-General, an individual elected by the General Assembly for a term of five years. The present Secretary-General is South Korea's Ban Ki-moon, who has served since 2007. In his position, Ban Ki-moon manages the UN's operations but works most effectively when persuading rather than pushing. Some Secretaries-General have been effective world diplomats; others have been primarily managers of the organization.

The United Nations has developed an important role as peacekeeper in local disputes where the states involved agree they want to lessen the likelihood of conflict. When acting as a peacekeeper, the United Nations organizes a corps of soldiers from states not involved in a conflict who go to the conflict site and separate the antagonists. Often this has involved establishment of a demilitarized buffer zone between two territories, which the antagonists agree to keep free of their own troops and which the United Nations peacekeeping force patrols. Over the years, the United Nations has mounted about sixty peacekeeping operations in conflicts, such as those between Israel and Lebanon, India and Pakistan, and to monitor agreements in the Darfur province of Sudan. Between 2004 and 2012 the number of soldiers involved in UN peacekeeping activities doubled, and it is now at the highest level ever. In 2013 the UN was operating seventeen separate peacekeeping operations around the world.[10]

Beyond its peacekeeping function, the United Nations operates a wide range of agencies that work to improve the condition of humanity in everything from helping refugees to encouraging trade and development. The scope of this work is large. The United Nations buys half of the world's vaccines for children, protects 30 million refugees in 50 countries, and is the world's largest customer for condoms.[11]

The United Nations might have been a great success if the victorious powers had remained united after World War II and had operated cooperatively as guardians of world peace. That was the purpose of its structure. Shortly after the establishment of the United Nations, however, the Cold War descended on the world. From then on, either the Soviet Union or the United States was likely to veto any important action of the organization, so the UN was for many years limited almost entirely to noncontroversial interventions.

With the end of the Cold War, it at first looked as though the United Nations could take on a more leading role in international affairs, since it would not be stymied by the Soviet-American rivalry. Its peacekeeping roles became more important and more demanding. However, the increased visibility of the United Nations soon conflicted with its own creaky bureaucracy, and with major states' unwillingness to cede it a leading role. A program to regulate Iraq's sale of oil was plagued by corruption, even involving the son of the Secretary-General. The organization developed severe financial problems, primarily because the United States refused to pay its dues for several years. New major powers like Japan, India, Brazil, and Germany began to ask why states like Britain or France should have permanent seats on the Security Council while they did not. Most seriously, the UN underwent a damaging crisis in 2003, when the United States wanted the United Nations to invade Iraq, but France and Russia (both permanent members of the Security Council) opposed the action. In the end the United States lost, after a nasty conflict that left the United Nations scarred and the U.S. resentful.

In the wake of all this, and most especially the corruption scandal involving his son and other United Nations officials, then Secretary-General Kofi Annan cleaned out a number of senior leaders in the organization and set further reforms on track. His successor Ban Ki-moon has continued these efforts very strenuously, but has expressed frustration at how little power he has to control staff and effect internal change.[12] The United Nations continue to play a useful, but modest, role in international politics.

---

[10] http://www.un.org/en/peacekeeping/resources/statistics
[11] "Pope Kofi's Unruly Flock," *The Economist,* August 8, 1998, p. 19.
[12] "UN's Ban Ki-moon on Nukes, Reform, His Image," *Wall Street Journal,* July 14, 2009.

The United Nations' website is http://www.un.org. A particularly interesting website is the United Nations Environmental Programme page of updates on negotiations in progress for international environmental agreements: http://www.unep.org.

↝ A PERSONAL NOTE

Let me close this book with a personal note. We tend, when analyzing politics, to think of it in the abstract and rather dispassionately. We analyze people's actions according to the resources available to them and according to a rational application of those resources to their goals. By and large, this analysis works well. We can usually tell which of two countries will be able to impose its will upon another, what sort of people will turn out to vote in greater numbers at election time, and how a change in party finance will affect candidates' strategies. Sometimes, however, passionate belief can cut through all this. Ideas and ideology can take on a power of their own, which transcends analysis. No political scientists in the early 1960s predicted the tumultuous events of the civil rights movement. Who would have thought that little Vietnam would be able to best the United States in a war, or that the democratic opposition would eventually triumph over the Communist Party in Eastern Europe and the Soviet Union?

As a small dog, if it is on its home ground, may be able to send a larger one running away with its tail down, so may the weaker side—even a very weak side—prevail in politics if its supporters believe strongly enough that they are right.

This book has emphasized the analysis of politics, and surely this is important, but I hope you will also remember the importance of passion and belief. As Marshall McLuhan put it, "Nothing is inevitable as long as one person is aware that it is happening."

KEY TERMS

international politics
global politics
NGOs
IGOs
International Criminal
    Court

United Nations
International Court of
    Justice
fiduciary role
diplomacy
consulates

ambassador
economic sanctions
democratic peace
terrorism
regime theory

FURTHER READING

Banks, William C., De Nevers, René, and Wallerstein, Mitchel B. *Combating Terrorism: Strategies and Approaches*. Washington, DC: CQ Press, 2008.

Bekou, Olympia, and Cryer, Robert, eds. *The International Criminal Court*. Burlington, VT: Ashgate, 2005.

420   PART V   INTERNATIONAL POLITICS

Breitmeier, Helmut, Young, Oran R., and Zurn, Michael. *Analyzing International Environmental Regimes.* Cambridge, MA: MIT Press, 2007.

Fortna, Virginia Page. *Does Peacekeeping Work? Shaping Belligerents' Choices After Civil War.* Princeton, NJ: Princeton University Press, 2008.

Gilpin, Robert. *Global Political Economy: Understanding the International Economic Order.* Princeton: Princeton University Press, 2001.

Keohane, Robert, and Nye, Joseph S. *Power and Interdependence,* 4th ed. New York: Pearson, 2012.

Leffler, Melvyn P., and Legro, Jeffrey W., eds. *To Lead the World: American Strategy After the Bush Doctrine.* New York: Oxford University Press, 2008.

Mearshimer, John J. *The Tragedy of Great Power Politics.* New York: W. W. Norton, 2001.

Murphy, John F. *The United States and the Rule of Law in International Affairs.* New York: Cambridge University Press, 2004.

Nye, Joseph S. *The Paradox of American Power.* New York: Oxford University Press, 2002.

_____. *Soft Power: The Means to Success in World Politics.* New York: Public Affairs Press, 2005.

Schiff, Benjamin. *Building the International Criminal Court.* New York: Cambridge University Press, 2008.

Senese, Paul D., and Vasquez, John A. *The Steps to War: An Empirical Study.* Princeton, NJ: Princeton University Press, 2008.

Stoessinger, John G. *Why Nations Go to War,* 11th ed. Beverly, MA: Wadsworth, 2010.

Weiss, Thomas G., and Daws, Sam, eds. *The Oxford Handbook of the United Nations.* New York: Oxford University Press, 2007.